START[ER KIT] for the IBM iSERIES & AS/400

SETUP

SECURITY

OPERATIONS

CL

GARY GUTHRIE & WAYNE MADDEN

NEWS/400 Books™ is a division of
DUKE COMMUNICATIONS INTERNATIONAL
A subsidiary of Penton Media, Inc.
221 E. 29th Street • Loveland, CO 80538 USA
(800) 650-1804 • (970) 663-4700 • www.as400networkstore.com

Library of Congress Cataloging-in-Publication Data

Guthrie, Gary, 1953-
Starter kit for the IBM iSeries and AS/400 / by Gary Guthrie and Wayne Madden.
p. cm.
Includes index.
ISBN 1-58304-084-6
1. IBM AS/400 (Computer)--Programming. 2. Linux. I. Madden, Wayne, 1960- II. Title.
QA76.8.I25919 G88 2001
005.4'445--dc21

2001001776

NEWS/400 Books™ is a division of
DUKE COMMUNICATIONS INTERNATIONAL
A subsidiary of Penton Media, Inc.
Loveland, Colorado USA

This book was printed and bound in Canada.

ISBN 1-58304-084-6

2003 2002 2001 WL 10 9 8 7 6 5 4 3 2 1

To my family,

Karen Sue, Josh, and Shannon.

I love you dearly.

— Gary Guthrie

To my beautiful children,

Rachel and Andrew.

— Wayne Madden

Acknowledgments

I'm humbled to be friend to the many people who made this book — the latest incarnation of Wayne Madden's classic *Starter Kit for the AS/400* — possible. I'd like to thank Wayne for the opportunity to work on this edition of the book and for entrusting me with the project. Over the years, he has afforded me numerous opportunities for which I am truly grateful.

Bryan Meyers and Debbie Saugen contributed material for the book. Bryan also reviewed the manuscript and provided helpful comments, as did Mel Beckman on the TCP/IP material. Editor Katie M. Tipton has always added a luster to my works, and this book is no exception. She is exceptionally talented and a true pleasure to work with, and her review of and revisions to the material have been invaluable. Martha Nichols worked on the production of the book. Kathy Wong provided administrative assistance. Matt Wiebe designed the engaging cover. Although Dale Agger didn't work directly on the book, she is largely responsible for getting me started in the writing business. Her encouragement and support throughout my tenure with *NEWS/400* are greatly appreciated, as are the many opportunities with which she has presented me.

Others not directly involved in production of the book deserve recognition as well. Closest of friends and industry expert, Don Kracke was always there to provide feedback. Other close friends Mark Marksbary, Charlie Sanchez, and Spiro Barouxis helped with their commentary and by providing various pieces of requested reference material. I want to extend a very special thanks to Dean Wagoner who, more than twenty years ago, took a chance by hiring a young man who knew virtually nothing about computers and introduced me to the industry. His mentoring and faith have been instrumental to my success.

My best friend and sweetheart, Karen Sue Nielsen, sacrificed much so that I could complete this project. She took over many responsibilities, giving me time to devote to the book. Her constant support and encouragement were welcome pillars throughout the process, and her cheers upon completion of each chapter kept me motivated. My children, Josh and Shannon, not only helped with several small tasks but also made things easier for me while I was busy with the book by maintaining their status as honor students through their own initiative.

I am in good company.

Gary Guthrie

About the Authors

Gary Guthrie is a *NEWS/400* technical editor and a technical support consultant with more than 20 years of progressive IT experience. He has written numerous articles for *NEWS/400*, is a frequent contributor to the magazine's Tech Corner department, and moderates the RPG Programmer and SQL/400 & Database communities at The AS400 Network. He also served as editor of the newsletter *The RPG Source*. Among Gary's many areas of expertise are problem determination and resolution, customer support, operating systems, languages, utilities, database, application development, operations integration, system migration, configuration, performance, security, work management, internals, and Client Access.

Wayne Madden is vice president and group publisher at Duke Communications International in Loveland, Colorado. He is also the editor-in-chief and publisher of *NEWS/400*, *Selling eServer Solutions*, and *Group Computing* magazines and The AS400 Network. Wayne is a well-known author and speaker in the IBM technology marketplace, has written more than 200 articles, and has authored three books, including the original *Starter Kit for the AS/400*. He has worked in the IBM midrange industry for more than 18 years as a programmer, manager, consultant, author, and speaker.

About the Contributing Authors

Bryan Meyers is vice president of PowerTech Group and head of the company's The 400 School division. He has served as a technical editor and writer for *NEWS/400* for many years. Bryan is also an accomplished author and sought-after speaker. His books include *RPG IV Jump Start, Third Edition* and *VisualAge for RPG by Example* (NEWS/400 Books) and the textbooks *Programming in RPG IV, Second Edition* and *Control Language Programming for the AS/400* (29th Street Press).

Debbie Saugen is the technical owner of iSeries 400 and AS/400 Backup and Recovery in IBM's Rochester, Minnesota, Development Lab. She is also a senior recovery specialist with IBM Business Continuity and Recovery Services. Debbie enjoys sharing her knowledge by speaking at COMMON, iSeries 400 and AS/400e Technical Conferences, and Business Continuity and Recovery Services Conferences and writing for various iSeries and AS/400e magazines and Web sites.

Table of Contents at a Glance

Table of Contents

[Italic type indicates a sidebar.]

SETUP

BASIC CL PROGRAMMING

THE NEW FACE OF THE SYSTEM

Introduction

Whether you're a programmer or a system operator, you'll find essential information in this book to help you understand some of the basic concepts and nuances of the iSeries and AS/400 — information that will make your job easier and increase your comfort working on these systems.

The strong suit of the iSeries and AS/400 is their operating system, OS/400. Compared with other operating systems in the industry, OS/400 delivers an unmatched level of functionality. However, with these many integrated functions also comes a complexity that you must learn and manage. We've written the chapters of this book to expose some of those complexities and help you learn how to manage them.

The book is arranged in logical order from basic system setup information — such as how to plan for installation, suggested actions to perform during installation, how to establish a basic work environment, how to create user profiles, and how to establish default public authorities — through some of the more important areas you need to understand to operate, program, and manage your system. At the same time, each section and chapter is tightly focused, so you can go directly to a particular topic and learn what you need to know without reading the entire book.

The book is divided into six sections. Following the chapters on system setup, we address the area of operations. This section offers you insight into basic system operation functions such as message handling, working with printer files and output queues, disk management, and job scheduling. You'll learn how to communicate with users on the system using messages; how to use OS/400 functions to automatically monitor for and answer specific messages; how to locate, work with, and secure spooled files on output queues; and how to move toward unattended operations using OS/400's job scheduler.

The next section focuses on system management and is tied closely to system operations with two chapters devoted to save and restore features and strategies. Anyone involved in system operation and application development needs to understand these concepts to take advantage of the save and restore capabilities that the iSeries and AS/400 offer. These chapters teach you both the technology and the strategies you'll find helpful as you plan and implement an effective backup and recovery approach for your systems.

The next three chapters of this section present practical help concerning iSeries and AS/400 work-management objects and functions. The concept of work management includes many objects — job descriptions, user profiles, subsystem descriptions, routing entries, and job queue entries — and the many relationships these objects share to process work through your system in a managed and efficient work environment. These chapters introduce you to both the key objects and those relationships. This complete description of work-management objects, together with sample work-management configurations, will give you a good taste for this often-feared area of the system while spurring your confidence and curiosity to learn more.

The section covering file basics tackles one of the most troublesome areas for those new to the iSeries and AS/400 architecture: file structure. Because of your previous experiences, the definition and administration of the OS/400 integrated database is something new and foreign to many of you. But you must master defining and using files on the system to ensure that your applications take advantage of OS/400's database functions. We've devoted several chapters to building your knowledge of iSeries and AS/400 files and how you can manipulate those files to use them effectively in your applications.

We've dedicated an entire section to basic CL programming tasks. This material, which covers everything from CL style, to using CL programs with display files and database files, to teaching programs to talk to each other, to using commands will certainly give you a firm foundation on which you can build your CL programming skills.

The final section of the book address two of the newer and increasingly used features of the system: TCP/IP connectivity and Operations Navigator. TCP/IP is the de facto standard in connectivity today, and we give you a basic understanding of the protocol. Operations Navigator offers you a graphical interface to iSeries and AS/400 operations; we introduce you to its functions as well.

The information presented in these 34 chapters will help you develop a basic working knowledge of some of the key concepts and functions you'll encounter on the iSeries and AS/400. With this foundation, you'll be solidly prepared to explore each subject in depth using the manuals and other resources mentioned in the Further Reading recommendations.

If this book makes you feel more comfortable with your new system, serves as a useful reference tool, and inspires you to further explore the iSeries and AS/400 systems, it will have served its purpose.

Chapter 1

Before the Power Is On

From its birth combining the power of the System/38 with the ease of use of the System/36 through today's race for server prominence, IBM's AS/400 — now reincarnated as the IBM eServer iSeries 400 — has sported a robust array of productivity features. Highly developed menu functions, extensive help text, and electronic customer support are just a few of the features that contribute to this system's user-friendliness.

Nevertheless, the system's ease of use stops short of "plug-and-go" installation. OS/400's complex structure of system objects — used to support security, work environment, performance tuning, backup, recovery, and a host of other functions — lets you configure a finely tuned and productive machine. However, these objects don't readily lend themselves to education on the fly. As a result, the iSeries and AS/400 require thought, foresight, planning, and preparation to ensure a successful installation.

Believe us, we know. We've experienced this planning and installation process as both customers and vendors, and we'd like to share what we've learned by suggesting a step-by-step approach for planning, installing, and configuring your system. First, we discuss the steps you can and should take before your system arrives. In subsequent chapters, we take you through your first session on the machine, address how to establish your work environment, and show you how to customize your system.

A Note About Names

In October 2000, IBM relaunched its AS/400 product line with the debut of its eServer family of e-business servers. The 270 and 8*xx* models introduced earlier that year — systems featuring IBM's silicon-on-insulator and copper processor technologies — were rechristened with the iSeries 400 name. The iSeries line now also includes IBM's Dedicated Server for Domino and the iSeries 400 model SB2/SB3.

Although IBM will continue to sell systems known as "AS/400s" through at least the end of 2001, the new name of the computer family that is the focus of this book is "iSeries." Throughout the book, therefore, we use the name iSeries to refer to both groups of systems (unless otherwise noted).

An Installation Checklist

The iSeries setup checklist in Figure 1.1 outlines the installation process. You might want to use this checklist as the cover page to a notebook you put together to keep track of your iSeries installation.

FIGURE 1.1
iSeries Setup Checklist

Action	Date completed
Before you install your system	
Develop overall installation plan	
Plan and schedule education	
Develop a migration plan	
Develop a security plan	
Develop an effective backup and recovery plan	
Establish a naming convention for devices and user profiles	
Signing on to the system for the first time	
Establish user ASPs	
Verify software and PTF levels	
Set the security level	
Set the password format control system values	
Change the system-supplied user profile passwords	
Enable/disable autoconfiguration	
Set general system values	
Establishing your work environment	
QMchPool — Machine pool size	
QBasPool — Minimum size of base storage pool	
QBasActLvl — Base pool activity level	
QMaxActLvl — Maximum activity level of the system	
QActJob — Active jobs for which to allocate storage	
QTotJob — Initial total number of jobs for which to allocate storage	
QAdlActJ — Additional number of active jobs to add	
QAdlTotJ — Additional number of jobs to add	
QCtlSbsD — Controlling subsystem	
Establish your subsystems	
Retrieve and modify the start-up program	
Creating user profiles that work	
Understanding user profile parameters	
User profile creation strategy	
User profile sign-on strategy	

Before You Install Your System

The first step in implementing anything complex — especially a computer system — is thorough planning. A successful iSeries installation begins long before your system rolls in the door. The first section of the setup checklist in Figure 1.1 lists tasks you should complete *before* you install your system — preferably even before it arrives.

These items may seem like a lot of work to do before you ever see your system, but this effort will save you and your company time and trouble when you finally begin installing, configuring, securing, and using your new system. Let's look at each item in this section of the checklist.

Develop an Installation Plan

A good installation plan serves as a road map. It guides you and your staff and keeps you focused on the work ahead. Figure 1.2 (page 4) shows a sample installation plan that lists installation details and lets you identify the person responsible for each task and track the schedule.

Note

Although the installation plan includes important considerations about the physical installation — such as electrical, space, and cooling requirements — these requirements are well documented by IBM, and we don't discuss them here.

An overall installation plan helps you put the necessary steps for a successful iSeries setup in writing and tailor these steps to your organization's specific needs. The plan also helps you identify and involve the right people and gives you a schedule with which to work.

Identifying and involving the right people is critical to creating an atmosphere that ensures a smooth transition to your new system. Management must commit itself to the installation process and must understand and agree to the project's priority. Other pending IT projects should be examined and assigned a priority based on staff availability in light of the iSeries installation schedule. Management and the departments you serve must understand and agree on these scheduling changes.

On the IT side, your staff must commit to learning about the iSeries in preparation for installation. Your staff must also commit itself to completing all assigned tasks, many of which (e.g., verifying any conversion of programs and data) may require extra hours.

The time frame outlined in your installation plan will probably change as the delivery date nears. However, even as the schedule changes and is refined, it provides a frame of reference for the total time you'll need to install, configure, and move to the new system.

Figure 1.2
Sample Installation Plan

Action	Person	Start date	Completion date
General			
Verify expected delivery date			
Determine education requirements and scheduling			
Physical requirements			
Plan physical location			
Complete electrical work			
Install UPS system			
Install additional cooling if required			
Physical installation			
Set installation date (delivery may change)			
Arrange physical installation with vendor			
Verify with vendor what system or program product software will be preloaded on the system			
Arrange with vendor or in-house personnel for installation of non-preloaded software			
Program/data migration (if applicable)			
Establish migration plan			
Contact appropriate personnel about involvement in migration, planning, work, and testing			
Identify and document objects to be migrated			
Identify and plan tests to test successful migration			
Operation/support			
Develop security plan			
Develop backup and recovery plan			
Develop strategy for creating appropriate user profiles			
Establish memory pools for the appropriate subsystems			
Determine how users will gain access to the system and the software they need to perform their tasks, and develop an initial sign-on program			

As part of your plan, you must also answer an important question: Can you run the old and new systems parallel for a period of time? If you can run parallel, you can greatly reduce the time needed for the installation process. Running parallel also reduces the risk factor involved in your conversion process.

Plan Education

We can hear you now: "We don't have *time* for classes! We're too *busy* to commit our people to any education." We're sure this will be your response to the suggestion that you plan for training now. We're also sure those statements are absolutely true. But education is a vital part of a successful iSeries installation. Realistically, then, you must schedule key personnel for education.

What key groups of personnel need training? The end users, for one. Their education should focus on the products with which they'll work, such as Client Access. You, your operations people, and your programming staff will also need some training. You must learn such things as security concepts, how to modify your work environment to improve performance, and how to control printer output. Training in relational database design and implementation will improve the applications you install or write, and learning something about the system's fast-path commands will help you feel more at home and productive.

If all this sounds complicated, you're getting the point: You need system-specific education for a smooth transition to the new system. Where can you get such education? Start by asking your vendor for educational offerings. If you buy from a third party, training support will vary from vendor to vendor. You can also arrange to attend courses at certain IBM locations.

In addition, you can find a variety of educational offerings in seminars, automated courses, study guides, one-on-one training sessions, and classroom training courses. The key to successful education is matching education to the user. Matching ensures productive use of the time that employees spend away from their daily duties.

Develop a Migration Plan

The next step in pre-installation planning is to develop a migration plan. It's almost certain that, at a minimum, you'll need to migrate data to your new system. If you're migrating to the iSeries from some other type of system, it's also a safe bet that this data will need to be reformatted for your new applications. A well-prepared plan can greatly reduce the time required to get your applications up and running, and it can increase the odds that your applications and data won't suffer from integrity problems.

Running parallel for a while greatly reduces the risk involved. You can migrate your applications in stages, testing and verifying each program as you go. If you can't run parallel, you must complete your migration process on the first try — a much trickier proposition. If you take this route, we recommend you seek an experienced outside source for help in the migration and conversion process.

If you decide to begin conversion immediately, be sure you know what you're getting into. Depending on your current system, conversion could involve one week to six months of work for your staff. Again, a good outside consultant, used in a way that provides educational benefits for your staff, could be an immense help. True, you could simply pay a consultant to convert your database and programs for you, but that approach doesn't educate your staff about the new system. Also, let us offer you a warning:

Caution

If you plan to replace your existing system and completely remove it before installing your iSeries, you are absolutely asking for trouble! If you find yourself forced into such a scenario, get help. Hire a consultant who has successfully migrated systems to the iSeries or the AS/400.

Develop a Security Plan

We can't overstate the importance of a sound security plan. You want to ensure system integrity, and implementing a robust security scheme from the outset is crucial to this endeavor. Figure 1.3 shows a basic security plan.

FIGURE 1.3
Sample Security Plan

Before iSeries installation:

1. Select security level (a minimum of 30 is recommended, with 40 suggested).
2. Determine password format rules.
3. Identify all system users.
4. List user roles (i.e., security groups, such as programmers, accounts receivable, accounts payable, operations).
5. Place users into role categories for user class and special authorities.
6. Examine application software (e.g., accounting packages, inventory packages) for specific security provisions, and determine whether users need specific authorities for these objects. Document methodologies for using application security provisions to ensure they fit with the system security plans you've developed.

After iSeries installation:

7. Set QSecurity system value to chosen level (10, 20, 30, 40, or 50).
8. IPL the system to activate chosen QSecurity level.
9. Change passwords of system-supplied profiles.
10. Set password format system values.
11. Create role (group) profiles (these should have no password assigned so that they can't be used when signing on to the system).
12. Create individual users' profiles, specifying the proper group profile where appropriate. Grant authority for group profiles to access objects on the system needed to perform tasks.
13. Grant or revoke specific individual user authorities as necessary.

System Security Level

The first and most significant step in planning your security is deciding which security level you need. The iSeries provides five levels of security: 10, 20, 30, 40, and 50.

Security Level 10

System security level 10 might more aptly be called security level zero, or "physical security only." At level 10, the physical security measures you take, such as locking the door to the computer room, are all you have. If a user has access to a workstation with a sign-on screen, he or she can simply press Enter and the system will create a user profile for the session and let the user proceed. The profile the system creates in this case has *AllObj (all object) special authority, which is sufficient for the user to change or delete any object on the system.

Although user profiles aren't required at level 10, you could still create and assign them and ask each user to enter his or her assigned user profile name at sign-on. You could then tailor the profiles to have the appropriate special authorities — you could even grant or revoke authorities to objects. However, level 10 provides no way to enforce the use of those assigned profiles and, thus, no way to enforce restricted special authorities or actual resource security.

Simply stated, level 10 provides no security. In fact, beginning with Version 4, Release 3 (V4R3) of OS/400, you can no longer set the security level to 10. (Level 10 was the default security level value shipped with earlier releases of OS/400.) If, however, your system is at security level 10 and you upgrade to V4R3 or a later release, the system will remain at security level 10. If you then change the security level to some other value, you won't be able to change it back to level 10.

Security Level 20

Security level 20 adds password security. At level 20, a user must have a user profile and a valid password to gain access to the system. Level 20 institutes minimum security by requiring users to know a user profile and password, thus deterring unauthorized access. However, as with level 10, the default special authorities for each user class include *AllObj special authority; therefore, resource security is, by default, bypassed.

At security level 20, only a security officer or a user with security administrator authority can create user profiles. Also, the limit capabilities feature is honored.

Although you can tailor the user profiles, the inherent weakness of level 20 remains: By default, resource security is not implemented. The *AllObj special authority assigned by default to every user profile bypasses any form of resource security. To implement resource security at level 20, you must remove the *AllObj special authority from any profiles that don't absolutely require it (only the security officer and the security administrator need *AllObj special authority). You then must remember to remove this special authority each time you create a new user profile.

This method of systematically removing *AllObj authority is pointless because, by default, level 30 security does this for you. On a production system, you must be able to explicitly authorize or deny user authority to specific objects. Therefore, level 20 security is inadequate in the initial configuration, requiring you to make significant changes to mimic what level 30 provides automatically.

Security Level 30

Level 30 supports resource security (users do not receive *AllObj authority by default). Resource security lets objects be accessed only by users who have authority to them. The authority to work with, create, modify, or delete objects must be either specifically granted or received as a result of existing default public authority.

All production systems should be set at security level 30 or higher (level 40 or 50). Production machines require resource security to effectively safeguard corporate data, programs, and other production objects and to prevent unintentional data loss or modification.

Security Level 40

Although security level 30 provides resource security, it's possible for programs to circumvent security in some instances. To address this shortcoming, level 40 adds a level of operating system integrity security. System integrity security strengthens level 30 security in four ways:

- by providing program states and object domains
- by preventing use of restricted machine interface (MI) instructions
- by validating job initiation authority
- by preventing restoration of invalid or modified programs

Level 40 provides the security necessary to prevent a vendor or an individual from creating or restoring programs on the system that might threaten system integrity at the MI level. This protection ensures an additional level of confidence when you work with products created by outside sources. Yet if the need arises to create a program that infringes on system integrity security, you can explicitly change the security level to 30. The advantage of using level 40 is that you control that decision.

Note

Some packaged software (e.g., some system tools) may require access to restricted MI instructions and will fail at level 40. In these cases, you can ask the vendor when the product will be compatible with level 40 and decide what to do based on the response.

Security Level 50

The primary purpose of security level 50 is to comply with the U.S. Department of Defense (DOD) C2 security requirements. IBM added specific features to OS/400 to comply with DOD C2 security, as well as to further enhance the system integrity security introduced in level 40. In addition to all the security features and functions found at all lower OS/400 security levels (e.g., 30, 40), level 50 adds

- restrictions for user domain object types — *UsrSpc (user space), *UsrIdx (user index), and *UsrQ (user queue)
- parameter validation
- restriction of message handling between user and system state programs
- prevention of modifications to internal control blocks
- provisions to make the QTemp library a temporary object

Because of the additional checking that the system performs at level 50, you may experience some performance degradation.

Those whose shops require DOD C2 compliance can find more information about security level 50 and other OS/400 security features (e.g., auditing capabilities) in the IBM manual *Security – Enabling for C2* (SC41-5303).

Password Format Rules

Your next task in security planning is to determine rules for passwords. In other words, what format restrictions should you apply for passwords? Without format requirements, you're likely to end up with passwords such as "joe," "sue," "xxx," and "12345." But are these passwords secret? Will they safeguard your system?

You can strengthen your security plan's foundation by instituting some rules that encourage users to create passwords that are *secret*, *hard to guess*, and *regularly changed*. However, know that "hard to guess" sometimes translates into "hard to remember" — and when that happens, users simply write down their passwords so they won't forget them. The following password rules will help establish a good starting point for controlling password formats.

Rule 1 says *passwords must be a minimum of seven characters and a maximum of 10 characters*. This rule deters users who lack the energy to think past three characters when conjuring up that secret, unguessable password.

Rule 2 builds on Rule 1: *Passwords must have at least one digit*. This rule ensures that passwords are more than just a familiar name, word, or place.

Rule 3 can deter those users who think they can remember only one or two characters and thus make their password something like "XXXXX6" or "X1X." Rule 3 simply states that *passwords can't use the same character more than once or can't use the same character consecutively*.

On a similar note, Rule 4 states that *passwords can't use adjacent digits*. This restriction prevents users from creating passwords such as "1111," "1234," or even their social security number.

With these four rules in place, you can feel more confident that only sound passwords will be used on the system. You can enhance your password security still further with one additional rule. Rule 5 says *you should assign passwords a time interval for expiration.* You can set this interval to let a password remain effective for from one to 366 days, thus ensuring that users change their passwords regularly.

Passwords are a part of *user profiles*, which you'll create to define the users to the system. Laying the groundwork for these user profiles is the next concern of your security plan.

Identifying System Users

Before you install the new machine, you should identify the people who will use the system. Obtain each user's full name and department and the basic applications he or she will require on the system. Some users, such as operators and programmers, will need to control jobs and execute save/restore functions on the system. Other users, such as accounts receivable personnel, need only to manipulate spooled files and execute applications from menus.

Once you identify the users and determine which system functions they need access to, you can assign each user to one of the following classes:

- *SecOfr — security officer
- *SecAdm — security administrator
- *Pgmr — programmer
- *SysOpr — system operator
- *User — user

To better understand these user classes, let's examine the special authorities you can assign to users. Figure 1.4 shows the default special authorities for each user class.

FIGURE 1.4
Default Special Authorities

	Default special authorities							
User class	***AllObj***	***Audit***	***IOSysCfg***	***JobCtl***	***SavSys***	***SecAdm***	***Service***	***SplCtl***
*SecOfr	✓	✓	✓	✓	✓	✓	✓	✓
*SecAdm	✓[1]			✓[1]	✓[1]	✓		
*Pgmr	✓[1]			✓[1]	✓[1]			
*SysOpr	✓[1]			✓	✓			
*User	✓[1]				✓[1]			

[1] Security levels 10 and 20 only

Special authorities let users perform certain system functions. Without the appropriate special authorities, these functions are unavailable to a user. The iSeries provides eight special authorities:

- *AllObj (all object) authority, as you've seen, lets users access any system object. This authority alone, however, doesn't let users create, modify, or delete user profiles.
- *Audit (audit) authority lets users start and stop security auditing and control security auditing characteristics.
- *IOSysCfg (system configuration) authority lets users change system configuration information. For example, they can configure I/O devices, work with TCP/IP servers, and configure communications.
- *JobCtl (job control) authority lets users change, display, hold, release, cancel, and clear all jobs on the system. Users can also control spooled files in output queues for which OprCtl(*Yes) is specified.
- *SavSys (save system) authority lets users save, restore, and free storage for all objects.
- *SecAdm (security administrator) authority lets users create, change, and delete user profiles.
- *Service (service) authority lets users perform functions from the System Service Tools, a group of executable programs used for various service functions (e.g., line traces, diagnostics).
- *SplCtl (spool control) authority lets users delete, display, hold, and release their own spooled files and spooled files owned by other users.

Keep in mind that the functions mentioned above are only a primary subset of the functions that special authorities permit.

Your IT staff members normally will be in either the *Pgmr or the *SysOpr class. Your end users should all reside in the *User class. Typically, the *User class carries no special authorities (as Figure 1.4 shows), which is appropriate for most users. These users can work within their own job and work with their own spooled files.

Caution

One rule of thumb when assigning classes is that you should never set up your system so that a user performs regular work with the *SecOfr class. The iSeries has a special QSecOfr user profile; when the security officer must perform a duty, the person responsible should sign on using this profile to perform the needed task. Using security officer authority to perform normal work is like playing with a loaded gun.

When you create user profiles, you can use the special authorities parameter to override the authorities granted by the user class. Doing so lets you tailor authorities as appropriate for specific users. For instance, a user profile might have a user class of *SysOpr, which grants the user special authorities for job control and save/restore functions. By entering only *SavSys for the special authorities parameter, you can instruct the system to grant only this special authority, ignoring the normal defaults for the *SysOpr user class.

In addition to considering special authorities, you must plan specific authorities, which control the objects a user can work with (e.g., job descriptions, data files, programs, menus). Going through the remainder of the pre-installation security planning process — checking your applications for security provisions — will help you decide which users need which specific authorities and will help you finish laying the groundwork for user profiles on your new system.

Of course, that's not the end of your security planning. You'll also need to address such issues as Internet- and TCP/IP-related concerns. You can find useful information about these topics in the following IBM documentation:

- *AS/400 Internet Security: Protecting Your AS/400 from HARM on the Internet* (SG24-4929)
- *An Implementation Guide for AS/400 Security and Auditing: Including C2, Cryptography, Communications, and PC Connectivity* (GG24-4200)
- *Tips and Tools for Securing Your AS/400* (SC41-5300)

Wizardry and Advice

To help with your security configuration, IBM provides automated assistance with two helpful tools: Security Wizard and Security Advisor. We suggest you take advantage of these options.

Security Wizard asks a series of questions, using the responses to generate reports with various security configuration suggestions. You can optionally apply the suggestions to your system's configuration automatically.

To use the wizard, you must connect to the iSeries using Client Access and a user profile with *AllObj, *Audit, *IOSysCfg, and *SecAdm special authorities. To begin using the wizard, take these steps:

1. In Client Access, open Operations Navigator.
2. If necessary, expand the tree for the system with which you want to work.
3. Right-click the Security folder, and select Configure.

Then simply follow the prompts to complete your session with Security Wizard.

If you're not using Operations Navigator, you can take advantage of Security Advisor. Security Advisor is a Web-based version of Security Wizard. Unlike the wizard, however, the advisor won't automatically configure your system (although it will create a CL program you can cut and paste onto the iSeries to do the task). You can access Security Advisor by pointing your browser to *http://www.as400.ibm.com/tstudio/secure1/index_av.htm* on the Internet. Simply answer the questions, and then click Calculate Recommendations.

Develop a Backup and Recovery Plan

Although it may seem premature to plan for backup and recovery on your as-yet-undelivered iSeries, we assure you it isn't. First, you shouldn't assume that the backup and recovery plan for your existing system will still work with the new system. Second, the iSeries has a variety of powerful backup and recovery options with which you may not be familiar. Some of these options are difficult and time-consuming to install if you wait until you've installed your applications and data on the new system.

The single-level storage of the iSeries minimizes disk-head contention and eliminates the need to track and manage the Volume Table of Contents. However, single-level storage can also create recovery problems. Because single-level storage fragments objects randomly among all the system's disks, the loss of any one disk can result in damage to every object on the system.

An *auxiliary storage pool (ASP)* is one of those features that are much easier to implement when you install your system rather than later. An ASP is a group of disk units. Your iSeries will be delivered with only the system ASP (ASP 1) installed. Figure 1.5A shows auxiliary storage configured only as the system ASP. The system ASP holds all system programs and most user data.

FIGURE 1.5A

Disk Configuration with Only a System ASP

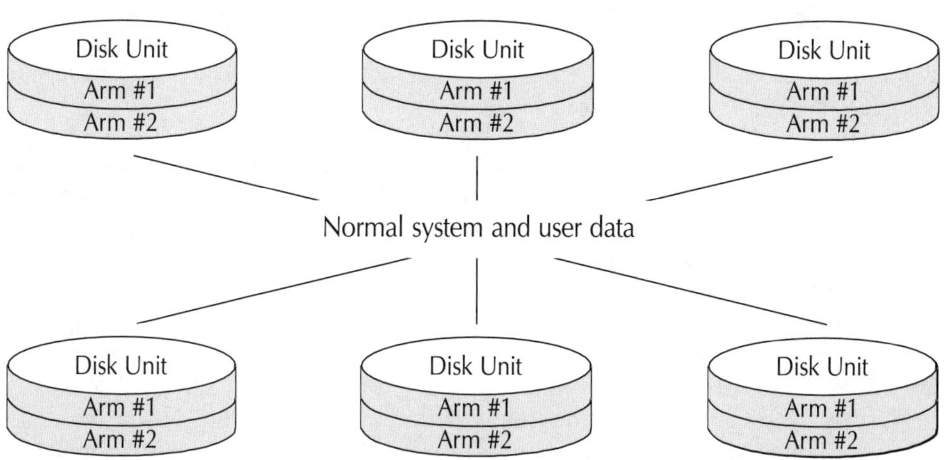

You can customize your disk storage configuration by partitioning some auxiliary storage into one or more user ASPs (Figure 1.5B).

FIGURE 1.5B
Disk Configuration Including User ASPs

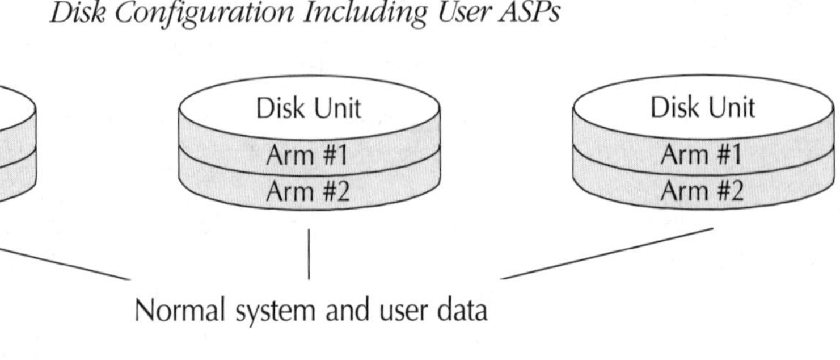

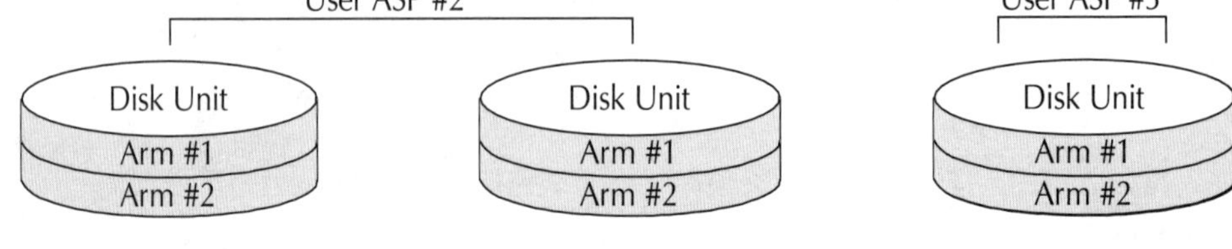

User ASPs provide protection from disk failures by segregating specific user data or backup data. Thus, if you lose a disk unit in the system ASP, your restore time is reduced to the minimum time of restoring the operating system and the objects in the system ASP, while data residing in the user ASPs will be available without any restore. If you lose a disk unit in a user ASP, your restore time will include only the time it takes to restore the user data in that user ASP.

You can use user ASPs for journaling and to hold save files. Journaling automatically creates a separate copy of file changes *as they occur*, thus letting you recover every change made to journaled files up to the instant of the failure. If you have online data entry — such as orders taken over the telephone — that lacks backup files for the entered data, you should strongly consider using journaling as part of your backup and recovery plan. Although you don't need user ASPs to implement journaling, they do make recovery (which is difficult under the best of circumstances) easier. If you don't journal to a user ASP, you should save your journal receivers (i.e., the objects that hold all file changes recorded by journaling) to media regularly and frequently.

User ASPs also protect save files from disk failures. A save file is a special type of physical file to which you can target your backup operation. Save files have two major advantages over backing up to media. The first is that you can back up "unattended" because you don't have to mount and dismount media. The second advantage is that backing up to disk is often much faster than backing up to tape or diskette. The major (and probably obvious) disadvantage is that save files require additional disk storage. Nevertheless, save files are worthwhile in many cases, and when used, isolating save files in a user ASP provides that extra measure of protection.

Two methods for safeguarding against disk failures and data loss are *mirrored protection* and *device parity protection*. Although there's an initial investment with either of these methods, the level of protection is significant for companies that rely on providing 24-hour service.

Mirrored protection is a software function designed to prevent data loss. It does so by using duplicates of disk-related hardware components. Should one of the components fail, your system remains available with no loss of data. Different levels of mirrored protection are available, depending on the hardware you duplicate. You can duplicate the following:

- disk units
- disk controllers
- disk I/O processors
- a bus

Like mirrored protection, device parity protection is designed to prevent data loss and to keep your system available in the case of a disk failure. Unlike mirrored protection, though, device parity protection is a hardware function. Device parity protection is similar to RAID-5 technology. Parity information is created and, for performance reasons, is spread across multiple units. When a disk failure occurs, the disk subsystem controller automatically reconstructs the data using the active units in the disk unit subsystem.

The point of this discussion is that you need to plan ahead and decide which type of disk protection you'll employ so you can be ready to implement your plan when the system is delivered, when the disk drives aren't yet full of information you'd have to save before making any storage configuration changes.

For more information about iSeries backup and recovery, see Chapters 15 and 16.

Establish Naming Conventions

Naming conventions vary greatly from one IT department to the next. The conventions you choose should result in names that are syntactically correct and consistent yet also easily remembered and understood by end users and programmers alike. A good standard does more than simply help you name files, programs, and other objects; it also helps you efficiently locate and identify objects and devices on your system. If your naming conventions are in place before you install your system, they'll help installation go smoothly and quickly.

Device Names

The naming convention you choose should be meaningful and should allow for growth of your enterprise. Let's look at an example:

- You have three locations for order entry: Montgomery, Alabama; Orlando, Florida; and Atlanta, Georgia.
- You have five order entry clerks at each location.
- You have one printer at each location.

You could let the system automatically configure all your workstations and printers, which would result in names such as DSP02, DSP03, and PRT02. But by configuring the devices yourself and assigning meaningful names, you could give your devices names such as ALDsp01, ALDsp02, FLDsp01, FLDsp02, and GAPrt01. Because these names contain a two-letter abbreviation for the state, they are more meaningful and useful than the names the iSeries would assign automatically. However, this convention would pose a problem if you had two offices in the same state. To allow for growth of the enterprise, you might instead incorporate the branch-office number into the names, resulting in names such as C01Dsp01 to identify a control unit for branch office 01, display station 01. Such a naming convention would help your operations personnel locate and control devices in multiple locations.

User Profile Names

You'll also need a standard for naming user profiles. There are those who believe a user profile name should be as similar as possible to the name of the person to whom it belongs (e.g., WMadden, MJones, MaryM, JohnZ). This approach can work well when there are only a few end users. This strategy lets operations personnel identify employees by their user profiles. The drawback to this method is that it results in profiles that are easily guessed and thus provides a door for unauthorized access, leaving only the password to figure out. For example, one of us once had a friend and co-worker, in a shop with such a strategy, whose Italian ancestry was of particular importance to her. It took only a few tries to sign on to the system under her user profile. Next, the focus shifted to the password. Let's see...TORTELLINI, CAPELLINI, RIGATONI — ah, there's the password! Good guess? No. Bad profile and password. There are only so many Italian pasta names.

Another opinion holds that user profile names should be completely meaningless (e.g., 2LR50M3ZT4, Q83S@06Y7B, SYS23431) and should be maintained in some type of user information file. The use of meaningless names makes profiles difficult to guess and doesn't link a name to a department or location that might change as the employee moves in the company. The user information file documents security-related information, such as the individual to whom the profile belongs and the department in which the user works. This naming method is the most secure, but it often meets with resistance from the users, who find their profiles difficult to remember.

A third approach is to use a naming standard that aids system administration. Under this strategy, each user profile name identifies the user's location and perhaps function to sharpen the ability to audit the system security plan. For instance, if you monitor the history log or use the security journal for auditing, this approach enables you to quickly identify users and the jobs they're doing.

To implement this strategy, your naming convention should incorporate the user's location or department and a unique identifier for the user's name. For example, if John E. Smith works as one of the order entry clerks at the Georgia location, you might assign one of the following profiles:

- GAJSmith — In this profile, the first two letters represent the location (GA for Georgia), and the remainder consists of the first letter of the user's first name followed by as much of the last name as will fit in the remaining seven characters.
- GAOEJES — This example is similar, but the location code is followed by the department (OE for order entry) and the user's initials. This method provides more departmental information while reducing the unique name identifier to initials.
- B12OEJES — This example is identical to the second, but the Georgia branch is identified by its branch number, B12.

When profile names provide this type of information, programs in your system that supply user menus or functions can resolve them at run time based on location, department, or group. As a result, both your security plan and your initial program drivers can be dynamic, flexible, and easily maintained. In addition, auditing is more effective because you can easily spot departmental trends. And user profile organization and maintenance tasks are enhanced by having a naming standard to follow. However, such profiles are less secure than meaningless profiles because they're easy to guess once someone understands the naming scheme. This leaves only the password to guess, thus rendering the system less secure.

As you'll discover in Chapter 3, we believe in maintaining user profiles in a user information file. Such a file makes it easy to maintain up-to-date user profile information, such as initial menu, initial values for programs (e.g., initial branch number, department number), and the user's full name formatted for use in outgoing invoices or order confirmations. When a user transfers to another location or moves to a new department, you should deactivate the old profile and assign a new one to maintain a security history. A user information file helps you keep what amounts to a user profile audit trail. Furthermore, your applications can retrieve information from the file and use it to establish the work environment, library list, and initial menu for a user.

A final consideration in choosing a naming convention for user profiles is whether your users will have access to multiple systems. If they will, you can simplify functions by using the same name for each user's profile on all systems. To do this, you must consider any limitations the other systems in the network place on user profile names and apply those limitations in creating the user profiles for your system. For instance, another platform in your network may limit the number of characters allowed for user profile names. To enable your user profiles to be valid across the network, you'll have to abide by that limitation.

You need to determine what user profile naming convention will work best for your environment. For the most secure environment, a meaningless profile name is best. User profiles that consist of the end user's name are the least secure and are often used in small shops where everyone knows (and is on good terms with) everyone else. A convention that incorporates the user's location and function is a compromise between security and system management and implementation that suits many shops.

What Next?

Okay, you've made it this far! You've planned and prepared, and then planned some more. You've planned education, scheduled classes, and started to prepare your users for things to expect with the iSeries. You've planned for security and for backup and recovery, and you know how you'll name the objects on your system. You feel ready to start the installation. But after your vendor helps you install the hardware, how do you implement all your carefully made plans? In the next chapter, we discuss what happens once the power is on.

Chapter 2

That Important First Session

Up to this point (if you've done your homework), you have committed, planned, and planned some more for your new iSeries system. Planning is a significant portion of the total installation process, but now the system is up and running! The microcode is all there, the operating system is installed, all your program products are loaded on the system, and the vendor is packing up the tools.

Once the power is on, it's time to take some immediate steps to put your carefully made plans into action. Figure 2.1 lists the steps you'll need to take once your system is installed.

FIGURE 2.1

First Steps After Installation

Signing on to the iSeries for the first time:

Establish user ASPs
Verify software and PTF levels
Set the security level
Set the password format control system values
Change the system-supplied user profile passwords
Enable/disable autoconfiguration
Set general system values

Establishing your work environment:

Set system values for work-management objects:

QMchPool	Machine pool size
QBasPool	Minimum size of base storage pool
QBasActLvl	Base pool activity level
QMaxActLvl	Maximum activity level of the system
QActJob	Active jobs for which to allocate storage
QTotJob	Initial total number of jobs for which to allocate storage
QAdlActJ	Additional number of active jobs to add
QAdlTotJ	Additional number of jobs to add

Establish your subsystems
Retrieve and modify the start-up program

Establish User ASPs

First, examine your backup and recovery plan to see whether you've decided to use auxiliary storage pools (ASPs). If you have, work with the installation team to remove disk units from the system ASP and configure them for a user ASP.

Allocate plenty of time for this process. It may take a long time to remove the units because the system must copy their contents to other units in the system ASP. If ASPs are part of your backup plans, you can begin breathing easier once this work is done, knowing that you're already better prepared for disasters.

Verify Software and PTF Levels

Next, verify that the program products you ordered are installed on the system. The vendor should help you load these products if they aren't already preloaded on the system. (If you don't have your program products and manuals, make sure you follow up on their delivery.)

Next, determine whether the latest available cumulative program temporary fix (PTF) package, as well as the appropriate group PTF packages, are installed on your system. The vendor should know the latest PTF level available and can help you determine whether that level exists on your system. If you don't have the latest PTFs, order them now so you can apply them before you move your iSeries into the production phase of installation.

For more information about PTFs and installing PTFs, see Chapter 6.

Signing On for the First Time

With ASPs configured and the latest PTFs installed, you're ready to sign on to your iSeries. Use the user profile QSecOfr to sign on, and enter **QSECOFR** — the preset password for that profile. Don't start playing with your new system yet, though! You have some important chores to do during your first session.

Set the Security Level

Your iSeries is shipped with the security level set at 40. We suggest you operate at least at this level. If you desire some level other than level 40, you need to reset the security level as the first step in implementing your security plan.

You can change the security level now by keying in the ChgSysVal (Change System Value) command:

```
ChgSysVal SysVal(QSecurity) Value(nn)
```

where *nn* is 20, 30, 40, or 50. The change will take effect when you perform an initial program load (IPL) of the system.

Because you must perform IPLs to implement several settings on your iSeries, you might as well practice one now to put the chosen security level into action. On the system panel, select a normal IPL from the B source, and then power down the system with an automatic restart by keying in

```
PwrDwnSys Option(*Immed) Restart(*Yes)
```

When the IPL is completed, your new security level will be in effect.

Set the Password Format Control System Values

The next important step in implementing your security plan is setting the system values that control password selection. You should have decided already on the password rules. Changing the system values to enforce those rules is relatively easy.

In Chapter 1, we recommended five rules to guarantee the use of secure passwords on your system. To implement Rule 1, that passwords must be at least seven characters and at most 10 characters, enter the commands

```
ChgSysVal SysVal(QPwdMinLen) Value(7)
ChgSysVal SysVal(QPwdMaxLen) Value(10)
```

The system value *QPwdMinLen* (Minimum password length) sets the minimum length of passwords used on the system. System value *QPwdMaxLen* (Maximum password length) specifies the maximum length of passwords used on the system.

To implement Rule 2, that passwords must contain at least one digit, enter

```
ChgSysVal SysVal(QPwdRqdDgt) Value('1')
```

Setting system value *QPwdRqdDgt* (Required digit in password) to 1 requires all passwords to include at least one digit.

For Rule 3, passwords cannot use the same character more than once or the same character consecutively, enter either

```
ChgSysVal SysVal(QPwdLmtRep) Value('1')
```

or

```
ChgSysVal SysVal(QPwdLmtRep) Value('2')
```

respectively. Setting system value *QPwdLmtRep* (Limit repeating characters in password) to 1 prevents characters from repeating at all. A value of 2 prevents characters from repeating consecutively.

For Rule 4, passwords cannot use adjacent digits, enter

```
ChgSysVal SysVal(QPwdLmtAjc) Value('1')
```

System value *QPwdLmtAjc* (Limit adjacent digits in password) prevents users from creating passwords with numbers next to each other, such as a social security number or a telephone number.

Rule 5 states that passwords should be assigned a time frame for expiration. You implement this rule by entering a ChgSysVal command such as

```
ChgSysVal SysVal(QPwdExpItv) Value(60)
```

System value *QPwdExpItv* (Password expiration interval) specifies the length of time, in days, that a user's password remains valid before the system instructs the user to change passwords. The value can range from 1 to 366. You also can set the password expiration interval individually for user profiles by using the PwdExpItv parameter of the user profile. This option is helpful because certain profiles, such as the QSecOfr profile, are particularly sensitive and should require a password change more often for additional security.

Change the System-Supplied User Profile Passwords

OS/400 provides several user profiles that serve various system functions. Some of these profiles, such as default-owner user profile QDftOwn, have no password, which means you can't sign on using that user profile. However, every iSeries is shipped with passwords for the system-supplied profiles listed below, and these passwords are preset to the profile name. For example, the preset password for the QSecOfr profile is QSecOfr. Therefore, one of your first steps should be to change the passwords for these profiles:

- QSecOfr (security officer)
- QSysOpr (system operator)
- QPgmr (programmer)
- QUser (user)
- QSrv (service representative)
- QSrvBas (basic service representative)

To enter the new passwords, sign on as the QSecOfr profile and execute the following command for each user profile listed above:

```
ChgUsrPrf UsrPrf(UserProfile) Password(NewPassword)
```

You can accomplish these changes more easily using the SETUP menu provided in OS/400. Type **Go Setup**, and then select option 11, "Change passwords for IBM-supplied users" to work with the panel shown in Figure 2.2.

FIGURE 2.2

Change Passwords for IBM-Supplied Users Panel

```
                    Change Passwords for IBM-Supplied Users
                                                          System:   AS400
Type new password below for IBM-supplied user, type password again to verify
  change, then press Enter.

New security officer (QSECOFR) password  . . . . . . . . . .
  New password (to verify) . . . . . . . . . . . . . . . . .

New system operator (QSYSOPR) password . . . . . . . . . . .
  New password (to verify) . . . . . . . . . . . . . . . . .

New programmer (QPGMR) password  . . . . . . . . . . . . . .
  New password (to verify) . . . . . . . . . . . . . . . . .

New user (QUSER) password  . . . . . . . . . . . . . . . . .
  New password (to verify) . . . . . . . . . . . . . . . . .

New service (QSRV) password  . . . . . . . . . . . . . . . .
  New password (to verify) . . . . . . . . . . . . . . . . .

                                                                    More...
F1=Help   F3=Exit   F5=Refresh   F12=Cancel
```

You can assign a password of *None (for any of the above profiles except QSecOfr), or you can assign new passwords that conform to the password rules you've just implemented. Once you change the passwords for the system-supplied profiles, write down the new passwords and store them in a secure place for future reference.

Enable/Disable Autoconfiguration

After you've taken steps to secure your system, the next important action concerns system value *QAutoCfg* (Automatic device configuration), which controls device autoconfiguration and helps you establish your naming convention.

When QAutoCfg is set to the value 1 (the shipped default), devices are configured automatically and are named according to the standard specified in system value *QDevNaming* (Device naming convention). The possible values for QDevNaming are *Normal, *S36, and *DevAdr. If QDevNaming is set to *Normal, the system assigns device names according to its own standard (e.g., DSP01 and DSP02 for workstations, PRT01 and PRT02 for printers). If the option *S36 is specified, the system automatically names devices according to System/36 naming conventions (e.g., W1 and W2 for workstations, P1 and P2 for printers). When QDevNaming's value is *DevAdr, device names are derived from their addresses (e.g., DSP010207, PRT010218).

Although automatic configuration gives you an easy way to configure new devices (you can plug in a new terminal, attach the cable, and — poof! — the system configures it), it can frustrate your efforts to establish a helpful naming convention for your new machine. Therefore, after the system has been IPLed and the initial configuration is complete, you should set the value of QAutoCfg to 0, which instructs the system not to autoconfigure devices. You can reset autoconfiguration by executing the command

```
ChgSysVal SysVal(QAutoCfg) Value('0')
```

This change takes effect when you IPL the system. (If you haven't done so already, you should IPL the system now to put into effect the changes you've made for security level, password rules, and autoconfiguration.) You must now configure devices yourself when needed.

Admittedly, configuring devices is much more of a pain than letting the system configure them for you. However, we recommend this approach because it usually requires more planning, better logic, better structure, a better naming convention, and better documentation. At times, you may want to enable autoconfiguration temporarily to create a configuration object automatically and then disable autoconfiguration again. Configuring devices is beyond the scope of this chapter, but you can find more information about it in *Basic System Operation, Administration, and Problem Handling* (SC41-5206).

Set General System Values

Several times now, you've set system values. The iSeries provides many such values to control basic system functions. To further familiarize you with your new system, let's take a look at a few of the most significant system values. (You can use the WrkSysVal, or Work with System Values, command to examine and change system values.)

System value *QAbnormSw* (Previous end of system indicator) isn't a value that you modify; the system itself maintains the proper value. When the system is IPLed, this system value contains a 0 if the previous end of system was normal (meaning you powered down the system and no error occurred). However, if the previous end of system was abnormal (meaning a power outage caused system failure, a hardware error stopped the system, or some other abnormal termination of the system occurred), QAbnormSw will be 1. The benefit of system value QAbnormSw is that during IPL, your initial start-up program can check this value. If the value is 1, meaning the previous end of system was abnormal, you might want to handle the IPL differently, such as in the start-up of the user subsystems.

System value *QCmnRcyLmt* (Communications recovery limits) controls the limits for automatic communications recovery. This system value is composed of two numbers. The first number controls how many times the system will try to recover from an error. The second indicates how many minutes will expire between attempts at recovery. The initial setting is '0' '0'. This setting instructs the system to perform no error recovery when a communications line or control unit fails. If left in this mode, the system prompts the operator with a system message asking whether to attempt error recovery. The value '5' '5' would instruct the system to attempt recovery five times and to wait five minutes between those attempts. Only if recovery had not been established at the end of those attempts would the system prompt the operator with a system message.

Note

A word about the use of QCmnRcyLmt: If you decide to use the system error recovery by setting this system value, you'll add some work overhead to your system because error recovery has a high priority on the iSeries. In other words, if a communications line or a control unit fails and error recovery kicks in, you may see a spike in your response time. If you experience severe communications difficulties, reset QCmnRcyLmt to the initial value of '0' '0' and respond manually to the failure messages.

System value *QMaxSign* (Maximum sign-on attempts allowed) specifies the number of invalid sign-on attempts to allow before the action specified in system value *QMaxSgnAcn* (Action to take for failed sign-on attempts) is taken. We recommend a QMaxSign value of 3 for reasonable security. Setting QMaxSign to 3 means that after a user tries unsuccessfully three times to sign on to the system (because of using an invalid user profile or password), the system will disable the device, the user profile being used, or both (the action performed depends on the value of QMaxSgnAcn). You'll have to re-enable the device or user profile to make it available again.

System value *QPrtDev* (Printer device description) specifies which printer device is the default system printer. The initial value is PRT01; however, you can change this value to specify a printer device of your choice.

These are just a few of the system values available on the iSeries. For a complete list of system values and their initial values, consult *OS/400 Work Management* (SC41-5306). It's worth your time to read about each of these values and determine which ones need to be modified for your installation.

Establishing Your Work Environment

Okay, you've covered a lot of ground so far. You've made the system secure, reset the autoconfiguration value, and looked at some general system values. However, it's not time for fun and games yet. Now, you should establish your work environment.

When the system is shipped, your work environment is simple. Memory is divided into a few basic storage pools. For instance, the machine pool provides storage for system jobs. The base storage pool contains storage that's not assigned to any other pool. In the simplest of environments, dividing storage between the machine pool, a storage pool for spool writers, and the base storage pool is adequate. Your interactive and batch jobs share the main storage from the base storage pool.

For many environments, this arrangement may be functional, but it's neither effective nor efficient. For example, if the system value that sets the machine pool size is too low, performance is slow; if the value is too high, you waste main storage. Thus, you need to tune your system for optimal performance.

Performance tuning, because of its complexities, usually evolves over time. You typically work to achieve a reasonably adequate performance model and then fine-tune as you go. It's beyond the scope of this chapter to teach you to tune your system. For that, we suggest you employ the help of performance experts, but we can introduce you to some important work-management system values that govern performance characteristics. You can learn more about these values in *OS/400 Work Management.*

QMchPool (Machine pool size) is the system value that specifies the amount of memory allocated to the machine (*Machine) pool. *OS/400 Work Management* provides a formula for calculating the amount of storage to reserve for the machine pool. You should consider performing the calculations and comparing your results with system value QMchPool.

QBasPool (Minimum size of base storage pool) specifies the minimum size of the base (*Base) storage pool. Memory not allocated to any other storage pool stays in the base storage pool. This pool is shared among many subsystems, and it supports system jobs (e.g., QSplMaint, QSysArb, QSysWrk, Scpf, and subsystem monitors) as well as system transients (e.g., file open/close operations). Enter the WrkSysSts (Work with System Status) command to see the amount of storage the machine has reserved for these functions.

QBasActLvl (Base pool activity level) sets the maximum activity level of the base storage pool. This value indicates how many system and user threads can concurrently compete for the base storage pool's storage.

QMaxActLvl (Maximum activity level of the system) sets the maximum activity level of the system by specifying the number of threads that can compete at the same time for main storage and processor resources. By examining each subsystem, you can establish the total number of activity levels; QMaxActLvl's value must at least equal that number or be set higher. We suggest you set QMaxActLvl to a value five above the total number of activity levels allowed in all subsystems. This setting will let you increase activity levels for individual subsystems for tuning purposes without having to increase QMaxActLvl. However, if the number of subsystem activity levels exceeds the value in QMaxActLvl, the system executes only the number of levels specified in QMaxActLvl, resulting in unnecessary waiting for your users. Therefore, if you increase the total number of activity levels in your subsystems or if you add subsystems, you must increase QMaxActLvl.

QActJob (Active jobs for which to allocate storage) is the system value that specifies the initial number of active jobs for which the system should allocate storage during IPL. This value should reflect the estimated number of jobs active during a period of typical heavy usage. We suggest you set this number to approximately 10 percent above this estimated number of active jobs. For example, if you have an average of 50 active jobs, set QActJob to 55. Setting QActJob and QTotJob (covered next) to values that closely match your requirements helps the iSeries correctly allocate resources for your users at system start-up time instead of continually having to allocate more work space (e.g., for jobs or workstations). It also provides more efficient performance.

QTotJob (Initial total number of jobs for which to allocate storage) specifies the initial number of jobs for which the system should allocate auxiliary storage during IPL. The number of jobs is the total possible number of jobs on the system at any one time (e.g., jobs in the job queue, active jobs, and jobs having spooled output in an output queue).

QAdlActJ (Additional number of active jobs to add) specifies the additional number of active jobs for which the system should allocate storage when the number of active jobs specified by system value QActJob is exceeded. Setting this value too low may result in delays if your system needs additional jobs; setting it too high increases the time needed to add the additional jobs.

QAdlTotJ (Additional number of jobs to add) specifies the additional number of jobs for which the system should allocate auxiliary storage when the initial value in QTotJob is exceeded. As with QAdlActJ, setting this value too low may result in delays and interruptions when your system needs additional jobs; setting it too high slows the system when new jobs are added. We recommend keeping the IBM-supplied default value.

You'll need to document changes you make to any of these system values. We suggest you record any commands that change the work-management system values (or any other IBM-supplied objects) by keying the same commands into a CL program that can be run each time you load a new release of the operating system. This ensures that your system's configuration remains consistent.

Establish Your Subsystems

The next task in establishing your work environment is selecting your controlling subsystem. A subsystem, defined by a subsystem description, is where the system brings together the resources needed to process work. IBM ships two complete subsystem configurations: QBase and QCtl. System value *QCtlSbsD* (Controlling subsystem description) determines which of these two configurations the system uses when you IPL.

When the iSeries is shipped, the controlling subsystem for operations is QBase. This configuration consists of the following subsystems:

- QBase — This is the controlling subsystem. It supports interactive, batch, and communications jobs. An autostart job starts subsystem QSpl.
- QSpl — This is the spool subsystem, supporting reader and writer jobs.
- QSysWrk — This is the system monitor subsystem. It contains jobs that support system functions started automatically at IPL time and when the system exits restricted state.
- QUsrWrk — This is the user work subsystem. Its jobs are started by servers to do work on behalf of users.
- QServer — This is the file server subsystem.

The QBase configuration is a simple configuration, with most main storage shared among subsystems. However, we recommend implementing separate subsystems for each type of job to provide separate memory pools for each activity. One memory pool can support all activities, but when long-running batch jobs run with interactive workstations that compete for the same memory, system performance is poor and the fight for activity levels and priority becomes hard to manage. Our experience with iSeries and AS/400 systems has taught us that establishing separate subsystems for batch, interactive, communications, and server jobs gives you much more control. Using QCtl as the controlling subsystem establishes separate subsystems for these types of jobs and can be the basis for various customized subsystems.

Use the following command to change the controlling subsystem from QBase to QCtl:

```
ChgSysVal SysVal(QCtlSbsD) Value('QCTL QGPL')
```

You can also use the WrkSysVal command to change the system value. The new value will take effect after the next IPL.

The QCtl configuration consists of the following subsystems:

- QCtl — This is the controlling subsystem. As shipped, QCtl supports sign-on only at the console. An autostart job starts subsystems QInter, QBatch, QCmn, and QSpl.
- QInter — This subsystem supports all interactive jobs, with the exception of the console.
- QBatch — This subsystem supports all batch jobs.
- QCmn — This subsystem supports all communications jobs.
- QSpl — This is the spool subsystem, supporting reader and writer jobs.
- QSNADS — This is the SNA Distribution Services (SNADS) subsystem. It supports jobs controlling the functions of the SNADS network, as well as IBM-supplied transaction programs such as document interchange and object distribution.
- QSysWrk — This is the system monitor subsystem. It contains jobs that support system functions started automatically at IPL time and when the system exits restricted state.

- QUsrWrk — This is the user work subsystem. Its jobs are started by servers to do work on behalf of users.
- QServer — This is the file server subsystem.

The QCtl configuration enables more granular control of your system. For instance, you can easily prevent users from signing on over the weekend yet permit batch jobs to continue to run by ending subsystem QInter and leaving subsystem QBatch active.

One advantage the QCtl configuration offers is the ability to allocate memory to each subsystem based on the need for each type of job and to set appropriate activity levels for each subsystem. No system values control the memory pools and activity levels for individual subsystems, but the subsystem description contains the parameters that control these functions. For example, when you create a subsystem description with the CrtSbsD (Create Subsystem Description) command, you specify the memory allocation and the number of activity levels. You can find more information about subsystem descriptions in Chapters 17, 18, and 19 and in *OS/400 Work Management.*

The QCtl configuration will also help if you decide to create your own subsystems. For instance, if your system supports many remote and local users, you may want to further divide the QInter subsystem into one subsystem for remote interactive jobs and another for local interactive jobs. Thus, you can establish appropriate execution priorities, time slices, and memory allocations for each type of job and greatly improve performance consistency.

Retrieve and Modify the Start-up Program

When you IPL your system, the controlling subsystem (QBase or QCtl, whichever you decide to use) submits an autostart job that runs the program specified in system value *QStrUpPgm* (Start-up program). The IBM-shipped default start-up program is QStrUp in library QSys. This program performs functions such as starting the appropriate subsystems and starting the print writers on your system.

However, you may want to modify the start-up program to perform custom functions. For instance, you may have created additional subsystems that need to be started at IPL, or you may want to run a job that checks the QAbnormSw system value each time the system is started. To retrieve the CL source code for QStrUp, execute the command

```
RtvCLSrc Pgm(QSys/QStrUp) SrcFile(YourLib/QCLSrc) SrcMbr(YourMember)
```

Notice that we suggest you retrieve the QStrUp source into a different member name. Because the new start-up program will be user created, it should have a name without the look of an IBM name.

Figure 2.3 shows the source code for program QStrUp.

FIGURE 2.3

CL Source Code for Start-up Program QStrUp

```
/********************************************************************/
/*                                                                  */
/* 5769SS1 V4R4M0 990521     RTVCLSRC Output     07/13/00 10:42:48  */
/*                                                                  */
/* Program name . . . . . . . . . . . . . . :   QSTRUP           PN*/
/* Library name . . . . . . . . . . . . . . :   QSYS             PL*/
/* Original source file . . . . . . . . . . :                    SN*/
/* Library name . . . . . . . . . . . . . . :                    SL*/
/* Original source member . . . . . . . . . :                    SM*/
/* Source file change                                              */
/*   date/time  . . . . . . . . . . . . . . :                    SC*/
/* Patch option . . . . . . . . . . . . . . :   *NOPATCH         PO*/
/* User profile . . . . . . . . . . . . . . :   *USER            UP*/
/* Text . . . :                                                  TX*/
/* Owner  . . . . . . . . . . . . . . . . . :   QSYS             OW*/
/* Patch change ID  . . . . . . . . . . . . :                    PC*/
/* Patch APAR ID  . . . . . . . . . . . . . :                    PA*/
/* User mod flag  . . . . . . . . . . . . . :   *NO              UM*/
/*                                                               ED*/
/********************************************************************/
     PGM
     DCL VAR(&STRWTRS) TYPE(*CHAR) LEN(1)
     DCL VAR(&CTLSBSD) TYPE(*CHAR) LEN(20)
     DCL VAR(&CPYR) TYPE(*CHAR) LEN(90) VALUE('5769-SS1 (C) COPYRIGHT-
 IBM CORP 1980, 1999. LICENSED MATERIAL - PROGRAM PROPERTY OF IBM')
     QSYS/STRSBS SBSD(QSPL)
     MONMSG MSGID(CPF0000)
     QSYS/STRSBS SBSD(QSERVER)
     MONMSG MSGID(CPF0000)
     QSYS/STRSBS SBSD(QUSRWRK)
     MONMSG MSGID(CPF0000)
     QSYS/RLSJOBQ JOBQ(QGPL/QS36MRT)
     MONMSG MSGID(CPF0000)
     QSYS/RLSJOBQ JOBQ(QGPL/QS36EVOKE)
     MONMSG MSGID(CPF0000)
     QSYS/STRCLNUP
     MONMSG MSGID(CPF0000)
     QSYS/RTVSYSVAL SYSVAL(QCTLSBSD) RTNVAR(&CTLSBSD)
     IF COND((&CTLSBSD *NE 'QCTL      QSYS      ') *AND (&CTLSBSD *NE-
 'QCTL      QGPL      ')) THEN(GOTO CMDLBL(DONE))
     QSYS/STRSBS SBSD(QINTER)
     MONMSG MSGID(CPF0000)
     QSYS/STRSBS SBSD(QBATCH)
     MONMSG MSGID(CPF0000)
     QSYS/STRSBS SBSD(QCMN)
     MONMSG MSGID(CPF0000)
DONE:
     QSYS/RTVSYSVAL SYSVAL(QSTRPRTWTR) RTNVAR(&STRWTRS)
     IF COND(&STRWTRS = '0') THEN(GOTO CMDLBL(NOWTRS))
     CALL PGM(QSYS/QWCSWTRS)
     MONMSG MSGID(CPF0000)
NOWTRS:
     RETURN
     CHGVAR VAR(&CPYR) VALUE(&CPYR)
     ENDPGM
```

After retrieving the source, you can modify it to perform additional functions. Figure 2.4 shows a sample user-modified start-up program you might use when QCtl is the controlling subsystem, with the addition of subsystems QPgmr, QRemote, and QLocal. The sample program also checks the status of the QAbnormSw system value and starts the subsystems only if the system previously ended in a normal fashion.

FIGURE 2.4

User-Modified Start-up Program

```
/* ================================================================ */
/* = Program....... StartSys                                      = */
/* = Source type... CLP                                           = */
/* = Description... System start-up                              = */
/* ================================================================ */

Pgm

/* ================================================================ */
/* = Variable declarations                                        = */
/* ================================================================ */

  Dcl        &StrWtrs    *Char     (    1    )
  Dcl        &AbnormSw   *Char     (    1    )

/* ================================================================ */
/* = Global error trapper                                         = */
/* ================================================================ */

  MonMsg     ( CPF0000 MCH0000 )

/* ================================================================ */
/* = Start basic subsystems                                       = */
/* ================================================================ */

  StrSbs     QSpl
  StrSbs     QServer
  StrSbs     QUsrWrk

/* ================================================================ */
/* = Start Operational Assistant cleanup operations               = */
/* ================================================================ */

  StrClnUp

/* ================================================================ */
/* = If system previously ended normally, start subsystems        = */
/* ================================================================ */

  RtvSysVal  QAbnormSw   ( &AbnormSw )
```

continued

FIGURE 2.4 CONTINUED

```
  If          ( &AbnormSw *Eq 'Ø' )                                        +
    Do
      StrSbs      QInter
      StrSbs      QBatch
      StrSbs      QCmn
      StrSbs      QPgmr
      StrSbs      QRemote
      StrSbs      QLocal
    EndDo

/*  ==============================================================  */
/*  =  Start writers if indicated                                 =  */
/*  ==============================================================  */

  RtvSysVal  QStrPrtWtr  ( &StrWtrs )
  If         ( &StrWtrs *Eq '1' )                                          +
    Call       QSys/QWCSWtrs

/*  ==============================================================  */
/*  =  Exit program                                               =  */
/*  ==============================================================  */

  Return

EndPgm
```

Once you've modified your new start-up program, recompile it into a user-created library. Before you change system value QStrUpPgm so that it reflects the fact that your new program is to be the system start-up program, be sure your program includes good error-handling techniques and that you test it well.

Now What?

You've made the most of your first session. You've secured your system, set the autoconfiguration values, customized your work environment, established the controlling subsystem, and modified the start-up program. Now, you need to create user profiles for your users and further customize your system. We'll tell you how in Chapter 3.

Chapter 3

Access Made Easy

If you've followed our recommendations about iSeries setup to this point, you planned carefully for installation, education, migration, security, backup, and recovery before you even received your system. You created consistent and meaningful naming conventions for system objects, and you established your work environment. Now that you've powered on the iSeries, it's time to start thinking about putting it to work. Your next step is to set up user profiles.

IBM supplies a few user profiles with which to maintain the iSeries, such as QDftOwn (default owner), QSecOfr (security officer), and QSrv (service, used by the customer engineer). In addition to these profiles, you need profiles for your users so they can sign on to the system and access their programs and data. For this aspect of setting up your iSeries, you first need to understand user profiles and their attributes. With that knowledge, you can, if you like, turn over to a program the job of creating profiles for your users.

What Is a User Profile?

To the iSeries, a user profile is an object. Although the object's name (e.g., Pgmr0234, WDavis) is what you normally think of as the user profile, a user profile is much more than a name. The attributes of a user profile object define the user to the system, enabling the system to establish a custom initial session (i.e., job) for that user at sign-on. To make the best use of user profiles, you must understand these attributes and how they can help you control access to your system.

You create a user profile using the CrtUsrPrf (Create User Profile) command. Only the security officer profile (QSecOfr) or another profile that has *SecAdm (security administrator) special authority can create, change, or delete user profiles. You should restrict authority to the CrtUsrPrf, ChgUsrPrf (Change User Profile), and DltUsrPrf (Delete User Profile) commands to those users responsible for creating and maintaining user profiles on your system.

The CrtUsrPrf and ChgUsrPrf commands have a parameter for each user profile attribute. If you prompt the CrtUsrPrf command and then press F10, the system displays the command's parameters (Figure 3.1).

FIGURE 3.1

CrtUsrPrf Command Prompt

```
                     Create User Profile (CRTUSRPRF)

Type choices, press Enter.

User profile . . . . . . . . . .   __________     Name
User password  . . . . . . . . .   *USRPRF___     Name, *USRPRF, *NONE
Set password to expired  . . . .   *NO_           *NO, *YES
Status . . . . . . . . . . . . .   *ENABLED_      *ENABLED, *DISABLED
User class . . . . . . . . . . .   *USER__        *USER, *SYSOPR, *PGMR...
Assistance level . . . . . . . .   *SYSVAL__      *SYSVAL, *BASIC, *INTERMED...
Current library  . . . . . . . .   *CRTDFT___     Name, *CRTDFT
Initial program to call  . . . .   *NONE_____     Name, *NONE
  Library  . . . . . . . . . . .     __________   Name, *LIBL, *CURLIB
Initial menu . . . . . . . . . .   MAIN______     Name, *SIGNOFF
  Library  . . . . . . . . . . .     *LIBL_____   Name, *LIBL, *CURLIB
Limit capabilities . . . . . . .   *NO____        *NO, *PARTIAL, *YES
Text 'description' . . . . . . .   *BLANK_____________________________________

Special authority  . . . . . . .   *USRCLS__      *USRCLS, *NONE, *ALLOBJ...
               + for more values   _________
Special environment  . . . . . .   *SYSVAL        *SYSVAL, *NONE, *S36
Display sign-on information  . .   *SYSVAL        *SYSVAL, *NO, *YES
Password expiration interval . .   *SYSVAL        1-366, *SYSVAL, *NOMAX
Limit device sessions  . . . . .   *SYSVAL        *SYSVAL, *YES, *NO
Keyboard buffering . . . . . . .   *SYSVAL___     *SYSVAL, *NO, *TYPEAHEAD...
Maximum allowed storage  . . . .   *NOMAX_____    Kilobytes, *NOMAX
Highest schedule priority  . . .   3              0-9
Job description  . . . . . . . .   QDFTJOBD__     Name
  Library  . . . . . . . . . . .     *LIBL_____   Name, *LIBL, *CURLIB
Group profile  . . . . . . . . .   *NONE_____     Name, *NONE
Owner  . . . . . . . . . . . . .   *USRPRF        *USRPRF, *GRPPRF
Group authority  . . . . . . . .   *NONE___       *NONE, *ALL, *CHANGE, *USE...
Group authority type . . . . . .   *PRIVATE       *PRIVATE, *PGP
Supplemental groups  . . . . . .   *NONE_____     Name, *NONE
               + for more values   __________
Accounting code  . . . . . . . .   *BLANK__________
Document password  . . . . . . .   *NONE___       Name, *NONE
Message queue  . . . . . . . . .   *USRPRF___     Name, *USRPRF
  Library  . . . . . . . . . . .     __________   Name, *LIBL, *CURLIB
Delivery . . . . . . . . . . . .   *NOTIFY        *NOTIFY, *BREAK, *HOLD, *DFT
Severity code filter . . . . . .   0______        0-99
Print device . . . . . . . . . .   *WRKSTN___     Name, *WRKSTN, *SYSVAL
Output queue . . . . . . . . . .   *WRKSTN___     Name, *WRKSTN, *DEV
  Library  . . . . . . . . . . .     __________   Name, *LIBL, *CURLIB
Attention program  . . . . . . .   *SYSVAL___     Name, *NONE, *SYSVAL, *ASSIST
  Library  . . . . . . . . . . .     __________   Name, *LIBL, *CURLIB
Sort sequence  . . . . . . . . .   *SYSVAL___     Name, *SYSVAL, *HEX...
  Library  . . . . . . . . . . .     __________   Name, *LIBL, *CURLIB
Language ID  . . . . . . . . . .   *SYSVAL        *SYSVAL...
Country ID . . . . . . . . . . .   *SYSVAL        *SYSVAL...
Coded character set ID . . . . .   *SYSVAL____    *SYSVAL, *HEX...
Character identifier control . .   *SYSVAL__      *SYSVAL, *DEVD, *JOBCCSID
Locale job attributes  . . . . .   *SYSVAL        *SYSVAL, *NONE, *CCSID...
               + for more values   ________
Locale . . . . . . . . . . . . .   *SYSVAL____________________________________

User options . . . . . . . . . .   *NONE____      *NONE, *CLKWD, *EXPERT...
               + for more values   _________
User ID number . . . . . . . . .   *GEN_______    1-4294967294, *GEN
Group ID number  . . . . . . . .   *NONE______    1-4294967294, *NONE, *GEN
Home directory . . . . . . . . .   *USRPRF____________________________________

Authority  . . . . . . . . . . .   *EXCLUDE__     *ALL, *CHANGE, *USE, *EXCLUDE
```

Before you create any user profiles, you should first decide how to name them. In Chapter 1, we stressed the importance of developing a strategic naming convention for user profiles. Once you've performed this task, you're ready to create a user profile for each person who needs access to your system.

Creating User Profiles

Figure 3.1 shows all the available parameters for creating a user profile. Except for the user profile name parameter, each parameter has a default value that will be used unless you supply a specific value to override the default. Following are the key user profile parameters that you'll frequently change to customize a user profile.

UsrPrf (User Profile)

The first parameter, UsrPrf, specifies the user profile name on which you decided. This is a required parameter; you enter the name of the user profile you're creating.

Password (User Password)

As we mentioned in Chapter 1, passwords should be secret, hard to guess, and regularly changed. You can't ensure that users keep their passwords secret, but you can help make passwords hard to guess by controlling password format, and you can make sure users change their passwords regularly.

This discussion assumes you let users select and maintain their own passwords. *No one in IT needs to know user passwords.* The iSeries doesn't let even the security officer view existing passwords. This would violate the first rule of passwords — that they be secret!

The CrtUsrPrf command's Password parameter lets you specify a value of *None, a value of *UsrPrf, or the password itself. *None, which means that the user profile can't sign on to the system, is recommended for group profiles, profiles of users who are on vacation and don't need access for a period of time, users who've been terminated but can't be deleted at the time of termination, and other situations in which you want to ensure that a profile isn't used. The default value, *UsrPrf, dictates that the password be the same as the user profile name.

Caution

You shouldn't use Password(*UsrPrf). If you do, you forfeit the layer of security that's provided by having a password that differs from the user profile name.

You can control the format of passwords by using one or more of the password-related system values discussed in Chapter 2 or by creating your own password validation program. For details about how to create such a program, see the discussion of system value QPwdVldPgm (Password validation program) in *OS/400 Security – Reference* (SC41-5302).

The password format you impose should encourage users to create hard-to-guess passwords but shouldn't result in passwords that are so cryptic that users can't remember them without writing them down within arm's reach of the keyboard. As we said in Chapter 1, we suggest the following guidelines:

- Enforce a minimum length of at least seven characters (use the QPwdMinLen system value).
- Require at least one digit (use the QPwdRqdDgt system value).
- Don't allow an alphabetic character to be repeated in a password (use the QPwdLmtRep system value).
- Don't allow adjacent numbers in a password (use the QPwdLmtAjc system value).

To ensure that users change their passwords regularly, use system value QPwdExpItv to specify the maximum number of days a password will remain valid before requiring a change. A good value for QPwdExpItv is 60 days or 90 days, which would require all users system-wide to change passwords every two or three months. You can specify a different password expiration interval for selected individual profiles using CrtUsrPrf's (or ChgUsrPrf's) PwdExpItv parameter, which we discuss later in this chapter.

PwdExp (Set Password to Expired)

The PwdExp parameter lets you set the password for a specific user profile to the expired state. When you create new user profiles, you may want to specify PwdExp(*Yes) to prompt new users to choose a secret password the first time they sign on. The same is true when you reset passwords for users who forget theirs.

Status (Status)

Parameter Status specifies whether a user profile is enabled or disabled for sign-on. When the value of Status is *Enabled, the system lets the user sign on to the system. When the value is *Disabled, the system doesn't let the user sign on until an authorized user re-enables the user profile (i.e., changes the Status value to *Enabled).

The primary use of this parameter is with the QMaxSgnAcn system value. If QMaxSgnAcn is set to 2 or 3, the system will disable a profile that exceeds the maximum number of invalid sign-on attempts (system value QMaxSign determines the maximum number of sign-on attempts allowed). When a profile is disabled, the system changes the value of Status to *Disabled. An authorized user must then reset the value to *Enabled before the user profile can be used again.

UsrCls (User Class) and SpcAut (Special Authority)

These two parameters work together to specify the special authorities granted to the user. Special authorities let users perform certain system functions, such as save/restore functions, job manipulation, spool file manipulation, and user profile administration. (For more information about user profile administration, see the discussion of user classes and special authorities in Chapter 1.)

Parameter UsrCls lets you classify users by type. Figure 3.2 (repeated from Chapter 1) shows the five classes of users recognized on the iSeries — *SecOfr, *SecAdm, *Pgmr, *SysOpr, and *User — and their default special authorities.

FIGURE 3.2
Default Special Authorities

User class	Default special authorities							
	*AllObj	*Audit	*IOSysCfg	*JobCtl	*SavSys	*SecAdm	*Service	*SplCtl
*SecOfr	✓	✓	✓	✓	✓	✓	✓	✓
*SecAdm	✓[1]			✓[1]	✓[1]	✓		
*Pgmr	✓[1]			✓[1]	✓[1]			
*SysOpr	✓[1]			✓	✓			
*User	✓[1]				✓[1]			

[1] Security levels 10 and 20 only

These classes represent the groups of users that are typical for an installation. By specifying a user class for each user profile, you can classify users based on their role on the system.

When you assign a user profile to a class, the profile inherits the special authorities associated with the class. Although you can override these special authorities using the SpcAut parameter, the default authorities are often sufficient.

The default value for the SpcAut parameter is *UsrCls, which instructs the system to refer to the UsrCls parameter and assign the predetermined set of special authorities that appears in Figure 3.2. You can override this default by typing from one to eight individual special authorities that you want to assign to the user profile. After sending a message that the special authorities assigned don't match the user class, the system creates the user profile as you requested.

Consider this example:

```
CrtUsrPrf UsrPrf(NielsenKar)    +
          Password(Password)    +
          UsrCls(*SysOpr)
```

Once this CrtUsrPrf command is executed, user profile NielsenKar will have *JobCtl and *SavSys special authorities. The command

```
CrtUsrPrf UsrPrf(NielsenKar)    +
          Password(Password)    +
          UsrCls(*SysOpr)       +
          SpcAut(*None)
```

creates user profile NielsenKar in the *SysOpr class but with no special authorities.

Figure 3.3 lists the allowed values for the SpcAut parameter and what each value means.

FIGURE 3.3
SpcAut Parameter Values

Special authority value	Description
*UsrCls	The default special authorities are based on the value specified for the UsrCls parameter.
*None	No special authorities are assigned.
*AllObj	All object authority. Lets users access any system object. This authority alone, however, doesn't let users create, change, or delete user profiles.
*Audit	Audit authority. Lets users start and stop security auditing and control security auditing characteristics.
*IOSysCfg	System configuration authority. Lets users change system configuration information. For example, users can configure I/O devices, work with TCP/IP servers, and configure communications.
*JobCtl	Job control authority. Lets users change, display, hold, release, cancel, and clear all jobs on the system. Users can also control spooled files in output queues for which OprCtl(*Yes) is specified.
*SavSys	Save system authority. Lets users save, restore, and free storage for all objects.
*SecAdm	Security administrator authority. Lets users create, change, and delete user profiles.
*Service	Service authority. Lets users perform functions from the System Service Tools, a group of executable programs used for various service functions (e.g., line traces, diagnostics).
*SplCtl	Spool control authority. Lets users delete, display, hold, and release their own spooled files and spooled files owned by other users.

Special authorities should be given to only a limited number of user profiles because some of the functions provided are powerful and exceed normal object authority. For instance, *AllObj special authority gives the user unlimited access to and control over any object on the system — a user with *AllObj special authority can perform virtually any function on virtually any object on your system. The danger in letting that power get into the wrong hands is clear.

Generally speaking, no profile other than QSecOfr should have *AllObj authority. This is why the security level of any development or production machine should be at least 30, where you can control resource security and *AllObj special authority with confidence.

Your security implementation should be designed so that it doesn't require *AllObj authority to administer most functions. Reserve this special authority for user profile QSecOfr, and use that profile to make any changes that require that level of authority.

The *SecAdm special authority is helpful in designing a security system that gives users no more authority than they need to do their jobs. *SecAdm special authority enables a user profile to create and maintain the system user profiles. Using *SecAdm, you can assign an individual to perform these functions without having to assign that person's profile to the *SecOfr user class.

The *SavSys special authority lets a user profile perform save/restore operations on any object on the system without having the authority to access or manipulate those objects. *SavSys shows clearly how the iSeries lets you grant only the authority a user needs to do a job. What would it do to your system security if your operations staff needed *AllObj special authority to perform save/restore operations? If that were the case, system operators could access such sensitive information as payroll and master files. *SavSys avoids that authorization problem while giving operators the functional authority to perform save/restore operations. (Be aware, though, that the ability to display information from the save media still makes it possible to view sensitive information.)

Special authority *SplCtl provides access to all spooled files on the system. Spooled files containing confidential information can't be protected from access by a user with *SplCtl special authority, so you'll want to be particularly careful when assigning this special authority to users.

*Service is another special authority that should be guarded. *Service special authority enables a user profile to use the System Service Tools. These tools provide the capability to trace data on communications lines and to actually view user profiles and passwords being transferred down the line when someone signs on to the system. The tools also provide the capability to display or alter any object on your system. So be stingy with *Service special authority. The QSrv and QSecOfr profiles provided with OS/400 have *Service authority. You should change the password to *None for system profile QSrv and assign a password only when a customer engineer needs to use the profile.

You should also carefully control *Audit special authority. OS/400 provides security-related auditing functions, and a user with *Audit special authority can start and stop this auditing and change the auditing characteristics. These abilities pose an obvious risk in environments that rely on security auditing functions.

To guard against changes to system configuration, you need to control special authority *IOSysCfg. This special authority gives a user the ability to change such things as the communications configuration, TCP/IP server characteristics, and the HTTP server.

Initial Sign-On Options

CurLib (Current library)
InlPgm (Initial program to call)
InlMnu (Initial menu)
LmtCpb (Limit capabilities)

Three user profile parameters work together to determine a user's initial sign-on options. The CurLib, InlPgm, and InlMnu parameters determine the user profile's current library, initial program, and initial menu, respectively. Why are these parameters significant to security? They establish how the user interacts with the system initially, and the menu or program executed at sign-on determines the menus and programs available to that user. Let's look at a couple of examples.

Consider the user profile User, which has the following values:

```
Current library . . . . . . . . . CURLIB          ICLIB_____
Initial program to call . . . . . INLPGM          *NONE_____
  Library . . . . . . . . . . .                     __________
Initial menu  . . . . . . . . . . INLMNU          ICMENU____
  Library . . . . . . . . . . .                     ICLIB_____
```

When User signs on to the system, the current library is set to ICLib, and the user receives menu ICMenu in library ICLib. Any other menus or programs that can be accessed through ICMenu and to which User is authorized are also available.

Here's another example:

```
Current library . . . . . . . . . CURLIB          ICLIB_____
Initial program to call . . . . . INLPGM          ICUSERON__
  Library . . . . . . . . . . .                     SYSLIB____
Initial menu  . . . . . . . . . . INLMNU          *SIGNOFF__
  Library . . . . . . . . . . .                     __________
```

With these values, when User signs on to the system, ICLib is the current library in the library list, and program ICUserOn in library SysLib is executed. Again, any other menus or programs accessible through ICUserOn and to which User is authorized are also available.

The value of *SignOff for the InlMnu parameter is worth some discussion. When a user signs on, OS/400 executes the program, if any, specified in the InlPgm parameter. If the user or user program hasn't actually executed the SignOff command when the initial program ends, the system executes the menu, if any, specified in parameter InlMnu. Thus, if the default value Main were given for InlMnu and program SysLib/ICUserOn were to end without signing off the user, the system would present the main menu. When *SignOff is the value for InlMnu, OS/400 signs off the user from the system when the initial program ends.

Parameters CurLib, InlPgm, and InlMnu are significant to security because users can change these parameter values at sign-on. Users can also execute OS/400 commands from the command line provided on iSeries menus. Obviously, allowing all users these capabilities is a bad idea from a security standpoint, and this is where parameter LmtCpb enters the picture. LmtCpb controls the user's ability to

- define (using the ChgUsrPrf command) or change (at sign-on) his or her own initial program
- define (using the ChgUsrPrf command) or change (at sign-on) his or her own initial menu
- define (using the ChgUsrPrf command) or change (at sign-on) his or her own current library
- define (using the ChgUsrPrf command) or change (at sign-on) his or her own attention key program
- execute OS/400 or user-defined commands from the command line on iSeries native menus

Figure 3.4 shows the effects of the possible values for the LmtCpb parameter.

FIGURE 3.4
LmtCpb Parameter Values

LmtCpb value	Change initial program	Change initial menu	Change current library	Change attention key program	Enter commands
	Functions allowed with LmtCpb				
*No	✓	✓	✓	✓	✓
*Partial		✓			✓
*Yes					✓[1]

[1] Users can execute only commands that allow limited-capability users. OS/400 is shipped with the following commands that allow limited-capability users: DspJob (Display Job), DspJobLog (Display Job Log), DspMsg (Display Messages), SignOff (Sign Off), SndMsg (Send Message), StrPCO (Start PC Organizer), and WrkMsg (Work with Messages).

Notice that LmtCpb(*Yes) prevents changing any of these values or executing any commands other than those that explicitly allow limited-capability users.

Production systems usually enforce LmtCpb(*Yes) for most user profiles. The profiles that typically need LmtCpb(*No) are IT personnel who frequently use the command line from OS/400 menus. You can still secure these user profiles from sensitive data by using resource security. Although you could specify LmtCpb(*Partial) for such IT personnel and thus ensure that they can't change their initial program, they could still change their initial menu, which would be executed at the conclusion of the initial program.

System Value Overrides

DspSgnInf (Display sign-on information)
PwdExpItv (Password expiration interval)
LmtDevSsn (Limit device sessions)

You can override the system values QDspSgnInf (Display sign-on information), QPwdExpItv, and QLmtDevSsn (Limit device sessions) through three user profile parameters that control these functions: DspSgnInf, PwdExpItv, and LmtDevSsn. You'll notice (in Figure 3.1) that each of these parameters has a default value of *SysVal. The default lets the system value control these functions. To override a system value, you specify the desired value in the user profile parameter. The available choices are the same as those for the system values themselves.

DspSgnInf controls whether the system displays the Sign-on Information panel after the user signs on. This panel shows

- the last sign-on date
- the number of invalid sign-on attempts
- the number of days until the password expires if it expires within seven days

The parameter can have the following values:

- 0 — Do not display sign-on information.
- 1 — Display sign-on information.

The Sign-on Information panel lets users monitor attempted uses of their profile and reminds users when a new password is about to be required.

PwdExpItv lets you specify, for each user, the number of days a password remains active before requiring a change. We suggest you set system value QPwdExpItv to a reasonable value that would apply to most of your users (for instance, 60 to 90 days). Then, for profiles with special considerations, such as increased security concerns, use parameter PwdExpItv in the profile itself to override the system value.

The LmtDevSsn parameter controls whether a user can sign on to more than one device at a time. As with PwdExpItv, you should assign system value QLmtDevSsn so that it applies to most users and use LmtDevSsn in the profile for special cases.

Group Profiles

GrpPrf (Group profile)
Owner (Owner)
GrpAut (Group authority)
SupGrpPrf (Supplemental groups)

All the parameters discussed up to this point are used to define profiles for individual users. The GrpPrf, Owner, and GrpAut parameters let you associate an individual with a group (or with several groups, using parameter SupGrpPrf) of user profiles via a *group profile*. When you authorize a group profile to objects on the system, the authorization applies to all profiles in the group.

How is this accomplished? You create a user profile for the group. The group profile should specify Password(*None) to prevent it from actually being used to sign on to the system — all members of the group should sign on using their own individual profiles. For instance, you might create a profile called DevPgmr to be the group profile for your programming staff. Then, for each user profile belonging to a member of the programming staff, use the ChgUsrPrf command and the GrpPrf, Owner, and GrpAut parameters to place the user in the DevPgmr group.

Parameter GrpPrf names the group profile with which the user profile will be associated. If you created the group profile DevPgmr, you'd specify DevPgmr as the GrpPrf value for the user profiles you put into that group.

Parameter Owner specifies who owns the objects created by the group profile. The parameter value determines whether the user profile or the group profile will own the objects created by profiles that belong to the group. There is an advantage to having the group profile own all objects created by its constituent user profiles: When the group profile owns the objects, every member of the group has *All authority to the objects. This arrangement is helpful, for instance, in a programming environment in which more than one programmer works on the same projects. However, there's a way to provide authority to group members without giving them *All authority. If you specify Owner(*UsrPrf), individual user profiles own the objects they create. If a user profile owns an object, the group profile and other members in the group have only the authority specified in the GrpAut parameter to the object.

Parameter GrpAut specifies the authority to be granted to the group profile and to members of the group when *UsrPrf is specified as the owner of the objects created. Valid values are *All, *Change, *Use, *Exclude, and *None. The first four of these values are authority classes, each of which represents a set of specific object and data authorities that will be granted. Chapter 4 discusses these values in detail as part of the discussion of specific authorities. If you specify one of the authority class values for GrpAut, the individual user profile that creates an object owns it, and the other members of the group, including the group profile, have the specified set of authorities to the object.

*None is the value required for GrpAut when *GrpPrf is specified as the owner of objects created by the user. Because the group profile automatically owns the object, all members of the group will share that authority.

You can assign a user to multiple group profiles using the SupGrpPrf parameter. The user then receives authorities to objects from the group profile as well as from all supplemental groups. To specify SupGrpPrf, you must also specify GrpPrf.

JobD (Job Description)

The JobD parameter on the CrtUsrPrf command determines the job description associated with the user profile. The job description specifies a set of attributes that determine how the system will process the job. Not only is the job description you specify used (as the default) when the user profile submits a batch job to the system, but values in the job description also determine the attributes of the user profile's workstation session. For instance, the initial library list that you specify for the job description becomes the user portion of the library list for the workstation session. If you don't specify a particular job description for the user profile on the JobD parameter, the system defaults to JobD(QDftJobD), an IBM-supplied job description that uses the QUsrLibL (User library list) system value to determine the user portion of the library list. The JobD parameter affects no other portion of the library list. After the user profile signs on, the initial program can manipulate the library list.

One way to manage the user portion of the library list is to use system value QUsrLibL to establish all user libraries. Then, when someone signs on to the system, QUsrLibL supplies all possible libraries, and users can always find the programs and data they need. However, this approach disregards security because it lets all users access all libraries, even those they don't need.

Another approach to setting up user libraries is to create a job description for each user type on the system. Then, when you create the user profile, you can specify the appropriate job description for the JobD parameter, and that job description's library list becomes the user library list when that profile signs on to the system.

The approach we recommend is to specify only general-purpose user libraries in QUsrLibL. These libraries should contain only general utility programs (e.g., date routines, extended math functions, a random number generator). Each profile's job description (and potentially initial program) should specify only the application libraries needed by that particular user profile. You can use department name or some other trigger kept in a database file to determine library needs.

Message Handling

MsgQ (Message queue)
Dlvry (Delivery)
Sev (Severity code filter)

When you create a user profile, the system automatically creates a message queue of the same name in library QUsrSys. The user receives job completion messages, system messages, and messages from other system users via this message queue. Three CrtUsrPrf parameters relate to handling user messages.

The MsgQ parameter specifies the message queue for the user. Except in very unusual circumstances, you should use the default value, *UsrPrf, for this parameter. If you keep the message queue name the same as the user profile name, system operators and other users can more easily remember the message queue name when sending messages.

The Dlvry parameter specifies how the system should deliver messages to the user. The value *Break specifies that the message will interrupt the user's job upon arrival. This interruption may annoy users, but it does help to ensure that they notice messages. The value *Hold causes the queue to hold messages until a user or program requests them. The value *Notify specifies that the system will notify the job of a message by sounding the alarm and displaying the message-waiting light. The user can then view messages at his or her convenience. The value *Dft specifies that the system will answer with the default reply any message that requires a response; informational messages are ignored.

The last parameter of the message group, Sev, specifies the lowest severity code of a message that the system will deliver when the message queue is in *Break or *Notify mode. Messages of lower severity are delivered to the user profile's message queue but don't interrupt the user or sound the alarm and turn on the message-waiting light. The default severity code is 0, meaning that the user will receive all messages. You should usually leave the Sev value at 0. But if you don't want certain users — because of their operational responsibilities, for instance — to be bothered by a lot of low-severity messages, you can assign another value (up to 99).

Printed Output Handling

PrtDev (Print device)
OutQ (Output queue)

Print direction on the iSeries is complex enough to be confusing to many. In Chapter 9, we unravel the chain of possibilities for print direction in detail. One of the links in that chain is the PrtDev and OutQ parameter pair found in the user profile. For the time being, simply know that the print device and output queue from the user profile are used when the printer file specifies that the job's attributes are to be used to determine print direction (the OutQ parameter value in the printer file is *Job) and the job description also specifies that the user profile should be used in deriving the print direction (the OutQ parameter value is *UsrPrf). Let's see how the system uses these values to further direct print.

PrtDev specifies the name of the printer (actually an output queue with the same name as the printer) to which output is directed. The PrtDev parameter allows the following values:

- *WrkStn — The printer assigned to the user's workstation (found in the device description) is used. This is the default value.
- *SysVal — The default system printer specified in system value QPrtDev is used.
- *PrintDeviceName* — If this device does not exist when referenced, the system directs print to the default system printer specified in system value QPrtDev.

Note that parameter PrtDev is used only when the OutQ parameter value is *Dev.

The OutQ parameter specifies the qualified name of the output queue to which output is directed. You can use the following values for OutQ:

- *WrkStn — The printer assigned to the user's workstation (found in the device description) is used. This is the default value.
- *Dev — The system directs output to an output queue with the same name as the value specified in the PrtDev parameter.
- *OutputQueueName* — The system directs output to the output queue herein named.

In our experience, print direction is typically derived from the OutQ information rather than from that found in PrtDev. For more in-depth information about print direction, refer to Chapter 9.

Text (Text Description)

The last parameter we'll look at on the CrtUsrPrf command is Text. Text gives you 50 characters in which to meaningfully describe the user profile. The information you include, as well as its format, should be consistent for each user profile to ensure readability and usability. You can retrieve, print, or display this text to identify who requests a report or uses a program.

Plan Your Profiles

Before you actually create any user profiles, consider each parameter and develop a plan to best use it. Once you determine your company's needs, devise standards for creating your user profiles. The CrtUsrPrf command shown in Figure 3.5 creates a sample user profile for an order entry clerk at branch location 01.

FIGURE 3.5
A Sample CrtUsrPrf Command

```
CrtUsrPrf   UsrPrf( NielsenKar )                                        +
            Password( *UsrPrf )                                         +
            PwdExp( *Yes )                                              +
            UsrCls( *User )                                             +
            CurLib( *CrtDft )                                           +
            InlPgm( QGPL/UserInlPgm )                                   +
            InlMnu( *SignOff )                                          +
            LmtCpb( *Yes )                                              +
            Text( 'Karen Nielsen, Branch Ø1, Order Entry' )             +
            SpcAut( *UsrCls )                                           +
            JobD( QGPL/OEJobD )                                         +
            GrpPrf( OEGroup )                                           +
            Owner( *GrpPrf )                                            +
            GrpAut( *None )                                             +
            MsgQ( *UsrPrf )                                             +
            Dlvry( *Break )                                             +
            PrtDev( *SysVal )                                           +
            OutQ( QUsrSys/BØ1OEOutQ )
```

It often helps to chart the various profile types and the parameter values you'll use when creating user profiles. Figure 3.6 shows a sample table that lists values you could use if your company had order entry, inventory control, accounting, personnel, IT operations, and IT programming departments. Such a table can serve as part of your security strategy and as a reference document for creating user profiles.

FIGURE 3.6
Sample Parameter Values for User Departments

User department	UsrCls	CurLib	InlPgm	LmtCpb	GrpPrf	OutQ
Order entry	*User	QGPL	UserInlPgm	*Yes	OEGroup	B*nn*OEOutQ
Inventory control	*User	QGPL	UserInlPgm	*Yes	ICGroup	B*nn*ICOutQ
Accounting	*User	QGPL	UserInlPgm	*Yes	AcGroup	B*nn*AcOutQ
Personnel	*User	QGPL	UserInlPgm	*Yes	PsGroup	B*nn*PsOutQ
IT operations	*SysOpr	*UserLib*	ITInlPgm	*No	OpGroup	*UserOutQ*
IT programming	*Pgmr	*UserLib*	ITInlPgm	*No	PgGroup	*UserOutQ*

nn = Location (e.g., 01 = Orlando, 02 = New York)
UserLib = Personal library with same name as user profile
UserOutQ = Personal output queue with same name as user profile

Maintaining User Profiles

After you've set up your user profiles, you'll need to maintain them as users come and go or as their responsibilities change. You can change a user profile with the ChgUsrPrf command. As with CrtUsrPrf, you must have *SecAdm special authority to use ChgUsrPrf. The ChgUsrPrf command is the same as the CrtUsrPrf command except that ChgUsrPrf has no Aut (Authority) parameter, and the parameter default values for ChgUsrPrf are the parameter values you assigned when you executed the CrtUsrPrf command.

Changing a User Password

Typically, you might employ ChgUsrPrf when a user forgets a password. Because the system won't display a password, you'd need to use ChgUsrPrf to change the forgetful user's password temporarily and require the user to choose a new password at the next sign-on. To accomplish this, execute the command

```
ChgUsrPrf UsrPrf(ProfileName)    +
          Password(Password)     +
          PwdExp(*Yes)
```

This command resets the password to a known value and sets the password expiration value to *Yes so that the system will prompt the user to choose a new secret password at the next sign-on.

Deleting a User Profile

Another user profile maintenance task you'll perform from time to time is deleting a user profile. For example, when an employee leaves, the security administrator should promptly remove the employee's profile from the system or at least set the password to *None.

Here are a few rules you should know:

- You can't delete a user profile that owns objects. You must first delete the objects or transfer their ownership to another profile.
- You can't delete a user profile if it's the primary group for any objects. You must first change or remove the primary group for objects.
- If the profile is a group profile, you can't delete it when it has members. You must first remove each member from the group by changing each member's GrpPrf or SupGrpPrf value.

The DltUsrPrf command has parameters that let you handle the objects owned by the profile as well as the objects for which the profile is the primary group, letting you address rules 1 and 2 above. For rule 3, you can list the members of a group profile using this DspUsrPrf (Display User Profile) command:

```
DspUsrPrf GroupProfileName *GrpMbr
```

DltUsrPrf's parameter OwnObjOpt (Owned object option) tells the system how to handle any objects owned by the user profile being deleted. The parameter can have one of three values:

- *NoDlt — The profile is not deleted if it owns objects.
- *Dlt — The owned objects and the profile are deleted.
- *ChgOwn — The owned objects are transferred to a new owner, and the profile is deleted.

Avoid the *Dlt option unless you've used the DspUsrPrf command to identify the owned objects and are sure you want to delete them. Remember, a backup of these objects is an easy way to protect yourself in case of error.

If you specify *ChgOwn for parameter OwnObjOpt, you must specify the new owner of these objects in the second part of the parameter. For instance, if a programmer owns some objects privately and you want to delete that programmer's profile, you might specify

```
DltUsrPrf UsrPrf(ProfileName) OwnObjOpt(*ChgOwn IT)
```

to transfer ownership of the objects to your IT group profile.

If you want to handle the owned objects individually, you can use command WrkObjOwn (Work with Objects by Owner). You can then selectively delete objects as well as change their ownership. This option makes it possible to specify different owners for different objects, if you so desire.

DltUsrPrf's PGpOpt (Primary group option) parameter tells the system how to handle objects for which the profile is the primary group. The parameter can have one of two values:

- *NoChg — The profile is not deleted if it is the primary group for objects.
- *ChgPGp — The objects for which the profile is the primary group are transferred to a newly specified primary group.

If you want to handle objects for which the profile is the primary group individually, you can use the WrkObjPGp (Work with Objects by Primary Group) command.

If you write a program to help you maintain user profiles, you may find the RtvUsrPrf (Retrieve User Profile) command helpful. You can use RtvUsrPrf to retrieve into a CL variable one or more of the parameter values associated with a user profile. For details about this command's parameters, see *OS/400 CL Reference – Part 4* (SC41-5726). You can also prompt this command on your screen and then use the help text to learn more about each variable you can retrieve.

Figure 3.7 shows the prompt screen for command RtvUsrPrf.

FIGURE 3.7
RtvUsrPrf Command Prompt

```
                     Retrieve User Profile (RTVUSRPRF)

Type choices, press Enter.

User profile . . . . . . . . . . . > *CURRENT__     Name, *CURRENT
CL var for RTNUSRPRF     (10) . .   __________     Character value
CL var for SPCAUT       (100) . .   __________     Character value
CL var for MAXSTG      (11 0) . .   __________     Number
CL var for STGUSED     (15 0) . .   __________     Number
CL var for PTYLMT         (1) . .   __________     Character value
CL var for INLPGM        (10) . .   __________     Character value
CL var for INLPGMLIB     (10) . .   __________     Character value
CL var for JOBD          (10) . .   __________     Character value
CL var for JOBDLIB       (10) . .   __________     Character value
CL var for GRPPRF        (10) . .   __________     Character value
```

continued

FIGURE 3.7 *CONTINUED*

```
CL var for OWNER       (10) . .   __________   Character value
CL var for GRPAUT      (10) . .   __________   Character value
CL var for ACGCDE      (15) . .   __________   Character value
CL var for MSGQ        (10) . .   __________   Character value
CL var for MSGQLIB     (10) . .   __________   Character value
CL var for OUTQ        (10) . .   __________   Character value
CL var for OUTQLIB     (10) . .   __________   Character value
CL var for TEXT        (50) . .   __________   Character value
CL var for PWDCHGDAT    (6) . .   __________   Character value
CL var for USRCLS      (10) . .   __________   Character value
CL var for ASTLVL      (10) . .   __________   Character value
CL var for SPCENV      (10) . .   __________   Character value
CL var for CURLIB      (10) . .   __________   Character value
CL var for INLMNU      (10) . .   __________   Character value
CL var for INLMNULIB   (10) . .   __________   Character value
CL var for LMTCPB      (10) . .   __________   Character value
CL var for DLVRY       (10) . .   __________   Character value
CL var for SEV        (2 0) . .   __________   Number
CL var for PRTDEV      (10) . .   __________   Character value
CL var for ATNPGM      (10) . .   __________   Character value
CL var for ATNPGMLIB   (10) . .   __________   Character value
CL var for USROPT     (240) . .   __________   Character value
CL var for DSPSGNINF    (7) . .   __________   Character value
CL var for PWDEXPITV  (5 0) . .   __________   Number
CL var for PWDEXP       (4) . .   __________   Character value
CL var for STATUS      (10) . .   __________   Character value
CL var for PRVSIGN     (13) . .   __________   Character value
CL var for NOTVLDSIGN (11 0) . .  __________   Number
CL var for LMTDEVSSN    (7) . .   __________   Character value
CL var for KBDBUF      (10) . .   __________   Character value
CL var for LANGID      (10) . .   __________   Character value
CL var for CNTRYID     (10) . .   __________   Character value
CL var for CCSID      (5 0) . .   __________   Number
CL var for SRTSEQ      (10) . .   __________   Character value
CL var for SRTSEQLIB   (10) . .   __________   Character value
CL var for OBJAUD      (10) . .   __________   Character value
CL var for AUDLVL     (640) . .   __________   Character value
CL var for GRPAUTTYP   (10) . .   __________   Character value
CL var for SUPGRPPRF  (150) . .   __________   Character value
CL var for UID       (10 0) . .   __________   Number
CL var for GID       (10 0) . .   __________   Number
CL var for SETJOBATR  (160) . .   __________   Character value
CL var for CHRIDCTL    (10) . .   __________   Character value
```

The prompt lists the length of each variable next to the parameter whose value is retrieved in that variable. The RtvUsrPrf command is valid only within a CL program because the parameters actually return variables to the program, and return variables can't be accepted when you enter a command from an interactive command line. You might use this command to retrieve specific user information and use this information to make application decisions. For example, the code segment in Figure 3.8 retrieves into variable &GrpPrf the group profile for the current user and tests to see whether it is OEGROUP.

When this condition is met, the code might display a certain menu or determine which application libraries to put in the user's library list.

FIGURE 3.8
RtvUsrPrf Example

```
RtvUsrPrf  UsrPrf( *Current)                                  +
           GrpPrf( &GrpPrf )
If         ( &GrpPrf *Eq 'OEGROUP' )                          +
  Do
  .
  .
  .
  EndDo
```

Integrity: The CpyUsr and CrtUsr Commands

An important characteristic of system administration is consistency. Consistency in both the approach to and the results of a task is key to shaping overall system integrity.

The automation of administrative tasks is a powerful approach to effective system administration. Not only does a programming solution effect consistency, but it also saves time and money — and user profile maintenance is a prime target for automation.

In planning your user profiles, you'll see that your users fall into one of a few general categories (such as those depicted in Figure 3.6) and that users within each group share the same general attributes. With the WrkUsrPrf (Work with User Profiles) command, you can use the copy option to duplicate user profiles. However, this approach requires manual interaction, relies on a person to supply valid and consistent input, and lacks the full control and flexibility of an automated process. Therefore, the first step in a programming solution to user profile maintenance is the creation of a routine to copy user profiles.

We've created user-defined command CpyUsr as a sample on which you can base your own command. Figure 3.9A shows the command source.

FIGURE 3.9A
CpyUsr Command Source

```
/*  ==============================================================  */
/*  = Command....... CpyUsr                                      =  */
/*  = CPP........... CpyUsr001                                   =  */
/*  = Description... Copy user                                   =  */
/*  ==============================================================  */

Cmd          Prompt( 'Copy User' )

  Parm         Kwd( FromUsrPrf )                                      +
               Type( *SName )                                         +
               Len( 10 )                                              +
               Min( 1 )                                               +
               Prompt( 'From user' )
```

continued

FIGURE 3.9A CONTINUED

```
  Parm        Kwd( ToUsrPrf )                                         +
              Type( *SName )                                          +
              Len( 10 )                                               +
              Min( 1 )                                                +
              Prompt( 'To user' )

  Parm        Kwd( Text )                                             +
              Type( *Char )                                           +
              Len( 50 )                                               +
              Min( 1 )                                                +
              Case( *Mixed )                                          +
              Prompt( 'Text description' )
```

The command accepts three input parameters:

- a user profile to be copied
- a user profile to be created
- a text description for the newly created user profile

With the exception of the text description, the newly created user profile's attributes are taken from the user profile being copied.

Figure 3.9B shows CpyUsr's CL command processing program, CpyUsr001.

FIGURE 3.9B

CpyUsr001 CLLE Source

```
/*  ============================================================  */
/*  = Program....... CpyUsr001                                 =  */
/*  = Description... Copy user                                 =  */
/*  =                Command processing program for CpyUsr     =  */
/*  ============================================================  */

Pgm         Parm(                                                  +
                 &FromUser                                         +
                 &ToUser                                           +
                 &Text                                             +
               )

/*  ============================================================  */
/*  = Variable definitions                                     =  */
/*  ============================================================  */

/*  ------------------------------------------------------------  */
/*  - Input parameters                                         -  */
/*  ------------------------------------------------------------  */

  Dcl         &FromUser    *Char   (   10    )
  Dcl         &ToUser      *Char   (   10    )
  Dcl         &Text        *Char   (   50    )
```

continued

FIGURE 3.9B *CONTINUED*

```
/*  -------------------------------------------------------------  */
/*  - Work variables                                             - */
/*  -------------------------------------------------------------  */

   Dcl          &TextA        *Char    (   52    )
   Dcl          &Cmd          *Char    ( 3000    )
   Dcl          &CmdLen       *Dec     (   15  5 )   ( 3000 )
   Dcl          &Counter      *Dec     (    5  0 )
   Dcl          &FromOffset   *Dec     (    5  0 )
   Dcl          &ToOffset     *Dec     (    5  0 )

/*  -------------------------------------------------------------  */
/*  - Retrieved user profile variables and their work variables  - */
/*  -------------------------------------------------------------  */

   Dcl          &SpcAut       *Char    (  100    )
   Dcl          &SpcAutA      *Char    (  120    )
   Dcl          &MaxStg       *Dec     (   11  0 )
   Dcl          &MaxStgA      *Char    (   11    )
   Dcl          &PtyLmt       *Char    (    1    )
   Dcl          &InlPgm       *Char    (   10    )
   Dcl          &InlPgmLib    *Char    (   10    )
   Dcl          &InlPgmA      *Char    (   21    )
   Dcl          &JobD         *Char    (   10    )
   Dcl          &JobDLib      *Char    (   10    )
   Dcl          &JobDA        *Char    (   21    )
   Dcl          &GrpPrf       *Char    (   10    )
   Dcl          &Owner        *Char    (   10    )
   Dcl          &GrpAut       *Char    (   10    )
   Dcl          &AcgCde       *Char    (   15    )
   Dcl          &OutQ         *Char    (   10    )
   Dcl          &OutQLib      *Char    (   10    )
   Dcl          &OutQA        *Char    (   21    )
   Dcl          &UsrCls       *Char    (   10    )
   Dcl          &AstLvl       *Char    (   10    )
   Dcl          &SpcEnv       *Char    (   10    )
   Dcl          &CurLib       *Char    (   10    )
   Dcl          &InlMnu       *Char    (   10    )
   Dcl          &InlMnuLib    *Char    (   10    )
   Dcl          &InlMnuA      *Char    (   21    )
   Dcl          &LmtCpb       *Char    (   10    )
   Dcl          &Dlvry        *Char    (   10    )
   Dcl          &Sev          *Dec     (    2  0 )
   Dcl          &SevA         *Char    (    2    )
   Dcl          &PrtDev       *Char    (   10    )
   Dcl          &AtnPgm       *Char    (   10    )
   Dcl          &AtnPgmLib    *Char    (   10    )
   Dcl          &AtnPgmA      *Char    (   21    )
   Dcl          &UsrOpt       *Char    (  240    )
   Dcl          &UsrOptA      *Char    (  270    )
   Dcl          &DspSgnInf    *Char    (    7    )
   Dcl          &PwdExpItv    *Dec     (    5  0 )
   Dcl          &PwdExpItvA   *Char    (    7    )
   Dcl          &LmtDevSsn    *Char    (    7    )
```

continued

FIGURE 3.9B CONTINUED

```
  Dcl          &KbdBuf      *Char    (   10     )
  Dcl          &LangID      *Char    (   10     )
  Dcl          &CntryID     *Char    (   10     )
  Dcl          &CCSID       *Dec     (    5   0 )
  Dcl          &CCSIDA      *Char    (    7     )
  Dcl          &SrtSeq      *Char    (   10     )
  Dcl          &SrtSeqLib   *Char    (   10     )
  Dcl          &SrtSeqA     *Char    (   21     )
  Dcl          &ObjAud      *Char    (   10     )
  Dcl          &AudLvl      *Char    (  640     )
  Dcl          &GrpAutTyp   *Char    (   10     )
  Dcl          &SupGrpPrf   *Char    (  150     )
  Dcl          &SupGrpPrfA  *Char    (  170     )
  Dcl          &ChrIDCtl    *Char    (   10     )

/*  ==============================================================  */
/*  = Global error trap                                          =  */
/*  ==============================================================  */

  MonMsg     ( CPF0000 MCH0000 ) Exec(                               +
    GoTo Error                        )

/*  ==============================================================  */
/*  = Put apostrophes around text                                =  */
/*  ==============================================================  */

  ChgVar     &TextA      ( '''' *TCat &Text *TCat '''' )

/*  ==============================================================  */
/*  = Retrieve existing user profile information                 =  */
/*  ==============================================================  */

  RtvUsrPrf  UsrPrf( &FromUser )                                     +
             SpcAut( &SpcAut )                                       +
             MaxStg( &MaxStg )                                       +
             PtyLmt( &PtyLmt )                                       +
             InlPgm( &InlPgm )                                       +
             InlPgmLib( &InlPgmLib )                                 +
             JobD( &JobD )                                           +
             JobDLib( &JobDLib )                                     +
             GrpPrf( &GrpPrf )                                       +
             Owner( &Owner )                                         +
             GrpAut( &GrpAut )                                       +
             AcgCde( &AcgCde )                                       +
             OutQ( &OutQ )                                           +
             OutQLib( &OutQLib )                                     +
             UsrCls( &UsrCls )                                       +
             AstLvl( &AstLvl )                                       +
             SpcEnv( &SpcEnv )                                       +
             CurLib( &CurLib )                                       +
             InlMnu( &InlMnu )                                       +
             InlMnuLib( &InlMnuLib )                                 +
             LmtCpb( &LmtCpb )                                       +
             Dlvry( &Dlvry )                                         +
```

continued

FIGURE 3.9B *CONTINUED*

```
                 Sev( &Sev )                                          +
                 PrtDev( &PrtDev )                                    +
                 AtnPgm( &AtnPgm )                                    +
                 AtnPgmLib( &AtnPgmLib )                              +
                 UsrOpt( &UsrOpt )                                    +
                 DspSgnInf( &DspSgnInf )                              +
                 PwdExpItv( &PwdExpItv )                              +
                 LmtDevSsn( &LmtDevSsn )                              +
                 KbdBuf( &KbdBuf )                                    +
                 LangID( &LangID )                                    +
                 CntryID( &CntryID )                                  +
                 CCSID( &CCSID )                                      +
                 SrtSeq( &SrtSeq )                                    +
                 SrtSeqLib( &SrtSeqLib )                              +
                 ObjAud( &ObjAud )                                    +
                 AudLvl( &AudLvl )                                    +
                 GrpAutTyp( &GrpAutTyp )                              +
                 SupGrpPrf( &SupGrpPrf )                              +
                 ChrIDCtl( &ChrIDCtl )

/*   ==============================================================   */
/*   = Extract and construct special case parameters              =   */
/*   ==============================================================   */

/*   --------------------------------------------------------------   */
/*   - Extract elements from list parameters and construct blank  -   */
/*   - separated list                                             -   */
/*   --------------------------------------------------------------   */

  ChgVar     &Counter    ( 1 )

SpcAutBeg:

  ChgVar     &FromOffset ( ( ( &Counter - 1 ) * 10 ) + 1 )
  ChgVar     &ToOffset   ( ( ( &Counter - 1 ) * 11 ) + 1 )

  If         (                                                        +
               ( &Counter *LE 10 )  *And                              +
               ( %Sst( &SpcAut &FromOffset 10 ) *NE ' ' )             +
             )                                                        +
    Do
      ChgVar     %Sst( &SpcAutA &ToOffset   10 )                      +
                 ( %Sst( &SpcAut  &FromOffset 10 ) )
      ChgVar     &Counter                                             +
                 ( &Counter + 1 )
      GoTo       SpcAutBeg
    EndDo

  ChgVar     &Counter    ( 1 )

UsrOptBeg:

  ChgVar     &FromOffset ( ( ( &Counter - 1 ) * 10 ) + 1 )
  ChgVar     &ToOffset   ( ( ( &Counter - 1 ) * 11 ) + 1 )
```

continued

FIGURE 3.9B *CONTINUED*

```
  If          (                                                          +
                ( &Counter *LE 24 )  *And                                +
                ( %Sst( &UsrOpt &FromOffset 10 ) *NE ' ' )               +
              )                                                          +
    Do
      ChgVar      %Sst( &UsrOptA &ToOffset   10 )                        +
                  ( %Sst( &UsrOpt  &FromOffset 10 ) )
      ChgVar      &Counter                                               +
                  ( &Counter + 1 )
      GoTo        UsrOptBeg
    EndDo

  ChgVar      &Counter    ( 1 )

SupGrpBeg:

  ChgVar      &FromOffset ( ( ( &Counter - 1 ) * 10 ) + 1 )
  ChgVar      &ToOffset   ( ( ( &Counter - 1 ) * 11 ) + 1 )

  If          (                                                          +
                ( &Counter *LE 15 )  *And                                +
                ( %Sst( &SupGrpPrf &FromOffset 10 ) *NE ' ' )            +
              )                                                          +
    Do
      ChgVar      %Sst( &SupGrpPrfA &ToOffset   10 )                     +
                  ( %Sst( &SupGrpPrf  &FromOffset 10 ) )
      ChgVar      &Counter                                               +
                  ( &Counter + 1 )
      GoTo        SupGrpBeg
    EndDo

/*  --------------------------------------------------------------  */
/*  - Convert special case parameters to appropriate values      -  */
/*  --------------------------------------------------------------  */

  If          ( &MaxStg *Eq -1 )                                         +
    ChgVar      &MaxStgA    ( '*NOMAX' )
  Else                                                                   +
    ChgVar      &MaxStgA    ( &MaxStg )



  If          ( &PwdExpItv *Eq 0 )                                       +
    ChgVar      &PwdExpItvA ( '*SYSVAL' )

  If          ( &PwdExpItv *Eq -1 )                                      +
    ChgVar      &PwdExpItvA ( '*NOMAX' )

  If          (                                                          +
                ( &PwdExpItv *NE 0 )  *And                               +
                ( &PwdExpItv *NE -1 )                                    +
              )                                                          +
    ChgVar      &PwdExpItvA ( &PwdExpItv )
```

continued

FIGURE 3.9B CONTINUED

```
  If          ( &CCSID *Eq -2 )                                        +
    ChgVar     &CCSIDA      ( '*SYSVAL' )
  Else                                                                 +
    ChgVar     &CCSIDA      ( CCSID )

/*  --------------------------------------------------------------  */
/*  - Construct qualified parameters                             -  */
/*  --------------------------------------------------------------  */

  If          ( &InlPgmLib *NE ' ' )                                   +
    ChgVar     &InlPgmA  ( &InlPgmLib *TCat '/' *TCat &InlPgm )
  Else                                                                 +
    ChgVar     &InlPgmA  ( &InlPgm )


  If          ( &InlMnuLib *NE ' ' )                                   +
    ChgVar      &InlMnuA ( &InlMnuLib *TCat '/' *TCat &InlMnu )
  Else                                                                 +
    ChgVar     &InlMnuA  ( &InlMnu )


  If          ( &OutQLib *NE ' ' )                                     +
    ChgVar      &OutQA  ( &OutQLib *TCat '/' *TCat &OutQ )
  Else                                                                 +
    ChgVar     &OutQA  ( &OutQ )


  If          ( &JobDLib *NE ' ' )                                     +
    ChgVar      &JobDA  ( &JobDLib *TCat '/' *TCat &JobD )
  Else                                                                 +
    ChgVar     &JobDA  ( &JobD )


  If          ( &AtnPgmLib *NE ' ' )                                   +
    ChgVar      &AtnPgmA  ( &AtnPgmLib *TCat '/' *TCat &AtnPgm )
  Else                                                                 +
    ChgVar     &AtnPgmA  ( &AtnPgm )


  If          ( &SrtSeqLib *NE ' ' )                                   +
    ChgVar      &SrtSeqA  ( &SrtSeqLib *TCat '/' *TCat &SrtSeq )
  Else                                                                 +
    ChgVar     &SrtSeqA  ( &SrtSeq )

/*  --------------------------------------------------------------  */
/*  - Convert numeric parameters to alpha                        -  */
/*  --------------------------------------------------------------  */

  ChgVar     &SevA         ( &Sev )
```

continued

FIGURE 3.9B ***CONTINUED***

```
/*  ============================================================  */
/*  = Create user profile                                      =  */
/*  ============================================================  */

  ChgVar     &Cmd       (                                          +
                          'CRTUSRPRF'   *BCat                      +
                          'USRPRF('     *TCat &ToUser     *TCat ')' +
                          *BCat                                    +
                          'PASSWORD('   *TCat '*USRPRF'   *TCat ')' +
                          *BCat                                    +
                          'PWDEXP('     *TCat '*YES'      *TCat ')' +
                          *BCat                                    +
                          'USRCLS('     *TCat &UsrCls     *TCat ')' +
                          *BCat                                    +
                          'ASTLVL('     *TCat &AstLvl     *TCat ')' +
                          *BCat                                    +
                          'CURLIB('     *TCat &CurLib     *TCat ')' +
                          *BCat                                    +
                          'INLPGM('     *TCat &InlPgmA    *TCat ')' +
                          *BCat                                    +
                          'INLMNU('     *TCat &InlMnuA    *TCat ')' +
                          *BCat                                    +
                          'LMTCPB('     *TCat &LmtCpb     *TCat ')' +
                          *BCat                                    +
                          'TEXT('       *TCat &TextA      *TCat ')' +
                          *BCat                                    +
                          'SPCAUT('     *TCat &SpcAutA    *TCat ')' +
                          *BCat                                    +
                          'SPCENV('     *TCat &SpcEnv     *TCat ')' +
                          *BCat                                    +
                          'DSPSGNINF('  *TCat &DspSgnInf  *TCat ')' +
                          *BCat                                    +
                          'PWDEXPITV('  *TCat &PwdExpItvA *TCat ')' +
                          *BCat                                    +
                          'LMTDEVSSN('  *TCat &LmtDevSsn  *TCat ')' +
                          *BCat                                    +
                          'KBDBUF('     *TCat &KbdBuf     *TCat ')' +
                          *BCat                                    +
                          'MAXSTG('     *TCat &MaxStgA    *TCat ')' +
                          *BCat                                    +
                          'PTYLMT('     *TCat &PtyLmt     *TCat ')' +
                          *BCat                                    +
                          'JOBD('       *TCat &JobDA      *TCat ')' +
                          *BCat                                    +
                          'GRPPRF('     *TCat &GrpPrf     *TCat ')' +
                          *BCat                                    +
                          'OWNER('      *TCat &Owner      *TCat ')' +
                          *BCat                                    +
                          'GRPAUT('     *TCat &GrpAut     *TCat ')' +
                          *BCat                                    +
                          'GRPAUTTYP('  *TCat &GrpAutTyp  *TCat ')' +
                          *BCat                                    +
                          'SUPGRPPRF('  *TCat &SupGrpPrfA *TCat ')' +
```

continued

FIGURE 3.9B CONTINUED

```
                                *BCat                                              +
                                'ACGCDE('      *TCat &AcgCde       *TCat ')'    +
                                *BCat                                              +
                                'MSGQ('        *TCat '*USRPRF'     *TCat ')'    +
                                *BCat                                              +
                                'DLVRY('       *TCat &Dlvry        *TCat ')'    +
                                *BCat                                              +
                                'SEV('         *TCat &SevA         *TCat ')'    +
                                *BCat                                              +
                                'PRTDEV('      *TCat &PrtDev       *TCat ')'    +
                                *BCat                                              +
                                'OUTQ('        *TCat &OutQA        *TCat ')'    +
                                *BCat                                              +
                                'ATNPGM('      *TCat &AtnPgmA      *TCat ')'    +
                                *BCat                                              +
                                'SRTSEQ('      *TCat &SrtSeqA      *TCat ')'    +
                                *BCat                                              +
                                'LANGID('      *TCat &LangID       *TCat ')'    +
                                *BCat                                              +
                                'CNTRYID('     *TCat &CntryID      *TCat ')'    +
                                *BCat                                              +
                                'CCSID('       *TCat &CCSIDA       *TCat ')'    +
                                *BCat                                              +
                                'CHRIDCTL('    *TCat &ChrIDCtl     *TCat ')'    +
                                *BCat                                              +
                                'USROPT('      *TCat &UsrOptA      *TCat ')'    +
                              )

  Call       Pgm( QCmdExc )                                                        +
             Parm(                                                                 +
                   &Cmd                                                            +
                   &CmdLen                                                         +
                 )

/*  ================================================================  */
/*  = Exit program                                                 =  */
/*  ================================================================  */

  Return

/*  ================================================================  */
/*  = Error handler                                                =  */
/*  ================================================================  */

Error:

  SndPgmMsg  MsgID( CPF9897 )                                                      +
             MsgF( QCPFMsg )                                                       +
             MsgDta( 'Error in CPYUSRPRF.' *BCat                                   +
                     'See job log for details.' )                                  +
             MsgType( *Escape )
  MonMsg     ( CPF0000 MCH0000 )

EndPgm
```

The program is quite simple. It performs the following basic tasks:

1. Format the text parameter.
2. Retrieve user profile information for the profile to be copied.
3. Format the retrieved parameters.
4. Construct the CrtUsrPrf command string.
5. Execute program QCmdExc (Execute Command) to create the new user profile.

CpyUsr001 implements global error trapping; if an error occurs, the program exits by sending an escape message up the program stack.

The CpyUsr command serves as a framework around which you can build a robust user profile maintenance application. For instance, you may decide that you want to maintain a database of past and current user profiles. In addition to serving as an audit trail, the contents of the database let you perform such tasks as set an initial environment when a user signs on to the system.

Figure 3.10 shows sample DDS for file UserInfo. With this file's information, you might provide the correct branch location in an inquiry program or identify the user requesting printed output by placing the user's name and department on the report.

FIGURE 3.10

DDS for File UserInfo

```
 *   ===============================================================
 *   = File.......... UserInfo                                     =
 *   = Description... User information for user profile audit      =
 *   =                and creation                                  =
 *   ===============================================================

A                                      UNIQUE
A          R USERINFOR

A            USRPRF        10A         COLHDG('User'             +
A                                             'Profile')
A            AUTDATE         L         COLHDG('Authorization'    +
A                                             'Date')
A            FIRSTNAME     15A         COLHDG('First'            +
A                                             'Name')
A            LASTNAME      15A         COLHDG('Last'             +
A                                             'Name')
A            LOCATION       2A         COLHDG('User'             +
A                                             'Location')
A            DEPARTMENT     2A         COLHDG('User'             +
A                                             'Department')

A          K USRPRF
A          K AUTDATE                   DESCEND
```

The UsrPrf and AutDate fields together serve as the primary key for the file. As a result, you can maintain a history for each user should a change occur, such as transferring to a new location. The sample assumes you don't need to maintain multiple records with the same date for a user. Note also that the AutDate key is in descending sequence. This order makes it easier for your applications to access the current (most recent) information for a user.

One good strategy for consistent user profile creation involves the use of a set of model user profiles that you copy. Consider the six user categories depicted in Figure 3.6 (page 46). For each of these categories, you can create a shell profile with parameter values set appropriately. The sole function of these shell profiles is to provide parameter values to a user profile creation application. These shell profiles should have their password set to *None so they can't be used. You should develop a naming scheme for the shell profiles that facilitates application development. For example, the categories shown in Figure 3.6 might result in the following user profiles:

- OECpy — order entry shell profile
- ICCpy — inventory control shell profile
- AcCpy — accounting shell profile
- PsCpy — personnel shell profile
- OpCpy — IT operations shell profile
- PgCpy — IT programming shell profile

Notice that each of these shell profiles has a name constructed by appending Cpy to a two-character department ID. It's now a simple task to create a command that uses a department ID to create a new user profile.

Figure 3.11A shows the source for such a user-defined command, CrtUsr.

FIGURE 3.11A

CrtUsr Command Source

```
/*  ============================================================  */
/*  = Command....... CrtUsr                                    =  */
/*  = CPP........... CrtUsrØØ1                                 =  */
/*  = Description... Create user profile and log to file UserInfo =  */
/*  ============================================================  */

  Cmd          Prompt( 'Create User' )

  Parm         Kwd( FirstName )                                     +
               Type( *Char )                                        +
               Len( 15 )                                            +
               Min( 1 )                                             +
               Case( *Mixed )                                       +
               Prompt( 'First name' )

  Parm         Kwd( LastName )                                      +
               Type( *Char )                                        +
               Len( 15 )                                            +
               Min( 1 )                                             +
               Case( *Mixed )                                       +
               Prompt( 'Last name' )
```

continued

FIGURE 3.11A *CONTINUED*

```
Parm        Kwd( Location )                                          +
            Type( *Char )                                            +
            Len( 2 )                                                 +
            Min( 1 )                                                 +
            Prompt( 'User location' )

Parm        Kwd( Department )                                        +
            Type( *Char )                                            +
            Len( 2 )                                                 +
            Min( 1 )                                                 +
            Rstd( *Yes )                                             +
            SpcVal( ( ORDER OE )                                     +
                    ( INVENTORY IC )                                 +
                    ( ACCOUNTING AC )                                +
                    ( PERSONNEL PS )                                 +
                    ( OPERATOR OP )                                  +
                    ( PROGRAMMER PG ) )                              +
            Prompt( 'User department' )

Parm        Kwd( UsrPrf )                                            +
            Type( *SName )                                           +
            Len( 10 )                                                +
            Dft( *GEN )                                              +
            SpcVal( ( *GEN ) )                                       +
            Prompt( 'User profile' )

Parm        Kwd( Password )                                          +
            Type( *SName )                                           +
            Len( 10 )                                                +
            Dft( *USRPRF )                                           +
            SpcVal( ( *USRPRF ) )                                    +
            Prompt( 'User password' )
```

The command accepts the following parameters as input:

- user's first name
- user's last name
- location code
- department code
- user profile name (optional)
- password (optional)

With this information and the shell profiles you've created, you can create your user profiles.

A closer look at CrtUsr's optional user profile name parameter reveals that you can supply a user profile name or accept its default special value, *Gen. This special value instructs the utility to generate the user profile name using the user's name (up to the first seven characters of the last name followed by up to the first three characters of the first name). You should let the utility generate the profile name whenever possible. In those cases when the result would duplicate an existing profile name, you should supply a user profile name based on some alternate naming scheme. For instance, you could replace the last character of the profile name with a number.

The password parameter is also optional; its default value of *UsrPrf instructs the system to set the password to the same value as the user profile name. The utility sets the password to an expired status so that the user must change the password at the next sign-on, but if this approach presents a security concern, you can supply a password to be used.

Figure 3.11B shows CrtUsr's CL command processing program, CrtUsr001.

FIGURE 3.11B

CrtUsr001 CLLE Source

```
/*  ================================================================  */
/*  = Program....... CrtUsr001                                     =  */
/*  = Description... Create user                                   =  */
/*  =                Command processing program for CrtUsr         =  */
/*  ================================================================  */

Pgm          Parm(                                                     +
                    &FirstName                                         +
                    &LastName                                          +
                    &Location                                          +
                    &Department                                        +
                    &UsrPrf                                            +
                    &Password                                          +
                  )

/*  ================================================================  */
/*  = Variable definitions                                         =  */
/*  ================================================================  */

/*  ----------------------------------------------------------------  */
/*  - Input parameters                                             -  */
/*  ----------------------------------------------------------------  */

  Dcl          &FirstName    *Char    (   15    )
  Dcl          &LastName     *Char    (   15    )
  Dcl          &Location     *Char    (    2    )
  Dcl          &Department   *Char    (    2    )
  Dcl          &Text         *Char    (   50    )
  Dcl          &UsrPrf       *Char    (   10    )
  Dcl          &Password     *Char    (   10    )

/*  ----------------------------------------------------------------  */
/*  - Work variables                                               -  */
/*  ----------------------------------------------------------------  */

  Dcl          &CpyPrf       *Char    (   10    )
  Dcl          &Text         *Char    (   50    )
  Dcl          &OutQ         *Char    (   10    )

/*  ================================================================  */
/*  = Global error trap                                            =  */
/*  ================================================================  */

  MonMsg      ( CPF0000 MCH0000 ) Exec(                                +
    GoTo Error                       )
```

continued

FIGURE 3.11B *CONTINUED*

```
/*  ================================================================  */
/*  = Generate user profile name when requested                     =  */
/*  ================================================================  */

  If          ( &UsrPrf *Eq '*GEN' )                                  +
    ChgVar      &UsrPrf                                               +
                (                                                     +
                  %Sst( &LastName 1 7 ) *TCat                         +
                  %Sst( &FirstName 1 3 )                              +
                )

/*  ================================================================  */
/*  = Generate text description                                     =  */
/*  ================================================================  */

  ChgVar      &Text        (                                          +
                             &FirstName *BCat                         +
                             &LastName  *TCat                         +
                             ','        *BCat                         +
                             'Loc.'     *BCat                         +
                             &Location  *TCat                         +
                             ','        *BCat                         +
                             'Dept.'    *BCat                         +
                             &Department                              +
                           )
/*  ================================================================  */
/*  = Copy user profile based on department                         =  */
/*  ================================================================  */

  ChgVar      &CpyPrf      ( &Department *TCat 'CPY' )

  CpyUsr      FromUsrPrf( &CpyPrf )                                   +
              ToUsrPrf( &UsrPrf )                                     +
              Text( &Text )

/*  ================================================================  */
/*  = Set output queue                                              =  */
/*  ================================================================  */

/*  ----------------------------------------------------------------  */
/*  - If member of IT, create and set personal output queue         -  */
/*  ----------------------------------------------------------------  */

  If          (                                                       +
                ( &Department *Eq 'PG' )  *Or                         +
                ( &Department *Eq 'OP' )                              +
              )                                                       +
    Do
      CrtOutQ     OutQ( QUsrSys/&UsrPrf )                             +
                  Text( 'Personal output queue' )
      MonMsg      ( CPF0000 MCH0000 )
      ChgVar      &OutQ       ( &UsrPrf )
    EndDo
```

continued

FIGURE 3.11B *CONTINUED*

```
/*  -------------------------------------------------------------   */
/*  - If not a member of IT, set location/department output queue -  */
/*  -------------------------------------------------------------   */

  If         (                                                      +
               ( &Department *NE 'PG' )  *And                       +
               ( &Department *NE 'OP' )                             +
             )                                                      +
    Do
      ChgVar     &OutQ        (                                     +
                                'B'          *TCat                  +
                                &Location    *TCat                  +
                                &Department *TCat                   +
                                'OUTQ'                              +
                              )
    EndDo

/*  -------------------------------------------------------------   */
/*  - Change user profile's output queue                        -   */
/*  -------------------------------------------------------------   */

  ChgUsrPrf  UsrPrf( &UsrPrf )                                      +
             OutQ( QUsrSys/&OutQ )
  MonMsg     ( CPF0000 MCH0000 )

/*  =============================================================   */
/*  = Log information to audit file UserInfo                    =   */
/*  =============================================================   */


  Call       Pgm( CrtUsr002 )                                       +
             Parm(                                                  +
                   &FirstName                                       +
                   &LastName                                        +
                   &Location                                        +
                   &Department                                      +
                   &UsrPrf                                          +
                 )

/*  =============================================================   */
/*  = Exit program                                              =   */
/*  =============================================================   */

  Return

/*  =============================================================   */
/*  = Error handler                                             =   */
/*  =============================================================   */

Error:

  SndPgmMsg  MsgID( CPF9897 )                                       +
             MsgF( QCPFMsg )                                        +
             MsgDta( 'Error in CPYUSRPRF.' *BCat                    +
                     'See job log for details.' )                   +
             MsgType( *Escape )
  MonMsg     ( CPF0000 MCH0000 )

EndPgm
```

CrtUsr001 performs the following basic tasks:

1. Generate user profile name when necessary.
2. Generate text description consisting of user name, location, and department.
3. Copy the departmental shell user profile.
4. Perform a special processing routine to set output queue.
5. Log the user profile to audit file UserInfo.

You can tailor this program as necessary. For instance, the special processing section described in step 4 is a likely candidate for enhancements. Like CpyUsr001, CrtUsr001 implements global error trapping; when an error occurs, it exits by sending an escape message up the program stack.

Logging the user profile is accomplished by RPG IV program CrtUsr002, shown in Figure 3.11C. This program simply sets the authorization date (field AutDate) to the system date and updates the UserInfo file. Figure 3.12 shows creation information for the CpyUsr and CrtUsr commands.

FIGURE 3.11C

CrtUsr002 RPGLE Source

```
 *   ==================================================================
 *   = Module........ CrtUsr002                                       =
 *   = Description... Log user profile information to audit file      =
 *   =                UserInfo                                        =
 *   ==================================================================

 *   ==================================================================
 *   = Files                                                          =
 *   ==================================================================

 *   ------------------------------------------------------------------
 *   - User information audit file                                    -
 *   ------------------------------------------------------------------

FUserInfo  UF A E           K Disk

 *   ==================================================================
 *   = Definitions                                                    =
 *   ==================================================================

 *   ------------------------------------------------------------------
 *   - Entry parameters                                               -
 *   ------------------------------------------------------------------

D EntryParms      PR                  ExtPgm( 'CRTUSR002' )
D  pFirstName                   15
D  pLastName                    15
D  pLocation                     2
D  pDepartment                   2
D  pUsrPrf                      10
```

continued

FIGURE 3.11C CONTINUED

```
D EntryParms      PI
D  FirstName                    15
D  LastName                     15
D  Location                      2
D  Department                    2
D  UsrPrf                       10

 *  ------------------------------------------------------------------
 *  - Work variables                                                 -
 *  ------------------------------------------------------------------

D  AutDate        S               D    DatFmt( *ISO )
D                                      Inz( *Sys )

 *  ==================================================================
 *  = Key lists                                                      =
 *  ==================================================================

C     UserInfoKey   Klist
C                   KFld                    UsrPrf
C                   KFld                    AutDate

 *  ==================================================================
 *  = Mainline                                                       =
 *  ==================================================================

C     UserInfoKey   Chain(E)  UserInfo

C                   If        %Found( UserInfo )
C                   Update    UserInfoR
C                   Else
C                   Write     UserInfoR
C                   EndIf

C                   Eval      *InLR = *On
```

FIGURE 3.12

Creating the CpyUsr and CrtUsr Objects

```
CrtPF       File( YourPgmLib/UserInfo )        +
            SrcFile( YourSrcLib/YourSrcFile )

CrtBndCL    Pgm( YourPgmLib/CpyUsr001 )        +
            SrcFile( YourSrcLib/YourSrcFile ) +
            DftActGrp( *No )                   +
            ActGrp( *Caller )

CrtCmd      Cmd( YourCmdLib/CpyUsr )           +
            Pgm( YourPgmLib/CpyUsr001 )        +
            SrcFile( YourSrcLib/YourSrcFile ) +
```

continued

FIGURE 3.12 CONTINUED

```
CrtBndCL    Pgm( YourPgmLib/CrtUsr001 )          +
            SrcFile( YourSrcLib/YourSrcFile ) +
            DftActGrp( *No )                  +
            ActGrp( *Caller )

CrtCmd      Cmd( YourCmdLib/CrtUsr )             +
            Pgm( YourPgmLib/CrtUsr001 )          +
            SrcFile( YourSrcLib/YourSrcFile )

CrtBndRPG   Pgm( YourPgmLib/CrtUsr002 )          +
            SrcFile( YourSrcLib/YourSrcFile ) +
            DftActGrp( *No )                  +
            ActGrp( *Caller )
```

With these examples, you should be able to develop a fully functional user profile maintenance application (with create, change, and delete features) that implements your rules. Should a rule change with time, requiring a change to one of the parameter values in a departmental shell profile, it's a snap to update all user profiles for the department. Simply include in your user profile maintenance application an UpdUsr command that retrieves the new user profile information from the shell profile, selects current users for the department from file UserInfo, and updates each of the selected profiles.

Keep in mind that there will be exceptions you'll need to handle individually. You should usually use these commands to create and maintain user profiles. Only in an exceptional case should you directly use the OS/400-supplied commands.

Making User Profiles Work for You

Whether you create user profiles with CL commands or employ user-written commands, planning is important. Careful planning will save literally hundreds of hours over your system's lifetime. Maintaining a database file such as UserInfo with the appropriate user information provides essential historical data for auditing and a way to extract significant information about the user profiles. You'll have a consistent method for creating and maintaining user profiles, and you can easily train others to create and maintain user profiles for their departments. Moreover, you'll be able to retrieve information from file UserInfo using a high-level language program, and you can use that information in applications to establish the work environment, library list, and initial menu for a user profile.

When you set up your iSeries, take the time to examine your current standards for establishing user profiles, and make your user profiles work for you!

Chapter 4

Public Authorities

High among the many strengths of the iSeries is a robust resource security mechanism. Resource security defines users' authority to objects. There are three categories of authority to an object:

- *Object authority* defines the operations that can be performed on an object. Figure 4.1A describes object authorities.
- *Data authority* defines the operations that can be performed on the object's contents. Figure 4.1B describes data authorities.
- *Field authority* defines the operations that can be performed on data fields. Figure 4.1C describes field authorities.

FIGURE 4.1A
Object Authorities

Authority	*Description*	*Allowed operations*
*ObjOpr	Object operational	• Examine object description • Use object as determined by data authorities
*ObjMgt	Object management	• Specify security for object • Move or rename object • All operations allowed by *ObjAlter and *ObjRef
*ObjExist	Object existence	• Delete object • Free storage for object • Save and restore object • Transfer object ownership
*ObjAlter	Object alter	• Add, clear, initialize, and reorganize database file members • Alter and add database file attributes • Add and remove triggers • Change SQL package attributes
*ObjRef	Object reference	• Specify referential constraint parent
*AutLMgt	Authorization list management	• Add and remove users and their authorities from authorization lists

FIGURE 4.1B
Data Authorities

Authority	*Description*	*Allowed operations*
*Read	Read	• Display object's contents
*Add	Add	• Add entries to object
*Upd	Update	• Modify object's entries
*Dlt	Delete	• Remove object's entries
*Execute	Execute	• Run a program, service program, or SQL package • Locate object in library or directory

FIGURE 4.1C
Field Authorities

Authority	*Description*	*Allowed operations*
*Mgt	Management	• Specify field's security
*Alter	Alter	• Change field's attributes
*Ref	Reference	• Specify field as part of parent key in referential constraint
*Read	Read	• Access field's contents
*Add	Add	• Add entries to data
*Update	Update	• Modify field's existing entries

Because of the number of options available, resource security is reasonably complex. It's important to examine the potential risks — as well as the benefits — of resource security's default public authority to ensure you maintain a secure production environment.

What Are Public Authorities?

Public authority to an object is that default authority given to users who have no specific, or private, authority to the object. That is, the users have no specific authority granted for their user profiles, are not on an authorization list that supplies specific authority, and are not part of a group profile with specific authority.

When you create an object, either by restoring an object to the system or by using one of the many Crt*Xxx* (Create) commands, public authorities are established. If an object is restored to the system, the public authorities stored with that object are the ones granted to the object. If a Crt*Xxx* command is used to create an object, the Aut (Authority) parameter of that command establishes the public authorities that will be granted to the object.

Public authority is granted to users in one of several standard authority sets described by the special values *All, *Change, *Use, and *Exclude. Following is a description of each of these values:

- *All — The user can perform all operations on the object except those limited to the owner or controlled by authorization list management authority. The user can control the object's existence, grant and revoke authorities for the object, change the object, and use the object. However, unless the user is also the owner of the object, he or she can't transfer ownership of the object.
- *Change — The user can perform all operations on the object except those limited to the owner or controlled by object management authority, object existence authority, object alter authority, and object reference authority. The user can perform basic functions on the object; however, he or she cannot change the attributes of the object. Change authority provides object operational authority and all data authority when the object has associated data.
- *Use — The user can perform basic operations on the object (e.g., open a file, read the records, and execute a program). However, although the user can read data records or entries, he or she will be prevented from adding, updating, or deleting data records or entries. This authority provides object operational authority, read data authority, and execute data authority.
- *Exclude — The user is specifically denied any access to the object.

Figure 4.2A shows the individual object authorities defined by the above authority sets. Figure 4.2B shows the individual data authorities.

FIGURE 4.2A
Individual Object Authorities

	Object authorities				
Authority set	***ObjOpr**	***ObjMgt**	***ObjExist**	***ObjAlter**	***ObjRef**
*All	✓	✓	✓	✓	✓
*Change	✓				
*Use	✓				
*Exclude					

FIGURE 4.2B
Individual Data Authorities

	Data authorities				
Authority set	***Read**	***Add**	***Upd**	***Dlt**	***Execute**
*All	✓	✓	✓	✓	✓
*Change	✓	✓	✓	✓	✓
*Use	✓				✓
*Exclude					

Creating Public Authority by Default

When your system arrives, OS/400 offers a means of creating public authorities. This default implementation uses the QCrtAut (Create default public authority) system value, the CrtAut (Create authority) attribute of each library, and the Aut (Public authority) parameter on each of the Crt*Xxx* commands that exist in OS/400.

System value QCrtAut provides a vehicle for system-wide default public authority. It can have the value *All, *Change, *Use, or *Exclude. *Change is the default for system value QCrtAut when OS/400 is loaded onto your iSeries. QCrtAut alone, though, doesn't control the public authority of objects created on your system.

The library attribute CrtAut found on the CrtLib (Create Library) and ChgLib (Change Library) commands defines the default public authority for all objects created in that library. Although the possible values for CrtAut include *All, *Change, *Use, *Exclude, and *AuthorizationListName*, the default for CrtAut is *SysVal, which references the value specified in system value QCrtAut. Therefore, when you create a library and don't specify a value for parameter CrtAut, the system uses the default value *SysVal. The value found in system value QCrtAut is then used to set the default public authority for objects created in the library. You should note, however, that the CrtAut value of the library isn't used when you create a duplicate object or move or restore an object in the library. Instead, the public authority of the existing object is used.

The Aut parameter of the Crt*Xxx* commands accepts the values *All, *Change, *Use, *Exclude, and *AuthorizationListName*, as well as the special value *LibCrtAut, which is the default value for most of the Crt*Xxx* commands. *LibCrtAut instructs OS/400 to use the default public authority defined by the CrtAut attribute of the library in which the object will exist. In turn, the CrtAut attribute might have a specific value defined at the library level, or it might simply reference system value QCrtAut to get the value.

Figure 4.3 shows the effect of the new default values provided for the CrtAut library attribute and the Aut object attribute. The lines and arrows on the right show how each object's Aut attribute references, by default, the CrtAut attribute of the library in which the object exists. The lines and arrows on the left show how each CrtAut attribute references, by default, the QCrtAut system value.

The values specified in Figure 4.3 for the QCrtAut system value, the CrtAut library attribute, and the Aut parameter are the shipped default values. Unless you change those defaults, every object you create on the system with the default value of Aut(*LibCrtAut) will automatically grant *Change authority to the public. (If you use the Replace(*Yes) parameter on the Crt*Xxx* command, the authority of the existing object is used rather than the CrtAut value of the library.)

If you look closely at Figure 4.3, you'll see that although this method may seem to make object authority easier to manage, it's a little tricky to grasp. First of all, consider that all libraries are defined by a library description that resides in library QSys (even the description of library QSys itself must reside in library QSys). Therefore, the QSys definition of the CrtAut attribute controls the default public authority for every library on

FIGURE 4.3
Effect of Data Values for CrtAut and Aut

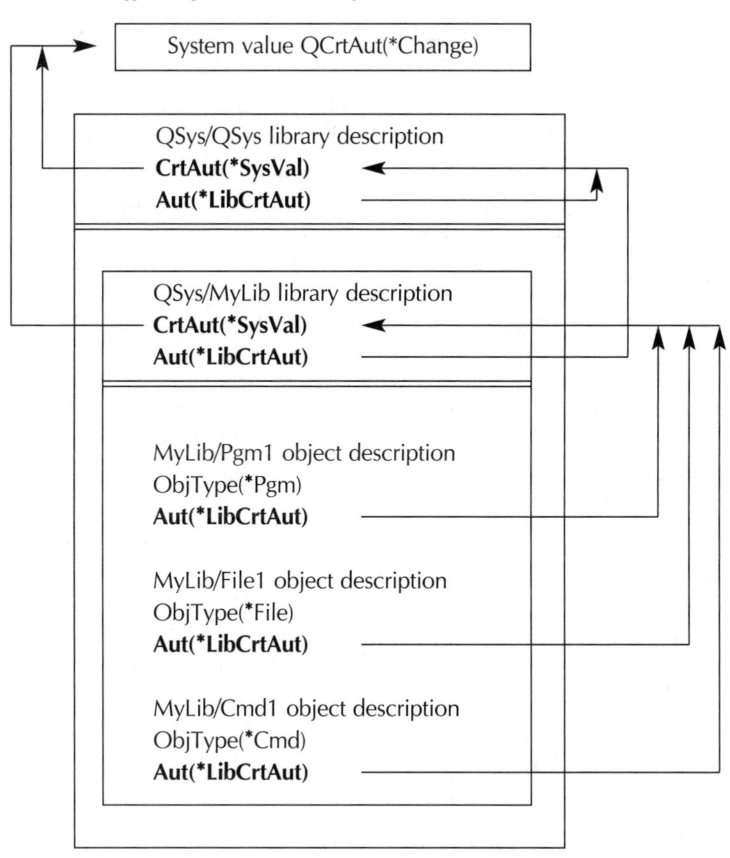

the system (not the objects in the libraries, just the library objects themselves) as long as each library uses the default value Aut(*LibCrtAut).

Executing the command

```
DspLibD QSys
```

displays the library description of QSys, which reveals that *SysVal is the value for CrtAut. Therefore, if you create a new library using the CrtLib command and specify Aut(*LibCrtAut), users will have the default public authority defined originally in the QCrtAut system value. Remember, at this point the Aut parameter on the CrtLib command is defining only the public authority to the library object.

As you can see in Figure 4.3, for each new object created in a library, the Aut(*LibCrtAut) value tells the system to use the default public authority defined by the CrtAut attribute of the library in which the object will exist.

When implementing default public authorities, consider these facts:

- You can use the CrtAut library attribute to determine the default public authority for any object created in a given library, provided the object being created specifies *LibCrtAut as the value for the Aut parameter of the Crt*Xxx* command.
- You can elect to override the *LibCrtAut value on the Crt*Xxx* command and still define the public authority using *All, *Change, *Use, *Exclude, or *AuthorizationListName*.
- The default value for the CrtAut library attribute for new libraries will be *SysVal, instructing the system to use the value found in system value QCrtAut (in effect, controlling new object default public authority at the system level).
- You can choose to replace the default value *SysVal with a specific default public authority value for that library (i.e., *All, *Change, *Use, *Exclude, or *AuthorizationListName*).

Limiting Public Authority

The fact that public authority can be created by certain default values brings us to an interesting point. The existence of default values indicates that they are the "suggested" or "normal" values for parameters. In terms of security, you may want to look at default values differently. Default values that define the public authority for objects created on your system are effective only if planned as part of your overall security implementation.

Your first inclination may be to change QCrtAut to *Use or even *Exclude to reduce the amount of public authority given to new libraries and objects. However, let us warn you that doing so could cause problems with some IBM-supplied functions.

Another tendency might be to change this system value to *All, hoping that every system object can then be "easily" accessed. Unfortunately, this would be like opening Pandora's box!

Let us make a few suggestions for effectively planning and implementing object security for your libraries and the objects in those libraries.

Public Authority by Design

The most significant threat of OS/400's default public authority implementation is the possible misuse of the QCrtAut system value. There is no doubt that changing this system value to *All would simplify security, but doing so would simply eliminate security for new libraries and objects — an unacceptable situation for any production machine. Therefore, leave this system value as *Change.

The first step in effectively implementing public authorities is to examine your user-defined libraries and determine whether the current public authorities are appropriate for the libraries and the objects within those libraries.

Then, modify the CrtAut attribute of your libraries to reflect the default public authority that should be used for objects created in each library. By doing so, you're providing the public authority at the library level instead of using the CrtAut(*SysVal) default, which references the QCrtAut system value. As a general rule, use the level of public authority given to the library object (the Aut library attribute) as the default value for the CrtAut library attribute. This is a good starting point for that library.

Consider this example. Perhaps a library contains only utility program objects that are used by various applications on your system (e.g., date-conversion programs, a binary-to-decimal conversion program, a check object or check authority program). Because all the programs should be available for execution, it's logical that the CrtAut attribute of this library be set to *Use so that any new objects created in the library will have *Use default public authority.

Suppose the library you're working with contains all the payroll and employee data files. You probably want to restrict access to this library and secure it by user profile, group profile, or an authorization list. Any new objects created in this library should probably also have *Exclude public authority unless the program or person creating the object specifically selects a public authority by using the object's Aut attribute. In this case, you would change the CrtAut attribute to *Exclude.

The point is this: Public authority at the library level and public authority for objects created in that library must be specifically planned and implemented — not just implemented by default via the QCrtAut system value.

Object-Level Public Authority

If you follow the suggestions above concerning the QCrtAut system value and the CrtAut library attribute, Aut(*LibCrtAut) will work well as the default for each object you create. In many cases, the level of public authority at the object level coincides with the public authorities established at the library level. However, it's important to plan this rather than simply use the default value to save time.

We hope you now recognize the significance of public authorities and understand the process of establishing them. If you've already installed OS/400, examine your user-defined libraries and objects to determine which, if any, changes to public authority are needed.

Chapter 5

Installing a New Release

One task you'll perform at some time on your system is installing a new release of OS/400 and your IBM licensed program products. The good news is that this process is a "piece of cake" today compared with the effort it required back when IBM first announced and delivered the AS/400 product family. No longer must you IPL the system more than a dozen times to complete the installation. When you load a new operating system release today, you can have the system perform an automatic installation or you can perform a manual installation — and either method normally requires only one machine IPL.

To prepare you for today's approach, this chapter provides a step-by-step guide to planning for and installing a new release of OS/400 and new IBM licensed program products. We cover the essential planning tasks you should accomplish before the installation, as well as the installation process itself.

Planning Is Preventive Medicine

Just as planning is important when you install your iSeries system the first time (as we covered in Chapter 1), planning for the installation of a new release offers the benefits of any preventive medicine — and it's painless! You'll no doubt be on a tight upgrade schedule, with little time for unexpected problems. By planning ahead and following the suggestions in this chapter, you can avoid having to tell your manager that the system will be down longer than expected while you recover the operating system because a missing or damaged item prevented completing the installation.

Before we describe the specific steps that will ensure a successful system upgrade, there's one other important preventive measure to note:

Caution

Unless it's impossible, don't perform a hardware upgrade and a software upgrade at the same time. If a new system model requires a particular release of OS/400 and that release is compatible with your older hardware, first install the new release on your older hardware, and then upgrade your hardware at another time to avoid compounding any problems you might encounter.

The Planning Checklist

Every good plan needs a checklist, and in this case the list of steps in Figure 5.1 is your guide. You can find a similar list in the manual *Software Installation* (SC41-5120).

FIGURE 5.1

Installation Planning Checklist

Pre–installation-day tasks

Step 1	When you receive the new release, verify your order (make sure you have the correct release, the right products on the media, and software keys for any locked licensed programs), and review the installation documents shipped with the release. If these documents weren't shipped with the release, you should order them; they may detail additional items you'll need to order before the installation.
Step 2	Determine whether you'll perform the automatic or the manual installation.
Step 3	Permanently apply any temporarily applied PTFs.
Step 4	A few days before installing the new release, remove unused objects from the system.
Step 5	Verify disk storage requirements.
Step 6	A few days before installation, document or save changes to IBM-supplied objects.
Step 7	A few days before installation, order the latest cumulative PTF package if you don't have it. You should also order the latest appropriate group packages, particularly the HIPER PTF group package.
Step 8	A day before or on the same day as the installation, save the system.

Installation-day tasks

Step 9	If your system participates in a network, resolve any pending database resynchronizations. If your system uses a 3995 optical library, check for and resolve any held optical files.
Step 10	If your system has an active Integrated Netfinity Server or Integrated xSeries Server, deactivate the server.
Step 11	Verify the integrity of system objects (user profiles QSecOfr and QLPInstall and the database cross-reference files).
Step 12	Verify and set appropriate system values.

Because IBM makes minor changes and improvements to the installation process for each release of OS/400, each new release means a new edition of the *Software Installation* manual. To ensure that you have the latest information about installing a new release, you should read this chapter in conjunction with the manual. Read the chapter entirely to get a complete overview of the process before performing the items on the checklist. If IBM's instructions conflict with those given here, follow IBM's instructions.

Pre–Installation-Day Tasks

The first group of tasks in Figure 5.1 (steps 1 through 8) should be accomplished *before* the day of the installation. By attending carefully to these items ahead of time, you'll be on firm footing when the time comes to perform the installation itself.

Step 1: Is Your Order Complete?

One of the first things you'll do is check the materials IBM shipped to you to make sure you have all the pieces you need for the installation. As of this writing, you should receive these items:

- distribution media (normally CD-ROM)
- Media Distribution Report
- Read This First
- Memo to Users for OS/400
- PTF Shipping Information Letter
- individual product documentation
- *Software Installation*

Don't underestimate the importance of each of these pieces.

Examine the CD-ROMs to make sure they're not physically damaged, and then use the Media Distribution Report to determine whether all listed volumes are actually present. For each item on the CD-ROMs, the Media Distribution Report identifies the version, release, and modification level; licensed program name; feature number (e.g., 5769SS1, 5769RG1); and language feature code. For V4R5, you'll find the version number listed as V4 (Version 4) in the product name; the release number and modification level are represented as R05M00 (Release 5, Modification Level 0) on the report.

Note that the Media Distribution Report lists only priced features. Some features, such as licensed internal code and base OS/400, are shipped with no additional charge. The report contains no entries for these items, nor does it contain entries for locked products.

The Read This First document is just what it sounds like: a document IBM wants you to read before you install the release, and preferably as soon as possible. This document contains any last-minute information that may not have been available for publication in the Memo to Users for OS/400 or in any manual.

The Memo to Users for OS/400 describes any significant changes in the new release that could affect your programs or system operations. You can use this memo to prepare for changes in the release. You'll find a specific section pertaining to licensed programs you have installed or plan to install on your system.

You'll want to read the PTF Shipping Information Letter for instructions about applying the cumulative PTF package. You also may receive additional documentation for some individual products; if you do, review those documents as well — they may contain information unique to a product that could affect its installation.

In addition to reviewing the deliverables listed above, you may want to review pertinent information found in the Preventive Service Planning Information document. This document lists additional preventive service planning documents you may want to order. To obtain it, order PTF SF98*vrm*, where *v* = version, *r* = release, and *m* = modification level for the new release. (For information about PTF ordering options, see Chapter 6.)

After reviewing this information, you should verify not only that you can read the CD-ROMs but also that they contain all necessary features. An automated procedure called Prepare for Install (available through an option on the Work with Licensed Programs panel) greatly simplifies this verification process compared with earlier releases, which involved considerable manual effort.

The panel in Figure 5.2 shows the installation-preparation procedures supported by Prepare for Install.

FIGURE 5.2

Prepare for Install Panel

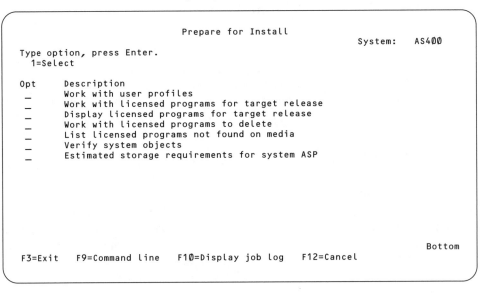

```
                          Prepare for Install
                                                        System:   AS400
 Type option, press Enter.
   1=Select

 Opt      Description
  _       Work with user profiles
  _       Work with licensed programs for target release
  _       Display licensed programs for target release
  _       Work with licensed programs to delete
  _       List licensed programs not found on media
  _       Verify system objects
  _       Estimated storage requirements for system ASP

                                                                  Bottom
 F3=Exit   F9=Command line   F10=Display job log   F12=Cancel
```

One of the panel's options compares the programs installed on your system with those on the CD-ROMs, generating a list of preselected programs that will be replaced during installation. You can inspect this list to determine whether you have all the necessary features.

To perform this verification, take these steps:

1. Arrange the CD-ROMs in the proper order. Chapter 3 of *Software Installation* contains a table specifying the correct order. You should refer to this table not only for sequencing information but also for any potential special instructions.
2. From the command line, execute the following ChgMsgQ (Change Message Queue) command to put the system operator's message queue in break mode:

   ```
   ChgMsgQ QSysOpr *Break Sev(95)
   ```

3. From the command line, enter the command

   ```
   Go LicPgm
   ```

4. You'll see the Work with Licensed Programs panel. Select option 5 (Prepare for install), and press Enter.
5. Select the option "Work with licensed programs for target release," and press Enter.
6. You'll see the Work with Licensed Programs for Target Release panel. You should

   a) load the first CD-ROM

   b) specify 1 (Distribution media) for the Generate list from prompt

   c) specify the appropriate value for the Optical device prompt

   d) specify the appropriate value for the Target release prompt

   e) press Enter

   When the system has read the CD-ROM, you'll receive a message asking you to load the next volume. If you have more CD-ROMs, load the next volume and reply G to the message to continue processing; otherwise, reply X to indicate that all CD-ROMs have been processed.
7. Once you've processed all the CD-ROMs, the Work with Licensed Programs for Target Release panel will display a list of the licensed programs that are on the distribution media and installed on your system. Preselected licensed programs (those with a 1 in the option column) indicate that a product on the distribution media can replace a product installed on your system. You can use F11 to display alternate views that provide more detail and use option 5 (Display release-to-release mapping) to see what installed products can be replaced.
8. Press Enter until the Prepare for Install panel appears.
9. Select the option "List licensed programs not found on media," and press Enter.
10. You'll see the Licensed Programs Not Found on Media panel. If no products appear in the panel's list, you have all the media necessary to replace your existing products. If products do appear in the list, you must determine whether they're necessary. If they're not, you can delete them (we describe this procedure later when we talk about cleaning up your system). If the products are necessary, you must obtain them before installation. Make sure you didn't omit any CD-ROMs during the verification process. If you didn't omit any CD-ROMs, compare your media labels with the product tables in *Software Installation* and check the Media Distribution Report to determine whether the products were shipped (or should have been shipped) with your order.
11. Exit the procedure.

Step 2: Manual or Automatic?

Before installing the new release, you need to determine whether you'll perform an automated or a manual installation. The automatic installation process is the recommended method and the one that minimizes the time required for installation. However, if you're performing any of the following tasks, you should use the manual installation process instead:

- adding a disk device using device parity protection, mirrored protection, or user auxiliary storage pools (ASPs)
- changing the primary language that the operating system and programs support (e.g., changing from English to French)
- creating logical partitions during the installation
- using tapes created with the SavSys (Save System) command
- changing the environment (AS/400 or System/36), system values, or configuration values. These changes differ from the others listed here because you can make them either during or after the new-release installation. To simplify the installation, it's best to automatically install the release and then manually make these changes.

The automatic installation will install the new release of the operating system and any currently installed licensed program products.

Step 3: Permanently Apply PTFs

One step that will save you time later is to permanently apply any PTFs that remain temporarily applied on your system. Doing so cleans up the disk space occupied by the temporarily applied PTFs. That disk space may not be much, but now is an opportune time to perform cleanup tasks. For more specific information about applying PTFs, see Chapter 6.

Step 4: Clean Up Your System

In addition to permanently applying PTFs, you should complete several other cleanup procedures. These tasks not only promote overall tidiness but also help ensure you have enough disk space for the installation. Consider these tasks:

- *Delete PTF save files and cover letters.* To delete these items, you'll use command DltPTF. Typically, you'll issue this command only for products 5769999 (licensed internal code) and 5769SS1 (OS/400).
- *Delete unnecessary spooled files, and reclaim associated storage.* Check all output queues for unnecessary spooled files. A prime candidate for housing unnecessary spooled files is output queue QEZJobLog. After deleting these spooled files, reclaim spool storage using command RclSplStg.
- *Have each user delete any unnecessary objects he or she owns.* You'd be surprised how much storage some users can unnecessarily consume. If possible, have users perform a bit of personal housekeeping by deleting spooled files and owned objects they no longer need.
- *Delete unnecessary licensed programs or optional parts.* Some licensed programs may be unnecessary for reasons such as lack of support at the target release. To review

candidates for deletion, you can use the Prepare for Install panel's "Work with licensed programs to delete" option. To reach this option, display menu LICPGM (type **Go LicPgm**) and select option 5 (Prepare for install). The "Work with licensed programs to delete" option preselects licensed programs to delete. You can use F11 (Display reasons) to determine why licensed programs are selected for deletion.

We rarely see a system that doesn't contain unused licensed programs or licensed program parts. For instance, it's not uncommon to see systems with many unused language dictionaries or unnecessary double-byte-character-set options. Prepare for Install's "Work with licensed programs to delete" option won't preselect such unnecessary options because they're valid options. If for any reason you can't use this procedure to delete licensed programs, you can use option 12 (Delete licensed programs) from menu LICPGM.

- *Delete unnecessary user profiles.* It's rarely necessary to delete user profiles as part of installation cleanup, but if this action is appropriate in your environment, consider taking care of it now. The Prepare for install option on menu LICPGM also offers procedures for cleaning up user profiles.
- *Use the automatic cleanup options in Operational Assistant.* These options provide a general method for tidying your system on a periodic basis.

For additional information about how to make more disk storage available to your system, see Chapter 12.

Step 5: Is There Enough Room?

Once you've cleaned up your system, you should verify that you have enough storage to complete the installation. Like most installation-related tasks today, this one is much easier than in earlier releases.

To determine whether you have adequate storage, perform these steps:

1. From the command line, enter **Go LicPgm**.
2. You'll see the Work with Licensed Programs panel. Select option 5 (Prepare for install), and press Enter.
3. Select the option "Estimated storage requirements for system ASP," and press Enter.
4. You'll see the Estimated Storage Requirements for System ASP panel. At the Additional storage required prompt, enter storage requirements for any additional software (e.g., third-party vendor software) that you'll be installing. Include storage requirements only for software that will be stored in the system ASP. Press Enter to continue.
5. You'll see the second Estimated Storage Requirements for System ASP panel. This panel displays information you can use to determine whether enough storage is available. Compare the value shown for "Storage required to install target release" with the value shown for "Current supported system capacity." If the value for "Current supported system capacity" is greater than the value for "Storage required to install target release," you can continue with the installation. Otherwise, you must make

additional storage available by removing items from your system or by adding DASD to your system.

6. Exit the procedure.

If you make changes to your system that affect the available storage, you should repeat these steps.

Step 6: Document System Changes

When you load a new release of the operating system, all IBM-supplied objects are replaced on the system. The installation procedure saves any changes you've made in libraries QUsrSys (e.g., message queues, output queues) and QGPL (e.g., subsystem descriptions, job queue descriptions, other work-management–related objects). However, any changes you make to objects in library QSys are lost because all those objects are replaced.

To minimize the possible loss of modified system objects, you should document any changes you make to these objects so that you can reimplement them after installing the new release. We strongly suggest maintaining a CL program that contains code to reinstate customized changes, such as command defaults; you can then execute this program with each release update.

When possible, implement these customizations in a user-created library rather than in QSys. Although the installation won't replace the user-created library's contents, you should regenerate the custom objects it contains to avoid potential problems. Such problems might occur, for example, if IBM adds a parameter to a command. Unless you duplicate the new command and then apply your customization, you'll be operating with an outdated command structure. In some cases, this difference could be critical. The CL program that customizes IBM-shipped objects should therefore first duplicate each object (when appropriate) and then change the newly created copy.

Step 7: Get the Latest Fixes

Normally, some time passes between the time you order and receive a new release and the date when you actually install it. During this elapsed time, PTFs to the operating system and licensed program products usually become available. To ensure you have the latest of these PTFs during installation, order PTFs for the new release the week before you install the release.

Obtain the latest cumulative PTF package and appropriate group packages. Of the group packages, you should at least order the HIPER group package. (IBM releases HIPER, or High-Impact PERvasive, PTFs regularly — often daily — as necessary to correct high-risk problems.) For more information about ordering PTFs, see Chapter 6.

Step 8: Save Your System

Just before installing the new release (either on installation day or the day before), you should save your system. To be safe, we recommend performing a complete system save (option 21 from the SAVE menu), but this isn't a requirement. We advise performing at least these two types of saves:

- SavSys — saves OS/400 and configuration and security information
- SavLib Lib(*IBM) — saves all IBM product libraries

It's also wise to schedule the installation so that it immediately follows your normally scheduled backup of data and programs. This approach guarantees that you have a current copy of all your most critical information in case any problems with the new installation require you to reinstall the old data and programs.

Installation-Day Tasks

Once you've completed step 8, you're nearly ready to start installing the new OS/400 release. The remaining steps (9 through 12) are best performed on the day of the installation (if they apply in your environment). They, together with the installation process itself, are the focus of the remainder of this chapter. (If you'll be using a tape drive on installation day, see "Installing from Tape?" on page 86 for some additional tips.)

Step 9: Resolve Pending Operations

First, if your system participates in a network and runs applications that use two-phase commit support, you should resolve any pending database resynchronizations before starting the installation. Two-phase commit support, used when an application updates database files on more than one system, ensures that the databases remain synchronized.

To determine whether your system uses two-phase commit support, issue the following WrkCmtDfn (Work with Commitment Definitions) command:

```
WrkCmtDfn Job(*All) Status(*Resync)
```

If the system responds with a message indicating that no commitment definitions are active, you need do nothing further. Because the typical iSeries environment isn't concerned with two-phase commit support, we don't provide details about database resynchronization here. For this information, refer to *Software Installation.*

Next, if your system has a 3995 optical library, check for and resolve any held optical files — that is, files that haven't yet been successfully written to media. Use the WrkHldOptF (Work with Held Optical Files) command to check for such files and either save or release the files.

Step 10: Shut Down the INS/IXS

If your system has an active Integrated Netfinity Server (INS) or Integrated xSeries Server (IXS), the installation may fail. You should therefore deactivate this server before starting the installation. To do so, access the Network Server Administration menu (enter **Go NwSAdm**) and select option 3.

Installing from Tape?

If you'll be using a tape drive during the new-release installation, be sure to clean the drive on installation day. Although this task sounds rather mundane, it can save you a lot of trouble. Cleaning the tape drive immediately before installing the release will minimize the chances of an interruption due to a simple problem such as the inability to read a tape because the tape drive is dirty.

In addition, if your tape drive has a history of problems such as this, clean the drive before mounting each tape during the install. Again, this step represents a small price to pay for valuable preventive medicine.

Step 11: Verify System Integrity

You should also verify the integrity of system objects required by the installation process. This includes the following:

- System distribution directory entries must exist for user profiles QSecOfr and QLPInstall.
- Database cross-reference files can't be in error.
- User profile QSecOfr can't contain secondary language libraries or alternate initial menus.

To verify the integrity of these objects, you can use the Prepare for install option on menu LICPGM. This option adds user profiles QSecOfr and QLPInstall to the system distribution directory if necessary and checks for errors in the database cross-reference files. To use the option, follow these steps:

1. From the command line, enter **Go LicPgm**.
2. The Work with Licensed Programs panel will appear. Select option 5 (Prepare for install), and press Enter.
3. From the resulting panel (Figure 5.2, shown on page 80), select the Verify system objects option, and press Enter.
4. If errors exist in the database cross-reference files, the system will issue message "CPI3DA3 Database cross-reference files are in error." Follow the instructions provided by this message to resolve the errors before continuing.
5. Exit the procedure.

A couple of items remain to check before you're finished with this step. If you're operating in the System/36 environment, check to see whether user profile QSecOfr has a menu or program specified. If so, you must remove the menu or program from the user profile before installing licensed programs.

Also, user profile QSecOfr can't have a secondary language library (named QSys29*xx*) at a previous release in its library list when you install a new release. If QSecOfr has an initial program, ensure that the program doesn't add a secondary language library to the system library list.

Step 12: Check System Values

Your next step is to check and set certain system values. Remove from system values QSysLibL (System library list) and QUsrLibL (User library list) any licensed program libraries and any secondary language libraries (QSys29*xx*). Do *not* remove library QGPL, QSys, QTemp, or QUsrSys from either of these system values.

In addition, set system value QAlwObjRst (Allow object restore) to *All. Once the installation is complete, you'll need to reset the QAlwObjRst value to ensure system security.

Ready, Set, Go!

With the planning behind you, you're ready to install your new release! The rest of this chapter provides basic instructions for the automatic installation procedure, which is the recommended method. If you must use the manual method (based on the criteria stated in planning step 2), see *Software Installation* for detailed instructions about this process.

When you perform an automatic installation of a new release of the operating system and licensed program products, the process retains the current operating environment (AS/400 or System/36), system values, and configuration while replacing these items:

- IBM licensed internal code
- OS/400 operating system
- licensed programs and optional parts of licensed programs currently installed on your system
- language feature code on the distribution media that's installed as the primary language on the system

Note

If, during the installation process, the System Attention light on the control panel appears, you should refer to Chapter 5 of *Software Installation* for a list of system reference codes (SRCs) and instructions about how to continue. The only exception is if the attention light comes on and the SRC begins with A6. The A6 codes indicate that the system is waiting for you to do something, such as reply to a message or make a device ready.

To install the new release, take the following steps.

Step 1. Arrange the CD-ROMs in the order you'll use them.

Step 2. Load the CD-ROM that contains the licensed internal code. Wait for the CD-ROM In-Use indicator to go out.

Step 3. At the control panel, set the mode to Normal.

Step 4. Execute the following PwrDwnSys (Power Down System) command:

```
PwrDwnSys *Immed Restart(*Yes) IPLSrc(D)
```

This command will start an IPL process. Note that SRC codes will continue to appear in the display area of the control panel.

Step 5. You'll see the Licensed Internal Code – Status panel. Upon 100 percent completion of the install, the display may be blank for approximately five minutes and the IPL in Progress panel may appear. You needn't respond to any of these panels.

Step 6. Load the next volume when prompted to do so. You'll receive this prompt several times during the installation process. After loading the volume, you must respond to the prompt to continue processing. The response value you specify depends on whether you have more volumes to process: A response of G instructs the installation process to continue with the next volume, and a response of X indicates that no more volumes exist.

Step 7. Next, the installation process loads the operating system followed by licensed programs. During this process, you may see panels with status information. One of these panels, Licensed Internal Code IPL in Progress, lists several IPL steps, some of which can take a long time (two hours or more). The amount of time needed depends on the amount of recovery your system requires. As the installation process proceeds, you needn't respond to the status information panels you see.

Once all your CD-ROMs have been read, be prepared to wait for quite some time while the installation process continues. The process is hands-free until the Sign On panel appears.

Step 8. When installation is complete, you'll see the Sign On panel. If you receive the message "Automatic installation not complete," you should sign on using the QSecOfr user profile and refer to Appendix A, "Recovery Procedures," in *Software Installation* for instructions about how to proceed. If the automatic installation process was completed normally, sign on using user profile QSecOfr and continue by verifying the installation, loading additional products, loading PTFs, and updating software license keys.

Verify the installation. To verify the installation, execute the Go LicPgm command. On the Work with Licensed Programs display, choose option 50 (Display log for messages). The Display Install History panel (Figure 5.3) will appear.

Press Enter on this panel, and scan the messages found on the History Log Contents display. If any messages indicate a failure or a partially installed product, refer to "Recovery Procedures" in *Software Installation.*

Next, verify the status and check the compatibility of the installed licensed programs. To do so, use option 10 (Display licensed programs) from menu LICPGM

FIGURE 5.3
Display Install History Panel

```
                          Display Install History

Type choices, press Enter.

  Start date . . . . . .   07/17/00    MM/DD/YY

  Start time . . . . . .   09:32:35    HH:MM:SS

  Output . . . . . . . .   *           *, *PRINT









F3=Exit   F12=Cancel
(C) COPYRIGHT IBM CORP. 1980, 1998.
```

to display the release and installed status values of the licensed programs. A status of *COMPATIBLE indicates a licensed program is ready to use. If you see a different status value for any licensed program, refer to the "Installed Status Values" section of Appendix E in *Software Installation.*

Load additional products. You're now ready to load any additional licensed programs and secondary languages. Return to the Work with Licensed Programs menu, and select option 11 (Install licensed programs). You'll see the Install Licensed Programs display that appears in Figure 5.4 (page 90).

The installation steps for loading additional products are similar to the steps you've already taken. Select a licensed program to install, and continue. If you don't see a desired product in the list, follow the specific instructions delivered with the distribution media containing the new product.

Load PTFs. Next, install the cumulative PTF package (either the one that arrived with the new release or a new one you ordered, as suggested in the planning steps we discussed earlier). The shipping letter that accompanies the PTF tape will have specific instructions about how to install the PTF package.

Note that to complete the installation process, you must IPL the system or install a cumulative PTF package, which will also perform an IPL. An IPL is required to start the Initialize System (InzSys) process. (The InzSys process can take two hours or more on some systems, but for most systems it's completed in a few

FIGURE 5.4
Install Licensed Programs Panel

```
                        Install Licensed Programs
                                                          System:   AS400
Type options, press Enter.
  1=Install

        Licensed  Installed
Option  Program   Status        Description
  _     5769SS1   *COMPATIBLE   OS/400 - Library QGPL
  _     5769SS1   *COMPATIBLE   OS/400 - Library QUSRSYS
  _     5769SS1   *COMPATIBLE   OS/400 - Extended Base Support
  _     5769SS1   *COMPATIBLE   OS/400 - Online Information
  _     5769SS1   *COMPATIBLE   OS/400 - Extended Base Directory Support
  _     5769SS1                 OS/400 - S/36 and S/38 Migration
  _     5769SS1                 OS/400 - System/36 Environment
  _     5769SS1                 OS/400 - System/38 Environment
  _     5769SS1   *COMPATIBLE   OS/400 - Example Tools Library
  _     5769SS1   *COMPATIBLE   OS/400 - AFP Compatibility Fonts
  _     5769SS1   *COMPATIBLE   OS/400 - *PRV CL Compiler Support
  _     5769SS1                 OS/400 - S/36 Migration Assistant
  _     5769SS1   *COMPATIBLE   OS/400 - Host Servers
                                                                    More...
F3=Exit   F11=Display release   F12=Cancel   F19=Display trademarks

(C) COPYRIGHT IBM CORP. 1980, 1998.
```

minutes.) In addition to installing a cumulative PTF package, you should install any group PTFs you have — particularly the HIPER PTFs group package. (For information about installing PTFs, see Chapter 6.)

After the cumulative PTF installation or IPL is completed, sign on as QSecOfr and check the install history (using option 50 on menu LICPGM) for status messages relating to the InzSys process. You should look for a message indicating that InzSys has started or a message indicating its completion. If you see neither message, wait a few minutes and try option 50 again. Continue checking the install history until you see the message indicating InzSys completion. If the message doesn't appear in a reasonable amount of time, refer to the "INZSYS Recovery Information" section of Appendix A in *Software Installation*.

Update software license keys. To install software license keys, use the WrkLicInf (Work with License Information) command. For each product, update the license key and the usage limit to match the usage limit you ordered. The license information is part of the upgrade media. You must install license keys within 70 days of your release installation.

Step 9. The installation of your new release is now complete! The only thing left to do before restarting production activities is to perform another SavSys to save the new release and the new IBM program products. Just think how much trouble it would be if you had a disk crash soon after loading the new release and, with no current SavSys, were forced to restore the old release and repeat the installation process. To make sure you don't suffer this fate, perform the SavSys and the SavLib Lib(*IBM) operations now.

Before starting the save, determine whether system jobs that decompress objects are running. You should start your save only if these jobs are in an inactive state. To make this determination, use the WrkActJob (Work with Active Jobs) command and check the status of QDCPOBJ*x* jobs (more than one may exist). You can ensure these jobs are inactive by placing the system in restricted state. Don't worry — the QDCPOBJ*x* jobs will become active again when the system is no longer in restricted state.

Final Advice

The only risk you take when installing a new release is not being prepared for failure. It's rare that a new-release installation must be aborted midway through, but it does happen. If you take the precautions mentioned in the planning suggestions in this chapter and turn to "Recovery Procedures" in *Software Installation* in the event of trouble, you won't find yourself losing anything but time should you encounter an unrecoverable error. For the most part, installing new releases is only an inconvenience in time.

Now that we've covered all the basic steps involved in planning and installing a new iSeries operating system release, in the next chapter we'll specifically address maintaining and installing PTFs.

Chapter 6

An Introduction to PTFs

Much as we'd like to think the iSeries is invincible, from time to time even the best of systems needs a little repair. IBM provides such assistance for the iSeries in the form of PTFs.

A PTF, or *program temporary fix*, is one or more objects (most often program code) that IBM creates to correct a problem in the IBM licensed internal code, in the OS/400 operating system, or in an IBM licensed program product. In addition to issuing PTFs to correct problems, IBM uses PTFs to add function or enhance existing function in these products. The fixes are called "temporary" because a PTF fixes a problem or adds an enhancement only until the next release of that code or product becomes available; at that time, the fix becomes part of the base product itself, or "permanent."

Hardware and software service providers distribute PTFs. Your hardware maintenance vendor is typically responsible for providing microcode PTFs, while your software service provider furnishes system software PTFs. Because IBM is both the hardware and the software provider for most shops, the focus here is on IBM distribution of PTFs.

In this chapter, you'll learn the necessary information to determine when PTFs are required on your system, what PTFs you need, how to order PTFs, and how to install and apply those PTFs.

When Do You Need a PTF?

Perhaps the most difficult hurdle to get over in understanding PTFs is knowing when you need one. Basically, there are three ways to determine when you need one or more PTFs. The first way is simple: You should regularly order and install the latest cumulative PTF package, group PTFs, Client Access service pack, and necessary individual HIPER PTFs.

A *cumulative PTF package* is an ever-growing collection of *significant* PTFs. You might wonder what criteria IBM uses to determine whether a PTF is significant. In general, a PTF is deemed significant, and therefore included in a cumulative package, when it has a large audience or is critical to operations. IBM releases cumulative packages on a regular basis, and you should stay up-to-date with them, loading each package fairly soon after it becomes available. You should also load the latest cumulative package any time you load a new release of OS/400. To order the latest cumulative PTF package, you use the special PTF identifier SF99*vrm*, where *v* = OS/400 version, *r* = release, and *m* = modification.

A *group PTF* is a logical grouping of PTFs related to a specific function, such as database or Java. Each group has a single PTF identifier assigned to it so that you can download all PTFs for the group by specifying only one identifier.

Client Access service packs are important if you access your system using Client Access. Like a group PTF, a service pack is a logical grouping of multiple PTFs available under a single PTF identifier for easy download.

HIPER, or High-Impact PERvasive, PTFs are released regularly (often daily) as necessary to correct high-risk problems. Ignore these important PTFs, and you chance catastrophic consequences, such as data loss or a system outage.

A second way you may discover you need a PTF is by encountering a problem. To identify and analyze the problem, you might use the AnzPrb (Analyze Problem) command, or you might investigate error messages issued by the system. If you report a system problem to IBM based on your analysis, you may receive a PTF immediately if someone else has already reported the problem and IBM has issued a PTF to resolve it.

The third way to discover you might need particular PTFs is by regularly examining the latest Preventive Service Planning (PSP) information. You can download PSP information by ordering special PTFs. (To learn more about PSP documents and for helpful guidelines for managing PTFs, see the section "Developing a Proactive PTF Management Strategy" on page 100.)

How Do You Order a PTF?

You can order individual PTFs, a set of PTFs (e.g., a cumulative PTF package, a group PTF), and PSP information from IBM by mail, telephone, fax, or electronic communications. Each PTF you receive has two parts: a cover letter that describes both the PTF and any prerequisites for loading it, and the actual fix.

You have two choices when ordering PTFs electronically. You can use Electronic Customer Support (ECS) and the CL SndPTFOrd (Send PTF Order) command, or you can order PTFs on the Internet.

Electronically ordered PTFs are delivered electronically only when they're small enough that they can be transmitted within a reasonable connect time. When electronic means are not practical, IBM send the PTFs via mail on selected media, as it does for PTFs ordered by non-electronic means.

SndPTFOrd Basics

The SndPTFOrd command is a simple command to use; however, a brief introduction here may point out a couple of the command's finer points to simplify its use. Figure 6.1 shows the prompted SndPTFOrd command.

For parameter PTFID, you enter one, or up to 20, PTF identifiers (e.g., SF98440, MF98440). The parameter actually has three elements or parts. First is the actual PTF identifier, a required entry. The second element is the Product identifier, which determines whether the PTF order is for a specific product or for all products installed on your system. The default value you see in Figure 6.1, *OnlyPrd, indicates that the order is for all products installed or supported on your system. Instead of this value, you can enter a specific product ID (e.g., 5769RG1, 5769PW1) to limit your order to PTFs specific to that product.

The third PTFID element, Release, determines whether the PTF order is for the current release levels of products on your system or for a specific release level, which may or may not be the current release level installed for your products. For example, you might order a different release-level PTF for products you support on remote systems. A Release value of *OnlyRls indicates that the order is for the release levels of the products installed or supported on your system. If you prefer, you can enter a specific release identifier (e.g., V4R4M0, V4R3M0) to limit the PTF order to that release.

FIGURE 6.1
SndPTFOrd Command Prompt

```
                              Send PTF Order (SNDPTFORD)
Type choices, press Enter.
PTF description:                     PTFID
  PTF identifier . . . . . . . .
  Product  . . . . . . . . . . .                   *ONLYPRD__
  Release  . . . . . . . . . . .                   *ONLYRLS__
                              + for more values
PTF parts  . . . . . . . . . . .PTFPART            *ALL______
Remote control point . . . . . .RMTCPNAME          *IBMSRV___
Remote network identifier  . . .RMTNETID           *NETADR___
                               Additional Parameters
Delivery method  . . . . . . . .DELIVERY           *LINKONLY
Order  . . . . . . . . . . . . .ORDER              *REQUIRED
Reorder  . . . . . . . . . . . .REORDER            *NO_

                                                                        Bottom
F3=Exit   F4=Prompt   F5=Refresh   F12=Cancel   F13=How to use this display
F24=More keys
```

Two restrictions apply to the Product and Release elements of the PTFID parameter. First, if you specify a particular product, you also must specify a particular release level. Second, if you specify *OnlyPrd for the product element, you also must specify *OnlyRls for the release element.

From time to time, you may want to download only a cover letter to determine whether a particular PTF is necessary for your system. The next SndPTFOrd parameter, PTFPart (PTF parts), makes this possible. Use value *All to request both PTF(s) and cover letter(s) or value *CvrLtr to request cover letter(s) only.

The next two parameters, RmtCPName (Remote control point) and RmtNetID (Remote network identifier), identify the remote service provider and the remote service provider network. You should change parameter RmtCPName (default value *IBMSrv) only if you are using a service provider other than IBM or are temporarily accessing another service provider to obtain application-specific PTFs. Parameter RmtNetID must correctly identify the remote service provider network. The value *NetAtr causes the system to refer to the system's network attributes to retrieve the local network identifier (you can view the network attributes using the DspNetA, or Display Network Attributes, command). If you change the local network identifier in the network attributes, you may then have to override this default value when you order PTFs. Your network provider can give you the correct RmtNetID if the default doesn't work.

SndPTFOrd's Delivery parameter determines how PTFs are delivered to you. A value of *LinkOnly tells ECS to deliver PTFs only via the electronic link. The value *Any specifies that the PTFs can be delivered using any available method. Most PTFs ordered using SndPTFOrd are downloaded immediately using ECS; however, PTFs that are too large for electronic download are instead shipped by mail.

The next parameter, Order, specifies whether only the ordered PTFs are sent or also any requisite PTFs you must apply before, or along with, the PTFs you're ordering. Value *Required requests the PTFs you're ordering as well as any other required PTFs that accompany them. Value *PTFID specifies that only those PTFs you're ordering are to be sent.

The last parameter, Reorder, specifies whether you want to reorder a PTF that's currently installed or ordered. Valid values are *No and *Yes. Reorder(*Yes) is necessary if you've previously sent for only the cover letter and now want to order the PTF itself. If you permit Reorder to default to *No in this case, OS/400 won't order the PTF because it thinks it's already done so, when, in fact, you've received only the cover letter.

Ordering PTFs on the Internet

IBM provides a detailed overview of the Internet PTF download process, along with detailed instructions, at the IBM iSeries and AS/400 Technical Support Web site, *http://www.as400service.ibm.com*. The service is free and available to all iSeries and AS/400 owners.

When you visit the site, select "Fixes and Updates" and then select "Internet PTF Downloads (iPTF)" to reach the Internet PTF Downloads page. Then simply complete the following few steps, and you're ready to download PTFs:

1. Register for the service.
2. Configure your system, and start the appropriate services.
3. Test your PC's Internet browser to ensure it supports the JavaScript programs used in the download process.
4. Log on, identify the PTFs you want to download, and begin the download.
5. After you've downloaded the PTFs, you simply continue normal PTF application procedures.

How Do You Install and Apply a PTF?

Installing a PTF includes two basic steps: loading the PTF and applying the PTF. The process we outline here performs both the loading and the application of the PTF. Note one caution concerning the process of loading and applying PTFs: *You must not interrupt any step in this process.* Interrupting a step can cause problems significant enough to require reloading the current version of the licensed internal code or the operating system. Make sure, for example, that your electrical power is protected with an uninterruptible power supply (UPS). Also note that for systems with logical partitions, the PTF process differs in some critical ways; if you have such a system, be sure to read "PTFs and Logical Partitioning (LPAR)" (page 97) for more information.

First, we'll look at loading and applying PTFs for the IBM licensed internal code. Then we'll examine the process for loading and applying PTFs for licensed program products.

Caution

Anytime you plan to add a significant number of PTFs to your system, you should have a current backup. Our preference is for a full system backup, but if that's not possible, you should at least have a current backup of system data (you can use option 22 on menu SAVE to back up system data). Applying even a single PTF can result in catastrophic problems that require you to reload the system. Fortunately, PTF application rarely causes such devastation, but if this does happen, you'll be relieved to know you have a backup with which you can recover your system.

PTFs and Logical Partitioning (LPAR)

Although the basic steps of installing PTFs are the same for a system with logical partitions, some important differences exist. Fail to account for these differences when you apply PTFs, and you could find yourself with an inoperable system requiring lengthy recovery procedures. For systems with logical partitions, heed the following warnings:

- When you load PTFs to a primary partition, shut down all secondary partitions before installing the PTFs.
- When using the Go PTF command on the primary partition, change the automatic IPL parameter from its default value of *Yes to *No unless the secondary partitions are powered down.

These warnings, however, are only the beginning with respect to the differences imposed by logical partitioning. There are also partition-sensitive PTFs that apply specifically to the lowest-level code that controls logical partitions. These PTFs have special instructions that you *must* follow *exactly*. These instructions include the following steps:

1. Permanently apply any PTFs superseded by the new PTFs.
2. Perform an IPL of all partitions from the A side.
3. Load the PTFs on all logical partitions using the LodPTF (Load PTF) command. *Do not* use the Go PTF command.
4. Apply the PTFs temporarily on all logical partitions using the ApyPTF (Apply PTF) command.
5. Power down all secondary partitions.
6. Perform a power down and IPL of the primary partition from side B in normal mode.
7. Perform normal-mode IPLs of all secondary partitions from side B.
8. Apply all the PTFs permanently using command ApyPTF.

When you receive partition-sensitive PTFs, *always* refer to any accompanying special instructions before loading the PTFs onto your system.

Installing Licensed Internal Code PTFs

Step 1. Print and review any cover letters that accompany the PTFs. Look especially for any specific pre-installation instructions. You can do this by entering the DspPTF (Display Program Temporary Fix) command and specifying the parameters CoverOnly(*Yes) and either Output(*) or Output(*Print), depending on whether you want to view the cover letter on your workstation or print the cover letter.

For example, to print the cover letter for PTF MF12345, you'd enter the following DspPTF command:

```
DspPTF LicPgm(5769999)   +
       Select(MF12345)   +
       CoverOnly(*Yes)   +
       Output(*Print)
```

Note

You can also access cover letters at the IBM Tech Support Web site by following the "Technical Information & Databases" link.

Step 2. Determine which storage area your machine is currently using. The system maintains two copies of all the IBM licensed internal code on your system. This lets your system maintain one permanent copy while you temporarily apply changes (PTFs) to the other area. Only when you're certain you want to keep the changes are those changes permanently applied to the control copy of the licensed internal code. The permanent copy is stored in system storage area A, and the copy considered temporary is stored in system storage area B. When the system is running, it uses the copy you selected at your last IPL. Except for rare circumstances, such as when serious operating system problems occur, the system should always run using storage area B.

To apply PTFs to the B storage area, the system must actually IPL from the A storage area and then IPL again on the B storage area to begin using those applied PTFs. On older releases of OS/400, you had to manually IPL to the A side, apply PTFs, and then manually IPL to the B side again. The system now handles this IPL process automatically during the PTF install and apply process.

To determine which storage area you're currently using, execute the command

```
DspPTF 5769999
```

and check the IPL source field to determine which storage area is current. You will see either ##MACH#A or ##MACH#B, which tells you whether you are running on storage area A or B, respectively. If you are not running on the B storage area, execute the following PwrDwnSys (Power Down System) command before continuing with your PTF installation

```
PwrDwnSys Option(*Immed) +
          Restart(*Yes)  +
          IPLSrc(B)
```

Step 3. Enter **Go PTF** and press Enter to reach the Program Temporary Fix (PTF) panel. Select the "Install program temporary fix package" option.

Step 4. Supply the correct value for the Device parameter, depending on whether you received the PTF(s) on media or electronically. If you received the PTF(s) on media, enter the name of the device you're using. If you received the PTF(s) electronically, enter the value *Service. Then press Enter.

Step 5. The system then performs the necessary steps to temporarily apply the PTFs and re-IPL to the B storage area. Once the IPL is complete, verify the PTF installation (for instructions about how to do so, see "Verifying Your PTF Installation," below).

Installing Licensed Program Product PTFs

Installing PTFs for licensed program products is almost identical to installing licensed internal code PTFs, except that you don't have to determine the storage area on which you're currently running. The abbreviated process for licensed program products is as follows.

Step 1. Review any cover letters that accompany the PTFs. Look especially for any specific pre-installation instructions.

Step 2. Enter **Go PTF** and press Enter to reach the Program Temporary Fix (PTF) panel. Select the "Install program temporary fix package" option.

Step 3. Supply the correct value for the Device parameter, depending on whether you received the PTF(s) on media or electronically. If you received the PTF(s) on media, enter the name of the device you're using. If you received the PTF(s) electronically, enter the value *Service. Then press Enter.

Step 4. After the IPL is complete, verify the PTF installation (see "Verifying Your PTF Installation").

Verifying Your PTF Installation

After installing one or more PTFs, you should verify the installation process before resuming either normal system operations or use of the affected product. Use the system-supplied history log to verify PTF installations by executing the DspLog (Display Log) command, specifying the time and date you want to start with in the log:

```
DspLog Log(QHst)                    +
       Period((StartTime StartDate))
```

Be sure to specify a starting time early enough to include your PTF installation information. On the Display Log panel, look for any messages regarding PTF installation. If you have messages that describe problems, see *Basic System Operation, Administration, and Problem Handling* (SC41-5206) for more information about what to do when your PTF installation fails.

When installing a cumulative PTF package, you can also use option 50, "Display log for messages," on the Work with Licensed Programs panel (to reach this panel, issue the command Go LicPgm). The message log will display messages that indicate whether the install was successful.

How Current Are You?

One last thing that will help you stay current with your PTFs is knowing what cumulative PTF package you currently have installed. To determine your current cumulative PTF package level, execute the command

```
DspPTF LicPgm(5769SS1)
```

The ensuing display panel shows the identifiers for PTFs on your system. The panel lists PTFs in decreasing sequence, showing cumulative package information first, before individual PTFs. Cumulative packages start with TC or TA and end with five digits that represent the Julian date (in *yyddd* format) for the particular package. PTF identifiers that start with TC indicate that the entire cumulative package has been applied; those starting with TA indicate that HIPER PTFs and HIPER licensed internal code fixes have been applied.

To determine the level of licensed internal code fixes on your system, execute the command

```
DspPTF LicPgm(5769999)
```

Identifiers beginning with the letters TL and ending with the five-digit Julian date indicate the cumulative level. Typically, you want the levels for TC, TA, and TL packages to match. This circumstance indicates that you've applied the cumulative package to licensed program products as well as to licensed internal code.

Developing a Proactive PTF Management Strategy

We can't overstate the importance of developing sound PTF management processes. A proactive PTF management strategy lessens the impact to your organization that can result from program failures by avoiding those failures, ensuring optimal performance, and maximizing availability.

Because environments vary, no single strategy applies to all scenarios. However, you should be aware of certain guidelines when evaluating your environment and establishing scheduled maintenance procedures. Your PTF maintenance strategy should include provisions for preventive service planning, preventive service, and corrective service.

Preventive Service Planning

Planning your preventive measures is the first step to effective PTF management. To help you with planning, IBM publishes several Preventive Service Planning documents in the form of informational PTFs. The easiest and fastest way to obtain these documents is from the IBM Service Web site. Following are some minimum recommendations for PSP review.

You should start with the software and hardware PSP information documents by ordering SF98*vrm* (Current Cumulative PTF Package) and MF98*vrm* (Hardware Licensed Internal Code Information), respectively. These documents contain service recommendations concerning critical PTFs or PTFs that are most likely to affect your system, as well as a list of the other PSP documents from which you can choose. You should order and review SF98*vrm* and MF98*vrm* at least monthly.

Between releases of cumulative PTF packages, you may need to order individual PTFs critical to sound operations. If you review no other additional PSP documents, review the information for HIPER PTFs and Defective PTFs. These documents contain information about critical PTFs. At a minimum, review this information weekly.

In years past, PSP documents contained enough detail to let you determine the nature of the problems that PTFs fixed. Unfortunately, that's no longer the case. With problem descriptions such as "Data Integrity" and "Usability of a Product's MAJOR Function," you often must do a little more work to determine the nature of problems described in the PSP documents by referring to PTF cover letters.

In addition to reviewing PSP documents, consider subscribing to IBM's AS/400 Alert offering. This service notifies you weekly about HIPER problems, defective PTFs, and the latest cumulative PTF package. You can receive this information by fax or mail. To learn more about this service, go to *http://www.ibm.com/services.*

Preventive Service

Preventive measures are instrumental to your system's health. Remember the old adage "An ounce of prevention…"? Suffice it to say we've seen situations where PTFs would have saved tens of thousands of dollars. Avoid problems, and you avoid their associated high costs.

Preventive maintenance includes regular application of cumulative and group PTF packages and Client Access service packs. Because all of these are collections of PTFs, your work is actually quite easy. There's no need to wade through thousands of PTFs to determine those you need. Instead, simply order and apply the packages.

Cumulative PTF packages are your primary preventive maintenance aid. Released on a periodic basis, they should be applied soon after they become available — usually every three to four months. This rule of thumb is especially true if you're using the latest hardware or software releases or making significant changes to your environment.

In conjunction with cumulative PTF packages, you should stay current with any group PTF packages applicable to your environment, as well as with Client Access service packs if appropriate. You can find Client Access service pack information and download service packs by following the links at *http://www.as400.ibm.com/clientaccess*.

Corrective Service

Even the most robust and aggressive scheduled maintenance efforts can't thwart all possible problems. When you experience problems, you need to find the corrective PTFs.

Ferreting out of PSP information about individual problems and fixes is without a doubt the most detailed of the tasks in managing PTFs. However, if you take the time to learn your way around PSP information and PTF cover letters, you'll be able to find timely resolution to your problems.

Your goal should be to minimize the corrective measures required. In doing so, your environment will be dramatically more stable operationally. With robust preventive service planning and preventive service measures, your corrective service issues will be minimal.

Chapter 7

Getting Your Message Across: User-to-User

Sooner or later, you'll want to use messages on your system. For instance, you might need to have a program communicate with a user or a workstation to request input, report a problem, or simply update a user or system operator about the status of the program (e.g., "Processing today's invoices"). Another time, your application might need to communicate with another program. Program-to-program messages can include informational, notification, status, completion, diagnostic, escape, and request messages, each of which aids in developing program function, problem determination, or application auditing. "File *YourLib/YourObj* not found" is an example of a diagnostic program-to-program message.

You or your users can also send messages to one or more users or workstations on the spur of the moment. Sometimes called impromptu messages, user-to-user messages aren't predefined in a message file. They might simply convey information, or they might require a response (e.g., "Joe, aliens have just landed and taken the programming manager hostage. What should we do???"). User-to-user messages can serve as a good introduction to iSeries messaging.

Sending Messages 101

To send user-to-user messages, you use one of three commands or a feature of Operational Assistant (an OS/400 facility that provides menus and displays to help end users perform common tasks). Commands SndMsg, SndBrkMsg, and SndNetMsg are similar, yet each offers its own unique features.

SndMsg (Send Message) is the most commonly used message command — you can use it even if LmtCpb(*Yes) is specified on your user profile — and the easiest to learn. Figure 7.1 shows the SndMsg prompt screen.

To access the SndMsg command, you can

- key **SndMsg** on a command line
- select option 5 (Send a message) on the System Request menu
- select option 3 (Send a message) on the User Task menu

The message string you enter in the SndMsg command's Msg (Message text) parameter can be up to 512 characters long. To specify the message destination, you enter a user profile name in the ToUsr (To user profile) parameter. ToUsr can have any of the following values:

- *UserProfileName* — to send the message to a user's message queue (which may or may not have the same name as the user profile)
- *SysOpr — to send the message to the system operator's message queue (QSys/QSysOpr)

FIGURE 7.1
Send Message (SNDMSG) Panel

```
                              Send Message (SNDMSG)

 Type choices, press Enter.

 Message text . . . . . . . . . .   ________________________________________
________________________________________________________________________
________________________________________________________________________
________________________________________________________________________
________________________________________________________________________
________________________________________________________________________
____________________________________________________________
 To user profile  . . . . . . . .   _________      Name, *SYSOPR, *ALLACT...

                           Additional Parameters

 To message queue . . . . . . . .   _________      Name, *SYSOPR, *HSTLOG
   Library  . . . . . . . . . . .     *LIBL____    Name, *LIBL, *CURLIB
              + for more values     _________
                                      *LIBL____
 Message type . . . . . . . . . .   *INFO          *INFO, *INQ
 Message queue to get reply . . .   *WRKSTN___     Name, *WRKSTN
   Library  . . . . . . . . . . .     _________    Name, *LIBL, *CURLIB
 Coded character set ID . . . . .   *JOB______     1-65535, *HEX, *JOB
```

- *AllAct — to send the message to the message queue of every user currently signed on to the system (note that *AllAct isn't valid when MsgType(*Inq) is also specified)
- *Requester — to send the message to either the requesting user profile's message queue (for interactive jobs) or the system operator message queue (when the command is executed from within a batch job)

For example, say you simply want to inform John Smith, a co-worker, of a meeting. You could enter

```
SndMsg Msg('John - Our meeting today will be at 4:00. Jim') +
       ToUsr(JSmith)
```

Another way to specify the message destination is to enter up to 50 message queue names in SndMsg's ToMsgQ (To message queue) parameter. You can specify any external message queue on your system, including the workstation, user profile, or system history log (QHst) message queue. (For more information about sending messages to QHst, see "Sending Messages into History," page 105.) Specifying more than one message queue is valid only for informational messages, with the exception that inquiry messages can specify two message queues if one of them is *HstLog.

The MsgType (Message type) parameter lets you specify whether the message you're sending is an informational (*Info, the default) or inquiry (*Inq) message. Like an informational message, an inquiry message appears on the destination message queue as text. However, an inquiry message also presents a response line to the user and waits for

Sending Messages into History

One feature of the SndMsg (Send Message) command is its ability to send a message to the system's history log, QHst. QHst automatically tracks high-level activities on your system, such as job starts and completions, device status changes, system operator messages and replies, and PTF activity. (For a more thorough description of QHst, see Chapter 14.)

Sending messages to QHst can enhance application auditing. For instance, say you want to monitor a certain report to determine who uses it and how often. In a CL program that submits or executes the report, you could simply add a statement such as

```
SndMsg Msg('Report ABCPRINT requested by user' *BCat +
           &UsrPrf)                                  +
       ToMsgQ(QHst)
```

where &UsrPrf is a CL variable that contains the current user profile name, which the program can retrieve by using the RtvUsrPrf (Retrieve User Profile) command. You could then use the DspLog (Display Log) command to display the contents of QHst.

This is just one example of the kind of tracking you can do. For instance, the SndPgmMsg (Send Program Message) command lets you perform this function as well. Experiment with these commands, and see how sending messages to QHst can give you insight into the way your applications are being used.

a reply. If you wanted to schedule a meeting with John and be sure he received your message, you could enter

```
SndMsg Msg('John - Will 4:00 be a good time for our meeting today? Jim') +
       ToUsr(JSmith)                                                      +
       MsgType(*Inq)
```

The RpyMsgQ (Message queue to get reply) parameter specifies which message queue should receive the response to the inquiry message. Because the default for RpyMsgQ is *Wrkstn, John's reply would be sent to your (the sender's) workstation message queue.

Message Delivery with SndMsg

As you can see, the SndMsg command provides a simple way to send a message or inquiry to someone else on the local system. However, it has one quirk. Although SndMsg can send a message to a message queue, it is the message queue delivery mode attribute, Dlvry (Delivery), that defines how the message will be received. The delivery mode can be any of the following values:

- *Break — This mode is typically used so that the user is interrupted with a message when it is received. When you specify *Break mode for the message queue, you also specify a program to process the message immediately upon its arrival in the message queue. You can specify special value *DspMsg for the program attribute, in which case the program is a system-supplied program that interrupts the user by displaying the message. Or, you can designate a user-written program to receive control when a message arrives on the message queue. This program can perform any desired processing, and, unless that processing includes a command to display the message, the user is not interrupted. It's possible to defeat the interruption by setting the job's BrkMsg (Break message handling) attribute to a value other than *Normal — namely, to *Notify or *Hold. In that case, the message is processed as if the message queue itself specified a delivery mode of *Notify or *Hold.

- *Notify — This mode causes a workstation alarm to sound and illuminates the "message wait" indicator on the display to alert the user to the fact that a message has arrived.
- *Hold — This mode causes the system to make no notification of the arrival of a message. The user must display the messages on the message queue to determine whether any messages have arrived.
- *Dft — This mode causes the system to reply to messages requiring a reply with their default reply value. No messages are added to the message queue unless the message queue is QSysOpr.

Each of these delivery modes is appropriate for specific circumstances, and the mode you select is largely a matter of personal preference.

I Break for Messages

With command SndMsg, the recipient determines the message delivery mode. The SndBrkMsg (Send Break Message) command, on the other hand, lets the message's sender specify that a message should interrupt the recipient regardless of the delivery mode, break-handling program, or severity filter specified by the recipient. This option is useful if you must send an urgent message to another user. There's a consideration, however: The recipient can prevent the interruption by setting his or her job's BrkMsg attribute to *Notify or *Hold.

Figure 7.2 shows the SndBrkMsg prompt screen. Three other differences exist between the SndBrkMsg command and the SndMsg command. First, SndBrkMsg provides only the ToMsgQ (To work station message queue) parameter on which to specify a destination (i.e., you can name only workstation message queues as destinations). Second, SndBrkMsg lets you specify the value *AllWs (all workstations) in parameter ToMsgQ to send a message to all workstation message queues. Third, when SndBrkMsg sends a message to a message queue whose delivery mode is *Dft, the message is added to the message queue.

The following is a sample message intended for all workstations on the system:

```
SndBrkMsg Msg('Please sign off the system immediately. The system +
               will be unavailable for the next 30 minutes.')     +
          ToMsgQ(*AllWs)
```

This message will go immediately to all workstation message queues and, when possible, will be displayed on all active workstations. If a workstation isn't active, the message will

FIGURE 7.2
Send Break Message (SNDBRKMSG) Panel

```
                     Send Break Message (SNDBRKMSG)

Type choices, press Enter.

Message text . . . . . . . . . .   ______________________________________
_____________________________________________________________________
_____________________________________________________________________
_____________________________________________________________________
_____________________________________________________________________
_____________________________________________________________________
______________________________________________________________
To work station message queue  .   __________   Name, *ALLWS
  Library  . . . . . . . . . . .     *LIBL_____  Name, *LIBL
             + for more values     __________
                                     *LIBL_____
Message type . . . . . . . . . .   *INFO         *INFO, *INQ
Message queue to get reply . . .   QSYSOPR___    Name
  Library  . . . . . . . . . . .     *LIBL_____  Name, *LIBL

                       Additional Parameters

Coded character set ID . . . . .   *JOB_______   1-65535, *HEX, *JOB
```

simply be added to the queue and displayed when the workstation becomes active and the message queue is allocated.

Messaging with Operational Assistant

OS/400's Operational Assistant provides perhaps the simplest user-to-user messaging interface. You can access the messaging feature either from the ASSIST menu (enter **Go Assist** and select option 4, Send messages) or by calling the menu option's system-supplied program, QEZSndMg. Figure 7.3 shows the resulting Send a Message panel.

You'll probably notice right away that this option is straightforward in its use. At its simplest, you type the message you want to send (up to 494 characters), list the users to whom you want to send the message, and then press F10 to send it. The system sends the message to the user message queue of each user you list.

If you require a reply to the message or you want to interrupt the users, you can specify so. Be aware, though, that QEZSndMg sports one characteristic that's less than straightforward: If you indicate that you want to interrupt the users, the message isn't actually sent to the user message queue of the selected users. Instead, for each listed user, the system sends the message to the workstation message queues of all workstations to which that user is signed on. If a user is signed on to four sessions, he or she will receive the message four times — once at each session. And if you've required a reply, you'll receive four responses! If the user isn't signed on to the system when the message is sent, the message is sent to the user message queue.

FIGURE 7.3
Send a Message Panel

```
                              Send a Message

Type information below, then press F10 to send.

  Message needs reply . . . . . .   N             Y=Yes, N=No

  Interrupt user . . . . . . . . .   N             Y=Yes, N=No

  Message text . . . . . . . . . .   __________________________________
______________________________________________________________________
______________________________________________________________________
______________________________________________________________________
______________________________________________________________________
______________________________________________________________________
__________________________________________

  Send to  . . . . . . . . . . . .  __________  Name, F4 for list
                                    __________
                                    __________
                                    __________
                                    __________
```

In Chapter 29, we discuss user-defined command SndBrkMsgU, which enhances the function provided by program QEZSndMg. The enhancements are primarily for use in programs, but you can also use SndBrkMsgU to send message to users if you prefer a command interface to that provided by the ASSIST menu.

Casting Network Messages

The remaining command available for sending messages to other users is SndNetMsg (Send Network Message), shown in Figure 7.4. As with SndMsg and SndBrkMsg, you can type an impromptu message in this command's Msg (Message text) parameter. However, with SndNetMsg, the maximum length of the message is 256 characters, rather than the 512-character limit of SndMsg and SndBrkMsg.

The distinguishing feature of the SndNetMsg command is its destination parameter, ToUsrID (User ID). The value you specify for ToUsrID must be either a valid network user ID or a valid distribution list name (i.e., the name of a list of network user IDs). You can specify up to 50 user IDs to receive the message, and you can mix user IDs with distribution lists if you like. If necessary, you can add network user IDs to the system network directory using the WrkDir (Work with Directory) command. Each network user ID is associated with a user profile on a local or remote system in the network.

There are two situations in which the SndNetMsg command is more appropriate than SndMsg or SndBrkMsg. First, you might need this command if your system is in a network, because SndMsg and SndBrkMsg can't send messages to a remote system. Second, you can use SndNetMsg to send messages to groups of users on a network (including users on your local system) using a distribution list. You create a distribution

FIGURE 7.4
Send Network Message (SNDNETMSG) Panel

```
                    Send Network Message (SNDNETMSG)

 Type choices, press Enter.

 Message text . . . . . . . . . .  ________________________________
___________________________________________________________________
___________________________________________________________________
_______________________________________
 User ID:                          _
   User ID  . . . . . . . . . . .  ______      Character value
   Address  . . . . . . . . . . .  ______      Character value
             + for more values _
```

list using the CrtDstL (Create Distribution List) command and add the appropriate network user IDs to the list using the AddDstLE (Add Distribution List Entry) command.

When you specify a distribution list as the message destination, the message is distributed to the message queue of each network user in the list. For example, if distribution list Pgmrs consists of network user IDs for Bob, Jim, Linda, and Sue, you could send the same message to each of these users (and give them reason to remember you on Boss's Day) by executing the following command:

```
SndNetMsg Msg('Thanks for your hard work on the order entry project. +
              Go home early today and enjoy a little time off.')    +
          ToUsrId(Pgmrs)
```

The only requirements for this method are that user profiles have valid network user IDs in the network directory and that SNA Distribution Services (SNADS) be active (you can start SNADS by starting the QSNADS subsystem).

As you can see, you have more than one option when sending user-to-user messages. You're ready now to move on to program-to-user and program-to-program messages, but these are topics for another day. Meanwhile, this introduction to messages should get you started and whet your appetite for learning more.

Chapter 8

Secrets of a Message Shortstop

by Bryan Meyers

What makes the OS/400 operating system tick? You could argue that messages are really at the heart of the iSeries. The system uses messages to communicate between processes. It sends messages noting the completion of jobs or updating the status of ongoing jobs. Messages tell when a job needs some attention or intervention. The computer dispatches messages to a problem log so the operator can analyze any problems the system may be experiencing. You send requests in the form of messages to the command processor when you execute commands. You can design screens and reports that use messages instead of constants, thus enabling multilingual support. And, of course, users can send impromptu messages to and receive them from other workstation users on the system.

With hundreds of messages flying around your computer at any given moment, it's important to have some way to catch those that relate to you — and that might require some action. IBM provides several facilities to organize and handle messages, and you can create programs to further define how to process messages. This chapter explores three methods of message processing:

- the system reply list
- break-handling programs
- default replies

The *system reply list* lets you specify that the operating system is to respond automatically to certain predefined inquiry messages without requiring that the user reply to them. A *break-handling program* lets you receive messages and process them according to their content. The reply list and the break-handling program have similar functions and can, under some conditions, accomplish the same result. The reply list tends to be easier to implement, while a break-handling program can be much more flexible in the way it handles different kinds of messages. The third message-handling technique, the *default reply*, lets you predefine an action that the computer will take when it encounters a specific message; the reply becomes a built-in part of the message description.

Return Reply Requested

The general concept of the system reply list is quite simple. The reply list primarily consists of message identifiers and reply values for each message. There's only one reply list on the system (hence the official name, "system reply list"). When a job using the reply list encounters a predefined inquiry message, OS/400 searches the reply list for an entry that matches the message ID (and the comparison data, covered later). When a matching entry exists, the system sends the listed reply without intervention from the user or the system operator. When the system finds no match, it sends the message to the user (for interactive jobs) or to the system operator (for batch jobs).

A job doesn't automatically use the system reply list; you must specify that the reply list will handle inquiry messages. To do so, indicate InqMsgRpy(*SysRpyL) within any of the following commands:

- BchJob (Batch Job)
- SbmJob (Submit Job)
- ChgJob (Change Job)
- CrtJobD (Create Job Description)
- ChgJobD (Change Job Description)

IBM ships the iSeries with the system reply list already defined as shown in Figure 8.1. This predefined reply list issues a "D" (job dump) reply for inquiry messages that indicate a program failure.

FIGURE 8.1

Shipped System Reply List

Sequence number (SeqNbr)	Message identifier (MsgID)	Comparison data (CmpDta)	Start (Start)	Reply (Rpy)	Dump (Dump)
10	CPA0700	*None	—	D	*Yes
20	RPG0000	*None	—	D	*Yes
30	CBE0000	*None	—	D	*Yes
40	PLI0000	*None	—	D	*Yes

Each entry in the system reply list consists of a unique sequence number (SeqNbr), a message identifier (MsgID), optional comparison data (CmpDta) and starting position (Start), a reply value (Rpy), and a dump attribute (Dump). Note that the reply list uses the same convention as the MonMsg (Monitor Message) command for indicating generic ranges of messages; for example, "RPG0000" matches all messages that begin with the letters "RPG," from RPG0001 through RPG9999.

You can modify the supplied reply list by adding your own entries using the following commands:

- WrkRpyLE (Work with Reply List Entries)
- AddRpyLE (Add Reply List Entry)
- ChgRpyLE (Change Reply List Entry)
- RmvRpyLE (Remove Reply List Entry)

Figure 8.2 lists some possibilities to consider for your own reply list. Let's look at each component of the system reply list individually.

FIGURE 8.2

Modified System Reply List

Sequence number (SeqNbr)	Message identifier (MsgID)	Comparison data (CmpDta)	Start (Start)	Reply (Rpy)	Dump (Dump)
8	CPF3773	*None	—	I	*No
9	CPF3130	*None	—	R	*No
10	CPA0700	*None	—	D	*Yes
15	CPA3394	PRT3816	41	C	*No
16	CPA3394	*None	—	*Rqd	*No
17	CPA4002	PRT3816	1	I	*No
18	CPA4002	PRTHPLASER	1	I	*No
19	CPA4002	*None	—	*Rqd	*No
20	RPG0000	*None	—	D	*Yes
30	CBE0000	*None	—	D	*Yes
40	PLI0000	*None	—	D	*Yes

A Table of Matches

The system searches the reply list in ascending sequence-number order. Therefore, if you have two list entries that would satisfy a match condition, the system uses the entry with the lowest sequence number. The message identifier can indicate a specific message (e.g., RPG1241) or a range of messages (e.g., RPG1200 for any RPG messages from RPG1201 through RPG1299), or you can use *Any as the message identifier for an entry that will match any inquiry message, regardless of its identifier.

Note

The reply list message identifiers are independent of the message files. If you have two message files with the message ID USR9876, for example (rarely a good idea), the system reply list treats both messages the same.

You should use the *Any message identifier with great care. It is a catch-all entry that ensures the system reply list handles all messages, regardless of their message identifier. If you use this identifier, it should be at the end of your reply list, with sequence number 9999. You should also be confident that the reply in the entry will be appropriate for any error condition that might occur. If the system reply list gets control of any message other than the listed ones, it performs a dump and then replies to the message using the default reply from the message description. If you don't use *Any, the system sends unmonitored messages to the operator.

The comparison data is an optional component of the reply list. You use comparison values when you want to send different replies for the same message, depending on the contents of the message data. The format of the message data is defined when you or IBM creates the message. To view the format, use the DspMsgD (Display Message Description) command. When a reply list entry contains comparison values, the system compares the values with the message data from the inquiry message. If you indicate a starting position in the system reply list, the comparison begins at that position in the message data. If the message data comparison value matches the list entry comparison value, the system uses the list entry to reply to the message; otherwise, it continues to search the list. For example, Figure 8.2 shows three list entries for the CPA4002 (Align forms) message. When the system encounters this message, it checks the message data for the name of the printer device. If the device name matches either the "PRT3816" or "PRTHPLASER" comparison data, the system automatically replies with the I (Ignore) response; otherwise, it requires the user or the system operator to respond to the message.

You use the reply value portion of the reply list entry to indicate how the system should handle the message in this entry. Your three choices are

- indicate a specific reply (up to 32 characters) that the system automatically returns to the job in response to the message (e.g., I, R, D, and C in Figure 8.2)
- use *Dft (Default) to have the system send the message default reply from the message description
- use *Rqd (Required) to require the user or system operator to respond to the message, just as if the job were not using the reply list

The system reply list's dump attribute tells the system whether to perform a job dump when it encounters a message matching this entry. Valid values are *Yes and *No. You can request a job dump no matter what you specify for a reply value. The system dumps the job before it replies to the message and returns control to the program that originated the message. The dump then serves as a snapshot of the conditions that caused a particular inquiry message to appear.

Although the reply list is a system-wide entity, you can use it with a narrower focus. Figure 8.3 shows parts of a CL program that temporarily changes the system reply list and then uses the changed list for message handling, checking for certain inquiry messages and issuing replies appropriate to the program. At the end, the program returns the system reply list to its original condition.

You should limit this approach to programs run on a dedicated or at least a fairly quiet system. Candidates for this method include such jobs as software installation or nightly processing.

Caution

Although this technique might be useful for certain conditions, it poses risks. For example, any jobs that use the system reply list may use the changed list while your program is active. In addition, should your program fail before removing the temporary entries, the system reply list will erroneously contain these entries until they're explicitly removed. When another technique will meet your requirements, you should strongly consider forgoing temporary modifications to the system reply list.

FIGURE 8.3

Temporarily Changing the System Reply List

```
/*  ===============================================================  */
/*  = Variable definitions                                        =  */
/*  ===============================================================  */

/*  ---------------------------------------------------------------  */
/*  - System reply list related variables                         -  */
/*  ---------------------------------------------------------------  */

  Dcl          &CPF3130Seq  *Dec     (     4  0 )
  Dcl          &CPF3773Seq  *Dec     (     4  0 )

  .
  .
  .

/*  ===============================================================  */
/*  = Add temporary system reply list entries                     =  */
/*  ===============================================================  */

/*  ---------------------------------------------------------------  */
/*  - Add CPF3130 entry                                           -  */
/*  ---------------------------------------------------------------  */

  ChgVar      &CPF3130Seq ( 9 )

AddCPF3130:

  AddRpyLE    SeqNbr( &CPF3130Seq )                                 +
              MsgID( CPF3130 )                                      +
              Rpy( R )
  MonMsg      ( CPF2555 ) Exec(                                     +
    Do                       )
      ChgVar      &CPF3130Seq ( &CPF3130Seq - 1 )
      If          ( &CPF3130 *GT 0 )                                +
        GoTo        AddCPF3130
    EndDo
```

continued

FIGURE 8.3 *CONTINUED*

```
/*  ------------------------------------------------------------------   */
/*  - Add CPF3773 entry                                             -   */
/*  ------------------------------------------------------------------   */

  ChgVar     &CPF3773Seq ( &CPF3130   1 )

AddCPF3773:

  AddRpyLE   SeqNbr( &CPF3773Seq )                                      +
             MsgID( CPF3773 )                                           +
             Rpy( I )
  MonMsg     ( CPF2555 ) Exec(                                          +
    Do                       )
      ChgVar     &CPF3773Seq ( &CPF3773Seq - 1 )
      If         ( &CPF3773 *GT 0 )                                     +
        GoTo       AddCPF3773
    EndDo

/*  ==================================================================   */
/*  = Set job to log CL commands and use system reply list          =   */
/*  ==================================================================   */

  ChgJob     LogCLPgm( *Yes )                                           +
             InqMsgRpy( *SysRpyL )

/*  ==================================================================   */
/*  = Nightly process                                               =   */
/*  ==================================================================   */

  .
  .
  .

/*  ==================================================================   */
/*  = Remove temporary system reply list entries                    =   */
/*  ==================================================================   */

/*  ------------------------------------------------------------------   */
/*  - Remove CPF3130 entry                                          -   */
/*  ------------------------------------------------------------------   */

  If         ( &CPF3130 *GT 0 )                                         +
    Do
      RmvRpyLE   SeqNbr( &CPF3130Seq )
      MonMsg     ( CPF2556 )
    EndDo

/*  ------------------------------------------------------------------   */
/*  - Remove CPF3773 entry                                          -   */
/*  ------------------------------------------------------------------   */

  If         ( &CPF3773 *GT 0 )                                         +
    Do
      RmvRpyLE   SeqNbr( &CPF3773Seq )
      MonMsg     ( CPF2556 )
    EndDo
```

Give Me a Break Message

Another way to process messages is to use a break-handling program, which processes messages arriving at a message queue in *Break mode. IBM supplies a default break-handling program; it's the same command processing program used by the DspMsg (Display Messages) command. If you want break messages to do more than just interrupt your normal work with the Display Messages panel, you can write your own break-handling program.

Both the system reply list and a break-handling program customize your shop's method of handling messages that arrive on a message queue, but there are several differences. The system reply list handles only inquiry messages, while a break handler can process any type of message (e.g., a completion message, an informational message). The system reply list has a specific purpose: to return a reply to a job in response to a specific message. The break handler's function, on the other hand, is limited only by your programming ability. It can send customized replies for inquiry messages, convert messages to status messages, process command request messages, initiate a conversational mode of messaging between workstations, redirect messages to another message queue — it can perform any number of functions. Unlike the system reply list, the break handler interrupts the job in which the message occurs and processes the message; it then returns control to the job. The interruption can, however, be transparent to the user.

Like the reply list, a break handler doesn't take control of break messages unless you first tell it to do so. To turn over control to a break-handling program, use the following command:

```
ChgMsgQ MsgQ(MessageQueueName) +
        Dlvry(*Break)          +
        Pgm(ProgramName)       +
        Sev(SeverityCode)
```

OS/400 calls the break handler if a message of high enough severity reaches the message queue. If you use a break handler in a job that's already using the system reply list, the reply list will receive control of the messages first, and it will pass to the break handler only those messages it can't process.

Take a Break

Figure 8.4 shows a sample break-handling program. OS/400 passes three parameters to such programs:

- the name of the message queue
- the library containing the message queue
- the reference key of the received message

You access the referenced message with the RcvMsg (Receive Message) command. Once you've received the message, you can do nearly anything you want with it before you end the break handler and let the original program resume. The example in Figure 8.4 displays any notify or inquiry messages, letting you send a reply, if appropriate. In addition, it monitors for and displays messages that could indicate potentially severe conditions, such as running out of DASD space. For any other messages, the program simply resends the message as a status message, which appears quietly at the bottom of the user's display without interrupting work (unless display of status messages is suppressed in the user profile, the job, or the system value QStsMsg, or Status messages).

FIGURE 8.4

Sample Break Message Handler

```
/*  ================================================================  */
/*  = Sample Break Message Handler                                 =  */
/*  ================================================================  */

Pgm           Parm(                                                  +
                    &MsgQ                                            +
                    &MsgQLib                                         +
                    &MsgKey                                          +
                  )

/*  ================================================================  */
/*  = Variable definitions                                         =  */
/*  ================================================================  */

/*  ----------------------------------------------------------------  */
/*  - Input parameters                                             -  */
/*  ----------------------------------------------------------------  */

  Dcl         &MsgQ         *Char    (    10    )
  Dcl         &MsgQLib      *Char    (    10    )
  Dcl         &MsgKey       *Char    (     4    )

/*  ----------------------------------------------------------------  */
/*  - Work variables                                               -  */
/*  ----------------------------------------------------------------  */

  Dcl         &Msg          *Char    (   132    )
  Dcl         &MsgID        *Char    (     7    )
  Dcl         &MsgDta       *Char    (   132    )
  Dcl         &RtnType      *Char    (     2    )

/*  ================================================================  */
/*  = Global error trap                                            =  */
/*  ================================================================  */

  MonMsg      ( CPF0000 MCH0000 ) Exec(                              +
    GoTo Error                         )

/*  ================================================================  */
/*  = Receive the message                                          =  */
/*  ================================================================  */

  RcvMsg      MsgQ( &MsgQLib/&MsgQ )                                 +
              MsgKey( &MsgKey )                                      +
              Rmv( *No )                                             +
              Msg( &Msg )                                            +
              MsgID( &MsgID )                                        +
              RtnType( &RtnType )
```

continued

FIGURE 8.4 CONTINUED

```
/*  ==================================================================  */
/*  = Display message when any of the following criteria is met:   =  */
/*  =    Inquiry message                                               =  */
/*  =    Notification message                                          =  */
/*  =    Serious condition message                                     =  */
/*  ==================================================================  */

  If        (                                                     +
              ( &RtnType *Eq 'Ø5' )        *Or                    +
              ( &RtnType *Eq '14' )        *Or                    +
              ( &MsgID   *Eq 'CPFØ9Ø7' )   *Or                    +
              ( &MsgID   *Eq 'CPIØ92Ø' )   *Or                    +
              ( &MsgID   *Eq 'CPIØ953' )   *Or                    +
              ( &MsgID   *Eq 'CPIØ954' )   *Or                    +
              ( &MsgID   *Eq 'CPIØ955' )   *Or                    +
              ( &MsgID   *Eq 'CPIØ964' )   *Or                    +
              ( &MsgID   *Eq 'CPIØ965' )   *Or                    +
              ( &MsgID   *Eq 'CPIØ966' )   *Or                    +
              ( &MsgID   *Eq 'CPIØ97Ø' )   *Or                    +
              ( &MsgID   *Eq 'CPIØ992' )   *Or                    +
              ( &MsgID   *Eq 'CPIØ996' )   *Or                    +
              ( &MsgID   *Eq 'CPIØ974' )   *Or                    +
              ( &MsgID   *Eq 'CPI22Ø9' )                          +
            )                                                     +
    DspMsg    MsgQ( &MsgQLib/MsgQ )
  Else                                                            +
    SndPgmMsg MsgID( CPF9897 )                                    +
              MsgF( QCPFMSG )                                     +
              MsgDta( &Msg )                                      +
              ToPgmQ( *Ext )                                      +
              MsgType( *Status )

/*  ==================================================================  */
/*  = Exit program                                                     =  */
/*  ==================================================================  */

  Return

/*  ==================================================================  */
/*  = Error handler                                                    =  */
/*  ==================================================================  */

Error:

  SndPgmMsg  MsgID( CPF9897 )                                     +
             MsgF( QCPFMsg )                                      +
             MsgDta( 'Error in break-handling program.' *BCat     +
                     'See job log for details.' )                 +
             MsgType( *Escape )
  MonMsg     ( CPFØØØØ MCHØØØØ )

EndPgm
```

Figure 8.5 shows part of an initial program that puts a break handler into action. The initial program first displays all messages that exist in a user's message queue and then clears all but unanswered messages from the queue and activates the break-handling program. Note that the initial program also checks whether the user is the system operator; if so, it activates the break handler for the system operator message queue.

FIGURE 8.5

Sample Initial Program

```
/*  ============================================================  */
/*  = Variable definitions                                     =  */
/*  ============================================================  */

/*  ------------------------------------------------------------  */
/*  - User profile related variables                           -  */
/*  ------------------------------------------------------------  */

   Dcl         &MsgQ         *Char    (   10    )
   Dcl         &MsgQLib      *Char    (   10    )
   Dcl         &GrpPrf       *Char    (   10    )

/*  ============================================================  */
/*  = Global error trap                                        =  */
/*  ============================================================  */

   MonMsg     ( CPF2400 CPF2534 )

/*  ============================================================  */
/*  = Retrieve user attributes                                 =  */
/*  ============================================================  */

   RtvUsrPrf  MsgQ( &MsgQ )                                          +
              MsgQLib( &MsgQLib )                                    +
              GrpPrf( &GrpPrf )

/*  ============================================================  */
/*  = Change message queues to *Break mode when possible       =  */
/*  ============================================================  */

/*  ------------------------------------------------------------  */
/*  - Change workstation message queue to *Break mode          -  */
/*  ------------------------------------------------------------  */

   ChgMsgQ    MsgQ( *WrkStn )                                        +
              Dlvry( *Break )
   ClrMsgQ    MsgQ( *WrkStn )                                        +
              Clear( *KeepUnans )
   ChgMsgQ    MsgQ( *WrkStn )                                        +
              Dlvry( *Break )                                        +
              Pgm( MngBrkMsg )
```

continued

FIGURE 8.5 CONTINUED

```
/*  ------------------------------------------------------------  */
/*  - Change user profile message queue to *Break mode          -  */
/*  ------------------------------------------------------------  */

   ChgMsgQ      MsgQ( &MsgQLib/&MsgQ )                             +
                Dlvry( *Break )
   ClrMsgQ      MsgQ( &MsgQLib/&MsgQ )                             +
                Clear( *KeepUnans )
   ChgMsgQ      MsgQ( &MsgQLib/&MsgQ )                             +
                Dlvry( *Break )                                    +
                Pgm( MngBrkMsg )

/*  ------------------------------------------------------------  */
/*  - Change system operator message queue to *Break mode if    -  */
/*  - member of QSYSOPR group                                   -  */
/*  ------------------------------------------------------------  */

   If          ( &GrpPrf *Eq 'QSYSOPR' )                           +
     Do
       ChgMsgQ      MsgQ( QSysOpr )                                +
                    Dlvry( *Break )
       ClrMsgQ      MsgQ( QSysOpr )                                +
                    Clear( *KeepUnans )
       ChgMsgQ      MsgQ( QSysOpr )                                +
                    Dlvry( *Break )                                +
                    Pgm( MngBrkMsg )
     EndDo
```

It's Your Own Default

One of the easiest ways to process message replies automatically is also one of the most often overlooked. The message descriptions for inquiry or notify messages can contain default replies, which you can tell the system to use when the system issues the message. The default reply must be among the valid replies for the message. You specify a message's default reply using either the AddMsgD (Add Message Description) or ChgMsgD (Change Message Description) command. You can display a message's default reply using the DspMsgD command. You can also use the WrkMsgD (Work with Message Descriptions) command to manage message descriptions.

The default reply is used under the following circumstances:

- when you use the system reply list and the list entry's reply for the message is *Dft
- when you've changed the delivery mode of the receiving message queue to *Dft, using the ChgMsgQ (Change Message Queue) command
- when the job's InqMsgRpy attribute value is *Dft

No messages are put in a message queue when the queue is in *Dft delivery mode (unless the message queue is QSysOpr); informational messages are ignored. Messages will be logged, however, in the system history log (QHst).

You can easily set up an unattended environment for your computer to use every night by having your system operator execute the following command daily when signing off:

```
ChgMsgQ MsgQ(QSysOpr) Dlvry(*Dft)
```

Your system will then use default replies instead of sending messages to an absent system operator. This technique may prevent your overnight batch processing from hanging up because of an unexpected error condition. You should take care, however, to ensure the suitability of the default replies for any messages that might be sent to the queue. You might also consider including the ChgMsgQ command within key CL programs, such as unattended backup procedures or program-installation procedures, for which default replies may be appropriate. Another good use for default replies is to have one message queue handle all printer messages. By defining default replies to these messages and placing that queue in *Dft delivery mode, you can have the system respond automatically to forms-loading and alignment messages.

Chapter 9

Printer Files, Job Logs, and Print Direction

To make printing operations run more smoothly, you need to understand a few basic concepts about printer files. In this chapter, we cover three items concerning printer files: changing printer file attributes, handling a specific type of printer file (the system-generated job log), and controlling print direction. A basic understanding of these topics will increase your power to customize your system by controlling output.

How Do You Make It Print Like This?

The iSeries does support direct printing — that is, output directly to a printer (which ties up a workstation or job while the printer device completes the task). However, you'll rarely use direct printing. The system uses *printer files* to create reports, and these reports are typically spooled to an *output queue.*

IBM ships the iSeries with many printer files, such as QSysPrt, which the system uses when you compile a CL program; QPQuPrFil, which the system uses when you run a query; and QPSuPrtF, which the system uses when you print a listing from a source file using Source Entry Utility (SEU). These printer files have predefined attributes that control printing features such as lines per inch, characters per inch, form size, overflow line number, and output queue.

In addition to the printer files that IBM provides, you can create two types of printer files within your applications. The first type uses the CrtPrtF (Create Printer File) command to define a printer file that has no external definition (i.e., the printer file has a set of defined attributes from the CrtPrtF command but only one record format with no details). Any program using this type of printer file must contain output specifications that describe the fields, positions, and edit codes used for printing.

The second type of printer file is externally described. When you use the CrtPrtF command to create this type of printer file, you specify a source member that describes the various record formats your program will use for printing. (For specifications that you can make in Data Description Specifications, or DDS, refer to *DDS Reference,* viewable online at *http://publib.boulder.ibm.com/pubs/html/as400/infocenter.htm.*) Whether you create an externally described printer file or a printer file that must be used with programs that internally describe the printing, you define certain printer file attributes (e.g., those controlling lines per inch, characters per inch, and form size) as part of the printer file object definition.

Let's examine a problem that often occurs when an iSeries installation is complete. All the IBM-supplied printer files are predefined for use with paper that's 11 inches long. If you've been using shorter paper (e.g., the 14-by-8½-inch size) and generate output (such as that produced by the command DspLib Output(*Print) or a Query/400 report) with a system-supplied printer file, the system will print the report through the page perforations. On your previous system, the overflow worked just right, but you weren't around when someone set up that system. How do you instruct the iSeries to print correctly on the short, wide paper?

First, you need to find out what the default values for printing are. To do so, enter the DspFD (Display File Description) command for the printer file QSysPrt:

```
DspFD QSysPrt
```

When you execute this command, you see the display represented in Figure 9.1.

FIGURE 9.1

Display File Description Panel

```
                              Display Spooled File
File  . . . . . :   QPDSPFD                             Page/Line   1/36
Control . . . . .   ________                            Columns     1 - 78
Find  . . . . . .   ______________________________
*...+....1....+....2....+....3....+....4....+....5....+....6....+....7....+...
   Creation date . . . . . . . . . . . . . . . . :            01/18/00
   Text 'description'  . . . . . . . . . . . . . : TEXT       System non-describ
   Spool the data  . . . . . . . . . . . . . . . : SPOOL      *YES
   Maximum devices . . . . . . . . . . . . . . . :              1
   User specified DBCS data  . . . . . . . . . . : IGCDTA     *NO
   Maximum file wait time  . . . . . . . . . . . : WAITFILE   *IMMED
   Share open data path  . . . . . . . . . . . . : SHARE      *NO
   Record format level check . . . . . . . . . . : LVLCHK     *NO
   Number of record formats  . . . . . . . . . . :                1
   User buffer length  . . . . . . . . . . . . . :                0
   Number of devices . . . . . . . . . . . . . . :              1
   Separate indicator area . . . . . . . . . . . : INDARA     No
   Coded character set identifier  . . . . . . . : CCSID          0
 Printer Attributes
   Device  . . . . . . . . . . . . . . . . . . . : DEV        *JOB
   Printer device type . . . . . . . . . . . . . : DEVTYPE    *SCS
   Page size                                       PAGESIZE
(A)  Length  . . . . . . . . . . . . . . . . . . :                 66
     Width . . . . . . . . . . . . . . . . . . . :                132
     Measurement Method  . . . . . . . . . . . . :            *ROWCOL
(B)Lines per inch  . . . . . . . . . . . . . . . : LPI        6
   Characters per inch . . . . . . . . . . . . . : CPI        10
   Front margin  . . . . . . . . . . . . . . . . : FRONTMGN   *DEVD
   Back margin . . . . . . . . . . . . . . . . . : BACKMGN    *FRONTMGN
(C)Overflow line number  . . . . . . . . . . . . : OVRFLW      60
   Fold records  . . . . . . . . . . . . . . . . : FOLD       *NO
   Degree of page rotation . . . . . . . . . . . : PAGRTT     *AUTO
   Hardware justification  . . . . . . . . . . . : JUSTIFY      0
   Print on both sides . . . . . . . . . . . . . : DUPLEX     *NO
   Defer Write . . . . . . . . . . . . . . . . . : DFRWRT     *YES
   Unprintable character action                    RPLUNPRT
     Replace character . . . . . . . . . . . . . :            *YES
     Replacement character . . . . . . . . . . . :            ' '    X'40'
   Print text  . . . . . . . . . . . . . . . . . : PRTTXT     *JOB
   Align page  . . . . . . . . . . . . . . . . . : ALIGN      *NO
   Control character . . . . . . . . . . . . . . : CTLCHAR    *NONE
```

continued

FIGURE 9.1 *CONTINUED*

```
  Channel values . . . . . . . . . . . . . . . . . : CHLVAL      *NORMAL
  Fidelity . . . . . . . . . . . . . . . . . . . . : FIDELITY    *CONTENT
  Printer quality . . . . . . . . . . . . . . . . : PRTQLTY     *STD
  Form feed . . . . . . . . . . . . . . . . . . . : FORMFEED    *DEVD
  Source drawer . . . . . . . . . . . . . . . . . : DRAWER      1
  Output bin . . . . . . . . . . . . . . . . . . . : OUTBIN      *DEVD
  Font                                              FONT
    Identifier . . . . . . . . . . . . . . . . . :             *CPI
    Point size . . . . . . . . . . . . . . . . . :             *NONE
  Character identifier . . . . . . . . . . . . . . : CHRID       *CHRIDCTL
  Decimal format . . . . . . . . . . . . . . . . . : DECFMT      *JOB
  Font character set . . . . . . . . . . . . . . . : FNTCHRSET   *FONT
  Coded font . . . . . . . . . . . . . . . . . . . : CDEFNT      *FNTCHRSET
  Table Reference Characters . . . . . . . . . . . : TBLREFCHR   *NO
  AFP Chars . . . . . . . . . . . . . . . . . . . : AFPCHARS    *NONE
  Page definition . . . . . . . . . . . . . . . . : PAGDFN      *NONE
  Form definition . . . . . . . . . . . . . . . . : FORMDF      *NONE
  Form type . . . . . . . . . . . . . . . . . . . : FORMTYPE    *STD
  Pages per side . . . . . . . . . . . . . . . . . : MULTIUP     1
  Reduce output . . . . . . . . . . . . . . . . . : REDUCE      *TEXT
  Unit of measure . . . . . . . . . . . . . . . . : UOM         *INCH
  Front side overlay . . . . . . . . . . . . . . . : FRONTOVL    *NONE
  Back side overlay . . . . . . . . . . . . . . . : BACKOVL     *FRONTOVL
  IPDS pass through . . . . . . . . . . . . . . . : IPDSPASTHR  *DEVD
  User resource library list . . . . . . . . . . . : USRRSCLIBL  *DEVD
  Corner staple . . . . . . . . . . . . . . . . . : CORNERSTPL  *NONE
  Edge stitch                                       EDGESTITCH
    Reference edge . . . . . . . . . . . . . . . :             *NONE
  Saddle stitch                                     SADLSTITCH
    Reference edge . . . . . . . . . . . . . . . :             *NONE
  Font resolution . . . . . . . . . . . . . . . . : FNTRSL      *DEVD
  DBCS extension characters . . . . . . . . . . . : IGCEXNCHR   *YES
  DBCS character rotation . . . . . . . . . . . . : IGCCHRRTT   *NO
  DBCS characters per inch . . . . . . . . . . . . : IGCCPI      *CPI
  DBCS SO/SI spacing . . . . . . . . . . . . . . . : IGCSOSI     *YES
  DBCS Coded font . . . . . . . . . . . . . . . . : IGCCDEFNT   *SYSVAL
Spooling Description
  Spooled output queue . . . . . . . . . . . . . . : OUTQ        *JOB
  Max spooled output records . . . . . . . . . . . : MAXRCDS        100000
  Spooled output schedule . . . . . . . . . . . . : SCHEDULE    *FILEEND      (D)
  Copies . . . . . . . . . . . . . . . . . . . . . : COPIES        1
  Page range to print                               PAGERANGE
    Starting page . . . . . . . . . . . . . . . . :                      1
    Ending page . . . . . . . . . . . . . . . . . :             *END
  File separators . . . . . . . . . . . . . . . . : FILESEP       0
  Hold spooled file . . . . . . . . . . . . . . . : HOLD        *NO           (E)
  Save spooled file . . . . . . . . . . . . . . . : SAVE        *NO
  Output priority (on OUTQ) . . . . . . . . . . . : OUTPTY      *JOB
  User data . . . . . . . . . . . . . . . . . . . : USRDTA      *SOURCE
  Spool file owner . . . . . . . . . . . . . . . . : SPLFOWN     *CURUSRPRF
  User defined option . . . . . . . . . . . . . . : USRDFNOPT   *NONE
  User defined data . . . . . . . . . . . . . . . : USRDFNDTA   *NONE
```

continued

FIGURE 9.1 CONTINUED

```
  User defined object                                    USRDFNOBJ
    Object  . . . . . . . . . . . . . . . . . :                   *NONE
      Library . . . . . . . . . . . . . . . . :
    Object type . . . . . . . . . . . . . . . :
Record Format List
                         Record  Format Level
 Format        Fields   Length  Identifier
 QSYSPRT            0        0  0000000000000
   Text . . . . . . . . . . . . . . . . . . . :
 Total number of formats  . . . . . . . . . . :                  1
 Total number of fields . . . . . . . . . . . :                  0
 Total record length  . . . . . . . . . . . . :                  0
```

Notice (at **A**, **B**, and **C**, respectively) the Page size parameter, PageSize(66 132); the Lines per inch parameter, LPI(6); and the Overflow line number parameter, OvrFlw(60). These default parameter values combine to determine the number of inches (i.e., 11) that the system considers to be a single page on the system-supplied objects.

In this example, though, your paper is only 8½ inches long, so you need to change the form size and overflow of each printer file (including all system-supplied printer files and those you create yourself) that generates reports on this short-stock paper. You can accomplish this task by identifying each printer file that needs to be modified and then executing this ChgPrtF (Change Printer File) command for each:

```
ChgPrtF File(LibraryName/FileName) +
        PageSize(51 132)           +
        OvrFlw(45)
```

If you need to change all printer files on the system, you can use the same command, but place the value *All in the File parameter:

```
ChgPrtF File(*All/*All)  +
        PageSize(51 132) +
        OvrFlw(45)
```

The page size can vary from one form type to the next, but you can easily compensate for differences by changing the appropriate printer files. Remember that changing the lines per inch, the page length, and the overflow line number requires no programming changes for programs that let the system check for overflow status (i.e., you don't need to have program logic count lines to control page breaks). Such programs will use the new attributes of the printer file at their next execution.

Controlling When a Report Is Printed

Once you've set up the page size you want and determined how a given report will be printed, you can start thinking about controlling when that report will be printed. The two parameters you can use to ensure that spooled data is printed at the time you designate are Schedule (Spooled output schedule) and Hold (Hold spooled file) — shown at **D** and **E**, respectively, in Figure 9.1.

The Schedule parameter specifies when the system should make the spooled output file available to a writer for printing. If the system finds the **Immed* value for Schedule, the file is available for a writer to begin printing the data as soon as the records arrive in the spooled file. This approach is helpful for short print items, such as invoices, receipts, or other output that's printed quickly. But when you generate long reports, allocating the writer as soon as data is available can tie up a single writer for a long time.

Entering the value **FileEnd* for Schedule specifies that the spooled output file is available to the writer as soon as the printer file is closed in the program. This value can be useful for long reports that you want available for printing only after the entire report is generated.

Specifying the value **JobEnd* for Schedule makes the spooled output file available only after the entire job (not just a program) is completed. One benefit of selecting this value is that you can ensure that all reports one job generates will be available at the same time and therefore will be printed in succession (unless the operator intervenes).

The Hold parameter works just like its name sounds. A Hold value of **Yes* specifies that when the system generates spooled output for a printer file, the output file stays on the output queue with a status of *Hld (held) until an operator releases the file to a writer.

Selecting the **No* value for Hold specifies that the system should not hold the spooled printer file on the output queue and should make the output available to a writer at the time the Schedule parameter indicates. For example, when a program generates a spooled file with the attributes Schedule(*FileEnd) and Hold(*No), the spooled file is available to the writer as soon as the file is closed.

As with the PageSize and OvrFlw parameters, you can change the Schedule and Hold parameter values for printer files by using the ChgPrtF command. You can also override printer file parameters at execution time using the OvrPrtF (Override with Printer File) command. In addition, you can change some printer file attributes at print time using the ChgSplFA (Change Spooled File Attributes) command or option 2 on the Work with Output Queue or Work with Spooled Files display. You should examine the various attributes associated with the CrtPrtF, ChgPrtF, and OvrPrtF commands to see whether you need to make other changes to customize your printed output needs. For more information about these parameters, see the discussion of the CrtPrtF command in *OS/400 CL Reference – Part 2* (SC41-5724).

Controlling Your Job Logs

After you have your printer files under control, the next step in customizing your system can prick a nasty thorn in the flesh of iSeries newcomers: learning how to manage all those job logs that the system generates as jobs are completed. A *job log* provides a record of job execution and contains informational, completion, diagnostic, and other messages. The reason these potentially useful job logs can be a pain is that the system generates a job log for each completed job on the system.

Fortunately, you can manage job logs. The three methods for job log management are

- controlling where the printed output for job logs is directed

- deciding whether to generate a printed job log for jobs that are completed normally or only for jobs that are completed abnormally
- determining how much information to include in the job logs

Controlling Where the Printed Output Is Directed

When your system is shipped, it's set up so that every job (interactive sessions as well as batch) generates a job log that records the job's activities and can vary in content according to the particular job description. To view a job log as the system creates it during a job's execution, you can use the DspJob (Display Job) or the DspJobLog (Display Job Log) command.

When a job is completed, the system spools the job log. When it generates a printed job log, the system uses printer file QSys/QPJobLog. It's typically a good idea to direct all printed job logs to one output queue that's not attached to a writer. Doing so leaves the job logs on the system so you can review or print them when necessary. You can choose to redirect this job log printer file in one of two ways.

The most popular redirection method is to use Operational Assistant, which not only can redirect your job logs to a single output queue but also can clean up old job logs automatically based on a number of retention days you supply. You can access the system cleanup option panel in three ways:

- from the Operational Assistant main menu (type **Go Assist**, select option 11 to display the SETUP menu, and then select option 2, Cleanup tasks)
- from the SETUP menu (type **Go Setup**, and then select option 2, Cleanup tasks)
- directly from the CLEANUP menu (type **Go Cleanup**)

Figure 9.2 shows the Cleanup Tasks menu.

Before starting cleanup, you need to define the appropriate cleanup options by selecting option 1 (Change cleanup options) from this menu. Figure 9.3 shows the resulting Change Cleanup Options panel, where you can enter the retention parameters for several automated cleanup functions and determine when you want the system to perform cleanup each day.

Chapter 12 provides a complete discussion of this panel and the automated cleanup process. For now, the key point is this: The first time you activate the automated cleanup function (by entering a Y for the "Allow automatic cleanup" option on this panel), OS/400 changes the job log printer file so that all job logs are directed to the system-supplied output queue QEZJobLog in library QUsrSys. Even if you don't start the actual cleanup process, or if you elect to stop the cleanup function at a later date, the job logs will continue to accumulate in output queue QEZJobLog.

FIGURE 9.2
Cleanup Tasks Menu

```
CLEANUP                          Cleanup Tasks
                                                             System:   AS400
To select one of the following, type its number below and press Enter:

     1. Change cleanup options
     2. Start cleanup at scheduled time
     3. Start cleanup immediately
     4. End cleanup

Type a menu option below
     _

F1=Help   F3=Exit   F9=Command line   F12=Cancel
```

FIGURE 9.3
Change Cleanup Options Panel

```
                          Change Cleanup Options                    AS400
                                                          09/18/00  10:50:02
Type choices below, then press Enter.

Allow automatic cleanup . . . . . . . . . . . . .   Y              Y=Yes, N=No

Time cleanup starts each day . . . . . . . . . .   22:00:00__     00:00:00-
                                                                   23:59:59,
                                                                   *SCDPWROFF,
                                                                   *NONE

Number of days to keep:
  User messages . . . . . . . . . . . . . . . . .   7____          1-366, *KEEP
  System and workstation messages . . . . . . . .   4____          1-366, *KEEP
  Job logs and other system output  . . . . . . .   7____          1-366, *KEEP
  System journals and system logs . . . . . . . .   30___          1-366, *KEEP
  OfficeVision for AS/400 calendar items  . . . .   30___          1-366, *KEEP

F1=Help   F3=Exit   F5=Refresh   F12=Cancel
```

The second method of redirecting printed job logs is to manually direct them to an output queue of your choice (we suggest QEZJobLog). To manually direct printed job logs, use the ChgPrtF command as follows:

```
ChgPrtF File(QPJobLog)            +
        OutQ(QUsrSys/QEZJobLog)
```

The job logs will now be redirected to the specified output queue. You might also want to specify Hold(*Yes) on the ChgPrtF command to place the spool files on hold in the output queue. However, unless a printer is assigned to that queue, the spool files won't be printed. The job logs will simply remain in the queue until you print or delete them.

Tip

When you think about managing job logs, remember that if you let job logs accumulate, they can reduce the system's performance efficiency because of the overhead incurred for each job on the system. If a job log exists, the system is maintaining information about the job. Therefore, it's important either to use the automated cleanup options available in Operational Assistant or to manually use the ClrOutQ (Clear Output Queue) command regularly to clear all the job logs from an output queue.

Deciding to Generate a Printed Job Log for Normally Completed Jobs

Another concern related to the overhead involved with job logs is how to control their content (size) and how to reduce the number of job logs the system spools. A job's *message-logging attributes* control the creation and contents of job logs. These attributes consist of three elements: the message level and the message severity, both of which control the number of messages the system writes to a job log, and the message text level, which controls the level (i.e., amount) of message text written to the job log when the first two values create an error message.

You set a job's message-logging attributes using the Log (Message logging) parameter found on the following commands:

- BchJob (Batch Job)
- SbmJob (Submit Job)
- ChgJob (Change Job)
- CrtJobD (Create Job Description)
- ChgJobD (Change Job Description)

Before discussing the three elements, we should define the term "message severity." Every message generated on the iSeries has an associated *severity*, which you can think of as the message's priority. Messages absolutely essential to the system's operation (e.g., inquiry messages that must be answered) have a severity of 99. Informational messages (e.g., messages that tell you a function is in progress) have a severity of 00. (For a detailed description of severity codes, refer to Appendix A, "Expanded Parameter Descriptions," in *OS/400 CL Reference – Part 4*, SC41-5726.)

The first message-logging element, message level, specifies one of the following five logging levels (note that a high-level message is one sent to the program message queue of the program that received the request or commands being logged from a CL program):

Message level	Description
0	No data is logged.
1	All messages sent to the job's external message queue with a severity level greater than or equal to the specified message severity are logged. This includes the indications of job start, job end, and job completion status.
2	In addition to the information logged at level 1: • Requests entered on a command line or commands being logged from a CL program that result in a high-level message with a severity code greater than or equal to the specified severity cause the request or command and all associated messages to be logged.
3	In addition to the information logged at level 1: • All requests entered on a command line or commands being logged from a CL program are logged. • Requests entered on a command line or commands being logged from a CL program that result in a high-level message with a severity code greater than or equal to the specified severity cause all associated messages to be logged.
4	The following information is logged: • All requests entered on a command line or commands being logged from a CL program and all messages with a severity code greater than or equal to the specified severity, including trace messages, are logged.

The second element of the Log parameter, message severity, determines which messages will be logged and which will be ignored. Messages with a severity greater than or equal to the severity specified in this element will be logged in the job log according to the logging level specified in the previous element.

For the third element of the Log parameter, the message text level, a value of **Msg* instructs the system to write only first-level message text to the job log. A value of **SecLvl* instructs the system to write both the message and the help text of the error message to the job log.

By setting the message text level value to **NoList*, you ensure that the job does not generate a job log if the job is completed normally. Jobs completed abnormally will generate a job log containing both message and help text. Eliminating job logs for jobs that are completed normally can greatly reduce the number of job logs written to the output queue.

Determining How Much Information to Include in Job Logs

You can cause any interactive or batch job initiated with the IBM-supplied default job description QDftJobD to withhold spooling of a job log if the job terminates normally. To do so, you simply create your user profiles using the default JobD (Job description) parameter value, QDftJobD, and enter the command

```
ChgJobD JobD(QDftJobD)              +
        Log(*Same *Same *NoList)
```

Is this approach wise? Interactive jobs almost always end normally. Therefore, changing the job description for such interactive sessions is effective. Do you need the information in those job logs? If you understand how your workstation sessions run (e.g., which menus are used and which programs are called), you probably don't need the information from sessions that end normally. You might need the information when errors occur, but you can generally re-create the errors at a workstation. With this approach, you can rest assured that jobs ending abnormally will still generate a job log and provide helpful diagnostic information.

Note

For interactive jobs, the Log parameter on the SignOff command overrides the value you specify for the job. For instance, if a job's attribute specifies *NoList in the Log parameter and the SignOff Log(*List) command is used to sign off from an interactive job, the system will spool a job log.

For batch jobs, the question of eliminating job logs is more complex than it is for interactive jobs. It's sometimes helpful to have job logs from batch jobs that end normally, as well as from those that end abnormally, so someone can re-create events chronologically. For instance, when many types of batch jobs (e.g., nightly routines) run unattended, job log information can be useful.

Remember, the job description controls job log generation, so you can use particular job descriptions when you want the system to generate a job log regardless of how a job ends. The job description includes the parameter LogCLPgm (Log CL program commands). This parameter affects the job log in that a value of *Yes instructs the system to write to the job log any candidate CL commands (which can happen only if you specify Log(*Job) or Log(*Yes) as an attribute of the CL program being executed). A value of *No specifies that commands in a CL program are not logged to the job log.

Job logs are a valuable information source when a job fails to perform, and handling job logs is a simple, but essential, part of managing system resources. When you neglect to control the number of job logs on the system, the system is forced to maintain information for an excessive number of jobs, which can hurt system performance.

Where Have All the Reports Gone?

One strength of the iSeries is its profusion of alternatives for implementing your business rules. One such area of abundant choice lies in defining the path reports can take in arriving at their destination. From printer file to printer, the path can be a winding one, though.

A frequent source of confusion, print direction is actually easier to understand than its complexity might first lead you to believe. To better understand print direction, you need a map of the path that printed output may potentially travel.

Device files are the interface between software and hardware, and printer files are the device files the system uses to communicate with printers. The system may examine many items to determine your output's destination, but the printer file is the first.

Printer files have many attributes that determine print characteristics. Three of these are essential in determining how the system directs printed output:

- Dev — names the printer device to use
- OutQ — defines the output queue to use
- Spool — determines whether the report will be spooled to an output queue

Although Dev and OutQ define where the system directs printed output, it is the Spool attribute that determines which of these attributes the system actually uses when resolving a report's destination:

- Spool(*No) — The system directs output to the printer device named in the Dev attribute.
- Spool(*Yes) — The system directs output to the output queue named in the OutQ attribute.

When you specify Spool(*No), the system prints directly to the printer. Spool(*Yes), on the other hand, results in the system placing the report in a "holding area" known as an output queue. From there, the report may or may not actually be printed based on user preference.

Let's reinforce these rules with a simple example. Consider printer file PayChecks, created with the following command:

```
CrtPrtF File(PayChecks)   +
        Dev(PayrollPrt)   +
        OutQ(PublicOutQ) +
        Spool(*No)
```

In this example, because the printer file's Spool attribute value is *No, the system obtains its print path from the Dev attribute and prints directly to the printer named PayrollPrt.

On the other hand, if you create printer file PayChecks with the command

```
CrtPrtF File(PayChecks)   +
        Dev(PayrollPrt)   +
        OutQ(PublicOutQ) +
        Spool(*Yes)
```

the system selects its print path from the OutQ attribute and spools the report into output queue PublicOutQ.

It's important to note that when the system examines the printer file attributes, any overridden attributes from the OvrPrtF command take precedence over the values found in the printer file itself. Using the PayChecks file just created, if an application issues the command

```
OvrPrtF File(PayChecks) +
        OutQ(PayOutQ)
```

before opening the printer file, the system places the report into output queue PayOutQ rather than in PublicOutQ as specified in the printer file.

So far, our examples all designate a specific printer device for the Dev attribute or a specific output queue for OutQ. Although this arrangement is simple, it's not very flexible. You need some way to direct printed output based on your business needs. Fortunately, the system lets you tailor print direction in a fashion that suits your environment.

Tailoring Print Direction

The system supports several special values you can specify for the printer device and output queue. These values instruct the system to derive print-direction information from something other than the printer file itself. Ultimately, these special values result in resolution to a specific printer device and output queue. Let's examine basic information for each of seven special values:

- *Job
- *JobD
- *Current
- *UsrPrf
- *WrkStn
- *SysVal
- *Dev

*Job

Typically, special value *Job is the most frequently used value within a printer file itself because within the job attributes, you can specify a variety of values to redirect your reports. *Job is often useful when you want your applications to have considerable control in determining the destination of your reports.

Jobs have many associated attributes, among which are printer device and output queue. When a job starts, the system initializes its printer device and output queue attribute values with values from such things as the job description used in starting the job or from commands such as BchJob and SbmJob. Remember that after a job starts, you can change the printer device and output queue attribute values.

Both the printer device and the output queue attributes of a printer file accept value *Job. This value instructs the system to derive the attribute value (or values) from the job's attributes. Consider the following example:

Job's printer device: PayPrt02

Job's output queue: PayOutQ17

```
CrtPrtF File(PayChecks) +
        Dev(*Job)       +
        OutQ(*Job)
```

Because both the Dev and OutQ attributes of printer file PayChecks contain special value *Job, both attributes derive their values from the job's attributes. In this example, the printer device is PayPrt02, and the output queue is PayOutQ17.

*JobD

Similar to special value *Job, *JobD can be specified on the BchJob and SbmJob commands. Like *Job, *JobD provides a variety of print-direction options and can be useful when you want applications to have considerable control over print direction.

Value *JobD results in the system deriving the printer device and output queue information from the values found in the job description specified in the BchJob or SbmJob command. Both the printer device and the output queue parameters on these commands accept value *JobD. Consider the following example:

Job description PayJobD printer device: PayPrt05

Job description PayJobD output queue: PayOutQ33

```
SbmJob Cmd(Call Pgm(PrtPayChks)) +
       JobD(PayJobD)             +
       PrtDev(*JobD)             +
       OutQ(*JobD)
```

Because both the PrtDev and OutQ parameters on the SbmJob command contain special value *JobD, the system derives the printer device and output queue values from the job description specified on the SbmJob command, PayJobD. In this example, those values are PayPrt05 and PayOutQ33, respectively.

*Current

This value, too, exhibits behavior characteristic of the *Job value. You can specify *Current on the SbmJob command. *Current is yet another value that's useful when you want your applications to exercise control in directing printed output.

Both the printer device and output queue parameters on the SbmJob command accept *Current as their value. This value instructs the system to obtain the printer device and output queue values from the job attributes of the job issuing the SbmJob command.

To exemplify:

Printer device of job issuing SbmJob command: PayPrt27

Output queue of job issuing SbmJob command: PayOutQ84

```
SbmJob Cmd(Call Pgm(PrtPayChks)) +
       PrtDev(*Current)          +
       OutQ(*Current)
```

Because both the PrtDev and OutQ parameters on the SbmJob command contain special value *Current, the system obtains the printer device and output queue values from the job attributes of the job that issued the SbmJob. Those values are PayPrt27 and PayOutQ84, respectively.

*UsrPrf

With value *UsrPrf, you can customize print direction at the user profile level. This is a reasonably popular approach to print direction because it lets you consider each user's individual needs and preferences in determining where printed output will go.

You can specify *UsrPrf in job-related objects (job description) and job-related commands (BchJob, ChgJob, SbmJob). Both printer device and output queue parameters accept this value. *UsrPrf instructs the system to examine the user profile to determine the printer device and output queue to use. For example:

Job submitted by user profile: GuthrieGar

Printer device in user profile GuthrieGar: PayPrt15

Output queue in user profile GuthrieGar: PayOutQ08

```
SbmJob Cmd(Call Pgm(PrtPayChks)) +
       PrtDev(*UsrPrf)           +
       OutQ(*UsrPrf)
```

Because both the PrtDev and OutQ parameters on the SbmJob command contain special value *UsrPrf, the system retrieves the printer device and output queue values from the user profile that submitted the job, GuthrieGar. In this example, the printer device is PayPrt15, and the output queue is PayOutQ08.

*WrkStn

Value *WrkStn is sometimes used when your environment is one in which you print interactively and want to direct your print based on proximity to a workstation. You can specify *WrkStn in job descriptions and on command ChgJob for both printer device and output queue. As a result, the job attributes contain the value *WrkStn. In addition, you can specify *WrkStn for both printer device and output queue in the user profile.

For interactive jobs, *WrkStn instructs the system to retrieve printer device and output queue information from the device description of the workstation where the job is running. For batch jobs, the value *WrkStn is meaningless because the job has no allocated workstation. If *WrkStn is encountered in a batch job, *WrkStn is replaced with the value *SysVal for the printer device and with *Dev for the output queue. Here's an example for an interactive job:

Printer device in display device description: PayPrt29

Output queue in display device description: PayOutQ47

Job's printer device: *WrkStn

Job's output queue: *WrkStn

```
CrtPrtF File(PayChecks) +
        Dev(*Job)       +
        OutQ(*Job)
```

Because both the Dev and OutQ parameters of printer file PayChecks contain special value *Job, both attributes derive their values from the job's attributes. In this example, the job's attributes contain yet another special value, *WrkStn, for both the printer device and the output queue. The system therefore examines the device description of the workstation where the job is running and finds that the printer device is PayPrt29 and the output queue is PayOutQ47.

This example not only demonstrates how special value *WrkStn functions but also points out the fact that print-direction resolution may require multiple steps. In other words, one special value can point to another.

*SysVal

In our experience, we've not encountered an environment in which value *SysVal was particularly useful. However, *SysVal is a supported special value, so you should be familiar with the rules that apply to it.

You can specify *SysVal for printer device only. You can use it in any of the objects or commands that contain printer device information. *SysVal instructs the system to retrieve the printer device value from system value QPrtDev, the system-wide, default printer device description. Consider the following example:

QPrtDev system value: PayPrt52

```
CrtPrtF File(PayChecks) +
        Dev(*SysVal)    +
        OutQ(PayOutQ31)
```

Notice that the OutQ parameter on the CrtPrtF command names a specific output queue, PayOutQ31. Therefore, the output queue will be that value. The Dev parameter, on the other hand, specifies special value *SysVal. Thus, the system examines system value QPrtDev and determines that the printer device value is PayPrt52.

*Dev

You can specify value *Dev for output queue only. Similar to *SysVal for printer device, *Dev can be specified in any object or command that contains output queue information.

*Dev instructs the system to examine the printer device (Dev) attribute of the printer file to determine the spooled file's destination output queue. Once the system resolves a specific value for the printer device, it places the report in an output queue with the same name as the resolved printer device name. The following example demonstrates use of the *Dev system value.

```
CrtPrtF File(PayChecks) +
        Dev(PayPrt21)   +
        OutQ(*Dev)
```

In this example, parameter Dev names printer device PayPrt21. The OutQ parameter specifies special value *Dev, thereby instructing the system to resolve the printer device name and assign it to the output queue value. In this case, the system determines that the output queue is PayPrt21.

Charting the Print Path

Figures 9.4A, 9.4B, and 9.4C chart the path that defines print direction. Remember that as a first step, the system determines whether to spool the report (Figure 9.4A). When the printer file (or override) specifies that the system should spool the report, the system follows the output queue path shown in Figure 9.4B to determine the spooled file's destination. The printer file (or override) can alternatively specify that the system should not spool the report and should instead print directly on the designated printer device. In this case, the system uses the printer device path denoted by Figure 9.4C.

When you peruse the charts in Figures 9.4B and 9.4C, be sure to examine the footnotes for additional information. For instance, Figure 9.4B explains in footnote 1 that when inspecting the printer file portion of the path, the system may derive the output queue value from the printer file itself or as the result of a printer file override.

Whether using the output queue path or the printer device path, the system begins the print-direction resolution process with the printer file (or override). Figures 9.4B and 9.4C imply this fact by placing the printer file at the top of each chart. Notice the arrows pointing from the printer file to various points in the chart. These arrows point to the possible values that the printer file's output queue attribute and printer device attribute can contain.

Let's examine the output queue path. In Figure 9.4B, you can see that the printer file can contain one of the following values for its output queue attribute:

- a specific output queue
- *Job
- *Dev

When the system is to derive the print-direction attributes from the printer file, the result can be that a specific output queue is named for use, that the system is to obtain the output queue from job attributes, or that the system is to examine the printer device attribute in the printer file to determine the output queue.

FIGURE 9.4A
Printer File Direction

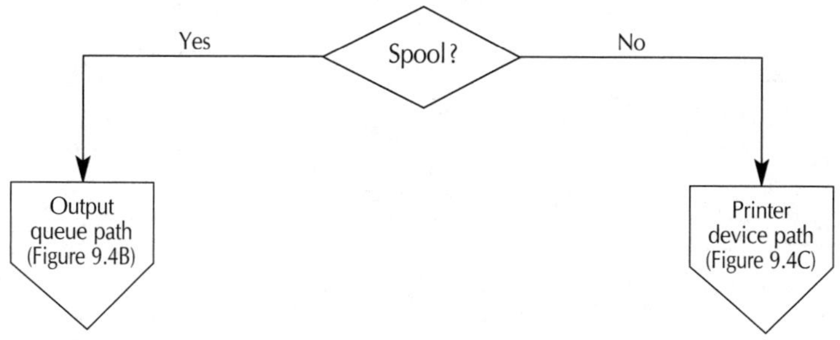

FIGURE 9.4B
Output Queue Path

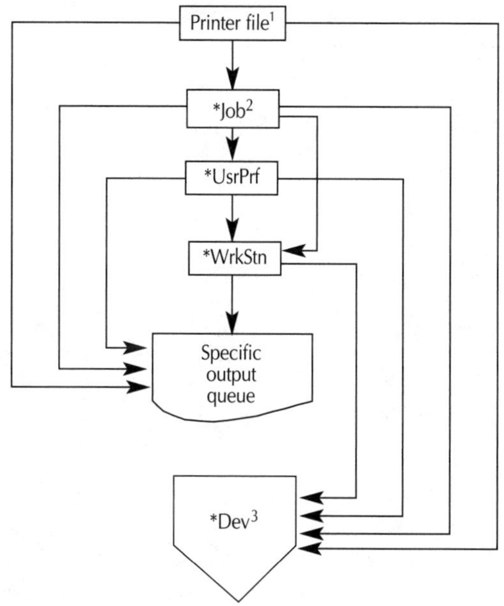

[1] Values derived from printer file description or OvrPrtF command.

[2] Commands BchJob and SbmJob can specify *JobD; in addition, SbmJob can specify *Current. In these cases, the output queue values result in the same path as *Job.

[3] See Figure 9.4C (printer device path).

FIGURE 9.4C
Printer Device Path

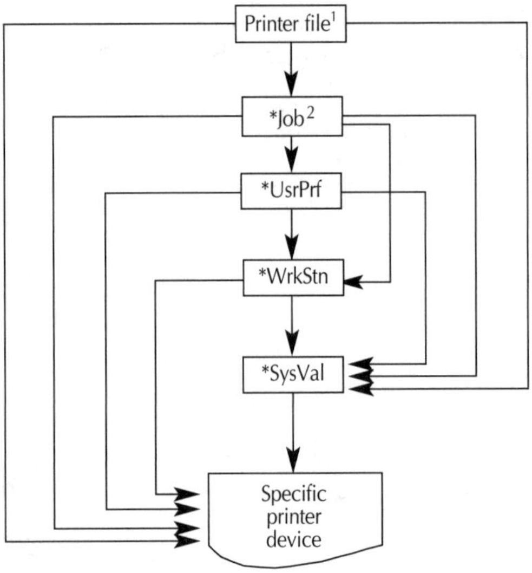

[1] Values derived from printer file description or OvrPrtF command.

[2] Commands BchJob and SbmJob can specify *JobD; in addition, SbmJob can specify *Current. In these cases, the printer device values result in the same path as *Job.

Let's assume the output queue value specifies *Job. Follow the arrows from the *Job box, and you can see that the job attributes can then

- name a specific output queue
- refer resolution to the user profile (value *UsrPrf)
- refer resolution to the printer device value specified in the printer file (value *Dev)
- refer resolution to the workstation device description (value *WrkStn)

Keep in mind that any time print-path resolution contains the value *Dev, resolution continues by examining the printer device attribute of the printer file, in which case you examine the path defined by Figure 9.4C. By following the arrows through the possible paths available in resolving a report's destination, you can see that resolving to a specific output queue or printer device can flow through numerous points.

Job QPrtJob and Print Direction

In addition to the seven special values we've just discussed, there's another factor you need to consider. There are times when the system generates spooled files during a job in which the current job's user is not the same as the user profile currently running. For example, suppose user GuthrieGar uses command SndNetSplF (Send Network Spooled File) to send a spooled file to user NielsenKar. Clearly, user NielsenKar should own the sent spooled file. However, a job running under user profile NielsenKar didn't initiate the spooled file's creation. Instead, a system job created the spooled file. To ensure that spooled file ownership is appropriate in such cases, the system generates a special job named QPrtJob for the user and associates the spooled file (or files) with this job. Thus, when user NielsenKar issues the WrkSplF (Work with Spooled File) command, she'll see the spooled file sent to her by user GuthrieGar.

A QPrtJob job can contain up to 9,999 spooled files. When a user's QPrtJob job has reached capacity, the system automatically creates another one for the user.

The system generates QPrtJob jobs for several system functions, including

- using the SndNetSplF or SndTCPSplF (Send TCP/IP Spooled File) command to send a spooled file to another user
- sending a spooled file from a VM or MVS system through a VM/MVS bridge to an iSeries system
- receiving a spooled file using TCP/IP or the line printer daemon (LPD) process
- using the QSpCrtSp (Create Spooled File) spool application programming interface (API) to create a spooled file for another user
- using the QWTSetP (Set Profile) security API to set the user profile to a different user and then creating a spooled file

Now that you know what QPrtJob is, let's see how it can affect print direction.

Before V4R4, storing a spooled file under a QPrtJob job could influence the spooled file's destination. If print direction revolved around a job-related special value (e.g., *Job in the output queue parameter of the printer file), the system obtained the output queue attribute from the QPrtJob job. The system would ignore the value in the output queue attribute for the current job. Starting with V4R4, the output queue of the current job controls the destination of the spooled file.

With special data-area support, you can instruct the system to use the information from QPrtJob rather than that from the current job. To do so, you must create a data area named QPrtJob and adhere to the following rules:

- The data area must exist in either QUsrSys or the first product library in the library list of the current job.
- User profile QSpl must own the data area.
- The data area must be of type logical.
- The data area must have a value of false (0).

If the system doesn't find the data area or there are any problems with it, the print-direction values come from the current job.

Some examples of problems with the data area are

- damage
- not owned by user QSpl
- incorrect type
- logical value of true (1)

You'll likely find that you don't take advantage of this special data-area support.

Ready for Action

As you can see, several things control the destination of printed output. With the information you've learned in this chapter, you're poised to customize settings to best fit your environment. You'll also be able to find those reports when a user calls and asks, "Where have all the reports gone?"

Chapter 10

Understanding Output Queues

Printing. It's one of the most common things any computer does, and it's relatively easy with the iSeries. What complicates this basic task is that the system provides many functions you can tailor for your printing needs. In Chapter 9, we introduced you to one such customization: print direction. That's only the beginning, though. You can use multiple printers to handle various types of forms. You can use printers that exist anywhere in your configuration — whether they're attached to local or remote machines or even on a network. You can let users view, hold, release, or cancel their own output, or you can design your system so that users' output is simply printed on a printer in their area without any operator intervention except to change and align the forms.

The cornerstone of all this capability is the iSeries output queue. Understanding how to create and use output queues can help you master iSeries print operations.

What Is an Output Queue?

An output queue is an object containing a list of spooled files that you can display on a workstation or write to a printer device. (You can also use output queues to write spooled output to a diskette device, but this chapter doesn't cover that function.) The iSeries object type identifier for output queues is *OutQ.

Figure 10.1A shows the display you see on a workstation when you enter the WrkOutQ (Work with Output Queues) command for the output queue QPrint:

```
WrkOutQ QPrint
```

As the figure shows, the Work with Output Queue panel lists each spooled file that exists on the queue you specify. For each spooled file, the display shows the spooled file name, the user of the job that created the spooled file, the user data identifier, the status of the spooled file on the queue, the number of pages in the spooled file, the number of copies requested, the form type, and the spooled file's output priority (which is defined in the job that generates the spooled file). You can use function key F11 (View 2) to view additional information (e.g., job name and number) about each spooled file entry.

The status of a spooled file can be any of the following:

- RDY (Ready) — The file is spooled and waiting to be printed when the writer is available. You can use option 3 to hold the spooled file.
- OPN (Open) — The file is being written and can't be printed at this time (i.e., the printer file's Schedule parameter value is *FileEnd or *JobEnd).
- DFR (Deferred) — The file has been deferred from printing.
- SND (Sending) — The file is being or has been sent to a remote system.

FIGURE 10.1A
Work with Output Queue Panel

```
                              Work with Output Queue

Queue:    QPRINT          Library:    QGPL            Status:    RLS/WTR

Type options, press Enter.
  1=Send   2=Change   3=Hold   4=Delete   5=Display   6=Release   7=Messages
  8=Attributes        9=Work with printing status

Opt  File         User         User Data    Sts    Pages    Copies   Form Type    Pty
 _   QSYSPRT      QSYSOPR                   WTR        6         1   *STD           5
 _   PRINTKEY     QSYSOPR                   RDY        1         1   *STD           5
 _   QQRYPRT      QSECOFR                   HLD        3         1   *STD           5

                                                                             Bottom
Parameters for options 1, 2, 3 or command
===> ______________________________________________________________________________
F3=Exit   F11=View 2   F12=Cancel   F20=Writers   F22=Printers
F24=More keys
```

- CLO (Closed) — The file is spooled and has been completely processed by a program but is unavailable for printing because Schedule(*JobEnd) was specified and the job that produced the file hasn't finished.
- HLD (Held) — The file is spooled and on hold in the output queue. You can use option 6 to release the spooled file for printing.
- SAV (Saved) — The file has been printed and is now saved in the output queue, from which it can be printed again if desired. (The spooled file attribute Save has a value of *Yes. In contrast, a spooled file with Save(*No) is removed from the queue after printing.)
- WTR (Writer) — The file is currently being printed. You can still use option 3 to hold the spooled file and stop the printing; do so, and the spooled file status will appear on the display as HLD.
- PND (Pending) — The file is waiting to be printed.
- PRT (Printing) — The file has been completely sent to the printer, but the printer hasn't yet returned an indication of completion.
- MSGW (Message waiting) — The file has a message that needs a reply or that indicates a necessary action.

We've mentioned two options for spooled files: option 3, which holds spooled files, and option 6, which releases them. The panel in Figure 10.1A shows all available options. Figure 10.1B explains each option.

FIGURE 10.1B

Output Queue Options

Option	Description
1=Send	Send a copy of the spooled file to someone in your network (local or remote).
2=Change	Change some or all of the spooled file's attributes.
3=Hold	Hold the spooled file.
4=Delete	Delete the spooled file.
5=Display	View the spooled file (spacing will differ from the printed version because blank lines aren't displayed).
6=Release	Release a spooled file and make ready for printing.
7=Messages	Work with any messages pending for the spooled file.
8=Attributes	Display the spooled file's attributes.
9=Work with printing status	Work with the spooled file's current printing status.

How to Create Output Queues

Now that you've seen that output queues contain spooled files and let you perform actions on those spooled files, we can focus on creating output queues. One common way output queues are created is through a printer device description. Yes, you've read correctly! When you create a printer device description using the CrtDevPtr (Create Device Description (Printer)) command or through automatic configuration, the system automatically creates an output queue in library QUsrSys of the same name as that assigned to that printer. This output queue is the default for that printer. In fact, the system places the description "Default output queue for printer *PrinterName*" in the output queue's Text attribute.

An alternative is to use the CrtOutQ (Create Output Queue) command. In this case, the parameter values for CrtOutQ determine the attributes of the output queue. When you use CrtOutQ, after entering the name of the output queue and library in which you want the queue to exist, you're presented with three categories of parameters:

- procedural parameters
- configuration-related parameters
- parameters with security implications

For a look at some of the parameters you can use, see the CrtOutQ panel in Figure 10.2.

FIGURE 10.2
Create Output Queue Panel

```
                        Create Output Queue (CRTOUTQ)

Type choices, press Enter.

Output queue . . . . . . . . . . OUTQ             __________
  Library  . . . . . . . . . . .                    *CURLIB___
Maximum spooled file size:       MAXPAGES   _
  Number of pages  . . . . . . .                  *NONE______
  Starting time  . . . . . . . .                  ________
  Ending time  . . . . . . . . .                  ________
                       + for more values _
Order of files on queue  . . . . SEQ              *FIFO__
Remote system  . . . . . . . . . RMTSYS           *NONE_________________________
________________________________________________________________________________
________________________________________________________________________________
__________________________________________________
Remote printer queue . . . . . . RMTPRTQ          *USER_________________________
________________________________________________________________________________
________________________________________________________________________________
__________________________________________________
Writers to autostart . . . . . . AUTOSTRWTR       *NONE_
Queue for writer messages  . . . MSGQ             QSYSOPR___
  Library  . . . . . . . . . . .                    *LIBL_____
Connection type  . . . . . . . . CNNTYPE          *SNA____
Destination type . . . . . . . . DESTTYPE         *OS400____
Host print transform . . . . . . TRANSFORM        *YES
User data transform  . . . . . . USRDTATFM        *NONE_____
  Library  . . . . . . . . . . .                    __________
Manufacturer type and model  . . MFRTYPMDL        *IBM42011_________
Workstation customizing object   WSCST            *NONE_____
  Library  . . . . . . . . . . .                    __________
Image configuration  . . . . . . IMGCFG           *NONE_____
Internet address . . . . . . . . INTNETADR        _______________
VM/MVS class . . . . . . . . . . CLASS            A
Forms Control Buffer . . . . . . FCB              *NONE___
Destination options  . . . . . . DESTOPT          *NONE_________________________
________________________________________________________________________________
____________________
Print separator page . . . . . . SEPPAGE          *YES
User defined option  . . . . . . USRDFNOPT        *NONE_____
                       + for more values          __________
User defined object:             USRDFNOBJ
  Object . . . . . . . . . . . .                  *NONE_____
    Library  . . . . . . . . . .                    __________
  Object type  . . . . . . . . .                  _______
User driver program  . . . . . . USRDRVPGM        *NONE_____
  Library  . . . . . . . . . . .                    __________
Spooled file ASP . . . . . . . . SPLFASP          *SYSTEM_
Text 'description' . . . . . . . TEXT             *BLANK________________________
__________________
```

continued

FIGURE 10.2 CONTINUED

```
                         Additional Parameters

Display any file . . . . . . . . . DSPDTA        *NO___
Job separators . . . . . . . . . . JOBSEP        0_____
Operator controlled  . . . . . . . OPRCTL        *YES
Data queue . . . . . . . . . . . . DTAQ          *NONE______
  Library  . . . . . . . . . . . .                ___________
Authority to check . . . . . . . . AUTCHK        *OWNER_
Authority  . . . . . . . . . . . . AUT           *USE______
```

Procedural Parameters

One of the CrtOutQ command's procedural parameters, Seq (Order of files on queue), controls the order of the spooled files on the output queue. You can choose a value of either *FIFO (first in, first out) or *JobNbr (job number). If you select *FIFO, the system places new spooled files on the queue following all other entries already on the queue that have the same output priority as the new spooled files (the job description you use during job execution determines the output priority).

Using *FIFO can be tricky because certain changes to an output queue entry cause the system to reshuffle the queue's contents and place the spooled file behind all others of equal priority:

- a change of output priority when you use the ChgJob (Change Job) or ChgSplFA (Change Spooled File Attributes) command
- a change in status from HLD, CLO, or OPN to RDY
- a change in status from RDY back to HLD, CLO, or OPN

The second possible value for the Seq parameter, *JobNbr, specifies that the system sort queue entries according to their priorities, using the date and time when the job that created the spooled file entered the system. We recommend using *JobNbr instead of *FIFO because with *JobNbr you don't have to worry about changes to an output queue entry affecting the order of the queue's contents.

Another procedural parameter, shown under Additional Parameters in Figure 10.2 (above), is JobSep (Job separators). You can specify a value from 0 to 9 to indicate the number of job separators (i.e., pages) the system should place at the beginning of each job's output. The job separator contains the job name, the job user's name, the job number, and the date and time when the job is run. This information can help in identifying jobs. If you'd rather not use a lot of paper, you can prevent job separators by selecting a JobSep value of 0. Or, you can enter special value *Msg for this parameter, and each time the end of a print job is reached, the system will send a message to the message queue for the writer.

Don't confuse the JobSep parameter with the FileSep (File separators) parameter, which is an attribute of printer files. When creating or changing printer files, you can specify a value for the FileSep parameter to control the number of file separators at the beginning of each spooled file. The information on the file separators is similar to that printed on the job separator but includes information about the particular spooled file.

When do you need the file separator, the job separator, or both? You need file separators to help operators separate the various printed reports within a single job. You need job separators to help separate the printed output of various jobs and to quickly identify the end of one report and the beginning of the next. However, if you program a header page for all your reports, job separators are probably wasteful. Another concern is that for output queues that handle only a specific type of form, such as invoices, a separator wastes an expensive form.

In reality, a person looking for a printed report usually pays no attention to separator pages but looks at the first page of the report to identify the contents and destination of the report. And, as you can imagine, a combination of file separators and job separators could quickly launch a major paper-recycling campaign. Understand, we're not saying these separators have no function. We're saying you should think about how helpful the separators are and explicitly choose the number you need.

Configuration Parameters

Among the several configuration-related CrtOutQ parameters are those that indicate whether the output queue is local or remote, as well as the type of connection used. For instance, using the RmtSys (Remote system) parameter, you can specify the system for a remote output queue. With parameter RmtPrtQ (Remote printer queue), you can specify the name of a remote system's output queue to associate with the local output queue being created. Spooled files placed in the local output queue are then printed at the specified remote location.

Other configuration parameters determine specific functionality. For example, parameters Transform (Host print transform), MfrTypMdl (Manufacturer type and model), and WsCst (Workstation customizing object) influence actual print characteristics, such as margins, font, and degree of rotation. Because they apply to printers that aren't "native" to the iSeries, you'll likely have occasion to use these parameters. Most often, you must specify these parameters for Printer Control Language (PCL) printers, such as many laser printers.

Security Parameters

The security-related CrtOutQ command parameters help control user access to particular output queues and particular spooled data. To appreciate the importance of controlling access, remember that you can use output queues not only to print spooled files but also to display them. What good is it to prevent people from watching as payroll checks are printed if they can simply display the spooled file in the output queue?

The DspDta (Display any file) parameter specifies what kind of access to the output queue is allowed for users who have *Read authority. A value of *Yes says that any user with *Read access to the output queue can display, copy, or send the data of any file on the queue. *No specifies that users with *Read authority to the output queue can display, copy, or send the output data only of their own spooled files unless they have some other special authority. (Special authorities that provide additional function are *JobCtl and *SplCtl.)

The OprCtl (Operator controlled) parameter specifies whether a user who has *JobCtl special authority can manage or control the files on an output queue. Allowable values are *Yes, which permits control of the queue and provides the ability to change queue entries, and *No, which blocks this control for users with the *JobCtl special authority.

One problem you might face relating to security is how to let users start, change, and end writers without having to grant them *JobCtl special authority, which also grants a user additional job-related authorities that might not be desirable (e.g., the ability to control any job on the system). One option is to write a program to perform such writer functions. You can specify that the program adopt the authority of its owner, and you'd make sure the owner has *JobCtl special authority. During program execution, the current user adopts the special and object-specific authorities of the owner. When the program ends, the user no longer has the adopted *JobCtl authority and thus can't take advantage of the functions this authority permits.

If a user doesn't have *JobCtl special authority or doesn't adopt this special authority, he or she must have a minimum of *Change authority to the output queue and *Use authority to the printer device to start the writer.

The AutChk (Authority to check) parameter specifies whether the commands that check the requester's authority to the output queue should check for ownership authority (*Owner) or just for data authority (*DtaAut). When the value is *Owner, the requester must have ownership authority to the output queue to pass the output queue authorization test. When the value is *DtaAut, the requester must have *Read, *Add, and *Delete authority to the output queue.

Last, the Aut (Authority) parameter specifies the initial level of authority allowed for *Public users. You can change this authority level by using the EdtObjAut (Edit Object Authority), GrtObjAut (Grant Object Authority), or RvkObjAut (Revoke Object Authority) command.

As you can see, creating output queues requires more than just choosing a name and pressing Enter. Given some appropriate attention, output queues can provide a proper level of support for procedural (e.g., finding printer files, establishing the order of printer files), configuration (e.g., type of printer, customizing object), and security (e.g., who can see what data) requirements.

Who Should Create Output Queues?

Who should create output queues? Although this seems like a simple question, it's important for two reasons: First, the owner of an output queue can change the output queue attributes and can grant and revoke authorities to the output queue, which means the owner controls who can view and work with spooled files on that queue. Second, the AutChk parameter checks the ownership of the output queue as part of the authorization test when an output queue is accessed. So ownership is a key to your ability to secure output queues.

Here are some suggestions. The system operator should be responsible for creating and controlling output queues that hold data considered public or non-secure. With this ownership and the various authority parameters on the CrtOutQ command, you can create an environment that lets users control their own printer files and print on various printers in their area of work. For secure data (e.g., payroll, human resources, financial statements), the department supervisor profile (or a similar one) should own the output queue. The person who owns the output queue is responsible for maintaining the security of the output queue and can even explicitly deny access to IT personnel.

How Spooled Files Get on the Queue

It's important to understand that all spooled output generated on the iSeries uses a printer file. Whether you enter the DspLib (Display Library) command using the Output(*Print) parameter to direct your output to a report, create and execute a query, or write a report-generating program, you're going to use a printer file to generate that output. A printer file is the means to spool output to a file that can be stored on a queue and printed as needed. Also, a printer file determines the attributes the printed output will have. This means you can create a variety of printer files on the system to accommodate various form requirements.

Another essential fact to understand about spooling on the iSeries is that, normally, all printed output is placed on an output queue to be printed. As we mentioned in Chapter 9, the system is capable of bypassing the spool process to perform direct printing, but this approach is normally avoided because of performance and work-management problems that arise when implementing direct printing. With that said, we can examine the spooling process more closely.

When a job generates a spooled file, the system places the file on an output queue. Recall from the discussion of print direction in Chapter 9 that numerous considerations apply in determining the output queue on which the file will be placed. A single job can place spooled files on different output queues. Figure 10.3 demonstrates this fact.
The job portrayed in the figure first spools the nightly corporate accounts receivable (AR) report to an output queue at the corporate office. Then the program creates a separate AR report for each branch office and places the report on the appropriate output queue.

FIGURE 10.3
One Job Placing Spooled Files on Different Output Queues

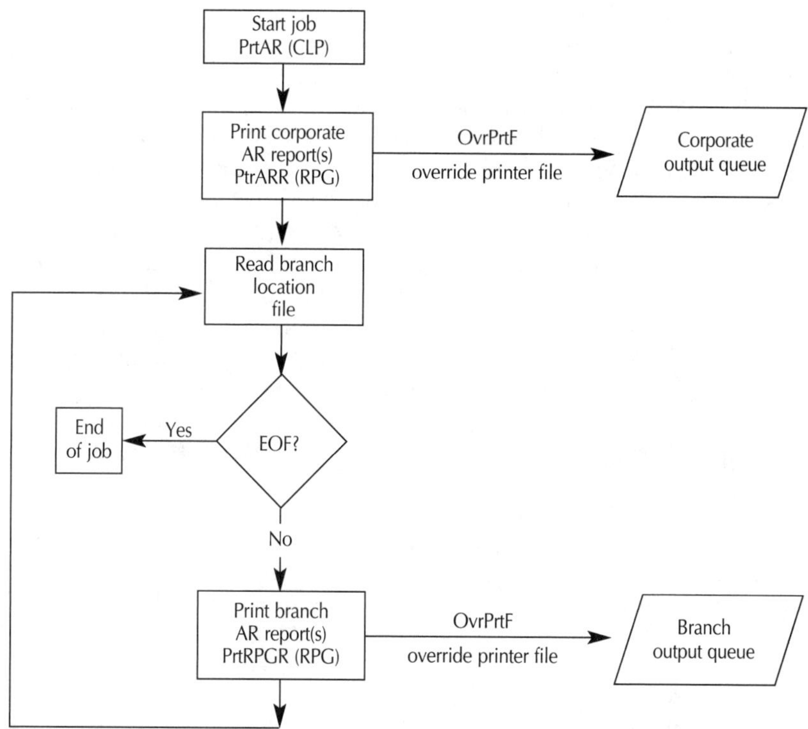

How Spooled Files Are Printed from the Queue

So how do the spooled files get printed from the queue? The answer is no secret. You must start (assign) a writer to an output queue. You make spooled files available to the writer by releasing the spooled file, using option 6 on the Work with Output Queue or Work with All Spooled Files panel. You then use the StrPrtWtr (Start Printer Writer) command for local printers or the StrRmtWtr (Start Remote Writer) command for remote printers. The OutQ parameter on these commands determines the output queue to be read by the printer.

When the writer is started to a specific output queue and you use the WrkOutQ command for that specific output queue, the letters WTR appear in the Status field at the top of the Work with Output Queue display to indicate that a writer is assigned to print available entries in that queue.

You can start a writer for any output queue. You don't have to worry about the name of the writer matching the name of the queue. For instance, to start printing the spooled files in output queue QPrint, you can execute the command

```
StrPrtWtr Writer(WriterName) +
          OutQ(QPrint)
```

(Messages for file control are sent to the message queue defined in the printer's device description unless you also specify the MsgQ parameter.)

When you IPL the system, your start-up program (specified in system value QStrUpPgm) can control whether the system starts the writers on the system. The IBM-supplied default start-up program (QSys/QStrUp) uses a single StrPrtWtr command to start all writers. When the start-up program starts all writers in this manner, each printer's device description determines both its output queue and its message queue. Of course, you can modify the start-up program so that it starts all writers, starts specific writers, or starts no writers. In addition, these changes can explicitly specify the output queue to assign when the system starts a writer. After a writer is started, you can redirect the writer to another output queue by using the ChgWtr (Change Writer) command or by ending the writer and restarting it, assigning a different output queue.

To list the writers on your system and their assigned output queues, type **WrkOutQ** on the command line and press Enter. You'll see a display similar to the one in Figure 10.4.

FIGURE **10.4**

Work with All Output Queues Panel

```
                        Work with All Output Queues

 Type options, press Enter.
   2=Change   3=Hold      4=Delete    5=Work with    6=Release    8=Description
   9=Work with Writers    14=Clear

 Opt     Queue          Library          Files      Writer          Status
  _      GRPOUTQ        GUTHRIE              0                       RLS
  _      USROUTQ        GUTHRIE              0                       RLS
  _      GUTHRIE        GUTHRIE              3      GGPRT            RLS
  _      QFAXOUTQ       QFAX                 0                       RLS
  _      QFQOUTQ        QFAX                 0                       RLS
  _      COMMON         QGPL                 0      PRT17            RLS
  _      QDKT           QGPL                 0                       RLS
  _      QPRINT         QGPL                34                       RLS
  _      QPRINTS        QGPL                 0                       RLS
  _      QPRINT2        QGPL                 0                       RLS
  _      QSCAPAROQ      QSC0640981           0                       RLS
  _      PRT01          QUSRSYS             17      PRT01            RLS
                                                                        More...
 Command
 ===> ____________________________________________________________________
 F3=Exit    F4=Prompt    F5=Refresh    F12=Cancel    F24=More keys
```

You can also use the WrkWtr (Work with Writers) command by typing **WrkWtr** and pressing Enter to see a display like the one in Figure 10.5.

FIGURE 10.5
Work with All Printers Panel

```
                         Work with All Printers

Type options, press Enter.
  1=Start   2=Change   3=Hold   4=End   5=Work with   6=Release
  7=Display messages   8=Work with output queue

Opt  Device      Sts   Sep    Form Type   File        User        User Data
 _   GGPRT       STR   *FILE  *ALL        QPDSPJOB    GUTHRIE
 _   KNPRT       END
 _   PRTØ1       STR   *FILE  *ALL        QSYSPRT     QSECOFR
 _   PRT17       STR   *FILE  *ALL





                                                                    Bottom
Parameters for options 1, 2, 3, 4, 6 or command
===> ____________________________________________________________________
F3=Exit   F11=View 2   F12=Cancel   F17=Top   F18=Bottom   F24=More keys
```

Note

It's important to understand that the output queue and the printer are independent objects, so output queues can exist with no printer assigned and can have entries. Operational Assistant illustrates some implications of this fact. Operational Assistant lets you create two output queues (QUsrSys/QEZJobLog and QUsrSys/QEZDebug) to store job logs and problem-related output, respectively. These output queues are not default queues for any printers. The people who manage the system can decide to print, view, move, or delete the entries stored in these queues.

A Different View of Spooled Files

The WrkOutQ command lets you work with all spooled files on a particular output queue. Another helpful command is WrkSplF (Work with Spooled Files). This command lets you work with all spooled files generated by your job, even if those spooled files are on multiple output queues. Figure 10.6 represents the WrkSplF command output for someone who works at the basic OS/400 assistance level. (A user's assistance level is determined first at the user profile level by the AstLvl parameter and then at the command level, based on the last use of the command or what the user enters for the AstLvl parameter on the command.)

FIGURE 10.6
Work with Printer Output — WrkSplF Basic Assistance Level

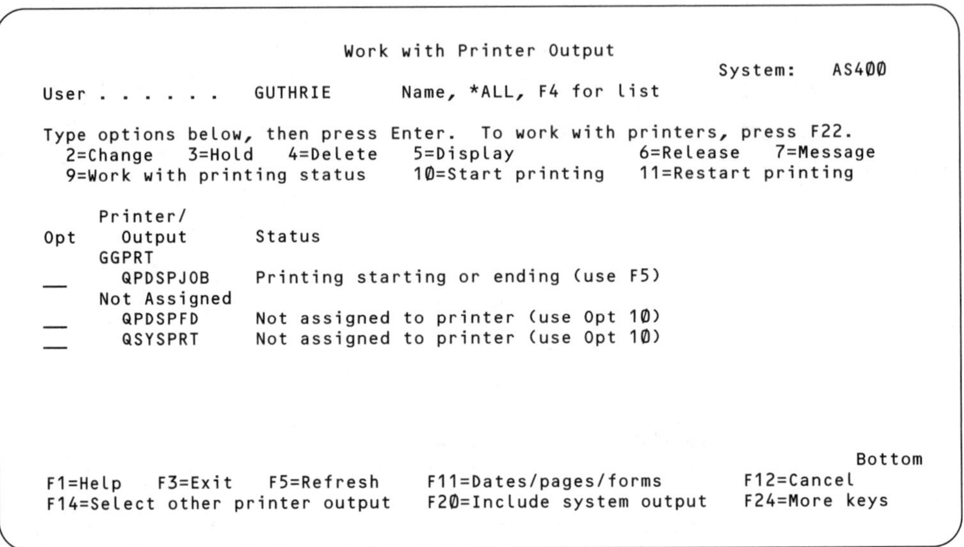

```
                         Work with Printer Output
                                                      System:   AS400
User . . . . . .   GUTHRIE      Name, *ALL, F4 for list

Type options below, then press Enter.  To work with printers, press F22.
  2=Change   3=Hold   4=Delete   5=Display          6=Release   7=Message
  9=Work with printing status    10=Start printing   11=Restart printing

     Printer/
Opt    Output       Status
     GGPRT
 _     QPDSPJOB     Printing starting or ending (use F5)
     Not Assigned
 _     QPDSPFD      Not assigned to printer (use Opt 10)
 _     QSYSPRT      Not assigned to printer (use Opt 10)

                                                                    Bottom
F1=Help   F3=Exit   F5=Refresh    F11=Dates/pages/forms       F12=Cancel
F14=Select other printer output   F20=Include system output   F24=More keys
```

Notice that one spooled file is assigned to the printer GGPrt, while the others are unassigned. They are definitely on an output queue, but because no writer is currently started for any of those output queues, the spooled files are listed as unassigned. The basic assistance level hides some of the technical details of spooled files and output queues unless you request more information by selecting option 9 (Work with printing status) to display the spooled file detail information.

Figure 10.7 represents the WrkSplF command output for someone who works at the intermediate assistance level. (There is no advanced assistance level for this command, so those at the advanced assistance level would also see this same panel.) Now, you can clearly see which user created each spooled file, which output queue the file is assigned to, the status, and the number of pages.

As you see, you have two methods for working with spooled files: the WrkOutQ and the WrkSplF commands. You'll find that you use both in your daily operations, but you'll probably find you use WrkSplF most when you're interested in a specific user's output and use WrkOutQ most when system operations is your concern.

FIGURE 10.7

Work with All Spooled Files—WrkSplF Intermediate Assistance Level

```
                         Work with All Spooled Files

 Type options, press Enter.
   1=Send   2=Change   3=Hold   4=Delete   5=Display   6=Release   7=Messages
   8=Attributes        9=Work with printing status

                                Device or                          Total      Cur
 Opt  File        User         Queue        User Data    Sts     Pages      Page  Copy
  _   QPDSPJOB    GUTHRIE      GUTHRIE                   WTR         6         3     1
  _   QPDSPFD     GUTHRIE      QPRINT                    RDY         4               1
  _   QSYSPRT     GUTHRIE      USROUTQ                   RDY         2               1

                                                                              Bottom
 Parameters for options 1, 2, 3 or command
 ===> ____________________________________________________________________________
 F3=Exit   F10=View 4   F11=View 2   F12=Cancel   F22=Printers   F24=More keys
```

How to Organize Output Queues

The organization of your output queues should be as simple as possible. To start, you can let the system create the default output queues for each printer you create. Of course, you may want to modify ownership and some output queue attributes. At this point, though, you can send output to an output queue and there will be a printer assigned to print from that queue.

How can you use output queues effectively? Each installation must discover its own answer, but we can give you a few ideas. If your installation generates relatively few reports, having one output queue per available printer is the most efficient way to use output queues.

Installations that generate large volumes of printed output need to control when and where these reports might be printed. For example, a staff of programmers might share a single printer. If you spool all compiled programs to the same queue and make them available to the writer, things could jam up fast, and important reports might get delayed behind compile listings being printed just because they were spooled to a queue with a writer. A better solution is to create an output queue for each programmer. Each programmer can then use a job description to route printed output to his or her own queue. When a programmer decides to print a spooled file, he or she moves the file to the output queue with the shared writer active. This means that the only reports printed are those specifically wanted. Also, you can better schedule printing of a large number of reports.

What about the operations department? Is it wise to have one output queue (e.g., QPrint, Prt01) to hold all the spooled files that nightly, daily, and monthly jobs generate? You should probably spend a few minutes planning for a better implementation.

For some end users, you may want to make the output queue invisible. You can direct requested printed output to an output queue with an available writer in the work area of the end user who made the request. The only things the user should have to do are change or add paper and answer occasional printer-related messages.

What a mountain of information! And we've only discussed a few concepts for managing output queues. But this information should be enough to get you started and on your way to mastering output queues.

Chapter 11

A Plug-and-Play Output Queue Monitor

In today's world, spooled files play a much larger part in day-to-day operations than their traditional role as the source of locally printed reports. For instance, rather than print a report, you now might want to fax it using host software or perhaps send it via e-mail. Undoubtedly, though, not all your applications were designed with an awareness that their output might be used in such ways.

Although adding the necessary support to your applications is an obvious solution, it's often better to integrate your applications with new, standalone programs that perform the new functions. Your applications continue to place spooled files on output queues, and the new programs process these spooled files. Not only does this approach typically limit application changes, but its modularity also makes it easy to integrate any of your applications with the new functions.

To implement this solution, though, you'll need some way to *automatically* determine when spooled files arrive on output queues, as well as a way to identify the spooled files so your new programs can then process them. You can easily accomplish these requirements using data queue support. With this support, you associate a data queue with an output queue, and as spooled files become ready, identifying information is sent to the data queue. Add a program to await the data queue entries, and you'll have everything you need for fully automated spooled file management.

We've mentioned how this technique might be used for automated fax systems or for sending a report to an e-mail recipient, but there are also many ways in which this approach can help with general spooled file management. For instance, you could use such a monitor system to automatically

- archive spooled files
- notify a user when a report is ready
- distribute copies of reports to users in a network
- transfer spooled files to a user on a remote system
- duplicate and distribute reports to a group of users
- page personnel when a particular job generates a job log, indicating abnormal termination

As you think about possible uses, we're sure the list will grow.

Setting the Stage

Setting up data queue support for an output queue is easy. You simply create a data queue using the CrtDtaQ (Create Data Queue) command and then specify the data queue name in the DtaQ (Data queue) parameter on the CrtOutQ (Create Output Queue) or ChgOutQ (Change Output Queue) command.

The entry sent to the data queue is 128 bytes long and contains information used to identify the spooled file and its output queue. Figure 11.1 shows the layout of the data queue entry. You can use this information on spooled-file–related commands, such as CpySplF (Copy Spooled File) and ChgSplFA (Change Spooled File Attributes), as well as in various spooled file application programming interfaces (APIs).

FIGURE 11.1

Data Queue Layout for Output Queue Entries

Position	*Type*	*Length*	*Description*
1	Character	10	*Function* Identifies the function that created the entry. For spooled files, the value is *SPOOL.
11	Character	2	*Record type* Identifies the record type within the function. The only defined valid value is '01', indicating a spooled file has arrived in a ready status.
13	Character	10	*Job name* Identifies the name of the job that created the spooled file.
23	Character	10	*Job user* Identifies the user that created the spooled file.
33	Character	6	*Job number* Identifies the job number of the job that created the spooled file.
39	Character	10	*Spooled file name* Identifies the spooled file name.
49	Binary	4	*Spooled file number* Identifies the spooled file number.
53	Character	10	*Output queue name* Identifies the output queue containing the spooled file.
63	Character	10	*Output queue library* Identifies the name of the library containing the output queue.
73	Unspecified	56	*Reserved* This portion of the data queue entry is unused.

Figure 11.2 shows the prompt screen for the CrtDtaQ command. A data queue associated with an output queue must have a MaxLen (Maximum entry length) value of at least 128. You can specify a larger value, but the data queue entry that describes the spooled file will occupy only the first 128 positions.

Figure 11.3 shows the prompt screen for the ChgOutQ command.

FIGURE 11.2
CrtDtaQ Command Prompt

```
                        Create Data Queue (CRTDTAQ)

   Type choices, press Enter.

   Data queue . . . . . . . . . . . > SAMPLE____     Name
     Library  . . . . . . . . . . .     *CURLIB___   Name, *CURLIB
   Type . . . . . . . . . . . . . .   *STD           *STD, *DDM
   Maximum entry length . . . . . . > 128_______     1-64512
   Force to auxiliary storage . . . > *YES           *NO, *YES
   Sequence . . . . . . . . . . . .   *FIFO_         *FIFO, *LIFO, *KEYED
   Include sender ID  . . . . . . .   *NO_           *NO, *YES
   Text 'description' . . . . . . .   Sample data queue___________________________
  ______

                                                                          Bottom
   F3=Exit   F4=Prompt   F5=Refresh   F10=Additional parameters   F12=Cancel
   F13=How to use this display        F24=More keys
```

FIGURE 11.3
ChgOutQ Command Prompt

```
                        Change Output Queue (CHGOUTQ)

   Type choices, press Enter.

   Output queue . . . . . . . . . . > QPRINT____     Name
     Library  . . . . . . . . . . .     *LIBL_____   Name, *LIBL, *CURLIB
                          Additional Parameters

   Display any file . . . . . . . .   *NO___         *SAME, *NO, *YES, *OWNER
   Job separators . . . . . . . . .   0_____         0-9, *SAME, *MSG
   Operator controlled  . . . . . .   *YES_          *SAME, *YES, *NO
   Data queue . . . . . . . . . . .   SAMPLE____     Name, *SAME, *NONE
     Library  . . . . . . . . . . .     OUTQMON___   Name, *LIBL, *CURLIB
   Authority to check . . . . . . .   *OWNER_        *SAME, *OWNER, *DTAAUT
                                                                         Bottom
   F3=Exit   F4=Prompt   F5=Refresh   F12=Cancel   F13=How to use this display
   F24=More keys
```

A value of *None for this command's DtaQ parameter indicates that no data queue is associated with the output queue. To cause OS/400 to send an entry to a data queue when a spooled file is ready on the associated output queue, specify a data queue name. The value *Same for the DtaQ parameter indicates no change to the existing parameter value.

Once you've created a data queue and associated it with an output queue, OS/400 will send a data queue entry for every spooled file that arrives in ready (RDY) status on that output queue until you execute the ChgOutQ command and specify DtaQ(*None) to stop the function. Noteworthy is the fact that the system sends a data queue entry not when the spooled file arrives on the output queue but rather when the spooled file goes to ready status. This point is important for two reasons. It's possible to specify that when a spooled file is created, the system should spool it in a held (HLD) status. In such a case, although the spooled file arrives on the output queue, the system sends no data queue entry because the spooled file never existed in the ready status. Consider also that after the system sends a data queue entry for a spooled file in ready status, a user might hold the spooled file. This action causes the spooled file to go to status HLD. Releasing the spooled file causes it to once again go to ready status, resulting in the system sending yet another related data queue entry.

The Output Queue Monitor Utility

At the heart of an output queue monitor system is a never-ending batch program that loops endlessly, executing a call to the QRcvDtaQ (Receive Data Queue) API. Each call of the API causes the system to wait indefinitely for an entry to arrive on the data queue. Once an entry arrives, the program parses the entry to obtain the spooled file identification information, and processing continues accordingly.

Fortunately, you needn't concern yourself with the details of the actual monitoring process because we've created a "plug-and-play" output queue monitor utility that handles all monitoring functions. You need only code for the function you want to perform. The monitor utility passes control to your program when a spooled file is ready.

Figure 11.4 contains a simple CL program, Sample, that interfaces to the output queue monitor utility. Notice that, with the exception of the function and the record type (both of which are unnecessary), the program's parameters correspond to the data queue information shown in Figure 11.1. All programs that interface to the utility must use this parameter structure. Program Sample simply executes the SndUsrMsg (Send User Message) command to notify the user that a spooled file is ready.

Tip

Unless the processing of your program is trivial, such as Sample's is, it should submit a new job to perform the actual processing. This approach lets your program exit quickly so that the monitor can continue receiving data queue entries, thereby preventing a backlog of entries.

FIGURE 11.4

Sample Output Queue Monitor Program

```
/*  ================================================================  */
/*  =  Program....... Sample                                      =  */
/*  =  Source type... CLLE                                        =  */
/*  =  Description... Output queue monitor processor to send      =  */
/*  =                 notification message to user                =  */
/*  =  -------------------------------------------------------   =  */
/*  =  Parameters                                                 =  */
/*  =                                                             =  */
/*  =    &Job          Input     Spooled file job name            =  */
/*  =    &User         Input     Spooled file user                =  */
/*  =    &JobNbr       Input     Spooled file job number          =  */
/*  =    &SplFName     Input     Spooled file name                =  */
/*  =    &SplFNbr      Input     Spooled file number              =  */
/*  =    &OutQName     Input     Spooled file OutQ name           =  */
/*  =    &OutQLib      Input     Spooled file OutQ library        =  */
/*  ================================================================  */

Pgm                                                                   +
          (                                                           +
            &Job                                                      +
            &User                                                     +
            &JobNbr                                                   +
            &SplFName                                                 +
            &SplFNbr                                                  +
            &OutQName                                                 +
            &OutQLib                                                  +
          )

/*  ================================================================  */
/*  =  Variable declarations                                      =  */
/*  ================================================================  */

  Dcl       &Job        *Char     (  10    )
  Dcl       &User       *Char     (  10    )
  Dcl       &JobNbr     *Char     (   6    )
  Dcl       &SplFName   *Char     (  10    )
  Dcl       &SplFNbr    *Dec      (   4  0 )
  Dcl       &OutQName   *Char     (  10    )
  Dcl       &OutQLib    *Char     (  10    )
```

continued

FIGURE 11.4 CONTINUED

```
/*  ================================================================  */
/*  =  Send notification message                                   =  */
/*  ================================================================  */

   SndUsrMsg  Msg( 'Spooled file'                                    +
                   *BCat                                             +
                   &SplFName                                         +
                   *BCat                                             +
                   'in output queue'                                 +
                   *BCat                                             +
                   &OutQLib                                          +
                   *TCat                                             +
                   '/'                                               +
                   *TCat                                             +
                   &OutQName                                         +
                   *BCat                                             +
                   'is ready.' )                                     +
              MsgType( *Info )                                       +
              ToUsr( &User )

   Return

/*  ================================================================  */
/*  =  End of program                                              =  */
/*  ================================================================  */

EndPgm
```

Configuring the Output Queue Monitor

Before you can monitor an output queue, you must first create a program, such as Sample, to perform the desired function. The utility requires you to place this program in the utility's product library. (For information about product libraries, see "Installing the Output Queue Monitor Utility," page 165.) Next, you must configure a monitor by creating a logical output queue monitor and defining the output queues on which this monitor is to operate. Following are the configuration commands and the basic sequence in which you'll use them.

CrtOutQMon (Create Output Queue Monitor)

This command defines a logical output queue monitor. Figure 11.5A (page 169) shows the prompt screen for CrtOutQMon. The command's single parameter, Monitor name, must be the name of the user-written program to which the utility passes control. CrtOutQMon creates a data queue and names it using this monitor name. The utility uses this data queue for the monitoring process.

Figures 11.5B through 11.5D (pages 169–174) show the source for the command and its associated programs.

AddOutQME (Add OutQ Monitor Entry)

This command defines up to 25 output queues on which a monitor is to operate. In the unlikely event that you need to monitor more than 25 output queues with one monitor, simply execute this command multiple times.

Figure 11.6A (page 174) shows the prompt screen for AddOutQME. Figures 11.6B through 11.6F (pages 175–183) show the source for the command and its associated programs.

RmvOutQME (Remove OutQ Monitor Entry)

This command lets you remove some or all of the output queue entries assigned to a monitor with the AddOutQME command. You can specify up to 25 output queues whose entries are to be removed, or you can specify the special value *All to remove all output queue entries.

Figure 11.7A (page 183) shows the prompt screen for RmvOutQME. Figures 11.7B through 11.7G (pages 184–193) show the source for the command and its associated programs.

DltOutQMon (Delete Output Queue Monitor)

This command deletes a previously created output queue monitor. The command removes all output queue entries and deletes the data queue associated with the monitor. The command does not delete the user-written program. Normally, you won't use this command. However, it does provide a mechanism for completely ridding your system of a monitor.

Figure 11.8A (page 194) shows the prompt screen for DltOutQMon. Figures 11.8B through 11.8D (pages 194–198) show the source for the command and its associated programs.

Using the Output Queue Monitor

Once you've created your program to process spooled file entries and you've completed the configuration steps, you can start using the monitor. The following commands start and stop the monitor.

StrOutQMon (Start Output Queue Monitor)

This command starts the monitoring process by submitting a job that calls the actual monitor program, OutQMon. CL program OutQMon, in turn, calls the user-written program (identified by the Monitor name parameter) that processes the spooled files. (We'll look at program OutQMon in a moment.) Figure 11.9A (page 199) shows the prompt screen for the StrOutQMon command.

Note that StrOutQMon submits the monitor job to the job queue specified in job description OutQMon found in the product library. Installation program Install creates this job description and assigns default values for all parameters. After installing the utility, you should change the job description, specifying the preferred job queue. We prefer to run monitor programs in the controlling subsystem.

Figures 11.9B through 11.9D (pages 199–204) show the source for command StrOutQMon and its associated programs.

EndOutQMon (End Output Queue Monitor)

This command stops the monitoring process for a specific monitor. To accomplish this, the command sends a special "shutdown" data queue entry to the monitor's data queue. Figure 11.10A (page 204) shows the prompt screen for EndOutQMon.

Note that EndOutQMon may not end the monitor immediately because other data queue entries may exist at the time you execute the command. You should also keep in mind that fact that spooled file entries may arrive in the data queue after the special shutdown entry arrives. In this case, the spooled file entries remain in the data queue, and the monitor processes these entries when it is started again.

Figures 11.10B through 11.10D (pages 204–209) show the source for command EndOutQMon and its associated programs.

Monitoring Program OutQMon

The source for the utility's monitoring program, OutQMon, appears in Figure 11.11 (page 209). You can see that program OutQMon accepts the monitor name (variable &MonName) as its only parameter. The program uses this variable in naming both the data queue to monitor and the user-written program to which the monitor should pass control. Like the other programs that make up the utility, OutQMon first calls API QUsrJobI (Retrieve Job Information) to retrieve the product library. The program uses variable &PrdLib to direct object references to a specific library — the product library.

After retrieving the product library, OutQMon allocates exclusively the data queue that the program monitors. This step yields a mechanism for preventing duplicate active instances of a particular output queue monitor. The program then enters the loop that calls API QRcvDtaQ to receive data queue entries. Because variable &Wait is set to special value –1 (negative one), the program will not continue until an entry arrives in the data queue.

After receiving a data queue entry, program OutQMon extracts the function information from the entry, placing the value in variable &Action. When &Action's value is *SPOOL, denoting a spooled file in ready status, the program parses the data queue entry into its specific fields and passes control to the user-written program specified in variable &MonName. When &Action's value is *ENDMON (the special value sent by command EndOutQMon), the program simply exits. If &Action's value is anything other than *SPOOL or *ENDMON, the program ignores the entry.

The utility stores information about the configured output queue monitor entries in physical file OutQMonE. In addition, the utility uses logical file OutQMonEL1. Figures 11.12A and 11.12B (page 212) contain the source for OutQMonE and OutQMonEL1, respectively. Should you want to enhance the utility by adding a WrkOutQMon (Work with Output Queue Monitor) or a WrkOutQME (Work with Output Queue Monitor Entries) command, you can use the information in these files to build the lists the commands present.

Installing the Output Queue Monitor Utility

A fair amount of code makes up the Output Queue Monitor Utility. To make installation easy and to prevent errors, we've created installation program Install (Figure 11.A, page 166) for your use. Follow the road map below, and you'll be monitoring output queues in no time.

1. *Create a product library.*

   A product library is more than a library containing a product. Not only does this library contain the product's objects, but the product library attribute for the product's commands is also specified. When you execute a command that has a product library specified, the system automatically places the product library in your library list. As long as all objects required by the execution of the command exist in the product library, the system will always find a referenced object.

   The output queue monitor utility takes this arrangement a step further, though. Rather than rely on the library list and run the risk that the system access the wrong object, the utility's programs use a system API to retrieve the product library name from the library list. The programs then qualify references to objects using the retrieved value. We suggest you place the utility in its own library to avoid conflict with any existing objects.

   Tip

   When using commands with their product library set, you can use the CrtDupObj (Create Duplicate Object) command to create copies of the commands in a library that is typically in users' library lists. This technique avoids the need to add the product library to the library list as well as the need to specify a library qualifier when a user wants to use a command. Here's a good strategy for such a setup:

   a) Create an alternate system library to contain the commands (as well as modified IBM-supplied objects).

   b) Place this library in system value QSysLibL (System part of the library list) so that it appears before library QSys.

   c) Copy the commands into the new system library.

2. *Create source files.*

   The Install program presumes standard IBM source file names. Execute the following commands, substituting your product library name:

   ```
   CrtSrcPF File(ProductLib/QCmdSrc)
   CrtSrcPF File(ProductLib/QCLSrc)
   CrtSrcPF File(ProductLib/QDDSSrc)
   CrtSrcPF File(ProductLib/QRPGLESrc) RcdLen(112)
   ```

3. *Populate source files.*

   Place the utility's source members (as well as program Install) in the appropriate source files. (The comment banner at the top of each member contains its source type.)

4. *Compile program Install.*

   Compile program Install into the product library. Execute the following command, substituting your product library name:

continued

(Installing the Output Queue Monitor Utility *Continued*)

```
CrtBndCL Pgm(ProductLib/Install)     +
         SrcFile(ProductLib/QCLSrc) +
         DftActGrp(*No)             +
         ActGrp(*New)
```

5. *Execute program Install.*

   Compile the utility's programs by executing program Install. This program requires you to pass the product library name as its parameter. You can avoid any potential interactive performance concerns by submitting the job to batch. Submit the following command, substituting your product library name:

```
Call Pgm(ProductLib/Install) Parm(ProductLib)
```

FIGURE 11.A

Installation Program Install

```
/*  ==============================================================  */
/*  =  Program....... Install                                    =  */
/*  =  Source type... CLLE                                       =  */
/*  =  Description... Create objects used by output queue        =  */
/*  =                 monitor utility                            =  */
/*  =  -------------------------------------------------------  =  */
/*  =  Parameters                                                =  */
/*  =                                                            =  */
/*  =    &PrdLib        Input     Product library for utility    =  */
/*  ==============================================================  */

Pgm         (                                                        +
              &PrdLib                                                +
            )

/*  ==============================================================  */
/*  =  Variable declarations                                     =  */
/*  ==============================================================  */

  Dcl        &PrdLib      *Char      (   10     )

/*  ==============================================================  */
/*  =  Add product library to library list                       =  */
/*  ==============================================================  */

  AddLibLE   &PrdLib
  MonMsg     CPF0000

/*  ==============================================================  */
/*  =  Create output monitor utility objects                     =  */
/*  ==============================================================  */

  DltF       &PrdLib/OutQMonEL1
  MonMsg     CPF0000

  DltF       &PrdLib/OutQMonE
  MonMsg     CPF0000

  CrtPF      File( &PrdLib/OutQMonE )                                +
             SrcFile( &PrdLib/QDDSSrc )

  CrtLF      File( &PrdLib/OutQMonEL1 )                              +
             SrcFile( &PrdLib/QDDSSrc )

  CrtJobD    JobD( &PrdLib/OutQMon )
```

continued

FIGURE 11.A CONTINUED

```
CrtCmd      Cmd( &PrdLib/AddOutQME )                                    +
            Pgm( &PrdLib/AddOutQM1A )                                   +
            SrcFile( &PrdLib/QCmdSrc )                                  +
            VldCkr( &PrdLib/AddOutQM2A )                                +
            PrdLib( &PrdLib )

CrtCmd      Cmd( &PrdLib/CrtOutQMon )                                   +
            Pgm( &PrdLib/CrtOutQM1A )                                   +
            SrcFile( &PrdLib/QCmdSrc )                                  +
            VldCkr( &PrdLib/CrtOutQM2A )                                +
            PrdLib( &PrdLib )

CrtCmd      Cmd( &PrdLib/DltOutQMon )                                   +
            Pgm( &PrdLib/DltOutQM1A )                                   +
            SrcFile( &PrdLib/QCmdSrc )                                  +
            VldCkr( &PrdLib/DltOutQM2A )                                +
            PrdLib( &PrdLib )

CrtCmd      Cmd( &PrdLib/EndOutQMon )                                   +
            Pgm( &PrdLib/EndOutQM1A )                                   +
            SrcFile( &PrdLib/QCmdSrc )                                  +
            VldCkr( &PrdLib/EndOutQM2A )                                +
            PrdLib( &PrdLib )

CrtCmd      Cmd( &PrdLib/RmvOutQME )                                    +
            Pgm( &PrdLib/RmvOutQM1A )                                   +
            SrcFile( &PrdLib/QCmdSrc )                                  +
            VldCkr( &PrdLib/RmvOutQM2A )                                +
            PrdLib( &PrdLib )

CrtCmd      Cmd( &PrdLib/StrOutQMon )                                   +
            Pgm( &PrdLib/StrOutQM1A )                                   +
            SrcFile( &PrdLib/QCmdSrc )                                  +
            VldCkr( &PrdLib/StrOutQM2A )                                +
            PrdLib( &PrdLib )

CrtBndCL    Pgm( &PrdLib/AddOutQM1A )                                   +
            SrcFile( &PrdLib/QCLSrc )                                   +
            DftActGrp( *No )                                            +
            ActGrp( *New )

CrtBndCL    Pgm( &PrdLib/AddOutQM2A )                                   +
            SrcFile( &PrdLib/QCLSrc )                                   +
            DftActGrp( *No )                                            +
            ActGrp( *New )

CrtBndCL    Pgm( &PrdLib/CrtOutQM1A )                                   +
            SrcFile( &PrdLib/QCLSrc )                                   +
            DftActGrp( *No )                                            +
            ActGrp( *New )

CrtBndCL    Pgm( &PrdLib/CrtOutQM2A )                                   +
            SrcFile( &PrdLib/QCLSrc )                                   +
            DftActGrp( *No )                                            +
            ActGrp( *New )

CrtBndCL    Pgm( &PrdLib/DltOutQM1A )                                   +
            SrcFile( &PrdLib/QCLSrc )                                   +
            DftActGrp( *No )                                            +
            ActGrp( *New )

CrtBndCL    Pgm( &PrdLib/DltOutQM2A )                                   +
            SrcFile( &PrdLib/QCLSrc )                                   +
            DftActGrp( *No )                                            +
            ActGrp( *New )
```

continued

(Installing the Output Queue Monitor Utility *Continued*)

Figure 11.A *Continued*

```
CrtBndCL    Pgm( &PrdLib/EndOutQM1A )                           +
            SrcFile( &PrdLib/QCLSrc )                           +
            DftActGrp( *No )                                    +
            ActGrp( *New )

CrtBndCL    Pgm( &PrdLib/EndOutQM2A )                           +
            SrcFile( &PrdLib/QCLSrc )                           +
            DftActGrp( *No )                                    +
            ActGrp( *New )

CrtBndCL    Pgm( &PrdLib/OutQMon )                              +
            SrcFile( &PrdLib/QCLSrc )                           +
            DftActGrp( *No )                                    +
            ActGrp( *New )

CrtBndCL    Pgm( &PrdLib/RmvOutQM1A )                           +
            SrcFile( &PrdLib/QCLSrc )                           +
            DftActGrp( *No )                                    +
            ActGrp( *New )

CrtBndCL    Pgm( &PrdLib/RmvOutQM2A )                           +
            SrcFile( &PrdLib/QCLSrc )                           +
            DftActGrp( *No )                                    +
            ActGrp( *New )

CrtBndCL    Pgm( &PrdLib/StrOutQM1A )                           +
            SrcFile( &PrdLib/QCLSrc )                           +
            DftActGrp( *No )                                    +
            ActGrp( *New )

CrtBndCL    Pgm( &PrdLib/StrOutQM2A )                           +
            SrcFile( &PrdLib/QCLSrc )                           +
            DftActGrp( *No )                                    +
            ActGrp( *New )

CrtBndRPG   Pgm( &PrdLib/AddOutQM1B )                           +
            SrcFile( &PrdLib/QRPGLESrc )                        +
            DftActGrp( *No )                                    +
            ActGrp( *Caller )

CrtBndRPG   Pgm( &PrdLib/AddOutQM2B )                           +
            SrcFile( &PrdLib/QRPGLESrc )                        +
            DftActGrp( *No )                                    +
            ActGrp( *Caller )

CrtBndRPG   Pgm( &PrdLib/RmvOutQM1B )                           +
            SrcFile( &PrdLib/QRPGLESrc )                        +
            DftActGrp( *No )                                    +
            ActGrp( *Caller )

CrtBndRPG   Pgm( &PrdLib/RmvOutQM1C )                           +
            SrcFile( &PrdLib/QRPGLESrc )                        +
            DftActGrp( *No )                                    +
            ActGrp( *Caller )

CrtBndRPG   Pgm( &PrdLib/RmvOutQM2B )                           +
            SrcFile( &PrdLib/QRPGLESrc )                        +
            DftActGrp( *No )                                    +
            ActGrp( *Caller )

/*  ==============================================================  */
/*  =  End of program                                            =  */
/*  ==============================================================  */

EndPgm
```

FIGURE 11.5A

CrtOutQMon Panel

```
                 Create Output Queue Monitor (CRTOUTQMON)

Type choices, press Enter.

Monitor name . . . . . . . . . .   SAMPLE____    Name

                                                                  Bottom
F3=Exit   F4=Prompt   F5=Refresh   F12=Cancel   F13=How to use this display
F24=More keys
```

FIGURE 11.5B

Command CrtOutQMon

```
/*  ===============================================================  */
/*  =  Command....... CrtOutQMon                                  =  */
/*  =  Source type... CMD                                         =  */
/*  =  Description... Create Output Queue Monitor                 =  */
/*  =                                                             =  */
/*  =  CPP........... CrtOutQM1A                                  =  */
/*  =  VCP........... CrtOutQM2A                                  =  */
/*  ===============================================================  */

           Cmd        Prompt( 'Create Output Queue Monitor' )

           Parm       Kwd( MonName )                                   +
                      Type( *Name )                                    +
                      Len( 10 )                                        +
                      Min( 1 )                                         +
                      Prompt( 'Monitor name' )
```

FIGURE 11.5C

CrtOutQMon Command Processing Program CrtOutQM1A

```
/*  ================================================================  */
/*  =  Program....... CrtOutQM1A                                   =  */
/*  =  Source type... CLLE                                         =  */
/*  =  Type.......... Command processing program for CrtOutQMon    =  */
/*  =  Description... Create output queue monitor                  =  */
/*  =  ----------------------------------------------------------  =  */
/*  =  Parameters                                                  =  */
/*  =                                                              =  */
/*  =    &MonName          Input      Monitor name                 =  */
/*  ================================================================  */

Pgm         (                                                          +
              &MonName                                                 +
            )

/*  ================================================================  */
/*  =  Variable declarations                                       =  */
/*  ================================================================  */

  Dcl        &MonName    *Char      (   10     )
  Dcl        &RcvVar     *Char      (  600     )
  Dcl        &RcvVarLen  *Char      (    4     )   ( X'00000258' )
  Dcl        &Format     *Char      (    8     )   ( 'JOBI0700' )
  Dcl        &QualJob    *Char      (   26     )   ( '*' )
  Dcl        &IntJobID   *Char      (   16     )
  Dcl        &PrdLib     *Char      (   10     )
  Dcl        &Offset     *Dec       (    4  0  )
  Dcl        &Nbr4       *Dec       (    4  0  )
  Dcl        &MsgID      *Char      (    7     )
  Dcl        &MsgDta     *Char      (  100     )
  Dcl        &MsgF       *Char      (   10     )
  Dcl        &MsgFLib    *Char      (   10     )

/*  ================================================================  */
/*  =  Global error monitor                                        =  */
/*  ================================================================  */

  MonMsg     ( CPF0000 MCH0000 ) Exec(                                 +
    GoTo       Error                 )

/*  ================================================================  */
/*  =  Retrieve product library name                               =  */
/*  ================================================================  */

  Call       QUsrJobI                                                  +
             (                                                         +
               &RcvVar                                                 +
               &RcvVarLen                                              +
               &Format                                                 +
               &QualJob                                                +
               &IntJobID                                               +
             )

  ChgVar     &Nbr4        ( %Bin( &RcvVar 65 4 ) )
  ChgVar     &Offset      ( ( &Nbr4 * 11 ) + 81 )
  ChgVar     &PrdLib      ( %Sst( &RcvVar &Offset 10 ) )

/*  ================================================================  */
/*  =  Create output queue monitor data queue                      =  */
/*  ================================================================  */

  CrtDtaQ    DtaQ( &PrdLib/&MonName )                                  +
             MaxLen( 128 )                                             +
             Force( *Yes )                                             +
             SenderID( *No )
```

continued

FIGURE 11.5C *CONTINUED*

```
/*  ================================================================  */
/*  =  Send completion message and exit                           =  */
/*  ================================================================  */

  SndPgmMsg  MsgID( CPF9898 )                                          +
             MsgF( QSys/QCPFMsg )                                      +
             MsgDta( 'Output queue monitor'                            +
                     *BCat                                             +
                     &MonName                                          +
                     *BCat                                             +
                     'created' )                                       +
             MsgType( *Comp )

  Return

/*  ================================================================  */
/*  =  Error handler                                              =  */
/*  ================================================================  */

Error:

  RcvMsg     MsgType( *Excp )                                          +
             MsgDta( &MsgDta )                                         +
             MsgID( &MsgID )                                           +
             MsgF( &MsgF )                                             +
             MsgFLib( &MsgFLib )

  MonMsg     ( CPF0000 MCH0000 )

  SndPgmMsg  MsgID( &MsgID )                                           +
             MsgF( &MsgFLib/&MsgF )                                    +
             MsgDta( &MsgDta )                                         +
             MsgType( *Escape )

  MonMsg     ( CPF0000 MCH0000 )

/*  ================================================================  */
/*  =  End of program                                             =  */
/*  ================================================================  */

EndPgm
```

FIGURE 11.5D

CrtOutQMon Validity-Checking Program CrtOutQM2A

```
/*  ================================================================  */
/*  =  Program....... CrtOutQM2A                                  =  */
/*  =  Source type... CLLE                                        =  */
/*  =  Type.......... Validity-checking program for CrtOutQMon    =  */
/*  =  Description... Create output queue monitor                 =  */
/*  =  ---------------------------------------------------------- =  */
/*  =  Parameters                                                 =  */
/*  =                                                             =  */
/*  =    &MonName          Input      Monitor name                =  */
/*  ================================================================  */

Pgm        (                                                           +
             &MonName                                                  +
           )
```

continued

FIGURE 11.5D CONTINUED

```
/*  ===============================================================  */
/*  =  Variable declarations                                      =  */
/*  ===============================================================  */

  Dcl        &MonName    *Char      (   10     )
  Dcl        &RcvVar     *Char      (  600     )
  Dcl        &RcvVarLen  *Char      (    4     )  ( X'00000258' )
  Dcl        &Format     *Char      (    8     )  ( 'JOBI0700' )
  Dcl        &QualJob    *Char      (   26     )  ( '*' )
  Dcl        &IntJobID   *Char      (   16     )
  Dcl        &PrdLib     *Char      (   10     )
  Dcl        &Offset     *Dec       (    4  0  )
  Dcl        &Nbr4       *Dec       (    4  0  )
  Dcl        &Msg        *Char      (  512     )
  Dcl        &MsgID      *Char      (    7     )
  Dcl        &MsgDta     *Char      (  100     )
  Dcl        &MsgF       *Char      (   10     )
  Dcl        &MsgFLib    *Char      (   10     )
  Dcl        &KeyVar     *Char      (    4     )

/*  ===============================================================  */
/*  =  Global error monitor                                       =  */
/*  ===============================================================  */

  MonMsg      ( CPF0000 MCH0000 ) Exec(                              +
    GoTo        Error                 )

/*  ===============================================================  */
/*  =  Retrieve product library name                              =  */
/*  ===============================================================  */

  Call       QUsrJobI                                                +
             (                                                       +
               &RcvVar                                               +
               &RcvVarLen                                            +
               &Format                                               +
               &QualJob                                              +
               &IntJobID                                             +
             )

  ChgVar     &Nbr4        ( %Bin( &RcvVar 65 4 ) )
  ChgVar     &Offset      ( ( &Nbr4 * 11 ) + 81 )
  ChgVar     &PrdLib      ( %Sst( &RcvVar &Offset 10 ) )

/*  ===============================================================  */
/*  =  Verify output queue monitor program existence              =  */
/*  ===============================================================  */

  ChkObj     Obj( &PrdLib/&MonName )                                 +
             ObjType( *Pgm )

  MonMsg     ( CPF9801 ) Exec(                                       +
    Do                        )
      ChgVar     &Msg         ( 'Output queue monitor program'       +
                                *BCat                                +
                                &MonName                             +
                                *BCat                                +
                                'does not exist in library'          +
                                *BCat                                +
                                &PrdLib                              +
                                *TCat                                +
                                '.' )
      GoTo       SendError
    EndDo
```

continued

FIGURE 11.5D *CONTINUED*

```
/*  ==============================================================  */
/*  =  Verify output queue monitor data queue non-existence      =  */
/*  ==============================================================  */

  ChkObj     Obj( &PrdLib/&MonName )                                 +
             ObjType( *DtaQ )

  MonMsg     ( CPF98Ø1 ) Exec(                                       +
    Return                   )

/*  ==============================================================  */
/*  =  Output queue monitor data queue already exists            =  */
/*  ==============================================================  */

  ChgVar     &Msg           ( 'Output queue monitor'                 +
                              *BCat                                  +
                              &MonName                               +
                              *BCat                                  +
                              'already exists'                       +
                              *TCat                                  +
                              '.' )
  GoTo       SendError

/*  ==============================================================  */
/*  =  Error handler                                             =  */
/*  ==============================================================  */

Error:

  RcvMsg     MsgType( *Excp )                                        +
             MsgDta( &MsgDta )                                       +
             MsgID( &MsgID )                                         +
             MsgF( &MsgF )                                           +
             MsgFLib( &MsgFLib )

  MonMsg     ( CPFØØØØ MCHØØØØ )

  SndPgmMsg  MsgID( &MsgID )                                         +
             MsgF( &MsgFLib/&MsgF )                                  +
             MsgDta( &MsgDta )                                       +
             ToPgmQ( *Same )                                         +
             KeyVar( &KeyVar )

  MonMsg     ( CPFØØØØ MCHØØØØ )

  RcvMsg     KeyVar( &KeyVar )                                       +
             Msg( &Msg )

  MonMsg     ( CPFØØØØ MCHØØØØ )

SendError:

  SndPgmMsg  MsgID( CPDØØØ6 )                                        +
             MsgF( QSys/QCPFMsg )                                    +
             MsgDta( 'ØØØØ' *TCat &Msg )                             +
             ToPgmQ( *Prv )                                          +
             MsgType( *Diag )

  MonMsg     ( CPFØØØØ MCHØØØØ )
```

continued

FIGURE 11.5D CONTINUED

```
  SndPgmMsg   MsgID( CPF0002 )                                             +
              MsgF( QSys/QCPFMsg )                                         +
              ToPgmQ( *Prv )                                               +
              MsgType( *Escape )

  MonMsg      ( CPF0000 MCH0000 )

/*  ==============================================================   */
/*  =  End of program                                            =   */
/*  ==============================================================   */

EndPgm
```

FIGURE 11.6A

AddOutQME Panel

```
                       Add OutQ Monitor Entry (ADDOUTQME)

 Type choices, press Enter.

 Monitor name . . . . . . . . . .   SAMPLE____     Name
 Output queues  . . . . . . . . .   QPRINT____     Name
   Library  . . . . . . . . . . .     *LIBL_____   Name, *LIBL, *CURLIB
               + for more values    __________
                                      *LIBL_____

                                                                      Bottom
 F3=Exit   F4=Prompt   F5=Refresh   F12=Cancel   F13=How to use this display
 F24=More keys
```

FIGURE 11.6B

Command AddOutQME

```
/*  ==============================================================  */
/*  =  Command....... AddOutQME                                  =  */
/*  =  Source type... CMD                                        =  */
/*  =  Description... Add Output Queue Monitor Entry             =  */
/*  =                                                            =  */
/*  =  CPP........... AddOutQM1A                                 =  */
/*  =  VCP........... AddOutQM2A                                 =  */
/*  ==============================================================  */

             Cmd        Prompt( 'Add OutQ Monitor Entry' )

             Parm       Kwd( MonName )                                +
                        Type( *Name )                                 +
                        Len( 10 )                                     +
                        Min( 1 )                                      +
                        Prompt( 'Monitor name' )

             Parm       Kwd( OutQ )                                   +
                        Type( QualOutQ )                              +
                        Min( 1 )                                      +
                        Max( 25 )                                     +
                        Prompt( 'Output queues' )

QualOutQ:    Qual       Type( *Name )                                 +
                        Len( 10 )
             Qual       Type( *Name )                                 +
                        Len( 10 )                                     +
                        Dft( *LibL )                                  +
                        SpcVal( ( *LibL     )                         +
                                ( *CurLib   ) )                       +
                        Prompt( 'Library' )
```

FIGURE 11.6C

AddOutQME Command Processing Program AddOutQM1A

```
/*  ==============================================================  */
/*  =  Program....... AddOutQM1A                                 =  */
/*  =  Source type... CLLE                                       =  */
/*  =  Type.......... Command processing program for AddOutQME   =  */
/*  =  Description... Add OutQ monitor entry                     =  */
/*  =  ------------------------------------------------------    =  */
/*  =  Parameters                                                =  */
/*  =                                                            =  */
/*  =    &MonName        Input     Monitor name                  =  */
/*  =                                                            =  */
/*  =    &OutQ           Input     List of up to 25 qualified    =  */
/*  =                              output queue names            =  */
/*  ==============================================================  */

Pgm         (                                                     +
              &MonName                                            +
              &OutQ                                               +
            )

/*  ==============================================================  */
/*  = Variable declarations                                       =  */
/*  ==============================================================  */

  Dcl         &MonName     *Char      (   10    )
  Dcl         &OutQ        *Char      (  502    )
  Dcl         &OutQName    *Char      (   10    )
  Dcl         &OutQLib     *Char      (   10    )
```

continued

FIGURE 11.6C CONTINUED

```
  Dcl        &OutQCount  *Char     (   2     )
  Dcl        &OutQCountN *Dec      (   2  0  )
  Dcl        &LoopCount  *Dec      (   3  0  )
  Dcl        &Offset     *Dec      (   3  0  )
  Dcl        &RcvVar     *Char     ( 600     )
  Dcl        &RcvVarLen  *Char     (   4     )   ( X'00000258' )
  Dcl        &Format     *Char     (   8     )   ( 'JOBI0700' )
  Dcl        &QualJob    *Char     (  26     )   ( '*' )
  Dcl        &IntJobID   *Char     (  16     )
  Dcl        &PrdLib     *Char     (  10     )
  Dcl        &Nbr4       *Dec      (   4  0  )
  Dcl        &Msg        *Char     ( 512     )
  Dcl        &MsgID      *Char     (   7     )
  Dcl        &MsgF       *Char     (  10     )
  Dcl        &MsgFLib    *Char     (  10     )
  Dcl        &MsgDta     *Char     ( 100     )
  Dcl        &KeyVar     *Char     (   4     )

/*  ==============================================================  */
/*  = Global error monitor                                       =  */
/*  ==============================================================  */

  MonMsg     ( CPF0000 MCH0000 ) Exec(                                +
    Goto       Error                    )

/*  ==============================================================  */
/*  =  Retrieve product library name                             =  */
/*  ==============================================================  */

  Call       QUsrJobI                                                 +
             (                                                        +
               &RcvVar                                                +
               &RcvVarLen                                             +
               &Format                                                +
               &QualJob                                               +
               &IntJobID                                              +
             )
  ChgVar     &Nbr4         ( %Bin( &RcvVar 65 4 ) )
  ChgVar     &Offset       ( ( &Nbr4 * 11 ) + 81 )
  ChgVar     &PrdLib       ( %Sst( &RcvVar &Offset 10 ) )

/*  ==============================================================  */
/*  = Parse number of output queues in list                      =  */
/*  ==============================================================  */

  ChgVar     &OutQCount  ( %Sst( &OutQ 1 2 ) )
  ChgVar     &OutQCountN ( %Bin( &OutQCount ) )

/*  ==============================================================  */
/*  =  Add data queue attribute to output queue(s) and add to    =  */
/*  =  control file                                              =  */
/*  ==============================================================  */

  ChgVar     &LoopCount  ( 0 )

Loop01:

  ChgVar     &LoopCount  ( &LoopCount + 1 )

  If         ( &LoopCount *GT &OutQCountN )                           +
    GoTo       End01

  ChgVar     &Offset       ( ( ( &LoopCount - 1 ) * 20 ) + 3 )
  ChgVar     &OutQName     ( %Sst( &OutQ &Offset 10 ) )
  ChgVar     &Offset       ( &Offset + 10 )
  ChgVar     &OutQLib      ( %Sst( &OutQ &Offset 10 ) )
```

continued

FIGURE 11.6C *CONTINUED*

```
  RtvObjD     Obj( &OutQLib/&OutQName )                                 +
              ObjType( *OutQ )                                          +
              RtnLib( &OutQLib )

  ChgOutQ     OutQ( &OutQLib/&OutQName )                                +
              DtaQ( &PrdLib/&MonName )

  Call        &PrdLib/AddOutQM1B                                        +
              (                                                         +
                &OutQName                                               +
                &OutQLib                                                +
                &MonName                                                +
              )

  GoTo        Loop01

End01:

/*  ============================================================   */
/*  =  Send completion message and exit                        =   */
/*  ============================================================   */

  SndPgmMsg   MsgID( CPF9898 )                                          +
              MsgF( QSys/QCPFMsg )                                      +
              MsgDta( 'Output queue entries added to monitor'           +
                      *BCat                                             +
                      &MonName )                                        +
              MsgType( *Comp )

  Return

/*  ============================================================   */
/*  = Error handler                                            =   */
/*  ============================================================   */

Error:

  RcvMsg      MsgType( *Excp )                                          +
              MsgDta( &MsgDta )                                         +
              MsgID( &MsgID )                                           +
              MsgF( &MsgF )                                             +
              MsgFLib( &MsgFLib )

  MonMsg      ( CPF0000 MCH0000 )

  SndPgmMsg   MsgID( &MsgID )                                           +
              MsgF( &MsgFLib/&MsgF )                                    +
              MsgDta( &MsgDta )                                         +
              MsgType( *Escape )

  MonMsg      ( CPF0000 MCH0000 )

/*  ============================================================   */
/*  = End of program                                           =   */
/*  ============================================================   */

EndPgm
```

FIGURE 11.6D

AddOutQME Command Processing Program AddOutQM1B — Add Control Record

```
 *  =================================================================
 *  =  Program....... AddOutQM1B                                    =
 *  =  Source type... RPGLE                                         =
 *  =  Description... Add OutQ Monitor Entry - add control record   =
 *  =================================================================

FOutQMonE  UF A E           K Disk

 *  =================================================================
 *  =  Entry parameters                                             =
 *  =================================================================

D EntryParms...
D                 PR                  ExtPgm( 'ADDOUTQM1B' )
D                               10
D                               10
D                               10
D EntryParms...
D                 PI
D  OutQName                     10
D  OutQLib                      10
D  MonName                      10

 *  =================================================================
 *  =  Key lists                                                    =
 *  =================================================================

 *  -----------------------------------------------------------------
 *  -  OutQMonE full key                                            -
 *  -----------------------------------------------------------------

C     Key           KList
C                   KFld                    OutQLib
C                   KFld                    OutQName

 *  =================================================================
 *  =  Add record to control file if necessary                      =
 *  =================================================================

C     Key           Chain     OutQMonE

C                   If        Not( %Found )
C                   Write     ROutQMonE
C                   EndIf

 *  =================================================================
 *  =  Exit program                                                 =
 *  =================================================================

C                   Eval      *InLR = *On
```

FIGURE 11.6E

AddOutQME Validity-Checking Program AddOutQM2A

```
/*  ==============================================================  */
/*  =  Program....... AddOutQM2A                                 =  */
/*  =  Source type... CLLE                                       =  */
/*  =  Type.......... Validity-checking program for AddOutQME    =  */
/*  =  Description... Add OutQ monitor entry                     =  */
/*  =  ---------------------------------------------------------  =  */
/*  =  Parameters                                                =  */
/*  =                                                            =  */
/*  =    &MonName        Input     Monitor name                  =  */
/*  =                                                            =  */
/*  =    &OutQ           Input     List of up to 25 qualified    =  */
/*  =                              output queue names            =  */
/*  ==============================================================  */

Pgm         (                                                      +
               &MonName                                            +
               &OutQ                                               +
            )

/*  ==============================================================  */
/*  = Variable declarations                                      =  */
/*  ==============================================================  */

  Dcl        &MonName    *Char     (   10     )
  Dcl        &OutQ       *Char     (  502     )
  Dcl        &OutQName   *Char     (   10     )
  Dcl        &OutQLib    *Char     (   10     )
  Dcl        &OtherMon   *Char     (   10     )
  Dcl        &OutQCount  *Char     (    2     )
  Dcl        &OutQCountN *Dec      (    2  0  )
  Dcl        &LoopCount  *Dec      (    3  0  )
  Dcl        &Offset     *Dec      (    3  0  )
  Dcl        &RcvVar     *Char     (  600     )
  Dcl        &RcvVarLen  *Char     (    4     )    ( X'00000258' )
  Dcl        &Format     *Char     (    8     )    ( 'JOBI0700' )
  Dcl        &QualJob    *Char     (   26     )    ( '*' )
  Dcl        &IntJobID   *Char     (   16     )
  Dcl        &PrdLib     *Char     (   10     )
  Dcl        &Nbr4       *Dec      (    4  0  )
  Dcl        &Msg        *Char     (  512     )
  Dcl        &MsgID      *Char     (    7     )
  Dcl        &MsgF       *Char     (   10     )
  Dcl        &MsgFLib    *Char     (   10     )
  Dcl        &MsgDta     *Char     (  100     )
  Dcl        &KeyVar     *Char     (    4     )

/*  ==============================================================  */
/*  = Global error monitor                                       =  */
/*  ==============================================================  */

  MonMsg      ( CPF0000 MCH0000 ) Exec(                            +
    Goto        Error                   )

/*  ==============================================================  */
/*  =  Retrieve product library name                             =  */
/*  ==============================================================  */

  Call        QUsrJobI                                             +
              (                                                    +
                &RcvVar                                            +
                &RcvVarLen                                         +
                &Format                                            +
                &QualJob                                           +
                &IntJobID                                          +
              )
```

continued

FIGURE 11.6E *CONTINUED*

```
  ChgVar      &Nbr4        ( %Bin( &RcvVar 65 4 ) )
  ChgVar      &Offset      ( ( &Nbr4 * 11 ) + 81 )
  ChgVar      &PrdLib      ( %Sst( &RcvVar &Offset 10 ) )

/*  ==============================================================  */
/*  =  Verify output queue monitor data queue existence          =  */
/*  ==============================================================  */

  ChkObj      Obj( &PrdLib/&MonName )                                +
              ObjType( *DtaQ )

  MonMsg      ( CPF9801 ) Exec(                                      +
    Do                         )
      ChgVar      &Msg           ( 'Output queue monitor'            +
                                   *BCat                             +
                                   &MonName                          +
                                   *BCat                             +
                                   'does not exist in library'       +
                                   *BCat                             +
                                   &PrdLib                           +
                                   *TCat                             +
                                   '.' )
      GoTo        SendError
    EndDo

/*  ==============================================================  */
/*  = Parse number of output queues in list                      =  */
/*  ==============================================================  */

  ChgVar      &OutQCount   ( %Sst( &OutQ 1 2 ) )
  ChgVar      &OutQCountN  ( %Bin( &OutQCount ) )

/*  ==============================================================  */
/*  = Validate output queues in list and make sure not already   =  */
/*  = monitored by another monitor                               =  */
/*  ==============================================================  */

  ChgVar      &LoopCount   ( 0 )

Loop01:

  ChgVar      &LoopCount   ( &LoopCount + 1 )

  If          ( &LoopCount *GT &OutQCountN )                         +
    GoTo        End01

  ChgVar      &Offset      ( ( ( &LoopCount - 1 ) * 20 ) + 3 )
  ChgVar      &OutQName    ( %Sst( &OutQ &Offset 10 ) )
  ChgVar      &Offset      ( &Offset + 10 )
  ChgVar      &OutQLib     ( %Sst( &OutQ &Offset 10 ) )

  RtvObjD     Obj( &OutQLib/&OutQName )                              +
              ObjType( *OutQ )                                       +
              RtnLib( &OutQLib )

  MonMsg      ( CPF9801 ) Exec(                                      +
    Do                         )
      ChgVar      &Msg           ( 'Output queue'                    +
                                   *BCat                             +
                                   &OutQName                         +
                                   *BCat                             +
                                   'does not exist in library'       +
                                   *BCat                             +
                                   &OutQLib                          +
                                   *TCat                             +
                                   '.' )
      GoTo        SendError
    EndDo
```

continued

FIGURE 11.6E *CONTINUED*

```
  Call        &PrdLib/AddOutQM2B                                       +
              (                                                        +
                &OutQName                                              +
                &OutQLib                                               +
                &MonName                                               +
                &OtherMon                                              +
              )

  If          ( &OtherMon *NE ' ' )                                    +
    Do
      ChgVar      &Msg          ( 'Output queue'                       +
                                  *BCat                                +
                                  &OutQLib                             +
                                  *TCat                                +
                                  '/'                                  +
                                  *TCat                                +
                                  &OutQName                            +
                                  *BCat                                +
                                  'is assigned to monitor'             +
                                  *BCat                                +
                                  &OtherMon                            +
                                  *TCat                                +
                                  '.' )
      GoTo        SendError
    EndDo

  GoTo        Loop01

End01:

/*  ============================================================  */
/*  =  Exit                                                     =  */
/*  ============================================================  */

  Return

/*  ============================================================  */
/*  = Error handler                                             =  */
/*  ============================================================  */

Error:

  RcvMsg      MsgType( *Excp )                                         +
              MsgDta( &MsgDta )                                        +
              MsgID( &MsgID )                                          +
              MsgF( &MsgF )                                            +
              MsgFLib( &MsgFLib )

  MonMsg      ( CPF0000 MCH0000 )

  SndPgmMsg   MsgID( &MsgID )                                          +
              MsgF( &MsgFLib/&MsgF )                                   +
              MsgDta( &MsgDta )                                        +
              ToPgmQ( *Same )                                          +
              KeyVar( &KeyVar )

  MonMsg      ( CPF0000 MCH0000 )

  RcvMsg      KeyVar( &KeyVar )                                        +
              Msg( &Msg )

  MonMsg      ( CPF0000 MCH0000 )
```

continued

FIGURE 11.6E *CONTINUED*

```
SendError:

  SndPgmMsg   MsgID( CPD0006 )                                          +
              MsgF( QSys/QCPFMsg )                                      +
              MsgDta( '0000' *TCat &Msg )                               +
              ToPgmQ( *Prv )                                            +
              MsgType( *Diag )

  MonMsg      ( CPF0000 MCH0000 )

  SndPgmMsg   MsgID( CPF0002 )                                          +
              MsgF( QSys/QCPFMsg )                                      +
              ToPgmQ( *PRV )                                            +
              MsgType( *Escape )

  MonMsg      ( CPF0000 MCH0000 )

/*  ============================================================  */
/*  = End of program                                            =  */
/*  ============================================================  */

EndPgm
```

FIGURE 11.6F

AddOutQME Validity-Checking Program AddOutQM2B — Confirm Output Queue

```
 *  ==================================================================
 *  =  Program....... AddOutQM2B                                     =
 *  =  Source type... RPGLE                                          =
 *  =  Description... Add OutQ Monitor Entry - confirm output queue  =
 *  =                 is not already being monitored                 =
 *  ==================================================================

FoutQMonE  IF   E           K Disk

 *  ==================================================================
 *  =  Entry parameters                                              =
 *  ==================================================================

D EntryParms...
D                 PR                  ExtPgm( 'ADDOUTQM2B' )
D                               10
D                               10
D                               10
D                               10
D EntryParms...
D                 PI
D  OutQName                     10
D  OutQLib                      10
D  MonNameIn                    10
D  OtherMon                     10

 *  ==================================================================
 *  =  Key lists                                                     =
 *  ==================================================================

 *  ------------------------------------------------------------------
 *  -  OutQMonE full key                                             -
 *  ------------------------------------------------------------------

C     Key           KList
C                   KFld                    OutQLib
C                   KFld                    OutQName
```

continued

FIGURE 11.6F CONTINUED

```
 *   ===================================================================
 *   =  Read record and determine if output queue is monitored by      =
 *   =  another monitor                                                =
 *   ===================================================================

C      Key            Chain     OutQMonE

C                     If        ( %Found ) and
C                               MonName <> MonNameIn
C                     Eval      OtherMon = MonName
C                     Else
C                     Eval      OtherMon = *Blank
C                     EndIf

 *   ===================================================================
 *   =  Exit program                                                   =
 *   ===================================================================

C                     Eval      *InLR = *On
```

FIGURE 11.7A

RmvOutQME Panel

```
                      Remove OutQ Monitor Entry (RMVOUTQME)

 Type choices, press Enter.

 Monitor name . . . . . . . . . . .   SAMPLE____    Name
 Output queues  . . . . . . . . . .   *ALL______    Name, *ALL
   Library  . . . . . . . . . . . .     *LIBL_____  Name, *LIBL, *CURLIB
               + for more values      __________
                                        *LIBL_____





                                                                      Bottom
 F3=Exit   F4=Prompt   F5=Refresh   F12=Cancel   F13=How to use this display
 F24=More keys
```

FIGURE 11.7B

Command RmvOutQME

```
/*  ==============================================================  */
/*  =  Command....... RmvOutQME                                  =  */
/*  =  Source type... CMD                                        =  */
/*  =  Description... Remove Output Queue Monitor Entry          =  */
/*  =                                                            =  */
/*  =  CPP........... RmvOutQM1A                                 =  */
/*  =  VCP........... RmvOutQM2A                                 =  */
/*  ==============================================================  */

             Cmd         Prompt( 'Remove OutQ Monitor Entry' )

             Parm        Kwd( MonName )                                +
                         Type( *Name )                                 +
                         Len( 10 )                                     +
                         Min( 1 )                                      +
                         Prompt( 'Monitor name' )

             Parm        Kwd( OutQ )                                   +
                         Type( QualOutQ )                              +
                         Min( 1 )                                      +
                         Max( 25 )                                     +
                         SngVal( ( *All ) )                            +
                         Prompt( 'Output queues' )

QualOutQ:    Qual        Type( *Name )                                 +
                         Len( 10 )
             Qual        Type( *Name )                                 +
                         Len( 10 )                                     +
                         Dft( *LibL )                                  +
                         SpcVal( ( *LibL    )                          +
                                 ( *CurLib  ) )                        +
                         Prompt( 'Library' )
```

FIGURE 11.7C

RmvOutQME Command Processing Program RmvOutQM1A

```
/*  ==============================================================  */
/*  =  Program....... RmvOutQM1A                                 =  */
/*  =  Source type... CLLE                                       =  */
/*  =  Type.......... Command processing program for RmvOutQME   =  */
/*  =  Description... Remove OutQ monitor entry                  =  */
/*  =  ---------------------------------------------------------  =  */
/*  =  Parameters                                                =  */
/*  =                                                            =  */
/*  =    &MonName         Input      Monitor name                =  */
/*  =                                                            =  */
/*  =    &OutQ            Input      List of up to 25 qualified  =  */
/*  =                                output queue names          =  */
/*  ==============================================================  */

Pgm         (                                                          +
              &MonName                                                 +
              &OutQ                                                    +
            )

/*  ==============================================================  */
/*  = Variable declarations                                      =  */
/*  ==============================================================  */

  Dcl         &MonName     *Char       (   10     )
  Dcl         &OutQ        *Char       (  502     )
  Dcl         &OutQName    *Char       (   10     )
  Dcl         &OutQLib     *Char       (   10     )
```

continued

FIGURE 11.7C *CONTINUED*

```
  Dcl        &OutQCount  *Char     (    2     )
  Dcl        &OutQCountN *Dec      (    2  0 )
  Dcl        &LoopCount  *Dec      (    3  0 )
  Dcl        &Offset     *Dec      (    3  0 )
  Dcl        &RcvVar     *Char     (  600     )
  Dcl        &RcvVarLen  *Char     (    4     )    ( X'00000258' )
  Dcl        &Format     *Char     (    8     )    ( 'JOBI0700' )
  Dcl        &QualJob    *Char     (   26     )    ( '*' )
  Dcl        &IntJobID   *Char     (   16     )
  Dcl        &PrdLib     *Char     (   10     )
  Dcl        &Nbr4       *Dec      (    4  0 )
  Dcl        &MsgID      *Char     (    7     )
  Dcl        &MsgF       *Char     (   10     )
  Dcl        &MsgFLib    *Char     (   10     )
  Dcl        &MsgDta     *Char     (  100     )

/*  ============================================================  */
/*  = Global error monitor                                     =  */
/*  ============================================================  */

  MonMsg     ( CPF0000 MCH0000 ) Exec(                            +
    Goto       Error              )

/*  ============================================================  */
/*  =  Retrieve product library name                           =  */
/*  ============================================================  */

  Call       QUsrJobI                                             +
             (                                                    +
               &RcvVar                                            +
               &RcvVarLen                                         +
               &Format                                            +
               &QualJob                                           +
               &IntJobID                                          +
             )

  ChgVar     &Nbr4         ( %Bin( &RcvVar 65 4 ) )
  ChgVar     &Offset       ( ( &Nbr4 * 11 ) + 81 )
  ChgVar     &PrdLib       ( %Sst( &RcvVar &Offset 10 ) )

/*  ============================================================  */
/*  = Remove all output queue entries                          =  */
/*  ============================================================  */

  If         ( %Sst( &OutQ 3 4 ) *Eq '*ALL' )                     +
    Do
      Call       &PrdLib/RmvOutQM1C                               +
                 (                                                +
                   &MonName                                       +
                   &OutQ                                          +
             )
    EndDo

/*  ============================================================  */
/*  = Parse number of output queues in list                    =  */
/*  ============================================================  */

  ChgVar     &OutQCount  ( %Sst( &OutQ 1 2 ) )
  ChgVar     &OutQCountN ( %Bin( &OutQCount ) )

/*  ============================================================  */
/*  =  Remove output queue entries from monitor control file   =  */
/*  =  and remove data queue attribute from output queues      =  */
/*  ============================================================  */

  ChgVar     &LoopCount  ( 0 )
```

continued

FIGURE 11.7C *CONTINUED*

```
Loop01:

  ChgVar     &LoopCount   ( &LoopCount + 1 )

  If         ( &LoopCount *GT &OutQCountN )                               +
    GoTo       End01

  ChgVar     &Offset      ( ( ( &LoopCount - 1 ) * 20 ) + 3 )
  ChgVar     &OutQName    ( %Sst( &OutQ &Offset 10 ) )
  ChgVar     &Offset      ( &Offset + 10 )
  ChgVar     &OutQLib     ( %Sst( &OutQ &Offset 10 ) )

  RtvObjD    Obj( &OutQLib/&OutQName )                                    +
             ObjType( *OutQ )                                             +
             RtnLib( &OutQLib )

  ChgOutQ    OutQ( &OutQLib/&OutQName )                                   +
             DtaQ( *None )

  Call       &PrdLib/RmvOutQM1B                                           +
             (                                                            +
               &OutQName                                                  +
               &OutQLib                                                   +
               &MonName                                                   +
             )

  GoTo       Loop01

End01:

/*  ==============================================================  */
/*  =  Send completion message and exit                          =  */
/*  ==============================================================  */

  SndPgmMsg  MsgID( CPF9898 )                                             +
             MsgF( QSys/QCPFMsg )                                         +
             MsgDta( 'Output queue entries removed from monitor'          +
                     *BCat                                                +
                     &MonName )                                           +
             MsgType( *Comp )

  Return

/*  ==============================================================  */
/*  = Error handler                                              =  */
/*  ==============================================================  */

Error:

  RcvMsg     MsgType( *Excp )                                             +
             MsgDta( &MsgDta )                                            +
             MsgID( &MsgID )                                              +
             MsgF( &MsgF )                                                +
             MsgFLib( &MsgFLib )

  MonMsg     ( CPF0000 MCH0000 )
  SndPgmMsg  MsgID( &MsgID )                                              +
             MsgF( &MsgFLib/&MsgF )                                       +
             MsgDta( &MsgDta )                                            +
             MsgType( *Escape )

  MonMsg     ( CPF0000 MCH0000 )

/*  ==============================================================  */
/*  = End of program                                             =  */
/*  ==============================================================  */

  EndPgm
```

FIGURE 11.7D

RmvOutQME Command Processing Program RmvOutQM1B — Update Control File

```
 *   ==================================================================
 *   =  Program....... RmvOutQM1B                                     =
 *   =  Source type... RPGLE                                          =
 *   =  Description... Remove OutQ Monitor Entry - update control file =
 *   ==================================================================

FOutQMonE  UF   E             K Disk

 *   ==================================================================
 *   =  Entry parameters                                              =
 *   ==================================================================

D EntryParms...
D                 PR                  ExtPgm( 'RMVOUTQM1B' )
D                               10
D                               10
D                               10
D EntryParms...
D                 PI
D  OutQName                     10
D  OutQLib                      10
D  MonNameIn                    10

 *   ==================================================================
 *   =  Key lists                                                     =
 *   ==================================================================

 *   ------------------------------------------------------------------
 *   -  OutQMonE full key                                             -
 *   ------------------------------------------------------------------

C     Key           KList
C                   KFld                    OutQLib
C                   KFld                    OutQName

 *   ==================================================================
 *   =  Delete record from control file if necessary                  =
 *   ==================================================================

C     Key           Chain     OutQMonE

C                   If        ( %Found ) and
C                             MonName = MonNameIn
C                   Delete    ROutQMonE
C                   EndIf

 *   ==================================================================
 *   =  Exit program                                                  =
 *   ==================================================================

C                   Eval      *InLR = *On
```

FIGURE 11.7E

RmvOutQME Command Processing Program RmvOutQM1C — Build OutQ List

```
 *   ================================================================
 *   =  Program....... RmvOutQM1C                                   =
 *   =  Description... Remove OutQ Monitor Entry - build OutQ list  =
 *   ================================================================

FOutQMonEL1IF   E           K Disk

 *   ================================================================
 *   =  Entry parameters                                            =
 *   ================================================================

D EntryParms...
D                 PR                  ExtPgm( 'RMVOUTQM1C' )
D                               10
D                              502
D EntryParms...
D                 PI
D  MonNameIn                    10
D  OutQOut                     502

D OutQ            DS
D  OutQCount                     5I 0 Inz( *Zero )
D  OutQs                       500    Inz( *Blank )

D Offset          S              5I 0

 *   ================================================================
 *   =  Key lists                                                   =
 *   ================================================================

 *   ----------------------------------------------------------------
 *   -  OutQMonEL1 full key                                         -
 *   ----------------------------------------------------------------

C     Key           KList
C                   KFld                    MonNameIn

 *   ================================================================
 *   =  Retrieve output queue list                                  =
 *   ================================================================

C     Key           SetLL     OutQMonEL1

C     Key           ReadE     OutQMonEL1
C                   DoW       Not( %EOF )
C                   Eval      OutQCount = OutQCount + 1
C                   Eval      Offset    = ( ( OutQCount -1 ) *20 ) + 1
C                   Eval      %Subst( OutQs  :
C                                     Offset :
C                                     10     ) =
C                             OutQName
C                   Eval      Offset = Offset + 10
C                   Eval      %Subst( OutQs  :
C                                     Offset :
C                                     10     ) =
C                             OutQLib
C     Key           ReadE     OutQMonEL1
C                   EndDo

C                   Eval      OutQOut = OutQ

 *   ================================================================
 *   =  Exit program                                                =
 *   ================================================================

C                   Eval      *InLR = *On
```

FIGURE 11.7F

RmvOutQME Validity-Checking Program RmvOutQM2A

```
/*  ============================================================  */
/*  =  Program....... RmvOutQM2A                                =  */
/*  =  Type.......... Validity-checking program for RmvOutQME   =  */
/*  =  Source type... CLLE                                      =  */
/*  =  Description... Remove OutQ monitor entry                 =  */
/*  =  -------------------------------------------------------  =  */
/*  =  Parameters                                               =  */
/*  =                                                           =  */
/*  =    &MonName        Input     Monitor name                 =  */
/*  =                                                           =  */
/*  =    &OutQ           Input     List of up to 25 qualified   =  */
/*  =                              output queue names           =  */
/*  ============================================================  */

Pgm          (                                                    +
               &MonName                                           +
               &OutQ                                              +
             )

/*  ============================================================  */
/*  = Variable declarations                                     =  */
/*  ============================================================  */

  Dcl         &MonName     *Char      (   10     )
  Dcl         &OutQ        *Char      (  502     )
  Dcl         &OutQName    *Char      (   10     )
  Dcl         &OutQLib     *Char      (   10     )
  Dcl         &OtherMon    *Char      (   10     )
  Dcl         &OutQCount   *Char      (    2     )
  Dcl         &OutQCountN  *Dec       (    2   0 )
  Dcl         &LoopCount   *Dec       (    3   0 )
  Dcl         &Offset      *Dec       (    3   0 )
  Dcl         &RcvVar      *Char      (  600     )
  Dcl         &RcvVarLen   *Char      (    4     )    ( X'00000258' )
  Dcl         &Format      *Char      (    8     )    ( 'JOBI0700' )
  Dcl         &QualJob     *Char      (   26     )    ( '*' )
  Dcl         &IntJobID    *Char      (   16     )
  Dcl         &PrdLib      *Char      (   10     )
  Dcl         &Nbr4        *Dec       (    4   0 )
  Dcl         &Msg         *Char      (  512     )
  Dcl         &MsgID       *Char      (    7     )
  Dcl         &MsgF        *Char      (   10     )
  Dcl         &MsgFLib     *Char      (   10     )
  Dcl         &MsgDta      *Char      (  100     )
  Dcl         &KeyVar      *Char      (    4     )

/*  ============================================================  */
/*  = Global error monitor                                      =  */
/*  ============================================================  */

  MonMsg      ( CPF0000 MCH0000 ) Exec(                           +
    Goto        Error                 )

/*  ============================================================  */
/*  =  Retrieve product library name                            =  */
/*  ============================================================  */

  Call        QUsrJobI                                            +
              (                                                   +
                &RcvVar                                           +
                &RcvVarLen                                        +
                &Format                                           +
                &QualJob                                          +
                &IntJobID                                         +
              )
```

continued

FIGURE 11.7F *CONTINUED*

```
  ChgVar     &Nbr4       ( %Bin( &RcvVar 65 4 ) )
  ChgVar     &Offset     ( ( &Nbr4 * 11 ) + 81 )
  ChgVar     &PrdLib     ( %Sst( &RcvVar &Offset 10 ) )

/*  ==============================================================  */
/*  =  Verify output queue monitor data queue existence          =  */
/*  ==============================================================  */

  ChkObj     Obj( &PrdLib/&MonName )                                +
             ObjType( *DtaQ )

  MonMsg     ( CPF9801 ) Exec(                                      +
    Do                        )
      ChgVar     &Msg         ( 'Output queue monitor'              +
                                *BCat                               +
                                &MonName                            +
                                *BCat                               +
                                'does not exist in library'         +
                                *BCat                               +
                                &PrdLib                             +
                                *TCat                               +
                                '.' )
      GoTo       SendError
    EndDo

/*  ==============================================================  */
/*  =  Ignore output queues when *ALL special value is chosen    =  */
/*  ==============================================================  */

  If         ( %Sst( &OutQ 3 4 ) *Eq '*ALL' )                       +
    Return

/*  ==============================================================  */
/*  = Parse number of output queues in list                      =  */
/*  ==============================================================  */

  ChgVar     &OutQCount  ( %Sst( &OutQ 1 2 ) )
  ChgVar     &OutQCountN ( %Bin( &OutQCount ) )

/*  ==============================================================  */
/*  = Validate output queues in list and make sure monitored by  =  */
/*  = this monitor                                               =  */
/*  ==============================================================  */

  ChgVar     &LoopCount  ( 0 )

Loop01:

  ChgVar     &LoopCount  ( &LoopCount + 1 )

  If         ( &LoopCount *GT &OutQCountN )                         +
    GoTo       End01

  ChgVar     &Offset     ( ( ( &LoopCount - 1 ) * 20 ) + 3 )
  ChgVar     &OutQName   ( %Sst( &OutQ &Offset 10 ) )
  ChgVar     &Offset     ( &Offset + 10 )
  ChgVar     &OutQLib    ( %Sst( &OutQ &Offset 10 ) )

  RtvObjD    Obj( &OutQLib/&OutQName )                              +
             ObjType( *OutQ )                                       +
             RtnLib( &OutQLib )

  MonMsg     ( CPF9801 ) Exec(                                      +
    Do                        )
```

continued

FIGURE 11.7F *CONTINUED*

```
      ChgVar      &Msg          ( 'Output queue'                  +
                                  *BCat                           +
                                  &OutQName                       +
                                  *BCat                           +
                                  'does not exist in library'     +
                                  *BCat                           +
                                  &OutQLib                        +
                                  *TCat                           +
                                  '.' )
      GoTo        SendError
    EndDo

  Call        &PrdLib/RmvOutQM2B                                  +
              (                                                   +
                &OutQName                                         +
                &OutQLib                                          +
                &MonName                                          +
                &OtherMon                                         +
              )

  If          ( &OtherMon *NE ' ' )                               +
    Do
      If          ( &OtherMon *NE '*' )                           +
        ChgVar      &Msg          ( 'Output queue'                +
                                    *BCat                         +
                                    &OutQLib                      +
                                    *TCat                         +
                                    '/'                           +
                                    *TCat                         +
                                    &OutQName                     +
                                    *BCat                         +
                                    'is assigned to monitor'      +
                                    *BCat                         +
                                    &OtherMon                     +
                                    *TCat                         +
                                    '.' )
      If          ( &OtherMon *Eq '*' )                           +
        ChgVar      &Msg          ( 'Output queue'                +
                                    *BCat                         +
                                    &OutQLib                      +
                                    *TCat                         +
                                    '/'                           +
                                    *TCat                         +
                                    &OutQName                     +
                                    *BCat                         +
                                    'is not assigned to monitor'  +
                                    *BCat                         +
                                    &MonName                      +
                                    *TCat                         +
                                    '.' )
      GoTo        SendError
    EndDo

  GoTo        Loop01

End01:

/*  =========================================================  */
/*  =  Exit                                                 =  */
/*  =========================================================  */

  Return
```

continued

Figure 11.7F *Continued*

```
/*  ================================================================  */
/*  = Error handler                                               =  */
/*  ================================================================  */

Error:

  RcvMsg     MsgType( *Excp )                                   +
             MsgDta( &MsgDta )                                  +
             MsgID( &MsgID )                                    +
             MsgF( &MsgF )                                      +
             MsgFLib( &MsgFLib )

  MonMsg     ( CPF0000 MCH0000 )

  SndPgmMsg  MsgID( &MsgID )                                    +
             MsgF( &MsgFLib/&MsgF )                             +
             MsgDta( &MsgDta )                                  +
             ToPgmQ( *Same )                                    +
             KeyVar( &KeyVar )

  MonMsg     ( CPF0000 MCH0000 )

  RcvMsg     KeyVar( &KeyVar )                                  +
             Msg( &Msg )

  MonMsg     ( CPF0000 MCH0000 )

SendError:

  SndPgmMsg  MsgID( CPD0006 )                                   +
             MsgF( QSys/QCPFMsg )                               +
             MsgDta( '0000' *TCat &Msg )                        +
             ToPgmQ( *Prv )                                     +
             MsgType( *Diag )

  MonMsg     ( CPF0000 MCH0000 )

  SndPgmMsg  MsgID( CPF0002 )                                   +
             MsgF( QSys/QCPFMsg )                               +
             ToPgmQ( *PRV )                                     +
             MsgType( *Escape )

  MonMsg     ( CPF0000 MCH0000 )

/*  ================================================================  */
/*  = End of program                                              =  */
/*  ================================================================  */

EndPgm
```

FIGURE 11.7G

RmvOutQME Validity-Checking Program RmvOutQM2B — Confirm Output Queue

```
 *  ================================================================
 *  =  Program....... RmvOutQM2B                                   =
 *  =  Source type... RPGLE                                        =
 *  =  Description... Remove OutQ Monitor Entry - confirm output   =
 *  =                 queue is being monitored                     =
 *  ================================================================

FoutQMonE  IF   E           K Disk

 *  ================================================================
 *  =  Entry parameters                                            =
 *  ================================================================

D EntryParms...
D                 PR                  ExtPgm( 'RMVOUTQM2B' )
D                               10
D                               10
D                               10
D                               10
D EntryParms...
D                 PI
D  OutQName                     10
D  OutQLib                      10
D  MonNameIn                    10
D  OtherMon                     10

 *  ================================================================
 *  =  Key lists                                                   =
 *  ================================================================

 *  ----------------------------------------------------------------
 *  -  OutQMonE full key                                           -
 *  ----------------------------------------------------------------

C     Key           KList
C                   KFld                    OutQLib
C                   KFld                    OutQName

 *  ================================================================
 *  =  Read record and determine if output queue is monitored by   =
 *  =  this monitor                                                =
 *  ================================================================

C     Key           Chain     OutQMonE

C                   Select
C                   When      ( %Found )
C                   If        MonName  = MonNameIn
C                   Eval      OtherMon = *Blank
C                   Else
C                   Eval      OtherMon = MonName
C                   EndIf
C                   Other
C                   Eval      OtherMon = '*'
C                   EndSl

 *  ================================================================
 *  =  Exit program                                                =
 *  ================================================================

C                   Eval      *InLR = *On
```

FIGURE 11.8A
DltOutQMon Panel

```
                    Delete Output Queue Monitor (DLTOUTQMON)

Type choices, press Enter.

Monitor name . . . . . . . . . .  SAMPLE____     Name











                                                                         Bottom
F3=Exit   F4=Prompt   F5=Refresh   F12=Cancel   F13=How to use this display
F24=More keys
```

FIGURE 11.8B
Command DltOutQMon

```
/*  ==============================================================  */
/*  =  Command....... DltOutQMon                                 =  */
/*  =  Source type... CMD                                        =  */
/*  =  Description... Delete Output Queue Monitor                =  */
/*  =                                                            =  */
/*  =  CPP........... DltOutQM1A                                 =  */
/*  =  VCP........... DltOutQM2A                                 =  */
/*  ==============================================================  */

             Cmd        Prompt( 'Delete Output Queue Monitor' )

             Parm       Kwd( MonName )                             +
                        Type( *Name )                              +
                        Len( 10 )                                  +
                        Min( 1 )                                   +
                        Prompt( 'Monitor name' )
```

FIGURE 11.8C

DltOutQMon Command Processing Program DltOutQM1A

```
/*  ================================================================  */
/*  =  Program....... DltOutQM1A                                  =  */
/*  =  Source type... CLLE                                        =  */
/*  =  Type.......... Command processing program for DltOutQMon  =  */
/*  =  Description... Delete output queue monitor                 =  */
/*  =  -------------------------------------------------------    =  */
/*  =                                                             =  */
/*  =  Parameters                                                 =  */
/*  =                                                             =  */
/*  =    &MonName         Input     Monitor name                  =  */
/*  ================================================================  */

Pgm         (                                                          +
              &MonName                                                 +
            )

/*  ================================================================  */
/*  =  Variable declarations                                      =  */
/*  ================================================================  */

  Dcl        &MonName    *Char     (   10     )
  Dcl        &RcvVar     *Char     (  600     )
  Dcl        &RcvVarLen  *Char     (    4     )   ( X'00000258' )
  Dcl        &Format     *Char     (    8     )   ( 'JOBI0700' )
  Dcl        &QualJob    *Char     (   26     )   ( '*' )
  Dcl        &IntJobID   *Char     (   16     )
  Dcl        &PrdLib     *Char     (   10     )
  Dcl        &Offset     *Dec      (    4  0  )
  Dcl        &Nbr4       *Dec      (    4  0  )
  Dcl        &MsgID      *Char     (    7     )
  Dcl        &MsgDta     *Char     (  100     )
  Dcl        &MsgF       *Char     (   10     )
  Dcl        &MsgFLib    *Char     (   10     )

/*  ================================================================  */
/*  =  Global error monitor                                       =  */
/*  ================================================================  */

  MonMsg     ( CPF0000 MCH0000 ) Exec(                                 +
    GoTo       Error                 )

/*  ================================================================  */
/*  =  Retrieve product library name                              =  */
/*  ================================================================  */

  Call       QUsrJobI                                                  +
             (                                                         +
               &RcvVar                                                 +
               &RcvVarLen                                              +
               &Format                                                 +
               &QualJob                                                +
               &IntJobID                                               +
             )

  ChgVar     &Nbr4        ( %Bin( &RcvVar 65 4 ) )
  ChgVar     &Offset      ( ( &Nbr4 * 11 ) + 81 )
  ChgVar     &PrdLib      ( %Sst( &RcvVar &Offset 10 ) )

/*  ================================================================  */
/*  =  Delete control records                                     =  */
/*  ================================================================  */

  RmvOutQME  MonName( &MonName )                                       +
             OutQ( *All )
```

continued

FIGURE 11.8C CONTINUED

```
/*  ================================================================  */
/*  =  Delete output queue monitor data queue                     =  */
/*  ================================================================  */

  DltDtaQ    DtaQ( &PrdLib/&MonName )

/*  ================================================================  */
/*  =  Send completion message and exit                           =  */
/*  ================================================================  */

  SndPgmMsg  MsgID( CPF9898 )                                          +
             MsgF( QSys/QCPFMsg )                                      +
             MsgDta( 'Output queue monitor'                            +
                     *BCat                                             +
                     &MonName                                          +
                     *BCat                                             +
                     'deleted' )                                       +
             MsgType( *Comp )
  Return

/*  ================================================================  */
/*  =  Error handler                                              =  */
/*  ================================================================  */

Error:

  RcvMsg     MsgType( *Excp )                                          +
             MsgDta( &MsgDta )                                         +
             MsgID( &MsgID )                                           +
             MsgF( &MsgF )                                             +
             MsgFLib( &MsgFLib )

  MonMsg     ( CPF0000 MCH0000 )

  SndPgmMsg  MsgID( &MsgID )                                           +
             MsgF( &MsgFLib/&MsgF )                                    +
             MsgDta( &MsgDta )                                         +
             MsgType( *Escape )

  MonMsg     ( CPF0000 MCH0000 )

/*  ================================================================  */
/*  =  End of program                                             =  */
/*  ================================================================  */

EndPgm
```

FIGURE 11.8D

DltOutQMon Validity-Checking Program DltOutQM2A

```
/*  ================================================================  */
/*  =  Program....... DltOutQM2A                                  =  */
/*  =  Source type... CLLE                                        =  */
/*  =  Type.......... Validity-checking program for DltOutQMon    =  */
/*  =  Description... Delete output queue monitor                 =  */
/*  =  -------------------------------------------------------    =  */
/*  =  Parameters                                                 =  */
/*  =                                                             =  */
/*  =    &MonName          Input      Monitor name                =  */
/*  ================================================================  */

Pgm        (                                                           +
             &MonName                                                  +
           )
```

continued

FIGURE 11.8D CONTINUED

```
/*  ===============================================================  */
/*  =  Variable declarations                                     =  */
/*  ===============================================================  */

  Dcl         &MonName    *Char      (   10     )
  Dcl         &RcvVar     *Char      (  600     )
  Dcl         &RcvVarLen  *Char      (    4     )    ( X'00000258' )
  Dcl         &Format     *Char      (    8     )    ( 'JOBI0700' )
  Dcl         &QualJob    *Char      (   26     )    ( '*' )
  Dcl         &IntJobID   *Char      (   16     )
  Dcl         &PrdLib     *Char      (   10     )
  Dcl         &Offset     *Dec       (    4   0 )
  Dcl         &Nbr4       *Dec       (    4   0 )
  Dcl         &Msg        *Char      (  512     )
  Dcl         &MsgID      *Char      (    7     )
  Dcl         &MsgDta     *Char      (  100     )
  Dcl         &MsgF       *Char      (   10     )
  Dcl         &MsgFLib    *Char      (   10     )
  Dcl         &KeyVar     *Char      (    4     )

/*  ===============================================================  */
/*  =  Global error monitor                                      =  */
/*  ===============================================================  */

  MonMsg      ( CPF0000 MCH0000 ) Exec(                              +
    GoTo        Error                  )

/*  ===============================================================  */
/*  =  Retrieve product library name                             =  */
/*  ===============================================================  */

  Call        QUsrJobI                                               +
              (                                                      +
                &RcvVar                                              +
                &RcvVarLen                                           +
                &Format                                              +
                &QualJob                                             +
                &IntJobID                                            +
              )

  ChgVar      &Nbr4          ( %Bin( &RcvVar 65 4 ) )
  ChgVar      &Offset        ( ( &Nbr4 * 11 ) + 81 )
  ChgVar      &PrdLib        ( %Sst( &RcvVar &Offset 10 ) )

/*  ===============================================================  */
/*  =  Verify output queue monitor data queue existence          =  */
/*  ===============================================================  */

  ChkObj      Obj( &PrdLib/&MonName )                                +
              ObjType( *DtaQ )

  MonMsg      ( CPF9801 ) Exec(                                      +
    Do                         )
      ChgVar      &Msg           ( 'Output queue monitor'            +
                                   *BCat                             +
                                   &MonName                          +
                                   *BCat                             +
                                   'does not exist in library'       +
                                   *BCat                             +
                                   &PrdLib                           +
                                   *TCat                             +
                                   '.' )
      GoTo        SendError
    EndDo

/*  ===============================================================  */
/*  =  Exit                                                      =  */
/*  ===============================================================  */

  Return
```

continued

FIGURE 11.8D CONTINUED

```
/*  ==============================================================  */
/*  =  Error handler                                             =  */
/*  ==============================================================  */

Error:

  RcvMsg      MsgType( *Excp )                                        +
              MsgDta( &MsgDta )                                       +
              MsgID( &MsgID )                                         +
              MsgF( &MsgF )                                           +
              MsgFLib( &MsgFLib )

  MonMsg      ( CPF0000 MCH0000 )

  SndPgmMsg   MsgID( &MsgID )                                         +
              MsgF( &MsgFLib/&MsgF )                                  +
              MsgDta( &MsgDta )                                       +
              ToPgmQ( *Same )                                         +
              KeyVar( &KeyVar )

  MonMsg      ( CPF0000 MCH0000 )

  RcvMsg      KeyVar( &KeyVar )                                       +
              Msg( &Msg )

  MonMsg      ( CPF0000 MCH0000 )

SendError:

  SndPgmMsg   MsgID( CPD0006 )                                        +
              MsgF( QSys/QCPFMsg )                                    +
              MsgDta( '0000' *TCat &Msg )                             +
              ToPgmQ( *Prv )                                          +
              MsgType( *Diag )

  MonMsg      ( CPF0000 MCH0000 )

  SndPgmMsg   MsgID( CPF0002 )                                        +
              MsgF( QSys/QCPFMsg )                                    +
              ToPgmQ( *Prv )                                          +
              MsgType( *Escape )

  MonMsg      ( CPF0000 MCH0000 )

/*  ==============================================================  */
/*  =  End of program                                            =  */
/*  ==============================================================  */

EndPgm
```

FIGURE 11.9A
StrOutQMon Panel

```
                    Start Output Queue Monitor (STROUTQMON)

 Type choices, press Enter.

 Monitor name . . . . . . . . . .   SAMPLE____    Name












                                                                     Bottom
F3=Exit   F4=Prompt   F5=Refresh   F12=Cancel   F13=How to use this display
F24=More keys
```

FIGURE 11.9B
Command StrOutQMon

```
/*  ===============================================================  */
/*  =  Command....... StrOutQMon                                  =  */
/*  =  Source type... CMD                                         =  */
/*  =  Description... Start Output Queue Monitor                  =  */
/*  =                                                             =  */
/*  =  CPP........... StrOutQM1A                                  =  */
/*  =  VCP........... StrOutQM2A                                  =  */
/*  ===============================================================  */

             Cmd         Prompt( 'Start Output Queue Monitor' )

             Parm        Kwd( MonName )                              +
                         Type( *Name )                               +
                         Len( 10 )                                   +
                         Min( 1 )                                    +
                         Prompt( 'Monitor name' )
```

FIGURE 11.9C

StrOutQMon Command Processing Program StrOutQM1A

```
/*  ==================================================================  */
/*  =  Program....... StrOutQM1A                                    =  */
/*  =  Source type... CLLE                                          =  */
/*  =  Type.......... Command processing program for StrOutQMon     =  */
/*  =  Description... Start output queue monitor                    =  */
/*  =  -------------------------------------------------------------  =  */
/*  =  Parameters                                                   =  */
/*  =                                                               =  */
/*  =    &MonName          Input      Monitor name                  =  */
/*  ==================================================================  */

Pgm          (                                                          +
               &MonName                                                 +
             )

/*  ==================================================================  */
/*  =  Variable declarations                                        =  */
/*  ==================================================================  */

  Dcl          &MonName     *Char      (   10     )
  Dcl          &RcvVar      *Char      (  600     )
  Dcl          &RcvVarLen   *Char      (    4     )   ( X'00000258' )
  Dcl          &Format      *Char      (    8     )   ( 'JOBI0700' )
  Dcl          &QualJob     *Char      (   26     )   ( '*' )
  Dcl          &IntJobID    *Char      (   16     )
  Dcl          &PrdLib      *Char      (   10     )
  Dcl          &Offset      *Dec       (    4  0  )
  Dcl          &Nbr4        *Dec       (    4  0  )
  Dcl          &MsgID       *Char      (    7     )
  Dcl          &MsgDta      *Char      (  100     )
  Dcl          &MsgF        *Char      (   10     )
  Dcl          &MsgFLib     *Char      (   10     )

/*  ==================================================================  */
/*  =  Global error monitor                                         =  */
/*  ==================================================================  */

  MonMsg       ( CPF0000 MCH0000 ) Exec(                                +
    GoTo         Error                 )

/*  ==================================================================  */
/*  =  Retrieve product library name                                =  */
/*  ==================================================================  */

  Call         QUsrJobI                                                 +
               (                                                        +
                 &RcvVar                                                +
                 &RcvVarLen                                             +
                 &Format                                                +
                 &QualJob                                               +
                 &IntJobID                                              +
               )

  ChgVar       &Nbr4         ( %Bin( &RcvVar 65 4 ) )
  ChgVar       &Offset       ( ( &Nbr4 * 11 ) + 81 )
  ChgVar       &PrdLib       ( %Sst( &RcvVar &Offset 10 ) )

/*  ==================================================================  */
/*  =  Start monitor job                                            =  */
/*  ==================================================================  */

  SbmJob       Cmd( Call &PrdLib/OutQMon ( &MonName ) )                 +
               Job( &MonName )                                          +
               JobD( &PrdLib/OutQMon )
```

continued

FIGURE 11.9C CONTINUED

```
/*  ============================================================  */
/*  =  Send completion message and exit                        =  */
/*  ============================================================  */

  SndPgmMsg  MsgID( CPF9898 )                                    +
             MsgF( QSys/QCPFMsg )                                +
             MsgDta( 'Output queue monitor'                      +
                     *BCat                                       +
                     &MonName                                    +
                     *BCat                                       +
                     'started' )                                 +
             MsgType( *Comp )

  Return

/*  ============================================================  */
/*  =  Error handler                                           =  */
/*  ============================================================  */

Error:

  RcvMsg     MsgType( *Excp )                                    +
             MsgDta( &MsgDta )                                   +
             MsgID( &MsgID )                                     +
             MsgF( &MsgF )                                       +
             MsgFLib( &MsgFLib )

  MonMsg     ( CPF0000 MCH0000 )

  SndPgmMsg  MsgID( &MsgID )                                     +
             MsgF( &MsgFLib/&MsgF )                              +
             MsgDta( &MsgDta )                                   +
             MsgType( *Escape )

  MonMsg     ( CPF0000 MCH0000 )

/*  ============================================================  */
/*  =  End of program                                          =  */
/*  ============================================================  */

EndPgm
```

FIGURE 11.9D

StrOutQMon Validity-Checking Program StrOutQM2A

```
/*  ============================================================  */
/*  =  Program....... StrOutQM2A                               =  */
/*  =  Source type... CLLE                                     =  */
/*  =  Type.......... Validity-checking program for StrOutQMon =  */
/*  =  Description... Start output queue monitor               =  */
/*  =  ------------------------------------------------------  =  */
/*  =  Parameters                                              =  */
/*  =                                                          =  */
/*  =    &MonName          Input      Monitor name             =  */
/*  ============================================================  */

Pgm        (                                                     +
             &MonName                                            +
           )
```

continued

FIGURE 11.9D *CONTINUED*

```
/*  ================================================================  */
/*  =  Variable declarations                                       =  */
/*  ================================================================  */

  Dcl         &MonName    *Char      (   10     )
  Dcl         &RcvVar     *Char      (  600     )
  Dcl         &RcvVarLen  *Char      (    4     )   ( X'00000258' )
  Dcl         &Format     *Char      (    8     )   ( 'JOBI0700' )
  Dcl         &QualJob    *Char      (   26     )   ( '*' )
  Dcl         &IntJobID   *Char      (   16     )
  Dcl         &PrdLib     *Char      (   10     )
  Dcl         &Offset     *Dec       (    4  0  )
  Dcl         &Nbr4       *Dec       (    4  0  )
  Dcl         &Msg        *Char      (  512     )
  Dcl         &MsgID      *Char      (    7     )
  Dcl         &MsgDta     *Char      (  100     )
  Dcl         &MsgF       *Char      (   10     )
  Dcl         &MsgFLib    *Char      (   10     )
  Dcl         &KeyVar     *Char      (    4     )

/*  ================================================================  */
/*  =  Global error monitor                                        =  */
/*  ================================================================  */

  MonMsg      ( CPF0000 MCH0000 ) Exec(                                +
    GoTo        Error                   )

/*  ================================================================  */
/*  =  Retrieve product library name                               =  */
/*  ================================================================  */

  Call        QUsrJobI                                                 +
              (                                                        +
                &RcvVar                                                +
                &RcvVarLen                                             +
                &Format                                                +
                &QualJob                                               +
                &IntJobID                                              +
              )

  ChgVar      &Nbr4         ( %Bin( &RcvVar 65 4 ) )
  ChgVar      &Offset       ( ( &Nbr4 * 11 ) + 81 )
  ChgVar      &PrdLib       ( %Sst( &RcvVar &Offset 10 ) )

/*  ================================================================  */
/*  =  Verify output queue monitor data queue existence            =  */
/*  ================================================================  */

  ChkObj      Obj( &PrdLib/&MonName )                                  +
              ObjType( *DtaQ )

  MonMsg      ( CPF9801 ) Exec(                                        +
    Do                        )
      ChgVar      &Msg          ( 'Output queue monitor'               +
                                  *BCat                                +
                                  &MonName                             +
                                  *BCat                                +
                                  'does not exist in library'          +
                                  *BCat                                +
                                  &PrdLib                              +
                                  *TCat                                +
                                  '.' )

      GoTo        SendError
    EndDo
```

continued

FIGURE 11.9D *CONTINUED*

```
/* ================================================================ */
/* =  Make sure output queue monitor is not already active       = */
/* ================================================================ */

  AlcObj     Obj( ( &PrdLib/&MonName *DtaQ *Excl ) )                +
             Wait( 1 )

  MonMsg     ( CPF1002 ) Exec(                                      +
    Do                       )
      ChgVar     &Msg          ( 'Output queue monitor'             +
                                 *BCat                              +
                                 &MonName                           +
                                 *BCat                              +
                                 'is already active'                +
                                 *TCat                              +
                                 '.' )
      GoTo       SendError
    EndDo

  DlcObj     Obj( ( &PrdLib/&MonName *DtaQ *Excl ) )

/* ================================================================ */
/* =  Exit                                                       = */
/* ================================================================ */

  Return

/* ================================================================ */
/* =  Error handler                                              = */
/* ================================================================ */

Error:

  RcvMsg     MsgType( *Excp )                                       +
             MsgDta( &MsgDta )                                      +
             MsgID( &MsgID )                                        +
             MsgF( &MsgF )                                          +
             MsgFLib( &MsgFLib )

  MonMsg     ( CPF0000 MCH0000 )

  SndPgmMsg  MsgID( &MsgID )                                        +
             MsgF( &MsgFLib/&MsgF )                                 +
             MsgDta( &MsgDta )                                      +
             ToPgmQ( *Same )                                        +
             KeyVar( &KeyVar )

  MonMsg     ( CPF0000 MCH0000 )

  RcvMsg     KeyVar( &KeyVar )                                      +
             Msg( &Msg )

  MonMsg     ( CPF0000 MCH0000 )

SendError:

  SndPgmMsg  MsgID( CPD0006 )                                       +
             MsgF( QSys/QCPFMsg )                                   +
             MsgDta( '0000' *TCat &Msg )                            +
             ToPgmQ( *Prv )                                         +
             MsgType( *Diag )

  MonMsg     ( CPF0000 MCH0000 )
```

continued

FIGURE 11.9D CONTINUED

```
  SndPgmMsg  MsgID( CPF0002 )                                           +
             MsgF( QSys/QCPFMsg )                                       +
             ToPgmQ( *Prv )                                             +
             MsgType( *Escape )
  MonMsg     ( CPF0000 MCH0000 )

/*  ===============================================================  */
/*  =  End of program                                             =  */
/*  ===============================================================  */

EndPgm
```

FIGURE 11.10A
EndOutQMon Panel

```
                     End Output Queue Monitor (ENDOUTQMON)

 Type choices, press Enter.

 Monitor name . . . . . . . . . .   SAMPLE____     Name

                                                                         Bottom
 F3=Exit   F4=Prompt   F5=Refresh   F12=Cancel   F13=How to use this display
 F24=More keys
```

FIGURE 11.10B
Command EndOutQMon

```
/*  ===============================================================  */
/*  =  Command....... EndOutQMon                                  =  */
/*  =  Source type... CMD                                         =  */
/*  =  Description... End Output Queue Monitor                    =  */
/*  =                                                             =  */
/*  =  CPP........... EndOutQM1A                                  =  */
/*  =  VCP........... EndOutQM2A                                  =  */
/*  ===============================================================  */

            Cmd        Prompt( 'End Output Queue Monitor' )

            Parm       Kwd( MonName )                                   +
                       Type( *Name )                                    +
                       Len( 10 )                                        +
                       Min( 1 )                                         +
                       Prompt( 'Monitor name' )
```

FIGURE 11.10C

EndOutQMon Command Processing Program EndOutQM1A

```
/*  ==============================================================  */
/*  =  Program....... EndOutQM1A                                 =  */
/*  =  Source type... CLLE                                       =  */
/*  =  Type.......... Command processing program for EndOutQMon  =  */
/*  =  Description... End output queue monitor                   =  */
/*  =  -------------------------------------------------------   =  */
/*  =  Parameters                                                =  */
/*  =                                                            =  */
/*  =    &MonName         Input     Monitor name                 =  */
/*  ==============================================================  */

Pgm         (                                                      +
              &MonName                                             +
            )

/*  ==============================================================  */
/*  =  Variable declarations                                     =  */
/*  ==============================================================  */

  Dcl         &MonName    *Char     (   10    )
  Dcl         &RcvVar     *Char     (  600    )
  Dcl         &RcvVarLen  *Char     (    4    )   ( X'00000258' )
  Dcl         &Format     *Char     (    8    )   ( 'JOBI0700' )
  Dcl         &QualJob    *Char     (   26    )   ( '*' )
  Dcl         &IntJobID   *Char     (   16    )
  Dcl         &PrdLib     *Char     (   10    )
  Dcl         &Offset     *Dec      (    4  0 )
  Dcl         &Nbr4       *Dec      (    4  0 )
  Dcl         &Data       *Char     (  128    )   ( '*ENDMON' )
  Dcl         &DataLen    *Dec      (    5  0 )   ( 128 )
  Dcl         &MsgID      *Char     (    7    )
  Dcl         &MsgDta     *Char     (  100    )
  Dcl         &MsgF       *Char     (   10    )
  Dcl         &MsgFLib    *Char     (   10    )

/*  ==============================================================  */
/*  =  Global error monitor                                      =  */
/*  ==============================================================  */

  MonMsg      ( CPF0000 MCH0000 ) Exec(                            +
    GoTo        Error               )

/*  ==============================================================  */
/*  =  Retrieve product library name                             =  */
/*  ==============================================================  */

  Call        QUsrJobI                                             +
              (                                                    +
                &RcvVar                                            +
                &RcvVarLen                                         +
                &Format                                            +
                &QualJob                                           +
                &IntJobID                                          +
              )

  ChgVar      &Nbr4         ( %Bin( &RcvVar 65 4 ) )
  ChgVar      &Offset       ( ( &Nbr4 * 11 ) + 81 )
  ChgVar      &PrdLib       ( %Sst( &RcvVar &Offset 10 ) )
```

continued

FIGURE 11.10C *CONTINUED*

```
/*  ================================================================  */
/*  =  Send signal to end output queue monitor                     =  */
/*  ================================================================  */

  Call       QSndDtaQ                                                  +
             (                                                         +
               &MonName                                                +
               &PrdLib                                                 +
               &DataLen                                                +
               &Data                                                   +
             )

/*  ================================================================  */
/*  =  Send completion message and exit                            =  */
/*  ================================================================  */

  SndPgmMsg  MsgID( CPF9898 )                                          +
             MsgF( QSys/QCPFMsg )                                      +
             MsgDta( 'Output queue monitor'                            +
                     *BCat                                             +
                     &MonName                                          +
                     *BCat                                             +
                     'ended' )                                         +
             MsgType( *Comp )

  Return

/*  ================================================================  */
/*  =  Error handler                                               =  */
/*  ================================================================  */

Error:

  RcvMsg     MsgType( *Excp )                                          +
             MsgDta( &MsgDta )                                         +
             MsgID( &MsgID )                                           +
             MsgF( &MsgF )                                             +
             MsgFLib( &MsgFLib )

  MonMsg     ( CPF0000 MCH0000 )

  SndPgmMsg  MsgID( &MsgID )                                           +
             MsgF( &MsgFLib/&MsgF )                                    +
             MsgDta( &MsgDta )                                         +
             MsgType( *Escape )

  MonMsg     ( CPF0000 MCH0000 )

/*  ================================================================  */
/*  =  End of program                                              =  */
/*  ================================================================  */

EndPgm
```

FIGURE 11.10D

EndOutQMon Validity-Checking Program EndOutQM2A

```
/*  ===============================================================  */
/*  =  Program....... EndOutQM2A                                 =  */
/*  =  Source type... CLLE                                       =  */
/*  =  Type.......... Validity-checking program for EndOutQMon   =  */
/*  =  Description... End output queue monitor                   =  */
/*  =  -------------------------------------------------------   =  */
/*  =  Parameters                                                =  */
/*  =                                                            =  */
/*  =    &MonName         Input     Monitor name                 =  */
/*  ===============================================================  */

Pgm         (                                                          +
              &MonName                                                 +
            )

/*  ===============================================================  */
/*  =  Variable declarations                                     =  */
/*  ===============================================================  */

  Dcl         &MonName    *Char     (   10    )
  Dcl         &RcvVar     *Char     (  600    )
  Dcl         &RcvVarLen  *Char     (    4    )    ( X'00000258' )
  Dcl         &Format     *Char     (    8    )    ( 'JOBI0700' )
  Dcl         &QualJob    *Char     (   26    )    ( '*' )
  Dcl         &IntJobID   *Char     (   16    )
  Dcl         &PrdLib     *Char     (   10    )
  Dcl         &Offset     *Dec      (    4  0 )
  Dcl         &Nbr4       *Dec      (    4  0 )
  Dcl         &Msg        *Char     (  512    )
  Dcl         &MsgID      *Char     (    7    )
  Dcl         &MsgDta     *Char     (  100    )
  Dcl         &MsgF       *Char     (   10    )
  Dcl         &MsgFLib    *Char     (   10    )
  Dcl         &KeyVar     *Char     (    4    )

/*  ===============================================================  */
/*  =  Global error monitor                                      =  */
/*  ===============================================================  */

  MonMsg      ( CPF0000 MCH0000 ) Exec(                                +
    GoTo        Error             )

/*  ===============================================================  */
/*  =  Retrieve product library name                             =  */
/*  ===============================================================  */

  Call        QUsrJobI                                                 +
              (                                                        +
                &RcvVar                                                +
                &RcvVarLen                                             +
                &Format                                                +
                &QualJob                                               +
                &IntJobID                                              +
              )

  ChgVar      &Nbr4       ( %Bin( &RcvVar 65 4 ) )
  ChgVar      &Offset     ( ( &Nbr4 * 11 ) + 81 )
  ChgVar      &PrdLib     ( %Sst( &RcvVar &Offset 10 ) )

/*  ===============================================================  */
/*  =  Verify output queue monitor data queue existence          =  */
/*  ===============================================================  */

  ChkObj      Obj( &PrdLib/&MonName )                                  +
              ObjType( *DtaQ )
```

continued

FIGURE 11.10D *CONTINUED*

```
  MonMsg      ( CPF9801 ) Exec(                                          +
    Do                            )
      ChgVar      &Msg          ( 'Output queue monitor'                   +
                                  *BCat                                  +
                                  &MonName                               +
                                  *BCat                                  +
                                  'does not exist in library'            +
                                  *BCat                                  +
                                  &PrdLib                                +
                                  *TCat                                  +
                                  '.' )
      GoTo        SendError
    EndDo

/*  ============================================================  */
/*  =  Make sure output queue monitor is active                =  */
/*  ============================================================  */

  AlcObj      Obj( ( &PrdLib/&MonName *DtaQ *Excl ) )                    +
              Wait( 1 )

  MonMsg      ( CPF1002 ) Exec(                                          +
    Return                    )

  ChgVar      &Msg          ( 'Output queue monitor'                     +
                              *BCat                                      +
                              &MonName                                   +
                              *BCat                                      +
                              'is not active'                            +
                              *TCat                                      +
                              '.' )

  DlcObj      Obj( ( &PrdLib/&MonName *DtaQ *Excl ) )

  GoTo        SendError

/*  ============================================================  */
/*  =  Error handler                                           =  */
/*  ============================================================  */

 Error:

  RcvMsg      MsgType( *Excp )                                           +
              MsgDta( &MsgDta )                                          +
              MsgID( &MsgID )                                            +
              MsgF( &MsgF )                                              +
              MsgFLib( &MsgFLib )

  MonMsg      ( CPF0000 MCH0000 )

  SndPgmMsg   MsgID( &MsgID )                                            +
              MsgF( &MsgFLib/&MsgF )                                     +
              MsgDta( &MsgDta )                                          +
              ToPgmQ( *Same )                                            +
              KeyVar( &KeyVar )

  MonMsg      ( CPF0000 MCH0000 )

  RcvMsg      KeyVar( &KeyVar )                                          +
              Msg( &Msg )

  MonMsg      ( CPF0000 MCH0000 )

 SendError:
```

continued

FIGURE 11.10D CONTINUED

```
  SndPgmMsg  MsgID( CPD0006 )                                  +
             MsgF( QSys/QCPFMsg )                              +
             MsgDta( '0000' *TCat &Msg )                       +
             ToPgmQ( *Prv )                                    +
             MsgType( *Diag )

  MonMsg     ( CPF0000 MCH0000 )

  SndPgmMsg  MsgID( CPF0002 )                                  +
             MsgF( QSys/QCPFMsg )                              +
             ToPgmQ( *Prv )                                    +
             MsgType( *Escape )
  MonMsg     ( CPF0000 MCH0000 )

/*  =============================================================  */
/*  =  End of program                                           =  */
/*  =============================================================  */

EndPgm
```

FIGURE 11.11

Output Queue Monitor Program OutQMon

```
/*  =============================================================  */
/*  =  Program....... OutQMon                                   =  */
/*  =  Source type... CLLE                                      =  */
/*  =  Description... Output queue monitor                      =  */
/*  =  -------------------------------------------------------  =  */
/*  =  Parameters                                               =  */
/*  =                                                           =  */
/*  =    &MonName        Input      Monitor name                =  */
/*  =============================================================  */

Pgm        (                                                    +
             &MonName                                           +
           )

/*  =============================================================  */
/*  =  Variable declarations                                    =  */
/*  =============================================================  */

  Dcl        &MonName    *Char     (  10    )
  Dcl        &Data       *Char     ( 128    )
  Dcl        &DataLen    *Dec      (   5  0 )
  Dcl        &Wait       *Dec      (   5  0 )  ( -1 )
  Dcl        &RcvVar     *Char     ( 600    )
  Dcl        &RcvVarLen  *Char     (   4    )  ( X'00000258' )
  Dcl        &Format     *Char     (   8    )  ( 'JOBI0700' )
  Dcl        &QualJob    *Char     (  26    )  ( '*' )
  Dcl        &IntJobID   *Char     (  16    )
  Dcl        &PrdLib     *Char     (  10    )
  Dcl        &Offset     *Dec      (   4  0 )
  Dcl        &Nbr4       *Dec      (   4  0 )
  Dcl        &Action     *Char     (  10    )
  Dcl        &Job        *Char     (  10    )
  Dcl        &User       *Char     (  10    )
  Dcl        &JobNbr     *Char     (   6    )
  Dcl        &SplFName   *Char     (  10    )
  Dcl        &SplFNbr    *Dec      (   4  0 )
  Dcl        &OutQName   *Char     (  10    )
  Dcl        &OutQLib    *Char     (  10    )
  Dcl        &MsgID      *Char     (   7    )
  Dcl        &MsgDta     *Char     ( 100    )
  Dcl        &MsgF       *Char     (  10    )
  Dcl        &MsgFLib    *Char     (  10    )
```

continued

FIGURE 11.11 CONTINUED

```
/*  ==============================================================  */
/*  =  Global error monitor                                     =  */
/*  ==============================================================  */

  MonMsg     ( CPF0000 MCH0000 ) Exec(                              +
    GoTo       Error                  )

/*  ==============================================================  */
/*  =  Retrieve product library name                            =  */
/*  ==============================================================  */

  Call       QUsrJobI                                               +
             (                                                      +
               &RcvVar                                              +
               &RcvVarLen                                           +
               &Format                                              +
               &QualJob                                             +
               &IntJobID                                            +
             )

  ChgVar     &Nbr4         ( %Bin( &RcvVar 65 4 ) )
  ChgVar     &Offset       ( ( &Nbr4 * 11 ) + 81 )
  ChgVar     &PrdLib       ( %Sst( &RcvVar &Offset 10 ) )

/*  ==============================================================  */
/*  =  Allocate output queue monitor data queue                 =  */
/*  ==============================================================  */

  AlcObj     Obj( ( &PrdLib/&MonName *DtaQ *Excl ) )                +
             Wait( 1 )

  MonMsg     ( CPF1002 ) Exec(                                      +
    SndPgmMsg  MsgID( CPF9898 )                                     +
               MsgF( QSys/QCPFMsg )                                 +
               MsgDta( 'Output queue monitor'                       +
                       *BCat                                        +
                       &MonName                                     +
                       *BCat                                        +
                       'is already active' )                        +
               MsgType( *Escape ) )

/*  ==============================================================  */
/*  =  Wait for a data queue entry                              =  */
/*  ==============================================================  */

Loop01:

  Call       QRcvDtaQ                                               +
             (                                                      +
               &MonName                                             +
               &PrdLib                                              +
               &DataLen                                             +
               &Data                                                +
               &Wait                                                +
             )

/*  ==============================================================  */
/*  =  Perform requested action                                 =  */
/*  ==============================================================  */

  If         ( &DataLen *GT 0 )                                     +
    Do
      ChgVar     &Action      ( %Sst( &Data 1 10 ) )
```

continued

FIGURE 11.11 *CONTINUED*

```
/*  --------------------------------------------------------------  */
/*  -  Spooled file arrived on output queue                      -  */
/*  --------------------------------------------------------------  */

      If         ( &Action *Eq '*SPOOL' )                             +
        Do
          ChgVar     &Job         ( %Sst( &Data 13 10 ) )
          ChgVar     &User        ( %Sst( &Data 23 10 ) )
          ChgVar     &JobNbr      ( %Sst( &Data 33  6 ) )
          ChgVar     &SplFName    ( %Sst( &Data 39 10 ) )
          ChgVar     &SplFNbr     ( %Bin( &Data 49  4 ) )
          ChgVar     &OutQName    ( %Sst( &Data 53 10 ) )
          ChgVar     &OutQLib     ( %Sst( &Data 63 10 ) )
          Call       &PrdLib/&MonName                                 +
                     (                                                +
                       &Job                                           +
                       &User                                          +
                       &JobNbr                                        +
                       &SplFName                                      +
                       &SplFNbr                                       +
                       &OutQName                                      +
                       &OutQLib                                       +
                     )
        EndDo

/*  --------------------------------------------------------------  */
/*  -  Request to end output queue monitor received              -  */
/*  --------------------------------------------------------------  */

      If         ( &Action *Eq '*ENDMON' )                            +
        Return
    EndDo

  GoTo       Loop01

/*  ==============================================================  */
/*  =  Error handler                                             =  */
/*  ==============================================================  */

Error:

  RcvMsg     MsgType( *Excp )                                         +
             MsgDta( &MsgDta )                                        +
             MsgID( &MsgID )                                          +
             MsgF( &MsgF )                                            +
             MsgFLib( &MsgFLib )

  MonMsg     ( CPF0000 MCH0000 )

  SndPgmMsg  MsgID( &MsgID )                                          +
             MsgF( &MsgFLib/&MsgF )                                   +
             MsgDta( &MsgDta )                                        +
             MsgType( *Escape )

  MonMsg     ( CPF0000 MCH0000 )

/*  ==============================================================  */
/*  =  End of program                                            =  */
/*  ==============================================================  */

EndPgm
```

FIGURE 11.12A

Control File OutQMonE

```
 *  ===================================================================
 *  =  Physical file. OutQMonE                                        =
 *  =  Source type... PF                                              =
 *  =  Description... Output Queue Monitor Entries control file       =
 *  ===================================================================

A          R ROUTQMONE

A            OUTQLIB       10
A            OUTQNAME      10
A            MONNAME       10

A          K OUTQLIB
A          K OUTQNAME
```

FIGURE 11.12B

Logical File OutQMonEL1

```
 *  ==============================================================
 *  =  Logical file.. OutQMonEL1                                 =
 *  =  Source type... LF                                         =
 *  =  Description... Output Queue Monitor Entries control file  =
 *  ==============================================================

A          R ROUTQMONE                 PFILE(OUTQMONE)

A          K MONNAME
```

Chapter 12

Disk Storage Cleanup

OS/400 is a sophisticated operating system that tracks almost everything that happens on the system. This tracking is useful, but it results in a messy byproduct of system-supplied database files, journal receivers, and message queues. Users add to the clutter with old messages, unused objects, out-of-date records, and unprinted spool files. If you do nothing about this disorder, it eventually will strangle your system. However, you can implement a few simple automated and manual procedures to keep your disk storage free of unwanted debris.

Automatic Cleanup Procedures

Operational Assistant (OA), part of OS/400, includes functions to automatically clean up some of the daily messes the system makes. OA's cleanup is a good place to start when you're trying to clean up your system's act.

To access the OA Cleanup Tasks menu, you can type **Go Cleanup** or, from the OA main menu (**Go Assist**), select option 11 (Customize your system, users, and devices) and then option 2 (Cleanup tasks). Figure 12.1 shows the CLEANUP menu, which you can use to start and stop automatic cleanup and to change cleanup parameters.

FIGURE 12.1

Cleanup Tasks Menu

```
CLEANUP                            Cleanup Tasks
                                                             System:   AS400
To select one of the following, type its number below and press Enter:

     1. Change cleanup options
     2. Start cleanup at scheduled time
     3. Start cleanup immediately
     4. End cleanup











Type a menu option below
     _

F1=Help   F3=Exit   F9=Command line   F12=Cancel
```

Selecting option 1, "Change cleanup options," on this menu brings up the Change Cleanup Options display (Figure 12.2). (To bypass the menus, you can just prompt and execute the ChgClnUp, or Change Cleanup, command.)

Note

To change cleanup options, you must have *AllObj, *JobCtl, and *SecAdm special authorities, as well as *Use authority to user profile QPgmr. If option 1 doesn't appear on the Cleanup Tasks menu, you don't have the proper authorities.

FIGURE 12.2

Change Cleanup Options Panel

```
                        Change Cleanup Options                         AS400
                                                             09/05/00  12:10:02
Type choices below, then press Enter.

Allow automatic cleanup . . . . . . . . . . . .   Y             Y=Yes, N=No

Time cleanup starts each day  . . . . . . . . .   22:00:00__    00:00:00-
                                                                23:59:59,
                                                                *SCDPWROFF,
                                                                *NONE

Number of days to keep:
  User messages . . . . . . . . . . . . . . . .   7____         1-366, *KEEP
  System and workstation messages . . . . . . .   4____         1-366, *KEEP
  Job logs and other system output  . . . . . .   7____         1-366, *KEEP
  System journals and system logs . . . . . . .   30___         1-366, *KEEP
  OfficeVision for AS/400 calendar items  . . .   30___         1-366, *KEEP




F1=Help   F3=Exit   F5=Refresh   F12=Cancel
```

Using the Change Cleanup Options screen, you can enable OA's automatic cleanup function and specify that cleanup should run either at a specific time each day or as part of any scheduled system power-off. To tell the system you want to enable automatic cleanup, specify Y for the AlwClnUp (Allow automatic cleanup) parameter. For parameter StrTime (Time cleanup starts each day), enter a specific time (e.g., 23:00:00) for the cleanup to start, or specify *ScdPwrOff to tell the system to run cleanup during a system power-off that you've scheduled using OA's power-scheduling function (the cleanup won't be run if you power off using any other method, such as the PwrDwnSys, or Power Down System, command). Although it's ideal to run cleanup procedures when the system is relatively free of other tasks, it's not required, and OA's cleanup won't conflict with application programs other than by competing for CPU cycles.

The other parameters on the Change Cleanup Options screen let you control which objects the procedure will try to clean up. Each parameter allows a value of either *Keep, which tells the system not to clean up the specified objects, or a number from 1 to 366 that indicates the number of days the objects or entries are allowed to stay on the system before the cleanup procedure removes them. The table in Figure 12.3 lists the cleanup options and the objects they automatically clean up.

FIGURE 12.3
Automatic Cleanup Functions

Cleanup option	***Cleans up***
User messages	• User message queues
System and workstation messages	• Workstation message queues • System operator message queue (QSysOpr)
Job logs and other system output	• Output queue QEZJobLog (job logs) • Output queue QEZDebug (service and program dumps)
System journals and system logs	• Journal receivers: QAOSDIAJRN Document Interchange Architecture (DIA) files QDSNX Distributed Systems Node Executive (DSNX) logs QSNADS SNA Distribution Services (SNADS) files QSNMP Simple Network Management Protocol (SNMP) QSXJRN Problem databases QLYJRN Application Development Manager transactions QPFRADJ Performance adjustment data QX400 Open Systems Interconnection (OSI) Message Services/400 QCQJMJRN Managed System Services/400 QO1JRN Application enabler OFC files ADJRNLO Application program driver files QLYPRJLOG Project logs QMAJRN Order assistance requests QZMF Mail server framework logging QVPN Virtual private networking support QZCAJRN SNMP database QACGJRN Job accounting data • History log • Problem log • Alerts database • PTF information
OfficeVision for AS/400 calendar items	• Calendar entries • RgzDLO and RgzPFM for some OfficeVision files is also run

Look closely at the list of objects cleaned up by the "Job logs and other system output" option. When you activate this option, the system places all job logs into output queue QUsrSys/QEZJobLog and places all dumps (e.g., system and program dumps) into output queue QUsrSys/QEZDebug. The cleanup procedure removes from these output queues any spool files that remain on the system beyond the maximum number of days.

OS/400 uses a variety of database files and journals to manage operating system functions (e.g., job accounting, performance adjustment, SNA Distribution Services, the problem log). Regular, hands-off cleanup of these journals and logs is the single most beneficial function of the automatic cleanup procedures. Without this automatic cleanup, you must locate the files and journals and write your own procedures to clean them up. This, along with the possibility that IBM could change or add to these objects in a future release of OS/400, makes this cleanup option the most helpful.

For OfficeVision users, the "OfficeVision for AS/400 calendar items" cleanup option is an effective way to manage the size of several OfficeVision production objects. This option cleans up old calendar items and reorganizes essential database files and document library objects (DLOs) to help maintain peak performance.

To enable automatic cleanup, execute option 2 (Start cleanup at scheduled time) from menu CLEANUP (Figure 12.1). If you ever want to stop the automatic daily cleanup, just select option 4 (End cleanup) to stop all automatic cleanup until you restart it using option 2.

Manual Cleanup Procedures

OA's automatic cleanup won't do everything for you. Figure 12.4 lists cleanup tasks you must handle manually. By "manually," we mean you must manually execute commands that clear entries or reorganize files or you must write a set of automated cleanup tools you can run periodically or along with OA's daily cleanup operations.

Let's take a closer look at each of these options.

FIGURE 12.4

Suggested Manual Cleanup Operations

Cleaning up system-supplied objects:	***Cleaning up user-defined objects:***
Detach, save, and clean up security audit journal receivers	Detach, save, and clean up journal receivers
Reclaim spool file storage	Reset user message queue size
Reclaim storage	Clean up spooled files
Clean up the recovery areas	Clear or delete save files no longer needed
Remove unused licensed program products	Delete unused objects
Permanently apply PTFs as necessary	Reorganize document library objects
	Purge and reorganize physical files
	Clean up OfficeVision for AS/400 objects
	Clean up hardware configuration

Detach, Save, and Clean Up Security Audit Journal Receivers

If you activate the security audit journaling process, the receiver associated with the security audit journal, QAudJrn, will grow continuously as long as it's attached to QAudJrn. In fact, if you select all possible auditing values, this receiver will grow rapidly. As with all journal receivers, you're responsible for receiver maintenance. Here are our recommendations.

First, don't place audit journal receivers in library QSys (QAudJrn itself must be in QSys, but receivers can reside in any library and in any auxiliary storage pool). Instead, place them in a library (e.g., one called AudLib) that you can save and maintain separately. Then, each week, use the ChgJrn (Change Journal) command to detach the old receiver from QAudJrn and attach a new one.

Also, make sure your regular backup procedure saves the security journal receivers (only detached receivers are fully saved). If you specify "System journals and system logs" on the Change Cleanup Options panel, OA's automated cleanup operation deletes old security audit journal receivers that are no longer attached to journals. Your backup strategy should include provisions for retaining several months of security journal receivers in case you need to track down a security problem.

Reclaim Spool File Storage

The iSeries has an operating-system–managed database in library QSpl that contains a member for every spooled file (e.g., job log, user report, Print key output) on the system. When you or the system creates a spooled file, OS/400 uses an empty member in the spool file database if one is available; otherwise, it creates a new member. Whenever a spooled file is deleted or printed, the operating system clears that file's database member, readying it for reuse. However, even empty database members occupy a significant amount of space. If you create many spooled files, this database can grow to the point of wasting considerable space.

The iSeries provides a couple of methods for cleaning up these empty database members. You can use system value QRclSplStg (Reclaim spool storage) to limit the number of days an empty member remains on the system. Valid values include whole numbers from 1 to 366; the default is eight days. When an empty member reaches the specified limit, the system deletes the member. *None is also a valid value, but it's impractical because it causes the system to generate a new database member for each spooled file you create, thus overburdening the system and impacting performance. A value of *NoMax tells the system to ignore automatic spool storage cleanup.

The RclSplStg (Reclaim Spool Storage) command provides a method of on-demand spooled file housecleaning. If you want to control spooled file cleanup yourself rather than have the system do it, you can enter a value of *NoMax for system value QRclSplStg and then execute the RclSplStg command whenever necessary.

Reclaim Storage and Clean Up Recovery Areas

You should use the RclStg (Reclaim Storage) command periodically to reclaim wasted space in your system's database cross-reference files. These files contain information about all files and fields on your system. Left unchecked, these cross-reference files typically become huge and contain a considerable amount of wasted space.

With RclStg, you can opt to run all reclaim functions, database cross-reference reclamation only, or all functions except the database cross-reference reclamation. Typically, you'll run only the database cross-reference portion. To do so, issue the command

```
RclStg Select(*DbXRef)
```

If you're experiencing lost or damaged objects, you'll need to reclaim the entire system or the entire system without the database cross-reference files portion. This process will find damaged or lost objects and ensure that all auxiliary storage is either used properly or available for use. Unexpected power failures, device failures, or other abnormal job endings can create unusual conditions in storage, such as damaged objects, objects with no owners, or even objects that exist in no library (i.e., the library name is absent). During a reclaim of storage, the system puts any damaged or lost objects it encounters into one of several recovery areas (detailed below) depending on the object type.

Tip

It's wise to delete or clear the recovery areas before running the RclStg command. If RclStg tries to place an object in the recovery area and there's an existing object with the same name and object type, the system generates meaningless names for the new object. The system does place the original name in the object text, but it's far better just to avoid the confusion of renamed objects and old objects that no longer apply. Cleaning up after a RclStg can be tasking enough without contributing to the confusion.

How RclStg Deals with Lost Objects

Let's turn our attention to the action RclStg takes with lost objects.

If the lost object normally resides in a library (i.e., in the QSys.Lib file system), the system tries to place the object in recovery library QRcl, using the following rules:

- If a lost object with the same name and object type already exists in the recovery library, the system renames the newly encountered object using the form QRcl*nnnnnn*, where *nnnnnn* is a unique number. To help you identify these objects, the system places the original object name in the object's text description.
- If the lost object is a physical file for which data exists, the system tries to rebuild the file in library QRcl. The object description's text value indicates that the file has been rebuilt. To recover the file, you can re-create the original file in the original library

and then copy data from the recovered object in library QRcl. Be aware that the data in the recovered file may be incomplete.

- If the lost object is a user domain object (object type *UsrSpc, *UsrIdx, or *UsrQ), it can be placed in library QRcl only if system value QAlwUsrDmn (Allow user domain objects) is *All or contains the value QRcl. If QAlwUsrDmn prevents placing the user domain object in library QRcl, the object is deleted.
- If the object has lost its owner, the system assigns the object to an IBM-supplied user profile based on object type. Most objects are assigned to user profile QDftOwn.
- If descriptions for objects in a library are not accessible, the system rebuilds the library.
- If the lost object is secured by a damaged authorization list or authority holder, the system assigns authorization list QRclAutL to the object. To determine the objects secured by QRclAutL, use command DspAutLObj (Display Authorization List Objects).

When a lost object resides in a file system other than QSys.Lib, the system performs recovery using the following rules:

- If the lost object was in the root file system, the object is placed in the /QReclaim directory.
- If the lost object was in the QOpenSys file system, it is placed in the /QOpenSys/QReclaim directory.
- If an object in a directory is damaged to the extent that it is unusable, the system deletes it.
- If the lost object was in a user-defined file system (UDFS), it is placed in the /QReclaim directory located in the root directory of the UDFS.
- If a lost object that was in a directory can't be placed in the appropriate /QReclaim directory, it is placed in the root directory of a special file system within the auxiliary storage pool (ASP) in which the object resides. The file system is named /dev/QASP*nn*/QReclaimFS.udfs, where *nn* is the ASP number.
- For objects in the root file system, the QOpenSys file system, or a user-defined file system, the system takes action for issues such as duplicate names and unidentified object owners in a fashion similar to the actions taken for objects in libraries (the QSys.Lib file system).

Recovering After RclStg

After storage is reclaimed, you should examine the recovery areas and perform any necessary recovery steps. The following recovery checklist can help guide you in finding and fixing problems. (The sidebar below lists the commands used in recovery area cleanup.)

1. Issue the **DspMsg QSysOpr** and **DspLog** commands, searching for messages about damaged objects. Using the information located, you should
   - delete unusable objects and then restore them from backup
   - re-create each necessary physical file and use the CpyF command to copy data from the file in library QRcl to the newly created file
2. Issue command **DspLib QRcl** to display the objects in the recovery library. If the RclStg command placed no objects in this recovery area, you may receive a message indicating the library doesn't exist. In that case, continue with the next step. Otherwise, using the information located, you should
   - move user-created objects (using command MovObj) from library QRcl to the correct library
   - if library QRcl contains IBM-supplied objects, contact your software support provider for assistance
3. Issue command **DspLnk** to display directory /QReclaim. If the RclStg command placed no objects in this recovery area, you may receive a message indicating the object doesn't exist. In that case, continue with the next step. Otherwise, using the information located, you should
   - move objects (using command Mov) from directory /QReclaim to the correct directory

Commands Used in Recovery Area Cleanup

AddMFS (Add Mounted File System)
CpyF (Copy File)
DspAutLObj (Display Authorization List Objects)
DspLib (Display Library)
DspLnk (Display Object Links)
DspLog (Display Log)
DspMsg (Display Messages)
Mov (Move)
MovObj (Move Object)
WrkObjOwn (Work with Objects by Owner)

4. Issue command **DspLnk** to display directory /QOpenSys/QReclaim. If the RclStg command placed no objects in this recovery area, you may receive a message indicating the object doesn't exist. In that case, continue with the next step. Otherwise, using the information located, you should
   - move objects (using command Mov) from directory /QOpenSys/QReclaim to the correct directory
5. Issue the command **DspMsg QSysOpr**, searching for message CPFA0D7. For each CPFA0D7 message that contains a directory name starting with /dev/QASP*nn*/ (where *nn* is the ASP number), perform the problem-resolution action. Using the information located, you should
   - issue command **AddMFS** to mount the user-defined file system specified in the CPFA0D7 message over a directory of your choice. Using command DspLnk, examine the contents of the UDFS. You should see reclaimed objects (beginning with QRcl) or directory /QReclaim. If you see directory /QReclaim, look therein to find the reclaimed objects.
   - move objects (using command Mov) to the correct directory. You may be able to obtain the original object name by examining the CPFA0D7 message. If the message doesn't contain the original object name, use the DspLnk command's Display attributes option and try to locate the original name in the object's attributes.
6. Issue the command **WrkObjOwn QDftOwn** to display objects owned by user profile QDftOwn.
   - From the Work with Objects by Owner display, use option 9 (Change owner) to transfer object ownership to the correct user profile.
7. Issue the command **DspAutLObj QRclAutL** to examine objects whose authorization list has been set to QRclAutL. If the RclStg command placed no objects in this recovery area, you may receive a message indicating the authorization list doesn't exist. In that case, ignore the message. Otherwise, you should
   - assign the object to the correct authorization list

When you're comfortable that you've completed your work with the recovery areas, you should delete or clear them.

Keep in mind that you can execute the RclStg command only when the system is in restricted state (i.e., all subsystems must be ended). You also need to check system value QAlwUsrDmn to make sure that its value is *All or that library QRcl is among the libraries listed. If neither of these is the case, document the current value and then use command ChgSysVal (Change System Value) to add library QRcl to the list of values. (Be sure to reset QAlwUsrDmn after you're finished reclaiming the system.)

You can use OA's disk analysis reports, which list the space taken up by damaged objects, objects without owners, and objects without libraries, to determine when you need to do a RclStg. For more information about the OS/400 RclStg function, see *OS/400 Backup and Recovery* (SC41-5304).

Remove Unused Licensed Program Products

Another way to reclaim disk storage is to remove unused licensed program products, such as product demos, old third-party products you no longer use, and IBM products once you're finished with them. After saving any libraries and objects you no longer need, delete the unnecessary products.

To begin, use the DspSfwRsc (Display Software Resources) command to print a list of software resources on your system:

```
DspSfwRsc Output(*Print)
```

On the printout, clearly mark the software products you want to delete.

Caution

As silly as this may sound, be certain you don't need a product before you delete it! You should seriously consider saving licensed programs before you delete them. Do so, and you'll save yourself considerable grief should you make a mistake.

You can use options on the LICPGM menu to save and delete unwanted licensed programs. Be sure to refer to your printed list of software resources because some products may not appear when using menu LICPGM. If a product doesn't appear on the menu, you can use the SavLicPgm and DltLicPgm commands to save and delete the licensed program, respectively.

Permanently Apply PTFs as Necessary

If disk consumption is high on your system, consider permanently applying any temporarily applied PTFs. This action cleans up temporary objects as well as the PTF index. To apply the PTFs, use command ApyPTF.

Detach, Save, and Clean Up Journal Receivers

If you use journaling on your system, you need to manage the journals you create. As with the security audit journal receivers, you should detach and save receivers as part of your normal backup and recovery strategy. Then you can delete receivers you no longer need. For more information about journaling and managing journals and receivers, refer to *OS/400 Backup and Recovery*.

Reset User Message Queue Size

User-created messages can also add to the clutter on the system. As messages accumulate, message queues grow to accommodate them. But queues don't become smaller as messages are removed. Although OA's automatic cleanup clears old messages from user and workstation message queues, it doesn't reset the message queue size.

To reset a queue to its original size, you must use the ClrMsgQ (Clear Message Queue) command to completely clear the message queue. Again, you can perform this task manually for specific message queues, or you can automate the process by writing a program.

Clean Up Spooled Files

What about user-created spooled output? OA's cleanup addresses job logs and certain service and program dump output. But when users create spooled files, these files also stay on the system until the user prints or deletes them. You need to either monitor user-created output queues or have users monitor their own.

Clear or Delete Unneeded Save Files

If you frequently use save files for ad hoc or regular backups, you may want to define a manual or automated procedure to periodically clear those save files and reclaim that storage. After you save a save file's data to media, clear the file by executing the ClrSavF (Clear Save File) command.

Delete Unused Objects

Old and unused objects of various kinds can accumulate on your system, unnecessarily consuming storage and degrading performance. You should evaluate objects that aren't used regularly to determine whether they should remain on the system. Remember to check development and test libraries as well as production libraries.

The description of each object on the system includes a "last used" timestamp as well as a "last used" days counter. The object description also contains "last changed" and "last saved" timestamps. You can use this information to help determine whether an object is obsolete.

To collect information about and analyze disk space utilization, you can use the Disk Space Tasks menu (Figure 12.5). You can reach this menu directly by typing **Go DiskTasks**, or you can access it through the main OA menu. As you can see, the menu options let you collect and print disk space information as well as actually work with libraries, folders, and objects.

When you select option 1 to collect disk space information, you'll see the prompt in Figure 12.6. You can collect disk space information at a specified date and time by selecting option 1 (Date/time). Selecting option 2 (Weekly) or option 3 (Monthly) tells the system to collect information at the specified interval.

FIGURE 12.5
Disk Space Tasks Menu

```
DISKTASKS                      Disk Space Tasks
                                                            System:   AS400
To select one of the following, type its number below and press Enter:

     1. Collect disk space information
     2. Print disk space information

    10. Work with libraries
    11. Work with folders
    12. Work with objects by owner









Type a menu option below
     __

F1=Help   F3=Exit   F9=Command line   F12=Cancel
```

FIGURE 12.6
Collect Disk Space Information Prompt

```
                        Collect Disk Space Information                 AS400
                                                            09/05/00
17:23:05

Information collected . . . . . . :


A job will be submitted to collect disk space information.  This job may
take several hours to complete, depending on the size of your system.


Type choice below, then press Enter.

  When to collect information . . .  _      1=Date/time
                                            2=Weekly
                                            3=Monthly





F1=Help   F3=Exit   F12=Cancel
```

Whichever option you choose, the system collects information about objects (e.g., database files, programs, commands, folders — including shared folders) and stores it in file QUsrSys/QAEZDisk. You can then select option 2 (Print disk space information) on the Disk Space Tasks menu to print reports that analyze disk space usage by library, folder, owner, or specific object. You can also print a disk information system summary report. Because the data is collected in a database file, you can also perform ad hoc interactive Structured Query Language (SQL) queries, use Query/400, or write high-level language programs to get the information you need.

Reorganize Document Library Objects

The RgzDLO (Reorganize Document Library Object) command reclaims unused space in document library objects. This command compresses documents, removing wasted space caused by editing changes. If your system has frequent document edit activity, reclaiming DLOs can return a significant amount of space.

Purge and Reorganize Physical Files

An active database environment can contribute to the system's sloppy habits. One problem is files in which records accumulate forever. You should examine your database to determine whether any files fit this description and then design a procedure to handle the "death" of active records.

In some situations, you can simply delete records that are no longer needed. In other situations, you might want to archive records before you delete them. In either case, you certainly won't want to delete or move records manually; instead, look for a public-domain or vendor-supplied file-edit utility or tool.

Deleting records doesn't increase your available disk space, though. Deleted records continue to occupy disk space until you execute a RgzPFM (Reorganize Physical File Member) command. You could search for files with a high percentage of deleted records and then manually reorganize those files. Or you could go one step further and write a custom utility that would search for those files and automatically reorganize them using the RgzPFM command. You should note that when you reorganize a file that is journaled, you must immediately save the file to preserve integrity.

Clean Up OfficeVision for AS/400 Objects

OfficeVision for AS/400 can devour disk space unless you clean up after it religiously. Encourage OfficeVision users to police their own documents and mail items and to delete items they no longer need. You can use the QryDocLib (Query Document Library) command as a reporting tool to monitor document and folder maintenance. You might also want to limit the auxiliary storage available to each user by using the MaxStg (Maximum allowed storage) parameter on each user profile.

In addition, consider reorganizing OfficeVision files. Candidate files begin with the letters QAO. Before trying to reorganize the files, be sure no users are using OfficeVision.

Clean Up Hardware Configuration

It's not uncommon for a system to have configuration descriptions for objects that no longer exist. You can save space and improve IPL performance by removing these descriptions from your system. Although the steps for doing so are documented in *Basic System Operation, Administration, and Problem Handling* (SC41-5206), we strongly suggest you contact your hardware service provider for assistance with this task.

Enhancing Your Manual Procedures

You can handle many of the manual tasks we've mentioned by using the system's QEZUsrClnp job to incorporate your own cleanup programs and commands into OA's automatic cleanup function. QEZUsrClnp is essentially an empty template that gives you a place to add your own cleanup code. Every time OA's automatic cleanup function runs, it calls QEZUsrClnp and executes your code.

To add your enhancements to QEZUsrClnp, first use the RtvCLSrc (Retrieve CL Source) command to retrieve the source statements for QEZUsrClnp (Figure 12.7) from library QSys. Then, insert your cleanup commands or calls to your cleanup programs into the QEZUsrClnp source. Be sure to add your statements between the two SndPgmMsg (Send Program Message) commands to ensure that when your cleanup job ends, the system sends a completion message to the system operator message queue. While you're editing the source, go ahead and add some style to the layout of the code — RtvCLSrc certainly lacks it!

Last, compile your copy of QEZUsrClnp into a library that appears before library QSys on the system library list. (You can change the system library list by editing system value QSysLibL.) We caution you against replacing the system-supplied version of the program by compiling your copy of QEZUsrClnp into QSys. By using a different library, you can preserve the original program and avoid losing your modified program the next time you load a new release of the operating system.

In OA's automated cleanup function, the iSeries gives you the services of a maid to solve some simple cleanup issues. Use the function. Your cleanup shouldn't stop there, though. You also need to develop and implement procedures to maintain system-supplied and user-defined objects, such as spool files and save files.

FIGURE 12.7
CL Program QEZUsrClnp

```
/*******************************************************************/
/*                                                                 */
/* 5769SS1 V4R4M0 990521     RTVCLSRC Output     01/05/01 17:19:49 */
/*                                                                 */
/* Program name . . . . . . . . . . . . . . :   QEZUSRCLNP      PN*/
/* Library name . . . . . . . . . . . . . . :   QSYS            PL*/
/* Original source file . . . . . . . . . . :                   SN*/
/* Library name . . . . . . . . . . . . . . :                   SL*/
/* Original source member . . . . . . . . . :                   SM*/
/* Source file change                                             */
/*   date/time  . . . . . . . . . . . . . . :                   SC*/
/* Patch option . . . . . . . . . . . . . . :   *NOPATCH        PO*/
/* User profile . . . . . . . . . . . . . . :   *USER           UP*/
/* Text . . . :                                                 TX*/
/* Owner  . . . . . . . . . . . . . . . . . :   QSYS            OW*/
/* Patch change ID  . . . . . . . . . . . . :                   PC*/
/* Patch APAR ID  . . . . . . . . . . . . . :                   PA*/
/* User mod flag  . . . . . . . . . . . . . :   *NO             UM*/
/*                                                              ED*/
/*******************************************************************/
     PGM
     DCL VAR(&COIBM) TYPE(*CHAR) LEN(128) VALUE('      5738-SS1 (C) -
COPYRIGHT IBM CORP. 1980, 1991 ALL RIGHTS RESERVED. LICENSED -
MATERIALS - PROPERTY OF IBM')
     QSYS/SNDPGMMSG MSGID(CPI1E91) MSGF(QCPFMSG) TOMSGQ(*SYSOPR) -
MSGTYPE(*INFO)
```

•
• *Insert your own cleanup code here*
•

```
     QSYS/SNDPGMMSG MSGID(CPI1E92) MSGF(QCPFMSG) TOMSGQ(*SYSOPR) -
MSGTYPE(*INFO)
     RETURN
COPYWRITE: +
     QSYS/CHGVAR VAR(&COIBM) VALUE(&COIBM)
PGM_END:
     QSYS/ENDPGM
```

Chapter 13

All Aboard the OS/400 Job Scheduler!

by Bryan Meyers

How many times have you plastered the side of your workstation with sticky notes containing scribbled reminders to run various jobs at various times? Or perhaps your shop is more sophisticated and has a run-book with instructions about which jobs to run and when. Although these "organizational" methods may work, they make it easy to make a mistake or to forget to perform some functions. And how many times have you missed one of your children's soccer games or some other important function because you needed to stay a little late at the office to start a job after everyone was gone for the day? Sound familiar? If so, OS/400's job-scheduling capabilities provide the relief you need.

OS/400's job-scheduling function lets you schedule jobs to run at dates and times you choose without performing any add-on programming. You can schedule jobs in two ways:

- using parameters on the SbmJob (Submit Job) command
- using the job schedule object

The job schedule function — system job QJobScd — starts automatically when you IPL the system. This job monitors scheduled job requirements and then submits and releases scheduled jobs at the appropriate date and time.

Arriving on Time

The SbmJob command places a job on a job queue for batch processing, apart from an interactive workstation session. The command's ScdDate (Schedule date) and ScdTime (Schedule time) parameters let you specify a date and time when the job should be run. This scheduling method is a one-time shot; you use it for a job that you want to run only once, at a later date and/or time. If you want a job to run more than once, you'll have to remember to submit the job each time (or use the job schedule object, as I discuss later).

When you use these parameters to indicate a schedule date and/or time, the SbmJob command places the job on a job queue in a scheduled state (SCD) until the date and time you specified; then the system releases the job on the job queue and processes it just like any other submitted job. If you specify Hold(*Yes) on the SbmJob command, at the appointed time the job's status on the queue will change from scheduled/held (SCD HLD) to held (HLD). You can then release the job when you choose.

The default value for the ScdDate and ScdTime parameters is *Current, which indicates that you want to submit the job immediately. Otherwise, you'll usually specify an exact date (in the same format as the job's date) and an exact time for the job to run. There are, however, other possible special values you may find useful for the ScdDate parameter.

If you specify value *MonthStr for parameter ScdDate, the job will be run at the scheduled time on the first day of the month. Value *MonthEnd specifies that the job should be run on the last day of the month (no more "Thirty days hath September..." or counting on your fingers!). Or you can specify a ScdDate value of *Mon, *Tue, *Wed, *Thu, *Fri, *Sat, or *Sun to run the job on the specified day of the week.

During which month, on which Monday, and so on, will your job be run? That depends. For example, if you've specified ScdDate(*MonthStr), and today is the first day of the month, and the current time is previous to the time in the ScdTime parameter... the job will be run today. Otherwise, it will wait until next month. Similar logic applies for other ScdDate and ScdTime possibilities.

If you remove a scheduled job from a job queue, the job won't be run, even when the scheduled date and time arrive. You can remove a job from a queue by using the ClrJobQ (Clear Job Queue) command or by using the WrkJobQ (Work with Job Queue) command and ending the job. Holding a job queue that includes a scheduled job can delay execution of the job, but it won't prevent the job from running when you release the job queue, even if the scheduled time has passed.

Running on a Strict Schedule

OS/400's job schedule object (type *JobScd) is a timetable that contains descriptive entries for jobs to be executed at a specific date, time, and frequency. It is most useful for jobs that you want to run repeatedly according to a set schedule. If a job is on the job schedule, you needn't remember to submit it for every execution; the operating system takes care of that chore. You can find information about job schedule entries in *OS/400 Work Management* (SC41-5306).

One job schedule object exists on the system: object QDftJobScd in library QUsrSys. Although its name indicates that this object is the default job schedule, it is in fact the only one. The operating system offers no commands to create, change, or delete your own customized job schedules... yet. You can manipulate the entries in the job schedule using the following CL commands:

- AddJobScdE (Add Job Schedule Entry)
- ChgJobScdE (Change Job Schedule Entry)
- HldJobScdE (Hold Job Schedule Entry)
- RlsJobScdE (Release Job Schedule Entry)
- RmvJobScdE (Remove Job Schedule Entry)
- WrkJobScdE (Work with Job Schedule Entries)

Figure 13.1 shows a sample list display like the one that appears when you run the WrkJobScdE command.

FIGURE 13.1
Work with Job Schedule Entries Panel

```
                        Work with Job Schedule Entries                 AS400
                                                           04/12/00  17:02:54

 Type options, press Enter.
   2=Change   3=Hold   4=Remove   5=Display details   6=Release
   8=Work with last submission    10=Submit immediately

                                                                     Next
                          -----Schedule------               Recovery  Submit
 Opt  Job          Status  Date        Time      Frequency   Action   Date
 __   BKPDLY       SCD     *ALL        21:00:00  *WEEKLY     *NOSBM   04/12/00
 __   QEZDKWKMTH   SCD     *SAT        03:00:00  *WEEKLY     *NOSBM   04/15/00
 __   PRTUSRINFO   SCD     04/17/00    01:30:00  *WEEKLY     *NOSBM   04/17/00
 __   VKEMBOSS     SCD     USER DEF    03:00:00  *WEEKLY     *NOSBM   04/17/00
 __   VKEMBOSS     SCD     USER DEF    03:15:00  *WEEKLY     *NOSBM   04/17/00
 __   VKEMBOSS     SCD     USER DEF    03:30:00  *WEEKLY     *NOSBM   04/17/00

                                                                       Bottom
 Parameters or command
 ===> _______________________________________________________________________
 F3=Exit   F4=Prompt            F5=Refresh   F6=Add    F9=Retrieve
 F11=Display job queue data     F12=Cancel   F17=Top   F18=Bottom
```

When you select option 5 (Display details) for an entry, you get a display such as the one in Figure 13.2. This example shows the details of a job that the system runs every weekday morning at 3:30.

Each job schedule entry is made up of many components that define the job to be run and describe the environment in which it will run. Figure 13.3 describes those components and lists the parameter keywords that the job-scheduling CL commands use.

FIGURE 13.2
Sample Job Schedule Entry Details Panel

```
                     Display Job Schedule Entry Details
                                                         System:   AS400
Job:   VKEMBOSS        Entry number:   000006      Status:   SCD

Last attempted submission:
  Status . . . . . . . . . . . . :   Job successfully submitted.

  Date . . . . . . . . . . . . . :   04/14/00
  Time . . . . . . . . . . . . . :   03:30:00
Last successful submission:
  Job  . . . . . . . . . . . . . :   VKEMBOSS
    User . . . . . . . . . . . . :     GUTHRIE
    Number . . . . . . . . . . . :     004580
  Date . . . . . . . . . . . . . :   04/14/00
  Time . . . . . . . . . . . . . :   03:30:00
Schedule day . . . . . . . . . . :   *MON  *TUE  *WED  *THU  *FRI
Schedule time  . . . . . . . . . :   03:30:00
Frequency  . . . . . . . . . . . :   *WEEKLY
Recovery action  . . . . . . . . :   *SBMHLD

Next submit date . . . . . . . . :   04/17/00
Command  . . . . . . . . . . . . :   CALL PGM(VKM085C) PARM('$VK' 6.00000 '*CURRE
NT' 'VALUE KARD' 'Y' 'SINCE' 'VJOBSCD003')

Job queue  . . . . . . . . . . . :   *JOBD
  Library  . . . . . . . . . . . :
Job queue status . . . . . . . . :
Job description  . . . . . . . . :   VJOBD
  Library  . . . . . . . . . . . :     VKMLIB
Scheduled by . . . . . . . . . . :   GUTHRIE
User profile . . . . . . . . . . :   QSYSOPR
Message queue  . . . . . . . . . :   QSYSOPR
  Library  . . . . . . . . . . . :     QSYS
Text . . . . . . . . . . . . . . :   Value Kard embossing - normal run
```

FIGURE 13.3
Job Schedule Entry Components

Entry component	*Command parameter*	*Description*
Job name	Job	Specifies the name of the job schedule entry.
Entry number	EntryNbr	Specifies the unique number of the job schedule entry.
Command to run	Cmd	Specifies the command the submitted job will execute.
Frequency	Frq	Controls how often the job will be submitted. Valid values are • *Once — Once only • *Weekly — Every week on the specified day(s) • *Monthly — Every month on the specified day(s)
Schedule date	ScdDate	Controls the date the job will be submitted. Valid values are • *Current — Today • *MonthStr — First day of month • *MonthEnd — Last day of month • *Date* — Specified date • *None — Submitted based on ScdDay parameter
Schedule day	ScdDay	Controls the day of the week on which the job will be submitted. Valid values are • *All — Every weekday • *Sun — Sunday • *Mon — Monday • *Tue — Tuesday • *Wed — Wednesday • *Thu — Thursday • *Fri — Friday • *Sat — Saturday • *None — Submitted based on ScdDate parameter
Schedule time	ScdTime	Controls the time of day when the job will be submitted. Valid values are • *Current — Immediately • *hhmmss* — Specified time
Relative day of month	RelDayMon	For Frq(*Monthly) entries submitted based on the ScdDay parameter, controls the relative day of the month when the job will be submitted. Valid values are • *n* — *n*th occurrence in the month • *Last — Last occurrence in the month
Save action	Save	For Frq(*Once) entries, controls whether the entry is saved after it is submitted. Valid values are • *Yes — Save entry after submission. • *No — Discard entry after submission.
Omit date	OmitDate	Specifies a list of up to 20 dates on which the job will not be submitted.
Recovery action	RcyAcn	Controls the action taken if a job cannot be submitted at the scheduled time. Valid values are • *SbmRls — Missed job is submitted in RLS (released) status. • *SbmHld — Missed job is submitted in HLD (held) status. • *NoSbm — Missed job is not submitted.

continued

FIGURE 13.3 CONTINUED

Entry component	*Command parameter*	*Description*
Job description	JobD	Contains the qualified job description name of the job description under which the job will be executed.
Job queue	JobQ	Specifies the name of the job queue to which the job will be submitted. Valid values are • *Name* — A qualified job queue name is used. • *JobD — The job queue found in the specified job description is used.
User profile	User	Specifies the name of the user profile under which the job is submitted. Valid values are • *Name* — The specified user profile is used. • *Current — The job is submitted using the user profile that added the job schedule entry. • *JobD — The user profile found in the specified job description is used.
Message queue	MsgQ	Provides the name of the message queue to which the submitted job sends messages. Valid values are • *Name* — The specified qualified message queue name is used. • *UsrPrf — Job uses message queue found in the user profile. • *None — Job does not send completion messages, and error messages are sent to QSysOpr.
Text description	Text	Text description of entry

You can print a list of your job schedule entries by entering the command

```
WrkJobScdE Output(*Print)
```

For detailed information about each job schedule entry on the list, use the command

```
WrkJobScdE Output(*Print) PrtFmt(*Full)
```

OS/400 gives each job schedule entry a sequence number to identify it uniquely. You usually refer to an entry by its job name, but if multiple entries exist with the same job name, you must also specify the sequence number to correctly refer to the entry. For example, Figure 13.1 shows three entries named VKEMBOSS. Displaying the details for each entry, however, would show that each has a unique sequence number.

The frequency component (Frq) of a schedule entry may seem confusing at first. It's obvious that you can schedule a job to run *Once, *Weekly, or *Monthly, but what if you want to schedule a daily job? In that case, you need to use an additional schedule entry element, the schedule day (ScdDay). To run a job every day, specify Frq(*Weekly) and ScdDay(*All). You can also run the job only on weekdays, using Frq(*Weekly) and ScdDay(*Mon *Tue *Wed *Thu *Fri). Just Thursdays? That's easy: Frq(*Weekly) and ScdDay(*Thu).

The schedule date component (ScdDate) of a schedule entry tells the system a specific date on which to run the job. If you use the ScdDay parameter, you can't use the ScdDate parameter; the two don't make sense together. The combination of Frq(*Monthly) and ScdDate(*MonthEnd) will run a job on the last day of each month, regardless of how many days each month has.

The relative day of the month component (RelDayMon) gives the job schedule even more flexibility. For instance, if you want to run a job on only the first Tuesday of each month, you indicate values for three parameters: Frq(*Monthly), ScdDay(*Tue), and RelDayMon(1).

Sometimes your computer can't run a job at the scheduled time; for example, your system may be powered off or in the restricted state at the time the job is to be submitted. In the recovery action component (RcyAcn) of the schedule entry, you can tell the computer to take one of three actions. RcyAcn(*SbmRls) submits the job to be run as soon as possible. RcyAcn(*SbmHld) submits the job but holds it until you explicitly release it for processing. RcyAcn(*NoSbm) is the "You snooze, you lose" option — the job scheduler won't try to submit the job after the scheduled time passes. Notice that this feature applies only to jobs scheduled from the job schedule, not to those you submit using SbmJob.

Two Trains on the Same Track

When setting up job schedule entries for your system, you may discover that some of the entries you need to make are similar. You may want to copy a job schedule entry to save yourself the drudgery of retyping long, error-prone command strings. Unfortunately, the job schedule commands don't offer such a function. Lucky for you, though, I provide such a command here.

The command, CrtDupScdE (Create Duplicate Job Schedule Entry), is easy to use. You simply supply the command with two things — the job name of the existing job schedule entry from which you want to copy and a name you want to give the copy:

```
CrtDupScdE FromJob(JobName) NewName(NewJobName)
```

The NewName parameter defaults to special value *FromJob, indicating that the new entry should have the same name as the original; the system will give the entry a unique sequence number.

Figure 13.4 provides the code for the CrtDupScdE command. Figure 13.5 shows the command processing program.

FIGURE 13.4

CrtDupScdE Command Source

```
/*  ==============================================================  */
/*  =  Command....... CrtDupScdE                                =  */
/*  =  Source type... CMD                                       =  */
/*  =  Description... Create Duplicate Job Schedule Entry       =  */
/*  =                                                           =  */
/*  =  CPP........... CrtDupSE1A                                =  */
/*  ==============================================================  */

            Cmd        Prompt( 'Create Dup Schedule Entry' )
```

continued

FIGURE 13.4 CONTINUED

```
             Parm          Kwd( FromJob )                                    +
                           Type( *Name )                                     +
                           Len( 10 )                                         +
                           Min( 1 )                                          +
                           Prompt( 'From job name' )

             Parm          Kwd( NewName )                                    +
                           Type( *Name )                                     +
                           Len( 10 )                                         +
                           Dft( *FromJob )                                   +
                           SpcVal( ( *FromJob ) )                            +
                           Prompt( 'New job name' )
```

FIGURE 13.5

CrtDupScdE Command Processing Program CrtDupSE1A

```
/*  ============================================================  */
/*  =  Program....... CrtDupSE1A                                =  */
/*  =  Source type... CLP                                       =  */
/*  =  Type.......... Command processing program for CrtDupScdE =  */
/*  =  Description... Create duplicate job schedule entry       =  */
/*  =  -------------------------------------------------------- =  */
/*  =  Parameters                                               =  */
/*  =                                                           =  */
/*  =    &JobName          Input     Job name of job to duplicate =  */
/*  =                                                           =  */
/*  =    &NewName          Input     Job name for duplicate entry =  */
/*  ============================================================  */

Pgm        (                                                          +
             &FromJob                                                 +
             &NewName                                                 +
           )

/*  ============================================================  */
/*  = Variable declarations                                     =  */
/*  ============================================================  */

  Dcl        &FromJob    *Char       (   10    )
  Dcl        &NewName    *Char       (   10    )
  Dcl        &Cmd        *Char       (  512    )
  Dcl        &CmdStr     *Char       ( 3000    )
  Dcl        &Continue   *Char       (   16    )
  Dcl        &EntLen     *Char       (    4    )
  Dcl        &Entry      *Char       ( 1156    )
  Dcl        &Frq        *Char       (   10    )
  Dcl        &Header     *Char       (  140    )
  Dcl        &JobD       *Char       (   20    )
  Dcl        &JobQ       *Char       (   20    )
  Dcl        &MsgQ       *Char       (   20    )
  Dcl        &NbrEnt     *Char       (    4    )
  Dcl        &Offset     *Char       (    4    )
```

continued

FIGURE 13.5 *CONTINUED*

```
   Dcl         &RcyAcn      *Char      (   10    )
   Dcl         &RelDayMon   *Char      (   50    )
   Dcl         &Save        *Char      (   10    )
   Dcl         &ScdDate     *Char      (   10    )
   Dcl         &ScdDay      *Char      (   70    )
   Dcl         &ScdTime     *Char      (    6    )
   Dcl         &StrPos      *Char      (    4    )
   Dcl         &Text        *Char      (   50    )
   Dcl         &User        *Char      (   10    )
   Dcl         &UsrSpc      *Char      (   20    )   ( 'ZZSCDL0200QTEMP' )
   Dcl         &MsgID       *Char      (    7    )
   Dcl         &MsgF        *Char      (   10    )
   Dcl         &MsgFLib     *Char      (   10    )
   Dcl         &MsgDta      *Char      (  100    )

/*  ==================================================================  */
/*  = Global error monitor                                           =  */
/*  ==================================================================  */

  MonMsg      ( CPF0000 MCH0000 ) Exec(                                  +
    Goto        Error                  )

/*  ==================================================================  */
/*  =  Substitute new name when special value *FromJob specified     =  */
/*  ==================================================================  */

  If          ( &NewName *Eq '*FROMJOB' )                                +
    ChgVar      &NewName     ( &FromJob )

/*  ==================================================================  */
/*  =  Create temporary user space to hold schedule entry list       =  */
/*  ==================================================================  */

  DltUsrSpc   %Sst( &UsrSpc 11 10 )/%Sst( &UsrSpc 1 10)
  MonMsg      ( CPF0000 )

  Call        QUSCrtUS                                                   +
              (                                                          +
                &UsrSpc                                                  +
                'CRTDUPSCDE'                                             +
                X'00000100'                                              +
                ' '                                                      +
                '*ALL'                                                   +
                ' '                                                      +
              )

/*  ==================================================================  */
/*  =  Retrieve schedule entry list to user space                    =  */
/*  ==================================================================  */

  Call        QWCLScdE                                                   +
              (                                                          +
                &UsrSpc                                                  +
                'SCDL0200'                                               +
                &FromJob                                                 +
                &Continue                                                +
                0                                                        +
              )
```

continued

FIGURE 13.5 CONTINUED

```
/*   ==============================================================   */
/*   =  Retrieve header                                            =   */
/*   ==============================================================   */

  Call        QUSRtvUS                                                  +
              (                                                         +
                &UsrSpc                                                 +
                X'00000001'                                             +
                X'0000008C'                                             +
                &Header                                                 +
              )

/*   ==============================================================   */
/*   =  Exit if list is incomplete or there are no entries         =   */
/*   ==============================================================   */

  If          ( %Sst( &Header 104 1 ) *Eq 'I' )                         +
    SndPgmMsg  MsgID( CPF9898 )                                         +
               MsgF( QSys/QCPFMsg )                                     +
               MsgDta( 'Job schedule entry list is incomplete' )        +
               MsgType( *Escape )

  ChgVar      &NbrEnt      ( %Sst( &Header 133 4 ) )

  If          ( %Bin( &NbrEnt ) *Eq 0 )                                 +
    SndPgmMsg  MsgID( CPF9898 )                                         +
               MsgF( QSys/QCPFMsg )                                     +
               MsgDta( 'No job schedule entries exist' )                +
               MsgType( *Escape )

/*   ==============================================================   */
/*   =  Get entry length and offset from header and calculate      =   */
/*   =  start position based on offset                             =   */
/*   ==============================================================   */

  ChgVar      &EntLen      ( %Sst( &Header 137 4 ) )
  ChgVar      &Offset      ( %Sst( &Header 125 4 ) )

  ChgVar      ( %Bin( &StrPos ) )   ( %Bin( &Offset ) + 1 )

/*   ==============================================================   */
/*   =  Retrieve first entry in the list                           =   */
/*   ==============================================================   */

  Call        QUSRtvUS                                                  +
              (                                                         +
                &UsrSpc                                                 +
                &StrPos                                                 +
                &EntLen                                                 +
                &Entry                                                  +
              )

/*   ==============================================================   */
/*   =  Extract parameters from the entry                          =   */
/*   ==============================================================   */

  ChgVar      &Cmd         ( %Sst( &Entry 645 512 ) )
  ChgVar      &Frq         ( %Sst( &Entry 108  10 ) )
```

continued

FIGURE 13.5 CONTINUED

```
  ChgVar     &ScdDate    ( %Sst( &Entry  22   10 ) )
  ChgVar     &ScdDay     ( %Sst( &Entry  32   70 ) )
  ChgVar     &ScdTime    ( %Sst( &Entry 102    6 ) )
  ChgVar     &RelDayMon  ( %Sst( &Entry 118   50 ) )
  ChgVar     &Save       ( %Sst( &Entry 577   10 ) )
  ChgVar     &RcyAcn     ( %Sst( &Entry 168   10 ) )

  If         ( %Sst( &Entry 537 10 ) *NE ' ' )                 +
    ChgVar     &JobD        ( %Sst( &Entry 537 10 )            +
                              *TCat                            +
                              '/'                              +
                              *TCat                            +
                              %Sst( &Entry 527 10 ) )
  Else
    ChgVar     &JobD        ( %Sst( &Entry 527 10 ) )

  If         ( %Sst( &Entry 208 10 ) *NE ' ' )                 +
    ChgVar     &JobQ        ( %Sst( &Entry 208 10 )            +
                              *TCat                            +
                              '/'                              +
                              *TCat                            +
                              %Sst( &Entry 198 10 ) )
  Else
    ChgVar     &JobQ        ( %Sst( &Entry 198 10 ) )

  ChgVar     &User       ( %Sst( &Entry 547 10 ) )

  If         ( %Sst( &Entry 567 10 ) *NE ' ' )                 +
    ChgVar     &MsgQ        ( %Sst( &Entry 567 10 )            +
                              *TCat                            +
                              '/'                              +
                              *TCat                            +
                              %Sst( &Entry 557 10 ) )
  Else
    ChgVar     &MsgQ        ( %Sst( &Entry 557 10 ) )

  ChgVar     &Text       ( 'Copy of'                           +
                           *BCat                               +
                           &FromJob )

/*  ==============================================================  */
/*  = Build command string to add new job schedule entry         =  */
/*  ==============================================================  */

  ChgVar     &CmdStr     ( 'ADDJOBSCDE'                        +
                           *BCat                               +
                           'JOB('                              +
                           *TCat                               +
                           &NewName                            +
                           *TCat                               +
                           ')'                                 +
                           *BCat                               +
                           'CMD('                              +
                           *TCat                               +
                           &Cmd                                +
                           *TCat                               +
                           ')'                                 +
```

continued

Figure 13.5 *Continued*

```
*BCat                                                  +
'FRQ('                                                 +
*TCat                                                  +
&Frq                                                   +
*TCat                                                  +
')'                                                    +
*BCat                                                  +
'SCDDATE('                                             +
*TCat                                                  +
&ScdDate                                               +
*TCat                                                  +
')'                                                    +
*BCat                                                  +
'SCDDAY('                                              +
*TCat                                                  +
&ScdDay                                                +
*TCat                                                  +
')'                                                    +
*BCat                                                  +
'SCDTIME('                                             +
*TCat                                                  +
&ScdTime                                               +
*TCat                                                  +
')'                                                    +
*BCat                                                  +
'RELDAYMON('                                           +
*TCat                                                  +
&RelDayMon                                             +
*TCat                                                  +
')'                                                    +
*BCat                                                  +
'SAVE('                                                +
*TCat                                                  +
&Save                                                  +
*TCat                                                  +
')'                                                    +
*BCat                                                  +
'RCYACN('                                              +
*TCat                                                  +
&RcyAcn                                                +
*TCat                                                  +
')'                                                    +
*BCat                                                  +
'JOBD('                                                +
*TCat                                                  +
&JobD                                                  +
*TCat                                                  +
')'                                                    +
*BCat                                                  +
'JOBQ('                                                +
*TCat                                                  +
&JobQ                                                  +
*TCat                                                  +
')'                                                    +
```

continued

FIGURE 13.5 *CONTINUED*

```
                             *BCat                                      +
                             'USER('                                    +
                             *TCat                                      +
                             &User                                      +
                             *TCat                                      +
                             ')'                                        +
                             *BCat                                      +
                             'MSGQ('                                    +
                             *TCat                                      +
                             &MsgQ                                      +
                             *TCat                                      +
                             ')'                                        +
                             *BCat                                      +
                             'TEXT('''                                  +
                             *TCat                                      +
                             &Text                                      +
                             *TCat                                      +
                             ''')' )

/*  ============================================================  */
/*  = Add new job schedule entry                               =  */
/*  ============================================================  */

  Call        QCmdExc                                               +
              (                                                     +
                &CmdStr                                             +
                3000                                                +
              )

/*  ============================================================  */
/*  =  Clean up, send completion message, and exit             =  */
/*  ============================================================  */

  DltUsrSpc   %Sst( &UsrSpc 11 10 )/%Sst( &UsrSpc 1 10)
  MonMsg      ( CPF0000 )

  SndPgmMsg   MsgID( CPF9898 )                                      +
              MsgF( QSys/QCPFMsg )                                  +
              MsgDta( 'New job schedule entry added for job'        +
                      *BCat                                         +
                      &NewName )                                    +
              MsgType( *Comp )

  Return

/*  ============================================================  */
/*  = Error handler                                            =  */
/*  ============================================================  */

Error:

  DltUsrSpc   %Sst( &UsrSpc 11 10 )/%Sst( &UsrSpc 1 10)
  MonMsg      ( CPF0000 MCH0000 )
```

continued

FIGURE 13.5 CONTINUED

```
  RcvMsg       MsgType( *Excp )                                        +
               MsgDta( &MsgDta )                                       +
               MsgID( &MsgID )                                         +
               MsgF( &MsgF )                                           +
               MsgFLib( &MsgFLib )

  MonMsg       ( CPF0000 MCH0000 )

  SndPgmMsg    MsgID( &MsgID )                                         +
               MsgF( &MsgFLib/&MsgF )                                  +
               MsgDta( &MsgDta )                                       +
               MsgType( *Escape )

  MonMsg       ( CPF0000 MCH0000 )

/*  ============================================================  */
/*  = End of program                                           =  */
/*  ============================================================  */

EndPgm
```

CrtDupScdE uses the IBM-supplied program QWCLScdE (List Job Schedule Entries), a system API that lists job schedule entries to a user space. After retrieving the "from" job schedule entry (which you specified in the FromJob parameter), the program breaks down the output from the API into the parameter values that describe the entry; then it uses those values in the AddJobScdE command to create a new entry based on the existing one. After that, it's a simple matter for you to use the ChgJobScdE command to make any minor changes the new entry needs. You can find documentation for QWCLScdE and the user space layouts used in CrtDupScdE in *OS/400 Work Management APIs* (SC41-5878). The command also uses two user space APIs: QUSCrtUS (Create User Space) and QUSRtvUS (Retrieve User Space). (For more information about using APIs in CL programs, see Chapter 25.)

In addition to being easy to use, command CrtDupScdE is very basic. To conserve space, it doesn't include some features that you might want to add. The command retrieves only the first instance of a schedule entry with the name you choose, even though the job schedule could contain multiple entries of the same name. If you have multiple same-name entries and you want to retrieve one other than the first, you'll need to add the code to loop through the data structure that returns the name. Last, the command doesn't duplicate the seldom-used OmitDate values from the original entry. If you find you need to include this value, you can add the appropriate support. I encourage you to experiment with enhancing this command to suit your own needs.

Derailment Dangers

Before we finish exploring the OS/400 job schedule object, a few cautionary comments are in order. There are a few situations for which documentation is inadequate.

Job Schedule Entries and the LDA

It's important to know that a job submitted by the job schedule won't retain the contents of the local data area (LDA) from the job that originally added it to the job schedule. When you submit a job with the SbmJob command, however, the system passes a copy of the LDA to the submitted job. In some shops, it's a common practice to store variable processing values in the LDA as a handy means of communicating between jobs or between programs within a job. If your application depends on specific values in the LDA, you may want to schedule jobs using the SbmJob command instead of creating a job schedule entry.

There's an alternate technique, however, that still lets you take advantage of a job schedule entry for recurring jobs that need the LDA: When you add the job schedule entry, also create a unique data area that contains the proper values in the proper locations, according to the specifications in the submitted program. It's then a simple matter to make a minor change to the submitted program so that the program either uses the new data area instead of the LDA or retrieves the new data area and copies it to the LDA using the RtvDtaAra (Retrieve Data Area) and/or ChgDtaAra (Change Data Area) command. The new data area should be a permanent object on the system as long as the dependent job schedule entry exists.

SbmJob vs. the Job Scheduler

As you play with the job scheduler, you might experience some seemingly odd and confusing behavior. For instance, when you submit a job using SbmJob, it works fine, finding all the objects it requires. Yet, your job *sometimes* terminates abnormally when run from the job scheduler because it can't find some of the objects it needs! You may scratch your head for some time before realizing the nature of the problem. An understanding of why the two methods behave differently not only will make you more effective in using the job scheduler but also will highlight the fact that SbmJob has several benefits that the job scheduler doesn't offer.

Let's unravel the problem in which intermittently the job scheduler can't find some of the objects the job needs. When you run a job from the job scheduler, the system retrieves the library list to use from the InlLibL (Initial library list) attribute of the job description specified in the job scheduler entry. On the other hand, when you use SbmJob to execute your program, the system retrieves the library list to use from the InlLibL parameter of the SbmJob command itself. The default value for this parameter is *Current, which instructs the system to derive the library list from the current (submitting) job's attributes. This may or may not match the library list specified in the job description! All along, the problem has been that the job sometimes runs using a different library list and all required libraries are not in that list. Of course, you could change the command defaults for SbmJob so that the default is InlLibL(*JobD) and the two methods would retrieve the same library list, but that surely would introduce problems throughout the system.

Several such oddities await your discovery because SbmJob supports several more parameters than the job scheduler does. Examine the differences between the parameters available when adding a job scheduler entry and those shown by the SbmJob command, and you'll find other areas that behave differently.

You can still use the job scheduler, avoiding the confusion and taking advantage of the many extra benefits afforded by SbmJob. When adding entries to the job scheduler, you can use SbmJob in the scheduler's Cmd parameter. Then, in SbmJob's Cmd parameter, specify the actual command. The following examples demonstrate how the same job can be run from the job scheduler:

```
AddJobScdE Job(YourJob) Cmd(Call Pgm(YourPgm))
AddJobScdE Job(YourJob) Cmd(SbmJob Cmd(Call Pgm(YourPgm)))
```

In the second example, the job scheduler submits a new job, and you can take advantage of all of SbmJob's benefits.

A Matter of Timing

It's also noteworthy that, just like the railroad, the job-scheduling function may not always run on time, whether you use SbmJob or the job schedule object. Although you can schedule a job to the second, the load on your system determines when the job actually runs. The system submits a job schedule entry to a job queue or releases a scheduled job already on a job queue approximately on time — usually within a few seconds. However, if many jobs are waiting on the job queue ahead of the scheduled job, the scheduled job will simply have to wait its turn.

If it's critical that a job run at a specific time, you can help by ensuring that the job's priority (parameter JobPty) puts the job ahead of other jobs on the queue, but the job may still have to wait for an available activity slot before it can begin. And, as I mentioned earlier, if your system is down or in a restricted state at the appointed time, the job schedule may not submit the job at all.

System Date and Time Changes

Changing your system's date or time can also affect your scheduled jobs. If you move the date or time system values backward, the effect is fairly straightforward: The system won't reschedule any job schedule entries that were run within the repeated time. For example, if at three o'clock you change your system's time back to one o'clock, the job you had scheduled to run at two o'clock won't repeat itself. The system stores a "next submission" date and time for each entry, which it updates each time the job schedule submits a job.

Changing the system's date or time forward, however, can be tricky. If the change causes the system to skip over a time when you had a job scheduled, the job schedule's action depends on whether the system is in restricted state when you make the change. If the system was not restricted, any missed job schedule entries are submitted immediately (only one occurrence of each missed entry is submitted even if, for example, you've scheduled a job to run daily and moved the system date ahead two days). If the system is in restricted state when you change the date or time system values, the system refers to the RcyAcn attributes of the missed job schedule entries to determine whether to submit the jobs when you bring the system out of its restricted state.

Detecting the Completion of Other Jobs

Last, the job-scheduling function doesn't offer job completion dependencies, regardless of which method you use. For example, if you use the job schedule to run a daily transaction posting and then a daily closing, you can't condition the closing job to be run only if the posting job goes through to a successful completion. Some third-party scheduling functions offer this capability. Without a third-party product, if you need to schedule jobs with such a completion requirement, your best bet is probably to incorporate the entire procedure into a single CL program with appropriate escape routes defined in case one or more functions fail.

Chapter 14

Keeping Up with the Past

For many of you, iSeries job processing is new, or at least different. There can be multiple subsystems, job queues, output queues, and messages flying all over the place at once. You can sign on to the system and submit several batch jobs for immediate processing, or you can submit jobs to be run at night. At the same time, the system operator can run jobs and monitor their progress, and users at various remote sites can sign on to the system. With so much going on, you might wonder how you can possibly manage and audit such activity.

The History Log

One valuable iSeries tool at your fingertips is the history log, which contains information about the operation of the system and system status. The history log tracks high-level activities such as the start and completion of jobs, device status changes, system operator messages and replies, attempted security violations, and other security-related events. It records this information in the form of messages, which are stored in files created by the system.

You can learn a lot from history — even your system's history. By maintaining an accurate history log, you can monitor specific system activities and reconstruct events to aid problem determination and debugging efforts. Note that history logs are different from job logs. Whereas job logs record the sequential events of a job, the history log records certain operational and status messages pertaining to all the jobs on the system. You can review the history log to find a particular point of interest and then refer to a job log to investigate further.

System Message Show and Tell

You can display the contents of the history log by executing the following DspLog (Display Log) command:

```
DspLog Log(QHst)
```

The resulting display resembles the screen in Figure 14.1. The DspLog command lets you look at the contents of the history log as you would messages in a message queue. Because system events, such as job completions, invalid sign-on attempts, and line failures, are listed as messages in file QHst, you can place the cursor on a particular message and press the Help key (F1) to display second-level help text for the message.

Several DspLog command parameters provide flexibility when inquiring into the history log. To prompt for parameters, type **DspLog** and press F4. The system displays the screen shown in Figure 14.2.

FIGURE 14.1
History Log Panel

```
                          Display History Log Contents

Job 160839/QPGMR/DCP100 released by user QPGMR.
Job 160839/QPGMR/DCP100 started on 10/09/00 at 06:00:04 in subsystem QBATCH
Receiver ACG0239 in JRNLIB never fully saved. (I C)
C
Job 160839/QPGMR/DCP100 completed on 10/09/00 at 06:02:05. 32 seconds process
Vary Configuration (VRYCFG) command completed for line EAST.
Line EAST varied on successfully.
Vary Configuration (VRYCFG) command completed for controller CHICAGO.
Vary Configuration (VRYCFG) command completed for device CHICAGO.
Job 160921/DALLMKW/DSP10 started on 10/09/00 at 06:50:23 in subsystem QINTER
Controller CHICAGO contracted on line CHICAGO.
Communications device CHICAGO was allocated to subsystem QCMN.
Password from device DSP23 not correct for user QSECOFR.
Writer 160934/QSPLJOB/PGMRWTR started.
Load form type '*STD' device PGMRWTR writer PGMRWTR.  (H CG I R)
A parity error or stop bit error detected while communicating with device CHIC
Password from device BPC01023S1 not correct for user DALLDDW.

                                                                       More...
Press Enter to continue.

F3=Exit   F10=Display all   F12=Cancel
```

FIGURE 14.2
DspLog Command Prompt

```
                             Display Log (DSPLOG)

Type choices, press Enter.

Log . . . . . . . . . . . . . .   QHST______     QHST
Time period for log output:
  Start time and date:
  Beginning time . . . . . . . .  *AVAIL__      Time, *AVAIL
  Beginning date . . . . . . . .  *CURRENT      Date, *CURRENT, *BEGIN
  End time and date:
  Ending time  . . . . . . . . .  *AVAIL__      Time, *AVAIL
  Ending date  . . . . . . . . .  *CURRENT      Date, *CURRENT, *END
Output . . . . . . . . . . . . .  *_______      *, *PRINT, *PRTWRAP






                                                                        More...
F3=Exit   F4=Prompt   F5=Refresh   F12=Cancel   F13=How to use this display
F24=More keys
```

The parameters for the DspLog command are as follows:

- Log — The system refers to the history log as QHst.
- Period — You can enter a specific time period or accept the defaults for the beginning and ending period of time for which you want to display messages. Notice that the default for "Beginning time" is the earliest available time (*Avail) and the default for "Beginning date" is the current date (*Current). To look at previous days, you must supply a value.
- Output — You're probably familiar with this parameter. The value * results in output to the screen, and *Print results in a printed spooled file.
- Job — You use the Job parameter (not shown in Figure 14.2) to search for a specific job or set of jobs. You can enter just the job name, in which case the system might find several jobs with the same name that ran during the selected period of time. Or you can enter a specific job name, user name, and job number to retrieve the history information for a particular job.
- MsgID — Like the Job parameter, parameter MsgID (not shown in Figure 14.2) helps narrow your search. You can specify one message or multiple messages. By specifying 00 as the last two digits of the message ID, you can retrieve related (generic) sets of messages. For example, if you enter the message ID CPF2200, the system retrieves all messages from CPF2200 to CPF2299 (these are all security-related messages).

History Log Housekeeping

The history log consists of a message queue and system files that store history messages. The files belong to library QSys and begin with the letters QHST, followed by a number derived as *yydddn*, where *yyddd* stands for the Julian date on which the log was created and *n* represents a sequence character appended to the Julian date (0 through 9 or A through Z). The text description maintained by the system contains the beginning and ending date and time for the messages contained in the file, which is helpful for tracking activities that occurred during a particular time period.

You can use the DspObjD (Display Object Description) command to display a list of history files. The command

```
DspObjD Obj(QSys/QHst*) ObjType(*File)
```

results in a display similar to the one shown in Figure 14.3.

FIGURE 14.3
DspObjD Panel

```
                         Display Object Description - Basic

 Library:    QSYS                                                   Library 1 of 1

 Type options, press Enter.
   5=Display full attributes    8=Display service attributes

 Opt  Object       Type      Attribute      Freed        Size   Text
  _   QHST90278A   *FILE     PF              NO        803328   0901005002917090
  _   QHST90278B   *FILE     PF              NO        803328   0901005151433090
  _   QHST90281A   *FILE     PF              NO        180736   0901008083436090

                                                                          Bottom
 F3=Exit   F12=Cancel   F17=Top   F18=Bottom
```

The system creates a new file each time the existing file reaches its maximum size limit, which the system value QHstLogSiz (History log size) controls. Because the system itself doesn't automatically delete files, it's important to develop a strategy for deleting the log files (to save disk space) and for using the data before you delete the files.

You should maintain enough recent history on disk to be able to easily inquire into the log to resolve problems. The best way to manage history logs on your system is to take advantage of the automatic cleanup capabilities of Operational Assistant (OA), which we covered in Chapter 12. The OA category "System journals and system logs" lets you specify the number of days' worth of information to keep in the history log. OA then deletes log files older than the specified number of days.

Keep in mind that OA provides no strategy for archiving the history logs to a media that you can easily retrieve. If you activate OA cleanup procedures, make sure that once each month you save a copy of the QHst files. If you're remiss in performing this save, OA will still delete the log files.

If you choose not to use the automatic cleanup that OA offers, you can set up your own cleanup schedule. Here's one potential schedule:

- On the first day of each month, save all QHst files in library QSys to media. For quick reference, record on the media label the names of the beginning and ending log files.
- View the existing log files on the system, and delete any that are more than 30 days old. (Hint: Remember that the text description contains the beginning and ending date and time to help you determine the age of the file.)

To determine how much history log information to keep, you should consider the disk space required to store the information and schedule your file saves accordingly. In most cases, it's a good idea to keep 30 days of online history, although large installations with heavy history-log activity may need to save and delete objects every 15 days.

Inside Information

Careful review of history logs can alert you to unusual system activity. If, for example, the message "Password from device DSP23 not correct for user QSECOFR" appears frequently in the log, you might be prompted to find out who uses DSP23 and why he or she is trying to sign on with the system security officer profile. Or you might notice the message "Receiver ACG0239 in JRNLIB never fully saved (I C)." The second-level help text would tell you which program was trying to delete the journal receiver. If such events are brought to your attention, you might be able to prevent the loss of important information.

Maintaining a history log lets you reconstruct events that have taken place on your system. We're familiar with one company that used the history log in discovering that a programmer had planted a system "virus." A history log can also alert you to less serious occurrences (e.g., a specific sequence of jobs wasn't performed exactly as planned). You can use the history log to review all completion messages to find out how many jobs are executed on your system each day or which jobs ended abnormally. As you monitor the history log, you'll soon start to recognize the messages that are most beneficial to you.

The history log is a management tool that lets you quickly analyze system activities. It provides a certain amount of security auditing and lets you determine whether and when specific jobs were executed and how they ended. Using and maintaining a history log isn't difficult and could prove to be time well spent.

Note

The security journaling capabilities that OS/400 offers using the audit journal QAudJrn provide additional event-monitoring capabilities specifically related to security. This journal can monitor for the security-related events recorded in QHst as well as additional events that QHst doesn't record. For more information about QAudJrn, see *OS/400 Security – Reference* (SC41-5302).

Chapter 15

Backup Basics

by Debbie Saugen

The most valuable component of any computer system isn't the hardware or software that runs the computer but, rather, the data that resides on the system. If a system failure or disaster occurs, you can replace the computer hardware and software that runs your business. Your company's data, however, is irreplaceable. For this reason, it's critical to have a good backup and recovery strategy. Companies go out of business when their data can't be recovered.

What should you be backing up? The simple answer to this question is that you should back up everything. A basic rule of backup and recovery is that if you don't save it, it doesn't get restored. However, you may have some noncritical data (e.g., test data) on your system that doesn't need to be restored and can be omitted from your backup.

When and how often do you need to back up? Ideally, saving your entire system every night is the simplest and safest backup strategy. This approach also gives you the simplest and safest strategy for recovery. Realistically, though, when and how you run your backup, as well as what you back up, depend on the size of your *backup window* — the amount of time your system can be unavailable to users while you perform a backup. To simplify recovery, you need to back up when your system is at a known point and your data isn't changing.

When you design a backup strategy, you need to balance the time it takes to save your data with the value of the data you might lose and the amount of time it may take to recover. Always keep your recovery strategy in mind as you design your backup strategy.

If your system is so critical to your business that you don't have a manageable backup window, you probably can't afford an unscheduled outage either. If this is your situation, you should seriously evaluate the availability options of the iSeries, including dual systems. For more information about these options, see "Availability Options" (page 255).

Designing and Implementing a Backup Strategy

You should design your backup strategy based on the size of your backup window. At the same time you design your backup strategy, you should also design your recovery strategy to ensure that your backup strategy meets your system recovery needs. The final step in designing a backup strategy is to test a full system recovery. This is the only way to verify that you've designed a good backup strategy that will meet your system recovery needs. Your business may depend on your ability to recover your system. You should test your recovery strategy at your recovery services provider's location.

When designing your backup and recovery strategy, think of it as a puzzle: The fewer pieces you have in the puzzle, the more quickly you can put the pieces of the puzzle together. The fewer pieces needed in your backup strategy, the more quickly you can recover the pieces.

Your backup strategy will typically be one of three types:

- Simple — You have a large backup window, such as an 8- to 12-hour block of time available daily with no system activity.
- Medium — You have a medium backup window, such as a 4- to 6-hour block of time available daily with no system activity.
- Complex — You have a short backup window, with little or no time of system inactivity.

A simple way to ensure you have a good backup of your system is to use the options provided on menu SAVE (Figure 15.1), which you can reach by typing **Go Save** on a command line. This command presents you with additional menus that make it easy either to back up your entire system or to split your entire system backup into two parts: system data and user data. In the following discussion of backup strategies, the menu options I refer to are from menu SAVE.

FIGURE 15.1
SAVE Menu Options

```
SAVE                                  Save
                                                    System:   AS400
Select one of the following:

  Save System and User Data
    20. Define save system and user data defaults
    21. Entire system
    22. System data only
    23. All user data

  Save Document Library Objects
    30. All documents, folders, and mail
    31. New and changed documents, new folders all ma
    32. Documents and folders
    33. Mail only
    34. Calendars
                                                              More...
Selection or command
===> ____________________________________________________________

F3=Exit  F4=Prompt  F9=Retrieve  F12=Cancel F13=Information Assistant
F16=AS/400 Main Menu
```

Availability Options

Availability options are a complement to a backup strategy, not a replacement. These options can significantly reduce the time it takes you to recover after a failure. In some cases, availability options can prevent the need for recovery. To justify the cost of using availability options, you need to understand the following:

- the value of the data on your system
- the cost of a scheduled or unscheduled outage
- your availability requirements

The following availability options can complement your backup strategy:

- journal management
- access-path protection
- auxiliary storage pools
- device parity protection
- mirrored protection
- dual systems
- clustered systems

You should compare these options and decide which are best suited to your business needs. For details about availability options, their benefits versus costs, and how to implement them, refer to IBM's iSeries Information Center at *http://publib.boulder.ibm.com/pubs/html/as400/infocenter.htm.*

We'll look more closely at each availability option in a moment, but first, it's helpful to be acquainted with the following terms, which are often used in discussing system availability:

- An *outage* is a period of time during which the system is unavailable to users. During a *scheduled outage,* you deliberately make your system unavailable to users. You might use a scheduled outage to run batch work, back up your system, or apply PTFs. An *unscheduled outage* is usually caused by a failure of some type.
- *High availability* means that the system has no unscheduled outages.
- In *continuous operations,* the system has no scheduled outages.
- *Continuous availability* means that the system has neither scheduled nor unscheduled outages.

Journal Management for Backup and Recovery

You can use journal management (often referred to as *journaling* a file or an access path) to recover the changes to database files (or other objects) that have occurred since your last complete backup. You use a journal to define which files and access paths you want to protect. A journal receiver contains the entries (called *journal entries*) that the system adds when events occur that are journaled, such as changes to database files, changes to other journaled objects, or security-related events.

continued

(Availability Options *Continued*)

You can use the *remote journal function* to set up journals and journal receivers on a remote iSeries system. These journals and journal receivers are associated with journals and journal receivers on the source system. The remote journal function lets you replicate journal entries from the source system to the remote system.

Access-Path Protection

An *access path* describes the order in which the records in a database file are processed. Because different programs may need to access the file's records in different sequences, a file can have multiple access paths. Access paths in use at the time of a system failure are at risk of corruption. If access paths become corrupted, the system must rebuild them before you can use the files again. This can be a very time-consuming process.

You should consider an access-path protection plan to limit the time required to recover corrupted access paths. The system offers two methods of access-path protection:

- system-managed access-path protection (SMAPP)
- explicit journaling of access paths

You can use these methods independently or together.

By using journal management to record changes to access paths, you can greatly reduce the amount of time it takes to recover access paths should doing so become necessary. Using journal entries, the system can recover access paths without the need for a complete rebuild. This can result in considerable time savings.

With SMAPP, you can let the system determine which access paths to protect. The system makes this determination based on access-path target recovery times that you specify. SMAPP provides a simple way to reduce recovery time after a system failure, managing the required environment for you.

You can use explicit journaling, even when using SMAPP, to ensure that certain access paths critical to your business are protected. The system evaluates the protected and unprotected access paths to develop its strategy for meeting your access-path recovery targets.

Auxiliary Storage Pools

Your system may have many disk units attached to it for auxiliary storage of your data that, to your system, look like a single unit of storage. When the system writes data to disk, it spreads the data across all of these units.

You can divide your disk units into logical subsets known as *auxiliary storage pools (ASPs)* which don't necessarily correspond to the physical arrangement of disks. You can then assign objects to particular ASPs, isolating them on particular disk units. When the system now writes to these objects, it spreads the information across only the units within the ASP.

ASPs provide a recovery advantage if the system experiences a disk unit failure that results in data loss. In such a case, recovery is required only for the objects in the ASP containing the failed disk unit. System objects and user objects in other ASPs are protected from the disk failure.

continued

In addition to the protection that isolating objects to particular ASPs provides, the use of ASPs provides a certain level of flexibility. When you assign the disk units on your system to more than one ASP, each ASP can have different strategies for availability, backup and recovery, and performance.

Device Parity Protection

Device parity protection is a hardware availability function that protects against data loss due to disk unit failure or damage to a disk. To protect data, the disk controller or input/output processor (IOP) calculates and saves a *parity value* for each bit of data. The disk controller or IOP computes the parity value from the data at the same location on each of the other disk units in the device parity set. When a disk failure occurs, the data can be reconstructed by using the parity value and the values of the bits in the same locations on the other disks. The system continues to run while the data is being reconstructed. The overall goal of device parity protection is to provide high availability and to protect data as inexpensively as possible.

If possible, you should protect all the disk units on your system with either device parity protection or mirrored protection (covered next). In many cases, your system remains operational during repairs.

Device parity protection is designed to prevent system failure and to speed the recovery process for certain types of failures, not as a substitute for a good backup and recovery strategy. Device parity protection doesn't protect you if you have a site disaster or user error. It also doesn't protect against system outages caused by failures in other disk-related hardware (e.g., disk controllers, disk I/O).

Mirrored Protection

Mirrored protection is a software availability function that protects against data loss due to failure or damage to a disk-related component. The system protects your data by maintaining two copies of the data on two separate disk units. When a disk-related component fails, the system continues to operate without interruption, using the mirrored copy of the data until repairs are complete on the failed component.

When you start mirrored protection or add disk units to an ASP that has mirrored protection, the system creates mirrored pairs using disk units that have identical capacities. The goal is to protect as many disk-related components as possible. To provide maximum hardware redundancy and protection, the system tries to pair disk units from different controllers, IOPs, and buses.

Different levels of mirrored protection are possible, depending on the duplicated hardware. For instance, you can duplicate

- disk units
- disk controllers
- disk IOPs
- a bus

If a duplicate exists for the failing component and attached hardware components, the system remains available during the failure.

continued

(Availability Options *Continued*)

Remote mirroring support lets you have one mirrored unit within a mirrored pair at the local site and the second mirrored unit at a remote site. For some systems, standard DASD mirroring will remain the best choice; for others, remote DASD mirroring provides important additional capabilities.

Dual Systems

System installations with very high availability requirements use a dual-systems approach, in which two systems maintain some or all data. If the primary system fails, the secondary system can take over critical application programs.

The most common way to maintain data on the secondary system is through journaling. The primary system transmits journal entries to the secondary system, where a user-written program uses them to update files and other journaled objects in order to replicate the application environments of the primary system. Users sometimes implement this by transmitting journal entries at the *application layer.* The remote journal function improves on this technique by transmitting journal entries to a duplicate journal receiver on the secondary system at the *licensed internal code layer.* Several software packages are available from independent software vendors to support dual systems.

Clustered Systems

A cluster is a collection or group of one or more systems that work together as a single system. The cluster is identified by name and consists of one or more cluster nodes. Clustering let you efficiently group your systems together to create an environment that approaches 100 percent availability.

Implementing a Simple Backup Strategy

The simplest backup strategy is to save everything daily whenever there is no system activity. You can use SAVE menu option 21 (Entire system) to completely back up your system (with the exception of queue entries such as spooled files). You should also consider using this option to back up the entire system after installing a new release, applying PTFs, or installing a new licensed program product. As an alternative, you can use SAVE menu option 22 (System data only) to save just the system data after applying PTFs or installing a new licensed program product.

Option 21 offers the significant advantage that you can schedule the backup to run unattended (with no operator intervention). Keep in mind that unattended save operations require you to have a tape device capable of holding all your data. (For more information about backup media, see "Preparing and Managing Your Backup Media," page 273.)

Even if you don't have enough time or enough tape-device capability to perform an unattended save using option 21, you can still implement a simple backup strategy:

Daily backup: Back up only user data that changes frequently.

Weekly backup: Back up the entire system.

A simple backup strategy may also involve SAVE menu option 23 (All user data). This option saves user data that can change frequently. You can also schedule option 23 to run without operator intervention.

If your system has a long period of inactivity on weekends, your backup strategy might look like this:

Friday night:	Entire system (option 21)
Monday night:	All user data (option 23)
Tuesday night:	All user data (option 23)
Wednesday night:	All user data (option 23)
Thursday night:	All user data (option 23)
Friday night:	Entire system (option 21)

Implementing a Medium Backup Strategy

You may not have a large enough backup window to implement a simple backup strategy. For example, you may have large batch jobs that take a long time to run at night or a considerable amount of data that takes a long time to back up. If this is your situation, you'll need to implement a backup and recovery strategy of medium complexity.

When developing a medium backup strategy, keep in mind that the more often your data changes, the more often you need to back it up. You'll therefore need to evaluate in detail how often your data changes.

Several methods are available to you in developing a medium backup strategy:

- saving changed objects
- journaling objects and saving the journal receivers
- saving groups of user libraries, folders, or directories

You can use one or a combination of these methods.

Saving Changed Objects

Several commands let you save only the data that has changed since your last save operation or since a particular date and time.

You can use the SavChgObj (Save Changed Objects) command to save only those objects that have changed since a library or group of libraries was last saved or since a particular date and time. This approach can be useful if you have a system environment in which program objects and data files exist in the same library. Typically, data files change very frequently, while program objects change infrequently. Using the SavChgObj command, you can save just the data files that have changed.

The SavDLO (Save Document Library Objects) command lets you save documents and folders that have changed since the last save or since a particular date and time. You can use SavDLO to save changed documents and folders in all your user auxiliary storage pools (ASPs) or in a specific user ASP.

You can use the Sav (Save) command to save only those objects in directories that have changed since the last save or since a particular date or time.

You can also choose to save only your changed data, using a combination of the SavChgObj, SavDLO, and Sav commands, if the batch workload on your system is heavier on specific days of the week. For example:

Day/time	*Batch workload*	*Save operation*
Friday night	Light	Entire system (option 21)
Monday night	Heavy	Changed data only*
Tuesday night	Light	All user data (option 23)
Wednesday night	Heavy	Changed data only*
Thursday night	Heavy	Changed data only*
Friday night	Light	Entire system (option 21)

* Use a combination of the SavChgObj, SavDLO, and Sav commands.

Journaling Objects and Saving the Journal Receivers

If your save operations take too long because your files are large, saving changed objects may not help in your system environment. For instance, if you have a file member with 100,000 records and one record changes, the SavChgObj command saves the entire file member. In this environment, journaling your database files and saving the journal receivers regularly may be a better solution. However, keep in mind that this approach will make your recovery more complex.

When you journal a database file, the system writes a copy of every changed record to a journal receiver. When you save a journal receiver, you're saving only the changed records in the file, not the entire file.

If you journal your database files and have a batch workload that varies, your backup strategy might look like this:

Day/time	*Batch workload*	*Save operation*
Friday night	Light	Entire system (option 21)
Monday night	Heavy	Journal receivers only
Tuesday night	Light	All user data (option 23)
Wednesday night	Heavy	Journal receivers only
Thursday night	Heavy	Journal receivers only
Friday night	Light	Entire system (option 21)

To take full advantage of journaling protection, you should detach and save the journal receivers regularly. The frequency with which you save the journal receivers depends on the number of journaled changes that occur on your system. Saving the journal receivers several times during the day may be appropriate for your system environment.

The way in which you save journal receivers depends on whether they reside in a library with other objects. Depending on your environment, you'll use either the SavLib (Save Library) command or the SavObj (Save Object) command. It's best to keep your journal receivers isolated from other objects so that your save/restore functions are simpler. Be aware that you must save a new member of a database file before you can apply journal entries to the file. If your applications regularly add new file members, you should consider using the SavChgObj strategy either by itself or in combination with journaling.

Saving Groups of User Libraries, Folders, or Directories

Many applications are set up with data files and program objects in different libraries. This design simplifies your backup and recovery procedures. Data files change frequently, and, on most systems, program objects change infrequently. If your system environment is set up like this, you may want to save only the libraries with data files on a daily basis. You can also save, on a daily basis, groups of folders and directories that change frequently.

Implementing a Complex Backup Strategy

If you have a very short backup window that requires a complex strategy for backup and for recovery, you can use some of the same techniques described for a medium backup strategy, but with a greater level of detail. For example, you may need to save specific critical files at specific times of the day or week.

Several other methods are available to you in developing a complex backup strategy. You can use one or a combination of these methods:

- save data concurrently using multiple tape devices
- save data in parallel using multiple tape devices
- use the save-while-active process

Before you use any of these methods, you must have a complete backup of your entire system.

Saving Data Concurrently Using Multiple Tape Devices

You can reduce the amount of time your system is unavailable by performing save operations on more than one tape device at a time. For example, you can save libraries to one tape device, folders to another tape device, and directories to a third tape device. Or you can save different sets of libraries, objects, folders, or directories to different tape devices. Later in this chapter, I provide more information about saving data concurrently using multiple tape devices.

Saving Data in Parallel Using Multiple Tape Devices

Starting with V4R4, you can perform a parallel save using multiple tape devices. A parallel save is intended for very large objects or libraries. With this method, the system "spreads" the data in the object or library across multiple tape devices. (This function is implemented with IBM's Backup, Recovery and Media Services; for more information, see Chapter 16.)

Save-While-Active

The save-while-active process can significantly reduce the time your system is unavailable during a backup. If you choose to use save-while-active, make sure you understand the process and monitor for any synchronization checkpoints before making your objects available for use. I provide more details about save-while-active later.

An Alternative Backup Strategy

Another option available to help implement your backup strategy is the Backup, Recovery and Media Services (BRMS) licensed program product. BRMS is IBM's strategic OS/400 backup and recovery product on the iSeries and AS/400.

BRMS is a comprehensive tool for managing the backup, archiving, and recovery environment for one or more servers in a site or across a network in which data exchange by tape is required. For more information about using BRMS to implement your backup strategy, see Chapter 16.

The Inner Workings of Menu SAVE

Menu SAVE contains many options for saving your data, but four are primary:

- 20 — Define save system and user data defaults
- 21 — Entire system
- 22 — System data only
- 23 — All user data

You can use these menu options to back up your system. Or, if your installation requires a more complex backup strategy, you can use OS/400's save commands in a CL program to customize your backup.

To help you make your decision, as well as to provide skeleton code that you can use as a guideline for your own backup programs, this section provides a look at some of the inner workings of these primary save options. For detailed instructions and a checklist on using these options, refer to *OS/400 Backup and Recovery* (SC41-5304). Figure 15.2 illustrates the save commands and the SAVE menu options you can use to save the parts of the system and the entire system.

FIGURE 15.2
Save Commands and Menu Options

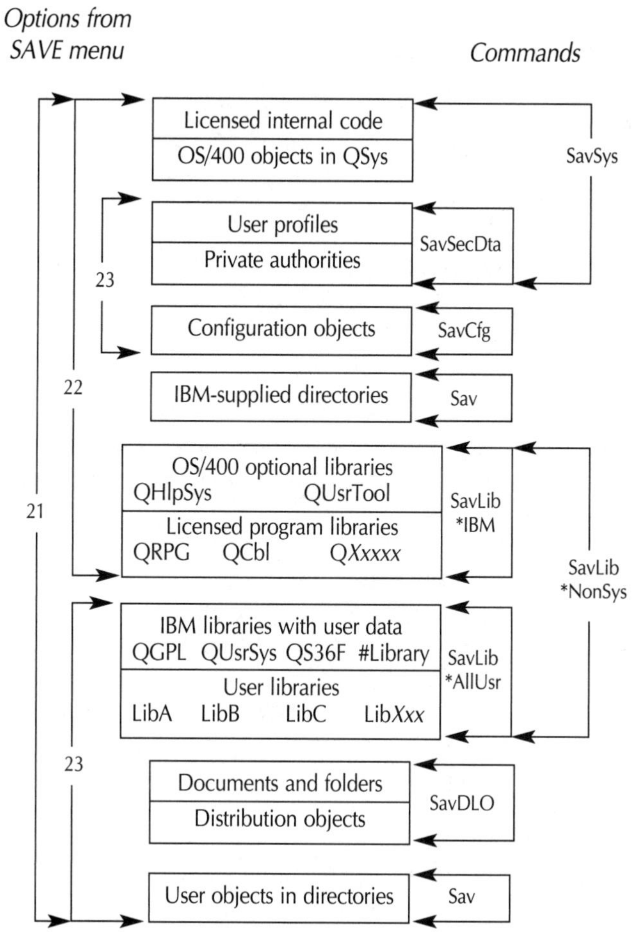

Entire System (Option 21)

SAVE menu Option 21 lets you perform a complete backup of all the data on your system, with the exception of backing up spooled files (I cover spooled file backup later). This option puts the system into a restricted state. This means no users can access your system while the backup is running. It's best to run this option overnight for a small system or during the weekend for a larger system.

Option 21 runs program QMNSave. The following program extract represents the significant processing that option 21 performs:

```
EndSbs Sbs(*All) Option(*Immed)
ChgMsgQ MsgQ(QSysOpr)                      +
        Dlvry(*Break or *Notify)
SavSys
SavLib Lib(*NonSys) AccPth(*Yes)
SavDLO DLO(*All) Flr(*Any)
Sav Dev('/QSYS.LIB/TapeDeviceName.DEVD') +
    Obj(('/*')                           +
        ('/QSYS.LIB' *Omit)              +
        ('/QDLS' *Omit))                 +
    UpdHst(*Yes)
StrSbs SbsD(ControllingSubsystem)
```

Note

The Sav command omits the QSys.Lib file system because the SavSys (Save System) command and the SavLib Lib(*NonSys) command save QSys.Lib. The Sav command also omits the QDLS file system because the SavDLO command saves QDLS.

System Data Only (Option 22)

Option 22 saves only your system data. It does not save any user data. You should run this option (or option 21) after applying PTFs or installing a new licensed program product. Like option 21, option 22 puts the system into a restricted state.

Option 22 runs program QSRSavI. The following program extract represents the significant processing that option 22 performs:

```
EndSbs Sbs(*All) Option(*Immed)
ChgMsgQ MsgQ(QSysOpr)                      +
        Dlvry(*Break or *Notify)
SavSys
SavLib Lib(*IBM) AccPth(*Yes)
Sav Dev('/QSYS.LIB/TapeDeviceName.DEVD') +
    Obj(('/QIBM/ProdData')               +
        ('/QOpenSys/QIBM/ProdData'))     +
    UpdHst(*Yes)
StrSbs SbsD(ControllingSubsystem)
```

All User Data (Option 23)

Option 23 saves all user data, including files, user-written programs, and all other user data on the system. This option also saves user profiles, security data, and configuration data. Like options 21 and 22, option 23 places the system in restricted state.

Option 23 runs program QSRSavU. The following program extract represents the significant processing that option 23 performs:

```
EndSbs Sbs(*All) Option(*Immed)
ChgMsgQ MsgQ(QSysOpr)                              +
        Dlvry(*Break or *Notify)
SavSecDta
SavCfg
SavLib Lib(*AllUsr) AccPth(*Yes)
SavDLO DLO(*All) Flr(*Any)
Sav Dev('/QSYS.LIB/TapeDeviceName.DEVD')    +
     Obj(('/*')                                    +
         ('/QSYS.LIB' *Omit)                       +
         ('/QDLS' *Omit)                           +
         ('/QIBM/ProdData' *Omit)                  +
         ('/QOpenSys/QIBM/ProdData' *Omit)) +
     UpdHst(*Yes)
StrSbs SbsD(ControllingSubsystem)
```

Note

The Sav command omits the QSys.Lib file system because the SavSys command, the SavSecDta (Save Security Data) command, and the SavCfg (Save Configuration) command save QSys.Lib. The Sav command also omits the QDLS file system because the SavDLO command saves QDLS. In addition, the Sav command executed by option 23 omits the /QIBM and /QOpenSys/QIBM directories because these directories contain IBM-supplied objects.

Setting Save Option Defaults

When you save information using option 21, 22, or 23, you can specify default values for some of the commands used by the save process. Figure 15.3 shows the Specify Command Defaults values used by these options. You can use SAVE menu option 20 (Define save system and user data defaults) to change the default values displayed on this panel for menu options 21, 22, and 23. Changing the defaults simplifies the task of setting up your backups. To change the defaults, you must have *Change authority to both library QUsrSys and the QSRDflts data area in QUsrSys.

When you select option 20, the system displays the default parameter values for options 21, 22, and 23. The first time you use option 20, the system displays the IBM-supplied default parameter values. You can change any or all of the parameter values to meet your needs. For example, you can specify additional tape devices or change the message queue delivery default. The system saves the new default values in data area QSRDflts in library QUsrSys for future use (the system creates QSRDflts only after you change the IBM-supplied default values).

Once you've defined new default values, you no longer need to worry about which, if any, options to change on subsequent backups. You can simply review the new default options and then press Enter to start the backup using the new default parameters.

FIGURE 15.3
Specify Command Defaults Panel

```
                         Specify Command Defaults

 Type choices, press Enter.

   Devices . . . . . . . . . . .   TAP01_____     Names
                                   __________
                                   __________
                                   __________

   Prompt for commands . . . . .   Y              Y=Yes, N=No

   Check for active files . . . .  Y              Y=Yes, N=No

   Message queue delivery . . . .  *BREAK_        *BREAK, *NOTIFY

   Start time . . . . . . . . . .  *CURRENT       *CURRENT, time

   Vary off network servers . . .  *NONE_____     *NONE, *ALL, *WINDOWSNT
                                   __________

   Unmount file systems . . . . .  N              Y=Yes, N=No

   Print system information . . .  N              Y=Yes, N=No

   Use system reply list . . . .   N              Y=Yes, N=No
                                                                    Bottom
 F3=Exit   F12=Cancel
```

If you have multiple, distributed systems with the same save parameters on each system, option 20 offers an additional benefit: You can simply define your default parameters using option 20 on one system and then save data area QSRDflts in library QUsrSys, distribute the saved data area to the other systems, and restore it.

Printing System Information

When you perform save operations using option 21, 22, or 23 from menu SAVE, you can optionally request a series of reports with system information that can be useful during system recovery. The Specify Command Defaults panel presented by these options provides a prompt for printing system information. You can also use command PrtSysInf (Print System Information) to print the system information. This information is especially useful if you can't use your SavSys media to recover and must use your distribution media.

Printing the system information requires *AllObj, *IOSysCfg, and *JobCtl authority and produces many spooled file listings. You probably don't need to print the information every time you perform a backup. However, you should print it whenever important information about your system changes.

The following lists and reports are generated when you print the system information (the respective CL commands are noted in parentheses):

- a library backup list with information about each library in the system, including which backup schedules include the library and when the library was last backed up (DspBckupL *Lib)
- a folder backup list with the same information for all folders in the system (DspBckupL *Flr)
- a list of all system values (DspSysVal)
- a list of network attributes (DspNetA)
- a list of edit descriptions (DspEdtD)
- a list of PTF details (DspPTF)
- a list of reply list entries (WrkRpyLE)
- a report of access-path relationships (DspRcyAP)
- a list of service attributes (DspSvrA)
- a list of network server storage spaces (DspNwSStg)
- a report showing the power on/off schedule (DspPwrScd)
- a list of hardware features on your system (DspHdwRsc)
- a list of distribution queues (DspDstSrv)
- a list of all subsystems (DspSbsD)
- a list of the IBM software licenses installed on your machine (DspSfwRsc)
- a list of journal object descriptions for all journals (DspObjD)
- a report showing journal attributes for all journals (WrkJrnA)
- a report showing cleanup operations (ChgClnup)
- a list of all user profiles (DspUsrPrf)
- a report of all job descriptions (DspJobD)

Saving Data Concurrently Using Multiple Tape Devices

As I mentioned earlier, one way to reduce the amount of time required for a complex backup strategy is to perform save operations to multiple tape devices at once. You can save data concurrently using multiple tape devices by saving libraries to one tape device, folders to another tape device, and directories to a third tape device. Or, you can save different sets of libraries, objects, folders, or directories to different tape devices.

Concurrent Saves of Libraries and Objects

You can run multiple save commands concurrently against multiple libraries. When you run multiple save commands, the system processes the request in several stages that overlap, improving save performance.

To perform concurrent save operations to different tape devices, you can use the OmitLib (Omit library) parameter with generic naming. For example:

```
SavLib Lib(*AllUsr)                   +
       Dev(FirstTapeDevice)           +
       OmitLib(A* B* $* #* @* ... L*)
SavLib Lib(*AllUsr)                   +
       Dev(SecondTapeDevice)          +
       OmitLib(M* N* ... Z*)
```

You can also save a single library concurrently to multiple tape devices by using the SavObj or SavChgObj command. This technique lets you issue multiple save operations using multiple tape devices to save objects from one large library. For example, you can save generic objects from one large library to one tape device and concurrently issue another SavObj command against the same library to save a different set of generic objects to another tape device.

You can use generic naming on the Obj (Object) parameter while performing concurrent SavChgObj operations to multiple tape devices against a single library. For example:

```
SavChgObj Obj(A* B* C* $* #* ... L*) +
          Dev(FirstTapeDevice)       +
          Lib(LibraryName)
SavChgObj Obj(M* N* O* ... Z*)       +
          Dev(SecondTapeDevice)      +
          Lib(LibraryName)
```

Concurrent Saves of DLOs (Folders)

You can run multiple SavDLO commands concurrently for DLO objects that reside in the same ASP. This technique allows concurrent saves of DLOs to multiple tape devices.

You can use the command's Flr (Folder) parameter with generic naming to perform concurrent save operations to different tape devices. For example:

```
SavDLO DLO(*All)              +
       Flr(DEPT*)             +
       Dev(FirstTapeDevice)   +
       OmitFlr(DEPT2*)
SavDLO DLO(*All)              +
       Flr(DEPT2*)            +
       Dev(SecondTapeDevice)
```

In this example, the system saves to the first tape device all folders starting with DEPT except those that start with DEPT2. Folders that start with DEPT2 are saved to the second tape device.

Note

Parameter OmitFlr is allowed only when you specify DLO(*All) or DLO(*Chg).

Concurrent Saves of Objects in Directories

You can also run multiple Sav commands concurrently against objects in directories. This technique allows concurrent saves of objects in directories to multiple tape devices.

You can use the Sav command's Obj (Object) parameter with generic naming to perform concurrent save operations to different tape devices. For example:

```
Sav Dev('/QSYS.LIB/FirstTapeDevice.DEVD')  +
    Obj(('/DIRA*'))                        +
    UpdHst(*Yes)
Sav Dev('/QSYS.LIB/SecondTapeDevice.DEVD') +
    Obj(('/DIRB*'))                        +
    UpdHst(*Yes)
```

Save-While-Active

To either reduce or eliminate the amount of time your system is unavailable for use during a backup (your *backup outage*), you can use the save-while-active process on particular save operations along with your other backup and recovery procedures. Save-while-active lets you use the system during part or all of the backup process. In contrast, other save operations permit either no access or only read access to objects during the backup.

How Does Save-While-Active Work?

OS/400 objects consist of units of storage called *pages*. When you use save-while-active to save an object, the system creates two images of the pages of the object. The first image contains the updates to the object with which normal system activity works. The second image is a "snapshot" of the object as it exists at a single point in time called a *checkpoint*. The save-while-active job uses this image — called the *checkpoint image* — to save the object. When an application makes changes to an object during a save-while-active job, the system uses one image of the object's pages to make the changes and, at the same time, uses the other image to save the object to tape.

The system locks objects as it obtains the checkpoint images, and you can't change objects during the checkpoint processing. After the system has obtained the checkpoint images, applications can once again change the objects.

The image that the system saves doesn't include any changes made during the save-while-active job. The image on the tape is an image of the object as it existed when the system reached the checkpoint. Rather than maintain two complete images of the object being saved, the system maintains two images only for the pages of the objects that are being changed as the save is performed.

Synchronization

When you back up more than one object using the save-while-active process, you must choose when the objects will reach a checkpoint in relationship to each other — a concept called *synchronization*. There are three kinds of synchronization:

- With *full synchronization*, the checkpoints for all the objects occur at the same time, during a time period in which no changes can occur to the objects. It's strongly recommended that you use full synchronization, even when you're saving objects in only one library.

- With *library synchronization*, the checkpoints for all the objects in a library occur at the same time.
- With *system-defined synchronization*, the system decides when the checkpoints for the objects occur. The checkpoints may occur at different times, resulting in a more complex recovery procedure.

How you use save-while-active in your backup strategy depends on whether you choose to reduce or eliminate the time your system is unavailable during a backup. Reducing the backup outage is much simpler and more common than eliminating it. It's also the recommended way to use save-while-active.

When you use save-while-active to reduce your backup outage, your system recovery process is exactly the same as if you performed a standard backup operation. Also, using save-while-active this way doesn't require you to implement journaling or commitment control.

To use save-while-active to reduce your backup outage, you can end any applications that change objects or end the subsystems in which these applications are run. After the system reaches a checkpoint for those objects, you can restart the applications. One save-while-active option lets you have the system send a message notification when it completes the checkpoint processing. Once you know checkpoint processing is completed, it's safe to start your applications or subsystems again. Using save-while-active this way can significantly reduce your backup outage.

Typically, when you choose to reduce your backup outage with save-while-active, the time during which your system is unavailable for use ranges anywhere from 10 minutes to 60 minutes. It's highly recommended that you use save-while-active to reduce your backup outage unless you absolutely cannot have your system unavailable for this time frame.

You should use save-while-active to eliminate your backup outage only if you have absolutely no tolerance for any backup outage. You should use this approach only to back up objects that you're protecting with journaling or commitment control.

When you use save-while-active to eliminate your backup outage, you don't end the applications that modify the objects or end the subsystems in which the applications are run. However, this method affects the performance and response time of your applications.

Keep in mind that eliminating your backup outage with save-while-active requires much more complex recovery procedures. You'll need to include these procedures in your disaster recovery plans.

Save Commands That Support the Save-While-Active Option

The following save commands support the save-while-active option:

Command	*Function*
SavLib	Save library
SavObj	Save object
SavChgObj	Save changed objects
SavDLO	Save document library objects
Sav	Save objects in directories

The following parameters are available on the save commands for the save-while-active process:

Parameter	*Description*
SavAct (Save-while-active)	You must decide whether you're going to use full synchronization, library synchronization, or system-defined synchronization. It's highly recommended that you use full synchronization in most cases.
SavActWait (Save active wait time)	You can specify the maximum number of seconds that the save-while-active operation will wait to allocate an object during checkpoint processing.
SavActMsgQ (Save active message queue)	You can specify whether the system sends you a message when it reaches a checkpoint.
SavActOpt (Save-while-active options)	This parameter has values that are specific to the Sav command.

For complete details about using the save-while-active process to either reduce or eliminate your backup outage, visit IBM's iSeries Information Center at *http://publib.boulder.ibm.com/pubs/html/as400/infocenter.htm.*

Backing Up Spooled Files

When you save an output queue, its description is saved but not its contents (the spooled files). With a combination of spooled file APIs, user space APIs, and list APIs, you can back up spooled files, including their associated advanced function attributes (if any).

The spooled file APIs perform the real work of backing up spooled files. These APIs include

- QUSLSpl (List Spooled Files)
- QUSRSplA (Retrieve Spooled File Attributes)
- QSpOpnSp (Open Spooled File)
- QSpCrtSp (Create Spooled File)
- QSpGetSp (Get Spooled File Data)
- QSpPutSp (Put Spooled File Data)
- QSpCloSp (Close Spooled File)

These APIs let you copy spooled file information to a user space for save purposes and copy the information back from the user space to a spooled file. Once you've copied spooled file information to user spaces, you can save the user spaces. For more information about these APIs, see *System API Reference* (SC41-5801).

One common misconception is that you can use the CpySplF (Copy Spooled File) command to back up spooled files. This command does let you copy information from a spooled file to a database file, but you shouldn't rely on this method for spooled file backup. CpySplF copies only textual data and not advanced function attributes such as graphics and variable fonts. CpySplF also does nothing to preserve print attributes such as spacing.

IBM does offer support for saving and restoring spooled files in its BRMS product. BRMS maintains all the advanced function attributes associated with the spooled files. For more information about BRMS, see Chapter 16.

Recovering Your System

Although the iSeries is very stable and disasters are rare, there are times when some type of recovery may be necessary. The extent of recovery required and the processes you follow will vary greatly depending on the nature of your failure.

The sheer number of possible failures precludes a one-size-fits-all answer to recovery. Instead, you must examine the details of your failure and recover accordingly. To help determine the best way to recover your system, you should refer to "Selecting the Right Recovery Strategy" in *OS/400 Backup and Recovery*, which categorizes failures and their associated recovery processes and provides checklists of recovery steps.

Before beginning your recovery, be sure to do the following:

- If you have to back up and recover because of some system problem, make sure you understand how the problem occurred so you can choose the correct recovery procedures.
- Plan your recovery.
- Make a copy of the *OS/400 Backup and Recovery* checklist you're using, and check off each step as you complete it. Keep the checklist for future reference. If you need help later, this record will be invaluable.
- If your problem requires hardware or software service, make sure you understand exactly what the service representative does. Don't be afraid to ask questions.

Starting with V4R5, the *OS/400 Backup and Recovery* manual includes a new appendix called "Recovering your AS/400 system," which provides step-by-step instructions for completely recovering your entire system to the same system (i.e., restoring to a system with the same serial number). You can use these steps *only* if you saved your entire system using either option 21 from menu SAVE or the equivalent SavSys, SavLib, SavDLO, and Sav commands.

Continue to use the Chapter 3 checklist titled "Recovering your entire system after a complete system loss (Checklist 17)" in *OS/400 Backup and Recovery* to completely recover your system in any of the following situations:

- Your system has logical partitions.
- Your system uses the Alternate Installation Device Setup feature that you can define through Dedicated Service Tools (DST) for a manual IPL from tape.
- Your system has mounted user-defined file systems before the save.
- You're recovering to a different system (a system with a different serial number).

One piece of advice warrants repeating: Test as many of the procedures in your recovery plan as you possibly can *before* disaster strikes. If any surprises await you, it's far better to uncover them in a test situation than during a disaster.

Preparing and Managing Your Backup Media

OS/400's save commands support different types of devices (including save file, tape, diskette, and optical). For a backup strategy, you should always back up to a tape device. Choose a tape device and tape media that has the performance capabilities and density capacity that will meet your backup window and any requirements you have for running an unattended backup.

Preparing and managing your tape media is an important part of your backup operations. You need to be able to easily locate the correct media to perform a successful system recovery.

You'll need to use sets of tapes and implement a rotation schedule. An important part of a good backup strategy is to have more than one set of backup media. When you perform a system recovery, you may need to go back to an older set of tape media if your most recent set is damaged or if you discover a programming error that has affected data on your most recent backup media.

At a minimum, you should rotate three sets of media, as follows:

Backup	***Media set***
Backup 1	Set 1
Backup 2	Set 2
Backup 3	Set 3
Backup 4	Set 1
Backup 5	Set 2
Backup 6	Set 3
.	.
.	.
.	.

You may find that the easiest method is to have a different set of media for each day of the week. This strategy makes it easier for the operator to know which set to mount for backup.

continued

(Preparing and Managing Your Backup Media *Continued*)

Cleaning Your Tape Devices

It's important to clean your tape devices regularly. The read-write heads can collect dust and other material that can cause errors when reading or writing to tape media. If you're using new tapes, it's especially important to clean the device because new tapes tend to collect more material on the read-write heads. For specific recommendations, refer to your tape drive's manual.

Preparing Your Tapes for Use

To prepare tape media for use, you'll need to use the InzTap (Initialize Tape) command. (Some tapes come pre-initialized.) When you initialize tapes, you're required to give each tape a new-volume identifier (using the InzTap command's NewVol parameter) and a density (Density parameter). The new-volume identifier identifies the tape as a standard-labeled tape that can be used by the system for backups. The density specifies the format in which to write the data on the tape based on the tape device you're using. You can use the special value *DevType to easily specify that the format be based on the type of tape device being used.

When initializing new tapes, you should also specify Check(*No); otherwise, the system tries to read labels from the volume on the specified tape device until the tape completely rewinds.

Here's a sample command to initialize a new tape volume:

```
InzTap Dev(Tap01)          +
       NewVol(A23001)      +
       Check(*No)          +
       Density(*DevType)
```

Tip

It's important to initialize each tape only once in its lifetime and give each tape volume a different volume identifier so tape-volume error statistics can be tracked.

Naming and Labeling Your Tapes

Initializing each tape volume with a volume identifier helps ensure that your operators load the correct tape for the backup. It's a good idea to choose volume-identifier names that help identify tape-volume contents and the volume set to which each tape belongs. The following table illustrates how you might initialize your tape volumes and label them externally in a simple backup strategy. Each label has a prefix that indicates the day of the week (A for Monday, B for Tuesday, and so on), the backup operation (option number from menu SAVE), and the media set with which the tape volume is associated.

continued

Volume Naming — Part of a Simple Backup Strategy

Volume name	External label
B23001	Tuesday–Menu SAVE, option 23–Media set 1
B23002	Tuesday–Menu SAVE, option 23–Media set 2
B23003	Tuesday–Menu SAVE, option 23–Media set 3
E21001	Friday–Menu SAVE, option 21–Media set 1
E21002	Friday–Menu SAVE, option 21–Media set 2
E21003	Friday–Menu SAVE, option 21–Media set 3

Volume names and labels for a medium backup strategy might look like this:

Volume Naming — Part of a Medium Backup Strategy

Volume name	External label
E21001	Friday–Menu SAVE, option 21–Media set 1
E21002	Friday–Menu SAVE, option 21–Media set 2
AJR001	Monday–Save journal receivers–Media set 1
AJR002	Monday–Save journal receivers–Media set 2
ASC001	Monday–Save changed data–Media set 1
ASC002	Monday–Save changed data–Media set 2
BJR001	Tuesday–Save journal receivers–Media set 1
BJR002	Tuesday–Save journal receivers–Media set 2
B23001	Tuesday–Menu SAVE, option 23–Media set 1
B23002	Tuesday–Menu SAVE, option 23–Media set 2

Tip

If your tapes don't come prelabeled, you should put an external label on each tape volume. The label should show the volume-identifier name and the most recent date the tape was used for a backup. Color-coded labels can help you locate and store your media — for example, yellow for set 1, red for set 2, and so on.

Verifying Your Tapes

Good backup procedures dictate that you verify you're using the correct tape volumes. Depending on your system environment, you can choose to manually verify your tapes or have the system verify your tapes:

- Manual verification — If you use the default value of *Mounted on the Vol (Volume) parameter of the save commands, telling the system to use the currently mounted volume, the operator must manually verify that the correct tape volumes are loaded in the correct order.

continued

(Preparing and Managing Your Backup Media *Continued*)

- System verification — By specifying a list of volume identifiers on the save commands, you can have the system verify that the correct tape volumes are loaded in the correct order. If the tape volumes aren't loaded correctly, the system will send a message telling the operator to load the correct volumes.

Another way to verify that the correct tape volumes are used is to specify expiration dates on the media files. If you rely on your operators to verify tape volumes, you can use the ExpDate (Expiration date) parameter and specify the value *Perm (permanent) for your save operations. This will prevent someone from writing over a file on the tape volume by mistake. When you're ready to use the tape volume again, specify Clear(*All) on the save operations.

If you want the system to verify your tape volumes, specify an ExpDate value that ensures you don't use the media again too soon. For example, if you rotate five sets of media for daily saves, specify an expiration date of the current day plus four on the save operation. Specify Clear(*None) on save operations so the system doesn't write over unexpired files.

Caution

It's important to try to avoid situations in which an operator must regularly respond to (and ignore) messages such as "Unexpired files on the media." If operators get into the habit of ignoring routine messages, they may miss important messages.

Storing Your Tapes

An important part of any recovery strategy is storing the tape volumes in a safe but accessible location. Ensure the tape volumes have external labels and are organized well so you can locate them easily.

To enable disaster recovery, you should store a complete set of your backups at a safe, accessible location away from your site. Consider contracting with a vendor that will pick up and store your tapes. When choosing off-site storage, consider how quickly you can retrieve the tapes. Also, consider whether you'll have access to your tapes on weekends and during holidays.

A complete recovery strategy keeps one set of tapes close at hand for immediate data recovery and keeps a duplicate set of tapes in off-site storage for disaster recovery purposes. To duplicate your tape volumes for off-site storage, you can use the DupTap (Duplicate Tape) command.

continued

Handling Tape Media Errors

When you're saving or restoring to tape, it's normal for some tape read/write errors to occur. Tape read/write errors fall into one of three categories:

- *Recoverable errors*: Some tape devices support recovering from read/write errors. The system repositions the tape automatically and tries the save or restore operation again.
- *Unrecoverable errors — processing can continue*: In some instances, the system can't continue to use the current tape but can continue processing on a new tape. The system will ask you to load another tape. You can still use the tape with the unrecoverable error for restore operations.
- *Unrecoverable errors — processing cannot continue*: In some cases, an unrecoverable read/write error will cause the system to end the save operation.

Tapes physically wear out after extended use. You can determine whether a tape is wearing out by periodically printing the error log. Use the PrtErrLog (Print Error Log) command, and specify Type(*VolStat). The printed output provides statistics about each tape volume. If you've used unique volume-identifier names for your tapes and you've initialized each volume only once, you can determine which tapes have excessive read/write errors. Refer to your tape-volume documentation to determine the error threshold for the tape volumes you're using. You should discard any bad tape volumes.

If you think you have a bad tape volume, you can use the DspTap (Display Tape) or the DupTap command to check the tape's integrity. Both of these commands read the entire tape volume and will detect any objects on the tape that the system can't read.

Chapter 16

Backup, Recovery and Media Services (BRMS) Overview

by Debbie Saugen

Backup, Recovery and Media Services (BRMS) is IBM's strategic backup and recovery product for the iSeries and AS/400. Packaged as licensed program 5769-BR1 (V4R5) or 5722-BR1 (V5R1), BRMS is a comprehensive tool for managing the backup, archive, and recovery environment for one or more systems in a site or across a network in which data exchange by tape is required.

BRMS lets you simplify and automate backups as well as manage your tape inventory. It keeps track of what you've saved, when you saved it, and where it is saved so that when recovery is necessary, BRMS restores the correct information from the correct tapes in the correct sequence.

In this chapter, you'll get a conceptual introduction to BRMS and some of its many features. With this information, you can determine whether BRMS is right for your backup strategy.

An Introduction to BRMS

BRMS lets you easily define, change, and execute simple, medium, or complex backup procedures. It offers full-function backup facilities, including keywords to match the OS/400 save keywords (e.g., *AllUsr, *IBM); exit commands to allow processing of user-defined routines; full, incremental, and noncumulative incremental saves; saves to save files; and save-while-active processing. BRMS even provides support for backing up spooled files, a save/restore feature sorely missing from OS/400.

You may be wondering, "What could be simpler than backing up the entire system every night?" Nothing is simpler, but not everyone can afford the outage that this type of save requires. BRMS is an effective solution in backing up only what's really required. BRMS also lets you easily schedule a backup that includes a SavSys (Save System) operation, which isn't so easy using just OS/400.

In addition to these capabilities, BRMS offers step-by-step recovery information, printed after backups are complete. Recovery no longer consists of operators clenching the desk with white knuckles at 4:00 a.m., trying desperately to recover the system in time for the users who'll arrive at 8:00 a.m., without any idea what's going on or how long it will take. With native OS/400 commands, the only feedback that recovery personnel get is the occasional change to the message line on line 25 of the screen as the recovery takes place. BRMS changes this with full and detailed feedback during the recovery process — with an auto-refresh screen, updated as each library is restored.

Following are some of the features that contribute to the robustness of BRMS:

- Data archive — Data archive is important for organizations that must keep large volumes of history data yet don't require rapid access to this information. BRMS can archive data from DASD to tape and track information about objects that have been archived. Locating data in the archives is easy, and the restore can be triggered from a work-with screen.
- Dynamic data retrieval — Dynamic retrieval for database files, document library objects, and stream files is possible with BRMS. Once archived with BRMS, these objects can be automatically restored upon access within user applications. No changes are required to user applications to initiate the restore.
- Media management — In a large single- or multisystem environment, control and management of tape media is critical. BRMS allows cataloging of an entire tape inventory and manages the media as they move from location to location. This comprehensive inventory-management system provides many reports that operators can use as instructions.
- Parallel save and restore — BRMS supports parallel save and restore, reducing the backup and recovery times of very large objects and libraries by "spreading" data across multiple tape drives. This method is in contrast to concurrent save and restore, in which the user must manage the splitting of data. With parallel save and restore, operations end at approximately the same time for all tape drives.
- Lotus Notes Servers backup — BRMS supports backup of online Lotus Notes Servers, including Domino and Quickplace Lotus Notes Servers.
- Flexible backup options — You can define different backup scenarios and execute the ones appropriate for particular circumstances.
- Spooled file backup — Unlike OS/400 save and restore functions, BRMS provides support for backing up spooled files. Spooled file backup is important to a complete backup, and BRMS lets you tailor spooled file backup to meet your needs.
- Storage alternatives — You can save to a tape device, a Media Library device, a save file, or a Tivoli Storage Manager server (previously known as an ADSM server).

It is these features, and more, that make BRMS a popular solution for many installations. Later, we'll take a closer look at some of these capabilities.

Getting Started with BRMS

BRMS brings with it a few new save/restore concepts as well as some new terminology. For instance, you'll find repeated references to the following terms when working with BRMS:

- media — a tape cartridge or save file that will hold the objects being backed up
- media identifier — a name given to a physical piece of media
- media class — a logical grouping of media with similar physical and/or logical characteristics (e.g., density)

- policy — a set of commonly used defaults (e.g., device, media class) that determine how BRMS performs its backup
- backup control group — a grouping of items (e.g., libraries, objects, stream files) to back up

You're probably thinking that "media" and "media identifier" aren't so new. True, but most people don't think of save files as media, and media identifier is typically thought to mean volume identifier.

Policies and backup control groups are concepts central to BRMS in that they govern the backup process. IBM provides default values in several policies and control groups. You can use these defaults or define your own for use in your save/restore operations.

Policies are templates for managing backups and media management operations. They act as a control point for defining operating characteristics. The standard BRMS package provides the following policies:

- System Policy — The System Policy is conceptually similar to system values. It contains general defaults for many BRMS operations.
- Backup Policy — The Backup Policy determines how the system performs backups. It contains defaults for backup operations.
- Recovery Policy — The Recovery Policy defines how the system typically performs recovery operations.
- Media Policies — Media Policies control media-related functionality. For instance, they determine where BRMS finds tapes needed for a backup.
- Move Policies — Move Policies define the way media moves through storage locations from creation time through expiration.

In pre-V5R1 releases of OS/400, BRMS is shipped with two default backup control groups, *SysGrp (system group) and *BkuGrp (backup group). The *SysGrp control group backs up all system data, and the *BkuGrp control group backs up all user data. You can back up your entire system using these two control groups, but doing so requires two backup commands, one for each group. To back up your entire system using a single control group, you can create a new backup control group that includes the following BRMS special values as backup items:

Seq	*Backup items*
10	*SavSys
20	*IBM
30	*AllUsr
40	*AllDLO
50	*Link

The time required to back up the system using this full backup control group is less than that required to use a combination of the *SysGrp and *BkuGrp backup control groups. The *SysGrp control group contains the special value *SavSys, which saves the licensed internal code, OS/400, user profiles, security data, and configuration data. The *BkuGrp control group contains the special values *SavSecDta and *SavCfg, which also save user profiles, security data, and configuration data. If you use the two control groups *SysGrp and *BkuGrp, you save the user profiles, security data, and configuration data twice. This redundancy in saved data contributes to the additional backup time when using control groups *SysGrp and *BkuGrp. Starting with V5R1, BRMS includes a new, full-system default backup control group, *System, that combines the function of groups *SysGrp and *BkuGrp.

Note

Note that none of the full backup control groups discussed so far saves spooled files. If spooled files are critical to your business, you'll need to create a backup list of your spooled files to be included in your full backup control group (more about how to do this later).

Saving Data in Parallel with BRMS

As I mentioned, BRMS supports parallel save/restore function. This support is intended for use with large objects and libraries. Its goal is to reduce backup and recovery times by evenly dividing data across multiple tape drives.

You typically define parallel resources when you work with backup control groups. You specify both a maximum number of resources (devices) and a minimum number of resources to be used during the backup. For example, you could specify 32 for maximum resources and 15 for minimum resources. When the backup is submitted, the system checks for available tape resources. If it can't find 32 available tape devices, the backup will be run with the minimum of 15. It's not a requirement that the number of devices used for the backup be used on the restore. However, to reduce the number of tape mounts, it's best to use the same number of tape devices on the restore.

Starting with V5R1, the special values *AllProd, *AllTest, *AllUsr, *ASP01–*ASP99, and *IBM are supported on BRMS parallel saves, with the objects being "spread" at the library level. Restores for objects saved in parallel with these special values are still done in a serial mode.

Online Backup of Lotus Notes Servers with BRMS

In today's working environment, users demand 24x7 access to their mail and other Lotus Notes databases, yet it's also critical that user data be backed up frequently and in a timely way. BRMS Online Lotus Notes Servers Backup support meets these critical needs.

With this support, you can save Lotus Notes databases while they're in use, without requiring users to exit the system. Prior save-while-active support required ending applications to reach a checkpoint or the use of commitment control or journaling.

Another alternative was to invest in an additional server, replicate the server data, and perform the backup from the second server. Online Lotus Notes Servers Backup with BRMS avoids these requirements.

Installation of BRMS automatically configures control groups and policies that help you perform online backup of your Lotus Notes Servers. The Online Lotus Notes Servers Backup process allows the collection of two backups into one entity. BRMS and Domino or Quickplace accomplish this using a BRMS concept called a *package*. The package is identified by the PkgID (Package identifier) parameter on the SavBRM (Save Object using BRM) command.

Domino or Quickplace will back up the databases while they are online and in use. When the backup is completed, a secondary file is backed up and associated with the first backup using the package concept. The secondary file contains all the changes that occurred during the online backup, such as transaction logs or journaling information.

When you need to recover a Lotus Notes Server database that was backed up using BRMS Online Backup, BRMS calls Domino or Quickplace through recovery exits that let Domino or Quickplace apply any changes from the secondary file backup to the database that was just restored. This recovery process maintains the integrity of the data.

Restricted-State Saves Using BRMS

You can use the console monitor function of BRMS to schedule unattended restricted-state saves. This support is meaningful because with OS/400 save functions, restricted-state saves must be run interactively from a display in the controlling subsystem.

BRMS's support means you can run an unattended SavSys operation to save the OS/400 licensed internal code and operating system (or other functions you want to run in a restricted state). You simply specify the special value *SavSys on the StrBkuBRM (Start Backup using BRM) command or within a BRMS control group to perform a SavSys. You can temporarily interrupt the console-monitoring function to enter OS/400 commands and then return the console to a monitored state.

Console monitoring lets users submit the SavSys job to the job scheduler instead of running the save interactively. You can use the Submit to batch parameter on the StrBkuBRM command to enter *Console as a value, thereby performing your saves in batch mode. Thus, you don't have to be nearby when the system save is processed. However, you must issue this command from the system console because BRMS runs the job in subsystem QCtl. If you try to start the console monitor from your own workstation, BRMS sends a message indicating that you're not in a correct environment to start the console monitor.

Backing Up Spooled Files with BRMS

With BRMS, you can create a backup list that specifies the output queues you want to save. You can then specify this backup list on your backup control groups.

You create a spooled file backup list using command WrkLBRM (Work with Lists using BRM). You simply add a list, specifying

- *Bku for the Use field
- a value for the List name (e.g., SaveSplF)
- *Spl for the Type field

When you press Enter, the Add Spooled File List panel (Figure 16.1) is displayed. (The figure shows the panel after backup information has been entered.)

FIGURE 16.1
Add Spooled File List Panel

```
                          Add Spooled File List                        AS400

Use . . . . . . . . . . :  *BKU
List name . . . . . . . .  SAVESPLF
Text  . . . . . . . . . .  Sample to save spooled files.

Type choices, press Enter.
                                                                      *INC/
  Seq Library     Outq      File       Job        User       User data *EXC

   10 QUSRSYS     PRT01     *ALL       *ALL       *ALL       *ALL      *INC









                                                                        Bottom

F3=Exit  F5=Refresh  F12=Cancel
```

Including Spooled File Entries in a Backup List

Now, you can update the backup list by adding the output queues you want to save. Within a spooled file list, you can save multiple output queues by selecting multiple sequence numbers. When you add an output queue to the list, you can filter the spooled files to save by specifying values for spooled file name, job name, user name, or user data. For example, if you want to save only spooled files that belong to user A, you can specify user A's name in the User field. Generic names are also allowed.

The sample setup in Figure 16.1 saves output queue Prt01 in library QUsrSys. If you leave the Outq field at its default value *All, BRMS saves all spooled files from all output queues in library QUsrSys. To exclude an output queue, you can use the *Exc value. Once you set up your backup list, you can add it to your daily, weekly, or monthly backup control group as a backup item with a list type of *Spl.

Note that BRMS doesn't support incremental saves of spooled files. If you specify an incremental save for a list type of *Spl, all spooled files in the list are saved. BRMS doesn't automatically clear the output queues after the spooled files are successfully saved.

After you've successfully saved your spooled files, you can use the WrkSplFBRM (Work with Spooled Files using BRM) command to display the status of your saves. The WrkSplFBRM panel displays your spooled files in the order in which they were created on the system.

Restoring Spooled Files Saved Using BRMS

BRMS doesn't automatically restore spooled files when you restore your user data during a system recovery. To restore saved spooled files, use the WrkSplFBRM command and select option 7 (Restore spooled file) on the resulting screen. From the Select Recovery Items panel that appears, you can specify the spooled files you want to restore.

By default, BRMS restores spooled file data in the output queue from which the data was saved. If necessary, you can change any of the BRMS recovery defaults by pressing F9 on the Select Recovery Items screen.

During the save and restore operations, BRMS retains spooled file attributes, names, user names, user data fields, and, in most cases, job names. During the restore operation, OS/400 assigns new job numbers, system dates, and times; the original dates and times aren't restored.

Be aware that BRMS saves spooled files as a single folder, with multiple documents (spooled members) within the folder. During the restore, BRMS searches the tape label for the folder and restores all the documents. If your spooled file save happens to span multiple tape volumes, you'll be prompted to load the first tape to read the label information before restoring the documents on the subsequent tapes. To help with recovery, consider saving your spooled files on a separate tape using the *Load exit in a control group, or split your spooled file saves so you use only one tape at a time.

The BRMS Operations Navigator Interface

With V5R1, BRMS has an Operations Navigator (OpsNav) interface that makes setting up and managing your backup and recovery strategy even easier (for more information about OpsNav, see Chapter 34). Using wizards, you can simplify the common operations you need to perform, such as creating a backup policy, adding tape media to BRMS, preparing the tapes for use, adding items to a backup policy, and restoring backed-up items.

If you're currently using BRMS, you may not find all the functionality in OpsNav that you have with the green-screen version. However, watch for additional features in future releases of BRMS Operations Navigator. You may still want to use the graphical interface to perform some of the basic operations. If so, you'll need to be aware of some differences between the green-screen and the OpsNav interfaces.

Terminology Differences

The OpsNav version of BRMS uses some different terminology than the green-screen BRMS. Here are some key terms:

New terminology	*Definition*
Backup history	Information about each of the objects backed up using BRMS. The backup history includes any items backed up using a backup policy. In the green-screen interface, the equivalent term is media information.
Backup policy	Defaults that control what data is backed up, how it is backed up, and where it is backed up. In the green-screen interface, a combination of a backup control group and a media policy would make up a backup policy. Also, there is no system policy in the OpsNav interface. All information needed to perform a backup is included in the backup policy.
Media pool	A group of media that has similar density and capacity characteristics. In the green-screen interface, this is known as a media class.

Functional Differences

As of this writing, the current version of BRMS Operations Navigator lets you

- run policies shipped with BRMS
- view the backup history
- view the backup and recovery log
- create and run a backup policy
- back up individual items
- restore individual items
- schedule items to be backed up and restored
- print a system recovery report
- customize user access to BRMS functions and components
- run BRMS maintenance activities
- add, display, and manage tape media

Some functions unavailable in the current release of BRMS Operations Navigator but included in the green-screen interface include

- move policies
- tape library support
- backup to save files
- backup of spooled files
- parallel backup
- networked systems support
- advanced functions, such as hierarchical storage management (HSM)
- BRMS Application Client for Tivoli Storage Manager

Backup and Recovery with BRMS OpsNav

BRMS Operations Navigator is actually a plug-in to OpsNav. A plug-in is a program that's created separately from OpsNav but, when installed, looks and behaves like the rest of the graphical user interface of OpsNav.

Backup Policies

One ease-of-use advantage offered by BRMS OpsNav is that you can create backup policies to control your backups. A backup policy is a group of defaults that controls what data is backed up, how it is backed up, and where it is backed up. Once you've defined your backup policies, you can run your backup at any time or schedule your backup to run whenever it fits into your backup window.

Three backup policies come with BRMS:

- *System — backs up the entire system
- *SysGrp — backs up all system data
- *BkuGrp — backs up all user data

If you have a simple backup strategy, you can implement your strategy using these three backup policies. If you have a medium or complex strategy, you create your own backup policies.

When you back up your data using a BRMS backup policy, information about each backed-up item is stored in the backup history. This information includes the item name, the type of backup, the date of the backup, and the volume on which the item is backed up. You can specify the level of detail you want to track for each item in the properties for the policy. You can then restore items by selecting them from the backup history. You also use the backup history information for system recoveries.

Creating a BRMS Backup Policy

You can use the New Backup Policy wizard in OpsNav to create a new BRMS backup policy. To access the wizard:

1. Expand Backup, Recovery and Media Services.
2. Right-click Backup policies, and select New policy.

The wizard gives you the following options for creating your backup policies:

Option	*Description*
Back up all system and user data	Enables you to do a full system backup of IBM-supplied data and all user data (spooled files are not included in this backup)
Back up all user data	Enables you to back up the data that belongs to users on your system, such as user profiles, security data, configuration data, user libraries, folders, and objects in directories
Back up Lotus server data online	Enables you to perform an online backup of Lotus Domino and Quickplace servers
Back up a customized set of objects	Enables you to choose the items you want to back up

After creating a backup policy, you can choose to run the backup policy immediately or schedule it to run later. If you want to change the policy later, you can do so by editing the properties of the policy. Many customization options that aren't available in the New Backup Policy wizard are available in the properties of the policy. To access the policy properties, right-click the policy and select Properties.

Backing Up Individual Items

In addition to using backup policies to back up your data, you can choose to back up individual files, libraries, or folders using the OpsNav hierarchy. You can also choose to back up just security or configuration data. Using OpsNav, simply right-click the item you want to back up and select Backup.

Restoring Individual Items

If a file becomes corrupted or accidentally deleted, you may need to restore individual items on your system. If you use backup policies to back up items on your system, you can restore those items from the backup history. When you restore an item from the backup history, you can view details about the item, such as when it was backed up and how large it is. If there are several versions of the item in the backup history, you can select which version of the item you want to restore.

You can also restore items that you backed up without using a backup policy. However, for these items, you don't have the benefit of using the backup history to make your selection. Fortunately, you can use the OpsNav Restore wizard to restore individual items on your system, whether they were backed up with a backup policy or not. To access the wizard in OpsNav, right-click Backup, Recovery and Media Services and select Restore.

Scheduling Unattended Backup and Restore Operations

Earlier, you saw how to schedule unattended restricted-state saves using the console monitor and the StrBkuBRM command. Of course, you can also schedule non–restricted-state save and restore operations.

In addition, you can use OpsNav to schedule your backup. To do so, you simply use the OpsNav New Policy wizard to create and schedule a backup. If you need to schedule an existing backup policy, you can do so by right-clicking its entry under Backup Policies in OpsNav and selecting Schedule. If the save operation requires a restricted-state system, you need only follow the console monitor instructions presented by OpsNav when you schedule the backup.

Tip

When you schedule a backup policy to be run, remember that only the items scheduled to be backed up on the day you run the policy will be backed up. For example, say you have a backup policy that includes the library MyLib. In the policy properties, you schedule MyLib for backup every Thursday. If you schedule the policy to run on Thursday, the system backs up MyLib. However, if you schedule the same policy to run on any other day, the system does not back up MyLib.

You can also schedule restore operations in much the same manner as backup operations using OpsNav. Restore operations, however, are scheduled less often than backup operations.

System Recovery Report

BRMS produces a complete system recovery report that guides you through an entire system recovery. The report lets you know exactly which tape volumes are needed to recover your system. When recovering your entire system, you should use the report in conjunction with *OS/400 Backup and Recovery* (SC41-5304). Keep the recovery report with your tape volumes in a secure and safe off-site location.

BRMS Security Functions

BRMS provides security functions via the Functional Usage Model, which lets you customize access to selected BRMS functions and functional components by user. You must use the OpsNav interface to access the Functional Usage Model feature. You can let certain users *use* specific functions and components while letting others *use* and *change* specific functions and components. You can grant various types of functional usage to all users or to specified users only.

Each BRMS function, functional component, and specific backup and media management item (e.g., policy, control group) has two levels of authority access:

- Access or No Access — At the first level of authority access using the Functional Usage Model, a user either has access to a BRMS function or component or has no access to it. If a user has access, he or she can use and view the function or component. With this basic level of access, a user can process a specific item (e.g., a library, a control group) in a backup operation but can't change the item.
- Specific Change or No Change — The second level of authority access lets a user change a specific function, component, or item. For example, to change a backup list, a user must have access to the specific backup list. Similarly, to change a media policy, a user must have access to the specific media policy.

The Functional Usage Model provides lists of existing items (e.g., control groups, backup lists, media and move policies) for which you can grant specific access. With the

Functional Usage Model, you can give a user both types of access (so the user can both use and change a particular function, component, or item) or only one type of access (e.g., access to use but not change a particular function, component, or item).

Security Options for BRMS Functions, Components, and Items

In the backup area, the following usage levels are available:

- Basic Backup Activities — Users with Basic Backup Activities access can use and view the backup policy, control groups, and backup lists. With use access, these users can also process backups by using backup control groups (i.e., using the StrBkuBRM command) or by saving libraries, objects, or folders (SavLibBRM, SavObjBRM, or SavFlrLBRM). A user without Basic Backup Activities access can't see backup menu options or command parameter options.
- Backup Policy — Users with Backup Policy access can change the backup policy (in addition to using and viewing it). Users without access to the backup policy cannot change it.
- Backup Control Groups — Users with Backup Control Groups access can change specific backup control groups (in addition to using and viewing them). A user can find a list of his or her existing backup control groups under the backup control groups heading in OpsNav. You can grant a user access to any number of specific control groups. Users without access to the backup control groups cannot change them.
- Backup Lists — Users with Backup Lists access can change specific backup lists (in addition to using and viewing them). A user can find a list of his or her existing backup lists under the backup lists heading in OpsNav. You can grant a user access to any number of specific backup lists. Users without access to a backup list cannot change it.

In the recovery area, the following usage levels are available:

- Basic Recovery Activities — Users with Basic Recovery Activities access can use and view the recovery policy. They can also use the WrkMedIBRM (Work with Media Information using BRM) command to process basic recoveries, command RstObjBRM (Restore Object using BRM), and command RstLibBRM (Restore Library using BRM). Users without Basic Recovery Activities access can't see recovery menu options or command parameter options.
- Recovery Policy — Users with Recovery Policy access can change the recovery policy (in addition to using and viewing it). Users without access to the recovery policy can't change it.

In the area of media management, the following usage levels are available:

- Basic Media Activities — Users with Basic Media Activities access can perform basic media-related tasks, such as using and adding media to BRMS. Users with this access can also use and view (but not change) media policies and media classes. Users without Basic Media Activities access can't see related menu options or command parameter options.

- Advanced Media Activities — Users with Advanced Media Activities access can perform media-related tasks such as expiring, removing, and initializing media.
- Media Policies — Users with Media Policies access can change specific media policies (in addition to using and viewing them). A user can find a list of his or her existing media policies under the media policies heading in OpsNav. You can grant a user access to any number of media policies. Users without access to a media policy cannot change it.
- Media Classes — Users with Media Classes access can change specific media classes (in addition to using and viewing them). A user can find a list of his or her existing media classes under the media classes heading in OpsNav. You can grant a user access to any number of media classes. Users without access to a media class cannot change it.
- Media Information — Users with Media Information access can change media information with command WrkMedIBRM (Work with Media Information).
- Basic Movement Activities — Users with Basic Movement Activities access can manually process or display MovMedBRM (Move Media using BRM) commands, but they can't change them.
- Move Verification — Users with Move Verification access can perform move verification tasks.
- Move Policies — Users with Move Policies access can change specific move policies (in addition to using and viewing them). A user can find a list of his or her existing move policies under the move policies heading in OpsNav. You can grant a user access to any number of move policies. Users without access to a move policy cannot change it.

In the system area, the following usage options are available:

- Basic System-related Activities — Users with Basic System-related Activities access can use and view device panels and commands. They can also view and display auxiliary storage pool (ASP) panels and commands. Users with this access level can also use and view the system policy.
- Devices — Users with Devices access can change device-related information. Users without this access can't change device-related information.
- Auxiliary Storage Pools — Users with ASP access can change information about BRMS ASP management.
- Maintenance — Users with Maintenance access can schedule and run maintenance operations.
- System Policy — Users with System Policy access can change system policy parameters.

- Log — Users with Log access can remove log entries. Any user can display log information, but only those with Log access can remove log entries.
- Initialize — Users with Initialize access can use the InzBRM (Initialize BRM) command.

Media Management

BRMS makes media management simple by maintaining an inventory of your tape media. It keeps track of what data is backed up on which tape and which tapes have available space. When you run a backup, BRMS selects the tape to use from the available pool of tapes. BRMS prevents a user from accidentally writing over active files or using the wrong tape.

Before you can use any tape media with BRMS, you need to add it to the BRMS inventory and initialize it. You can do this using OpsNav's Add media wizard (under Media, right-click Tape Volumes and select Add). You can also use the green-screen BRMS command AddMedBRM (Add Media to BRM).

Once you've added tape media to the BRMS inventory, you can view the media based on criteria you specify, such as the volume name, status, media pool, or expiration date. This gives you the capability to manually expire a tape and make it available for use in the BRMS media inventory.

To filter which media you see in the list, under Media, right-click Tape Volumes and select Include. To view information about a particular tape volume or perform an action on that volume, right-click the volume and select the action you want to perform from the menu.

BRMS Housekeeping

You should perform a little BRMS housekeeping on a daily basis. The BRMS maintenance operation automatically performs BRMS cleanup on your system, updates backup information, and runs reports. BRMS maintenance performs these functions:

- expires media
- removes media information
- removes migration information (180 days old)
- removes log entries (from beginning entry to within 90 days of current date)
- runs cleanup
- retrieves volume statistics
- audits system media
- changes journal receivers
- prints expired media report

- prints version report
- prints media information
- prints recovery reports

You can run BRMS maintenance using OpsNav (right-click Backup, Recovery and Media Services and select Run Maintenance) or using BRMS command StrMntBRM (Start Maintenance for BRM).

Check It Out

As you can see, BRMS provides some powerful features for simplifying and managing many aspects of iSeries backup and recovery. Keep in mind that BRMS isn't a replacement for your backup and recovery strategy; rather, it's a tool that can help you implement and carry out such a strategy.

There's a lot more to BRMS than what's been covered here. For the complete details, see *Backup, Recovery and Media Services* (SC41-5345), as well as the BRMS home page (*http://www.as400.ibm.com/service/brms.htm*) and IBM's iSeries Information Center (*http://publib.boulder.ibm.com/pubs/html/as400/infocenter.htm*).

Chapter 17

Defining a Subsystem

We've all found ourselves lost at some time or other. It's not that we're stupid. We're simply in an unfamiliar place without the proper orientation.

You may have experienced a similar feeling of discomfort the first few times you signed on to your system. Perhaps you submitted a job and then wondered, "How do I find that job?" or "Where did it go?" Although we're sure you've progressed beyond these initial stages of bewilderment, you may still need a good introduction to the concepts of work management on the iSeries.

Work management on the iSeries refers to the set of objects that define jobs and how the system processes those jobs. With a good understanding of work-management concepts, you can easily perform such tasks as finding a job on the system, solving problems, improving performance, and controlling job priorities. We can't imagine anyone operating an iSeries in a production environment without having basic work-management skills to facilitate problem solving and operations. Let us illustrate two situations in which work management could enhance system operations.

Perhaps you're plagued with end users who complain that the system takes too long to complete short jobs. You investigate, and you discover that, indeed, the system is processing short jobs slowly because those jobs are spending too much time in the job queue behind long-running end-user batch jobs, operator-submitted batch jobs, and even program compiles. You could tell your operators not to submit jobs, or you could have your programmers compile interactively, but these approaches are impractical and unnecessary. The answer lies in understanding the work-management concepts of multiple subsystems and multiple job queues.

Or perhaps when your "power users" and your programmers share a subsystem, excessive peaks and valleys in performance occur due to the heavy interaction of these users. Maybe you'd like to use separate storage pools (i.e., memory pools) based on user profiles so you can place your power users in one pool, your programmers in another, and everyone else in a third pool, thereby creating consistent performance for each user group. You could do this if you knew the work-management concepts of memory management.

Learning work-management skills means learning how to maximize system resources. Our goal for this and the next two chapters is to teach you the basic skills you need to effectively and creatively manage all the work processed on your system.

Getting Oriented

Just as a road map gives you the information you need to find your way in an unfamiliar city, Figure 17.1 serves as a guide to understanding work management. It shows the basic work-management objects and how they relate to one another.

FIGURE 17.1
Work-Management Objects

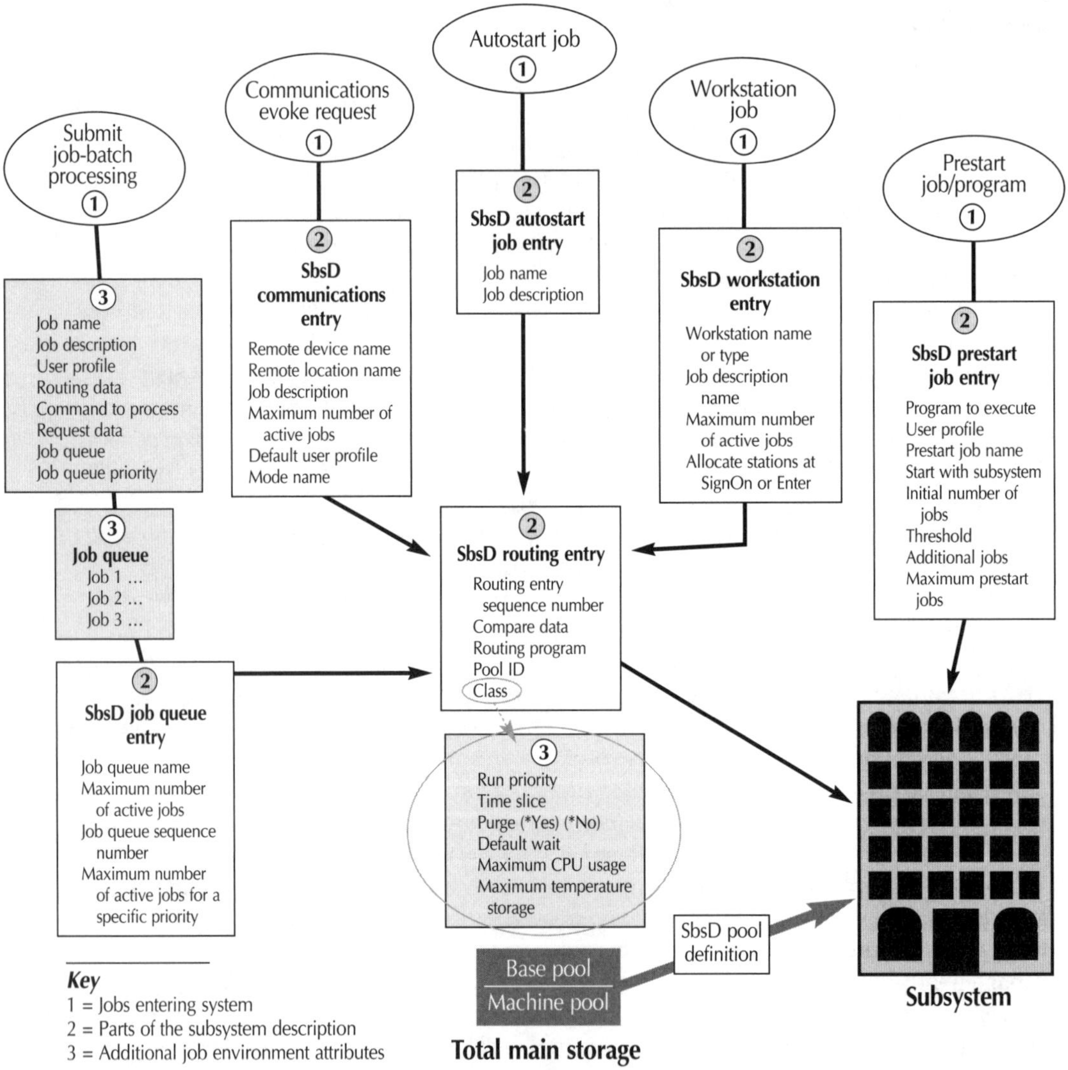

Autostart job ①

Communications evoke request ①

Submit job-batch processing ①

Workstation job ①

Prestart job/program ①

③
Job name
Job description
User profile
Routing data
Command to process
Request data
Job queue
Job queue priority

② **SbsD communications entry**
Remote device name
Remote location name
Job description
Maximum number of active jobs
Default user profile
Mode name

② **SbsD autostart job entry**
Job name
Job description

② **SbsD workstation entry**
Workstation name or type
Job description name
Maximum number of active jobs
Allocate stations at SignOn or Enter

② **SbsD prestart job entry**
Program to execute
User profile
Prestart job name
Start with subsystem
Initial number of jobs
Threshold
Additional jobs
Maximum prestart jobs

③ **Job queue**
Job 1 ...
Job 2 ...
Job 3 ...

② **SbsD routing entry**
Routing entry sequence number
Compare data
Routing program
Pool ID
Class

② **SbsD job queue entry**
Job queue name
Maximum number of active jobs
Job queue sequence number
Maximum number of active jobs for a specific priority

③
Run priority
Time slice
Purge (*Yes) (*No)
Default wait
Maximum CPU usage
Maximum temperature storage

SbsD pool definition

Base pool
Machine pool

Total main storage

Subsystem

Key
1 = Jobs entering system
2 = Parts of the subsystem description
3 = Additional job environment attributes

The objects designated by a 1 in the figure represent jobs that enter the system. Those designated by a 2 represent parts of the subsystem description. And those designated by a 3 represent additional job environment attributes (e.g., job description, user profile) that affect the way a job interacts with the system.

In the Roman Empire, all roads led to Rome. You'll notice that all the paths in Figure 17.1 lead to one destination: the subsystem. On the iSeries, all jobs must be processed in a subsystem. So what better place to start our study of work management than the subsystem?

Defining a Subsystem

A subsystem, defined by a subsystem description, is where the system brings together the resources needed to process work. As Figure 17.2 shows, the subsystem description contains seven parts that fall into three categories.

FIGURE 17.2
Subsystem Description Components

Subsystem attributes
- Storage pool definitions

Work entries
- Autostart job entries
- Workstation entries
- Job queue entries
- Communications entries
- Prestart job entries

Routing entries

Let us briefly introduce you to these components of the subsystem description.

- *Subsystem attributes* provide the general definition of the subsystem and control its main storage allocations. The general definition includes the subsystem name, the subsystem description, and the maximum number of jobs allowed in the subsystem.
  - *Storage pool definitions* are the most significant subsystem attributes. A subsystem's storage pool definition determines how the subsystem uses main storage to process work. The storage pool definition lets a subsystem either share an existing pool of main storage (e.g., *Base, *Interact) with other subsystems, establish a private pool of main storage, or both. The storage pool definition also lets you establish the activity level — the maximum number of jobs allowed in the subsystem — for a particular storage pool.
- *Work entries* define how jobs enter the subsystem and how the subsystem processes that work. They consist of autostart job entries, workstation entries, job queue entries, communications entries, and prestart job entries.
  - *Autostart job entries* let you predefine any jobs you want the system to start automatically when it starts the subsystem.
  - *Workstation entries* define which workstations the subsystem will use to receive work. You can use a workstation entry to initiate an interactive job when a user

signs on to the system or when a user transfers an interactive job from another subsystem. You can create workstation entries for specific workstation names (e.g., Dsp10, OH0123), for generic names (e.g., Dsp*, DP*, OH*), or by the type of workstations (e.g., 5251, 3476, 3477).

- ◦ *Job queue entries* define the specific job queues from which to receive work. A job queue, which submits jobs to the subsystem for processing, can be allocated by only one active subsystem. A single subsystem, however, can allocate multiple job queues, prioritize them, and specify for each a maximum number of active jobs.
- ◦ *Communications entries* define the communications device associated with a remote location name from which you can receive a communications evoke request.
- ◦ *Prestart job entries* define jobs that start on a local system before a remote system sends a communications request. When a communications evoke request requires the program running in the prestart job, the request attaches to that prestart job, thereby eliminating all overhead associated with initiating a job and program.

- *Routing entries* identify which programs to call to control routing steps that will be executed in the subsystem for a given job. Routing entries also define in which storage pool the job will be processed and which basic execution attributes (defined in a job class object associated with a routing entry) the job will use for processing.

All these components of the subsystem description determine how the system uses resources to process jobs within a subsystem. We'll expand on our discussion of work entries in Chapter 18 and on the discussion of routing entries in Chapter 19.

Now that we've covered some basic terms, let's take a closer look at subsystem attributes and how subsystems can use main storage to process work.

Main Storage and Subsystem Pool Definitions

When the iSeries is shipped, all of main storage resides in two system pools: the machine pool (*Machine) and the base pool (*Base). You must define the machine pool to support your system hardware; the amount of main storage you allocate to the machine pool is hardware dependent and varies with each system. For more information about calculating the required machine pool size, see *OS/400 Work Management* (SC41-5306).

The base pool is the main storage that remains after you reserve the machine pool. You can designate *Base as a shared pool for all subsystems to use to process work, or you can divide it into smaller pools of shared and private main storage. A shared pool is an allocation of main storage where multiple subsystems can process work. *Machine and *Base are both examples of shared pools. Other shared storage pools you can define include *Interact (for interactive jobs), *Spool (for printers), and *ShrPool1 through *ShrPool60 (for pools you can define for your own purposes).

You can control shared pool sizes by using the ChgShrPool (Change Shared Storage Pool) or WrkShrPool (Work with Shared Pools) command. Figure 17.3 shows a WrkShrPool screen, where you can modify the pool size or activity level simply by changing the entries.

FIGURE 17.3
Work with Shared Pools Panel

```
                           Work with Shared Pools
                                                          System:   AS400
Main storage size (M)  . :            64.00

Type changes (if allowed), press Enter.

             Defined     Max   Allocated    Pool   -Paging Option--
Pool         Size (M)  Active  Size (M)      ID    Defined   Current
*MACHINE        36.62   +++++      36.62      1    *FIXED    *FIXED
*BASE           10.95       5      10.95      2    *FIXED    *FIXED
*INTERACT       15.38       6      15.38      3    *FIXED    *FIXED
*SPOOL           1.03       1       1.03      4    *FIXED    *FIXED
*SHRPOOL1         .00       0                      *FIXED
*SHRPOOL2         .00       0                      *FIXED
*SHRPOOL3         .00       0                      *FIXED
*SHRPOOL4         .00       0                      *FIXED
*SHRPOOL5         .00       0                      *FIXED
*SHRPOOL6         .00       0                      *FIXED
                                                                  More...
Command
===>
F3=Exit   F4=Prompt   F5=Refresh   F9=Retrieve   F11=Display tuning data
F12=Cancel
```

The iSeries default controlling subsystem, QBase, and the default spooling subsystem, QSpl, are configured to take advantage of shared pools. QBase uses the *Base pool and the *Interact pool, while QSpl uses *Base and *Spool.

To see what pools a subsystem is using, you use the DspSbsD (Display Subsystem Description) command. For instance, when you execute the command

```
DspSbsD QBase Output(*Print)
```

you'll find the following pool definitions for QBase listed (if the defaults haven't been changed):

```
QBASE   ((1 *BASE) (2 *INTERACT))
```

Parentheses group together two definitions, each of which can contain two distinct parts (the subsystem pool number and size). In this example, the (1 *BASE) represents the subsystem pool number 1 and a size of *Base, meaning that the system will use all of the *Base pool as a shared pool. A third part of the pool definition, the activity level, doesn't appear for *Base because system value QBasActLvl (Base pool activity level, covered in Chapter 2) maintains the activity level.

The second pool definition for QBase in this example is (2 *INTERACT). Because you can use the ChgShrPool or WrkShrPool command to change the activity level for shared pool *Interact, the activity level isn't listed as part of the subsystem description, nor is it specified when you use the CrtSbsD or ChgSbsD command.

Be careful not to confuse subsystem pool numbering with *system* pool numbering. The two predefined system pools for the iSeries, *Machine and *Base, are defined as system pool 1 and system pool 2, respectively. Pool numbering within a subsystem is unique to that subsystem, and only the routing entries in that subsystem use it to determine which pool jobs will use, based on the routing data associated with each job. As subsystems define new storage pools (shared or private) in addition to the two predefined system pools, the system simply assigns the next available system pool number to use as a reference on the WrkSysSts display.

For example, with the above pools for QBase and the following pools for QSpl

```
QSPL   ((1 *BASE) (2 *SPOOL))
```

the system pool numbering might correspond to the subsystem pool numbering as shown in Figure 17.4.

FIGURE 17.4

System and Subsystem Pool Numbering

System pool number	Subsystem pool number *QBase*	*QSpl*
1 Machine pool		
2 *Base pool	1	1
3 *Interact shared pool	2	
4 *Spool shared pool		2

A private pool is a specific allocation of main storage reserved for one subsystem. It's common to use a private pool when the system uses the controlling subsystem QCtl instead of QBase. If you change your controlling subsystem to QCtl, at IPL the system start-up program starts several subsystems (QInter, QBatch, QCmn, and QSpl) that are designed to support specific types of work. Although using QBase as the controlling subsystem lets you divide main storage into separate pools, using QCtl is inherently easier to manage and administer in terms of controlling the number of jobs and performance tuning.

IBM ships the following pool definitions for the multiple-subsystem approach:

```
QCTL   ((1 *BASE))
QINTER ((1 *BASE) (2 *INTERACT))
QBATCH ((1 *BASE))
QCMN   ((1 *BASE))
QSPL   ((1 *BASE) (2 *SPOOL))
```

As you can see, the initial configuration of these subsystems is like the initial configuration of subsystem QBase in that shared pools reserve areas of main storage for specific types of jobs. However, pool sharing doesn't provide optimum performance in a diverse operations environment where various types of work are processed simultaneously. In such cases, subsystems with private pools may be necessary to improve performance.

Look at the pool definitions in Figure 17.5, in which two interactive subsystems (QInter and QPgmr) provide private pools for both end users and programmers.

FIGURE 17.5
Sample Subsystem Pool Definitions

Controlling subsystem
```
   QCTL       ((1 *BASE))
```
Interactive subsystems
```
   QINTER     ((1 *BASE) (2 20000 50))
   QPGMR      ((1 *BASE) (2 2000 5))
```
Batch subsystems
```
   QBATCH     ((1 *BASE))
   DAYQ       ((1 *BASE) (2 1000 2))
   QPGMRB     ((1 *BASE) (2 500 1))
```
Communications subsystem
```
   QCMN       ((1 *BASE))
```
Spooling subsystem
```
   QSPL       ((1 *BASE) (2 *SPOOL))
```

Both QInter and QPgmr define specific amounts of main storage to be allocated to the subsystem instead of sharing the *Interact pool. Also, both storage definitions require a specific activity level, whereas shared pool activity levels are maintained as part of the shared pool definitions (using the ChgShrPool or WrkShrPool command). The private pool configuration in this example, with private main storage and private activity levels, prevents unwanted contention for resources between end users and programmers.

Figure 17.5 also demonstrates how you can use multiple batch subsystems. Three batch subsystems — QBatch, DayQ, and QPgmrB — provide, respectively, for daytime and nighttime processing of operator-submitted batch jobs, daytime end-user processing of short jobs, and program compiles. A separate communications subsystem, QCmn, is configured to handle any communications requests, and QSpl handles spooling.

The decision about whether to use shared pools or private pools should depend on the storage capacity of your system. On one hand, because shared pools ensure efficient use of main storage by letting more than one subsystem share a storage pool, it's wise to use shared pools if you have a system with limited main storage. On the other hand, private pools provide a reserved pool of main storage and activity levels that are constantly available to a subsystem without contention from any other subsystem. They're easy to manage when you're dealing with multiple subsystems. Therefore, private pools are a wise choice for a system with ample main storage.

Starting a Subsystem

A subsystem definition is only that — a definition. To start a subsystem, you use the StrSbs (Start Subsystem) command. Figure 17.6 outlines the steps your system takes to activate a subsystem after you execute a StrSbs command.

FIGURE 17.6
Starting a Subsystem

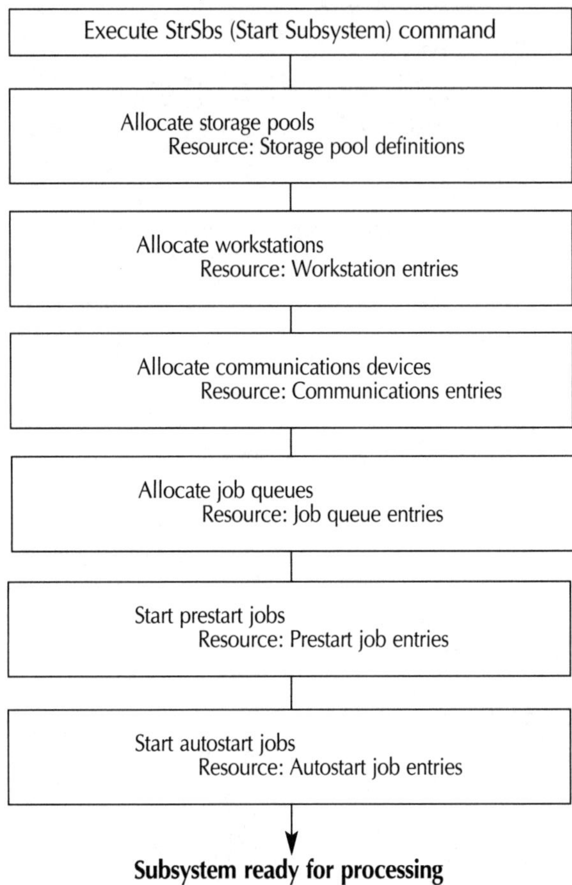

First, the system uses the storage pool definitions to allocate main storage for job processing. Next, it uses the workstation entries to allocate workstation devices and present the workstation sign-on displays. If the system finds communications entries, it uses them to allocate the named devices. The system then allocates job queues so that when the subsystem completes the start-up process, the subsystem can receive jobs from the job queues. Next, the system starts any defined prestart or autostart jobs. When the system has completed all these steps, the subsystem is finally ready to begin processing work.

The Next Step

With this introduction to subsystems under your belt, look over *OS/400 Work Management* and make a sketch of your system's main storage pool configuration to see how your subsystems work. Chapter 18 examines work entries and where jobs come from, and Chapter 19 discusses routing and where jobs go. When we're done with all that, you'll find yourself on Easy Street — with the skills you need to implement a multiple-subsystem work environment.

Chapter 18

Where Jobs Come From

One of OS/400's most elegant features is the concept of a "job" — a unit of work with a tidy package of attributes that lets you easily identify and track work throughout your system. The iSeries defines this unit of work with a job name, a user profile associated with the job, and a computer-assigned job number; it is these three attributes that give a job a unique identifier. For example, when a user signs on to a workstation, the resulting job might be known to the system as

Job name: DSP10

User profile: KNIELSEN

Job number: 003459

Any transaction that OS/400 completes is associated with an active job executing on the system. But where do these jobs come from? A job can be initiated at times such as when

- you sign on to the system from a workstation
- you submit a batch job
- your system receives a communications evoke request from another system
- you submit a prestart job
- you create autostart job entries that the system automatically executes when it starts the associated subsystem

Understanding how jobs get started on the system is crucial to grasping iSeries work-management concepts. So let's continue Chapter 17's look at the subsystem description by focusing on work entries, the part of the description that defines how jobs gain access to the subsystem for processing.

Types of Work Entries

There are five types of work entries:

- workstation
- job queue
- communications
- prestart job
- autostart job

Let's look more closely at each of these entry types now.

Workstation Entries

The easiest work-entry type to understand is the *workstation entry*, which describes how a user gains access to a particular subsystem (for interactive jobs) using a workstation. To define a workstation entry, you use the AddWSE (Add Work Station Entry) command. A subsystem can have as many workstation entries as you need. Each one has the following attributes:

- WrkStnType (workstation type) or WrkStn (workstation name)
- JobD (job description name)
- MaxAct (maximum number of active workstations)
- At (when to allocate workstation)

When defining a workstation entry, you can use either the WrkStnType attribute or the WrkStn attribute to specify which workstation(s) the system should allocate. For instance, if you want to allocate all workstations, you specify WrkStnType(*All) in the workstation entry. This entry tells the system to allocate all workstations, regardless of the type (e.g., 5250, 5291, 3476, 3477). You can also specify a special workstation type using WrkStnType(*Cons), WrkStnType(*ASCII), or WrkStnType(*NonASCII) to define the console device, ASCII devices, or non-ASCII devices, respectively. Or you can use the WrkStnType attribute in one or more workstation entries to tell the system to allocate a specific type of workstation — for example, WrkStnType(3477).

You can also define workstation entries using the WrkStn attribute to specify that the system allocate workstations by name. You can enter either a specific name or a generic name. For example, an entry defining WrkStn(Dsp01) tells the subsystem to allocate device Dsp01. The generic entry WrkStn(Ohio*) tells the subsystem to let any workstation whose name begins with OHIO establish an interactive job.

The JobD workstation entry attribute specifies the job description for the workstation entry. You can give this attribute a value of *UsrPrf (the default) to tell the system to use the job description named in the user profile of the person who signs on to the workstation. Or you can specify a value of *SbsD to tell the system to use the job description with the same name as that of the subsystem. You can also use the qualified name of an existing job description.

Caution

For security reasons, it's wise to use the default value *UsrPrf for the workstation entry's JobD attribute so that a user profile is required to sign on to the workstation. If you use the value *SbsD or a job description name, and a valid user profile is associated with the job description through the job description's User attribute, any user can simply press Enter and sign on to the subsystem. In such a situation, the user then assumes the user ID associated with the default job description named on the workstation entry.

There may be times when you want to define a workstation entry so that one user profile is always used when someone accesses the system using a particular workstation (e.g., if you wanted to disseminate public information at a courthouse, mall, or school). In such cases, be sure to construct such configurations so that only certain workstation entries have a job description that provides this type of access.

The workstation entry's MaxAct attribute determines the maximum number of workstations (using this work entry) allowed in the subsystem at one time. When this limit is reached, the subsystem must deallocate one workstation before it can allocate another. The value you should normally use for this attribute is the default, *NoMax, because you typically control (i.e., you physically limit) the number of devices. In fact, supplying a number for the MaxAct attribute could cause confusion if one day the limit is reached and some poor soul has to figure out why certain workstations aren't functioning. It could take days to find this seldom-used attribute and change the value.

The At attribute tells the system when to allocate the workstation. The default value, *SignOn, tells the system to allocate the workstation (i.e., initiate a sign-on screen at the workstation) when the subsystem is started. Value *Enter tells the system to let jobs enter the subsystem only via the TfrJob (Transfer Job) command. (Before a job can be transferred into an interactive subsystem, a job queue and a subsystem description job queue entry must exist.)

Using Workstation Entries

Now you're acquainted with the workstation entry attributes, but how can you use workstation entries? Let's say you want to process all your interactive jobs in subsystem QInter. When you look at the default workstation entries for QInter, you see the following:

```
WRKSTNTYPE    JOBD       MAXACT    AT
*ALL          *USRPRF    *NOMAX    *SIGNON
*CONS         *USRPRF    *NOMAX    *ENTER
```

The first set of values tells the system to allocate all workstations to subsystem QInter when the subsystem is started. The second set of values tells the system to let the console transfer into the subsystem but not to allocate the device.

What about a multiple-subsystem environment for interactive jobs? Let's say you want to configure three subsystems: one for programmers (Pgmrs), one for local end-user workstations (Local), and one for remote end-user workstations (Remote). How can you make sure the system allocates the workstations to the correct subsystem?

Perhaps you're thinking you can create individual workstation entries for each device. You can, but such a method would be a nightmare to maintain. Likewise, it would be impractical to use the WrkStnType attribute because defining types doesn't necessarily define specific locations for certain workstations.

You have only two good options for ensuring that the correct subsystem allocates the devices. One is to name your various workstations so you can use generic WrkStn values in the workstation entry. For example, you could allocate programmers' workstations to the proper subsystem by first giving them names such as Pgmr01 and Pgmr02 and then creating a workstation entry that specifies WrkStn(Pgmr*). You might prefix all local end-user workstation names with Admn and Loc and then create workstation entries in the local subsystem using WrkStn(Admn*) and WrkStn(Loc*). For the remote subsystem, you could continue to create workstation entries using generic names such as the ones described above, or simply specify WrkStnType(*All), which would cause the subsystem to allocate the remaining workstations. However, you'll need to read on to learn how subsystems allocate workstations to ensure that the workstations in the programmer and local subsystems are allocated properly.

Your second option for ensuring that the correct subsystem allocates the devices is to use *routing entries* to reroute workstation jobs to the correct subsystem. (We'll explain how to do this in Chapter 19.)

Conflicting Workstation Entries

Can workstation entries in different subsystems conflict with each other? You bet they can! Consider what happens when two different subsystems have workstation entries that allocate the same device. If At(*SignOn) is specified in the workstation entry, the first active subsystem will allocate the device, and the device will show a sign-on display. When the system starts another subsystem with a workstation entry that applies to that same device (with At(*SignOn) specified), the subsystem will try to allocate it. If no user is signed on to the workstation, the second subsystem will allocate the device.

This arrangement isn't all bad. In fact, you can make it work for you. Imagine that you want to establish an interactive environment for two subsystems: QInter (for all end-user workstations) and QPgmr (for all programmer workstations). You supply WrkStnType(*All) for subsystem QInter and WrkStn(Pgmr*) for subsystem QPgmr.

To ensure that each workstation is allocated to the proper subsystem, you should start QInter first. As a consequence, the system will allocate all workstations to QInter. After a brief delay, start QPgmr, which then will allocate (from QInter) only the workstations whose names begin with "PGMR". Every workstation has its rightful place by simply using the system to do the work.

What about you? Can you see how your configuration is set up to let interactive jobs be processed? Take a few minutes to examine the workstation entries in your system's subsystems. You can use the DspSbsD (Display Subsystem Description) command to display the work entries that are part of the subsystem description.

Job Queue Entries

Job queue entries control job initiation on your system and define how jobs enter the subsystem for processing. To submit jobs for processing, you must assign one or more job queues to a subsystem. A job queue entry associates a job queue with a subsystem. The attributes of a job queue entry are

- JobQ (job queue name)
- MaxAct (maximum number of active jobs from this job queue)
- SeqNbr (sequence number used to determine the order of selection among all of a subsystem's job queues)
- MaxPty*n* (maximum number of active jobs with the specified job queue priority)

The JobQ attribute, which is required, defines the name of the job queue you're attaching to the subsystem. The subsystem will search this job queue to receive jobs for processing. You can name only one job queue for a job queue entry, but you can define multiple job queue entries for a subsystem.

Attribute MaxAct defines the maximum number of jobs that can be active in the subsystem from the job queue named in this entry. This attribute controls *only* the maximum number of jobs allowed into the subsystem from the named job queue. The default MaxAct value is 1, which lets only one job at a time from this job queue be processed in the subsystem.

Caution

Don't confuse the job queue entry's attribute with the MaxAct (yes, same name) attribute of the subsystem description. The subsystem description's MaxAct attribute controls the maximum number of jobs in the subsystem from all entries (e.g., job queue entries and communications entries).

You can use the SeqNbr attribute to sequence multiple job queue entries associated with the subsystem. The subsystem searches each job queue in the order specified by the SeqNbr attribute of each job queue entry. The default for this attribute is 10, which you can use to define only one subsystem job queue entry; however, when defining multiple job queue entries, you should determine the appropriate sequence numbers desired to prioritize the job queues.

The job queue entry's MaxPty*n* attribute is similar to the MaxAct attribute except that MaxPty*n* controls the number of active jobs from a job queue that have the same job queue priority (e.g., MaxPty1 defines the maximum number of jobs with job queue priority 1, MaxPty2 defines the maximum number of jobs with job queue priority 2). The default for MaxPty1 through MaxPty9 is *NoMax.

To illustrate how job queue entries work together to create a proper batch environment, Figure 18.1 shows a scheme that includes three subsystems: DaySbs, NightSbs, and BatchSbs. DaySbs processes daytime, short-running end-user batch jobs. NightSbs processes nighttime, long-running end-user batch jobs. BatchSbs processes operator-submitted requests and program compiles.

FIGURE 18.1
Sample Batch Work Environment

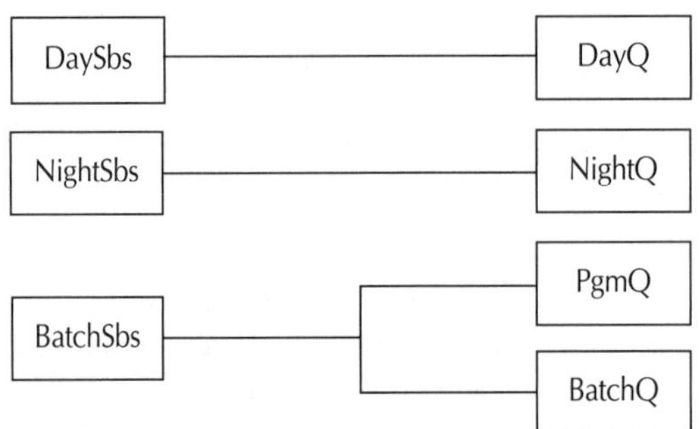

To create the batch work environment depicted in the figure, you first create the subsystems using the following CrtSbsD (Create Subsystem Description) commands:

```
CrtSbsD SbsD(QGPL/DaySbs) Pool((1 *Base) (2 400 1)) MaxAct(1)
CrtSbsD SbsD(QGPL/NightSbs) Pool((1 *Base) (2 2000 2)) MaxAct(2)
CrtSbsD SbsD(QGPL/BatchSbs) Pool((1 *Base) (2 1500 3)) MaxAct(3)
```

Notice that each subsystem has an established maximum number of active jobs (MaxAct(*n*)). The maximum limit matches the activity level specified in the subsystem pool definition so that each active job is assigned an activity level without having to wait for one.

The next step is to create the appropriate job queues using the following CrtJobQ (Create Job Queue) commands:

```
CrtJobQ JobQ(QGPL/DayQ)
CrtJobQ JobQ(QGPL/NightQ)
CrtJobQ JobQ(QGPL/PgmQ)
CrtJobQ JobQ(QGPL/BatchQ)
```

Then, use the AddJobQE (Add Job Queue Entry) command to add the job queue entries to associate the job queues with the subsystems:

```
AddJobQE SbsD(DaySbs) JobQ(DayQ) MaxAct(*NoMax) SeqNbr(10)
AddJobQE SbsD(NightSbs) JobQ(NightQ) MaxAct(*NoMax) SeqNbr(10)
AddJobQE SbsD(BatchSbs) JobQ(PgmQ) MaxAct(1) SeqNbr(10)
AddJobQE SbsD(BatchSbs) JobQ(BatchQ) MaxAct(2) SeqNbr(20)
```

Now let's walk through this batch work environment. Subsystem DaySbs is a simple configuration that lets one job queue feed jobs into the subsystem. Because the MaxAct attribute value of DaySbs is 1, only one job filters into the subsystem at a time, despite the fact that we specified the attribute MaxAct(*NoMax) for the DayQ job queue entry. Later, we can change the subsystem pool size and activity level, along with the MaxAct subsystem attribute, to let more jobs from the job queue be processed without having to re-create the job queue entry to modify MaxAct.

The configuration of NightSbs is similar to the configuration of DaySbs, except that the NightSbs configuration lets two jobs be processed at the same time. This subsystem is inactive during the day and is started at night via the StrSbs (Start Subsystem) command. When a subsystem is inactive, no job queues are allocated and no jobs are processed. Therefore, application programs can send batch jobs to the NightQ job queue, where they wait to be processed at night. When NightSbs is started, the system allocates job queue NightQ, and jobs can be processed.

To show you how job queues can work together to feed into one subsystem, we configured the BatchSbs subsystem with two job queue entries. Notice that BatchSbs supports a maximum of three jobs (MaxAct(3)). Job queue entry PgmQ lets one job from that queue be active (MaxAct(1)), while job queue entry BatchQ lets two jobs be active (MaxAct(2)).

As with workstation entries, job queue entries can conflict if you define the same job queue as an entry for more than one subsystem. When a subsystem is started, the job queues defined in the job queue entries are allocated. And when a job queue is allocated to an active subsystem, that job queue can't be allocated to another subsystem until the first subsystem is ended. In other words, first come, first served!

Communications Entries

Workstation entries enable local workstations to start interactive jobs. You may also need to establish entries to enable the initiation of jobs from a remote work site. After you establish a workstation and a physical connection between remote sites, you need a *communications entry*, which enables the subsystem to process the program start request. If no communications entries exist, the system rejects any program start request. There's no real pizzazz to this entry; you simply need it to link the remote system with your subsystem.

A communications entry has the following attributes:

- Dev (name or type of communications device)
- RmtLocName (remote location name)
- JobD (job description name)
- DftUsr (default user profile name)
- Mode (mode description name)
- MaxAct (maximum number of jobs active with this entry)

The Dev attribute specifies the particular device (e.g., CommDev, RemSys) or device type (e.g., *APPC) needed for communications. The RmtLocName attribute specifies the remote location name you define when you use the CrtDev*Xxx* (Create Device

Description (*Xxx*)) command to create the communications device. There is no default for the Dev or RmtLocName attribute. In addition, you must specify one attribute or the other, but not both.

The next two attributes, JobD and DftUsr, are crucial. JobD specifies the job description to associate with this entry. As you do with the workstation entry, you should use the default value *UsrPrf to ensure that a user profile is used and that the system uses the job description associated with the user making the program start request. As with workstation entries, using a specific job description can cause a security problem if that job description names a default user.

Attribute DftUsr defines the default user for the communications entry. You should specify *None for this attribute to ensure that any program start request supplies a valid user profile and password.

The Mode attribute defines specific communications boundaries and variables. For more information about this attribute, see *OS/400 Communications Configuration* (SC41-5401).

The MaxAct attribute defines the maximum number of program start requests that can be active at any time in the subsystem for this communications entry.

You can add a communications entry with the AddCmnE (Add Communications Entry) command, as in this example:

```
AddCmnE SbsD(CommSbs)        +
        RmtLocName(NewYork) +
        JobD(*UsrPrf)       +
        DftUsr(*None)       +
        Mode(*Any)          +
        MaxAct(*NoMax)
```

If you're communicating already and you want to know what entries are configured, use the DspSbsD command to find out.

Prestart Job Entries

The *prestart job entry* goes hand-in-hand with the communications entry, telling the subsystem which program to start when the subsystem itself is started. The program isn't executed — the system simply performs all the opens, initializes the job named in the prestart job entry, and then waits for a program start request for that particular program. When the system receives a program start request, it starts a job by using the prestart program that's ready and waiting, thus saving valuable time in program initialization.

For example, consider an order entry program that requires considerable initialization time due to the need to open many files. If remote sales personnel communicate with the system and use the order entry program to enter their orders, they'll experience much better response time if a prestart job opens the files in advance of their requests to use the program.

The prestart job entry is the only work entry that defines an actual program and job class to be used. (Other jobs get their initial routing program from the routing data entries that are part of the subsystem description.) The two key attributes of the prestart job entry are Pgm and JobD. The Pgm attribute specifies the program to use, and the JobD attribute specifies the job description to be used.

To add a prestart job entry, use an AddPJE (Add Prestart Job Entry) command similar to the following:

```
AddPJE SbsD(CommSbs) +
       Pgm(OEPgm)    +
       JobD(OEJobD)
```

Then, when the communications entry receives a program start request (an evoke) and processes the request, it will compare the program evoke to the prestart job program defined. In the example above, if the program evoke is also OEPgm, the system has no need to start a job because the prestart job is already started.

Autostart Job Entries

An *autostart job entry* specifies the job to be executed when the subsystem is started. For instance, if you want to print a particular history report each time the system is IPLed, you can use the AddAJE (Add Autostart Job Entry) command to add the following autostart job entry to the controlling subsystem description:

```
AddAJE SbsD(SbsName)             +
       Job(History)              +
       JobD(YourLib/HistJobD)
```

The Job and JobD attributes are the only ones the autostart job entry defines, which means that the job description must use the request data or the routing data to execute a command or a program. In the example above, job description HistJobD would have the correct RqsDta (Request data) attribute to call the program that generates the history report (e.g., RqsDta('Call HistPgm')). The History job, defined in the autostart job entry, is started each time the associated subsystem is started, ensuring that the job runs whether or not anyone remembers to submit it.

OS/400 uses an autostart job entry to assist the IPL process. If you examine either the QBase or QCtl subsystem description (using the DspSbsD command), you'll find that an autostart job entry exists to submit the QStrUpJD job using the job description QSys/QStrUpJD. This job description uses the request data to call a program used in the IPL process.

Where Jobs Go

Now you've seen where jobs come from on the iSeries — but where do they go? We'll address that question in Chapter 19 when we look at how routing entries provide the final gateway to subsystem processing.

One reminder: If you decide to create or change the system-supplied work-management objects, such as subsystem descriptions and job queues, you should place the new objects in a user-defined library. When you're ready to start using the new objects, you can change the system start-up program to use the new objects to establish your work environment. (To change the system start-up program, you modify the CL source and recompile the program.) Placing the new objects in your own library enables easy documentation of any changes.

Chapter 19

Demystifying Routing

So far, we've explained how jobs are defined and started on the iSeries. You've seen that jobs are processed in a subsystem, which is where the system combines all the resources needed to process work. And you've seen how work entries control the way jobs gain access to the subsystem. Now we need to talk about *routing*, which determines how jobs are processed after they reach the subsystem.

Through the years, routing has been kept shrouded in mystery. It's almost as if routing were some secret whose meaning only a few are meant to know. In this chapter, we concentrate on subsystem routing entries to prove to you, once and for all, that you have nothing to fear!

The iSeries uses routing to determine where jobs go. The system uses the following routing concepts to process each and every job:

- *routing data* — a character string, up to 80 characters long, that determines the routing entry that the subsystem will use to establish the routing step
- *routing entry* — a subsystem description entry, which you create, that determines the program and the job class that the subsystem will use to establish a routing step
- *routing step* — the processing that starts when the routing program is executed

To understand routing, it might help to think of highway signs, which control the flow of traffic from one place to another. A job's routing data is like the driving directions, and the subsystem routing entries are like the highway exits. The routing step is like the trip itself.

To be executed in a subsystem, iSeries jobs (except prestart jobs) must have routing data. Routing data determines which routing entry the subsystem will use. For most jobs, routing data is defined either by the RtgDta (Routing data) parameter of the job description associated with the job or by the RtgDta parameter of the SbmJob (Submit Job) command.

The Importance of Routing Data

When a job enters a subsystem, the subsystem looks for routing data that matches the *compare value* in one or more routing entries of the subsystem description — similar to the way you would check your written directions to see which highway exit to take. The subsystem seeks a match to determine which program to use to establish the routing step for that job. Routing entries, typically defined when you create a subsystem, are defined as part of the subsystem description via the AddRtgE (Add Routing Entry) command.

Before we take a closer look at the various attributes of a routing entry, let us explain how routing entries relate to routing data. Figure 19.1 shows how the subsystem uses routing data for an interactive job.

FIGURE 19.1

Use of Routing Data for an Interactive Job

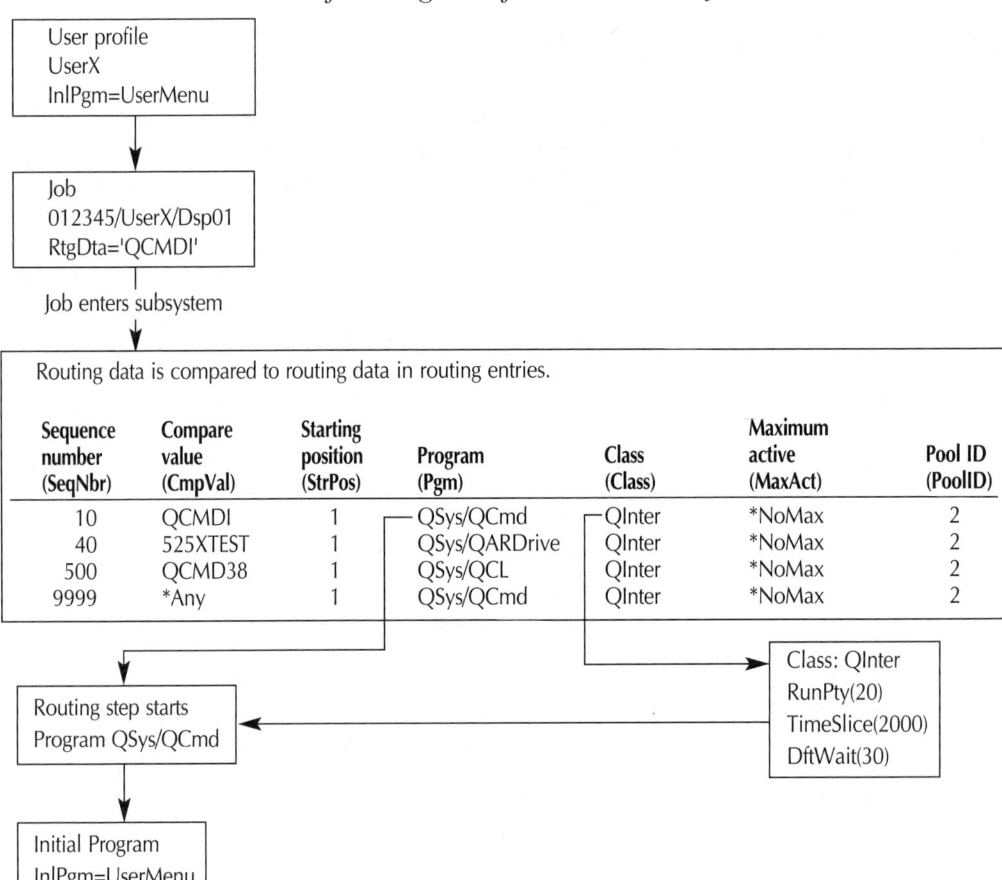

Sequence number (SeqNbr)	Compare value (CmpVal)	Starting position (StrPos)	Program (Pgm)	Class (Class)	Maximum active (MaxAct)	Pool ID (PoolID)
10	QCMDI	1	QSys/QCmd	QInter	*NoMax	2
40	525XTEST	1	QSys/QARDrive	QInter	*NoMax	2
500	QCMD38	1	QSys/QCL	QInter	*NoMax	2
9999	*Any	1	QSys/QCmd	QInter	*NoMax	2

When UserX signs on to workstation Dsp01, the interactive job is started and the routing data (QCMDI) is established. When the job enters the subsystem, the system compares the routing data in the job with the routing data of each routing entry until it finds a match. (The search is based on the starting position specified in the routing entry and the literal specified as the compare value.)

In Figure 19.1, the compare value for the first routing entry (SeqNbr(10)) and the routing data for job 012345/UserX/Dsp01 are the same. Because the system has found a match, it executes the program defined in the routing entry (QCmd in library QSys) to establish the routing step for the job in the subsystem. In addition to establishing the routing step, the routing entry provides the job with specific runtime attributes based on the specified job class. In this case, the specified class is QInter.

Jobs that require routing data (all but prestart jobs) follow this same procedure when being started in the subsystem. Now that you have a feel for how this process works, let's talk about routing entries and associated job classes.

Routing Entry Attributes

In Chapter 18, we said that routing entries identify which programs to call, define which storage pool the job will be processed in, and specify the execution attributes that the job will use for processing. As shown in Figure 19.1, a routing entry consists of several attributes: sequence number, compare value, starting position, program, class, maximum active, and pool ID. You define each attribute when you use the AddRtgE command to add a routing entry to a subsystem description. It's important that you understand these attributes and how you can use them to create the routing entries you need for your subsystems.

The sequence number is simply a basic numbering device that determines the order in which routing entries will be compared against routing data to find a match. When assigning a sequence number, you need to remember two rules. First, always reserve SeqNbr(9999) for use with the compare value *Any so it will be used only when no other match can be found. (Notice that routing entry SeqNbr(9999) in Figure 19.1 has a compare value of *Any.) Second, when using similar compare values, use the sequence numbers to order the values from most specific to least specific. For example, you would arrange the values PGMR, PGMRS, and PGMRS1 this way:

Sequence number	*Compare value*
10	PGMRS1
20	PGMRS
30	PGMR

Placing the least specific value (PGMR) first would cause a match to occur even when the intended value (e.g., PGMRS1) is more specific.

The system uses the compare value and starting position attributes together to search a job's routing data for a match. For example, if you specify a compare value of ROUTE and a starting position of 5, the system searches the job's routing data beginning in position 5 for the value ROUTE. The compare value can be any characters you want (up to 80 characters in length). The important thing is to use a compare value that matches some routing data that identifies a particular job or job type. Why go to this trouble? Because you can use this matching routing entry to determine a lot about the way a job is processed on the system (e.g., subsystem storage pool, run priority, time slice).

A routing entry's Pgm attribute determines which program is called to establish the routing step for the job being processed. Remember, a routing step simply starts the program named in the routing entry. Normally, this program is QCmd (the IBM CL processor), but it can be any program. When QCmd is the routing program, it waits for a request message to process. For an interactive job, the request message would be the initial program or menu request; for a batch job, it would be the request data (i.e., the command or program to execute). If the routing program is a user-defined program, the program is simply executed. The routing entry program is the first program executed in the routing step. You can use the routing entry to make sure a specific program is executed when certain routing data is found, regardless of the initial program or specific request data for a job. Later in this chapter, we explain how this might be beneficial to you.

Runtime Attributes

The Class (job class) object is an important performance-related object that defines the run priority of the job as well as the time slice for the job. (The time slice is the length of time, in CPU milliseconds, that a job will be processed before being bumped from the activity level to wait while another job executes a time slice.) A routing entry establishes a job's run priority and time slice much the way speed limit or yield signs control the flow of traffic. For more information about these performance-related attributes of the Class object, see *OS/400 Work Management* (SC41-5306).

In Figure 19.1, all the routing entries use class QInter, which is defined to represent the run priority and time slice typical for an interactive job. Because you wouldn't want to process a batch job using these same values, the system also has an IBM-supplied class, called QBatch, that defines attributes more typical for batch-job processing. If you look at the subsystem description for QBase, you'll find the following routing entry:

Sequence number	*Compare value*	*Program*	*Class*
10	QCMDB	QSys/QCmd	QBatch

This entry uses program QCmd and directs the system to use class QBatch to define the runtime attributes for jobs having routing data QCMDB. To route jobs with the correct routing program and job class, the system-supplied routing data for the default batch job description QBatch is QCMDB. You can use different classes to create the right performance mix.

Attribute MaxAct determines the maximum number of active jobs that can use a particular routing entry. You'll rarely need to change this attribute's default, which is *NoMax.

The last routing entry attribute is PoolID (Subsystem storage pool ID). As we explained in Chapter 17, the subsystem definition includes the specific storage pools the subsystem will use. These storage pools are numbered in the subsystem, and these numbers are used only within that particular subsystem description; they do not match the numbering scheme of the system pools. The routing entry attribute PoolID tells the system which subsystem storage pool to use to process this job. Look at the following pool definition and abbreviated routing entry:

Pool definition		
((1 *BASE) (2 10000 20))		
Sequence number	***Compare value***	***Pool ID***
10	QCMDI	1

This routing entry tells the system to use subsystem pool 1 (*BASE). Considering that 10,000 K of storage is set aside in pool 2, this routing entry is probably incorrectly specifying pool 1. Beginners commonly make the mistake of leaving the default value in the routing entry definition when creating their own subsystems and defining their own routing entries. Just remember to compare the pool definition with the routing entry definition to ensure that the correct subsystem pool is being used.

Routing Data for Interactive Jobs

Users gain access to a given subsystem for interactive jobs through workstations, defined by workstation entries. The key to determining routing data for an interactive job is the JobD (Job description) parameter of the workstation entry that the subsystem uses to allocate the workstation being used. If the value of the JobD parameter is *UsrPrf, the routing data defined on the job description associated with the user profile is used as the routing data for the interactive job. If the value of the workstation entry's JobD parameter is *SbsD (which instructs the system to use the job description of the same name as the subsystem description) or an actual job description name, the routing data of the specified job description will be used as the routing data for the interactive job. Let's consider a couple of examples.

Let's say you create a user profile using the CrtUsrPrf (Create User Profile) command and do not enter a specific job description. In that case, the system uses the default job description, QDftJobD, for that user profile. Executing the command

```
DspJobD QDftJobD
```

reveals that the RtgDta attribute has the value QCMDI. When a user signs on to a workstation that uses a subsystem workstation entry whose JobD attribute is defined as *UsrPrf, the routing data for that interactive job is the routing data defined on the job description associated with the user profile; in this case, the JobD value would be QDftJobD, and the routing data would be QCMDI.

Now look at Figure 19.2, in which the workstation entry defines SpJobD as the job description. Instead of using the job description associated with the user profile, the subsystem uses job description SpJobD to establish job attributes, including the RtgDta value of SPECIAL.

FIGURE 19.2
Workstation Entry Using SpJobD Job Description

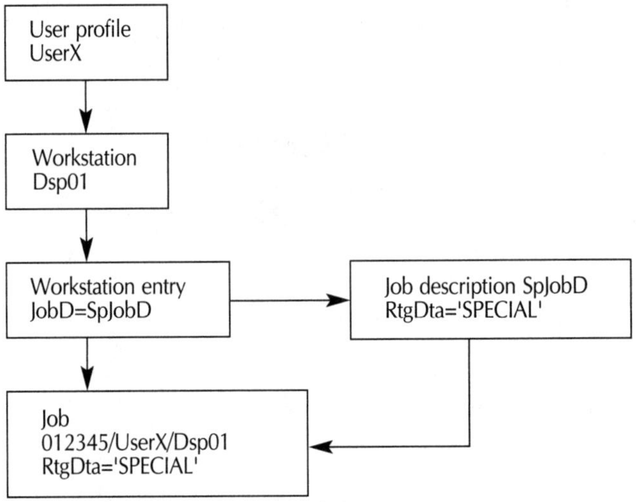

Routing Data for Batch Jobs

Establishing routing data for a batch job is simple: You use the RtgDta parameter of the SbmJob command. On this command, RtgDta has four possible values:

- *JobD — the routing data of the job description
- *RqsDta — the value specified in the RqsDta (Request data) parameter on the SbmJob command. (Because the request data represents the actual command or program to process, specifying *RqsDta is practical only if specific routing entries have been established in a subsystem to start specific routing steps based on the command or program being executed by a job.)
- QCMDB — the default routing data used by certain IBM-supplied subsystems (e.g., QBase, QPgmr) to route batch jobs to the CL processor QCmd (more about this later)
- *RoutingData* — up to 80 characters of user-defined routing data

Keeping these values in mind, let's look at a SbmJob command. To submit a batch job that sends the operator the message "hi," you would enter the command

```
SbmJob Job(Message)                              +
       Cmd('SndMsg "hi" ToMsgQ(QSysOpr)')
```

This batch job would use the routing data of QCMDB. How do we know that? Because, as the list above states, the value QCMDB is the default. If you submit a job using the SbmJob command without changing the default value for the RtgDta parameter, the routing data is always QCMDB (as long as this default hasn't been changed via the ChgCmdDft, or Change Command Default, command).

Now, examine another SbmJob command:

```
SbmJob Job(Priority)              +
       Cmd('Call UserPgm')        +
       RtgDta('high-priority')
```

In this example, a routing data character string ('high-priority') is defined. By now, you're probably wondering just how changing the routing data might change the way a job is processed. We'll get to that in a minute.

Figure 19.3 provides an overview of how the routing data for a batch job is established.

FIGURE 19.3

Method for Determining Batch Job Routing Data

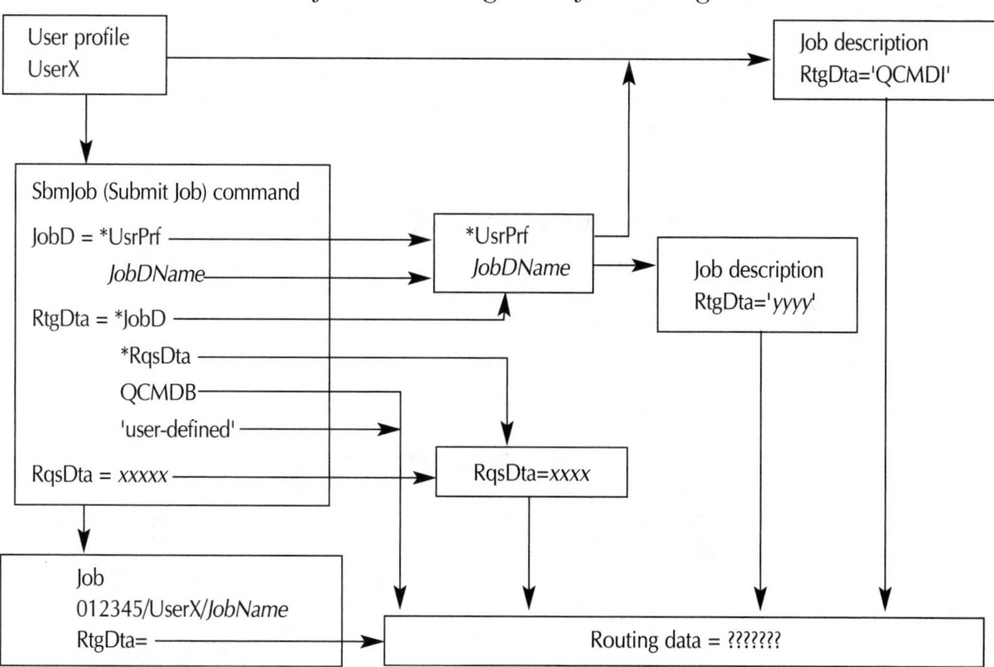

A user submits a job via the SbmJob command. The RtgDta parameter of the SbmJob command determines the routing data, and the resulting job (012345/UserX/*JobName*) is submitted to be processed in a subsystem. We can pick any of the four possible values for the RtgDta attribute on the SbmJob command and follow the path to see how that value eventually determines the routing data for the submitted batch job.

If you specify RtgDta(*JobD), the system examines the JobD parameter of the SbmJob command and then uses either the user profile's job description or the actual job description named in the parameter. If you specify RtgDta(*RqsDta), the job uses the value specified in the RqsDta parameter of the SbmJob command as the routing data. Last, if you define the RtgDta parameter value as QCMDB or any user-defined routing data, that value becomes the routing data for the job.

Routing Data for Autostart, Communications, and Prestart Jobs

As you may recall from Chapter 18, an autostart job entry in the subsystem description consists of just two attributes: the job name and the specific job description to be used for processing. The routing data of a particular job description is the only source for the routing data of an autostart job.

For communications jobs (communications evoke requests), the subsystem builds the routing data from the program start request. The routing data isn't taken from a permanent object on the system but is instead derived from the program start request that the communications entry in the subsystem receives and processes.

Prestart jobs use no routing data. The prestart job entry attribute, Pgm, specifies the program to be started in the subsystem. The processing of this program is the routing step for that job.

Is There More Than One Way to Get There?

So far, we've discussed how routing data is created, how routing entries are established to search for that routing data, and how routing entries establish a routing step for a job and control specific runtime attributes of a job.

Now for one more hurdle.... A job can have more than one routing step. But why would you want it to? One reason might be to use a new class to change the runtime attributes of the job.

After a job is started, you can reroute it using the RrtJob (Reroute Job) command or transfer it to another subsystem using the TfrJob (Transfer Job) command. Both commands provide the RtgDta parameter, which lets you change the job's current routing data to establish a new routing step.

Suppose you issue the following command during the execution of a job:

```
RrtJob RtgDta('FASTER') RqsDta(*None)
```

Your job would be rerouted in the same subsystem but would use the value FASTER as the value to be compared in the routing entries.

Do-It-Yourself Routing

To reinforce your understanding of routing and tie together some of the facts you've learned about work management, consider the following example.

Let's say you want to place programmers, OfficeVision for AS/400 (OV/400) users, and general end users in certain subsystems based on their locations or functions. You need to do more than just separate the workstations; you need to separate the users, no matter what workstation they're using at the time. Figures 19.4A through 19.4F describe the objects and attributes needed to define such an environment.

Figure 19.4A lists three job descriptions that have distinct routing data.

FIGURE 19.4A

Sample Job Descriptions

Job descriptions	*Routing data*
`InterJobD`	`('QINTER')`
`OfficeJobD`	`('QOFFICE')`
`PgmrJobD`	`('QPGMR')`

Note: Only the RtgDta parameter of the job descriptions is addressed for the purpose of this example. You'll need to supply the desired values for the remaining parameters on the CrtJobD (Create Job Description) command. One easy way to establish these job descriptions is to use the CrtDupObj (Create Duplicate Object) command to duplicate the QDftJobD job description and then simply change the routing entry.

InterJobD has QINTER as its routing data. OfficeJobD and PgmrJobD have QOFFICE and QPGMR specified, respectively, as their routing data. (Note that the routing data needn't match the job description name.) To enable users to work in separate subsystems, you first need to create or change user profiles and supply the appropriate job description based on the subsystem in which each user should work. In our example, general end users would have job description InterJobD, OV/400 users would have OfficeJobD, and programmers would have PgmrJobD.

Next, you must build subsystem descriptions that use the routing entries associated with the job descriptions. Figure 19.4B shows some sample subsystem definitions. All three subsystems use the WrkStnType (Workstation type) entry with the value *All. However, only the workstation entry in QInter uses the At(*SignOn) entry to tell the subsystem to allocate the workstations. This means that subsystem QInter allocates all workstations, and QOffice and QPgmr (both with At(*Enter)) allocate workstations only as jobs are transferred into those subsystems. Also, notice that each workstation entry specifies JobD(*UsrPrf) so that the routing data from the job descriptions of the user profiles will be the routing data for the job.

After a user signs on to a workstation in subsystem QInter, the routing entries do all the work. The first routing entry looks for the compare value QOFFICE. When it finds QOFFICE, program QOffice in library SysLib is called to establish the routing step. In Figure 19.4C, program QOffice simply executes the TfrJob command to transfer this particular job into subsystem QOffice.

FIGURE 19.4B
Sample Subsystem Descriptions

QInter — General end-user subsystem

Workstation entries

```
WrkStnType(*All) JobD(*UsrPrf) At(*SignOn) MaxAct(*NoMax)
```

Job queue entries

```
JobQ(QInter) SeqNbr(10) MaxAct(*NoMax)
```

Routing entries

```
SeqNbr(10)   CmpVal('QOFFICE') Pgm(SysLib/QOffice) Class(QInter)
SeqNbr(20)   CmpVal('QPGMR')   Pgm(SysLib/QPgmr)   Class(QInter)
SeqNbr(30)   CmpVal('QCMDI')   Pgm(QSys/QCmd)      Class(QInter)
SeqNbr(9999) CmpVal(*Any)      Pgm(QSys/QCmd)      Class(QInter)
```

QOffice — OfficeVision end-user subsystem

Workstation entries

```
WrkStnType(*All) JobD(*UsrPrf) At(*Enter) MaxAct(*NoMax)
```

Job queue entries

```
JobQ(QOffice) SeqNbr(10) MaxAct(*NoMax)
```

Routing entries

```
SeqNbr(10)   CmpVal('QINTER') Pgm(SysLib/QInter) Class(QOffice)
SeqNbr(20)   CmpVal('QPGMR')  Pgm(SysLib/QPgmr)  Class(QOffice)
SeqNbr(30)   CmpVal('QCMDI')  Pgm(QSys/QCmd)     Class(QOffice)
SeqNbr(9999) CmpVal(*Any)     Pgm(QSys/QCmd)     Class(QOffice)
```

QPgmr — Programmer subsystem

Workstation entries

```
WrkStnType(*All) JobD(*UsrPrf) At(*Enter) MaxAct(*NoMax)
```

Job queue entries

```
JobQ(QPgmr) SeqNbr(10) MaxAct(*NoMax)
```

Routing entries

```
SeqNbr(10)   CmpVal('QINTER')  Pgm(SysLib/QInter)  Class(QPgmr)
SeqNbr(20)   CmpVal('QOFFICE') Pgm(SysLib/QOffice) Class(QPgmr)
SeqNbr(30)   CmpVal('QCMDI')   Pgm(QSys/QCmd)      Class(QPgmr)
SeqNbr(9999) CmpVal(*Any)      Pgm(QSys/QCmd)      Class(QPgmr)
```

FIGURE 19.4C

Program QOffice

```
/*  ==========================================================  */
/*  =  Program....... QOffice                                =  */
/*  =  Description... Transfer users to QOffice subsystem    =  */
/*  ==========================================================  */

Pgm

/*  ==========================================================  */
/*  =  Transfer to QOffice subsystem. If error occurs, reroute to =  */
/*  =  current subsystem.                                    =  */
/*  ==========================================================  */

  TfrJob     JobQ( QOffice )                                    +
             RtgDta( 'QCMDI' )
  MonMsg     ( CPF0000 MCH0000 ) Exec(                          +
    RrtJob     RtgDta( 'QCMDI' )     )

EndPgm
```

However, if you look carefully at Figure 19.4C, you'll see that the TfrJob command also changes the routing data to QCMDI, so that when the job enters subsystem QOffice, routing data QCMDI matches the corresponding routing entry and uses program QCmd and class QOffice. If an error occurs on the TfrJob command, the command

```
MonMsg CPF0000 Exec(RrtJob RtgDta('QCMDI'))
```

reroutes the job in the current subsystem. Figure 19.4D shows how class QOffice might be created to provide the performance differences needed for OV/400 users.

FIGURE 19.4D

Sample Class Object Definitions

```
QInter     RunPty(20)
           TimeSlice(2000)
           DftWait(30)
           Text('General interactive user job class')

QOffice    RunPty(21)
           TimeSlice(3000)
           DftWait(30)
           Text('OfficeVision user job class')

QPgmr      RunPty(20)
           TimeSlice(2500)
           DftWait(30)
           Text('Programmer job class')
```

Note: These are only sample values for RunPty, TimeSlice, and DftWait. When configuring for your system, you should research these parameters to determine the values that best suit your environment.

Look again at Figure 19.4B. The next routing entry in the QInter subsystem looks for compare value QPGMR. When it finds QPGMR, it calls program QPgmr (Figure 19.4E) to transfer the job into subsystem QPgmr. Routing data QCMDI calls program QCmd and then processes the initial program or menu of the user profile. The same is true for routing data *Any.

FIGURE 19.4E

Program QPgmr

```
/*  ==============================================================  */
/*  =  Program....... QPgmr                                      =  */
/*  =  Description... Transfer users to QPgmr subsystem          =  */
/*  ==============================================================  */

Pgm

/*  ==============================================================  */
/*  =  Transfer to QPgmr subsystem. If error occurs, reroute to  =  */
/*  =  current subsystem.                                        =  */
/*  ==============================================================  */

   TfrJob      JobQ( QPgmr )                                        +
               RtgDta( 'QCMDI' )
   MonMsg      ( CPF0000 MCH0000 ) Exec(                            +
     RrtJob      RtgDta( 'QCMDI' )     )

EndPgm
```

In our example, subsystems QOffice and QPgmr use similar routing entries to make sure each job enters the correct subsystem. Notice that each of these subsystems has a routing entry that searches for QINTER. If this compare value is found, program QInter (Figure 19.4F) is called to transfer the job into subsystem QInter.

FIGURE 19.4F

Program QInter

```
/*  ==============================================================  */
/*  =  Program....... QInter                                     =  */
/*  =  Description... Transfer users to QInter subsystem         =  */
/*  ==============================================================  */

Pgm

/*  ==============================================================  */
/*  =  Transfer to QInter subsystem. If error occurs, reroute to =  */
/*  =  current subsystem.                                        =  */
/*  ==============================================================  */

   TfrJob      JobQ( QInter )                                       +
               RtgDta( 'QCMDI' )
   MonMsg      ( CPF0000 MCH0000 ) Exec(                            +
     RrtJob      RtgDta( 'QCMDI' )     )

EndPgm
```

As intimidating as they may at first appear, routing entries are really plain and simple. Basically, you can use them to intercept jobs as they enter the subsystem and then control the jobs using various runtime variables. We strongly recommend that you take the time to learn how your system uses routing entries. Start by studying subsystem descriptions to learn what each routing entry controls. Once you understand entries, you'll find you can use them as solutions to many work-management problems.

Chapter 20

File Structures

Getting a handle on iSeries file types can be puzzling. If you count the various types of files the system supports, how many do you get? The answer is five — and 10.

The iSeries supports five types of files: database files, source files, device files, Distributed Data Management (DDM) files, and save files. So if you count types, you get five. However, if you count the file subtypes — all the objects designated as ObjType(*File) — you get 10. Still puzzled? Figure 20.1 lists the five file types that exist on the iSeries, as well as the 10 subtypes and the specific Crt*Xxx*F (Create *Xxx* File) commands used to create them. (Keep in mind that in addition to using these Crt*Xxx*F commands, you can create some types of files using alternate methods, such as SQL's Create Table statement.)

FIGURE 20.1

iSeries File Types and Subtypes

File type	*Subtype*	*File description*	*Create command*
Database file	PF	Physical file	CrtPF
	LF	Logical file	CrtLF
Source file	PF	Physical source file	CrtSrcPF
Device file	DSPF	Workstation display file	CrtDspF
	PRTF	Printer file	CrtPrtF
	TAPF	Tape file	CrtTapF
	DKTF	Diskette file	CrtDktF
	ICFF	Intersystem Communications Function (ICF) file	CrtICFF
DDM file	DDMF	Distributed Data Management (DDM) file	CrtDDMF
Save file	SAVF	Save file	CrtSavF

Each file type (and subtype) has unique characteristics that provide unique functions on the system. In this chapter, we discuss the various types of files and describe the way each file type functions.

Structure Fundamentals

If there is any one iSeries concept that is the key to unlocking a basic understanding of application development, it is the concept of iSeries file structure. It's not that this concept is difficult to grasp; it's just that there are quite a few facts to digest. Let's start by looking at how files are described.

On the iSeries, all files are described at four levels, depicted in Figure 20.2.

FIGURE 20.2
File Description Levels

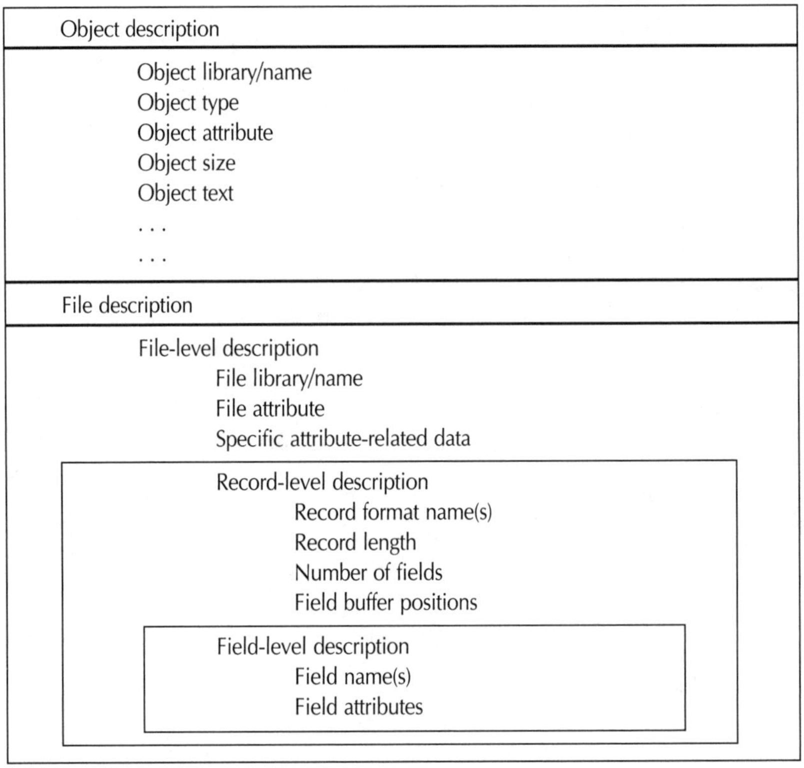

First is the object-level description. A file is an iSeries object whose object type is *File. The iSeries maintains the same object description information for a file (e.g., its library and size) as it does for any other object on the system. You can view the object-level information with the DspObjD (Display Object Description) command.

The second level of description the system maintains for *File objects is a file-level description. The file description is created along with the file when you execute a Crt*Xxx*F command. It describes the attributes or characteristics of a particular file and is embedded within the file itself. You can display or print a file description using the DspFD (Display File Description) command.

One of the attributes maintained as part of the file description is the file *subtype*. The subtype gives OS/400 the ability to determine which commands can operate on which types of files. For instance, the DltF (Delete File) command works for any type of file on the system, but the AddPFM (Add Physical File Member) command works only for physical files. OS/400 uses the description of the file to maintain and enforce each file's object identity.

The third level of descriptive information the system maintains for files is the record-level description. This level describes the various (if more than one) *record formats* that exist in the file. A record format describes a set of fields that make a record. If the fourth level of description — field descriptions — isn't used when creating the file, the record format is described by a specific record length.

All files have at least one record format, and logical files can have multiple record formats (we'll cover this topic in a later chapter). Applications perform I/O by using specific record formats. An application can further break the record format into fields either by explicitly defining those fields within the application or by working with external field definitions if they are defined for a record format. Although the iSeries provides the DspObjD command and the DspFD command, there is no Display Record Description command. To display or print a file's record-level information, you use the DspFD command and the DspFFD (Display File Field Description) command.

The final level of descriptive information that the system maintains for files is the field-level description. Field descriptions don't exist for all types of files; tape files, diskette files, DDM files, and save files have no field descriptions because they have no fields. For the remaining files — physical, logical, source, display, printer, and Intersystem Communications Function (ICF) — a description of each field and field attribute is maintained. You can use the DspFFD command to display or print the field-level descriptions for a file.

Data Members

There's yet another organizational element that applies only to database and source files, the two types of files that actually contain records of data: The iSeries sports the *data member*. This additional element of file organization has, at times, caused even the best application programmers to squirm.

Examine Figure 20.3, which introduces you to the concept of the file data member. You traditionally think of a file as containing a set of records, and usually an iSeries database file has a description and a data member that contains all the records that exist in that database file. If you create a physical file using the CrtPF (Create Physical File) command and accept the defaults for member name and maximum number of members — Mbr(*File) and MaxMbrs(1), respectively — you'll create a file that contains only one data member, and the name of that member will be the same name as the file itself.

So far, so good. Now comes the tricky part. Believe it or not, iSeries database and source files can be void of data members. If you create a physical file and specify Mbr(*None), the system creates the file without any data member in which to place records. If you try to add records to this file, the system will issue an error stating that no data member exists. In such a case, you must use the AddPFM (Add Physical File Member) command to create a data member in the file before you can add records to the file.

At the other end of the scale is the fact that you can have multiple data members in a file. A source file offers a good example. Figure 20.4 depicts the way a source file is organized.

FIGURE 20.3
Usual Database File Organization

File name: TEST

File-level description
Record-level description
Field-level description

Data member	Member name: TEST
Record 1	....
Record 2	....
Record 3	....
Record 4	....
Record 5	....
Record 6	....
Record 7	....
Record 8	....
Record 9	....
Record 10.	....

Each source member is a different data member in the file. When you create a new source member, you're actually creating another data member in this physical source file. For instance, when you specify the name of the source member you want to work with using Programming Development Manager (PDM), you're instructing the software to override the file to use that particular member for its record manipulations.

Consider another example: a user application that views both current and historical data by year. Each year represents a unique set of records. This type of application might use a database file to store each year's records in separate data members, using the year itself to construct the name of the data member. Figure 20.5 shows how this application might use a single physical file to store these records. As you can see, each year has a unique data member, and each member has a certain number of records. All members have the same description in terms of record format and fields, but each member contains unique data. The applications that access this data must use the OvrDbF (Override with Database File) command to open the correct data member for record retrieval.

Wow! One database member, no database members, multiple database members… . Why? That's a fair question. With multiple data members, it's possible to handle data that uses the same record format and same field descriptions while segregating groups of data for business reasons. One set of software can be written to support the effort, but the data can be maintained — even saved — separately.

FIGURE 20.4
Source File Organization

Source file: QRPGSrc

File-level description
Record-level description
Field-level description

Data member   Member name: INLT01

Source data record 1 . . . .
Source data record 2 . . . .
Source data record 3 . . . .
Source data record 4 . . . .
Source data record 5 . . . .

Data member   Member name: INLT02

Source data record 1 . . . .
Source data record 2 . . . .
Source data record 3 . . . .
Source data record 4 . . . .
Source data record 5 . . . .

Data member   Member name: INLT03

Source data record 1 . . . .
Source data record 2 . . . .
Source data record 3 . . . .
Source data record 4 . . . .
Source data record 5 . . . .

FIGURE 20.5
Physical File with Multiple Data Members

File name: YEARS

File-level description
Record-level description
Field-level description

Data member   Member name: YR1997
Number of records: 134,564

Data member   Member name: YR1998
Number of records: 125,000

Data member   Member name: YR1999
Number of records: 142,165

Data member   Member name: YR2000
Number of records: 46,243

iSeries File Types

Having sorted through the structure of iSeries files and dealt with data members, let's now look specifically at the types of files and how they're used.

Database Files

Database files are iSeries objects that actually contain data or provide access to data. Two types of files are considered database files: physical files and logical files. A physical file, denoted as Type(*File) and Attr(PF), has file-, record-, and field-level descriptions and can be created with or without using externally described source specifications (or, alternatively, SQL's Create Table instruction). Physical files — so called because they contain your actual data (e.g., customer records) — can have only one record format. As records are added, the data entered into the physical file is assigned a relative record number based on arrival sequence. As we indicated earlier, database files can have multiple data members, and special program considerations must be implemented to ensure that applications work with the correct data members. You can view the data that exists in a specific data member of a file using the DspPFM (Display Physical File Member) command.

A logical file (or "view" in SQL parlance), denoted as Type(*File) and Attr(LF), is created in conjunction with physical files to determine how data will be presented to the requester. Logical files contain no data but instead are used to specify key fields, select/omit logic, field selection, and field manipulation. The key fields serve to specify the access paths to use for accessing the actual data records that reside in physical files. A logical file must be externally described using Data Description Specifications (DDS) or created as a view using SQL's Create View statement. If you use DDS to describe a logical file, the physical file on which the logical file is based can even be program described (no external definition)!

Source Files

A source file (such as QCLSrc, where CL source members are maintained) is simply a customized form of a physical file; as such, source files are denoted as Type(*File) and Attr(PF). (Note: If you work with objects using PDM, physical data files and physical source files are distinguished by using two specific attributes: PF-DTA and PF-SRC.)

All source files created using the CrtSrcPF (Create Source Physical File) command have similar record formats. Each source file has the same fields, but the field to contain your source statements, SrcDta, can differ in length from one source file to another. This is made possible by the fact that the CrtSrcPF command lets you specify a record length.

When you use the CrtSrcPF command, the system creates a physical file that allows multiple data members. When you edit a particular source member, you're simply editing a specific data member in the file.

Some iSeries commands are specific to source files and can't be used with data files. Likewise, some commands are specific to data files yet do not operate on source files.

Device Files

Device files contain no actual data. Their function is to define a protocol for presenting application-supplied information to a physical device, such as a workstation or printer. The types of device files are display, printer, tape, diskette, and ICF.

Display files, denoted by the system as Type(*File) and Attr(DspF), provide specific information about how an application can interact with a workstation. Although a display file contains no data, it does contain various record formats that represent the screens the application will present to the workstation. You can view and maintain each specific record format using IBM's Screen Design Aid (SDA), which is part of the Application Development Tools licensed program product. SDA generates DDS source for the display file. Programmers often edit display file DDS source directly rather than use SDA to generate display files.

Interactive high-level language (HLL) programs include the workstation display file as one of the files to be used in the application. The HLL program writes a display file record format to the screen to present the user with formatted data and then reads that format from the screen when the end user presses Enter or another appropriate function key. Whereas I/O to a database file accesses disk storage, I/O to a display file accesses a workstation.

Printer files, denoted by the system as Type(*File) and Attr(PrtF), provide specific information about how an application can create data for output to a writer. The printer file can be created with a specified maximum record length and a single format to be used with an HLL program for program-described printing, or it can be created from external source statements that define the formats to be used for printing. Like display files, printer files themselves contain no data and therefore have no data member associated with them. When an application program performs output operations to a printer file, the output becomes spooled data that can be printed on a writer device or is printed directly from the application to the writer device.

Tape files, denoted by the system as Type(*File) and Attr(TapF), provide specific information about how an application can read or write data using tape media. The description of the tape file contains information such as the device name for tape read/write operations, the tape volume requested (if a specific volume is desired), the density of the tape to be processed, the record and block length to be used, and other essential information related to tape processing. Without the use of a tape file, HLL programs cannot access tape media devices.

Diskette files, denoted by the system as Type(*File) and Attr(DktF), are much like tape files, except diskette files support diskette devices. For example, diskette files have attributes that describe the volume to be used as well as the record and block length.

Intersystem Communications Function files, denoted by the system as Type(*File) and Attr(ICFF), provide specific attributes to describe the physical communications device used for application peer-to-peer communications programming. When a local application wants to communicate with an application on a remote system, the local application turns to the ICF file for information about the physical device to use for those communications.

The ICF file also contains record formats used to read data from and write data to the device as well as the peer program.

DDM Files

Distributed Data Management files, denoted by the system as Type(*File) and Attr(DDMF), are objects that represent files that exist on a remote system. For instance, if your customer file exists on a remote system, you can create a DDM file on the local system that specifically points to that customer file on the remote system. DDM files provide an interface that lets you access the remote file just as if it were on your local system. You can compile programs using the file, read records, write records, and update records while the system handles the communications. Figure 20.6 represents a typical DDM file implementation.

FIGURE 20.6
DDM File Implementation

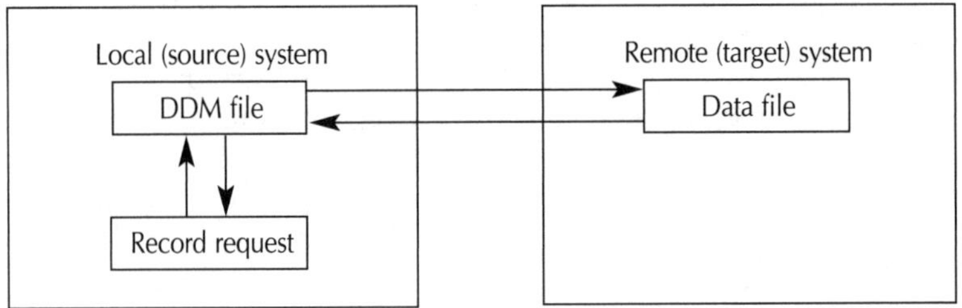

Save Files

Save files, denoted by the system as Type(*File) and Attr(SavF), are a special form of file designed specifically to handle save/restore data. You can't determine the file-, record-, and field-level descriptions for a save file. The system creates a specific description used for all save files to make them compatible with save/restore operations.

Save files can be used to receive the output from a save operation and then be used as input for a restore operation. The process works just the same as performing save/restore operations with tape or diskette, except that the saved data is maintained on disk. Save file data can be transmitted electronically or transported via a sneaker network or overnight courier network to another system and then restored.

With that, we've looked briefly at the various types of files that exist on the system. Understanding these objects is critical to effective application development and maintenance on the iSeries.

Chapter 21

So You Think You Understand File Overrides

In Chapter 20, we discussed the various kinds of files that exist on the iSeries, each of which has unique characteristics or attributes. These attributes not only provide the file definition; they also determine how the system controls the file. In this chapter, we introduce file overrides, which you can use to temporarily change the attributes (i.e., the definition) of a file during program execution.

Caution

If you're considering skipping this chapter because you already understand file overrides, read the chapter title again! We know many AS/400 and iSeries programmers, some excellent, who sincerely believe they understand file overrides — after all, they've been using file overrides in their applications for years. But we wouldn't be at all surprised to learn that, given a comprehensive test on file overrides, each and every one of these programmers would come up short in some way.

What Do Overrides Do?

You use file overrides to temporarily, and dynamically, change the attributes of a file that your programs use so that you don't need to create permanent files or programs for every combination of attributes your applications might need. When you consider the number of attributes supported by the various types of files, it's easy to see how overrides might be necessary from time to time.

To perform an override, you use a specific override command designed to override the particular type of file you want to access. Figure 21.1 lists the file override commands and some of the reasons for performing each type of override. As the figure shows, override commands exist for most *File objects on the iSeries. Each override command has specific parameters that correspond to the file attributes of the file type on which the command is designed to operate. For instance, you can't use the OvrTapF (Override with Tape File) command to specify a data member because tape files don't support members. Likewise, the OvrDbF (Override with Database File) command can't specify a tape-volume number because a database file doesn't require a tape when you access the file directly. You get the idea — a command for each type of file and appropriate override parameters for each command.

FIGURE 21.1
File Override Commands and Their Functions

Override command	*File types*	*Possible reasons to use*
OvrDbF (Override with Database File)	Database Source	• Select data member to process • Change Share attribute to share ODP
OvrDktF (Override with Diskette File)	Device	• Select device to associate with file • Establish record and block length
OvrDspF (Override with Display File)	Device	• Change DfrWrt (Defer write) attribute • Change RstDsp (Restore display) attribute
OvrICFF (Override with ICF File)	Device	• Select device to associate with file • Select communications type
OvrPrtF (Override with Printer File)	Device	• Select output queue • Select font, CPI, LPI, and form type
OvrSavF (Override with Save File)	Save	• Select whether to delete previous records
OvrTapF (Override with Tape File)	Device	• Select device to associate with file • Establish record and block length

Suppose you want to override a tape file so you can write records from a physical file to tape using a high-level language (HLL) program. You can specify this override in a CL program before calling the HLL program. The override and call would appear as follows:

```
OvrTapF File(QSysTap)    +
        Dev(Tap01)       +
        RcdLen(256)      +
        BlkLen(5120)     +
        EndOpt(*Unload)
Call    HLLProgram
```

This override provides the attributes for device, record length, block length, and end-of-process tape options. The HLL program opens file QSysTap using the new attributes, reads records from the physical file, and writes the records to tape.

Consider another example. Suppose you need an override to a printer file to correctly set the number of copies you want to print. Because the number of copies will vary depending on each particular job, you want to specify the desired number of copies as a parameter to a CL program that calls the HLLPrint program. The code in the CL program would use the OvrPrtF (Override with Printer File) command and would look something like this:

```
OvrPrtF File(Report)     +
        ToFile(QPrint)   +
        Copies(&Copies)
Call    HLLPrint
```

Because of the override, program HLLPrint opens file QPrint rather than file Report and generates the specified number of reports.

Yet another useful example of an override is selecting a specific member of a multimember file for processing. For instance, to process member Ord200011 (orders for November of the year 2000) in file Orders, which contains a member for each month's orders, you would specify

```
OvrDbF  File(Orders)    +
        Mbr(Ord200011)
Call    HLLPgm
```

When program HLLPgm opens file Orders, it opens member Ord200011.

Prerequisites

Before examining file overrides closely, you need to be familiar with the parts of a job's anatomy integral to the function of overrides. The *call stack* and *activation groups* both play a key role in determining the effect that overrides have in your applications.

The Call Stack and Job Call Levels

Jobs typically consist of a chain of active programs, with one program calling another. The call stack is simply an ordered list of these active programs. When a job starts, the system routes it to the beginning program to execute and designates that program as the first entry in the call stack. If that program then calls another program, the system assigns the newly called program to the second call stack entry. This process can continue, with the second program calling a third, the third calling a fourth, and so on, each time adding the new program to the end of the call stack. The call stack therefore reflects the *depth* of program calls.

Consider the following call stack:

ProgramA
ProgramB
ProgramC
ProgramD

You can see four active programs in this call stack. In this example, the system called ProgramA as its first program when the job started. ProgramA then called ProgramB, which in turn called ProgramC. Last, ProgramC called ProgramD. Because these are nested program calls, each program is at a different layer in the call stack. These layers are known as *call levels.* In the example, ProgramA is at call level 1, indicating the fact that it is the first program called when the job started. ProgramB, ProgramC, and ProgramD are at call levels 2, 3, and 4, respectively.

As programs end, the system removes them from the call stack, reducing the number of call levels. For instance, when ProgramD ends, the system removes it from the call stack, and the job will then consist of only three call levels. If ProgramC then ends, the job consists of only two call levels, with ProgramA and ProgramB making up the call stack. This process continues until ProgramA ends, at which time the job ends.

So far, you've seen that when one program calls another, the system creates a new, higher call level at which the called program runs. The called program then begins execution, and when it ends, the system removes the program from the call stack, returning control to the calling program at the previous call level.

That's the simple version. But there's a little more to the picture. First, it's possible for one program to pass control to another program *without* the newly invoked program running at a higher call level. For instance, with CL's TfrCtl (Transfer Control) command, the system replaces (in the call stack) the program issuing the command with the program to which control is to be transferred. Not only does this action result in the invoked program running at the same call level as the invoking program, but the invoking program is also completely removed from the chain of programs making up the call stack. Hence, control cannot be returned to the program that issued the TfrCtl command. Instead, when the newly invoked program ends, control returns to the program at the immediately preceding call level.

You may recall that earlier we said that as programs end, the system removes them from the call stack. In reality, when a program ends, the system removes from the call stack not only the ending program but also all programs at a call level higher than that of the ending program. You might be thinking about our example and scratching your head, wondering, "How can ProgramB end before ProgramC"? Consider the fact that ProgramD can send an escape message to ProgramB's program message queue. This event results in the system returning control to ProgramB's error handler. This return of control to ProgramB results in the system removing all programs at a call level higher than ProgramB — namely, ProgramC and ProgramD — from the call stack. ProgramB's design then determines whether it is removed from the call stack. If it handles the exception, ProgramB is not removed from the call stack; instead, processing continues in ProgramB.

You should also note that under normal circumstances, the call stack begins with several system programs before any user-written programs appear. In fact, system programs will likely appear throughout your call stack. This point is important only to demonstrate that the call stack isn't simply a representation of user-written programs as they are called.

Activation Groups

In addition to an understanding of a job's call levels, you need a basic familiarity with activation groups to comprehend file overrides. You're probably familiar with the fact that a job is a structure with its own allocated system resources, such as open data paths (ODPs) and storage for program variables. These resources are available to programs executed within that job but are not available to other jobs. Activation groups, introduced with the Integrated Language Environment (ILE), are a further division of jobs into smaller substructures.

As is the case with jobs, activation groups consist of private system resources, such as ODPs and storage for program variables. An activation group's allocated resources are available only to program objects that are assigned to, and running in, that particular activation group within the job. You assign ILE program objects to an activation group when you create the program objects. Then, when you execute these programs, the system creates the activation group (or groups) to which the programs are assigned. A job can consist of multiple activation groups, none of which can access the resources unique to the other activation groups within the job. For example, although multiple activation groups within a job may open the same file, each activation group can maintain its own private ODP. In such a case, programs assigned to the *same* activation group can use the ODP, but programs assigned to a *different* activation group wouldn't have access to the same ODP.

A complete discussion of activation groups could span volumes. For this chapter's purposes, it's sufficient simply to note that activation groups exist, that they are substructures of a job, and that they can contain their own set of resources not available to other activation groups within the job.

Override Rules

The rules governing the effect that overrides have on your applications fall into three primary areas: the override scope, overrides to the same file, and the order in which the system processes overrides. After we examine the details of each of these areas, we'll look at a few miscellaneous rules.

Scoping an Override

An override's *scope* determines the range of influence that the override will have on your applications. You can scope an override to the following levels:

- Call level — A call-level override is at the level of the process that issues the override, except that if the override is issued using a call to program QCmdExc, the call level is that of the process that called QCmdExc. A call-level override remains in effect from the time it is issued until the system replaces or deletes it or until the call level in which the override was issued ends.
- Activation group level — An activation-group–level override applies to all programs running in the activation group associated with the issuing program, regardless of the call level in which the override is issued. In other words, only the most recently issued activation-group–level override is in effect. An activation-group–level override remains in effect from the time the override is issued until the system replaces it, deletes it, or deletes the activation group. *These rules apply only if the override is issued from an activation group other than the default activation group. Activation-group–level overrides issued from the default activation group are scoped to call-level overrides.*
- Job level — A job-level override applies to all programs running in the job, regardless of activation group or call level in which the override is issued. Only the most

recently issued job-level override is in effect. A job-level override remains in effect from the time it is issued until the system replaces or deletes it or until the job in which the override was issued ends.

You specify an override's scope when you issue the override, by using the override command's OvrScope (Override scope) parameter. Figure 21.2 depicts an ILE application's view of a job's structure, along with the manner in which you can specify overrides.

First, notice that two activation groups, the default activation group and a named activation group, make up the job. All jobs have as part of their structure the default activation group and can optionally have one or more named activation groups.

Original Program Model (OPM) programs can run only in the default activation group. Figure 21.2 shows two OPM programs, Program1 and Program2, both running in the default activation group. Because OPM programs can't be assigned to a named activation group, jobs that run only OPM programs consist solely of the default activation group.

ILE program objects, on the other hand, can run in either the default activation group or a named activation group, depending on how you assign the program objects to activation groups. If any of a job's program objects are assigned to a named activation group, the job will have as part of its structure that named activation group. In fact, if the job's program objects are assigned to different named activation groups, the job will have each different named activation group as part of its structure. Figure 21.2 shows five ILE programs: Program3 and Program4 are both running in the default activation group, and Program5, Program6, and Program7 are running in a named activation group.

The figure not only depicts the types of program objects that can run in the default activation group and in a named activation group; it also shows the valid levels to which you can scope overrides. Programs running in the default activation group, whether OPM or ILE, can issue overrides scoped to the job level or to the call level. ILE programs running in a named activation group can scope overrides not only to these two levels but to the activation group level as well. Figure 21.2 portrays each of these possibilities.

Overriding the Same File Multiple Times

One feature of call-level overrides is the ability to combine multiple overrides for the same file so that each of the different overridden attributes applies. Consider the following program fragments:

ProgramA:

```
OvrPrtF File(Report) OutQ(SalesØ1) OvrScope(*CallLvl)
Call    Pgm(ProgramB)
```

ProgramB:

```
OvrPrtF File(Report) Copies(3) OvrScope(*CallLvl)
Call    Pgm(PrintPgm)
```

When program PrintPgm opens and spools printer file Report, the overrides from both programs are combined, resulting in the spooled file being placed in output queue Sales01 with three copies set to print.

FIGURE 21.2
Scoping Overrides

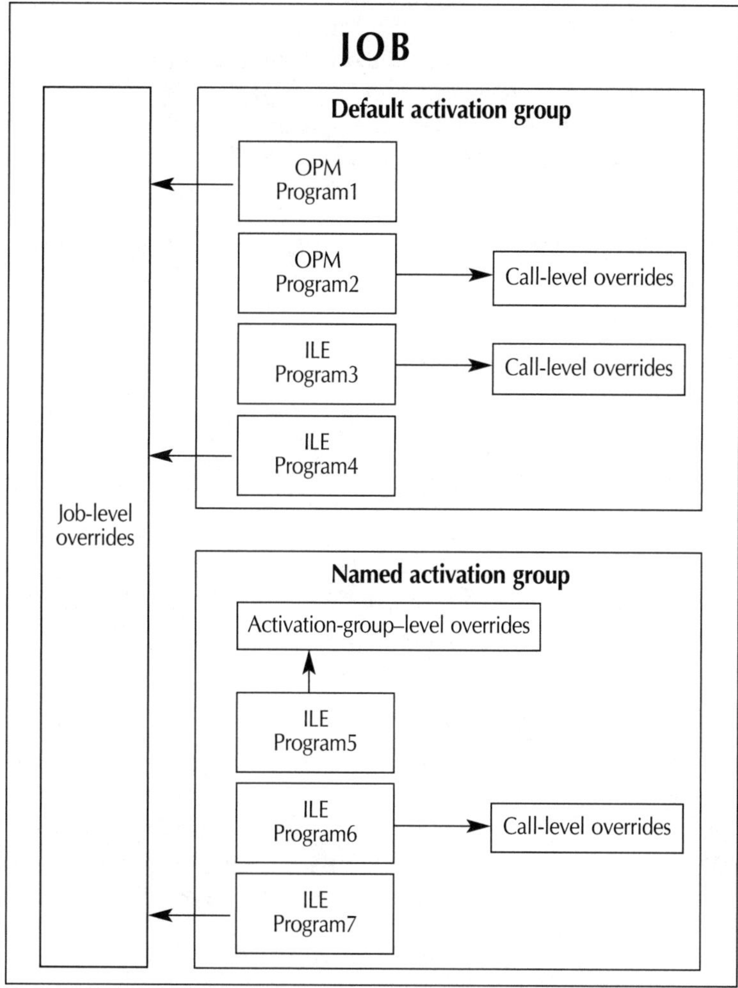

Now, consider the following program fragment:

ProgramC:

```
OvrPrtF File(Report) OutQ(Sales01) OvrScope(*CallLvl)
OvrPrtF File(Report) Copies(3) OvrScope(*CallLvl)
Call    Pgm(PrintPgm)
```

What do you think happens? You might expect this program to be functionally equivalent to the two previous programs, but it isn't. Within a single call level, only the most recent override is in effect. In other words, the most recent override replaces the previous override in effect. In the case of ProgramC, the Copies(3) override is in effect, but the OutQ(Sales01) override is not. This feature provides a convenient way to replace an override within a single call level without the need to first delete the previous override. It's also fun to show programmers ProgramA and ProgramB and explain that things worked flawlessly and then ask them to help you figure out why things didn't work right after you modified the application to look like ProgramC! When they finally figure out that only the most recent override within a program is in effect, show them your latest modification —

ProgramA:

```
OvrPrtF File(Report) OutQ(Sales01) OvrScope(*CallLvl)
TfrCtl  Pgm(ProgramB)
```

ProgramB:

```
OvrPrtF File(Report) Copies(3) OvrScope(*CallLvl)
Call    Pgm(PrintPgm)
```

— and watch them go berserk again! This latest change is identical to the first iteration of ProgramA and ProgramB, except that rather than issue a Call to ProgramB from ProgramA, you use TfrCtl to invoke ProgramB. Remember, TfrCtl doesn't start a new call level. ProgramB will simply replace ProgramA on the call stack, thereby running at the same call level as ProgramA. Because the call level doesn't change, the overrides aren't combined.

You may need to point out to the programmers that they didn't really figure it out at all when they determined that only the most recent override within a *program* is in effect. The rule is: Only the most recent override within a *call level* is in effect.

The Order of Applying Overrides

You've seen the rules concerning the applicability of overrides. In the course of a job, many overrides may be issued. In fact, many may be issued for a single file. When many overrides are issued for a single file, the system constructs a single override from the overridden attributes in effect from all the overrides. This type of override is called a *merged override.* Merged overrides aren't simply the result of accumulating the different overridden file attributes, though. The system must also modify, or replace, applicable attributes that have been overridden multiple times, as well as remove overrides when an applicable request to delete overrides is issued.

To determine the merged override, the system follows a distinct set of rules that govern the order in which overrides are processed. You should first note that the system processes the overrides for a file when it opens the file. The system uses the following sequence to check and apply overrides:

1. call-level overrides up to and including the call level of the oldest procedure in the activation group containing the file open (beginning with the call level that opens the file and progressing in decreasing call-level sequence)

2. the most recent activation-group–level overrides for the activation group containing the file open
3. call-level overrides lower than the call level of the oldest procedure in the activation group containing the file open (beginning with the call level immediately preceding the call level of the oldest procedure in the activation group containing the file open and progressing in decreasing call-level sequence)
4. the most recent job-level overrides

Caution

This ordering of overrides can get tricky! It is without a doubt the least-understood aspect of file overrides and the source of considerable confusion and errors.

Let's look at an example. Figure 21.3A shows a job with 10 call levels, programs in the default activation group as well as in two named activation groups, and overrides within each call level and each activation group. Before we show you how the system processes these overrides, see whether you can determine the file that ProgramJ at call level 10 will open, as well as the attribute values that will be in effect due to the job's overrides. In fact, try the exercise twice, the first time without referring to the ordering rules.

Figure 21.3B reveals the results of the job's overrides. Did you arrive at these results in either of your tries? Let's walk, step by step, through the process of determining the overrides in effect for this example.

Step 1 — call-level overrides up to and including the call level of the oldest procedure in the activation group containing the file open

Checking call level 10 shows that the system opens file Report1 in activation group AG1. The oldest procedure in activation group AG1 appears at call level 2. Therefore, in step 1, the system processes call-level overrides beginning with call level 10 and working up the call stack through call level 2. When the system processes call level 2, step 1 is complete.

a. There is no call-level override for file Report1 at call level 10.
b. There is no call-level override for file Report1 at call level 9.
c. There is no call-level override for file Report1 at call level 8.
d. There is no call-level override for file Report1 at call level 7.
e. Call level 6 contains a call-level override for file Report1. The Copies attribute for file Report1 is overridden to 7.

Active overrides at this point: Copies(7)

FIGURE 21.3A
Ordering Overrides Example 1

Program	*Call level*	*Activation group*	*Source*		
ProgramA	1	Default	`OvrPrtF`	`File(Report1)`	+
				`OutQ(Prt01)`	+
				`Copies(2)`	+
				`OvrScope(*CallLvl)`	
			`Call`	`Pgm(ProgramB)`	
ProgramB	2	AG1	`OvrPrtF`	`File(Report1)`	+
				`LPI(7.5)`	+
				`FormType(FormB)`	+
				`Copies(3)`	+
				`OvrScope(*ActGrpDfn)`	
			`Call`	`Pgm(ProgramC)`	
ProgramC	3	AG2	`OvrPrtF`	`File(Report1)`	+
				`LPI(9)`	+
				`Copies(4)`	+
				`OvrScope(*CallLvl)`	
			`Call`	`Pgm(ProgramD)`	
ProgramD	4	Default	`OvrPrtF`	`File(Report1)`	+
				`LPI(8)`	+
				`PrtQlty(*NLQ)`	+
				`Copies(5)`	+
				`OvrScope(*Job)`	
			`Call`	`Pgm(ProgramE)`	
ProgramE	5	Default	`OvrPrtF`	`File(Report1)`	+
				`CPI(13.3)`	+
				`Copies(6)`	+
				`OvrScope(*ActGrpDfn)`	
			`Call`	`Pgm(ProgramF)`	
ProgramF	6	AG1	`OvrPrtF`	`File(Report1)`	+
				`Copies(7)`	+
				`OvrScope(*CallLvl)`	
			`Call`	`Pgm(ProgramG)`	
ProgramG	7	AG2	`OvrPrtF`	`File(Report1)`	+
				`Copies(8)`	+
				`OvrScope(*Job)`	
			`Call`	`Pgm(ProgramH)`	
ProgramH	8	AG1	`OvrPrtF`	`File(Report1)`	+
				`LPI(12)`	+
				`FormFeed(*Cut)`	+
				`Copies(9)`	+
				`OvrScope(*ActGrpDfn)`	
			`Call`	`Pgm(ProgramI)`	
ProgramI	9	AG2	`OvrPrtF`	`File(Report1)`	+
				`LPI(4)`	+
				`Copies(10)`	+
				`OvrScope(*ActGrpDfn)`	
			`Call`	`Pgm(ProgramJ)`	
ProgramJ	10	AG1	File specification from RPG IV program: `FReport1   O    F  132         Printer`		

FIGURE 21.3B

Merged Override Values for Ordering Overrides Example 1

From step	From call level	Merged override value
2	8	LPI(12)
1	5	CPI(13.3)
2	8	FormFeed(*Cut)
3	1	OutQ(Prt01)
4	7	Copies(8)

f. Call level 5 shows an activation-group–level override, but the program is running in the default activation group. Remember, activation-group–level overrides issued from the default activation group are scoped to call-level overrides. Therefore, the system processes this override as a call-level override. The CPI attribute for file Report1 is overridden to 13.3, and the previous Copies attribute value is replaced with this latest value of 6.

Active overrides at this point: CPI(13.3) Copies(6)

g. There is no call-level override for file Report1 at call level 4.

h. Call level 3 contains a call-level override for file Report1. The LPI attribute for file Report1 is overridden to 9, and the previous Copies attribute value is replaced with this latest value of 4.

Active overrides at this point: LPI(9) CPI(13.3) Copies(4)

i. There is no call-level override for file Report1 at call level 2.

Step 1 is now complete. Call level 2 contains the oldest procedure in activation group AG1 (the activation group containing the file open).

Step 2 — the most recent activation-group–level overrides for the activation group containing the file open

The system now checks for the most recently issued activation-group–level override within activation group AG1, where file Report1 was opened.

a. There is no activation-group–level override for file Report1 at call level 10.

b. There is no activation-group–level override for file Report1 in activation group AG1 at call level 9. The activation-group–level override in call level 9 is in activation group AG2 and is therefore not applicable.

c. Call level 8 contains an activation-group–level override in activation group AG1 for file Report1. The FormFeed attribute for file Report1 is overridden to *Cut. The previous LPI attribute value is replaced with this latest value of 12, and the previous Copies attribute value is replaced with this latest value of 9.

*Active overrides at this point: LPI(12) CPI(13.3) FormFeed(*Cut) Copies(9)*

Step 2 is now complete. The system discontinues searching for activation-group–level overrides because this is the most recently issued activation-group–level override in activation group AG1.

Step 3 — call-level overrides lower than the call level of the oldest procedure in the activation group containing the file open

Remember, call level 2 is the call level of the oldest procedure in activation group AG1. The system begins processing call-level overrides at the call level preceding call level 2. In this case, there is only one call level lower than call level 2.

a. Call level 1 contains a call-level override for file Report1. The OutQ attribute for Report1 is overridden to Prt01, and the previous Copies attribute value is replaced with this latest value of 2.

*Active overrides at this point: LPI(12) CPI(13.3) FormFeed(*Cut) OutQ(Prt01) Copies(2)*

Step 3 is now complete. The call stack has been processed through call level 1.

Step 4 — the most recent job-level overrides

The system finishes processing overrides by checking for the most recently issued job-level override for file Report1.

a. There is no job-level override for file Report1 at call level 10.

b. There is no job-level override for file Report1 at call level 9.

c. There is no job-level override for file Report1 at call level 8.

d. Call level 7 contains a job-level override for file Report1. Notice that the program runs in activation group AG2 rather than AG1. Job-level overrides can come from any activation group. The previous Copies attribute value is replaced with this latest value of 8.

*Active overrides at this point: LPI(12) CPI(13.3) FormFeed(*Cut) OutQ(Prt01) Copies(8)*

Step 4 is now complete. The system discontinues searching for job-level overrides because this is the most recently issued job-level override.

This completes the application of overrides. The final merged override that will be applied in call level 10 is

```
LPI(12) CPI(13.3) FormFeed(*Cut) OutQ(PrtØ1) Copies(8)
```

All other attribute values come from the file description for printer file Report1. It's easy to see how this process could be confusing and lead to the introduction of errors in applications!

Now, let's make the process even more confusing! In the previous example, our HLL program (ProgramJ) opened file Report1, and no programs issued an override to the file name. What do you think happens when you override the file name to a different file using the ToFile parameter on the OvrPrtF command? Once the system issues an override that changes the file, it searches for overrides to the new file, not the original. Let's look at a slightly modified version of our example. Figure 21.3C contains the new programs.

Only two of the original programs have been changed in this new example. In ProgramC at call level 3, the ToFile parameter has been added to the OvrPrtF, changing the file to be opened from Report1 to Report2. And ProgramB at call level 2 now overrides printer file Report2 rather than Report1

. Figure 21.3D shows the results of the overrides. Let's once again walk, step by step, through the process of determining the overrides in effect for this new example.

FIGURE 21.3C
Ordering Overrides Example 2

Program	*Call level*	*Activation group*	*Source*		
ProgramA	1	Default	`OvrPrtF`	`File(Report1)`	+
				`OutQ(Prt01)`	+
				`Copies(2)`	+
				`OvrScope(*CallLvl)`	
			`Call`	`Pgm(ProgramB)`	
ProgramB	2	AG1	`OvrPrtF`	`File(Report2)`	+
				`LPI(7.5)`	+
				`FormType(FormB)`	+
				`Copies(3)`	+
				`OvrScope(*ActGrpDfn)`	
			`Call`	`Pgm(ProgramC)`	
ProgramC	3	AG2	`OvrPrtF`	`File(Report1)`	+
				`ToFile(Report2)`	+
				`LPI(9)`	+
				`Copies(4)`	+
				`OvrScope(*CallLvl)`	
			`Call`	`Pgm(ProgramD)`	
ProgramD	4	Default	`OvrPrtF`	`File(Report1)`	+
				`LPI(8)`	+
				`PrtQlty(*NLQ)`	+
				`Copies(5)`	+
				`OvrScope(*Job)`	
			`Call`	`Pgm(ProgramE)`	
ProgramE	5	Default	`OvrPrtF`	`File(Report1)`	+
				`CPI(13.3)`	+
				`Copies(6)`	+
				`OvrScope(*ActGrpDfn)`	
			`Call`	`Pgm(ProgramF)`	
ProgramF	6	AG1	`OvrPrtF`	`File(Report1)`	+
				`Copies(7)`	+
				`OvrScope(*CallLvl)`	
			`Call`	`Pgm(ProgramG)`	
ProgramG	7	AG2	`OvrPrtF`	`File(Report1)`	+
				`Copies(8)`	+
				`OvrScope(*Job)`	
			`Call`	`Pgm(ProgramH)`	
ProgramH	8	AG1	`OvrPrtF`	`File(Report1)`	+
				`LPI(12)`	+
				`FormFeed(*Cut)`	+
				`Copies(9)`	+
				`OvrScope(*ActGrpDfn)`	
			`Call`	`Pgm(ProgramI)`	
ProgramI	9	AG2	`OvrPrtF`	`File(Report1)`	+
				`LPI(4)`	+
				`Copies(10)`	+
				`OvrScope(*ActGrpDfn)`	
			`Call`	`Pgm(ProgramJ)`	
ProgramJ	10	AG1	File specification from RPG IV program: `FReport1   O    F  132           Printer`		

FIGURE 21.3D

Merged Override Values for Ordering Overrides Example 2

From step	From call level	Merged override value
1	3	ToFile(Report2)
2	2	LPI(7.5)
1	5	CPI(13.3)
2	2	FormType(FormB)
2	2	Copies(3)

Step 1 — call-level overrides up to and including the call level of the oldest procedure in the activation group containing the file open

Checking call level 10 shows that the system opens file Report1 in activation group AG1. The oldest procedure in activation group AG1 appears at call level 2. Therefore, in step 1, the system processes call-level overrides beginning with call level 10 and working up the call stack through call level 2. When the system processes call level 2, step 1 is complete.

a. There is no call-level override for file Report1 at call level 10.

b. There is no call-level override for file Report1 at call level 9.

c. There is no call-level override for file Report1 at call level 8.

d. There is no call-level override for file Report1 at call level 7.

e. Call level 6 contains a call-level override for file Report1. The Copies attribute for file Report1 is overridden to 7.

Active overrides at this point: Copies(7)

f. Call level 5 shows an activation-group–level override, but the program is running in the default activation group. Again, activation-group–level overrides issued from the default activation group are scoped to call-level overrides. Therefore, the system processes this override as a call-level override. The CPI attribute for file Report1 is overridden to 13.3, and the previous Copies attribute value is replaced with this latest value of 6.

Active overrides at this point: CPI(13.3) Copies(6)

g. There is no call-level override for file Report1 at call level 4.

h. Call level 3 contains a call-level override for file Report1. The LPI attribute for file Report1 is overridden to 9, and the previous Copies attribute value is replaced with this latest value of 4. Notice that the printer file has also been overridden to Report2. This is especially noteworthy because the system will now begin searching for overrides to file Report2 rather than file Report1.

Active overrides at this point: ToFile(Report2) LPI(9) CPI(13.3) Copies(4)

i. There is no call-level override for file Report2 at call level 2.

Step 1 is now complete. Call level 2 contains the oldest procedure in activation group AG1 (the activation group containing the file open).

Step 2 — the most recent activation-group–level overrides for the activation group containing the file open

The system now checks for the most recently issued activation-group–level override within activation group AG1 where file Report1 (actually Report2 now) was opened.

a. There is no activation-group–level override for file Report2 at call level 10.
b. There is no activation-group–level override for file Report2 in activation group AG1 at call level 9. The activation-group–level override in call level 9 is in activation group AG2 and is therefore not applicable.
c. There is no activation-group–level override for file Report2 at call level 8.
d. There is no activation-group–level override for file Report2 at call level 7.
e. There is no activation-group–level override for file Report2 at call level 6.
f. There is no activation-group–level override for file Report2 at call level 5.
g. There is no activation-group–level override for file Report2 at call level 4.
h. There is no activation-group–level override for file Report2 at call level 3.
i. Call level 2 contains an activation-group–level override in activation group AG1 for file Report2. The FormType attribute for file Report2 is overridden to FormB. The previous LPI attribute value is replaced with this latest value of 7.5, and the previous Copies attribute value is replaced with this latest value of 3.

Active overrides at this point: ToFile(Report2) LPI(7.5) CPI(13.3) FormType(FormB) Copies(3)

Step 2 is now complete. The system discontinues searching for activation-group–level overrides because this is the most recently issued activation-group–level override in activation group AG1.

Step 3 — call-level overrides lower than the call level of the oldest procedure in the activation group containing the file open

Again, call level 2 is the call level of the oldest procedure in activation group AG1. The system begins processing call-level overrides at the call level preceding call level 2 (i.e., call level 1).

a. There is no call-level override for file Report2 at call level 1.

Step 3 is now complete. The call stack has been processed through call level 1.

Step 4 — the most recent job-level overrides

The system finishes processing overrides by checking for the most recently issued job-level override for file Report2.

a. There is no job-level override for file Report2 at call level 10.
b. There is no job-level override for file Report2 at call level 9.
c. There is no job-level override for file Report2 at call level 8.
d. There is no job-level override for file Report2 at call level 7.
e. There is no job-level override for file Report2 at call level 6.
f. There is no job-level override for file Report2 at call level 5.
g. There is no job-level override for file Report2 at call level 4.
h. There is no job-level override for file Report2 at call level 3.
i. There is no job-level override for file Report2 at call level 2.
j. There is no job-level override for file Report2 at call level 1.

Step 4 is now complete. There are no job-level overrides for file Report2.

This completes the application of overrides. The final merged override that will be applied to printer file Report2 in call level 10 is

```
LPI(7.5) CPI(13.3) FormType(FormB) Copies(3)
```

All other attribute values come from the file description for printer file Report2.

Protecting an Override

In some cases, you may want to protect an override from the effect of other overrides to the same file. In other words, you want to ensure that an override issued in a program is the override that will be applied when you open the overridden file. You can protect an override from being changed by overrides from lower call levels, the activation group level, and the job level by specifying Secure(*Yes) on the override command.

Figure 21.4 shows excerpts from two programs, ProgramA and ProgramB, running in the default activation group and with call-level overrides only. ProgramA simply issues an override to set the output queue attribute value for printer file Report1 and then calls ProgramB. ProgramB in turn calls two HLL programs, HLLPrtPgm1 and HLLPrtPgm2, both of which function to print report Report1. Before the call to each of these HLL programs, ProgramB issues an override to file Report1 to change the output queue attribute value.

FIGURE 21.4
Protecting Overrides

Program	*Call level*	*Activation group*	*Source*

ProgramA	1	Default	`OvrPrtF File(Report1) +`
			`OutQ(Prt01) +`
			`OvrScope(*CallLvl)`
			`Call Pgm(ProgramB)`

ProgramB	2	Default	`OvrPrtF File(Report1) +`
			`OutQ(Prt02) +`
			`Secure(*Yes) +`
			`OvrScope(*CallLvl)`
			`Call Pgm(HLLPrtPgm1)`
			
			`OvrPrtF File(Report1) +`
			`OutQ(Prt03) +`
			`OvrScope(*CallLvl)`
			`Call Pgm(HLLPrtPgm2)`

When you call ProgramA, the system first issues a call-level override that sets Report1's output queue attribute to value Prt01. Next, ProgramA calls ProgramB, thereby creating a new call level. ProgramB begins by issuing a call-level override, setting Report1's output queue attribute value to Prt02. Notice that the OvrPrtF command specifies the Secure parameter with a value of *Yes. ProgramB then calls HLL program HLLPrtPgm1 to open and print Report1. Because this call-level OvrPrtF command specifies Secure(*Yes), the system does not apply call-level overrides from lower call levels — namely, the override in ProgramA that sets the output queue attribute value to Prt01. HLLPrtPgm1 therefore places the report in output queue Prt02.

ProgramB continues with yet another call-level override, setting Report1's output queue attribute value to Prt03. Because this override occurs at the same call level as the first override in ProgramB, the system replaces the call level's override. However, this new override doesn't specify Secure(*Yes). Therefore, the system uses the call-level override from call level 1. This override changes the output queue attribute value from Prt03 to Prt01. ProgramB finally calls HLLPrtPgm2 to open and spool Report1 to output queue Prt01. These two overrides in ProgramB clearly demonstrate the behavioral difference between an unsecured and a secured override.

Explicitly Removing an Override

The system automatically removes overrides at certain times, such as when a call level ends, when an activation group ends, and when the job ends. However, you may want to remove the effect of an override at some other time. The DltOvr (Delete Override) command makes this possible, letting you explicitly remove overrides.

With this command, you can delete overrides at the call level, the activation group level, or the job level as follows:

Call level:	`DltOvr File(File1) OvrScope(*)`
Activation group level:	`DltOvr File(File2) OvrScope(*ActGrpDfn)`
Job level:	`DltOvr File(File3) OvrScope(*Job)`

Value *ActGrpDfn is the default value for the DltOvr command's OvrScope (Override scope) parameter. If you don't specify parameter OvrScope on the DltOvr command, this value is used.

The command's File parameter also supports special value *All, letting you extend the reach of the DltOvr command. This option gives you a convenient way to remove overrides for several files with a single command.

Miscellanea

We've covered quite a bit of ground with these rules of overriding files. In addition to the rules you've already seen, we'd like to introduce you to a few tidbits you might find useful.

You've probably grown accustomed to CL programs letting you know when you've coded something erroneously — the program crashes with an exception! However, specify a valid, yet wrong, file name on an override, and the system gives you no warning that you've done so. This seemingly odd behavior is easily explained. Consider the following code:

```
OvrPrtF File(Report1) OutQ(Prt01)
Call    Pgm(HLLPrtPgm)
```

However, HLLPrtPgm opens file Report2, not Report1. The system happily spools Report2 without any regard to the override. Although this is clearly a mistake in that you've specified the wrong file name in the OvrPrtF command, the system has no way of knowing this. The system can't know your intentions. Remember, this override could be used somewhere else in the job, perhaps even in a different call level.

The second tidbit involves a unique override capability that exists with the OvrPrtF command. OvrPrtF's File parameter supports special value *PrtF, letting you extend the reach of an override to all printer files (within the override scoping rules, of course). All rules concerning the application of overrides still apply. Special value *PrtF simply gives you a way to include multiple files with a single override command.

Also, you may recall an earlier reference to program QCmdExc and how its use affects the scope of an override. This program's primary purpose is to serve as a vehicle that lets HLL programs execute system commands. You can therefore use QCmdExc from within a HLL program to issue a file override. Remember that when you issue an override using this method, the call level is that of the process that invoked QCmdExc.

You should note that override commands may or may not have an effect on system commands. For more information about overrides and system commands, see "Overrides and System Commands" (page 358).

Important Additional Override Information

With the major considerations of file overrides covered, let's now take a brief look at some additional override information of note.

Overriding the Scope of Open Files

At times, you'll want to share a file's ODP among programs in your application. For instance, when you use the OpnQryF (Open Query File) command, you must share the ODP created by OpnQryF or your application won't use the ODP created by OpnQryF. To share the ODP, you specify Share(*Yes) on the OvrDbF command.

You can also explicitly control the scope of open files (ODPs) using the OpnScope (Open scope) parameter on the OvrDbF command. You can override the open scope to the activation group level and the job level.

Non-File Overrides

In addition to file overrides, the system provides support for overriding message files and program device entries used in communications applications.

You can override the message file used by programs by using the OvrMsgF (Override with Message File) command. However, the rules for applying overrides with OvrMsgF are quite different from those with other override commands. You can override only the name of the message file used, not the attributes.

During the course of normal operations, the system frequently sends various types of messages to various types of message queues. OvrMsgF provides a way for you to specify that when sending a message for a particular message ID, the system should first check the message file specified in the OvrMsgF for the identified message. If the message is found, the system sends the message using the information from this message file. If, on the other hand, the message isn't found, the system sends the message using the information from the original message file.

Using the OvrICFDevE (Override ICF Program Device Entry) command, you can issue overrides for program device entries. Overrides for program device entries let you override attributes of the Intersystem Communications Function (ICF) file that provides the link between your programs and the remote systems or devices with which your program communicates.

Overrides and Multithreaded Jobs

The system provides limited support for overrides in multithreaded jobs. Some restrictions apply to the provided support. The system supports the following override commands:

- OvrDbF — You can issue this command from the initial thread of a multithreaded job. Only overrides scoped to the job level or an activation group level affect open operations performed in a secondary thread.
- OvrPrtF — You can issue this command from the initial thread of a multithreaded job. As with OvrDbF, only overrides scoped to the job level or an activation group level affect open operations performed in a secondary thread.
- OvrMsgF — You can issue this command from the initial thread of a multithreaded job. This command affects only message file references in the initial thread. Message file references performed in secondary threads are not affected.
- DltOvr — You can issue this command from the initial thread of a multithreaded job.

The system ignores any other override commands in multithreaded jobs.

File Redirection

You can use overrides to redirect input or output to a file of a different type. For instance, you may have an application that writes directly to tape using a tape file. If at some time you'd like to print the information that's written to tape, you can use an override to accomplish your task. When you redirect data to a different file type, you use the override appropriate for the new target file. In the case of our example, you would override from the tape file to a printer file using the OvrPrtF command.

Because file redirection is rarely used, we don't provide detailed information here. We mention file redirection so that you know it's a possibility. Of course, many restrictions apply when using file redirection, so if you decide you'd like to use the technique, refer to the documentation. You can find more information about file redirection in the *File Management* book at IBM's iSeries Information Center (*http://publib.boulder.ibm.com/pubs/html/as400/infocenter.htm*).

Is All This Really Necessary?

Strictly speaking, it's possible to develop applications without using overrides. However, try to do so, and you undoubtedly will create an unmanageable nightmare. As experienced application developers, we can unequivocally state that overrides provide needed flexibility.

Overrides and System Commands

Overrides may or may not have an effect on a system command, or they may have limited effect on a system command. The following information will help you determine the effect that overrides will have on many system commands.

Commands That Ignore Overrides

AddLFM (Add Logical File Member)
AddPFM (Add Physical File Member)
AlcObj (Allocate Object)
ApyJrnChg (Apply Journaled Changes)
ChgObjOwn (Change Object Owner)
ChgPtr (Change Pointer)
ChgSbsD (Change Subsystem Description)
Chg*Xxx*F[1] (Change *Xxx* File)
ClrPFM (Clear Physical File Member)
ClrSavF (Clear Save File)
CpyIGCTbl (Copy DBCS Font Table)
CrtAutHlr (Create Authority Holder)
CrtDktF (Create Diskette File)
CrtDupObj (Create Duplicate Object)
CrtSbsD (Create Subsystem Description)
CrtTapF (Create Tape File)
DlcObj (Deallocate Object)
DltAutHlr (Delete Authority Holder)
DltF (Delete File)
DspDbR (Display Database Relations)
DspFD (Display File Description)
DspFFD (Display File Field Description)
DspJrn (Display Journal)
EdtDLOAut (Edit Document Library Object Authority)
EdtObjAut (Edit Object Authority)
EndJrnPF (End Journal Physical File)
GrtObjAut (Grant Object Authority)
InzPFM (Initialize Physical File Member)
MovObj (Move Object)
RgzPFM (Reorganize Physical File Member)
RmvJrnChg (Remove Journaled Changes)
RmvM (Remove Member)
RnmObj (Rename Object)
RtvMbrD (Retrieve Member Description)
RvkObjAut (Revoke Object Authority)
SbmDbJob (Submit Database Jobs)
SignOff (Sign Off)
StrDbRdr (Start Database Reader)
StrJrnPF (Start Journal Physical File)

[1] *All change file commands*

Commands That Allow Overrides Only for SrcFile and SrcMbr

CrtCmd (Create Command)
CrtDspF (Create Display File)
CrtICFF (Create ICF File)
CrtLF (Create Logical File)
CrtPF (Create Physical File)
CrtPrtF (Create Printer File)
CrtSrcPF (Create Source Physical File)
CrtTbl (Create Table)
Crt*Xxx*Pgm[2] (Create *Xxx* Program)

[2] *All create program object commands*

Commands That Allow Overrides Only for ToFile, Mbr, SeqOnly, LvlChk, and InhWrt

OpnQryF (Open Query File)

continued

Commands That Allow Overrides but Not Mbr(*All)

CpyFrmPCD (Copy From PC Document) CpyToPCD (Copy To PC Document)

Save and Restore Operations

Save and restore operations ignore all file overrides related to the respective media (e.g. tape, diskette, save file).

Files Opened as Part of an End-of-Routing Step or End-of-Job Processing

The system does not apply overrides to system files that are opened as part of an end-of-routing step or end-of-job processing. For instance, you cannot override the printer file for job logs, QPJobLog.

Chapter 22

Logical Files

As you learned in Chapter 20, the iSeries provides two kinds of database files: physical files and logical files. Physical files contain data; logical files do not. Logical files control how data in physical files is presented, most commonly using key fields so that data can be retrieved in key-field sequence. However, the use of key fields isn't the only function logical files provide. In this chapter, we introduce you to the following basic logical file concepts:

- record format definition/physical file selection
- key fields
- select/omit logic
- multiple logical file members

We discuss only the Data Description Specifications (DDS) interface to logical file creation. Keep in mind that you can also create logical files using SQL's Create View statement.

Record Format Definition/Physical File Selection

To define a logical file, you must select the record formats to be used and the physical files to be referenced. You can use the record format found in the physical file, or you can define a new record format. If you use the physical file record format, every field in that record format is accessible through the logical file. If you create a new record format, you must specify which fields will exist in the logical file. A logical file field must either reference a field in the physical file record format or be derived by using concatenation or substring functions.

Because the logical file doesn't contain any data, it must know which physical file to access for the requested data. You use the DDS PFile keyword to select the physical file referenced by the logical file record format. You specify the physical file in the PFile keyword as a qualified name (i.e., *LibraryName/FileName*) or as the file name alone.

Figure 22.1A lists the DDS for physical file HREMFP, and Figure 22.1B shows the DDS for logical file HREMFL1.

FIGURE 22.1A

DDS for Physical File HREMFP

```
*...1....+....2....+....3....+....4....+....5....+....6....+....7....
 *   =================================================================
 *   =  File.......... HREMFP                                        =
 *   =  File type..... Physical                                      =
 *   =  Description... Employee Master File                          =
 *   =================================================================

A          R HREMFR                    TEXT('Employee Master')

A            EMPID          6          TEXT('Employee ID')
A            FIRSTNAME     15          TEXT('First Name')
A            MIDDLEINIT     1          TEXT('Middle Initial')
A            LASTNAME      15          TEXT('Last Name')
A            SOCIALSEC      9          TEXT('Social Security No.')
A            STREETADDR    30          TEXT('Street Address')
A            CITY          20          TEXT('City')
A            STATEABBR      2          TEXT('State Abbreviation')
A            ZIPCODE        9          TEXT('Zip Code')
A            TELEPHONE     20          TEXT('Telephone Number')
A            DEPTID         4          TEXT('Department ID')
A            STARTDATE       L         TEXT('Start Date')
A                                      ALWNULL
A            TERMDATE        L         TEXT('Termination Date')
A                                      ALWNULL
A            TYPE           1          TEXT('Employee Type')
A            PAYRATE        9  2       TEXT('Pay Rate')
```

FIGURE 22.1B

DDS for Logical File HREMFL1

```
*...1....+....2....+....3....+....4....+....5....+....6....+....7....
 *   =================================================================
 *   =  File.......... HREMFL1                                       =
 *   =  File type..... Logical                                       =
 *   =  Description... Employee Master File with primary key         =
 *   =                                                               =
 *   =  Key fields.... EMPID - Employee ID (Unique)                  =
 *   =================================================================

A                                      UNIQUE
A          R HREMFR                    PFILE(HREMFP)

A          K EMPID
```

Notice that the logical file references the physical file's record format (HREMFR) and does not list fields individually. As a consequence, every field in the physical file will be presented in logical file HREMFL1. Also notice that the PFile keyword in Figure 22.1B references physical file HREMFP.

In Figure 22.1C, logical file HREMFL2 defines a record format not found in PFile-referenced HREMFP. Therefore, this logical file must define each physical file field it will use.

Figure 22.1C

DDS for Logical File HREMFL2

```
*...1....+....2....+....3....+....4....+....5....+....6....+....7....
 *  ================================================================
 *  =  File.......... HREMFL2                                      =
 *  =  File type..... Logical                                      =
 *  =  Description... Employee Master File alternate keys and      =
 *  =                 selected fields                              =
 *  =                                                              =
 *  =  Key fields.... LASTNAME   - Employee Last Name              =
 *  =                 FIRSTNAME  - Employee First Name             =
 *  =                 MIDDLEINIT - Employee Middle Initial         =
 *  ================================================================

A          R HREMFR2                   PFILE(HREMFP)

A            FIRSTNAME
A            MIDDLEINIT
A            LASTNAME
A            STREETADDR
A            CITY
A            STATEABBR
A            ZIPCODE
A            DEPTID
A            STARTDATE
A            TERMDATE
A            TYPE

A          K LASTNAME
A          K FIRSTNAME
A          K MIDDLEINIT
```

A logical file can thus be a projection of the physical file — that is, contain only selected physical file fields. Notice that fields EmpID, SocialSec, Telephone, and PayRate all appear in the physical file but are not included in file HREMFL2.

Tip

Although a logical file can use the record format name of the physical file on which it is based and still use explicitly named fields to restrict the fields contained in the logical file, we suggest you not use the physical file's record format name. Instead, for each group of selected fields, supply a unique record format name.

Key Fields

Let's look at Figures 22.1B and 22.1C again to see how key fields are used. File HREMFL1 identifies field EmpID as a key field (in DDS, key fields are denoted by a K in position 17 and the name of the field in positions 19–28). When you access this logical file by key, the records will be presented in employee ID sequence. The logical file simply defines an access path for the access sequence — it doesn't physically sort the records.

The Unique keyword specified in this source member tells the system to require a unique value for EmpID for each record in the file, thus establishing EmpID as the primary key to physical file HREMFP. Should the logical file be deleted, records could be added to the physical file with a non-unique key — giving rise to a question that has been debated over the years: Is it better to use a keyed physical file or a keyed logical file to establish a file's primary key?

You could specify EmpID as the key in the DDS for physical file HREMPF and enforce it as the primary key by using keyword Unique. Making the primary key part of the physical file has a distinct advantage: The primary key is always enforced because the physical file can't be deleted without deleting the data. Even if all dependent logical files were deleted, the primary key would be enforced. However, placing the key in the physical file also has a disadvantage: Should the access path for a physical file data member be damaged (a rare, but possible, occurrence), the damaged access path prevents access to the data. Depending on the type and severity of the damage, you may be forced to delete the member and restore it from a backup.

Placing the primary key in a logical file, as we do in Figure 22.1B, ensures that access path damage results only in the need to recompile the logical file — the physical file remains intact. This method also means you can access the physical file in arrival sequence. As we mentioned earlier, the negative effect is that deleting the logical file results in leaving the physical file without a primary key.

Let us make a few more comments concerning the issue of where to place the primary key. Access path maintenance is costly; when records are updated, the system must determine whether any key fields have been changed, requiring the access path to be updated. In an interactive environment where changes are made randomly based on business demands, the overhead for this operation is relatively small. But when batch purges or updates result in many access path updates for files, the overhead can be quite detrimental to performance.

With these points in mind, you should investigate the potential performance gains that the following suggestions might provide:

- For work files, which are frequently cleared and reloaded, create the physical file with no keys, and place the primary and alternate keys in logical files. Then delete the logical files (access paths) before you clear and reload the file. The update will occur much faster with no access path maintenance to perform. After the update, rebuild or restore the logical files.

- For very large files, consider the same method as that for work files. When you need to update the entire file, you can delete the logical files, perform the update, and then rebuild or restore the logical files.
- For files updated primarily through interactive maintenance programs, putting the key in the physical file poses no performance problems.

The Unique keyword is also expensive in terms of system overhead, so you should use it only to maintain the primary key. Logical file HREMFL2 specifies three key fields — LastName (employee last name), FirstName (employee first name), and MiddleInit (employee middle initial). Keyword Unique is not used here because the primary key is the employee ID and because there is no advantage to requiring unique names (even if you could ensure that no two employees had the same name). A primary key protects the integrity of the file, while alternative keys provide additional views of the same data.

Select/Omit Logic

Another feature logical files offer is the ability to select or omit records from the referenced physical file. You can use DDS keywords Comp, Values, and Range to provide select or omit statements when you build logical files.

Figure 22.2 shows logical file HREMFL3.

FIGURE 22.2

DDS for Logical File HREMFL3

```
*...1....+....2....+....3....+....4....+....5....+....6....+....7....
 *  ===============================================================
 *  =  File.......... HREMFL3                                     =
 *  =  File type..... Logical                                     =
 *  =  Description... Employee Master File primary key and        =
 *  =                 selected records                            =
 *  =                                                             =
 *  =  Key fields.... EMPID - Employee ID                         =
 *  =                                                             =
 *  =  Selection..... Current employees                           =
 *  ===============================================================

A          R HREMFR                     PFILE(HREMFP)

A          K EMPID
A          S TERMDATE                   COMP(EQ *NULL)
```

Field TermDate (employee termination date) is used with keyword Comp to compare values, forming a Select statement (notice the S in position 17). This DDS line tells the system to select records from the physical file in which field TermDate is equal to *Null (i.e., no termination date has been entered for that employee). Therefore, when you create logical file HREMFL3, OS/400 builds indexed entries in the logical file only for records in which the employee termination date is *Null, thus selecting only current employees. When a program accesses the logical file, it reads only the selected records.

Using Select/Omit Statements

Before looking at some more examples, let's go over some of the basic rules for using select/omit statements:

1. You can use select/omit statements only if the logical file specifies key fields (the value *None in positions 19–23 satisfies the requirement for a key field) or if the logical file uses the DynSlt keyword. (We provide more detail about keyword DynSlt later.)
2. To locate the field definitions for fields named on a select/omit statement, OS/400 first checks the field name specified in positions 19–28 in the record format definition and then checks fields specified as parameters on ConCat (concatenate) or Rename keywords. If the field name is found in more than one place, OS/400 uses the first occurrence of the field name.
3. Select/omit statements are designated by an S or an O in position 17. Multiple statements coded with an S or an O form an OR connective relationship. The first true statement is used for select/omit purposes.
4. You can follow a select/omit statement with other statements containing a blank in position 17. Such additional statements form an AND connective relationship with the initial select or omit statement. All related statements must be true before the record is selected or omitted.
5. You can specify both select and omit statements in the same file, but the following rules apply:
   a. If you specify both select and omit for a record format, OS/400 processes the statements only until one of the conditions is met. Thus, if a record satisfies the first statement or group of related statements, the record is processed without being tested against the subsequent select/omit statements.
   b. If you specify both select and omit, you can use the All keyword to specify whether records that do not meet any of the specified conditions should be selected or omitted.
   c. If you don't use the All keyword, the action taken for records not satisfying any of the conditions is the converse of the last statement specified. For example, if the last statement was an omit, the record is selected.

Now, let's work through a few select/omit examples to see how some of these rules apply. Consider the statements in Figure 22.3.

FIGURE 22.3

Statements Forming an OR Relationship

```
*...1....+....2....+....3....+....4....+....5....+....6....+....7....
A            S TERMDATE                 COMP(EQ *NULL)
A            S TYPE                     COMP(EQ 'H')
```

Based on rule 3, OS/400 selects any record in which the employee termination date equals *Null or the employee type equals H (i.e., hourly). Both statements have an S coded in position 17, representing an OR connective relationship.

Contrast the statements in Figure 22.3 with those in Figure 22.4.

FIGURE 22.4

Statements Forming an AND Relationship

```
*...1....+....2....+....3....+....4....+....5....+....6....+....7....
A            S TERMDATE                      COMP(EQ *NULL)
A              TYPE                          COMP(EQ 'H')
```

Notice that the second statement in Figure 22.4 does not have an S or an O in position 17. According to rule 4, this statement is related to the previous statement by an AND connective relationship. Therefore, both comparisons must be true for a record to be selected, so all current hourly employees will be selected.

To keep things interesting, let's change the statements to appear as they do in Figure 22.5.

FIGURE 22.5

An Incorrect Variation of Figure 22.4

```
*...1....+....2....+....3....+....4....+....5....+....6....+....7....
A            S TYPE                          COMP(EQ 'H')
A            O TERMDATE                      COMP(NE *NULL)
```

At first glance, you might think this combination of select and omit would provide the same result as the statements in Figure 22.4. However, it doesn't — for two reasons. As rule 5a explains, the order of the statements is significant. In Figure 22.5, the first statement determines whether the employee type equals H. If it does, the record is selected and the second test is not performed, thus letting records for terminated hourly employees be selected.

The second reason the statements in Figures 22.4 and 22.5 produce different results is because of the absence of the All keyword, which specifies how to handle records that don't meet either condition. According to rule 5c, records that don't meet either comparison are selected because the system performs the converse of the last statement listed (i.e., the omit statement).

Figure 22.6 shows the correct way to select records for current hourly employees using both select and omit statements.

FIGURE 22.6

A Correct Use of Select and Omit

```
*...1....+....2....+....3....+....4....+....5....+....6....+....7....
A            O TERMDATE                      COMP(NE *NULL)
A            S TYPE                          COMP(EQ 'H')
A            O                               ALL
```

The All keyword in the last statement tells the system to omit records that don't meet the conditions specified by the first two statements.

In general, however, it's best to use only one type of statement (either select or omit) when you define a logical file. By limiting your definitions this way, you'll avoid introducing errors that result when the rules governing the use of select and omit are violated.

Dynamic Selection with Select/Omit

Select/omit statements give you dynamic selection capabilities through the DDS DynSlt keyword. DynSlt lets you defer the select/omit process until a program requests input from the logical file. When the program reads the file, OS/400 presents only the records that meet the select/omit criteria. Figure 22.7 shows how to code the DynSlt keyword.

FIGURE 22.7

Coding the DynSlt Keyword

```
*...1....+....2....+....3....+....4....+....5....+....6....+....7....
 *  ==============================================================
 *  =  File.......... HREMFL4                                    =
 *  =  File type..... Logical                                    =
 *  =  Description... Employee Master File primary key and       =
 *  =                 dynamically selected records               =
 *  =                                                            =
 *  =  Key fields.... EMPID - Employee ID                        =
 *  =                                                            =
 *  =  Selection..... Current employees                          =
 *  ==============================================================

A                                      DYNSLT
A          R HREMFR                    PFILE(HREMFP)

A          K EMPID
A          S TERMDATE                  COMP(EQ *NULL)
```

You're probably wondering just how this differs from an example without the DynSlt keyword. It differs in one significant way: performance. Without keyword DynSlt, the system uses access path select/omit. With access path select/omit, the access path contains keys only for those records that meet the logical file's select/omit criteria. This access path is maintained by the system when you add records to or update records in the physical file on which the logical file is based. This approach results in faster access than with dynamic select/omit, but at the cost of increased overhead.

With dynamic select/omit, a key exists for all records in the file, not just for those that meet the select/omit criteria. Only when you access the file does the system perform the record selection. This removes the overhead of performing the select/omit logic as records are added to or updated in the physical file. Dynamic select/omit also allows more access path sharing, which can improve performance.

One scenario in which dynamic select/omit might be appropriate is when you have a file that is updated frequently, yet read infrequently. In such a case, you may not need to update the access path for select/omit purposes until a program reads the file.

For example, consider a physical file with a field that you want to use for select/omit processing in a logical file, and assume that this field changes frequently. Further, assume that you infrequently read the logical file to produce a report. In such a case, dynamic select/omit may be more efficient than performing access path maintenance on an ongoing basis as the field is changed.

As a guideline, if you have a select/omit logical file that uses more than 75 percent of the records in the physical file member, keyword DynSlt can reduce the overhead required to maintain that logical file without significantly affecting the retrieval performance of the file because most records will be selected anyway. If the logical file uses less than 75 percent of the records in the physical file member, you can usually maximize performance by omitting keyword DynSlt and letting the select/omit process occur when the file is created.

Multiple Logical File Members

The last basic logical file concept you should understand is the way logical file members work. The CrtLF (Create Logical File) command has several parameters related to establishing the member or members that will exist in the logical file. These parameters are Mbr (the logical file member name), DtaMbrs (the physical file data members upon which the logical file member is based), and MaxMbrs (the maximum number of data members the logical file can contain). The default values for these parameters are *File, *All, and 1, respectively. Typically, a physical file has one data member. When you create a logical file to reference such a physical file, these default values instruct the system to create a logical file member with the same name as the logical file itself, base this logical file member on the single physical file data member, and specify that a maximum of one logical file member can exist in this file.

When creating applications with multiple-data-member physical files, you often don't know precisely what physical and logical members you eventually will need. For example, for each user, you might add members to a temporary work file for each session when the user signs on. Obviously, you (or, more accurately, your program) don't know in advance what members to create. In such a case, you would normally

- create the physical file with no members:

```
CrtPF File(TestPF) +
      Mbr(*None)
```

- create the logical file with no members:

```
CrtLF File(TestLF) +
      Mbr(*None)
```

- for every user that signs on, add a physical file member to the physical file:

```
AddPFM File(TestPF)            +
       Mbr(TestMbr)            +
       Text('Test PF Member')
```

- for every physical file member, add a member to the logical file and specify the physical file member on which to base the logical member:

```
AddLFM File(TestLF)                +
       Mbr(TestMbr)                +
       DtaMbrs((TestPF TestMbr))  +
       Text('Test LF Member')
```

When a logical file member references more than one physical file member and your application finds duplicate records in the multiple members, the application processes those records in the order in which the members are specified on the DtaMbrs parameter. For instance, if the CrtLF command specifies

```
CrtLF File(TestLib/TestLF)    +
      Mbr(AllYears)           +
      DtaMbrs((YrPF DT1998)  +
              (YrPF DT1999)  +
              (YrPF DT2000))
```

a program that performs sequential-by-key processing on logical file member AllYears first reads the records in member DT1998, then in member DT1999, and finally in member DT2000.

Keys to the iSeries Database

Logical files on the iSeries provide the flexibility needed to build a database for an interactive multiuser environment. Understanding logical files will take you a long way toward creating effective database implementations.

Because this chapter has introduced only the basic concepts, we strongly recommend that you spend some time in the manuals to increase your knowledge about logical files. You can find more information about logical files in *OS/400 DDS Reference* (SC41-5712) and in *DB2 UDB for AS/400 Database Programming* (available at IBM's iSeries Information Center, *http://publib.boulder.ibm.com/pubs/html/as400/infocenter.htm*). As you master the methods presented there, you'll discover many ways in which logical files can enhance your applications.

Chapter 23

File Sharing

You may already be familiar with the general concept of file sharing, a common feature of many operating systems that lets more than one program concurrently open a file. The iSeries provides this support automatically. When a program opens a file, the system allocates the file and the file's resources in a way that prevents conflict with other jobs and programs that may be using the file. This is true even if the file open occurs multiple times in a single program within a job!

This is just one level of file sharing provided by OS/400, though. In this chapter, we focus on another level — that provided by the Share (Share open data path) file attribute. As you further examine the Share attribute, you'll see that this additional level of sharing not only enables programs within a job to interact in ways not otherwise possible but also provides a mechanism for enhancing program performance.

Sharing Fundamentals

When a program opens a file, the system creates a path from the program to the data or device associated with the file through which the program performs all I/O operations for the file. This path, called the *open data path (ODP)*, contains such things as file status information (i.e., the general and file-dependent I/O feedback areas), the file cursor (i.e., the current record position in a file), and storage areas.

Even if a file is used multiple times within a job, the system creates a new ODP for each open operation. This approach lets a job's programs perform independent I/O operations to the same file. For instance, for each ODP, the system maintains a unique database file cursor that determines which record the system reads next. This unique file cursor means that when multiple programs within a job open the same file, each program can be assured that its I/O operations will be applied to the correct record within the file.

However, the behavior associated with a unique ODP isn't always the most desirable, as you'll soon see. Fortunately, the system provides a method that enables multiple programs within a job to share an ODP created when the job initially opened a file. This sharing of an ODP is controlled by a file's Share attribute.

The Share attribute is valid for database, source, device, Distributed Data Management (DDM), and save files. You establish the Share attribute or change it for a file using any of the Crt*Xxx*F (Create *Xxx* File), Chg*Xxx*F (Change *Xxx* File), or Ovr*Xxx*F (Override with *Xxx* File) commands. The valid values for the Share attribute are *Yes and *No.

The default Share value *No instructs the system to establish a unique ODP each time a job opens the file. We advise you to always use this default value in the file object itself (i.e., don't set Share to *Yes using the Crt*Xxx*F or Chg*Xxx*F command). Instead, you should issue the appropriate override command and specify Share(*Yes) only when you want to share an ODP for a specific application. Specifying within the file object that the file's ODP should be shared means that unless you issue an override in your jobs to prevent sharing, *all* opens for that file will be shared opens. This approach is counterintuitive and sure to introduce programming errors. Now is an opportune time to introduce you to a few fundamentals that will help you better understand the sharing of ODPs and prevent such application problems.

First, you should be aware that there's only a slight difference between jobs running in the Original Program Model (OPM) environment and jobs running in the Integrated Language Environment (ILE). In the OPM environment, shared opens let multiple programs within a job share an ODP. ILE, on the other hand, lets you scope a file open to either the job level or the activation group level using the OpnScope (Open scope) parameter on the appropriate override command. Therefore, when you scope a file open to the job level specifying Share(*Yes) in ILE, all program objects within the job use the ODP created by the first file open operation. When an ILE job uses shared opens scoped to the activation group level, the system creates an ODP for each activation group that opens the file. Program objects running within any activation group can share open files that are scoped to the job level. However, only programs running within the same activation group can share open files scoped to the activation group level. To simplify further discussion, we refer primarily to open files scoped to the job level. Just remain aware that in ILE, the scope may really be to the activation group level.

You should also note that when a program opens a file, the system establishes open options that control the operations the program can perform for the file. The options specified on the OpnDbF (Open Database File) command or by the high-level language definition of the file (e.g., RPG's F-spec) determine the open options. The open options are

- input only (*Inp on the OpnDbF command)
- output only (*Out on the OpnDbF command)
- input, output, update, and delete (*All on the OpnDbF command)

These options are significant when you share an ODP. If you specify Share(*Yes) for a file, the first program to open the file determines these options. This program must therefore specify all the open options required for any subsequent programs in the same job. For example, if program Program1 performs a shared open of file Test with the open option *Inp (for input only) and the job then calls program Program2, which requires the open option *All (for an update or delete function), Program2 will fail.

In addition to sharing open options, programs also share the file cursor. This means that each program within a job does not maintain its own position within a file (i.e., the record that will be read next). For instance, if Program1 performs sequential reads of file Test, reading records 1 and 2, and then calls Program2 to perform two sequential reads of file Test, Program2 reads records 3 and 4 rather than rereading records 1 and 2. If control then returns to Program1 and this program performs two reads of file Test, it reads records 5 and 6. This capability, although powerful, can be problematic. If your programs need to maintain their own individual positions within a file, you must code the programs accordingly. Upon return from a called program that reads records from a shared file, calling programs cannot presume that they will be pointing to the same record they were pointing to when they issued the call.

Last, there is a common misconception that the use of Share(*Yes) alters the way in which the database manager performs record locking. This is not the case. The system performs record locking on files with Share(*Yes) specified in the same manner it performs record locking on files with Share(*No) specified.

With these fundamentals under your belt, it's time to look at a few examples. These examples will show you the differing behavior when you share an ODP and when you do not. We'll also point out a few reasons you might consider sharing ODPs in your applications.

Sharing Examples

Let's look at two examples that illustrate how sharing an ODP lets your programs interact in ways not otherwise possible. We'll show you an example using a shared database file ODP, as well as an example using a shared device file ODP.

Shared Database File Example

The first example demonstrates the behavior of the file cursor when you share the ODP for a database file. This example also illustrates sharing an ODP within an activation group. The example uses activation groups AG1 and AG2 for this purpose.

Figure 23.1A shows the data contained in physical file ShrDb, and Figures 23.1B, 23.1C, and 23.1D show sample code for processing this file using a shared ODP. Notice that the comment banner at the top of the code in Figure 23.1D indicates that the source code is for four programs. In other words, this same source applies to each of the four programs. Programs ShrDb03A1 and ShrDb03A2 will share an ODP for file ShrDb within activation group AG1, while programs ShrDb03B1 and ShrDb03B2 will share an ODP for file ShrDb within activation group AG2.

FIGURE 23.1A

Shared Database File Example — Data for File ShrDb

```
Record 1
Record 2
Record 3
Record 4
Record 5
Record 6
Record 7
Record 8
```

FIGURE 23.1B

Shared Database File Example — Program ShrDb01A

```
/*  ====================================================================  */
/*  = Program....... ShrDbØ1A                                          =  */
/*  = Source type... CLLE                                              =  */
/*  = Description... Shared database file example                      =  */
/*  = Comments...... Runs in default activation group                  =  */
/*  ====================================================================  */

Pgm

/*  ====================================================================  */
/*  = Share ODP for file ShrDb                                         =  */
/*  ====================================================================  */

  OvrDbF      File( ShrDb )                                               +
              Share( *Yes )                                               +
              OpnScope( *ActGrpDfn )

/*  ====================================================================  */
/*  = Call main RPG driver                                             =  */
/*  ====================================================================  */

  Call        ShrDbØ2A

/*  ====================================================================  */
/*  = Clean up activation groups                                       =  */
/*  ====================================================================  */

  RclActGrp   AG1
  RclActGrp   AG2

EndPgm
```

FIGURE 23.1C

Shared Database File Example — Program ShrDb02A

```
 *  ======================================================================
 *  =  Program....... ShrDbØ2A                                           =
 *  =  Source type... RPGLE                                              =
 *  =  Comments...... Runs in default activation group                   =
 *  ======================================================================

C                   Do        4
C                   Call      'SHRDBØ3A1'
C                   Call      'SHRDBØ3A2'
C                   Call      'SHRDBØ3B1'
C                   Call      'SHRDBØ3B2'
C                   EndDo
C                   Eval      *InLR = *On
```

FIGURE 23.1D

Shared Database File Example — Programs to Read ShrDb

```
 *  ==================================================================
 *  =  Program....... ShrDbØ3A1   (assign to activation group AG1)    =
 *  =                 ShrDbØ3A2   (assign to activation group AG1)    =
 *  =                 ShrDbØ3B1   (assign to activation group AG2)    =
 *  =                 ShrDbØ3B2   (assign to activation group AG2)    =
 *  =  Source type... RPGLE                                           =
 *  =  Comments...... This source is used to compile all programs     =
 *  =                 listed above                                    =
 *  ==================================================================

FShrDb     IF   E             Disk

C                   Read      ShrDb
C                   Return
```

Program ShrDb01A (Figure 23.1B) is the main CL program that drives the process. This program runs in the default activation group. The program begins by issuing an OvrDbF (Override with Database File) command for file ShrDb. The override indicates that the system is to share the ODP and is to set the file's open scope to the activation group. This statement causes the system to create one ODP per activation group for file ShrDb when the system opens the file.

Next, the program calls the main RPG driver program, ShrDb02A, which calls all programs that actually read file ShrDb. When control returns from the RPG programs to CL program ShrDb01A, the program finishes by cleaning up the resources for activation groups AG1 and AG2. This cleanup closes the open instances (both ODPs) of file ShrDb.

Figure 23.1C shows the main RPG driver program that calls all programs that read file ShrDb. This program, like CL program ShrDb01A, runs in the default activation group. Program ShrDb02A simply calls the four programs to read file ShrDb (within a loop executed four times).

The source shown in Figure 23.1D applies to all four of the programs that ShrDb02A calls. These programs do nothing more than read one record from file ShrDb and return control to ShrDb02A.

The table in Figure 23.1E shows the results of this example. You can see that within each activation group, each program reads a record and skips a record. The record is skipped because a different program read it!

FIGURE 23.1E

Shared Database File Example — Results

Loop iteration in program ShrDb02A	Program	ODP used	Record read
1	ShrDb03A1	AG1	Record 1
	ShrDb03A2	AG1	Record 2
	ShrDb03B1	AG2	Record 1
	ShrDb03B2	AG2	Record 2
2	ShrDb03A1	AG1	Record 3
	ShrDb03A2	AG1	Record 4
	ShrDb03B1	AG2	Record 3
	ShrDb03B2	AG2	Record 4
3	ShrDb03A1	AG1	Record 5
	ShrDb03A2	AG1	Record 6
	ShrDb03B1	AG2	Record 5
	ShrDb03B2	AG2	Record 6
4	ShrDb03A1	AG1	Record 7
	ShrDb03A2	AG1	Record 8
	ShrDb03B1	AG2	Record 7
	ShrDb03B2	AG2	Record 8

Shared Printer File Example

Now, let's look at an example that demonstrates the use of a shared ODP for a device file — namely, a printer file. This example shows how you can use multiple programs to write a single spooled file. As with the previous example, you'll see how multiple activation groups influence the process.

Figure 23.2A shows the DDS for printer file ShrPrt, which produces a simple name list. The printer file contains two record formats: Hdg01 to print headings and Dtl01 to print the detail lines containing the names. The main driver program is CL program ShrPrt01A (Figure 23.2B).

FIGURE 23.2A

Shared Printer File Example — Printer File ShrPrt

```
  *  =================================================================
  *  = File.......... ShrPrt                                         =
  *  = Source type... PRTF                                           =
  *  = Description... Shared printer file example printer file       =
  *  =================================================================

A          R HDG01
A                                      SKIPB(1)
A                                     1'Name List'
A                                      SPACEA(3)
A                                     1'Name'
A                                      SPACEA(2)

A          R DTL01
A                                      SPACEA(1)
A            NAME          10         1
```

FIGURE 23.2B

Shared Printer File Example — Program ShrPrt01A

```
/*  ================================================================  */
/*  = Program....... ShrPrt01A                                     =  */
/*  = Source type... CLLE                                          =  */
/*  = Description... Shared printer file example                   =  */
/*  = Comments...... Runs in default activation group              =  */
/*  ================================================================  */

Pgm

/*  ================================================================  */
/*  = Share print file ShrPrt                                      =  */
/*  ================================================================  */

  OvrPrtF    File( ShrPrt )                                          +
             Share( *Yes )

/*  ================================================================  */
/*  = Open print file ShrPrt in each activation group              =  */
/*  ================================================================  */

  Call       ShrPrt02A
  Call       ShrPrt02B

/*  ================================================================  */
/*  = Write reports                                                =  */
/*  ================================================================  */

  Call       ShrPrt03A

/*  ================================================================  */
/*  = Clean up activation groups                                   =  */
/*  ================================================================  */

  RclActGrp  AG1
  RclActGrp  AG2

EndPgm
```

This program begins by overriding print file ShrPrt to share its ODP. Next, ShrPrt01A calls RPG programs ShrPrt02A (running in activation group AG1) and ShrPrt02B (running in activation group AG2) to open print file ShrPrt in each activation group. Because there are two ODPs (one for each activation group), two spooled files will be produced. After opening the printer files, ShrPrt01A calls program ShrPrt03A, the main RPG program that calls the actual print programs. Last, ShrPrt01A cleans up the activation groups, closing the printer files.

Figure 23.2C shows the source used to create programs ShrPrt02A and ShrPrt02B.

FIGURE 23.2C

Shared Printer File Example — Programs to Open ShrPrt

```
 *  ===================================================================
 *  =  Program....... ShrPrt02A   (assign to activation group AG1)    =
 *  =                 ShrPrt02B   (assign to activation group AG2)    =
 *  =  Source type... RPGLE                                           =
 *  =  Comments...... This source is used to compile all programs     =
 *  =                 listed above                                    =
 *  ===================================================================

FShrPrt    O    E             Printer

C                   Return
```

These programs may seem a little odd to you. A glance at the C-specs reveals that these programs simply return to their caller! That's true. It's the F-spec that does all the work in these programs. Programs ShrPrt02A and ShrPrt02B serve only to open print file ShrPrt in activation group AG1 and AG2, respectively. We chose this method of opening the printer files to demonstrate that once you open a file scoped to the activation group level, that open is available for all programs in the activation group.

Program ShrPrt03A (Figure 23.2D) runs in the default activation group (it could be any activation group, though) and serves to call the actual print programs.

FIGURE 23.2D

Shared Printer File Example — Program ShrPrt03A

```
 *  ===================================================================
 *  =  Program....... ShrPrt03A                                       =
 *  =  Source type... RPGLE                                           =
 *  =  Comments...... Runs in default activation group                =
 *  ===================================================================

C                   Call      'SHRPRT04A'
C                   Call      'SHRPRT04C'
C                   Call      'SHRPRT04D'
C                   Call      'SHRPRT04B'
C                   Return
```

Programs ShrPrt04A and ShrPrt04B share the ODP in activation group AG1, while programs ShrPrt04C and ShrPrt04D share the ODP in activation group AG2. You might notice that ShrPrt03A calls these programs in a seemingly strange sequence. We've purposely used this sequence to highlight the fact that the ODPs are shared within an activation group. First, we call an activation group AG1 print program. Next, we call two activation group AG2 print programs. Last, we call the second activation group AG1 program. When you examine the resulting output later, you'll see that the reports are indeed correct.

Figures 23.2E through 23.2H shows print programs ShrPrt04A, ShrPrt04B, ShrPrt04C, and ShrPrt04D, respectively. Each of these programs simply prints headings and two detail lines. The resulting spooled file for activation group AG1 appears in Figure 23.2I, while Figure 23.2J shows the spooled file for activation group AG2.

FIGURE 23.2E

Shared Printer File Example — Program ShrPrt04A

```
 *  ====================================================================
 *  =  Program....... ShrPrt04A                                        =
 *  =  Source type... RPGLE                                            =
 *  =  Comments...... Runs in activation group AG1                     =
 *  ====================================================================

FShrPrt    O    E              Printer

C                        Write     Hdg01
C                        Eval      Name = 'Gary'
C                        Write     Dtl01
C                        Eval      Name = 'Karen'
C                        Write     Dtl01
C                        Return
```

FIGURE 23.2F

Shared Printer File Example — Program ShrPrt04B

```
 *  ====================================================================
 *  =  Program....... ShrPrt04B                                        =
 *  =  Source type... RPGLE                                            =
 *  =  Comments...... Runs in activation group AG1                     =
 *  ====================================================================

FShrPrt    O    E              Printer

C                        Write     Hdg01
C                        Eval      Name = 'Josh'
C                        Write     Dtl01
C                        Eval      Name = 'Shannon'
C                        Write     Dtl01
C                        Return
```

FIGURE 23.2G

Shared Printer File Example — Program ShrPrt04C

```
 *   ===================================================================
 *   =  Program....... ShrPrtØ4C                                       =
 *   =  Source type... RPGLE                                           =
 *   =  Comments...... Runs in activation group AG2                    =
 *   ===================================================================

FShrPrt    O    E             Printer

C                   Write     HdgØ1
C                   Eval      Name = 'Don'
C                   Write     DtlØ1
C                   Eval      Name = 'Mark'
C                   Write     DtlØ1
C                   Return
```

FIGURE 23.2H

Shared Printer File Example — Program ShrPrt04D

```
 *   ===================================================================
 *   =  Program....... ShrPrtØ4D                                       =
 *   =  Source type... RPGLE                                           =
 *   =  Comments...... Runs in activation group AG2                    =
 *   ===================================================================

FShrPrt    O    E             Printer

C                   Write     HdgØ1
C                   Eval      Name = 'Charlie'
C                   Write     DtlØ1
C                   Eval      Name = 'Spiro'
C                   Write     DtlØ1
C                   Return
```

FIGURE 23.2I

Spooled File Produced for Activation Group AG1

```
Name List


Name

Gary
Karen
Josh
Shannon
```

FIGURE 23.2J
Spooled File Produced for Activation Group AG2

```
Name List


Name

Don
Mark
Charlie
Spiro
```

How Sharing ODPs Can Help

Now that you've seen the examples, you may be wondering why you would ever do such a thing. Perhaps the best answer is that the shared ODP technique sometimes makes it easier to write more modular applications. For example, consider an application that maintains a set of database files with current customer information as well as database files with historical customer information. Often, applications summarize current information before archiving it to history files. The result is that the history database typically has completely different files with completely different layouts than the current files. You may need to produce a report that contains both current information and historical customer information. The information in the report is the same whether the source of the information is current or historical, but the processing required for current information differs greatly from that required for historical information.

A modular application might have one program to process and print current customer information and another program to process and print historical customer information. Using a shared ODP, you can call both programs yet generate a single spooled file with all the necessary information. This modular approach means you can

- call Program1 to generate a spooled file with current customer information
- call Program2 to generate a spooled file with historical customer information
- share the ODP and call both programs to generate a spooled file with all information

We're sure you can think of many ways you can use this technique to your advantage.

Share and Enhance Program Performance

Sharing ODPs can also play an important role in boosting application performance. In fact, this is perhaps the most common reason applications employ shared ODPs.

One of the most popular uses of the Share attribute is opening files at the menu level when users frequently enter and exit applications on that menu. Figure 23.3A illustrates a simple order entry menu (OEMenu) with five options, each of which represents a program that uses one or more of the listed files. If Share(*No) is defined for each file, then each time one of these programs is called, an ODP is created for each file the program uses. File-open processing is considerably expensive in terms of performance, and if users frequently switch between menu options, they experience a delay each time a file is opened. In applications with a considerable number of files to open, this delay can be significant.

The coding example in Figure 23.3B provides a solution to this problem. For this example, assume that program OEMenu runs in activation group OE and that all programs it calls run in activation group *Caller. This lets file opens be scoped to the activation group level. Program OEMenu first issues an OvrDbF command specifying Share(*Yes) for each file identified. The program then uses OpnDbF to open each file with the maximum open options required for the various applications. This moves the overhead of opening the file to the menu program itself rather than each application program. Users therefore experience the delay in opening the files only once, when the menu program is executed. When a user selects an option on the menu, the respective program need not perform a full open of the file, and thus the programs are initiated more quickly. Remember, however, to plan carefully when using shared ODPs, keeping in mind the above-mentioned guidelines about placing the file cursor.

FIGURE 23.3A
Sample Order Entry Menu

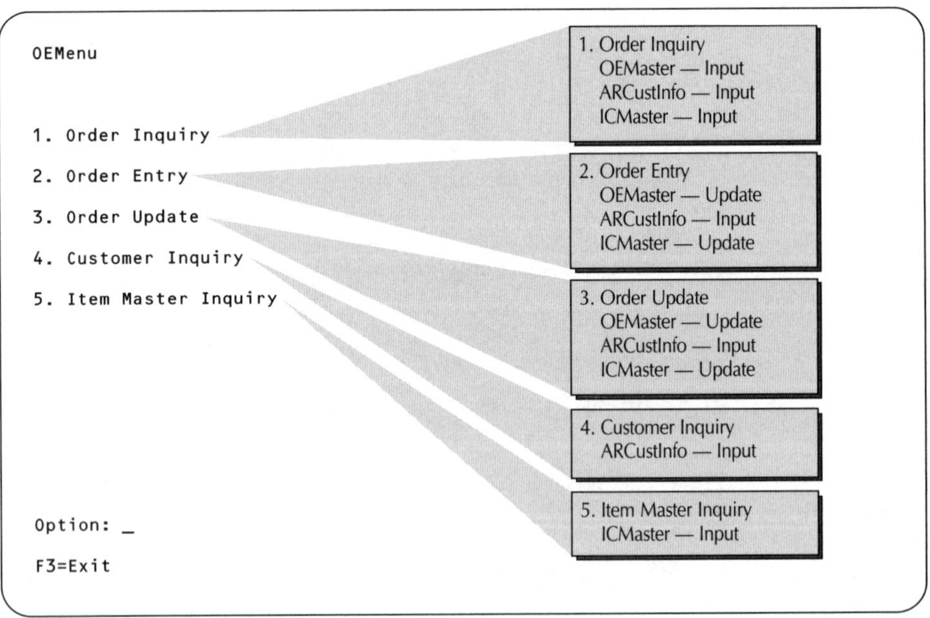

FIGURE 23.3B

Sample Order Entry Menu Program

```
/*  ==================================================================  */
/*  = Program....... OEMenu                                           =  */
/*  = Source type... CLLE                                             =  */
/*  = Description... Order Entry Menu                                 =  */
/*  ==================================================================  */

Pgm

/*  ==================================================================  */
/*  = Declarations                                                    =  */
/*  ==================================================================  */

  DclF        OEMenu

/*  ==================================================================  */
/*  = Open files for application programs                             =  */
/*  ==================================================================  */

  OvrDbF      File( OEMaster )                                        +
              Share( *Yes )                                           +
              OpnScope( *ActGrpDfn )
  OvrDbF      File( ARCustInfo )                                      +
              Share( *Yes )                                           +
              OpnScope( *ActGrpDfn )
  OvrDbF      File( ICMaster )                                        +
              Share( *Yes )                                           +
              OpnScope( *ActGrpDfn )

  OpnDbF      File( OEMaster )                                        +
              Option( *All )
  OpnDbF      File( ARCustInfo )                                      +
              Option( *Inp )
  OpnDbF      File( ICMaster )                                        +
              Option( *All )

/*  ==================================================================  */
/*  = Display menu and process selected option                        =  */
/*  ==================================================================  */

Menu:

  SndRcvF     RcdFmt( OEMenu )

  If          ( &In03 )                                               +
    GoTo Exit
  If          ( &Option *Eq 1 )                                       +
    Call OrdInquiry
  If          ( &Option *Eq 2 )                                       +
    Call OrdEntry
  If          ( &Option *Eq 3 )                                       +
    Call OrdUpdate
```

continued

FIGURE 23.3B CONTINUED

```
  If          ( &Option *Eq 4 )                                        +
    Call CstInquiry
  If          ( &Option *Eq 5 )                                        +
    Call ItmInquiry

  GoTo        Menu

/*  ============================================================  */
/*  = Clean up activation group and exit program                =  */
/*  ============================================================  */

Exit:

  RclActGrp  OE

EndPgm
```

The Share attribute also comes in handy when you write applications that provide online inquiries into related files. Figure 23.4A outlines an order entry program that opens several files and lets the user call a customer inquiry program or item master inquiry program to look up specific customers or items. Both of these inquiry programs use a file already opened by the initial program.

FIGURE 23.4A
Structure of Order Entry Program

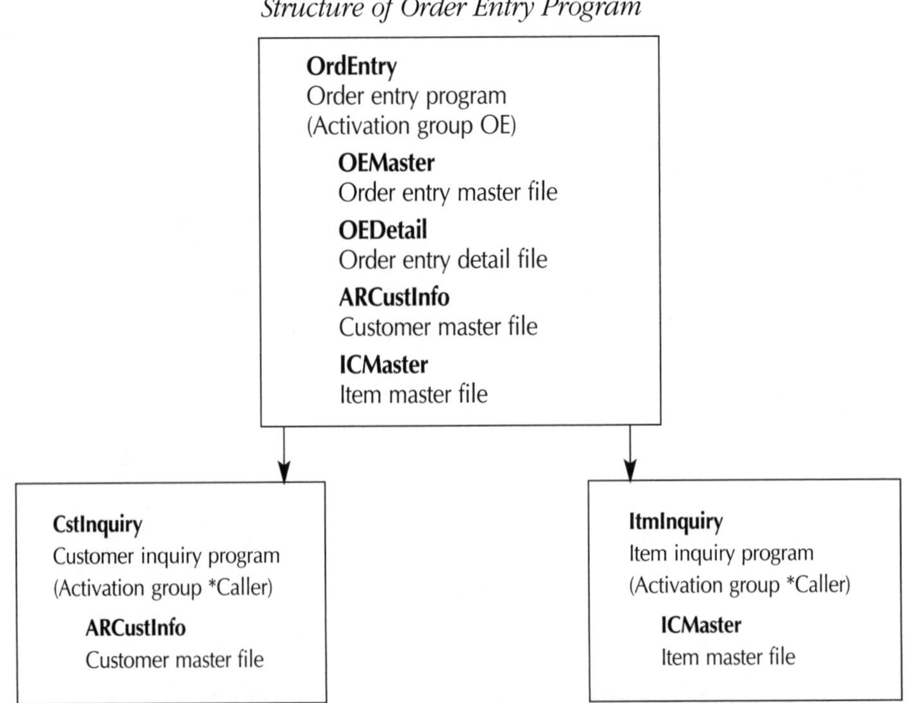

By including the statements in Figure 23.4B in a CL program that calls the order entry program, you can ensure that the ODP for these files is shared, reducing the time needed to access the two inquiry programs.

FIGURE 23.4B

Sharing ODPs for Order Entry

```
OvrDbF      File( ARCustInfo )                                  +
            Share( *Yes )                                       +
            OpnScope( *ActGrpDfn )
OvrDbF      File( ICMaster )
            Share( *Yes )                                       +
            OpnScope( *ActGrpDfn )

Call        OrdEntry
```

There's no doubt that the Share attribute is powerful. Sharing ODPs lets programs perform functions not otherwise possible, can shorten program initiation steps, and can let programs share vital I/O feedback information. If you're considering highly modular programming designs, sharing ODPs is a must.

Chapter 24

CL Programming: You're Stylin' Now!

There's much to be said for individuality, but when it comes to code, it's usually unwise to have as many styles as there are programmers. A single style based on a set of standards helps ensure your code is easy to read, understand, and maintain. Although adhering to standards may initially slow you down, within a short time you'll find that it actually results in faster development. Beyond this boost in productivity, though, is the fact that good coding style transcends any one language. It's a matter of professionalism, of doing your work to the best of your abilities and with pride.

Although most CL programs are short and to the point, a consistent programming style is as essential to CL as it is to any other language. When we started writing CL, we used the prompter to enter values for command parameters. Today, we still use the prompter for more complex commands or to prompt for valid values when we're not sure what to specify. The prompter produces a standard of sorts: Every command begins in column 14, labels are to the left of the commands, and the editor wraps the parameters onto continuation lines the way a word processor wraps words when you've reached the margin. But although using the prompter is convenient, code generated this way can be extremely difficult to read and maintain.

Apples and Oranges

Apples and oranges? Let's look at CL program EZCHGDFTC (Figure 24.1), a utility program for changing command defaults. Don't get hung up on what the code is doing (it's a bit complicated). Simply pay attention to its look. Take a quick glance at this code, and make note of your first-impression "comfort level."

FIGURE 24.1

Styleless CL Program EZCHGDFTC

```
/* PROGRAM EZCHGDFTC */
             PGM        PARM(&CMDSTR)

/* VARIABLE DECLARATIONS */
             DCL        VAR(&CMDSTR) TYPE(*CHAR) LEN(2088)
             DCL        VAR(&CMDSTRLENA) TYPE(*CHAR) LEN(2)
             DCL        VAR(&CMDSTRLEN) TYPE(*DEC) LEN(4 0)
             DCL        VAR(&CMDSTRPOS) TYPE(*DEC) LEN(4 0)
             DCL        VAR(&CHGSTR) TYPE(*CHAR) LEN(3000) +
                          VALUE('CHGCMDDFT ')
             DCL        VAR(&CHGSTRLEN) TYPE(*DEC) LEN(4 0) VALUE(10)
             DCL        VAR(&CHGSTRPOS) TYPE(*DEC) LEN(4 0)
             DCL        VAR(&CMD) TYPE(*CHAR) LEN(10)
             DCL        VAR(&CMDLIB) TYPE(*CHAR) LEN(10)
             DCL        VAR(&CMDPOS) TYPE(*DEC) LEN(4 0)
```

continued

FIGURE 24.1 *CONTINUED*

```
            DCL         VAR(&LEN) TYPE(*DEC) LEN(4 0)
            DCL         VAR(&USR) TYPE(*CHAR) LEN(10)
            DCL         VAR(&MSGID) TYPE(*CHAR) LEN(7)
            DCL         VAR(&MSGDTA) TYPE(*CHAR) LEN(100)
            DCL         VAR(&MSGF) TYPE(*CHAR) LEN(10)
            DCL         VAR(&MSGFLIB) TYPE(*CHAR) LEN(10)
            DCL         VAR(&ERRORSW) TYPE(*LGL)
            MONMSG      MSGID(CPF0000 MCH0000) EXEC(GOTO CMDLBL(ERROR))

/* GET USER */
            RTVJOBA     USER(&USR)
            IF          COND(&USR *EQ 'QSECOFR') THEN(CALL +
                          PGM(EZCHGDFTC1))
            ELSE        CMD(CALL PGM(EZCHGDFTC2))  /* NOT QSECOFR */

/* BUILD COMMAND */
            CHGVAR      VAR(&CMDSTRLENA) VALUE(%SST(&CMDSTR 1 2))
            CHGVAR      VAR(&CMDSTRLEN) VALUE(%BIN(&CMDSTRLENA))
            CHGVAR      VAR(&CMDSTR) VALUE(%SST(&CMDSTR 3 &CMDSTRLEN))
            CHGVAR      VAR(&CMDLIB) VALUE('*LIBL')
            CHGVAR      VAR(&CMDPOS) VALUE(1)
            CHGVAR      VAR(&CMDSTRPOS) VALUE(1)
 GETCMDEND: CHGVAR      VAR(&CMDSTRPOS) VALUE(&CMDSTRPOS + 1)
            IF          COND(%SST(&CMDSTR &CMDSTRPOS 1) *EQ '/') +
                          THEN(DO)
            CHGVAR      VAR(&LEN) VALUE(&CMDSTRPOS - 1)
            CHGVAR      VAR(&CMDLIB) VALUE(%SST(&CMDSTR 1 &LEN))
            CHGVAR      VAR(&CMDPOS) VALUE(&CMDSTRPOS + 1)
            ENDDO
            IF          COND(%SST(&CMDSTR &CMDSTRPOS 1) *NE ' ') +
                          THEN(GOTO CMDLBL(GETCMDEND))
            CHGVAR      VAR(&LEN) VALUE(&CMDSTRPOS - &CMDPOS)
            CHGVAR      VAR(&CMD) VALUE(%SST(&CMDSTR &CMDPOS &LEN))
            CHGVAR      VAR(&CMDPOS) VALUE(&CMDSTRPOS)
            RTVOBJD     OBJ(&CMDLIB/&CMD) OBJTYPE(*CMD) RTNLIB(&CMDLIB)
            CHGVAR      VAR(&CHGSTRPOS) VALUE(&CHGSTRLEN)
            CHGVAR      VAR(&CMDSTRPOS) VALUE(0)
 ADDNXT:    CHGVAR      VAR(&CMDSTRPOS) VALUE(&CMDSTRPOS + 1)
            IF          COND(&CMDSTRPOS *GT &CMDSTRLEN) THEN(GOTO +
                          CMDLBL(ADDENDDFT))
            CHGVAR      VAR(&CHGSTRPOS) VALUE(&CHGSTRPOS + 1)
            IF          COND(&CHGSTRPOS *GT 3000) THEN(GOTO +
                          CMDLBL(STRLENERR))
            IF          COND(&CMDSTRPOS *EQ &CMDPOS) THEN(DO)
            CHGVAR      VAR(&CHGSTRPOS) VALUE(&CHGSTRPOS + 1)
            CHGVAR      VAR(%SST(&CHGSTR &CHGSTRPOS 1)) VALUE('(')
            CHGVAR      VAR(&CHGSTRPOS) VALUE(&CHGSTRPOS + 1)
            CHGVAR      VAR(%SST(&CHGSTR &CHGSTRPOS 1)) VALUE('''')
            GOTO        CMDLBL(ADDNXT)
            ENDDO
            CHGVAR      VAR(%SST(&CHGSTR &CHGSTRPOS 1)) +
                          VALUE(%SST(&CMDSTR &CMDSTRPOS 1))
            IF          COND(%SST(&CHGSTR &CHGSTRPOS 1) *EQ '''') +
                          THEN(DO)
```

continued

FIGURE 24.1 CONTINUED

```
            CHGVAR     VAR(&CHGSTRPOS) VALUE(&CHGSTRPOS + 1)
            IF         COND(&CHGSTRPOS *GT 3000) THEN(GOTO +
                         CMDLBL(STRLENERR))
            CHGVAR     VAR(%SST(&CHGSTR &CHGSTRPOS 1)) VALUE('''')
            ENDDO
            GOTO       CMDLBL(ADDNXT)
 ADDENDDFT: CHGVAR     VAR(&CHGSTRPOS) VALUE(&CHGSTRPOS + 1)
            IF         COND(&CHGSTRPOS *GT 3000) THEN(GOTO +
                         CMDLBL(STRLENERR))
            CHGVAR     VAR(%SST(&CHGSTR &CHGSTRPOS 1)) VALUE('''')
            CHGVAR     VAR(&CHGSTRPOS) VALUE(&CHGSTRPOS + 1)
            IF         COND(&CHGSTRPOS *GT 3000) THEN(GOTO +
                         CMDLBL(STRLENERR))
            CHGVAR     VAR(%SST(&CHGSTR &CHGSTRPOS 1)) VALUE(')')

/* CHANGE COMMAND DEFAULTS */
 EXECUTE:   RMVMSG     CLEAR(*ALL)
            CALL       PGM(QCMDEXC) PARM(&CHGSTR 3000)
            MONMSG     MSGID(CPF0000) EXEC(GOTO CMDLBL(CHGCMDERR))
            CHGVAR     VAR(&MSGDTA) VALUE(&CMD *CAT &CMDLIB)
            SNDPGMMSG  MSGID(CPC6260) MSGF(QSYS/QCPFMSG) +
                         MSGDTA(&MSGDTA) MSGTYPE(*COMP)
            RETURN
 STRLENERR: RMVMSG     CLEAR(*ALL)
            SNDPGMMSG  MSGID(CPF9897) MSGF(QSYS/QCPFMSG) +
                         MSGDTA('Command string is too long.') +
                         MSGTYPE(*DIAG)
            RETURN
 CHGCMDERR: RCVMSG     MSGTYPE(*DIAG) RMV(*YES) MSGDTA(&MSGDTA) +
                         MSGID(&MSGID)
            IF         COND((&MSGID *EQ 'CPD6260') *OR (&MSGID *EQ +
                         'CPD6261') *OR (&MSGID *EQ 'CPD6262')) +
                         THEN(DO)
            CALL       PGM(EZCHGDFTC3) PARM(&CHGSTR &MSGDTA)
            GOTO       CMDLBL(EXECUTE)
            ENDDO
            IF         COND(&MSGID *EQ 'CPD6273') THEN(DO)
            CALL       PGM(EZCHGDFTC4) PARM(&CHGSTR &MSGDTA)
            GOTO       CMDLBL(EXECUTE)
            ENDDO
            IF         COND((&MSGID *EQ 'CPD1013') *OR (&MSGID *EQ +
                         'CPD1014')) THEN(DO)
            RMVMSG     CLEAR(*ALL)
            SNDPGMMSG  MSGID(CPF9897) MSGF(QSYS/QCPFMSG) MSGDTA('No +
                         parameters selected for change.') +
                         MSGTYPE(*DIAG)
            RETURN
            ENDDO
            GOTO       CMDLBL(ERROR)
```

continued

FIGURE 24.1 CONTINUED

```
/* ERROR ROUTINE */
 ERROR:      IF         COND(&ERRORSW) THEN(SNDPGMMSG MSGID(CPF9897) +
                          MSGF(QSYS/QCPFMSG) MSGDTA('An unexpected +
                          error occurred. See job log.') +
                          MSGTYPE(*ESCAPE))
             CHGVAR     VAR(&ERRORSW) VALUE('1')
             RCVMSG     MSGTYPE(*EXCP) MSGDTA(&MSGDTA) MSGID(&MSGID) +
                          MSGF(&MSGF) MSGFLIB(&MSGFLIB)
             SNDPGMMSG  MSGID(&MSGID) MSGF(&MSGFLIB/&MSGF) +
                          MSGDTA(&MSGDTA) MSGTYPE(*DIAG)
             ENDPGM
```

Now, compare the code in Figure 24.1 with the version of this program shown in Figure 24.2. How's your first-impression comfort level now?

The programs' styles are dramatically different, aren't they? Figure 24.1's code is crowded and difficult to read, primarily because of the CL prompter's default layout. In addition, this style lacks elements such as helpful spacing, code alignment, and comments that help you break the code down into logical, readable chunks. Figure 24.2's code is much more readable and comprehensible. An informative program header relates the program's purpose and basic functions. The program also features more-attractive code alignment, spacing that divides the code into distinct sections, indentation for nested Do-EndDo groups, and mnemonic variable names. Apples and oranges!

Developing Stylistic Standards

In developing your standards, it's important to keep in mind some key considerations. Among these are psychological constraints, such as the fact that we're conditioned to read in mixed case and to associate words that are next to or close to each other. There are also physical constraints, such as the size of your screen — you want to add white space for readability, but not so much that you can see only a few commands and parameters at a time. You'll be happier with the results of your efforts to develop standards if you take some time to think about considerations such as these before you begin.

Let's look at some suggestions to consider as you develop standards for your CL environment. We'll present guidelines for CL style in the following areas:

- comments
- statement alignment
- variable names and case
- use of shortcuts

As you peruse these guidelines, refer to Figure 24.2 for illustration.

(Text resumes on page 397 following Figure 24.2.)

FIGURE 24.2
Stylin' CL Program EZChgDftC

```
/*  ==================================================================  */
/*  =  Program....... EZChgDftC                                      =  */
/*  =  Type.......... Command processing program for EZChgDft        =  */
/*  =  Description... EZ Change command defaults                     =  */
/*  =                                                                =  */
/*  =                 This program receives a command string and     =  */
/*  =                 for each parameter specified attempts to       =  */
/*  =                 change the command defaults.                   =  */
/*  =                                                                =  */
/*  =                 Because the prompter requires that all         =  */
/*  =                 required parameters be specified, it is not    =  */
/*  =                 possible to omit required parameters from      =  */
/*  =                 the command string this program receives       =  */
/*  =                 as input. Instead, these parameters must       =  */
/*  =                 be stripped from the command string. The       =  */
/*  =                 program monitors for error messages that       =  */
/*  =                 are returned from ChgCmdDft to identify        =  */
/*  =                 the parameters that must be stripped. This     =  */
/*  =                 also applies not only to those parameters      =  */
/*  =                 that are required but also to errors that      =  */
/*  =                 might result from such actions as trying       =  */
/*  =                 to change the default value for parameters     =  */
/*  =                 that have no default value.                    =  */
/*  =  ------------------------------------------------------------  =  */
/*  =  Parameter interface                                           =  */
/*  =                                                                =  */
/*  =  Parameter         Type        Description                     =  */
/*  =                                                                =  */
/*  =  &CmdStr           Input       Command string for which to     =  */
/*  =                                change command defaults         =  */
/*  ==================================================================  */

  Pgm         (                                                          +
                &CmdStr                                                  +
              )

/*  ==================================================================  */
/*  = Variable declarations                                          =  */
/*  ==================================================================  */

  Dcl         &CmdStr      *Char     ( 2000     )
  Dcl         &CmdStrLenA  *Char     (    2     )
  Dcl         &CmdStrLen   *Dec      (    4  0  )
  Dcl         &CmdStrPos   *Dec      (    4  0  )
  Dcl         &ChgStr      *Char     ( 3000     )    ( 'CHGCMDDFT ' )
  Dcl         &ChgStrLen   *Dec      (    4  0  )    ( 10 )
  Dcl         &ChgStrPos   *Dec      (    4  0  )
  Dcl         &Cmd         *Char     (   10     )
  Dcl         &CmdLib      *Char     (   10     )
  Dcl         &CmdPos      *Dec      (    4  0  )                        (A)
  Dcl         &Len         *Dec      (    4  0  )
  Dcl         &Usr         *Char     (   10     )
  Dcl         &MsgID       *Char     (    7     )
  Dcl         &MsgDta      *Char     (  100     )
  Dcl         &MsgF        *Char     (   10     )
  Dcl         &MsgFLib     *Char     (   10     )
  Dcl         &ErrorSw     *Lgl
```

continued

Figure 24.2 Continued

```
/*  ==============================================================  */
/*  = Global error monitor                                      =   */
/*  ==============================================================  */

(B)  MonMsg      ( CPF0000 MCH0000 ) Exec(                            +
       Goto        Error                   )

/*  ==============================================================  */
/*  = Set logging options based on user profile                 =   */
/*  ==============================================================  */

     RtvJobA     User( &Usr )

     If          ( &Usr *Eq 'QSECOFR' )                               +
(C)    Call        EzChgDftC1
     Else                                                             +
       Call        EzChgDftC2

/*  ==============================================================  */
/*  = Parse command string into length and actual command string =  */
/*  ==============================================================  */

     ChgVar      &CmdStrLenA ( %Sst( &CmdStr 1 2 ) )
     ChgVar      &CmdStrLen  ( %Bin( &CmdStrLenA ) )
     ChgVar      &CmdStr     ( %Sst( &CmdStr 3 &CmdStrLen ) )

/*  ==============================================================  */
/*  = Get command name and library name for completion message  =   */
/*  ==============================================================  */

     ChgVar      &CmdLib     ( '*LIBL' )
     ChgVar      &CmdPos     ( 1 )
     ChgVar      &CmdStrPos  ( 1 )

   GetCmdEnd:

     ChgVar      &CmdStrPos  ( &CmdStrPos + 1 )

     If          ( %Sst( &CmdStr &CmdStrPos 1 ) *Eq '/' )             +
       Do
         ChgVar      &Len         ( &CmdStrPos - 1 )
         ChgVar      &CmdLib      ( %Sst( &CmdStr 1 &Len ) )
(D)      ChgVar      &CmdPos      ( &CmdStrPos + 1 )
       EndDo

     If          ( %Sst( &CmdStr &CmdStrPos 1 ) *NE ' ' )             +
       GoTo        GetCmdEnd

     ChgVar      &Len        ( &CmdStrPos - &CmdPos )
(E)  ChgVar      &Cmd        ( %Sst( &CmdStr &CmdPos &Len ) )
     ChgVar      &CmdPos     ( &CmdStrPos )

     RtvObjD     Obj( &CmdLib/&Cmd )                                  +
                 ObjType( *Cmd )                                      +
                 RtnLib( &CmdLib )
```

continued

FIGURE 24.2 CONTINUED

```
/*  ==============================================================  */
/*  = Build change command string one character at a time        =  */   (F)
/*  ==============================================================  */

  ChgVar     &ChgStrPos   ( &ChgStrLen )
  ChgVar     &CmdStrPos   ( 0 )

AddNxt:

/*  --------------------------------------------------------------  */
/*  - Check to see if end of command has been reached            -  */   (G)
/*  --------------------------------------------------------------  */

  ChgVar     &CmdStrPos   ( &CmdStrPos + 1 )

  If         ( &CmdStrPos *GT &CmdStrLen )                             +
    GoTo       AddEndDft

/*  --------------------------------------------------------------  */
/*  - Check to see if within maximum length for change command   -  */
/*  --------------------------------------------------------------  */

  ChgVar     &ChgStrPos   ( &ChgStrPos + 1 )

  If         ( &ChgStrPos *GT 3000 )                                   +
    GoTo       StrLenErr

/*  --------------------------------------------------------------  */
/*  - If at end of command name, insert beginning delimiter of ('  -  */
/*  - for parameters                                              -  */
/*  --------------------------------------------------------------  */

  If         ( &CmdStrPos *Eq &CmdPos )                                +
    Do
      ChgVar     &ChgStrPos                         ( &ChgStrPos + 1 )
      ChgVar     ( %Sst( &ChgStr &ChgStrPos 1 ) )   ( '(' )
      ChgVar     &ChgStrPos                         ( &ChgStrPos + 1 )
      ChgVar     ( %Sst( &ChgStr &ChgStrPos 1 ) )   ( '''' )
      GoTo       AddNxt
    EndDo

/*  --------------------------------------------------------------  */
/*  - Copy character from command to change command. If the      -  */
/*  - character is ' then add another ' character to the change  -  */
/*  - command string. Also, make sure change command is within   -  */
/*  - maximum length.                                            -  */
/*  --------------------------------------------------------------  */

  ChgVar     ( %Sst( &ChgStr &ChgStrPos 1 ) )                          +
             ( %Sst( &CmdStr &CmdStrPos 1 ) )

  If         ( %Sst( &ChgStr &ChgStrPos 1 ) *Eq '''' )                 +
    Do
      ChgVar     &ChgStrPos   ( &ChgStrPos + 1 )

      If         ( &ChgStrPos *GT 3000 )                               +
        GoTo       StrLenErr
```

continued

FIGURE 24.2 *CONTINUED*

```
      ChgVar      ( %Sst( &ChgStr &ChgStrPos 1 ) )  ( '''' )
    EndDo
  GoTo        AddNxt

/*  -----------------------------------------------------------------  */
/*  - Insert ending delimiter of ') for parameters and make sure    -  */
/*  - change command is within maximum length                       -  */
/*  -----------------------------------------------------------------  */

AddEndDft:

  ChgVar      &ChgStrPos  ( &ChgStrPos + 1 )

  If          ( &ChgStrPos *GT 3000 )                                  +
    GoTo        StrLenErr

  ChgVar      ( %Sst( &ChgStr &ChgStrPos 1 ) )  ( '''' )
  ChgVar      &ChgStrPos                        ( &ChgStrPos + 1 )

  If          ( &ChgStrPos *GT 3000 )                                  +
    GoTo        StrLenErr

  ChgVar      ( %Sst( &ChgStr &ChgStrPos 1 ) )  ( ')' )

/*  =================================================================  */
/*  = Execute the ChgCmdDft command                                 =  */
/*  =================================================================  */

Execute:

  RmvMsg      Clear( *All )
  Call        QCmdExc                                                  +
              ( &ChgStr 3000 )
  MonMsg      ( CPF0000 ) Exec(                                        +
    GoTo        ChgCmdErr     )

/*  -----------------------------------------------------------------  */
/*  - ChgCmdDft command succeeded. Send a completion message and    -  */
/*  - exit.                                                         -  */
/*  -----------------------------------------------------------------  */

  ChgVar      &MsgDta     ( &Cmd *Cat &CmdLib )

  SndPgmMsg   MsgID( CPC6260 )                                         +
              MsgF( QSys/QCPFMsg )                                     +
              MsgDta( &MsgDta )                                        +
              MsgType( *Comp )
  Return

/*  =================================================================  */
/*  = Generated command string is too long                          =  */
/*  =================================================================  */
```

continued

FIGURE 24.2 CONTINUED

```
StrLenErr:

  RmvMsg      Clear( *All )
  SndPgmMsg   MsgID( CPF9897 )                                       +
              MsgF( QSys/QCPFMsg )                                   +
              MsgDta( 'Command string is too long.' )                +
              MsgType( *Diag )
  Return

/*  =============================================================  */
/*  = Error in ChgCmdDft - try to handle                        =  */
/*  =============================================================  */

ChgCmdErr:

  RcvMsg      MsgType( *Diag )                                       +
              Rmv( *Yes )                                            +
              MsgDta( &MsgDta )                                      +
              MsgID( &MsgID )

/*  -------------------------------------------------------------  */
/*  - If ChgCmdDft command fails with one of the following       -  */
/*  - diagnostic messages, strip the parameter out of the command -  */
/*  - string. This can occur if the parameter does not have a    -  */
/*  - default value (such as a required parameter), for a list   -  */
/*  - item with no default value, or for a qualifier (such as a  -  */
/*  - library name) with no default value. After removing the    -  */
/*  - parameter, execute the ChgCmdDft command again.            -  */
/*  -------------------------------------------------------------  */

  If          ( ( &MsgID *Eq 'CPD6260' )                             +
  *Or           ( &MsgID *Eq 'CPD6261' )                             +
  *Or           ( &MsgID *Eq 'CPD6262' ) )                           +
    Do
      Call        EZChgDftC3                                         +
                  ( &ChgStr &MsgDta )
      Goto        Execute
    EndDo

/*  -------------------------------------------------------------  */
/*  - If ChgCmdDft command fails with the following diagnostic   -  */
/*  - message, add a null placeholder for the missing entry.     -  */
/*  - This can occur when a single value is specified in a list  -  */
/*  - (such as the Size parameter with value *NoMax specified on -  */
/*  - the ChgPF command). After adding the null placeholder,     -  */
/*  - execute the ChgCmdDft command again.                       -  */
/*  -------------------------------------------------------------  */

  If          ( &MsgID *Eq 'CPD6273' )                               +
    Do
      Call        EZChgDftC4                                         +
                  ( &ChgStr &MsgDta )
      Goto        Execute
    EndDo
```

continued

FIGURE 24.2 CONTINUED

```
/*  --------------------------------------------------------------   */
/*  - If ChgCmdDft command fails with one of the following       -   */
/*  - diagnostic messages, just ignore the change request. This  -   */
/*  - can occur when the request results in no parameters being  -   */
/*  - changed. This can happen due to the data entered by the    -   */
/*  - user or as a result of stripping out parameters with no    -   */
/*  - default value (for instance, all parameters may be stripped -  */
/*  - out).                                                      -   */
/*  --------------------------------------------------------------   */

  If          ( ( &MsgID *Eq 'CPD1Ø13' )                             +
  *Or           ( &MsgID *Eq 'CPD1Ø14' ) )                           +
    Do
      RmvMsg      Clear( *All )
      SndPgmMsg   MsgID( CPF9897 )                                   +
                  MsgF( QSys/QCPFMsg )                               +
                  MsgDta( 'No parameters selected for change.' )     +
                  MsgType( *Diag )
      Return
    EndDo

/*  --------------------------------------------------------------   */
/*  - ChgCmdDft command failed for an unknown reason. Let normal -   */
/*  - error processing take control.                             -   */
/*  --------------------------------------------------------------   */

  Goto        Error

/*  ==============================================================   */
/*  = Error handler                                              =   */
/*  ==============================================================   */

Error:

  If          ( &ErrorSw )                                           +
    SndPgmMsg  MsgID( CPF9897 )                                      +
               MsgF( QSys/QCPFMsg )                                  +
               MsgDta( 'An unexpected error occurred. See job log.' ) +
               MsgType( *Escape )

  ChgVar      &ErrorSw     ( '1' )

  RcvMsg      MsgType( *Excp )                                       +
              MsgDta( &MsgDta )                                      +
              MsgID( &MsgID )                                        +
              MsgF( &MsgF )                                          +
              MsgFLib( &MsgFLib )
  SndPgmMsg   MsgID( &MsgID)                                         +
              MsgF( &MsgFLib/&MsgF )                                 +
              MsgDta( &MsgDta )                                      +
              MsgType( *Diag )

/*  ==============================================================   */
/*  = End of program                                             =   */
/*  ==============================================================   */

  EndPgm
```

1.0 Comments

No doubt the notion of including comments in your code has been drilled into you more times than you care to remember. However, a closer look at some specific commenting guidelines might help you improve your technique.

1.1 *Use comments to clarify — not echo — your code.* Remember that sometimes less is more. Good coding techniques help document your program, so simply repeating the code in your comments adds no value. Use comments to

- provide a brief program summary
- group logical sections of code
- explain a technique that isn't readily apparent
- explain any business rules that aren't readily apparent

1.2 *Always include a brief summary at the beginning of a program.* The program summary should include

- the program name
- the program type (e.g., command processing program, validity-checking program)
- a description of the program's purpose
- a description of any special circumstances that exist
- a description of the program's interface (any input, update, and output parameters)
- any special program-creation information

There's a school of thought that says the program summary should also contain a chronology of changes that includes the date, programmer, and purpose of each change. You can include this information if you like, but, in our experience, this information is often ignored or erroneous. If you need to track program changes, a better alternative is to institute a change management system.

1.3 *Use consistent "comment boxes" to divide major sections of code.* To clearly divide sections of code by using comments, enclose the comments inside a "comment box." Never use one-line comments or comments embedded on the same line as code. Such comments tend to be overlooked, and they often lead to a cluttered appearance. Instead, start comments in column 1, and make them a standard length. Use a hierarchy of box styles. For instance, construct the boxes for major sections out of equal signs (=), as at **F** in Figure 24.2 (page 393), and construct those for a subordinate level out of hyphens (-), as at **G** (page 393). Use a third box style if you have yet another subordinate level, but normally two box styles will suffice.

1.4 *Use blank lines to group related code and heighten readability.* When comments are unnecessary but you still want to divide sections of code, blank lines can be useful. Used in the right place, white space also makes your code easier to read.

2.0 Statement Alignment

Well-laid-out comments are only the first step in adding style to your CL programs. You can also take steps to maximize the readability of the CL statements in your code by improving on the way the prompter aligns statements.

2.1 *Begin statements near the left margin.* To accommodate labels in column 2, the prompter begins statements in column 14. You should instead relegate labels to their own line and start them in column 1. Begin CL commands in column 3 (or at the appropriate indentation level if the code is part of a Do structure or the continuation of a previous line). This practice maximizes the space you have for entering useful code on a line.

2.2 *Align command parameters by allowing space for the maximum command length.* When a command is shorter than the 10-byte maximum, leave sufficient blanks after the command to pad to the maximum length. Skip one more space, and then start the first parameter. For example, when a command begins in column 3, start the first parameter in column 14.

2.3 *Use indentation to highlight dependencies.* Use a consistent indentation factor (we prefer two spaces) for all statements you want to indent. For each nested level, increase the indentation by this factor.

2.3.1 *If statements.* Place each If condition on a line by itself (or on multiple lines if the condition uses *And or *Or). On a continuation line, indent the command to be executed when the If condition is true. If only one command is to be executed as the result of a test, don't follow the If with a Do group; instead, execute the actual command. When an If statement has an associated Else statement, align Else with If. The segments of code at **C** and **D** (page 392) and **H** (page 396) in Figure 24.2 illustrate these guidelines.

2.3.2 *MonMsg/Exec statements.* When you use the MonMsg (Monitor Message) command's Exec parameter, follow an alignment standard that indents the command to be executed in case of error on the line following the MonMsg, as at **B** (page 392) in Figure 24.2. It would be nice if you could simply drop the Exec keyword; unfortunately, it's required. By positioning Exec and its parentheses as shown in the figure, you further enhance your code's readability.

2.3.3 *Do groups.* Indent each statement that occurs between the Do and EndDo commands of a Do group. Grouping statements this way makes it easy to tell which ones belong to the Do group.

2.4 *Align command parameters.* In many cases, you can fit a command and all its parameters on one line. When this isn't possible, place the first parameter on the line with the command. Code a continuation line for each subsequent parameter, and align it directly beneath the first one. Place the continuation character (+) to the right, aligned with the last character of your comment boxes.

2.5 *For repeated one-line commands, align the commands and their parameters.* Some commands (e.g., ChgVar, Dcl) are often repeated in succession and fit on a single line. When this is the case, align the commands and their parameters in columns (see **A** on page 391).

2.6 *Align continuation characters in a consistent column at the end of each line.* This style not only gives your program a tidy appearance but also makes it easy to distinguish which commands are continued on subsequent lines. A quick glance lets you know whether a command is continued — no more hunt-and-peck missions looking for continuation characters.

3.0 Variable Names and Case

Many schools of thought exist on variable naming and whether to use upper, lower, or mixed case for various programming entities. Proper variable naming and proper case use greatly enhance your code's appearance and readability.

3.1 *Avoid special characters in variable names.* It's wise to avoid special characters (e.g., $, #) in variable names for several reasons. First, special characters can differ from language to language, and their use can lead to problems if your software ever runs on systems with different or multiple language features. Special characters don't "read" well, either — isn't CstNbr (or CstNo) easier to interpret than Cst#? Likewise, don't prefix field names with special characters to signify information such as the fact that a field is from a display file. Not only is DspCstNbr or DspCstNo easier to read than $Cst#, but a prefix of Dsp rather than $ more clearly says that the field comes from a display file.

If those reasons aren't enough for you, consider that special characters are harder to find on the keyboard! Okay, so that's not the greatest reason, but you get the point.

3.2 *Construct meaningful variable names.* Devise a naming convention that relies on abbreviations to represent particular entities. Then combine these abbreviations to construct meaningful variable names. OS/400 commands provide a good example of this type of structure with their verb/subject construction.

3.3 *Use mixed case.* NEVER USE ALL UPPER CASE! It is perhaps the most difficult case style to read. If this chapter were presented in all upper case, you wouldn't even be reading this sentence — you'd have given up long ago! Likewise, code written all in lower case can be hard to interpret.

Some stylists suggest using all lower case for variables and all upper case for everything else. Others suggest some other variant — upper case for this, lower case for that, mixed case for something else. But your goal should be to create readable code, not to emphasize the fact that a variable is a variable — you know it's a variable by its context!

We suggest you use mixed case for everything. Code written this way looks neat and is by far the easiest to read. When you break down entities into multiple abbreviations, capitalize only the first character of each piece (e.g., variable &CmdStr

for command string); when a name consists of only one element, capitalize just the first character of the name (e.g., variable &User for user).

4.0 Shortcut Dos and Don'ts

Shortcuts have their place in program code, but be sure to use them thoughtfully. For starters, never use a shortcut out of laziness. This tendency is a sure sign of a drop in quality. On the other hand, some shortcuts don't detract from quality and can actually make some parts of your CL programs easier to read.

4.1 *Don't use shorthand symbols for concatenation operations.* Avoid using the shorthand symbols ||, |>, and |< for CL's *Cat, *BCat, and *TCat concatenation operators. The vertical bar character (|) isn't readily available with some keyboard mappings. More important, though, the meanings of these symbols aren't as clear as the reserved words.

4.2 *Simplify commands with obvious keywords.* Some commands, such as the following, have obvious keywords and are easier to interpret when you omit the keywords altogether.

4.2.1 *Simplifying Pgm.* Drop the Parm keyword on the Pgm (Program) command, enclose the parameter list in parentheses, and place one parameter to a line.

4.2.2 *Simplifying Dcl.* On Dcl (Declare CL Variable) commands, drop the Var, Type, Len, and Value keywords. Define the keyword values positionally, and enclose the Len and Value parameters in parentheses. Leave enough space between the parentheses to enable Len to contain the largest value possible (a four-digit number, a space, and two decimal positions). Figure 24.2 illustrates this rule at **A** (page 391).

4.2.2 *Simplifying MonMsg.* Drop the MonMsg command's MsgID keyword, and use parentheses to enclose the list of message IDs for which you're monitoring (**B**, page 392).

4.2.3 *Simplifying ChgVar.* Omit the ChgVar (Change Variable) command's Var and Value keywords, and enclose the Value parameter in parentheses.

4.2.4 *Simplifying If.* Drop the Cond and Then keywords from If statements, and follow the alignment guidelines given above.

4.2.5 *Simplifying Else.* Drop the Else command's Cmd keyword, and follow the alignment guidelines given above.

4.2.6 *Simplifying GoTo.* Drop the GoTo command's CmdLbl keyword.

5.0 Miscellaneous Suggestions

Several other general techniques can help make your CL programs more readable and maintainable. Here are some ideas.

5.1 *Insert a blank after each opening parenthesis and before each closing parenthesis.* This rule may seem trite, but it makes your code easier to read.

5.2 Develop a standard error-handling routine, and place it at the end of your code. It's wise to insulate your users from abnormal terminations. Toward that end, you should always include a standard error-handling routine in your programs. Use a global MonMsg statement to trap any unforeseen errors, and handle the errors gracefully in the error-handling section. Tuck this section of code out of the way, at the end of your code.

5.3 Extract single values from multivalue variables before referring to the values. When a variable contains more than one value, such as a qualified object name or the contents of a data structure, extract the individual values before using them in your program. Declare individual fields and then use the ChgVar command with the %Sst built-in function to extract the fields (**E**, page 392). Then use these individual fields in your program.

Start Stylin'!

You can use the guidelines in this chapter as the foundation for a style that lets you write CL code that's easy to read, understand, and maintain. Try out these style suggestions, share your ideas about what works with others, and implement your own set of standards to give your CL more style.

CL Coding Suggestions

- Use comments to clarify — not echo — your code.
- Always include a brief summary at the beginning of a program.
- Use consistent "comment boxes" to divide major sections of code.
- Use blank lines to group related code and heighten readability.
- Begin statements near the left margin.
- Align command parameters by allowing space for the maximum command length.
- Use indentation to highlight dependencies.
- Align command parameters.
- For repeated one-line commands, align the commands and their parameters.
- Align continuation characters in a consistent column at the end of each line.
- Avoid special characters in variable names.
- Construct meaningful variable names.
- Use mixed case.
- Don't use shorthand symbols for concatenation operations.
- Simplify commands with obvious keywords.
- Insert a blank after each opening parenthesis and before each closing parenthesis.
- Develop a standard error-handling routine, and place it at the end of your code.
- Extract single values from multivalue variables before referring to the values.

Chapter 25

Extend CL's Reach with APIs

The fact that CL programs consist of the very OS/400 commands used in day-to-day operation is good news for those wanting to automate system-related tasks. The bad news is that not all of those commands used in day-to-day operations lend themselves to automated, programmatic solutions. For instance, a command may let you display or print a particular item of interest but provide no way for a program to retrieve the same information in a useful form.

One common scenario for such a case is the need to determine programmatically a particular job's status. No OS/400 command exists to retrieve this information in a form useful to programs. Some programmers use a programming technique that issues the appropriate job-related command (e.g., DspJob, WrkActJob) to create a spooled file containing the necessary information. After creating the spooled file, the program copies it to a physical file and extracts the information that the program needs to continue processing. Such techniques, however, often perform poorly and are risky in a production environment. Even if a program's design accounts for all possible scenarios during the information-extraction process, applying PTFs or upgrading the operating system may change the layout of the spooled file, thereby invalidating the extraction rules and producing incorrect results.

We have seen many such techniques employed and have seen many of them fail to function correctly after a change to the system. We've also seen the resulting mayhem that occurred when these techniques were relied on in a production environment. A better, more stable solution often lies in the use of application programming interfaces (APIs) to perform the desired tasks. In addition to exhibiting better performance characteristics, APIs provide for compatibility with future releases.

OS/400 APIs are simply IBM-supplied programs designed to interface with user-written programs. The system sports numerous APIs that perform a variety of functions. Typically, you'll use these APIs in high-level language programs, but you can also use many of them in CL programs. In this chapter, we assume you have some familiarity with APIs as we discuss concerns unique to CL when using APIs.

Know Your Limitations

Make no mistake about it — limitations apply when you use APIs in CL programs. Even so, many APIs are suitable for use. Familiarize yourself with the limitations, and you'll be successful in determining which APIs you can effectively use in your CL programs.

When you call an API, you use parameters to communicate information between it and your program. The various APIs accept as parameters various data types, some of which CL does not support. Figure 25.1 shows common data types and constructs used by APIs, along with the level of support provided by Original Program Model (OPM) CL and Integrated Language Environment (ILE) CL.

FIGURE 25.1

CL Data Support

	Character	Packed decimal	Zoned decimal	Floating point	Binary 2	Binary 4	Pointer	Structures	Arrays
OPM CL	✓	✓			✓[1]	✓[1]		✓[3]	✓[3]
ILE CL	✓	✓			✓[1]	✓[1]	✓[2]	✓[3]	✓[3]

[1] CL has no binary data type. However, you can use built-in function %Bin to convert decimal data to character data with the equivalent binary value, and vice versa.

[2] CL has no pointer data type. However, pointers passed to an ILE CL program are preserved.

[3] CL has no structure or array support. However, you can use the substring function to simulate structures and arrays.

Of the data types listed in the figure, only two (character and packed decimal) have full, direct support. Nor does direct support exist for structures or arrays. Fortunately, there are techniques you can use in CL to relax some of these limitations.

The CL built-in function %Bin is very important to using APIs in CL. This built-in function converts decimal data into character data that has the equivalent binary value and converts character data representing a binary value into decimal data. Because of the prevalence of binary parameters in APIs, you could all but forget about using APIs in CL without %Bin. Consider the following code:

```
Dcl  Var(&LengthNbr) Type(*Dec) Len(4 0)
Dcl  Var(&LengthChr) Type(*Char) Len(4)

ChgVar Var(&LengthNbr) Value(10)
ChgVar Var(%Bin(&LengthChr)) Value(&LengthNbr)
.
. Call to API with input parameter &LengthChr
.
```

This example shows how you can use %Bin to place a numeric variable's value into a character field so that the character field contains the binary representation of the numeric value. You can then specify this character field as an API's binary input parameter.

Now, let's look at another use for %Bin in conjunction with APIs. Consider the following code:

```
Dcl  Var(&LengthNbr) Type(*Dec) Len(4 0)
Dcl  Var(&LengthChr) Type(*Char) Len(4)
.
. Call to API with output parameter &LengthChr
.
ChgVar Var(&LengthNbr) Value(%Bin(&LengthChr))
```

This example shows how you can use %Bin to place the value of an API's binary output parameter into a numeric variable.

As you investigate APIs, you'll probably discover two important pieces of information. First, many APIs use only character and four-byte binary parameters. You're also likely to find that much of the time, the APIs you want to use fall into this category.

APIs also frequently use structures. Although CL doesn't provide support for structures or arrays, CL can simulate both with the substring string function, %Sst. This function lets you construct and decompose structures and arrays. Let's look at a simple example for a name structure that contains the following subfields:

15-byte first name subfield &FirstName

1-byte middle initial subfield &MiddleInit

20-byte last name subfield &LastName

You can use the subfields to construct a structure in variable &FullName with the following code:

```
Dcl  Var(&FullName)   Type(*Char) Len(36)
Dcl  Var(&FirstName)  Type(*Char) Len(15)
Dcl  Var(&MiddleInit) Type(*Char) Len(1)
Dcl  Var(&LastName)   Type(*Char) Len(20)

ChgVar Var(%Sst(&FullName  1 15)) Value(&FirstName)
ChgVar Var(%Sst(&FullName 16  1)) Value(&MiddleInit)
ChgVar Var(%Sst(&FullName 17 20)) Value(&LastName)
```

You use this construction technique before calling an API when you need to pass a structure as input to the API.

Let's now look at decomposing a structure into its subfields. To decompose the name structure from the previous example, you simply reverse the operands in the ChgVar (Change Variable) commands as follows:

```
ChgVar Var(&FirstName)  Value(%Sst(&FullName  1 15))
ChgVar Var(&MiddleInit) Value(%Sst(&FullName 16  1))
ChgVar Var(&LastName)   Value(%Sst(&FullName 17 20))
```

You use this decomposition technique after calling an API when you need to parse a structure returned by the API (output parameter).

You should also be aware that there are two ways the system passes parameters: by reference and by value. When you pass a parameter by reference, you simply pass a pointer to the data that the parameter references (the field's address). When you pass a parameter by value, you pass the actual contents of the field. Some APIs (notably Unix-type APIs) require you to pass parameters by value. CL, however, supports passing only by reference. Obviously, you won't be able to call such APIs from CL programs. The good news here is that these aren't among the most commonly used APIs.

Reporting Errors with APIs

As with any program, APIs can encounter error conditions. When an API fails with an error, a well-designed application should take notice of the failure and handle the exception gracefully rather than let the application terminate abnormally.

APIs use three basic error-reporting mechanisms:

- feedback codes and conditions
- an error number (errno)
- an API error structure

The API's category determines the error-reporting mechanism used. For example, ILE CEE APIs use feedback codes and conditions, while Unix-type APIs use an error number that you can optionally use to retrieve error text. The most commonly used error-reporting mechanism, though, is the API error structure; hence, it is the focus of this discussion.

The API error structure can be one of two formats, ERRC0100 or ERRC0200, each of which is variable in length and contains information relating to an error condition. ERRC0100 is the most frequently used of these formats. Typically, only when convertible character support is required is ERRC0200 used. The general principles that apply and the techniques you will use in CL programs are the same regardless of the format; therefore, we'll look solely at format ERRC0100.

Figure 25.2 shows the layout for format ERRC0100. The output subfields return error details. The single input subfield determines how much error information is returned and whether the system issues an exception message.

FIGURE 25.2

API Error Format ERRC0100

From	*To*	*Type*	*Use*	*Description*
1	4	Binary	Input	*Bytes Provided* Length of API error structure to pass to the API. Valid values are 0 — The API returns no error details. The system issues an exception message. 8 — The API returns no error details (except the length of returned message data indicating an error occurred). The system does not issue an exception message. >8 — The API returns error details. This value specifies the maximum amount of error information to return. The system does not issue an exception message.
5	8	Binary	Output	*Bytes Available* Length of returned API error structure information when the API encounters an error (the value is 16 plus the length of the message data returned). If the API does not encounter an error, 0 (zero) is returned.
9	15	Character	Output	*Message ID* Message ID returned when the API encounters an error.
16	16	Character	Output	Reserved
17	*n*	Character	Output	*Message Data* Message data associated with the message ID returned when the API encounters an error. This field is variable in length to a maximum of 32,767 bytes (i.e., a value of 32,783 for *n*).

The first two subfields, Bytes Provided and Bytes Available, confuse a fair share of programmers. The decision to refer to these subfields as Bytes Provided and Bytes Available in the documentation contributes to the confusion. Both of these subfields designate a length, and labeling them as such would have been a better choice. The Bytes Provided subfield simply specifies the length of the entire API structure that the application is passing to the API. The Bytes Available subfield returned by the API indicates the length of the returned API error structure (i.e., 16 plus the length of the returned message data). IBM probably chose the terms "provided" and "available" because the API error structure is variable in length and the programmer determines how large a structure to "provide." This in turn influences the amount of error data that the API can return and make "available" to the calling program. Because the programmer determines the length of the structure, it's possible that the space available to hold the returned error data isn't large enough to hold the data in its entirety. In such a case, the API truncates the error data accordingly.

Handling API Errors

The Bytes Provided subfield is responsible for determining what occurs when an API encounters an error. The following three basic methods represent your options:

Method 1: Bytes Provided = 0

The API does not return error information and instead issues an exception message. In such a case, you must use normal CL error-handling techniques (i.e., the MonMsg, or Monitor Message, command) to trap any errors the API may issue. This is a common method for handling API errors in CL programs.

Method 2: Bytes Provided = 8

The API does not issue an exception message and returns only the Bytes Available subfield portion of the error details. Your program can check for a nonzero Bytes Available value to determine whether an error occurred in the API, but specific identifying information (message ID and message data) are not returned by the API. This method is sufficient if you need to determine only that an error of some kind occurred. You can accomplish the same thing using method 1 along with a MonMsg statement to monitor for any message (CPF0000); therefore, method 2 is not commonly used.

Method 3: Bytes Provided > 8

The API does not issue an exception message, and it returns as much of the error details as will fit in the API error structure. Your program can check for a nonzero Bytes Available value to determine whether an error occurred in the API. This method makes it possible to examine the message ID for the error that generated the exception and to react accordingly. You can accomplish the same thing using method 1 and a RcvMsg (Receive Message) command to obtain the error details, but letting the API furnish the information is simpler. This is another common method for handling API errors in CL programs.

Figure 25.3 demonstrates these three methods of handling API errors.

FIGURE 25.3
API Error Structure Alternatives

```
/*  ==================================================================  */
/*  =  API error methods                                             =  */
/*  ==================================================================  */

Pgm

/*  ==================================================================  */
/*  =  Variable declarations                                         =  */
/*  ==================================================================  */

/*  ------------------------------------------------------------------  */
/*  -  API error fields                                              -  */
/*  ------------------------------------------------------------------  */

  Dcl      &APIError     *Char     (  272     )
  Dcl      &AEBytesPrv   *Char     (    4     )
  Dcl      &AEBytesAvl   *Char     (    4     )
  Dcl      &AEMsgID      *Char     (    7     )
  Dcl      &AEMsgDta     *Char     (  256     )
  Dcl      &AEMsgDtaLn   *Dec      (    3  0  )

/*  ------------------------------------------------------------------  */
/*  -  Global error handler fields                                   -  */
/*  ------------------------------------------------------------------  */

  Dcl      &MsgID        *Char     (    7     )
  Dcl      &MsgDta       *Char     (  256     )
  Dcl      &MsgF         *Char     (   10     )
  Dcl      &MsgFLib      *Char     (   10     )

/*  ------------------------------------------------------------------  */
/*  -  Global error trap                                             -  */
/*  ------------------------------------------------------------------  */

  MonMsg      ( CPF0000 MCH0000 ) Exec(                                 +
    GoTo        Error                    )
/*  ------------------------------------------------------------------  */
/*  -  Call API                                                      -  */
/*  ------------------------------------------------------------------  */

/*  : : : : : : : : : : : : : : : : : : : : : : : : : : : : : : : : :  */
/*  :  Method 1 - Bytes Provided = 0                                 :  */
/*  :             Exception occurs. If explicit MonMsg statements    :  */
/*  :             follow the call to the API, they are checked       :  */
/*  :             to determine whether they handle the exception.    :  */
/*  :             If explicit MonMsg statements do not exist or      :  */
/*  :             do not handle the exception, the global error      :  */
/*  :             monitor receives control if one exists.            :  */
/*  : : : : : : : : : : : : : : : : : : : : : : : : : : : : : : : : :  */

  ChgVar      %Bin( &AEBytesPrv )     ( 0 )
  ChgVar      %Sst( &APIError 1 4 )   ( &AEBytesPrv )
```

continued

FIGURE 25.3 CONTINUED

```
  Call        SomeAPI                                                  +
              ( &SomeParm                                              +
                &APIError )

  .
  .
  .

/*  : : : : : : : : : : : : : : : : : : : : : : : : : : : : : : : : :  */
/*  :  Method 2 - Bytes Provided = 8                                 :  */
/*  :             No exception occurs. The program continues and     :  */
/*  :             optionally can check the return value in the       :  */
/*  :             bytes available portion of the API error           :  */
/*  :             structure to determine whether some exception      :  */
/*  :             occurred. Error details (MsgID and MsgDta) are     :  */
/*  :             not available.                                     :  */
/*  : : : : : : : : : : : : : : : : : : : : : : : : : : : : : : : : :  */

  ChgVar      %Bin( &AEBytesPrv )      ( 8 )
  ChgVar      %Sst( &APIError 1 4 )    ( &AEBytesPrv )

  Call        SomeAPI                                                  +
              ( &SomeParm                                              +
                &APIError )

  ChgVar      &AEBytesAvl  ( %Sst( &APIError 5 4 ) )

  If          ( %Bin( &AEBytesAvl ) *NE 0 )                            +
    Do
  .
  . Insert code for condition where some error occurred
  .
    EndDo

  .
  .
  .

/*  : : : : : : : : : : : : : : : : : : : : : : : : : : : : : : : : :  */
/*  :  Method 3 - Bytes Provided > 8                                 :  */
/*  :             No exception occurs. The program continues and     :  */
/*  :             optionally can check the return value in the       :  */
/*  :             bytes available portion of the API error           :  */
/*  :             structure to determine whether some exception      :  */
/*  :             occurred. Error details (MsgID and MsgDta) are     :  */
/*  :             available (if sufficient space is allocated),      :  */
/*  :             providing granular control. The program can        :  */
/*  :             optionally examine error details and take the      :  */
/*  :             appropriate action. For example, it can check      :  */
/*  :             for specific errors (by examining the MsgID        :  */
/*  :             portion of the API error structure) and handle     :  */
/*  :             them in a specific manner. The program can also    :  */
/*  :             easily percolate the exception to the calling      :  */
/*  :             program.                                           :  */
/*  : : : : : : : : : : : : : : : : : : : : : : : : : : : : : : : : :  */
```

continued

FIGURE 25.3 CONTINUED

```
ChgVar      %Bin( &AEBytesPrv )       ( 272 )
ChgVar      %Sst( &APIError 1 4 )     ( &AEBytesPrv )

Call        SomeAPI                                                    +
            ( &SomeParm                                                +
              &APIError )

ChgVar      &AEBytesAvl  ( %Sst( &APIError  5 4 ) )
ChgVar      &AEMsgDtaLn  ( %Bin( &AEBytesAvl)   16 )
ChgVar      &AEMsgID     ( %Sst( &APIError  9 7 ) )
ChgVar      &AEMsgDta    ( %Sst( &APIError 17 &AEMsgDtaLn ) )

If          ( %Bin( &AEBytesAvl ) *NE 0 )                              +
  Do
    If          ( ( &AEMsgID *NE 'MsgID01' ) *And                      +
                  ( &AEMsgID *NE 'MsgID02' ) )                         +
      Do
        ChgVar      &MsgID        ( &AEMsgID )
        ChgVar      &MsgDta       ( &AEMsgDta )
        ChgVar      &MsgF         ( 'QCPFMSG' )
        ChgVar      &MsgFLib      ( 'QSYS' )
        GoTo        SndError
      EndDo

    If          ( &AEMsgID *Eq 'MsgID01' )                             +
      Do
   .
   . Insert code for specific error condition
   .
      EndDo

    If          ( &AEMsgID *Eq 'MsgID02' )                             +
      Do
   .
   . Insert code for specific error condition
   .
      EndDo

  EndDo

.
.
.

/*  -------------------------------------------------------------  */
/*  -   Exit program                                             -  */
/*  -------------------------------------------------------------  */

Return
```

continued

FIGURE 25.3 CONTINUED

```
/*  ---------------------------------------------------------------  */
/*  -  Error handler (percolate error message to caller)          -  */
/*  ---------------------------------------------------------------  */

Error:

  RcvMsg      MsgType( *Excp )                                       +
              Rmv( *Yes )                                            +
              MsgDta( &MsgDta )                                      +
              MsgID( &MsgID )                                        +
              MsgF( &MsgF )                                          +
              MsgFLib( &MsgFLib )
  MonMsg      ( CPF0000 MCH0000 )

SndError:

  SndPgmMsg   MsgID( &MsgID )                                        +
              MsgF( &MsgFLib/&MsgF )                                 +
              MsgDta( &MsgDta )                                      +
              MsgType( *Escape )
  MonMsg      ( CPF0000 MCH0000 )

EndPgm
```

The example uses variable &APIError as the API error structure. Notice that we declare this variable with a length of 272. This lets the API return up to 256 bytes of message data. We use 272-byte structures for all the API calls in the example, but note that this structure could be shorter for methods that don't need the error details. Also, notice that we've defined a global error trap to handle any errors that aren't handled explicitly.

In each of the methods, the program first initializes the API error structure's Bytes Provided subfield and then calls the API. In method 1, the program initializes the subfield to 0 (zero) so that any API error generates an exception message. The example relies on the global MonMsg statement to handle any errors produced by the API. However, you can follow the API call with any MonMsg statements appropriate to your requirements and explicitly handle any errors.

Method 2 initializes the Bytes Provided subfield to 8, thereby preventing any exception messages when an error occurs in the API. After the call to the API, the program checks to determine whether an error of any kind occurred and explicitly handles any such error.

Method 3 in the example demonstrates granular control when an API encounters an error. The example explicitly handles *MsgID01* and *MsgID02* errors. The example percolates any other errors to the calling program. This section begins by initializing the Bytes Provided subfield to the full length (i.e., 272) of the declared API error structure. After the call to the API, the program decomposes the API error structure into its subfields. Next, the program determines whether an error occurred. When an error occurs and the message ID is neither *MsgID01* nor *MsgID02*, the program sets values needed by the SndPgmMsg (Send Program Message) command to percolate the message to the calling program. The program then branches to the portion of the global error handler that sends the message. When the error is either *MsgID01* or *MsgID02*, the program explicitly handles the error.

As you can see, you have a choice when it comes to handling errors encountered by APIs. For consistency's sake, you may want to select either method 1 or method 3 as the standard technique to use in all your CL programs.

Retrieve an IP Address

With the basics under your belt, let's now take a look at an API in action in a CL program. We often hear of the need to know the IP address associated with a device. This information is handy both for application reasons and for operational reasons. This need is a classic example of a situation where an API provides a solution when no system-supplied command exists do so.

With format DEVD0600 of API QDCRDevD (Retrieve Device Description), you can retrieve a device's IP address. We've encapsulated this function in command RtvIPAddr (Retrieve IP Address). Figure 25.4A shows the RtvIPAddr panel.

FIGURE 25.4A

Retrieve IP Address (RTVIPADDR) Panel

```
                     Retrieve IP Address (RTVIPADDR)

Type choices, press Enter.

Device . . . . . . . . . . . . . . > *REQUESTER      Name, *REQUESTER
CL Var for IPADDR        (15)        ___________      Character value













                                                                   Bottom
F3=Exit   F4=Prompt   F5=Refresh   F12=Cancel   F13=How to use this display
F24=More keys
```

The command has a single input parameter, Dev, in which you specify the name of the device whose IP address you want to retrieve. You can enter a specific device name, or you can accept the default special value, *Requester, which specifies that the command is to retrieve the IP address of the device from which the command was issued. The command also has a return value parameter, IPAddr, in which you specify the CL variable to contain the retrieved IP address. Figure 25.4B shows the command source. Figure 25.4C shows command processing program RtvIPAddrC.

FIGURE 25.4B

RtvIPAddr Command Source

```
/*  ==============================================================  */
/*  =  Command....... RtvIPAddr                                 =  */
/*  =  Description... Retrieve device IP address                =  */
/*  =  ------------------------------------------------------   =  */
/*  =  CrtCmd  Cmd( YourLib/RtvIPAddr )    +                     =  */
/*  =          Pgm( YourLib/RtvIPAddrC )   +                     =  */
/*  =          Allow( *IPgm *IMod *IRexx )                       =  */
/*  ==============================================================  */

           Cmd        Prompt( 'Retrieve IP Address' )

           Parm       Kwd( Dev )                                    +
                      Type( *Name )                                 +
                      Len( 10 )                                     +
                      Dft( *Requester )                             +
                      SpcVal( ( *Requester ) )                      +
                      Expr( *Yes )                                  +
                      Prompt( 'Device' )

           Parm       Kwd( IPAddr )                                 +
                      Type( *Char )                                 +
                      Len( 15 )                                     +
                      RtnVal( *Yes )                                +
                      Prompt( 'CL Var for IPADDR        (15)' )
```

FIGURE 25.4C

RtvIPAddr Command Processing Program RtvIPAddrC

```
/*  ==============================================================  */
/*  =  Program....... RtvIPAddrC                                =  */
/*  =  Description... Retrieve device IP address                =  */
/*  =  ------------------------------------------------------   =  */
/*  =  CrtCLPgm  Pgm( YourLib/RtvIPAddrC )  +                    =  */
/*  =            SrcFile( YourLib/YourSrcF )                     =  */
/*  ==============================================================  */

Pgm       (                                                        +
            &Dev                                                   +
            &IPAddr                                                +
          )

/*  --------------------------------------------------------------  */
/*  -  Variable declarations                                     -  */
/*  --------------------------------------------------------------  */

  Dcl     &Dev          *Char     (   10    )
  Dcl     &IPAddr       *Char     (   15    )
  Dcl     &RcvVar       *Char     (  892    )
  Dcl     &RcvVarLen    *Char     (    4    )
  Dcl     &Format       *Char     (    8    )
```

continued

FIGURE 25.4C CONTINUED

```
  Dcl      &APIError    *Char    (    8     )
  Dcl      &AEBytesPrv  *Char    (    4     )
  Dcl      &NoIPAddr    *Char    (   15     )
  Dcl      &MsgID       *Char    (    7     )
  Dcl      &MsgDta      *Char    (  256     )
  Dcl      &MsgF        *Char    (   10     )
  Dcl      &MsgFLib     *Char    (   10     )

/*  -------------------------------------------------------------  */
/*  -  Global error trap                                        -  */
/*  -------------------------------------------------------------  */

  MonMsg      ( CPF0000 MCH0000 ) Exec(                           +
    GoTo        Error                 )
/*  -------------------------------------------------------------  */
/*  -  Initialize information                                   -  */
/*  -------------------------------------------------------------  */

  ChgVar      &NoIPAddr            ( X'000000000000000000000000000000' )
  ChgVar      &Format              ( 'DEVD0600' )
  ChgVar      %Bin( &RcvVarLen )   ( 892 )
  ChgVar      %Bin( &AEBytesPrv ) ( 0 )

/*  -------------------------------------------------------------  */
/*  -  Retrieve current device name if necessary                -  */
/*  -------------------------------------------------------------  */

  If          ( &Dev *Eq '*REQUESTER' )                           +
    RtvJobA     Job( &Dev )

/*  -------------------------------------------------------------  */
/*  -  Retrieve dotted IP address                               -  */
/*  -------------------------------------------------------------  */

  ChgVar      %Sst( &APIError 1 4)  ( &AEBytesPrv )

  Call        QDCRDevD                                            +
              ( &RcvVar                                           +
                &RcvVarLen                                        +
                &Format                                           +
                &Dev                                              +
                &APIError )

  ChgVar      &IPAddr  ( %Sst( &RcvVar 878 15 ) )

  If          ( ( &IPAddr *Eq &NoIPAddr ) *Or                     +
                ( &IPAddr *Eq ' ' ) )                             +
    ChgVar      &IPAddr  ( '*None' )

  Return
```

continued

FIGURE 25.4C *CONTINUED*

```
/*  ----------------------------------------------------------------  */
/*  -  Error handler (percolate error message to caller)           -  */
/*  ----------------------------------------------------------------  */

Error:

  RcvMsg      MsgType( *Excp )                                        +
              Rmv( *Yes )                                             +
              MsgDta( &MsgDta )                                       +
              MsgID( &MsgID )                                         +
              MsgF( &MsgF )                                           +
              MsgFLib( &MsgFLib )
  MonMsg      ( CPF0000 MCH0000 )

  SndPgmMsg   MsgID( &MsgID )                                         +
              MsgF( &MsgFLib/&MsgF )                                  +
              MsgDta( &MsgDta )                                       +
              MsgType( *Escape )
  MonMsg      ( CPF0000 MCH0000 )

EndPgm
```

First, notice the definition for the API error structure, variable &APIError, in the variable declarations section of the program. We've defined this structure as only eight bytes in length because the program is to use a global error handler to trap any error that may occur and percolate it back to the calling program.

In the initialization section, we set variable &NoIPAddr's value to the hexadecimal string that API QDCRDevD returns for an applicable device that is not currently using an IP address. Notice that we also set the Bytes Provided subfield, &AEBytesPrv, to 0 (zero) to indicate that the API is to issue an exception if it encounters an error. The program continues by retrieving the current device name when special value *Requester is specified.

Before calling the API, the program constructs the API error structure variable by placing the Bytes Provided value in the structure's first four bytes. The program then calls API QDCRDevD to retrieve the selected device's IP address. If the API encounters an error, control is passed to the global error handler, which receives the exception and percolates it back to the calling program. When no error occurs, the program continues by extracting the IP address stored in bytes 878–892 of the information returned by the API. If the returned IP address value matches the aforementioned hex string or if the address is blank, the program sets the return IP address to value *None.

One application requirement that can make good use of command RtvIPAddr is an application that uses the RunRmtCmd (Run Remote Command) command to initiate a program on a TCP/IP-attached PC. You specify the PC to which the RunRmtCmd command applies by specifying the PC's IP address as a parameter on RunRmtCmd. Your application program can use command RtvIPAddr to capture the needed IP address.

Displaying IP Addresses

At times, operations personnel may need to know the IP address associated with one or more devices to diagnose and solve an operational problem or perhaps simply to locate particular devices. The RtvIPAddr command can help when such needs arise.

Command DspIPAddr (Display IP Address) displays the IP address of up to 25 selected devices. Figure 25.5A shows a sample of the command's output.

FIGURE 25.5A
DspIPAddr Output

```
                           Display IP Address

Device        IP Address

AS400PRT      Incompatible device category
CMN01TCP      Incompatible device category
DSP01         *None
DSP99         *None
LT001         *None
OPT01         Incompatible device category
PC002         Incompatible device category
PC002A        *None
PC002B        *None
PC002C        *None
PC002D        *None
QPADEV0001    192.168.0.1
PC002E        *None
PC002F        *None
PRT01         Incompatible device category
QCONSOLE      *None
QESPAP        Incompatible device category                              +

F3=Exit
```

```
                           Display IP Address

Device        IP Address

QIADSP        Incompatible device category
QPADEV0004    192.168.0.2
QQAHOST       Incompatible device category
QTIDA         Incompatible device category
Q1SHARE400    Incompatible device category
TAP01         Incompatible device category

F3=Exit
```

Notice that the output spans two screens. Believe it or not, the output is a subfile that is loaded and displayed by a CL program. Let's see how DspIPAddr takes advantage of a handy technique to display, in a subfile, the output from command RtvIPAddr.

Figure 25.5B shows the source for display file DspIPAddrD. DspIPAddr uses this display file to display the retrieved IP addresses (as shown in Figure 25.5A).

FIGURE 25.5B

Display File DspIPAddrD

```
 * ==============================================================
 * = Display file... DspIPAddrD                                 =
 * = Description.... Display IP Addresses                       =
 * ==============================================================

 * --------------------------------------------------------------
 * - Headings                                                   -
 * --------------------------------------------------------------

A          R DSPHDG                    CLRL(*NO)
A                                     1 32'Display IP Address'
A                                          COLOR(BLU)
A                                     3  2'Device'
A                                          COLOR(BLU)
A                                     3 14'IP Address'
A                                          COLOR(BLU)

 * --------------------------------------------------------------
 * - Function key legend                                        -
 * --------------------------------------------------------------

A          R DSPFTR                    OVERLAY
A                                      SLNO(23)
A                                      CLRL(*NO)
A                                      CF03(03)
A                                     1  2'F3=Exit'

 * --------------------------------------------------------------
 * - Message subfile to show IP addresses                       -
 * --------------------------------------------------------------

A          R MSGSFL                    SFL
A                                      SFLMSGRCD(5)
A            MSGKEY                    SFLMSGKEY
A            PGMQ                      SFLPGMQ

A          R MSGCTL                    SFLCTL(MSGSFL)
A                                      KEEP
A                                      SFLSIZ(18)
A                                      SFLPAG(17)
A  99                                  SFLINZ
A  99                                  SFLEND
A                                      SFLDSPCTL
A                                      SFLDSP
A            PGMQ                      SFLPGMQ
```

Four record formats make up the display file. Format DspHdg contains the headings, and format DspFtr contains the function key legend displayed at the bottom of the display. The other two formats, MsgSfl and MsgCtl, make up a message subfile used to display the IP address information. You may be familiar with message subfiles that display error messages on the bottom of the display. It is standard design to load all error messages in the message subfile, display one of them, and allow scrolling through the list of messages. Nothing says that message subfiles must contain only error messages or that the subfile page size must be 1 and be displayed on the bottom line of the display, though. In record format MsgSfl, we use the SflMsgRcd keyword to specify line 5 as the line on which to begin the message subfile; a glance at record format MsgCtl shows that the subfile contains 17 entries per page. Notice that we set the subfile size to 18, one more than the number of entries per page, to enable scrolling.

Now, let's see how to load the subfile for display. Figure 25.5C shows the DspIPAddr panel, where you can enter up to 25 devices or accept the default special value *Requester for the command's single parameter, Dev.

FIGURE 25.5C

Display IP Address (DSPIPADDR) Panel

```
                        Display IP Address (DSPIPADDR)

 Type choices, press Enter.

 Device . . . . . . . . . . . . . > AS400PRT__      Name, *REQUESTER
                                  > CMN01TCP__
                                  > DSP01_____
                                  > DSP99_____
                                  > LT001_____
                                  > OPT01_____
                                  > PC002_____
                                  > PC002A____
                                  > PC002B____
                                  > PC002C____
                                  > PC002D____
                                  > QPADEV0001
                                  > PC002E____
                                  > PC002F____
                                  > PRT01_____

                                                                    More...
 F3=Exit   F4=Prompt   F5=Refresh   F12=Cancel   F13=How to use this display
 F24=More keys
```

continued

FIGURE 25.5C *CONTINUED*

```
                      Display IP Address (DSPIPADDR)

 Type choices, press Enter.

 Device . . . . . . . . . . . . . > QCONSOLE__     Name, *REQUESTER
                                  > QESPAP____
                                  > QIADSP____
                                  > QPADEV0004
                                  > QQAHOST___
                                  > QTIDA_____
                                  > Q1SHARE400
                                  > TAP01_____

                                                                    Bottom
 F3=Exit   F4=Prompt   F5=Refresh   F12=Cancel   F13=How to use this display
 F24=More keys
```

The source for command DspIPAddr appears in Figure 25.5D.

FIGURE 25.5D

DspIPAddr Command Source

```
/*  ===========================================================  */
/*  =  Command....... DspIPAddr                              =  */
/*  =  Description... Display IP Address                     =  */
/*  =  ----------------------------------------------------- =  */
/*  =  CrtCmd  Cmd( YourLib/DspIPAddr )     +                =  */
/*  =          Pgm( YourLib/DspIPAddrC )    +                =  */
/*  =          VldCkr( YourLib/DspIPAddrV ) +                =  */
/*  =          Allow( *Interact *IPgm *IMod *IRexx )         =  */
/*  ===========================================================  */

            Cmd          Prompt( 'Display IP Address' )

            Parm         Kwd( Dev )                              +
                         Type( *Name )                           +
                         Len( 10 )                               +
                         Dft( *Requester )                       +
                         SngVal( ( *Requester ) )                +
                         Max( 25 )                               +
                         Expr( *Yes )                            +
                         Prompt( 'Device' )
```

Validity-checking program DspIPAddrV (Figure 25.5E) simply loops through the list of selected devices, ensuring that each entry is indeed a device. Once the devices have been validated, command processing program DspIPAddrC (Figure 25.5F) is executed. DspIPAddrC declares display file DspIPAddrD for use, specifying that all its record formats are to be available. As part of standard design, the program sets a global error trap to prevent abnormal termination. If the error handler receives control, it percolates the exception back to the calling program.

FIGURE 25.5E

DspIPAddr Validity-Checking Program DspIPAddrV

```
/*  ================================================================  */
/*  =                                                              =  */
/*  =  Program....... DspIPAddrV                                   =  */
/*  =  Type.......... Validity checking program for DspIPAddr      =  */
/*  =  Description... Display IP Address                           =  */
/*  =                                                              =  */
/*  =  ----------------------------------------------------------  =  */
/*  =                                                              =  */
/*  =  Parameters                                                  =  */
/*  =                                                              =  */
/*  =    &Dev               Input     List of up to 25 device names =  */
/*  =                                                              =  */
/*  ================================================================  */

   Pgm          (                                                     +
                  &Dev                                                +
                )

/*  ================================================================  */
/*  = Variable declarations                                        =  */
/*  ================================================================  */

   Dcl          &Dev         *Char      (  252     )
   Dcl          &DevName     *Char      (   10     )
   Dcl          &DevCount    *Char      (    2     )
   Dcl          &DevCountN   *Dec       (    2  0  )
   Dcl          &LoopCount   *Dec       (    3  0  )
   Dcl          &Offset      *Dec       (    3  0  )
   Dcl          &Msg         *Char      (  512     )
   Dcl          &MsgID       *Char      (    7     )
   Dcl          &MsgF        *Char      (   10     )
   Dcl          &MsgFLib     *Char      (   10     )
   Dcl          &MsgDta      *Char      (  100     )
   Dcl          &KeyVar      *Char      (    4     )

/*  ================================================================  */
/*  = Global error monitor                                         =  */
/*  ================================================================  */

   MonMsg       ( CPF0000 MCH0000 ) Exec(                             +
     Goto         Error                )

/*  ================================================================  */
/*  = Parse number of devices in list                              =  */
/*  ================================================================  */

   ChgVar       &DevCount    ( %Sst( &Dev 1 2 ) )
   ChgVar       &DevCountN   ( %Bin( &DevCount ) )
```

continued

FIGURE 25.5E *CONTINUED*

```
/*  ===============================================================  */
/*  = Validate devices in list                                     =  */
/*  ===============================================================  */

  ChgVar      &LoopCount  ( 0 )

Loop01:

  ChgVar      &LoopCount  ( &LoopCount + 1 )

  If          ( &LoopCount *GT &DevCountN )                          +
    GoTo        End01

  ChgVar      &Offset     ( ( ( &LoopCount - 1 ) * 10 ) + 3 )
  ChgVar      &DevName    ( %Sst( &Dev &Offset 10 ) )

  If          ( &DevName *Eq '*REQUESTER' )                          +
    RtvJobA     Job( &DevName )

  ChkObj      Obj( &DevName )                                        +
              ObjType( *DevD )

  GoTo        Loop01

End01:

/*  ===============================================================  */
/*  =  Exit                                                        =  */
/*  ===============================================================  */

  Return

/*  ===============================================================  */
/*  = Error handler                                                =  */
/*  ===============================================================  */

Error:

  RcvMsg      MsgType( *Excp )                                       +
              MsgDta( &MsgDta )                                      +
              MsgID( &MsgID )                                        +
              MsgF( &MsgF )                                          +
              MsgFLib( &MsgFLib )
  MonMsg      ( CPF0000 MCH0000 )

  SndPgmMsg   MsgID( &MsgID )                                        +
              MsgF( &MsgFLib/&MsgF )                                 +
              MsgDta( &MsgDta )                                      +
              ToPgmQ( *Same )                                        +
              KeyVar( &KeyVar )
  MonMsg      ( CPF0000 MCH0000 )

  RcvMsg      KeyVar( &KeyVar )                                      +
              Msg( &Msg )
  MonMsg      ( CPF0000 MCH0000 )
```

continued

FIGURE 25.5E CONTINUED

```
  SndPgmMsg   MsgID( CPD0006 )                                        +
              MsgF( QSys/QCPFMsg )                                    +
              MsgDta( '0000' *TCat &Msg )                             +
              ToPgmQ( *Prv )                                          +
              MsgType( *Diag )
  MonMsg      ( CPF0000 MCH0000 )

  SndPgmMsg   MsgID( CPF0002 )                                        +
              MsgF( QSys/QCPFMsg )                                    +
              ToPgmQ( *PRV )                                          +
              MsgType( *Escape )
  MonMsg      ( CPF0000 MCH0000 )

/*  =============================================================  */
/*  = End of program                                            =  */
/*  =============================================================  */

EndPgm
```

FIGURE 25.5F

DspIPAddr Command Processing Program DspIPAddrC

```
/*  =============================================================  */
/*  =                                                           =  */
/*  =  Program....... DspIPAddrC                                =  */
/*  =  Type.......... Command processing program for DspIPAddr  =  */
/*  =  Description... Display IP Address                        =  */
/*  =                                                           =  */
/*  =  -------------------------------------------------------  =  */
/*  =                                                           =  */
/*  =  Parameters                                               =  */
/*  =                                                           =  */
/*  =    &Dev            Input     List of up to 25 device names =  */
/*  =                                                           =  */
/*  =============================================================  */

  Pgm         (                                                       +
                &Dev                                                  +
              )

/*  =============================================================  */
/*  = Variable declarations                                     =  */
/*  =============================================================  */

  Dcl         &Dev         *Char      (  252     )
  Dcl         &DevName     *Char      (   10     )
  Dcl         &DevCount    *Char      (    2     )
  Dcl         &DevCountN   *Dec       (    2   0 )
  Dcl         &IPAddr      *Char      (   15     )
  Dcl         &IPAddrInfo  *Char      (   60     )
  Dcl         &LoopCount   *Dec       (    3   0 )
  Dcl         &Offset      *Dec       (    3   0 )
  Dcl         &Msg         *Char      (  512     )
  Dcl         &MsgID       *Char      (    7     )
```

continued

FIGURE 25.5F CONTINUED

```
  Dcl         &MsgF        *Char      (   10     )
  Dcl         &MsgFLib     *Char      (   10     )
  Dcl         &MsgDta      *Char      (  100     )
  Dcl         &KeyVar      *Char      (    4     )

/*  ================================================================  */
/*  = File declaration                                             =  */
/*  ================================================================  */

  DclF        DspIPAddrD                                                +
              RcdFmt( *All )

/*  ================================================================  */
/*  = Global error trap                                            =  */
/*  ================================================================  */

  MonMsg      ( CPF0000 MCH0000 ) Exec(                                 +
    Goto        Error                  )

/*  ================================================================  */
/*  = Initialize error subfile information                         =  */
/*  ================================================================  */

  ChgVar      &PgmQ        ( 'DSPIPADDRC' )

/*  ================================================================  */
/*  = Parse number of devices in list                              =  */
/*  ================================================================  */

  ChgVar      &DevCount    ( %Sst( &Dev 1 2 ) )
  ChgVar      &DevCountN   ( %Bin( &DevCount ) )

/*  ================================================================  */
/*  =  Retrieve IP addresses and send as message                   =  */
/*  ================================================================  */

  ChgVar      &LoopCount   ( 0 )

Loop01:

  ChgVar      &LoopCount   ( &LoopCount + 1 )

  If          ( &LoopCount *GT &DevCountN )                             +
    GoTo        DspInfo

  ChgVar      &Offset      ( ( ( &LoopCount - 1 ) * 10 ) + 3 )
  ChgVar      &DevName     ( %Sst( &Dev &Offset 10 ) )

  If          ( &DevName *Eq '*REQUESTER' )                             +
    RtvJobA     Job( &DevName )

  ChgVar      &IPAddrInfo ( &DevName )

  RtvIPAddr   Dev( &DevName )                                           +
              IPAddr( &IPAddr )
```

continued

FIGURE 25.5F CONTINUED

```
MonMsg      ( CPF2625 ) Exec(                                          +
  Do                      )
    RcvMsg     MsgType( *Excp )                                        +
               Rmv( *Yes )
    ChgVar     %Sst( &IPAddrInfo 13 48 )                               +
               ( 'Cannot allocate device description' )
  EndDo

MonMsg      ( CPF2634 ) Exec(                                          +
  Do                      )
    RcvMsg     MsgType( *Excp )                                        +
               Rmv( *Yes )
    ChgVar     %Sst( &IPAddrInfo 13 48 )                               +
             ( 'Not authorized to device description' )
  EndDo
MonMsg      ( CPF26A7 ) Exec(                                          +
  Do                      )
    RcvMsg     MsgType( *Excp )                                        +
               Rmv( *Yes )
    ChgVar     %Sst( &IPAddrInfo 13 48 )                               +
               ( 'Incompatible device category' )
  EndDo

MonMsg      ( CPF27Ø2 ) Exec(                                          +
  Do                      )
    RcvMsg     MsgType( *Excp )                                        +
               Rmv( *Yes )
    ChgVar     %Sst( &IPAddrInfo 13 48 )                               +
               ( 'Device description not found' )
  EndDo

MonMsg      ( CPF81Ø5 ) Exec(                                          +
  Do                      )
    RcvMsg     MsgType( *Excp )                                        +
               Rmv( *Yes )
    ChgVar     %Sst( &IPAddrInfo 13 48 )                               +
               ( 'Device description damaged' )
  EndDo

If          ( %Sst( &IPAddrInfo 13 48 ) *Eq ' ' )                      +
  ChgVar      %Sst( &IPAddrInfo 13 48 ) ( &IPAddr )

SndPgmMsg   MsgID( CPF9897 )                                           +
            MsgF( QSys/QCPFMsg )                                       +
            MsgDta( &IPAddrInfo )                                      +
            ToPgmQ( *Same * )                                          +
            MsgType( *INFO )

GoTo        LoopØ1
```

continued

FIGURE 25.5F *CONTINUED*

```
/*  ===============================================================  */
/*  =  Display IP addresses                                       =  */
/*  ===============================================================  */

DspInfo:

  ChgVar     &In99        ( '1' )

  SndF       RcdFmt( MsgCtl )
  SndF       RcdFmt( DspHdg )
  SndRcvF    RcdFmt( DspFtr )
  If         ( &In03 *NE '1' )                                     +
    GoTo       DspInfo

/*  ===============================================================  */
/*  =  Exit                                                       =  */
/*  ===============================================================  */

  Return

/*  ===============================================================  */
/*  = Error handler                                               =  */
/*  ===============================================================  */

Error:

  RcvMsg     MsgType( *Excp )                                      +
             MsgDta( &MsgDta )                                     +
             MsgID( &MsgID )                                       +
             MsgF( &MsgF )                                         +
             MsgFLib( &MsgFLib )
  MonMsg     ( CPF0000 MCH0000 )

  SndPgmMsg  MsgID( &MsgID )                                       +
             MsgF( &MsgFLib/&MsgF )                                +
             MsgDta( &MsgDta )                                     +
             MsgType( *Escape )
  MonMsg     ( CPF0000 MCH0000 )

/*  ===============================================================  */
/*  = End of program                                              =  */
/*  ===============================================================  */

EndPgm
```

DspIPAddrC begins by initializing the display file field (&PgmQ) that identifies the call message queue that the message subfile uses. The program indicates that the message subfile is to use the program's own call message queue.

Next, DspIPAddrC processes the list of selected devices. For each entry in the list, the program sends a message containing the device name along with the retrieved IP address information to its call message queue. This, of course, causes the information to be displayed in the message subfile. The program builds the message in variable &IPAddrInfo. Notice that immediately before executing RtvIPAddr, the program initializes variable &IPAddrInfo with the device name. DspIPAddrC adds to this information based on the result of the attempt to retrieve the device's IP address.

DspIPAddrC explicitly monitors for five of the possible exceptions that RtvIPAddr may cause. This lets the program tailor the message it sends to its call message queue for display. If RtvIPAddr signals any exception other than the monitored five, the global error handler receives control. After the five MonMsg statements, the program checks variable &IPAddrInfo to determine whether it contains error information. When it doesn't, no errors occurred and the program adds the retrieved IP address to the variable. Finally, DspIPAddrC sends the message it constructed in variable &IPAddrInfo to its call message queue for display.

Once the program finishes processing the entire list of selected devices, it displays the results by setting control indicator 99's value and writing the record formats from the display file. The sequence in which the program writes the record formats is important for ensuring that all information is displayed properly and that function key F3 is active. To exit the display, the user must press F3.

EndPgm

Although CL has its limitations, it's a good language when your programs need to interface to the system. And with APIs, you have additional capabilities not inherent to CL. The information in this chapter will help you determine whether CL is a viable language to use with an API, and the techniques used in the examples will help you more easily integrate APIs with CL programs.

Chapter 26

CL Programs and Database Files

Once you learn to write basic CL programs, you'll probably try to find more ways to use CL as part of your iSeries applications. In contrast to operations languages such as a mainframe's Job Control Language (JCL), which is used primarily to control steps, sorts, and parameters in a job stream, CL offers more. CL is more procedural, provides support for database file (read-only) and display file (both read and write) processing, and lets you extend the operating system command set with your own user-written commands.

In this chapter, we examine one of those fundamental differences of CL: its ability to process database files. We explain how to declare a file, extract the field definitions from a file, read a file sequentially, and position a file by key to read a specific record. With this overview, you should be able to process database files in your next CL program.

Why CL?

Before we talk about how to process database files in a CL program, let us address the question you're probably asking yourself: "Why would I want to read records in CL instead of in a high-level language program?" In most cases, you probably wouldn't. But sometimes, such as when you want to use data from a database file as a substitute value in a CL command, reading records in CL is a sensible programming solution.

Say you want to perform a DspObjD (Display Object Description) command to an output file and then read the records from that output file and process each object using another CL command, such as DspObjAut (Display Object Authority) or MovObj (Move Object). Because executing a CL command is much easier and clearer from a CL program than from a high-level language (HLL) program, you'd probably prefer to write a single CL program that can handle the entire task. We'll show you just such a program a little later.

I DCLare!

Perhaps the most crucial point in understanding how CL programs process database files is knowing when you need to declare a file in the program. The rule is simple: If your CL program uses the RcvF (Receive File) command to read the file, you must use the DclF (Declare File) command to declare that file to your program. DclF tells the compiler to retrieve the file and field descriptions during compilation and make the field definitions available to the program. The command has only one required parameter: the file name. To declare a file, you need only code in your program either

```
DclF File(YourFile)
```

or

```
DclF File(YourLib/YourFile)
```

When using the DclF command, you must remember three implementation rules. First, you can declare only one file — either a database file or a display file — in any CL program. This doesn't mean your program can't operate on other files — for example, using the CpyF (Copy File), OvrDbF (Override with Database File), or OpnQryF (Open Query File) command; it can. However, you can use the RcvF command to process only the file named in the DclF statement.

Second, the DclF statement must be placed after the Pgm (Program) command in your program and must precede all executable commands (the Pgm and Dcl, or Declare CL Variable, commands are not executable). The third rule is that the declared file must exist when you compile your CL program. If you don't qualify the file name, the compiler must be able to find the file in the current library list during compilation.

Extracting Field Definitions

When you declare a file to a CL program, the program can access the fields associated with that file. Fields in a declared file automatically become available to the program as CL variables — there's no need to declare the variables separately.

When the file is externally described, the compiler uses the external record-format definition associated with the file object to identify each field and its data type and length. Figure 26.1 shows the Data Description Specifications (DDS) for sample file TestPF.

FIGURE 26.1

DDS for Sample File TestPF

```
 *  ==============================================================
 *  = File.......... TestPF                                       =
 *  = Source type... PF                                           =
 *  = Description... Sample file for reading files in CL          =
 *  ==============================================================

A            R TESTPFR                     TEXT('Test Record')
A              CODE            1           TEXT('Test Code')
A              NUMBER          5S Ø        TEXT('Test Number')
A              FIELD          3Ø           TEXT('Test Field')
```

To declare this file in a program, you code

```
DclF TestPF
```

The system then makes the following variables available to the program:

Variable	*Type*
&Code	*Char 1
&Number	*Dec 5,0
&Field	*Char 30

Your program can then use these variables in spite of the fact that they're not explicitly declared. For instance, you could include in the program the statements

```
If       ((*Code *Eq 'A') *And +
          (&Number *GT 10))    +
  ChgVar      &Code     ('B')
```

Notice that when you refer to the field in the program, you must prefix the field name with the ampersand (&) character. All CL variables, including those implicitly defined using the DclF command and the file field definitions, require the & prefix when referenced in a program.

What about program-described files — that is, files with no external data definition? Suppose you create the following file using the CrtPF (Create Physical File) command

```
CrtPF File(DiskFile) RcdLen(258)
```

and then declare file DiskFile in your CL program. As it does with externally defined files, the CL compiler automatically provides access to program-described files. Because there is no externally defined record format, however, the compiler recognizes each record in the file as consisting of a single field. That field is always named *&FileName*, where *FileName* is the name of the file. Therefore, if you code

```
DclF DiskFile
```

your CL program recognizes one field, &DiskFile, with a length equal to DiskFile's record length. You can then extract the subfields with which you need to work. In CL, you extract the fields using the built-in function %Sst (or %Substring). The statements

```
ChgVar &Field1 (%Sst(&DiskFile  1 10))
ChgVar &Field2 (%Sst(&DiskFile 11 25))
ChgVar &Field3 (%Sst(&DiskFile 50  1))
```

extract three subfields from &DiskFile's single field.

You'll need to remember two rules when using program-described files. First, you must extract the subfields every time you read a record from the file. Unlike RPG, CL has no global data-structure concept that can be applied for every read. With each read cycle, you must use the %Sst function to retrieve the subfields.

Second, the %Sst function supports only character data. If a certain range of positions holds numeric data, you must retrieve that data as a character field and then move the data into a numeric field. You can use command ChgVar (Change Variable) to move character data to a numeric field. You must also ensure that the variable's data type matches that of the data you're extracting.

Assume that positions 251–258 in file DiskFile hold a numeric date field eight digits long. To extract that date into a numeric CL variable requires the following Dcl statements and operations:

```
Dcl     &DateChar    *Char    (   8   )
Dcl     &DateNbr     *Dec     (   8  Ø)
    .
    .
    .
ChgVar &DateChar (%Sst(&DiskFile 251 8))
ChgVar &DateNbr  (&DateChar)
```

The first ChgVar command extracts the substring from the single &DiskFile field and places it in variable &DateChar. The second ChgVar places the contents of field &DateChar into numeric field &DateNbr.

Caution

When you use this technique, be sure that the substring contains only numeric data. If it doesn't, the system will send your program a distinctly unfriendly error message, and your program will end abnormally.

Reading the Database File

Reading a database file in CL is straightforward. The only complication is that you need a program loop to process records one at a time from the file, and CL doesn't directly support structured operations such as Do-While or Do-Until. However, CL does offer the primitive GoTo command and lets you put labels in your code. Using these two capabilities, you can write the necessary loop.

Figure 26.2 shows part of a program to process file TestPF. Notice that the program uses a manual loop to return to the ReadBegin label and process the next record in the file. The first time through the loop, the RcvF command opens the file and processes the first record. The loop continues until the RcvF statement causes the system to send error message "CPF0864 End of file detected." When the MonMsg (Monitor Message) command traps this message, control skips to ReadEnd, thus ending the loop.

FIGURE 26.2

CL Fragment for Processing a Database File

```
/*  ==============================================================  */
/*  =  Program....... TestCL                                    =  */
/*  =  Description... Process database file                     =  */
/*  ==============================================================  */

Pgm

/*  ==============================================================  */
/*  =  Variable declarations                                    =  */
/*  ==============================================================  */

   Dcl         &MsgFlag    *Lgl
   Dcl         &RtnCode    *Char      (    1    )
```

continued

FIGURE 26.2 CONTINUED

```
/*  ================================================================  */
/*  =  File declaration                                            =  */
/*  ================================================================  */

   DclF        TestPF

   .
   .
   .

/*  ================================================================  */
/*  =  Read database file                                          =  */
/*  ================================================================  */

ReadBegin:

   RcvF        RcdFmt(TestPFR)
   MonMsg      ( CPF0864 ) Exec(                                        +
     GoTo        ReadEnd       )

   .
   .
   .

   GoTo        ReadBegin

ReadEnd:

   .
   .
   .
```

Unlike HLLs, CL doesn't let you reposition the file for additional processing after the program receives an end-of-file message. Although you can execute an OvrDbF command containing a Position parameter after your program receives an end-of-file message, any ensuing RcvF command simply elicits another end-of-file message. Two possible workarounds to this potential problem exist, but each has its restriction.

You can use the first workaround if, and only if, you can ensure that the data in the file will remain static for the duration of the read cycles. The technique involves the use of the RtvMbrD (Retrieve Member Description) command. Using this command's NbrCurRcd (CL variable for NBRCURRCD) parameter, you can retrieve into a program variable the number of records currently in the file. Then, in your loop to read records, you can use another variable to count the number of records read, comparing it with the number of records currently in the file. When the two numbers are equal, the program has read the last record in the file.

Although the program has read the last record, the end-of-file condition is not yet set. The system sets this condition and issues the CPF0864 message indicating end-of-file only *after* attempting to read a record *beyond* the last record. Therefore, this technique gives you a way to avoid the end-of-file condition. You can then use the PosDbF (Position

Database File) command to set the file cursor back to the beginning of the file. Simply specify *Start for the Position parameter, and you can read the file again! Remember, use this technique only when you can ensure that the data will in no way change while you're reading the file.

The second circumvention is perhaps even trickier because it requires a little application design planning. Consider a simple CL program that does nothing more than perform a loop that reads all the records in a database file and exits when the end-of-file condition occurs (i.e., when the system issues message CPF0864). If you replace the statement

```
MonMsg (CPF0864) Exec(GoTo End)
```

with

```
MonMsg     (CPF0864) Exec(Do)
  If         (&Stop *Eq 'Y') GoTo End
  ChgVar     &Stop ('Y')
  TfrCtl     Pgm(YourPgm) Parm(&Stop)
EndDo
```

where *YourPgm* is the name of the program containing the command, the system starts the program over again, thereby reading the file again. Notice that with this technique, you must add code to the program to prevent an infinite loop. In addition to the changes shown above, the program should accept the &Stop parameter. Fail to add these groups of code, and each time the system detects end-of-file, the process restarts. You also must add code to ensure that only those portions of the code you want to execute do so.

When possible, we advise that if you need to read a database file multiple times, you construct your application in such a way that you can call multiple CL programs (or one program multiple times, as appropriate). Each of these programs (or instances of a program) can then process the file once. This approach is the clearest and least error-prone method.

File Positioning

One well-kept secret of CL file processing is that you can use it to retrieve records by key…sort of. The OvrDbF command's Position parameter lets you specify the position from which to start retrieving database file records. You can position the file to *Start or *End (you can also use the PosDbF command to position to *Start or *End), to a particular record using relative record number, or to a particular record using a key.

To retrieve records by key, you supply four search values in the Position parameter: a key-search type, the number of key fields, the name of the record format that contains the key fields, and the key value. The key-search type determines where in the file the read-by-key begins by specifying which record the system is to read first. The key-search value specifies one of the following five key-search types:

- *KeyB (key-before) — The first record retrieved is the one that immediately precedes the record identified by the other Position parameter search values.

- *KeyBE (key-before or equal) — The first record retrieved is the one identified by the search values. If no record matches those values, the system retrieves the record that matches the largest previous value.
- *Key (key-equal) — The first record retrieved is the one identified by the search values. (If your CL program calls an HLL program that issues a read-previous operation, the called program will retrieve the preceding record.)
- *KeyAE (key-after or equal) — The first record retrieved is the one identified by the search values. If no record matches those values, the system retrieves the record with the next highest key value.
- *KeyA (key-after) — The first record retrieved is the one that immediately follows the record identified by the search values.

As a simple example, let's assume that file TestPF has one key field, Code, and contains the following records:

Code	*Number*	*Field*
A	1	Text in Record 1
B	100	Text in Record 2
C	50	Text in Record 3
E	27	Text in Record 4

The statements

```
OvrDbF Position(*Key 1 TestPFR 'B')
RcvF   RcdFmt(TestPFR)
```

specify that the record to be retrieved has one key field as defined in DDS record format TestPFR (Figure 26.1) and that the key field contains the value B. These statements will retrieve the second record (Code = B) from file TestPF. If the key-search type were *KeyB instead of *Key, the same statements would cause the RcvF command to retrieve the first record (Code = A). Key-search types *KeyBE, *KeyAE, and *KeyA would cause the RcvF statement to retrieve records 2 (Code = B), 2 (Code = B), and 3 (Code = C), respectively.

Rules for Database File Processing in CL

- If your CL program uses the RcvF (Receive File) command to read a database file, you must use the DclF (Declare File) command to declare that file to your program.
- You can declare only one file — either a database file or a display file — in any CL program.
- The DclF statement must appear after the Pgm command and precede all executable commands (Pgm and Dcl are not executable commands).
- The declared file must exist when you compile your CL program.
- When using program-described files, you must extract the subfields every time you read a record from the file.
- The CL substring operation supports only character data.

Now let's suppose that the program contains these statements:

```
OvrDbF Position(&KeySearch 1 TestPFR 'D')
RcvF   RcdFmt(TestPFR)
```

The following matrix shows how each *&KeySearch* value affects the RcvF results.

- *KeyB — returns record 3 (Code = C)
- *KeyBE — returns record 3 (Code = C)
- *Key — causes an exception error because no match was found
- *KeyAE — returns record 4 (Code = E)
- *KeyA — returns record 4 (Code = E)

Using the Position parameter with a key consisting of more than one field gets tricky, especially when one of the key fields is a packed numeric field. You must code the key string to match the key's definition in the file, and if any key field is other than a character or signed-decimal field, you must code the key string in hexadecimal form.

For example, suppose the key consists of two fields: a one-character field and a five-digit packed numeric field with two decimals. You must code the key value in the Position parameter as a hex string equal in length to the length of the two key fields together (i.e., 1 + 3 — a packed 5,2 field occupies three positions). For instance,

```
Position(*Key 2 YourFormat X'C323519F')
```

tells the system to retrieve the record that contains values for the character and packed-numeric key fields of C and 235.19, respectively.

As we've mentioned, a CL program can position the database file and then call an HLL program to process the records. For instance, the CL program can use OvrDbF's Position parameter to set the starting point in a file and then call an RPG program that issues a read or read-previous to start reading records at that position.

Having this capability doesn't necessarily mean you should use it, though. One of our fundamental rules of programming is this: Make your program explicit and its purpose clear. Thus, we avoid using the OvrDbF or PosDbF command to position a file before we process it with an HLL program when we can more explicitly and clearly position the file within the HLL program itself. There's just no good reason to hide the positioning function in a CL program that may not clearly belong with the program that actually reads the file. However, when you process a file in a CL program, positioning the file therein can simplify the solution.

What About Record Output?

Just about the time you get the hang of reading database files, you suddenly realize that your CL program can't perform any other form of I/O with them. CL provides no direct support for updating, writing, or printing records in a database file. Some programmers use command StrQMQry (Start Query Management Query) to execute a query management query or use the RunSQLStm (Run SQL Statements) command to effect one of these operations from within CL. To use these techniques, you must first create the query management query or enter the SQL source statements to execute with RunSQLStm.

A Useful Example

Now that you know how to process database files in a CL program, let's look at a practical example. Security administrators would likely find a program that prints the object authorities for selected objects in one or more libraries useful. Figure 26.3A shows the command definition for the PrtObjAut (Print Object Authorities) command, which does just that. Figure 26.3B shows PrtObjAut's command processing program (CPP), PrtObjAut1.

FIGURE 26.3A

Command PrtObjAut

```
/*  ============================================================  */
/*  =   Command....... PrtObjAut                               =  */
/*  =   Source type... CMD                                     =  */
/*  =   Description... Print Object Authorities                =  */
/*  =                                                          =  */
/*  =   CPP........... PrtObjAut1                              =  */
/*  ============================================================  */

             Cmd        Prompt( 'Print Object Authorities' )

             Parm       Kwd( Obj )                                    +
                        Type( QualObj )                               +
                        Min( 1 )                                      +
                        Prompt( 'Object' )

             Parm       Kwd( ObjType )                                +
                        Type( *Char )                                 +
                        Len( 8 )                                      +
                        Rstd( &Yes )                                  +
                        Dft( *All )                                   +
                        Values(                                       +
                               *AlrTbl     *AutL       *BndDir        +
                               *CfgL       *ChtFmt     *CLD           +
                               *Cls        *Cmd        *CnnL          +
                               *CoSD       *CRG        *CRQD          +
                               *CSI        *CSPMap     *CSPTbl        +
                               *CtlD       *DevD       *Doc           +
                               *DtaAra     *DtaDct     *DtaQ          +
                               *EdtD       *ExitRg     *FCT           +
                               *File       *Flr        *FntRsc        +
                               *FntTbl     *FormDf     *Ftr           +
                               *GSS        *IPXD       *JobD          +
                               *JobQ       *JobScd     *Jrn           +
                               *JrnRcv     *Lib        *LinD          +
                               *Locale     *MedDfn     *Menu          +
                               *MgtCol     *ModD       *Module        +
                               *MsgF       *MsgQ       *M36           +
                               *M36Cfg     *NodGrp     *NodL          +
                               *NtBD       *NwID       *NwSD          +
```

continued

Figure 26.3A Continued

```
                                     *OutQ           *Ovl            *PagDfn         +
                                     *PagSeg         *PDG            *Pgm            +
                                     *PnlGrp         *PrdAvl         *PrdDfn         +
                                     *PrdLod         *PSFCfg         *QMForm         +
                                     *QMQry          *QryDfn         *RCT            +
                                     *SbsD           *SchIdx         *SpADct         +
                                     *SQLPkg         *SQLUDT         *SrvPgm         +
                                     *SsnD           *SrvStg         *S36            +
                                     *Tbl            *UsrIdx         *UsrPrf         +
                                     *UsrQ           *UsrSpc         *VldL           +
                                     *WsCst                                          +
                                 )                                                   +
                            SpcVal( ( *All ) )                                       +
                            Prompt( 'Object type' )

QualObj:        Qual        Type( *Generic )                                         +
                            Len( 10 )                                                +
                            SpcVal( ( *All ) )
                Qual        Type( *Name )                                            +
                            Len( 10 )                                                +
                            Dft( *LibL )                                             +
                            SpcVal(                                                  +
                                     ( *LibL    )                                    +
                                     ( *UsrLibL )                                    +
                                     ( *CurLib  )                                    +
                                     ( *All )                                        +
                                     ( *AllUsr )                                     +
                                 )                                                   +
                            Prompt( 'Library' )
```

Notice that the CPP declares file QADspObj in the DclF statement. This IBM-supplied file resides in library QSys and is a model for the output file that the DspObjD command creates. In other words, when you use DspObjD to create an output file, that output file is modeled on QADspObj's record format and associated fields. In the CPP, the DspObjD command creates output file ObjList, whose file description includes record format QLiDObjD and fields from the QADspObj file description.

Because we declare file QADspObj in the program, that's the file we must process. (Remember: You can declare only one file in the program, and file ObjList did not exist at compile time.) The CPP uses OvrDbF to override QADspObj to newly created file ObjList in library QTemp. When the RcvF command reads record format QLiDObjD, the override causes the RcvF to read records from file ObjList.

As it reads each record, the CL program substitutes data from the appropriate fields into the DspObjAut command and prints a separate authority report for each object represented in the file.

Now, you're ready to begin processing those database files with CL. Using CL programs to process display files is the next logical step and is the topic of Chapter 27.

FIGURE 26.3B

PrtObjAut Command Processing Program PrtObjAut1

```
/*  ===================================================================  */
/*  =  Program....... PrtObjAut1                                     =  */
/*  =  Source type... CLP                                            =  */
/*  =  Type.......... Command processing program for PrtObjAut       =  */
/*  =  Description... Print Object Authorities                       =  */
/*  =  -------------------------------------------------------------  =  */
/*  =  Parameters                                                    =  */
/*  =                                                                =  */
/*  =    &Obj             Input     Qualified object name            =  */
/*  =                                                                =  */
/*  =    &ObjType         Input     Object type                      =  */
/*  ===================================================================  */

Pgm         (                                                            +
              &Obj                                                       +
              &ObjType                                                   +
            )

/*  ===================================================================  */
/*  = Variable declarations                                          =  */
/*  ===================================================================  */

  Dcl         &Obj         *Char      (   20    )
  Dcl         &ObjType     *Char      (   10    )
  Dcl         &ObjName     *Char      (   10    )
  Dcl         &MsgID       *Char      (    7    )
  Dcl         &MsgF        *Char      (   10    )
  Dcl         &MsgFLib     *Char      (   10    )
  Dcl         &MsgDta      *Char      (  100    )
  Dcl         &ErrorFlag   *Lgl

/*  ===================================================================  */
/*  = File declaration                                               =  */
/*  ===================================================================  */

  DclF        QADspObj

/*  ===================================================================  */
/*  = Global error monitor                                           =  */
/*  ===================================================================  */

  MonMsg      ( CPF0000 MCH0000 ) Exec(                                  +
    GoTo        Error                  )

/*  ===================================================================  */
/*  =  Retrieve list of objects to a file                            =  */
/*  ===================================================================  */

  ChgVar      &ObjName     ( %Sst( &Obj  1 10 ) )
  ChgVar      &ObjLib      ( %Sst( &Obj 11 10 ) )

  DspObjD     Obj( &ObjLib/&ObjName )                                    +
              ObjType( &ObjType )                                        +
              Detail( *Basic )                                           +
              Output( *OutFile )                                         +
              OutFile( QTemp/ObjList )
```

continued

FIGURE 26.3B CONTINUED

```
/*  ==============================================================  */
/*  =  Read records in file ObjList and print authorities        =  */
/*  ==============================================================  */

  OvrDbF      File( QADspObj )                                      +
              ToFile( QTemp/ObjList )

ReadBegin:

  RcvF        RcdFmt( QLiDObjD )
  MonMsg      ( CPF0864 ) Exec(                                     +
    GoTo        Exit          )

  DspObjAut   Obj( &ODLbNm/&ODObNm )                                +
              ObjType( &ODObTp )                                    +
              Output( *Print )

  GoTo        ReadBegin

/*  ==============================================================  */
/*  = Error handler                                              =  */
/*  ==============================================================  */

Error:

  If          ( &ErrorFlag )                                        +
    Do
      SndPgmMsg  MsgID( CPF9897 )                                   +
                 MsgF( QSys/QCPFMsg )                               +
                 MsgDta( 'Error in PrtObjAut. See joblog.' )        +
                 MsgType( *Escape )
      MonMsg     ( CPF0000 MCH0000 ) Exec(                          +
        Return                             )
    EndDo

  ChgVar      &ErrorFlag  ( '1' )

  RcvMsg      MsgType( *Excp )                                      +
              MsgDta( &MsgDta )                                     +
              MsgID( &MsgID )                                       +
              MsgF( &MsgF )                                         +
              MsgFLib( &MsgFLib )

  MonMsg      ( CPF0000 MCH0000 )

  SndPgmMsg   MsgID( &MsgID )                                       +
              MsgF( &MsgFLib/&MsgF )                                +
              MsgDta( &MsgDta )                                     +
              MsgType( *Escape )

  MonMsg      ( CPF0000 MCH0000 )
```

continued

FIGURE 26.3B *CONTINUED*

```
/*  ==================================================================  */
/*  = Clean up and exit program                                     =  */
/*  ==================================================================  */

Exit:

  DltF        QTemp/ObjList
  MonMsg      ( CPFØØØØ MCHØØØØ )

/*  ==================================================================  */
/*  = End of program                                                =  */
/*  ==================================================================  */

EndPgm
```

Chapter 27

CL Programs and Display Files

In Chapter 26, we talked about processing database files using a CL program. We discussed declaring a file, extracting field definitions (both externally described and program-described), and processing database records. In this chapter, we discuss how CL programs work with display files.

CL is an appropriate choice for certain situations that require displays. For example, CL works well with display files for menus because CL is the language most commonly used to override files, change a user's library list, submit jobs, and check authorities — all common tasks in a menu environment.

CL is also a popular choice for implementing a friendly interface at which users can enter parameters for commands or programs that print reports or execute inquiries. For example, a CL program can present an easily understood panel to prompt the user for a beginning and ending date for use in a query management query. The program can then format and substitute those dates into a StrQMQry (Start Query Management Query) command to produce a report covering a certain period. When you want users to enter substitution values for use in a complex command such as OpnQryF (Open Query File), it's almost imperative that you let them enter selections in a format they understand (e.g., a prompt screen) and then build the command string in CL.

CL Display File Basics

As with a database file, you must use the DclF (Declare File) command to identify the display file with which you want to work in CL (for more details about declaring a file, see Chapter 26). Declaring the file lets the compiler locate it as well as retrieve the field and format definitions.

Figure 27.1 shows the Data Description Specifications (DDS) for a sample display file, UserMenuF, and Figure 27.2 (page 444) shows part of a compiler listing for a CL program that declares UserMenuF.

FIGURE 27.1

DDS for Display File UserMenuF

```
 *   ====================================================================
 *   = File.......... UserMenuF                                         =
 *   = Source type... DSPF                                              =
 *   = Description... Display file for UserMenu menu example            =
 *   ====================================================================

A                                       ERRSFL                              (A)
A                                       MSGLOC(24)
A                                       CA03(03)
A                                       PRINT
```

continued

FIGURE 27.1 CONTINUED

```
  *  ------------------------------------------------------------------
  *  - Main menu format                                               -
  *  ------------------------------------------------------------------

A          R MENU
A                                           KEEP
A                                           OVERLAY
A                                       1  2'USERMENU'
A                                           COLOR(BLU)
A                                       1 3Ø'Sample User Menu'
A                                           DSPATR(HI)
A                                       3  2'Select one of the following:'
A                                           COLOR(BLU)
A                                       5  7'1. Submit Batch Report 1'
A                                       6  7'2. Submit Batch Report 2'
A                                       7  7'3. Submit Batch Report 3'
A                                       8  7'4. Work with printed output'
A                                      19  2'Selection'
A                                      2Ø  2'===>'
A            OPTION         2Y ØI 2Ø  7
A                                      22  2'F3=Exit'
A                                           COLOR(BLU)

  *  ------------------------------------------------------------------
  *  - Message subfile                                                -
  *  ------------------------------------------------------------------

A          R MSGSFL                         SFL
A                                           SFLMSGRCD(24)
A            MSGKEY                         SFLMSGKEY
A            PGMQ                           SFLPGMQ
A          R MSGCTL                         SFLCTL(MSGSFL)
A                                           KEEP
A                                           SFLSIZ(1Ø)
A                                           SFLPAG(1)
A 4Ø                                        SFLINZ
A 4Ø                                        SFLEND
A                                           SFLDSPCTL
A                                           SFLDSP
A            PGMQ                           SFLPGMQ

  *  ------------------------------------------------------------------
  *  - Prompt for menu option 1                                       -
  *  ------------------------------------------------------------------

A          R PROMPTØ1                       CA12(12)
A                                       1  2'PROMPTØ1'
A                                           COLOR(BLU)
A                                       1 3Ø'Submit Batch Report 1'
A                                           DSPATR(HI)
A                                       4  2'Type the following, then press Ent-
A                                           er.'
A                                           COLOR(BLU)
A                                       7  4'Territory ID . . . . . . . . . . .'
```

(B) marks the MSGSFL record lines; (C) marks the two 4Ø lines (SFLINZ, SFLEND).

continued

Figure 27.1 *Continued*

```
A            TERRID         3   B  7 40
A  61                                  ERRMSG('Territory ID required.' 61)
A  62                                  ERRMSG('Invalid Territory ID.' 62)
A                                  8  4'Sales Rep ID . . . . . . . . . . .'
A            SLSREPID       3   B  8 40
A  63                                  ERRMSG('Sales Rep ID required.' 63)
A  64                                  ERRMSG('Invalid Sales Rep ID.' 64)
A                                 10  4'Ordered by . . . . . . . . . . . .'
A            ORDER          1   B 10 40VALUES('D' 'C' 'A')
A                                 10 44'(D)ate'
A                                 11 44'(C)ustomer'
A                                 12 44'(A)mount - Decreasing'
A                                 14  4'Detail type  . . . . . . . . . . .'
A            DETAIL         1   B 14 40VALUES('D' 'S')
A                                 14 44'(D)etail'
A                                 15 44'(S)ummary'
A                                 23  2'F3=Exit   F12=Cancel'
A                                      COLOR(BLU)
```

The default for DclF's RcdFmt (Record format) parameter, *All, tells the compiler to identify and retrieve the descriptions for all record formats in the file. Notice that the field and format definitions immediately follow the DclF statement on the compiler listing.

If your display file has many formats and you plan to use only one or a few of them, you can specify up to 99 different record formats in the RcdFmt parameter instead of using the *All default value. Doing so reduces the size of the compiled program object by eliminating unnecessary definitions.

After you declare a display file, you can output record formats to a display device using the SndF (Send File) command, read formats from the display device using the RcvF (Receive File) command, or perform both functions with the SndRcvF (Send/Receive File) command. These commands parallel RPG's Write, Read, and ExFmt opcodes, respectively.

For instance, to present a record format named Prompt on the display, you could code your CL as either

```
SndF RcdFmt(Prompt)
RcvF RcdFmt(Prompt)
```

or

```
SndRcvF RcdFmt(Prompt)
```

To send more than one format to the screen at once — for example, a standard header format, a function key format, and an input-capable format — you use a combination of the SndF and SndRcvF commands as you'd use a combination of Write and ExFmt in RPG:

```
SndF    RcdFmt(Header)
SndF    RcdFmt(FKeys)
SndRcvF RcdFmt(Detail)
```

Notice that the RcdFmt parameter value in each statement specifies the particular format for the operation. If only one format exists in the file, you can use RcdFmt's default value, *File, and then simply use the SndF, RcvF, or SndRcvF command without coding a parameter.

FIGURE 27.2

Partial CL Compiler Listing

```
5769SS1 V4R4M0  990521                    Control Language                        USER/USERMENU
Program . . . . . . . . . . . . . . . . . . . . :   USERMENU
  Library . . . . . . . . . . . . . . . . . . . :     USER
Source file . . . . . . . . . . . . . . . . . . :   QCLSRC
  Library . . . . . . . . . . . . . . . . . . . :     USER
Source member name  . . . . . . . . . . . . . . :   USERMENU   10/02/00 14:23:34
Source printing options . . . . . . . . . . . . :   *SOURCE  *XREF  *GEN  *NOSE
Program generation options  . . . . . . . . . . :   *NOLIST  *NOXREF  *NOPATCH
User profile  . . . . . . . . . . . . . . . . . :   *USER
Program logging . . . . . . . . . . . . . . . . :   *JOB
Allow RTVCLSRC command  . . . . . . . . . . . . :   *YES
Replace program . . . . . . . . . . . . . . . . :   *YES
Target release  . . . . . . . . . . . . . . . . :   V4R4M0
Authority . . . . . . . . . . . . . . . . . . . :   *LIBCRTAUT
Sort sequence . . . . . . . . . . . . . . . . . :   *HEX
Language identifier . . . . . . . . . . . . . . :   *JOBRUN
Text  . . . . . . . . . . . . . . . . . . . . . :
Compiler  . . . . . . . . . . . . . . . . . . . :   IBM AS/400 Control Language
                                       Control Language Source
SEQNBR  *...+... 1 ...+... 2 ...+... 3 ...+... 4 ...+... 5 ...+... 6 ...+...
   100- /*  ===========================================================
   200- /*  =  Program....... UserMenu                                 =
   300- /*  =  Description... Sample CL menu program                   =
   400- /*  ===========================================================
   500-
   600- Pgm
   700-
   800- /*  ===========================================================
   900- /*  =  File declaration                                        =
  1000- /*  ===========================================================
  1100-
  1200-   DclF       File( UserMenuF )
  1300               RcdFmt( *All )
        QUALIFIED FILE NAME - USER/USERMENUF
           RECORD FORMAT NAME - MENU
             CL VARIABLE      TYPE     LENGTH     PRECISION     TEXT
              &IN03           *LGL        1
              &OPTION         *DEC        2           0
           RECORD FORMAT NAME - MSGSFL
             CL VARIABLE      TYPE     LENGTH     PRECISION     TEXT
              &IN03           *LGL        1
              &MSGKEY         *CHAR       4
              &PGMQ           *CHAR      10
           RECORD FORMAT NAME - MSGCTL
             CL VARIABLE      TYPE     LENGTH     PRECISION     TEXT
              &IN03           *LGL        1
              &IN40           *LGL        1
              &PGMQ           *CHAR      10
           RECORD FORMAT NAME - PROMPT01
             CL VARIABLE      TYPE     LENGTH     PRECISION     TEXT
              &IN03           *LGL        1
              &IN12           *LGL        1
              &IN61           *LGL        1                     Territory ID required.
              &IN62           *LGL        1                     Invalid Territory ID.
              &IN63           *LGL        1                     Sales Rep ID required.
              &IN64           *LGL        1                     Invalid Sales Rep ID.
              &TERRID         *CHAR       3
              &SLSREPID       *CHAR       3
              &ORDER          *CHAR       1
              &DETAIL         *CHAR       1
```

CL Display File Examples

Let's look at an example of how to use CL with a display file for a menu and a prompt screen. Figure 27.3 shows a menu based on the DDS in Figure 27.1 (page 441).

FIGURE 27.3
Sample User Menu

```
USERMENU                          Sample User Menu

Select one of the following:

      1. Submit Batch Report 1
      2. Submit Batch Report 2
      3. Submit Batch Report 3
      4. Work with printed output










Selection
===> __

F3=Exit
```

From the DDS, you can see that record format Menu displays the list of menu options, and record formats MsgSfl and MsgCtl control the message subfile function that sends messages to the program message queue. Record format Prompt01 is a panel that lets the user enter selection values for Batch Report 1.

Figure 27.4 shows CL program UserMenu, the driving program for this menu. As you can see, UserMenu sets up variable &PgmQ to hold the program message queue name, displays the menu, and then, depending on user input, either executes the code that corresponds to the selected menu option or exits the menu.

The sample menu's options, option selection field, and function key description are all part of the Menu record format on the DDS. To display this information to the user and allow input, program UserMenu uses the SndRcvF command. Should the user enter an invalid menu option, the program displays an error message at the bottom of the screen by displaying message subfile record format MsgCtl (at **C**). (We discuss this record format in more detail in a moment.) Figure 27.5 (page 449) shows a completion message at the bottom of the sample menu.

FIGURE 27.4

CL Menu Driver

```
/*  ================================================================  */
/*  =  Program....... UserMenu                                    =  */
/*  =  Description... Sample CL menu program                      =  */
/*  ================================================================  */

Pgm

/*  ================================================================  */
/*  =  File declaration                                           =  */
/*  ================================================================  */

  DclF        File( UserMenuF )                                      +
              RcdFmt( *All )

/*  ================================================================  */
/*  =  Global error monitor                                       =  */
/*  ================================================================  */

  MonMsg      ( CPF0000 MCH0000 ) Exec(                              +
    GoTo        DspMsg             )

/*  ================================================================  */
/*  =  Initialize program message queue control field             =  */
/*  ================================================================  */

(A)  ChgVar      &PgmQ        ( 'USERMENU' )

/*  ================================================================  */
/*  =  Display menu                                               =  */
/*  ================================================================  */

DspMenu:

  SndRcvF     RcdFmt( Menu )

(B)  RmvMsg      PgmQ( *Same * )                                     +
              Clear( *All )

  ChgVar      &In40        ( '0' )

/*  ----------------------------------------------------------------  */
/*  -  Exit selected with F3                                      -  */
/*  ----------------------------------------------------------------  */

  If          ( &In03 )                                              +
    GoTo        Exit

/*  ----------------------------------------------------------------  */
/*  -  Option 1                                                   -  */
/*  ----------------------------------------------------------------  */

  If          ( &Option *Eq 1 )                                      +
    Do
      ChgVar      &TerrID      ( ' ' )
      ChgVar      &Order       ( 'D' )
      ChgVar      &Detail      ( 'D' )
```

continued

FIGURE 27.4 CONTINUED

```
Prompt01:

      SndRcvF     RcdFmt( Prompt01 )

      If          ( &In03 )                                          +
        GoTo        Exit

      If          ( &In12 )                                          +
        Do
          SndPgmMsg  MsgID( CPF9897 )                                +
                     MsgF( QSys/QCPFMsg )                            +
                     MsgDta( 'User cancelled request.' )             +
                     ToPgmQ( *Same * )                               +
                     MsgType( *Diag )
          GoTo       DspMsg
        EndDo

      If          ( &TerrID *Eq ' ' )                                +
        ChgVar      &In61        ( '1' )

      If          ( %Sst( &TerrID 1 1 ) *NE 'T' )                    +
        ChgVar      &In62        ( '1' )

      If          ( &SlsRepID *Eq ' ' )                              +
        ChgVar      &In63        ( '1' )

      If          ( %Sst( &SlsRepID 1 1 ) *NE 'S' )                  +
        ChgVar      &In64        ( '1' )

      If          ( ( &In61 ) *Or                                    +
                    ( &In62 ) *Or                                    +
                    ( &In63 ) *Or                                    +
                    ( &In64 ) )                                      +
        GoTo        Prompt01

      SbmJob      Cmd( Call Batch01 ( &TerrID &Order &Detail ) )     +
                  Job( UserMenu01 )                                  +
                  JobD( QBatch )

    EndDo

/*  -------------------------------------------------------------   */
/*  -  Option 2                                                 -   */
/*  -------------------------------------------------------------   */

  If          ( &Option *Eq 2 )                                      +
    Do
    .
    .
    .
    EndDo

/*  -------------------------------------------------------------   */
/*  -  Option 3                                                 -   */
/*  -------------------------------------------------------------   */

  If          ( &Option *Eq 3 )                                      +
    Do
    .
    .
    .
    EndDo
```

continued

FIGURE 27.4 CONTINUED

```
/*  -----------------------------------------------------------------   */
/*  -  Option 4                                                     -   */
/*  -----------------------------------------------------------------   */

  If          ( &Option *Eq 4 )                                          +
    Do
    .
    .
    .
    EndDo

/*  -----------------------------------------------------------------   */
/*  -  Invalid option                                               -   */
/*  -----------------------------------------------------------------   */

  If          ( ( &Option *NE 1 ) *And                                   +
                ( &Option *NE 2 ) *And                                   +
                ( &Option *NE 3 ) *And                                   +
                ( &Option *NE 4 ) )                                      +
    Do
      SndPgmMsg  MsgID( CPF9897 )                                        +
                 MsgF( QSys/QCPFMsg )                                    +
                 MsgDta( 'Invalid option.' )                             +
                 ToPgmQ( *Same * )                                       +
                 MsgType( *Diag )
    EndDo

/*  =================================================================   */
/*  = Display messages                                              =   */
/*  =================================================================   */

DspMsg:

  ChgVar      &In40         ( '1' )

  SndF        RcdFmt( MsgCtl )
  MonMsg      ( CPF0000 MCH0000 ) Exec(                                  +
    Do                                 )
      SndPgmMsg  MsgID( CPF9897 )                                        +
                 MsgF( QSys/QCPFMsg )                                    +
                 MsgDta( 'Error in UserMenu. See joblog.' )              +
                 MsgType( *Escape )
      MonMsg     ( CPF0000 MCH0000 ) Exec(                               +
        Return                                 )
    EndDo

  GoTo        DspMenu

/*  =================================================================   */
/*  = Exit program                                                  =   */
/*  =================================================================   */

Exit:

EndPgm
```

Ⓒ

FIGURE 27.5
Sample Message Subfile Display

```
USERMENU                    Sample User Menu

Select one of the following:

     1. Submit Batch Report 1
     2. Submit Batch Report 2
     3. Submit Batch Report 3
     4. Work with printed output








Selection
===> __

F3=Exit

Job 006073/GUTHRIE/USERMENU01 submitted to job queue QBATCH in library QGPL.
```

Using a Message Subfile

The message subfile is a special form of subfile whose definition includes some predefined variables and special keywords. The message subfile record format is format MsgSfl (**B** in Figure 27.1, page 442). The keyword SflMsgRcd(24) tells the display file to display the messages in this subfile beginning on line 24 of the panel. You can specify any line number for this keyword that is valid for the panel you're displaying.

The associated SflMsgKey keyword and the variable MsgKey support the tasks of retrieving a message from the program message queue associated with the SflPgmQ keyword (i.e., the message queue named in variable &PgmQ) and displaying the message in the form of a subfile. The CL program assigns the value USERMENU to variable &PgmQ (at **A** in Figure 27.4, page 446), thus specifying that the program message queue to be displayed is the one associated with program UserMenu.

MsgCtl, the next record format in the DDS, uses the standard subfile keywords (e.g., SflSiz, SflInz, SflDsp) along with the SflPgmQ keyword. This record format establishes the message subfile for this display file with the SflSiz value of 10 and the SflPag value of 1. In other words, the message subfile will hold up to 10 messages and will display one message on each page. Because of the value of the SflMsgRcd keyword in the MsgSfl format, the message will be displayed on line 24. You can alter the SflMsgRcd and SflPag values to display as many messages as you like and have room for on the screen. If more than one page of messages exists, the user can scroll through the pages by pressing Page up and Page down.

You might be asking, "What does program UserMenu have to do to fill the message subfile?" The answer: absolutely nothing! This fact often confuses programmers new to message subfiles because they can't figure out how to load the subfile. You can think of the message subfile as simply a mechanism by which you can view the messages on the program message queue. By changing the value of variable &PgmQ to USERMENU, we specified which program message queue to associate with the message subfile. That's all it takes.

At **C** in Figure 27.4 (page 448), you can see that we change indicator 40 (variable &In40) to '1' (on) and then output format MsgCtl using the SndF command. In the DDS, indicator 40 controls the SflInz and SflEnd keywords (**C** in Figure 27.1, page 442) to initialize the subfile before loading it and to display the appropriate plus sign (+) or blank to let the user know whether more subfile records exist beyond those currently displayed. (You can specify SflEnd(*More) if you prefer to have the message subfile use the "More..." and "Bottom" text).

When the program outputs the MsgCtl format, the &PgmQ and &MsgKey variables coded in the MsgSfl record format cause all messages to be retrieved from the program message queue and presented in the subfile. The user can move the cursor onto a message and press the Help key to get secondary text (when it is available) and can scroll through all the error messages in the subfile.

At **B** in Figure 27.4 (page 446), the RmvMsg (Remove Message) command clears all (*All) messages from the current program queue (i.e., queue UserMenu). Clearing the queue at the beginning of the program ensures that old messages from a previous invocation do not remain in the queue.

Using an Error Subfile

Figure 27.6 shows a prompt screen a user might receive to specify selections for a menu option that submits a report program to batch. The user keys the appropriate values and presses Enter to submit the report. If the program encounters an error when validating the entered values, the display file uses an error subfile to display the error message at the bottom of the screen, like the error message shown in Figure 27.7.

To indicate an error subfile, you use the ErrSfl keyword in the DDS (**A** in Figure 27.1, page 441). An error subfile provides a different function than a message subfile. The error subfile automatically presents any error messages generated as a result of DDS message or validity-checking keywords (e.g., Check, ErrMsg, SflMsg, Values). The purpose of the error subfile is to group error messages generated by these keywords for a particular record format, not to view messages on the program message queue.

FIGURE 27.6
Prompt Screen to Specify Selections

```
PROMPT01                      Submit Batch Report 1

Type the following, then press Enter.

  Territory ID . . . . . . . . . . . .  T01
  Sales Rep ID . . . . . . . . . . . .  S04

  Ordered by . . . . . . . . . . . . .  D   (D)ate
                                            (C)ustomer
                                            (A)mount - Decreasing

  Detail type  . . . . . . . . . . . .  D   (D)etail
                                            (S)ummary




F3=Exit   F12=Cancel
```

FIGURE 27.7
Sample Error Subfile Display

```
PROMPT01                      Submit Batch Report 1

Type the following, then press Enter.

  Territory ID . . . . . . . . . . . .  T01
  Sales Rep ID . . . . . . . . . . . .  ___

  Ordered by . . . . . . . . . . . . .  D   (D)ate
                                            (C)ustomer
                                            (A)mount - Decreasing

  Detail type  . . . . . . . . . . . .  D   (D)etail
                                            (S)ummary




F3=Exit   F12=Cancel
Sales Rep ID required.
```

Considerations

CL's lack of support for user-written subfiles limits the usefulness of display files within CL in applications that require user interaction. However, in many common situations, CL's strengths more than offset these limitations. CL's command-processing, message-handling, and string-manipulation capabilities make it a good choice for menus, prompt screens, and other nondatabase-related screen functions.

Although it's not always appropriate, for many basic interactive applications CL offers a simple alternative to a high-level language for display file processing. With this knowledge under your belt, you can choose the best and easiest language for applications that use display files.

Chapter 28

OpnQryF Fundamentals

The basic function of the OpnQryF (Open Query File) command is to open one or more database files and present records in response to a query request. Under the covers, OpnQryF creates an open data path (ODP) that programs can then use in obtaining input. This ODP appears to programs as a single database file containing only the records that satisfy the query selection criteria. In essence, OpnQryF works as a filter that determines the way your programs see the file or files being opened.

You can use the OpnQryF command to perform a variety of database functions, including to

- join records from more than one file
- group records
- perform aggregate calculations such as sum and average
- select records before or after grouping
- sort records by one or more key fields
- calculate new fields using numeric or character string operations

Although OpnQryF is powerful, its syntax can be confusing. In this chapter, we provide the foundation for OpnQryF use. You'll want to spend some time studying OpnQryF so you can maximize the benefit the command provides.

First Things First

One crucial point to remember when using OpnQryF is that you must share the ODP the command creates so your programs can use the ODP to obtain their input. To share the ODP, you must use the Share(*Yes) file attribute for each file opened by the OpnQryF command. When you specify Share(*Yes), subsequent opens of the same file will share the original ODP and thus see the file as presented by the OpnQryF process. If OpnQryF opens a file using the Share(*No) attribute, the next open of the file will not use the ODP created by the OpnQryF command but instead will perform another full open of the file. You must also be aware of the file open scope. You must properly scope the open so your programs will work properly. (If you've not done so yet, this would be a good time to read Chapter 23, where we discuss sharing ODPs and the scope of file opens.)

Tip

Don't assume the file description already has the Share(*Yes) value when you use the OpnQryF command. Instead, always use the OvrDbF (Override with Database File) command just before executing OpnQryF to explicitly specify Share(*Yes) for each file to be opened. Be aware that the OpnQryF command ignores any parameters on the OvrDbF command other than ToFile, Mbr, LvlChk, WaitRcd, SeqOnly, InhWrt, and Share.

The Command

Figure 28.1 shows the entire OpnQryF command. OpnQryF has five major groups of parameters — specifications for file, format, key field, join field, and mapped field — plus a few extra parameters not in a group. Using the OpnQryF command is easier once you master the parameter groups.

Some strong (but awkwardly structured) parallels exist between OpnQryF parameters and specific Structured Query Language (SQL) concepts. For instance:

- OpnQryF's file and format specifications parallel the more basic functions of the SQL Select and From statements.
- OpnQryF's query selection expression parallels SQL's Where statement.
- OpnQryF's key field specifications parallel SQL's Order By statement.
- OpnQryF's grouping field names expression parallels SQL's Group By statement.
- OpnQryF's group selection parallels SQL's Having statement.

If you compare OpnQryF with SQL, you'll see that the OpnQryF command is basically a complicated SQL front end that offers a few extra parameters.

Start with a File and a Format

For every query, there must be data — and for data, there must be a file. OpnQryF's File specifications parameters identify the file or files that contain the data. A simple OpnQryF command might name a single file, like this:

```
OpnQryF File(MyLib/MyFile) ...
```

This partial command identifies MyLib/MyFile as the file to be queried. Notice that the File parameter in Figure 28.1 has three separate parameter elements: the qualified file name, data member, and record format. A specified file must be a physical or logical file, an SQL view, or a Distributed Data Management (DDM) file. In the sample command above, we've specified the qualified file name only and have not entered a specific value for the second and third elements of the File parameter. Therefore, the default values of *First and *Only are used for the member and record format, respectively.

FIGURE 28.1
OpnQryF Command Panel

```
                        Open Query File (OPNQRYF)

Type choices, press Enter.

File specifications:              FILE            _
  File . . . . . . . . . . . . .                    __________
    Library  . . . . . . . . . .                      *LIBL_____
  Member . . . . . . . . . . . .                    *FIRST____
  Record format  . . . . . . . .                    *ONLY_____
                         + for more values        _
Open options . . . . . . . . . . OPTION             *INP
                         + for more values          ____
Format specifications:            FORMAT
  File . . . . . . . . . . . . .                    *FILE_____
    Library  . . . . . . . . . .                      __________
  Record format  . . . . . . . .                    __________
Query selection expression . . . QRYSLT             *ALL___________________________
_______________________________________________________________________________
_______________________________________________________________________________
_______________________________________________________________________________
_______________________________________________________________________________
_______________________________________________________________________________
_______________________________________________________________________________
_ ...
Key field specifications:         KEYFLD          _
  Key field  . . . . . . . . . .                    *NONE_____
    File or element  . . . . . .                      __________
  Key field order  . . . . . . .                    ________
  Order by absolute value  . . .                    _______
                         + for more values        _
Unique key fields  . . . . . . . UNIQUEKEY          *NONE_
Join field specifications:        JFLD            _
  From field . . . . . . . . . .                    *NONE_____
    File or element  . . . . . .                      __________
  To field . . . . . . . . . . .                    __________
    File or element  . . . . . .                      __________
  Join operator  . . . . . . . .                    ___
                         + for more values        _
Join with default values . . . . JDFTVAL            *NO______
Join file order  . . . . . . . . JORDER             *ANY_
Grouping field names . . . . . . GRPFLD             *NONE_____
  File or element  . . . . . . .                      __________
                         + for more values          __________
                                                      __________
Group selection expression . . . GRPSLT             *ALL___________________________
_______________________________________________________________________________
_______________________________________________________________________________
_______________________________________________________________________________
_______________________________________________________________________________
_______________________________________________________________________________
_______________________________________________________________________________
_ ...
```

continued

FIGURE 28.1 *CONTINUED*

```
Mapped field specifications:     MAPFLD         _
  Mapped field . . . . . . . . .                *NONE_____
  Field definition expression  .                ______________________________
_______________________________________________________________________________
_______________________________________________________________________________
_________________________________________________________________________

  Mapped field type  . . . . . .                _________
  Length . . . . . . . . . . . .                ______
  Decimal positions  . . . . . .                ______
  Mapped field CCSID . . . . . .                ___________
                   + for more values            _
Ignore decimal data errors . . . IGNDECERR      *NO_
Open file identifier . . . . . . OPNID          *FILE_____
Limit to sequential only:        SEQONLY
  Sequential only  . . . . . . .                *YES
  Number of records  . . . . . .                ______
Commitment control active  . . . COMMIT         *NO_
Open scope . . . . . . . . . . . OPNSCOPE       *ACTGRPDFN
Duplicate key check  . . . . . . DUPKEYCHK      *NO_
Allow copy of data . . . . . . . ALWCPYDTA      *YES
Performance optimization:        OPTIMIZE
  Performance optimization . . .                *ALLIO__
  Number of records  . . . . . .                ___________
Optimize all access paths  . . . OPTALLAP       *NO_
Sort sequence  . . . . . . . . . SRTSEQ         *JOB______
  Library  . . . . . . . . . . .                  __________
Language ID  . . . . . . . . . . LANGID         *JOB______
Final output CCSID . . . . . . . CCSID          *JOB_______

                          Additional Parameters

Type of open . . . . . . . . . . TYPE           *NORMAL
```

You can select a particular data member to query by supplying a member name. You can also select a specific record format. The default value of *Only for record format tells the iSeries database manager to use the only record format named in the file. When the file has more than one record format, you must use the record format element of the File parameter to name the particular record format to use.

You can enter a plus sign (+) in the "+ for more values" field and enter multiple file specifications to be dynamically joined (as opposed to creating a permanent join logical file on the system). When joining more than one record format, you must enter values in the Join field specifications parameter (JFld) to specify the field (or fields) the database manager will use to perform the join.

OpnQryF's Format parameter specifies the format for records made available by the command. The fields defined in this record format must be different from those named in the File and MapFld (Mapped field) parameters. When you use the default value of *File for the Format parameter, the record format of the file defined in the File parameter is used for the records selected. You cannot use Format(*File) when the File parameter references more than one file, member, or record format.

To return to our example, if you used

```
OpnQryF File(MyLib/MyFile) ...
```

the record format of file MyFile would be used for the records presented by the OpnQryF command. On the other hand, if you used the command

```
OvrDbF File(MyJoin)          +
       ToFile(MyLib/MyFile) +
       Share(*Yes)
```

with this OpnQryF command

```
OpnQryF File(MyLib/MyFile) +
        Format(MyJoin)
```

the database manager would use the record format for file MyJoin.

The Format parameter can specify a qualified file name and a record format (e.g., (MyLib/MyJoin JoinR)), or it can simply name the file containing the format to be used (e.g., (MyJoin)). Although you can select (via the QrySlt parameter) any fields defined in the record format of the file named in the File parameter, OpnQryF will make available only those fields defined by the record format named in the Format parameter. In the previous example, the high-level language (HLL) program would open file MyJoin, and the OvrDbF command would redirect the open to the queried file, MyLib/MyFile. The format for MyJoin would present records from MyFile. Later, in the discussion of field mapping, we'll explain why you might want to do this.

Because this chapter is only an introduction to OpnQryF, we don't discuss join files further. Instead, we focus on creating queries for single-file record selection, sorting, mapping fields, and HLL processing.

Record Selection

As we said earlier, the record selection portion of the OpnQryF command parallels SQL's Where statement. The system performs record selection before it performs record grouping (the GrpFld parameter controls record grouping). The query selection expression, specified in parameter QrySlt, can be up to 5,000 characters long, must be enclosed in apostrophes (') — it constitutes a character expression — and can consist of one or more logical expressions connected by *And or *Or. Each logical expression must use at least one field. The OpnQryF command also offers built-in functions you can include in your expressions (e.g., %Range, %Sst, %Values, and %Wildcard).

The simple logical expression

```
QrySlt('DltCde = "D"')
```

instructs the database manager to select only records for which the field DltCde contains the constant value D. A more complex query might use the following expression:

```
QrySlt('CstNbr *Eq %Range(10000 49999) *And +
        CurDue *GT CrdLim              *And +
        CrdFlg *Eq "Y"')
```

In this example, CstNbr (customer number), CurDue (current due), and CrdLim (credit limit) are numeric fields, and CrdFlg (credit flag) is a character field. The QrySlt expression uses the %Range function to determine whether the CstNbr field is in the range of 10000 to 49999 and then checks whether CurDue is greater than the credit limit. Last, it tests field CrdFlg against the value Y. When all tests are true for a record in the file, that record is selected.

QrySlt Guidelines

You can minimize trips to the manual by remembering a few rules about the QrySlt parameter. The following guidelines can help you avoid many common CL programming mistakes.

QrySlt and Constants

When the system parses the QrySlt expression, it determines whether a constant is character or numeric by the absence or presence of enclosing apostrophes or quotation marks ("). Consider the following examples:

Example 1:

```
'CustID *Eq 123'
```

Example 2:

```
'CustID *Eq "123"'
```

In example 1, the system compares a numeric customer ID field with the constant value 123. The value 123 is numeric because it doesn't appear within surrounding apostrophes or quotation marks (the apostrophes at the beginning and end of the expression apply to the QrySlt parameter expression itself). Example 2 shows the syntax to use when you want to compare a character customer ID field. Notice that quotation marks surround the value 123, making it a character constant. The rules regarding constants state that you don't enclose numeric constants within apostrophes or quotation marks and you must enclose character constants within apostrophes or quotation marks.

In reality, the use of constants in QrySlt expressions usually isn't a major source of confusion. This is true because not only are the rules easy to remember, but the syntax is intuitive as well. One look at the examples and this is reasonably obvious.

The most important thing you can learn from this discussion about using constants in the QrySlt expression is the *form* of the expression. Understanding QrySlt's form is essential to understanding how to use variables — where the real source of confusion lies — in the expression. A quick dissection of the QrySlt parameter reveals that its form is quite simply

```
'Expression'
```

Right about now, you're probably thinking, "No kidding?" We're not, though. Our point is that mastering the QrySlt parameter can be quite simple if you methodically pick apart its syntax piece by piece. The lesson here is that there are three elements to the QrySlt parameter: the opening apostrophe, the expression, and the closing apostrophe. In the case of the two examples above, the *Expression* element is

In Example 1:

```
CustID *Eq 123
```

In Example 2:

```
CustID *Eq "123"
```

From this, you can see that *Expression* consists of three elements:

```
Field Operator Operand
```

In both examples, *Field* is CustID and *Operator* is *Eq. *Operand* can take one of two forms, either numeric (123) or character ("123") in the examples. (For brevity's sake, we discuss only numeric and character values here.) The lesson in this step is that the complete QrySlt statement takes the form

```
'Field Operator Operand'
```

and that the data type of *Operand* determines the syntax used in specifying it (i.e., with or without quotation marks).

The final lesson in this section is that OpnQryF *always* sees the QrySlt parameter in this form, even when you use variable substitution in the QrySlt parameter. That's because CL performs the variable substitution before OpnQryF processes the QrySlt expression.

QrySlt and Variables

Without a doubt, the use of variables in the QrySlt expression introduces an added level of complexity, which leads to confusion, which in turn leads to errors. For example, assume you want to use variable substitution with the two examples we just discussed. The most common mistake is to construct the QrySlt statement as

```
'CustID *Eq &SelectID'
```

It's natural to make this mistake. After all, it sure looks right! The problem with this expression is that the system interprets &SelectID as a constant because it's part of the expression enclosed within apostrophes.

It's interesting that this mistake is so common when you consider that programmers rarely make the same mistake on other commands that function similarly with respect to variable substitution. One such command is the ChgVar (Change Variable) command. For example, consider a scenario in which the value of CL variable &SelectID is "A47" and you want to set another variable, &Prompt, to the value "Selection: A47" using variable substitution. Few would code the following erroneous statement

```
ChgVar Var(&Prompt)                +
       Value('Selection: &SelectID')
```

which would produce the value "Selection: &SelectID" for variable &Prompt. Instead, most would correctly code

```
ChgVar Var(&Prompt)                        +
       Value('Selection:' *BCat &SelectID)
```

setting &Prompt's value to "Selection: A47".

The first rule when using variable substitution in the QrySlt parameter is that you must *concatenate* variables into the expression, just as you concatenate variables on the ChgVar command when using compound values. Just how you concatenate the variables is the most confusing aspect of constructing the QrySlt parameter. For instance, as is the case with the ChgVar command, you can concatenate only character variables. If you need to substitute a numeric value into the QrySlt expression, you must first place the value in a character field (using the ChgVar command) and then concatenate the character field into the expression.

The trickiest part of concatenating variables into the QrySlt expression is making sure you have the expression's form correct, as we previously mentioned. Again, breaking down the expression into its individual components makes it much easier to construct the string properly. Let's take another look at our two examples, this time with an eye to using variable substitution rather than constants. Assume that the goal is to select records in which field CustID is equal to the value in CL variable &SelectID. Let's see how to code the QrySlt statement for numeric and for character fields.

Recall that the expression's form is

```
'Field Operator Operand'
```

Let's break this down into its components. First, there's the opening and closing apostrophe. You might find it useful to actually code the expression piece by piece, so you might enter the following in your source:

```
'                          '
```

The other known, nonvariable elements are the database field (CustID) and the operator (*Eq). Let's insert these into the line above as follows:

```
'CustID *Eq                '
```

Now, all that's left to code is the variable portion of the expression. Because we have only variable information left to insert into the expression, we can rid the statement of the extraneous spaces appearing after the *Operator* element. Our statement now is

```
'CustID *Eq'
```

So far, we've coded all elements of the QrySlt expression except the *Operand* element. Everything we've shown to this point will work regardless of the data type of the variable to be concatenated into the expression. Next, let's see how to insert a numeric variable into the QrySlt expression. First, look at the following CL declarations:

```
Dcl  Var(&CustIDNbr) Type(*Dec) Len(3 0)
Dcl  Var(&SelectID) Type(*Char) Len(3)
```

Variable &CustIDNbr contains the numeric customer ID for which we want to select records. Remember, though, that you can concatenate only character variables. For that reason, we've defined character variable &SelectID, into which we can place the value of &CustIDNbr. After you issue the command

```
ChgVar   &SelectID   &CustIDNbr
```

you can concatenate variable &Select ID into the QrySlt expression. There must be a blank between *Operator* (*Eq) and *Operand*, so you use function *BCat as follows to insert into the QrySlt expression the customer ID for which to select records:

```
'CustID *Eq' *BCat &SelectID
```

We now have the final QrySlt expression. Your OpnQryF statement resembles the following:

```
OpnQryF File(CstHist)                            +
        QrySlt('CustID *Eq' *BCat &SelectID)
```

That wasn't so bad, was it?

Now, let's examine the most confusing case — when the customer ID field is a character field. The confusion lies in the fact that when *Operand* is character, you must enclose it within apostrophes or quotation marks.

Remember, the first few steps of constructing the QrySlt expression are the same regardless of the type of variable we want to insert. Let's begin this example after those steps that construct the following portion of the expression:

```
'CustID *Eq'
```

All that remains is to concatenate the variable portion. First, we concatenate the opening quotation mark for the character data, remembering to insert a blank first. The expression is now

```
'CustID *Eq' *BCat '"'
```

Next, we concatenate the variable, so that the expression is

```
'CustID *Eq' *BCat '"' *Cat &SelectID
```

Last, we add the closing quotation mark. The expression is now

```
'CustID *Eq' *BCat '"' *Cat &SelectID *Cat '"'
```

and the QrySlt expression is complete. It resembles

```
OpnQryF File(CstHist)                                        +
        QrySlt('CustID *Eq' *BCat '"' *Cat &SelectID *Cat '"')
```

Some programmers find it easier to avoid the literal quotation marks in the expression. You can do this by setting a program variable's value to the quotation mark and using this variable as you construct the QrySlt expression. For example, the statements

```
Dcl  Var(&Quote) Type(*Char) Len(1) Value('"')
OpnQryF File(CstHist)                                               +
        QrySlt('CustID *Eq' *BCat &Quote *Cat &SelectID *Cat &Quote)
```

result in the same QrySlt expression as the previous example. This is simply a matter of preference.

Note

The examples so far have all shown character variables enclosed within quotation marks. You may remember that we said apostrophes work as well. If you prefer to use apostrophes, you must code two of them to replace a quotation mark. In other words, rather than coding apostrophe-quote-apostrophe, you code apostrophe-apostrophe-apostrophe-apostrophe. Be careful if you decide to use apostrophes. You can code apostrophe-apostrophe-apostrophe, and the combination will pass Source Entry Utility's (SEU's) syntax checker. However, the QrySlt expression won't function in the intended manner. We prefer to use the quotation mark method exclusively because it is more intuitive and less error-prone.

Tip

If OpnQryF is failing in one of your programs, using the ChgJob (Change Job) command, set the LogCLPgm (Log CL program commands) attribute for your job to value *Yes. Then after you try to execute the OpnQryF command, display the job log, and you can see how your OpnQryF command's parameters look after variable substitution. Remember this tip. It will save you considerable time!

Differentiate Between Upper- and Lowercase Data

Character data in the QrySlt expression are case sensitive. You must therefore be careful to make sure your comparisons are coded in a way that accounts for this. If your data can be either upper or lower case, or is in mixed case, you might find the %Xlate function useful. This function lets you translate data using a translation table. Table QSysTrnTbl translates lowercase data to upper case. For instance, if CustID in our example is in mixed case, with some records containing customer ID ABC, some AbC, some aBC, and so on, the %Xlate function lets you select all these records. The syntax is as follows:

```
QrySlt('%Xlate(CustID QSysTrnTbl)...
```

That does it for the guidelines for using the QrySlt parameter. OpnQryF's GrpSlt (Group Selection expression) parameter functions exactly like the QrySlt parameter, except that the system performs selection after grouping records. The same QrySlt functions are available for the GrpSlt expression, and the same rules apply.

Key Fields

Besides selecting records, you can establish the order of the records OpnQryF presents to your HLL program by entering one or more key fields in the Key field specifications. The

KeyFld parameter consists of several elements. You must specify the field name, whether to sequence the field in ascending or descending order, whether to use absolute values for sequencing, and whether to enforce uniqueness.

Let's look at a couple of examples. The OpnQryF command

```
OpnQryF File(MyLib/MyFile) +
        QrySlt('...')      +
        KeyFld(CstNbr)
```

causes the selected records to appear in ascending order by customer number (because *Ascend is the default for the key field order). The command

```
OpnQryF File(MyLib/MyFile)                    +
        QrySlt('...')                         +
        KeyFld((CurBal *Descend) (CstNbr))
```

presents the selected records in descending order by current balance and then in ascending order by customer number.

Any key field you name in the KeyFld parameter must exist in the record format referenced by the Format parameter. The key fields specified in the KeyFld parameter can be mapped from existing fields, as long as the referenced field definition exists in the referenced record format. The KeyFld default value of *None tells the database manager to present the selected records in any order. Entering the value *File tells the query to use the access path definition of the file named in the File parameter to order the records.

Note

In Data Description Specifications (DDS), you can specify only fields from the primary file as key fields for a join logical file. With OpnQryF, however, you can use fields from any of the joined files as key fields.

Mapping Virtual Fields

One of the richer features of the OpnQryF command is its support of field mapping. The Mapped field specifications let you derive new fields (known as "virtual" fields in relational database terms) from fields in the queried record format. You can map fields using a variety of powerful built-in functions. For example, %Sst returns a substring of the field argument, %Digits converts numbers to characters, and %Xlate performs character translation using a translation table. You can use the resulting fields to select records and to sequence the selected records.

Look at the following OpnQryF statement:

```
OpnQryF File(InpDtl)                          +
        Format(Detail)                        +
        QrySlt('LinTot *GT 10000')            +
        KeyFld((CstNbr) (InvDte))             +
        MapFld((LinTot 'InvQty * IPrice'))
```

Fields InvQty (invoice item quantity) and IPrice (invoice item price) exist in physical file InpDtl. Mapped field LinTot (line total) exists in the Detail format, which is used as the format for the selected records. As each record is read from the InpDtl file, the calculation defined in the MapFld parameter ('InvQty * IPrice') is performed, and the value is placed in field LinTot. The database manager then uses the value in LinTot to determine whether to select or reject the record.

OpnQryF Command Performance

Whenever possible, the OpnQryF command uses an existing access path for record selection and sequencing. In other words, if you select all customer numbers in a specific range and an access path exists for CstNbr, the database manager will use that access path to perform the selection, thus enhancing the performance of the OpnQryF command. However, if the system finds no usable access path, it creates a temporary one — and creating an access path can take a long time at the machine level, especially if the file is large. Likewise, when you specify one or more key fields in your query, the database manager will use an existing access path if possible; otherwise, the database manager must create a temporary one, again potentially degrading performance.

Overall, the OpnQryF command provides flexibility that is sometimes difficult to emulate using only HLL programming and the native database. However, OpnQryF is a poor performer when the system must create many temporary access paths to fulfill the query request. You may also need to weigh flexibility against performance to decide which record-selection method is best for a particular application. To help you make a decision, you can use these guidelines:

- If the application is interactive, use OpnQryF sparingly. And unless the file is relatively small (i.e., fewer than 10,000 records), ensure that existing access paths support the selection and sequencing.
- If the application is a batch application run infrequently or only at night, you can use OpnQryF without hesitation, especially if it eliminates the need for logical files used only to support those infrequent or night jobs.
- If the application is run frequently and in batch during normal business hours, use OpnQryF when existing access paths support the selection and sequencing or when the files are relatively small. Use native database and HLL programming when the files are large (greater than 10,000 records) or when many (more than three or four) temporary access paths are required.

The next time a user requests a report that requires more than a few selections and whose records must be in four different sequences, use the OpnQryF command to do the work, and write one HLL program to do the reporting. . . . But remember, to be on the safe side, run the report at night!

Chapter 29

Teaching Programs to Talk

In Chapter 7, we covered the commands you can use to send impromptu messages from one user to another: SndMsg (Send Message), SndBrkMsg (Send Break Message), and SndNetMsg (Send Network Message). Programs can also use these commands to send an informational message to a user, but because these commands provide no means for the sending program to receive a user response, their use for communication between programs and users is limited.

In contrast, IBM-supplied command SndUsrMsg (Send User Message) and user-written command SndBrkMsgU both let a CL program send a message to a user and then receive a reply. Your program can then use this reply in its processing.

Putting SndUsrMsg to Work

Figure 29.1 shows the SndUsrMsg command screen.

FIGURE 29.1
SndUsrMsg Command Screen

```
                     Send User Message (SNDUSRMSG)

 Type choices, press Enter.
 Message text, or . . . . . . . . MSG              ______________________
_________________________________________________________________________
_________________________________________________________________________
_________________________________________________________________________
_________________________________________________________________________
__________
 Message identifier . . . . . . . MSGID            _______
 Message file . . . . . . . . . . MSGF             __________
   Library  . . . . . . . . . . .                   *LIBL
 Message data field values  . . . MSGDTA           ______________________
_________________________________________________________________________
_________________________________________________________________________
_________________________________________________________________________
_________________________________________________________________________
__________
 Valid reply values . . . . . . . VALUES           *NONE
______________
                       + for more values
______________
 Default reply value  . . . . . . DFT              *MSGDFT
______________
 Message type . . . . . . . . . . MSGTYPE          *INQ
 To message queue . . . . . . . . TOMSGQ           *
   Library  . . . . . . . . . . .                   __________
 To user profile  . . . . . . . . TOUSR            __________
 CL var for message reply . . . . MSGRPY           __________
 Translate table  . . . . . . . . TRNTBL           QSYSTRNTBL
   Library  . . . . . . . . . . .                   *LIBL
```

The message you send can be an impromptu message or one you've defined in a message file. To send an impromptu message, just type a message of up to 512 characters in the Msg (Message text) parameter. To use a predefined message, enter a message ID in the MsgID (Message identifier) parameter. The message you identify must exist in the message file named in the MsgF parameter.

The MsgDta (Message data field values) parameter lets you specify values to take the place of substitution variables in a predefined message. For example, message CPF2105, which is

```
Object &1 in &2 type *&3 not found
```

has three data substitution variables: &1, &2, and &3. When you use the SndUsrMsg command to send this message, you can also send a MsgDta string that contains the substitution values for these variables. If you supply the following in the MsgDta string

```
'CSTMAST   ARLIB     FILE   '
```

the message appears as

```
Object CSTMAST in ARLIB type *FILE not found
```

If you don't supply any MsgDta values, the message is sent without values (e.g., "Object in type * not found").

The character string specified in the MsgDta parameter is valid only for messages that have data substitution variables. It's important that the character string you supply is the correct length and that each substitution variable is positioned properly within the string. The previous example assumes that the message is expecting three variables (&1, &2, and &3) and that the expected length of each variable is 10, 10, and 7, respectively, making the entire MsgDta string 27 characters long. How do we know that? Because each system-defined message has a message description that includes detailed information about substitution variables, and we used the DspMsgD (Display Message Description) command to get this information for message CPF2105.

Every iSeries system is shipped with file QCPFMsg (a message file for OS/400 messages) and several other message files that support particular products. You can also create your own message files and message IDs that your applications can use to communicate with users or other programs. For more information about creating and using messages, see *OS/400 CL Programming* (SC41-5721).

The next parameter on the SndUsrMsg command is Values (Valid reply values), which lets you specify the value or values that will be accepted as the response to your message, if a response is requested. When you specify MsgType(*Inq) and specify a CL variable in the MsgRpy parameter (discussed later), the system automatically supplies a prompt for a response when it displays the message. The system then verifies the response against the valid values listed in the Values parameter. If the user enters an invalid value, the system displays a message saying that the reply was not valid and resends the inquiry message. To make sure the user knows which values are valid, you should list the valid values as part of your inquiry message.

In the Dft (Default reply value) parameter, you can supply a default reply to be used for an inquiry message when the message queue that receives the message is in the *Dft delivery mode or when an unanswered message is deleted from the message queue. The default value in the SndUsrMsg command overrides defaults specified in the message description of predefined messages. The system uses the default value when the message is sent to a message queue that is in the *Dft delivery mode, when the message is inadvertently removed from a message queue without a reply, or when a system reply list entry is used that specifies the *Dft reply.

Oddly enough, this value need not match any of the supplied values in the Values parameter. This oddity presents some subtle problems for programmers. If the system supplies a default value not listed in the Values parameter, the value is accepted. However, if a user types the default value as a reply and the default is not listed in the Values parameter, the system will notify the user that the reply was invalid. To avoid such a mess, we strongly recommend that you use only valid values (those listed in the Values parameter) when you supply a default value.

The MsgType (Message type) parameter lets you specify whether the message you're sending is an *Info (informational, the default) or *Inq (inquiry) message. Both kinds appear on the destination message queue as text, but an inquiry message also supplies a response line and waits for a reply.

The ToMsgQ (To message queue) parameter names the message queue that will receive the message. You can enter the name of any message queue on the local system, or you can use one of the following special values:

- * — instructs the system to send the message to the external message queue (*Ext) if the job is interactive or to message queue QSys/QSysOpr if the program is being executed in batch.
- *SysOpr — tells the system to send the message to the system operator message queue, QSys/QSysOpr.
- *Ext — instructs the system to send the message to the job's external message queue. Inquiry messages to batch jobs will automatically be answered with the default value or with a null value (*N) if no default is specified. Keep in mind that although messages can be up to 512 characters long for first-level text, only the first 76 characters will be displayed when messages are sent to *Ext.

The ToUsr (To user profile) parameter is similar to ToMsg but lets you specify the recipient by user profile instead of by message queue. You can enter the recipient's user profile, specify *SysOpr to send the message to the system operator at message queue QSys/QSysOpr, or enter *Requester to send the message to the current user profile for an interactive job or to the system operator message queue for a batch job.

One problem emerges when using the SndUsrMsg command to communicate with a user from the batch job environment. In the interactive environment, both the ToUsr and ToMsgQ parameters supply values that let you communicate easily with the external user of the job. In the batch environment, the only values provided for ToUsr and ToMsgQ direct messages to the system operator as the external user. There are no parameters to communicate with the user who submitted the job.

The CL code in Figure 29.2 solves this problem. When you submit a job, the MsgQ parameter on the SbmJob (Submit Job) command tells the system where to send a job completion message. You can retrieve this value using the RtvJobA (Retrieve Job Attributes) command and the SbmMsgQ and SbmMsgQLib return variables. The program in Figure 29.2 uses the RtvJobA command to retrieve the name of the message queue and then tests variable &Type to determine whether the current job is a batch job. If so, SndUsrMsg sends the message to the message queue defined by the &SbmMsgQ and &SbmMsgQLib variables. If the job is interactive, the SndUsrMsg command simply directs the message to the external user by specifying ToUsr(*Requester).

FIGURE 29.2

Sample CL Code for Communicating with the User of a Batch Job

```
/*  ==============================================================  */
/*  =  Program....... MsgSample1                                 =  */
/*  =  Source type... CLP                                        =  */
/*  =  Description... SndUsrMsg demonstration                    =  */
/*  ==============================================================  */

Pgm

/*  ==============================================================  */
/*  =  Variable declarations                                     =  */
/*  ==============================================================  */

  Dcl         &SbmMsgQ     *Char     (  10   )
  Dcl         &SbmMsgQLib  *Char     (  10   )
  Dcl         &Type        *Char     (   1   )

/*  ==============================================================  */
/*  =  Retrieve environment information                          =  */
/*  ==============================================================  */

  RtvJoBA     Type( &Type )                                          +
              SbmMsgQ( &SbmMsgQ )                                    +
              SbmMsgQLib( &SbmMsgQLib )

  .
  .
  .

/*  ==============================================================  */
/*  =  Send message to external user or submitter                =  */
/*  ==============================================================  */

/*  --------------------------------------------------------------  */
/*  -  If job is running in batch, send the message to the       -  */
/*  -  message queue retrieved from job attributes               -  */
/*  --------------------------------------------------------------  */

  If          ( &Type *Eq '0' )                                      +
    SndUsrMsg  Msg( 'The daily report is available for printing.' )  +
               MsgType( *Info )                                      +
               ToMsgQ( &SbmMsgQLib/&SbmMsgQ )
```

continued

FIGURE 29.2 CONTINUED

```
/*  ------------------------------------------------------------  */
/*  -  If job is running interactively, send the message to   -  */
/*  -  *Requester                                              -  */
/*  ------------------------------------------------------------  */

  If          ( &Type *Eq '1' )                                      +
    SndUsrMsg  Msg( 'The daily report is available for printing.' )  +
               MsgType( *Info )                                      +
               ToUsr( *Requester )

/*  ============================================================  */
/*  =  End of program                                          =  */
/*  ============================================================  */

EndPgm
```

You can use the SndUsrMsg command's MsgRpy (CL variable for message reply) parameter to specify a CL character variable (up to 132 characters long) to receive the reply to an inquiry message. Make sure the length of the variable is at least as long as the expected length of the reply; if the reply is too short, it will be padded with blanks to the right, but if the reply exceeds the length of the variable, it will be truncated. The first result causes no problem, but a truncated reply may cause an unexpected glitch in your program.

An inquiry message reply must be a character (alphanumeric) reply. If your application requires the retrieval of a numeric value, it's best to use Data Description Specifications (DDS) and a CL or high-level language (HLL) program to prompt the user for a reply. This approach ensures that validity checking is performed for numeric values.

Alas, the SndUsrMsg command also exhibits another oddity: If you don't specify a MsgRpy variable but do specify MsgType(*Inq), the command causes the job to wait for a reply from the message queue but doesn't retrieve the reply into your program.

The last parameter on the SndUsrMsg command is TrnTbl (Translate table), which lets you specify a translation table to process the response automatically. The default translation table is QSysTrnTbl, which translates lowercase characters (X'81' through X'A9') to uppercase characters. This option makes it possible for you to check only for uppercase replies (e.g., Y or N) rather than having to code painstakingly for all lowercase and uppercase possibilities (e.g., Y, y, N, n).

Figure 29.3 shows how the SndUsrMsg command might be implemented in a CL program. Notice that SndUsrMsg is first used for an inquiry message. The message is sent to *Requester to make sure the entire message text is displayed on the queue. The job determines whether the daily report has already been run for that day and, if it has, prompts the user to verify that the report should indeed be run again. The program checks for a valid reply of Y or N and takes appropriate action.

Also notice that the SndUsrMsg command is used again in Figure 29.3 to send informational messages that let the user know which action the program has completed (the completion of the task or the cancellation of the request to process the daily report, depending on the user reply). You'll find that supplying informational program-to-user messages will endear you to your users and help you avoid headaches (e.g., multiple submissions of the same job because a user wasn't sure the first job submission worked).

FIGURE 29.3

Sample CL Program Using SndUsrMsg

```
/*  ==============================================================  */
/*  =  Program....... MsgSample2                                 =  */
/*  =  Source type... CLP                                        =  */
/*  =  Description... SndUsrMsg demonstration                    =  */
/*  ==============================================================  */

Pgm

/*  ==============================================================  */
/*  =  Variable declarations                                     =  */
/*  ==============================================================  */

  Dcl        &Reply      *Char      (    1    )
  Dcl        &DailySts   *Char      (    1    )

/*  ==============================================================  */
/*  =  Retrieve daily report status                              =  */
/*  ==============================================================  */

  RtvDtaAra  DtaAra( DailyLib/DailyRpt )                              +
             RtnVar( &DailySts )

/*  ==============================================================  */
/*  =  If daily report has already run, prompt user to verify    =  */
/*  =  that the daily report should be executed again            =  */
/*  ==============================================================  */

  If         ( &DailySts *Eq 'Y' )                                    +
    Do

SendMsg:

      SndUsrMsg  Msg( 'The daily report has already been run today.'  +
                      *BCat                                           +
                      'Do you want to run it again? (Y,N)' )          +
                 Values( 'Y' 'N' )                                    +
                 Dft( 'N' )                                           +
                 MsgType( *Inq )                                      +
                 ToUsr( *Requester )                                  +
                 MsgRpy( &Reply )

      If         ( &Reply *Eq 'Y' )                                   +
        GoTo       RunRpt

      If         ( &Reply *Eq 'N' )                                   +
        GoTo       CnlRpt

      GoTo       SendMsg

    EndDo
```

continued

FIGURE 29.3 CONTINUED

```
/*  ==============================================================  */
/*  =  Run report                                                =  */
/*  ==============================================================  */

RunRpt:

  Call        DlyRpt
  SndUsrMsg   Msg( 'The daily report is available for printing.' )     +
              MsgType( *Info )                                         +
              ToUsr( *Requester )
  GoTo        End

/*  ==============================================================  */
/*  =  Cancel report                                             =  */
/*  ==============================================================  */

CnlRpt:

  SndUsrMsg   Msg( 'The daily report request has been canceled.' )     +
              MsgType( *Info )                                         +
              ToUsr( *Requester )

/*  ==============================================================  */
/*  =  End of program                                            =  */
/*  ==============================================================  */

End:

EndPgm
```

Send Break Messages to a User with SndBrkMsgU

One feature missing from the iSeries potpourri of messaging commands is the ability to direct a message to a user so that it interrupts him or her. Users, as message recipients, can choose to place their message queue in a delivery mode that causes messages to break; however, the message sender, whether an interactive user or a program, has no system-supplied command for doing so.

When you consider that users can sign on to multiple workstations, along with the nuances of object allocation, you can understand why the system doesn't provide this type of support. Where would the system actually display a break message if the user has multiple sessions? And, how could the system allocate the user's message queue properly with multiple sessions using it? For such reasons, the system sends break messages only to workstation message queues, where it knows there is a one-to-one relationship between message queue and physical device — no object allocation problems and no question as to where the system should display the message.

Although you can't send a break message to a user message queue, the QEZSndMg (Send Message) API lets you send a break message to a specified user. The API directs the message to the workstation message queue of any workstation to which the user is signed on. If the user isn't signed on at the time the system sends the message, the message is placed in the user message queue.

API QEZSndMg combines the functions of the SndMsg (Send Message) and SndBrkMsg (Send Break Message) commands. With it, you can

- send a message to one or more users or display stations
- send an inquiry message to more than one user
- send a break message to users
- send a break or inquiry message to all active users
- send an inquiry message to display stations

QEZSndMg requires no parameters, but 12 optional parameters determine

- the type of message sent (informational or inquiry)
- the delivery mode of the message (break or normal)
- the message text
- the users or display stations to receive the message
- the message queue to receive the reply to an inquiry message
- whether the Operational Assistant's Send a Message display is shown
- whether user profile names or display station names have been specified

Figure 29.4 describes the 12 QEZSndMg parameters and their possible values.

You can use QEZSndMg interactively from the command line or within a program. For instance, if you call the program from the command line and pass no parameters, the system presents the Operational Assistant Send a Message panel (Figure 29.5, page 475) where you can enter the message you want to send, along with its recipients and presentation information.

A user-written command interface to QEZSndMg brings an air of user-friendliness to the API. Fashioned after IBM's SndBrkMsg command, the SndBrkMsgU (Send Break Message to User) command (Figures 29.6A through 29.6C) makes it a snap to send break messages to users (i.e., to their workstation message queues). The command also adds the ability to send predefined messages based on a message ID. API QEZSndMg, by itself, supports only impromptu messages.

To keep the command simple, only one value is allowed for the ToUsr (To user profile) parameter. You may want to modify the command to accept a list of users or a generic name. Notice that in addition to the special values API QEZSndMg allows (*All, *SysOpr, and *AllAct), command SndBrkMsgU adds *Requester. When you specify this value, the message is sent to the user profile of the job containing the command.

FIGURE 29.4
API QEZSndMg Parameters

Two optional parameter groups make up the 12 parameters for API QEZSndMg (Send Message). If a batch job uses the API, you must specify all the parameters from both groups.

Optional Parameter Group 1

API QEZSndMg's first optional parameter group has nine parameters. If you specify any of these parameters, you must specify all nine.

Message type. This 10-byte character input field determines whether an informational (*Info) or inquiry (*Inq) message is sent. When an inquiry message is sent, the system appends the name of the user profile providing the reply to the beginning of the reply text.

Delivery mode. This 10-byte character input field determines how the message is delivered. Valid values are *Break and *Normal. In break (*Break) mode, the message interrupts the recipient at each workstation to which he or she is signed on. If the recipient isn't signed on, the message is sent to the user message queue. If the sender isn't authorized to send break messages, normal (*Normal) mode is used; in this mode, the delivery mode of the target message queue determines how the message is delivered.

Message text. This variable-length character input field contains the message to be sent. The maximum length of the text is 494 bytes. This parameter cannot be blank when used in a batch job or when the value of QEZSndMg's Show Send a Message display parameter (covered below) is N.

Length of message text. This four-byte binary input field specifies the number of bytes in the Message text parameter. Valid values are 0 through 494. The parameter value must be greater than 0 when used in a batch job or when the value of the Show Send a Message display parameter is N.

List of user profiles or displays. This parameter is an array of 10-byte character input fields containing the list of message queues to which the message is to be sent. The list can contain from 0 to 299 entries. QEZSndMg's Name type indicator parameter (covered below) indicates whether the list contains user profiles or workstations; the default is user profiles. You must specify at least one entry for this parameter when using it in a batch job or when the Show Send a Message display parameter value is N. You can also specify the following special values for this parameter:

- *All (all user message queues): When you use *All, it must be the only value in the list and the Name type indicator value cannot be *Dsp. Using *All requires *JobCtl special authority.
- *AllAct (all active user or workstation message queues): You can use *AllAct in combination with specific users or workstations, as well as with the special value *SysOpr.
- *SysOpr (the system operator message queue, QSysOpr): You can use *SysOpr in combination with specific users or workstations, as well as with special value *AllAct.

When the message is sent to workstation message queues, the system uses the library list to locate them.

continued

FIGURE 29.4 CONTINUED

Number of user profiles or displays. This four-byte binary input field specifies the number of user or workstation message queues specified. Valid values are 0 through 299. The parameter's value must be 1 when the value of the List of user profiles or displays parameter is *All. The value must be greater than 0 when the parameter is used in a batch job or when the Show Send a Message display parameter value is N.

Message sent indicator. This four-byte binary output field indicates whether the user pressed F10 to send a message from the Send a Message display. The return value will be one of the following:

- 0 No messages were sent.
- 1 One or more messages were sent.
- 2 One or more messages were sent, but one or more message queues specified are invalid.

Function requested. This four-byte binary output field indicates how the user exited the Send a Message display. The return value will be one of the following:

- –4 The user pressed the Exit key (F3).
- –8 The user pressed the Cancel key (F12).
- 0 The Send a Message display was not used.

Error code. This variable-length input/output structure contains the standard API error information.

Optional Parameter Group 2

API QEZSndMg's second optional parameter group has the following three parameters:

Show Send a Message display. This one-byte character input field determines whether the Send a Message display is to be displayed before the message is sent. Valid values are Y (the default) and N. Batch jobs must specify N for this parameter.

Qualified message queue name. This 20-byte character input field specifies the message queue to receive the reply for an inquiry message. The field contains a 10-byte message queue name followed by a 10-byte library name. If the parameter is blank or not specified, the reply is sent to the message queue specified in the sender's user profile. If the message is not an inquiry message, the parameter is ignored. Special values *LibL and *CurLib are valid for the library portion of the message queue name.

Name type indicator. This four-byte character input field specifies whether the message is being sent to user or workstation message queues. Valid values are *Usr (the default) and *Dsp. You cannot specify *Dsp when the Show Send a Message display parameter value is Y.

FIGURE 29.5

Operational Assistant Send a Message Panel

```
                              Send a Message

 Type information below, then press F10 to send.

   Message needs reply . . . . . .   N             Y=Yes, N=No

   Interrupt user . . . . . . . . .  N             Y=Yes, N=No

   Message text . . . . . . . . . .  ______________________________________
 ________________________________________________________________________
 ________________________________________________________________________
 ________________________________________________________________________
 ________________________________________________________________________
 ________________________________________________________________________
 _______________________________________________

   Send to . . . . . . . . . . . .  __________  Name, F4 for list
                                    __________
                                    __________
                                    __________
                                    __________
                                                                 More...
 F1=Help   F3=Exit   F10=Send   F12=Cancel
```

Although SndBrkMsgU supports inquiry messages, as does SndUsrMsg, the reply mechanism works differently. With SndUsrMsg, you receive the reply in a program variable. SndBrkMsgU, on the other hand, requires you to designate a message queue to receive the reply. Your program can access the reply by receiving messages from this designated message queue.

FIGURE 29.6A

SndBrkMsgU Command Source

```
/*  =================================================================  */
/*  =  Command....... SndBrkMsgU                                    =  */
/*  =  Source type... CMD                                           =  */
/*  =  Description... Send Break Message to User                    =  */
/*  =                                                               =  */
/*  =  CPP........... SndBrkMsgC                                    =  */
/*  =  VCP........... SndBrkMsgV                                    =  */
/*  =================================================================  */

             Cmd         Prompt( 'Send Break Message to User' )

             Parm        Kwd( Msg )                                     +
                         Type( *Char )                                  +
                         Len( 494 )                                     +
                         Vary( *Yes *Int4 )                             +
                         Prompt( 'Message text, or' )
```

continued

FIGURE 29.6A

```
           Parm       Kwd( MsgID )                                        +
                      Type( *Name )                                       +
                      Len( 7 )                                            +
                      Full( *Yes )                                        +
                      Prompt( 'Message identifier' )

           Parm       Kwd( MsgF )                                         +
                      Type( QMsgF )                                       +
                      Prompt( 'Message file' )

           Parm       Kwd( MsgDta )                                       +
                      Type( *Char )                                       +
                      Len( 494 )                                          +
                      Dft( *None )                                        +
                      SpcVal( ( *None ' ') )                              +
                      Prompt( 'Message data' )

           Parm       Kwd( ToUsr )                                        +
                      Type( *Name )                                       +
                      Len( 10 )                                           +
                      Dft( *Requester )                                   +
                      SpcVal(                                             +
                              ( *All )                                    +
                              ( *SysOpr )                                 +
                              ( *AllAct )                                 +
                              ( *Requester )                              +
                            )                                             +
                      Prompt( 'To user profile' )

           Parm       Kwd( MsgType )                                      +
                      Type( *Char )                                       +
                      Len( 5 )                                            +
                      Rstd( *Yes )                                        +
                      Dft( *Info )                                        +
                      Values(                                             +
                              *Info                                       +
                              *Inq                                        +
                            )                                             +
                      Prompt( 'Message type' )

           Parm       Kwd( RpyMsgQ )                                      +
                      Type( QRpyMsgQ )                                    +
                      Prompt( 'Message queue to get reply' )

QMsgF:     Qual       Type( *Name )                                       +
                      Len( 10 )                                           +
                      Min( 1 )

           Qual       Type( *Name )                                       +
                      Len( 10 )                                           +
                      Dft( *LibL )                                        +
                      SpcVal(                                             +
                              ( *LibL )                                   +
                              ( *CurLib )                                 +
                            )                                             +
                      Prompt( 'Library' )
```

continued

FIGURE 29.6A

```
QRpyMsgQ:     Qual      Type( *Name )                                      +
                        Len( 10 )                                          +
                        Dft( QSysOpr )

              Qual      Type( *Name )                                      +
                        Len( 10 )                                          +
                        Dft( *LibL )                                       +
                        SpcVal(                                            +
                                ( *LibL )                                  +
                                ( *CurLib )                                +
                              )                                            +
                        Prompt( 'Library' )

              Dep       Ctl( &Msg *Eq ' ' )                                +
                        Parm( ( MsgID ) )                                  +
                        MsgID( CPD2536 )

              Dep       Ctl( &Msg *NE ' ' )                                +
                        Parm(                                              +
                              ( MsgID )                                    +
                              ( MsgF )                                     +
                              ( MsgDta )                                   +
                            )                                              +
                        NbrTrue( *NE 1 )                                   +
                        MsgID( CPD2443 )

              Dep       Ctl( &Msg *NE ' ' )                                +
                        Parm(                                              +
                              ( MsgID )                                    +
                              ( MsgF )                                     +
                              ( MsgDta )                                   +
                            )                                              +
                        NbrTrue( *NE 2 )                                   +
                        MsgID( CPD2443 )

              Dep       Ctl( &Msg *NE ' ' )                                +
                        Parm(                                              +
                              ( MsgID )                                    +
                              ( MsgF )                                     +
                              ( MsgDta )                                   +
                            )                                              +
                        NbrTrue( *NE 3 )                                   +
                        MsgID( CPD2443 )

              Dep       Ctl( &Msg *NE ' ' )                                +
                        Parm( ( MsgID ) )                                  +
                        NbrTrue( *NE 1 )                                   +
                        MsgID( CPD2536 )

              Dep       Ctl( &MsgID *NE '       ' )                        +
                        Parm( ( MsgF ) )                                   +
                        NbrTrue( *EQ 1 )                                   +
                        MsgID( CPD2441 )
```

FIGURE 29.6B

Validity-Checking Program SndBrkMsgV

```
/*  ===============================================================  */
/*  =  Program....... SndBrkMsgV                                  =  */
/*  =  Source type... CLP                                         =  */
/*  =  Type.......... Validity-checking program for SndBrkMsgU    =  */
/*  =  Description... Send Break Message to User                  =  */
/*  =  ---------------------------------------------------------  =  */
/*  =  Parameters                                                 =  */
/*  =                                                             =  */
/*  =    &Msg            Input     Message                        =  */
/*  =                                                             =  */
/*  =    &MsgID          Input     Message ID                     =  */
/*  =                                                             =  */
/*  =    &MsgF           Input     Qualified message file         =  */
/*  =                                                             =  */
/*  =    &MsgDta         Input     Message data                   =  */
/*  =                                                             =  */
/*  =    &ToUsr          Input     To user profile                =  */
/*  =                                                             =  */
/*  =    &MsgType        Input     Message Type                   =  */
/*  =                                                             =  */
/*  =    &RpyMsgQ        Input     Message queue to get reply     =  */
/*  ===============================================================  */

Pgm          (                                                      +
               &Msg                                                 +
               &MsgID                                               +
               &MsgF                                                +
               &MsgDta                                              +
               &ToUsr                                               +
               &MsgType                                             +
               &RpyMsgQ                                             +
             )

/*  ===============================================================  */
/*  = Variable declarations                                       =  */
/*  ===============================================================  */

  Dcl        &Msg        *Char      (  498    )
  Dcl        &MsgID      *Char      (    7    )
  Dcl        &MsgF       *Char      (   2Ø    )
  Dcl        &MsgDta     *Char      (  494    )
  Dcl        &ToUsr      *Char      (   1Ø    )
  Dcl        &MsgType    *Char      (    5    )
  Dcl        &RpyMsgQ    *Char      (   2Ø    )
  Dcl        &MsgFNm     *Char      (   1Ø    )
  Dcl        &MsgFLib    *Char      (   1Ø    )
  Dcl        &RpyMsgQN   *Char      (   1Ø    )
  Dcl        &RpyMsgQL   *Char      (   1Ø    )
  Dcl        &EMsgID     *Char      (    7    )
  Dcl        &EMsgF      *Char      (   1Ø    )
  Dcl        &EMsgFLib   *Char      (   1Ø    )
  Dcl        &EMsgDta    *Char      (  2ØØ    )
  Dcl        &EMsg       *Char      (  5Ø8    )
  Dcl        &EKeyVar    *Char      (    4    )
```

continued

FIGURE 29.6B CONTINUED

```
/*  ==============================================================  */
/*  = Global error monitor                                       =  */
/*  ==============================================================  */

  MonMsg     ( CPF0000 MCH0000 ) Exec(                               +
    GoTo       Error                  )

/*  ==============================================================  */
/*  =  If ToUsr is special value *Requester, retrieve user       =  */
/*  ==============================================================  */

  If         ( &ToUsr *Eq '*REQUESTER' )                             +
    RtvJobA    User( &ToUsr )

/*  ==============================================================  */
/*  =  Validate ToUsr parameter                                  =  */
/*  ==============================================================  */

  If         ( ( &ToUsr *NE '*ALL' )                                 +
  *And         ( &ToUsr *NE '*SYSOPR' )                              +
  *And         ( &ToUsr *NE '*ALLACT' ) )                            +
    ChkObj     &ToUsr       *UsrPrf

/*  ==============================================================  */
/*  =  Parse message file name                                   =  */
/*  ==============================================================  */

  ChgVar     &MsgFNm     ( %Sst( &MsgF 1 10 ) )

/*  --------------------------------------------------------------  */
/*  -  If message file specified, parse and validate             -  */
/*  --------------------------------------------------------------  */

  If         ( &MsgFNm *NE ' ' )                                     +
    Do
      ChgVar     &MsgFLib    ( %Sst( &MsgF 11 10 ) )
      ChkObj     &MsgFLib/&MsgFNm    *MsgF
    EndDo

/*  ==============================================================  */
/*  =  If message type is *INQ, parse and validate reply queue   =  */
/*  ==============================================================  */

  If         ( &MsgType *Eq '*INQ' )                                 +
    Do
      ChgVar     &RpyMsgQN   ( %Sst( &RpyMsgQ  1 10 ) )
      ChgVar     &RpyMsgQL   ( %Sst( &RpyMsgQ 11 10 ) )
      ChkObj     &RpyMsgQL/&RpyMsgQN    *MsgQ
    EndDo

/*  ==============================================================  */
/*  =  If message type is not *INQ default reply queue so a valid =  */
/*  =  value will be passed to the QEZSndMg program. Even if an  =  */
/*  =  inquiry message is not being sent, this parameter must be =  */
/*  =  a valid message queue name.                               =  */
/*  ==============================================================  */

  Else                                                               +
    Do
      ChgVar     &RpyMsgQ    ( 'QSYSOPR   *LIBL' )
    EndDo

  Return
```

continued

FIGURE 29.6B CONTINUED

```
/*  ================================================================  */
/*  = Error handler                                                =  */
/*  ================================================================  */

Error:

  RcvMsg      MsgType( *Excp )                                        +
              MsgDta( &EMsgDta )                                      +
              MsgID( &EMsgID )                                        +
              MsgF( &EMsgF )                                          +
              MsgFLib( &EMsgFLib )

  MonMsg      ( CPF0000 MCH0000 )

  SndPgmMsg   MsgID( &EMsgID )                                        +
              MsgF( &EMsgFLib/&EMsgF )                                +
              MsgDta( &EMsgDta )                                      +
              ToPgmQ( *Same )                                         +
              KeyVar( &EKeyVar )

  MonMsg      ( CPF0000 MCH0000 )

  RcvMsg      KeyVar( &EKeyVar )                                      +
              Msg( &EMsg )

  MonMsg      ( CPF0000 MCH0000 )

  SndPgmMsg   MsgID( CPD0006 )                                        +
              MsgF( QSys/QCPFMsg )                                    +
              MsgDta( '0000' *TCat &EMsg )                            +
              ToPgmQ( *Prv )                                          +
              MsgType( *Diag )

  MonMsg      ( CPF0000 MCH0000 )

  SndPgmMsg   MsgID( CPF0002 )                                        +
              MsgF( QSys/QCPFMsg )                                    +
              ToPgmQ( *PRV )                                          +
              MsgType( *Escape )

  MonMsg      ( CPF0000 MCH0000 )

/*  ================================================================  */
/*  = End of program                                               =  */
/*  ================================================================  */

 EndPgm
```

FIGURE 29.6C

Command Processing Program SndBrkMsgC

```
/*  ==============================================================  */
/*  =  Program....... SndBrkMsgC                                 =  */
/*  =  Source type... CLP                                        =  */
/*  =  Type.......... Command processing program for SndBrkMsgU  =  */
/*  =  Description... Send Break Message to User                 =  */
/*  =  ------------------------------------------------------    =  */
/*  =  Parameters                                                =  */
/*  =                                                            =  */
/*  =    &Msg             Input      Message                     =  */
/*  =                                                            =  */
/*  =    &MsgID           Input      Message ID                  =  */
/*  =                                                            =  */
/*  =    &MsgF            Input      Qualified message file      =  */
/*  =                                                            =  */
/*  =    &MsgDta          Input      Message data                =  */
/*  =                                                            =  */
/*  =    &ToUsr           Input      To user profile             =  */
/*  =                                                            =  */
/*  =    &MsgType         Input      Message Type                =  */
/*  =                                                            =  */
/*  =    &RpyMsgQ         Input      Message queue to get reply  =  */
/*  ==============================================================  */

Pgm         (                                                       +
              &Msg                                                  +
              &MsgID                                                +
              &MsgF                                                 +
              &MsgDta                                               +
              &ToUsr                                                +
              &MsgType                                              +
              &RpyMsgQ                                              +
            )

/*  ==============================================================  */
/*  = Variable declarations                                      =  */
/*  ==============================================================  */

  Dcl         &Msg        *Char      (  498    )
  Dcl         &MsgID      *Char      (    7    )
  Dcl         &MsgF       *Char      (   20    )
  Dcl         &MsgDta     *Char      (  494    )
  Dcl         &ToUsr      *Char      (   10    )
  Dcl         &MsgType    *Char      (    5    )
  Dcl         &RpyMsgQ    *Char      (   20    )
  Dcl         &KeyVar     *Char      (    4    )
  Dcl         &MsgToSnd   *Char      (  494    )
  Dcl         &MsgLenA    *Char      (    4    )
  Dcl         &MsgTypeA   *Char      (   10    )
  Dcl         &Delivery   *Char      (   10    )    ( '*BREAK' )
  Dcl         &NbrUsers   *Char      (    4    )    ( X'00000001' )
  Dcl         &NbrMsgsSnt *Char      (    4    )
  Dcl         &RqsFnc     *Char      (    4    )
  Dcl         &APIErr     *Char      (   16    )                    +
                                  ( X'00000000000000004040404040404040' )
```

continued

FIGURE 29.6C CONTINUED

```
  Dcl        &UseSndDsp  *Char      (    1    )   ( 'N' )
  Dcl        &SndToTyp   *Char      (    4    )   ( '*USR' )
  Dcl        &MsgFNm     *Char      (   10    )
  Dcl        &MsgFLib    *Char      (   10    )
  Dcl        &EMsgID     *Char      (    7    )
  Dcl        &EMsgF      *Char      (   10    )
  Dcl        &EMsgFLib   *Char      (   10    )
  Dcl        &EMsgDta    *Char      (  200    )

/*  ===============================================================  */
/*  = Global error monitor                                        =  */
/*  ===============================================================  */

  MonMsg     ( CPF0000 MCH0000 ) Exec(                                +
    GoTo       Error                 )

/*  ===============================================================  */
/*  = Parse message into length and message                       =  */
/*  ===============================================================  */

  ChgVar     &MsgLenA    ( %Sst( &Msg 1   4 ) )
  ChgVar     &MsgToSnd   ( %Sst( &Msg 5 494 ) )

/*  ===============================================================  */
/*  = Change message type to length required by QEZSndMg          =  */
/*  ===============================================================  */

  ChgVar     &MsgTypeA   &MsgType

/*  ===============================================================  */
/*  = If ToUsr is special value *Requester, retrieve user         =  */
/*  ===============================================================  */

  If         ( &ToUsr *Eq '*REQUESTER' )                              +
    RtvJobA    User( &ToUsr )

/*  ===============================================================  */
/*  = If MsgID specified, retrieve message and set length         =  */
/*  ===============================================================  */

  If         ( &MsgID *NE ' ' )                                       +
    Do
      ChgVar     &MsgFNm     ( %Sst( &MsgF  1 10 ) )
      ChgVar     &MsgFLib    ( %Sst( &MsgF 11 10 ) )

      SndPgmMsg  MsgID( &MsgID )                                      +
                 MsgF( &MsgFLib/&MsgFNm )                             +
                 MsgDta( &MsgDta )                                    +
                 ToPgmQ( *Same )                                      +
                 KeyVar( &KeyVar )

      RcvMsg     MsgKey( &KeyVar )                                    +
                 Msg( &MsgToSnd )

      ChgVar     &MsgLenA    ( X'000001EE' )
    EndDo
```

continued

FIGURE 29.6C *CONTINUED*

```
/*  ==============================================================  */
/*  = Send the message                                           =  */
/*  ==============================================================  */

  Call       QEZSndMg                                                +
             (                                                       +
               &MsgTypeA                                             +
               &Delivery                                             +
               &MsgToSnd                                             +
               &MsgLenA                                              +
               &ToUsr                                                +
               &NbrUsers                                             +
               &NbrMsgsSnt                                           +
               &RqsFnc                                               +
               &APIErr                                               +
               &UseSndDsp                                            +
               &RpyMsgQ                                              +
               &SndToTyp                                             +
             )
  Return

/*  ==============================================================  */
/*  = Error handler                                              =  */
/*  ==============================================================  */

Error:

  RcvMsg     MsgType( *Excp )                                        +
             MsgDta( &EMsgDta )                                      +
             MsgID( &EMsgID )                                        +
             MsgF( &EMsgF )                                          +
             MsgFLib( &EMsgFLib )

  MonMsg     ( CPF0000 MCH0000 )

  SndPgmMsg  MsgID( &EMsgID )                                        +
             MsgF( &EMsgFLib/&EMsgF )                                +
             MsgDta( &EMsgDta )                                      +
             MsgType( *Escape )

  MonMsg     ( CPF0000 MCH0000 )

/*  ==============================================================  */
/*  = End of program                                             =  */
/*  ==============================================================  */

EndPgm
```

Knowing When to Speak

As shown in the CL program example, using command SndUsrMsg to prompt the user for a simple reply makes good use of the command's capabilities. This function differs somewhat from prompting for data when you submit a job. We don't recommend using the SndUsrMsg command to retrieve data for program execution (e.g., branch number, order number range, date range) because SndUsrMsg offers minimal validity checking and isn't as user-friendly as a DDS-coded display file prompt can be. Instead, you should create prompts for data as display files (using DDS) and process them with either a CL or an HLL program.

In a nutshell, the SndUsrMsg command is best suited to sending an informational message to the user to relate useful information (e.g., "Your job has been submitted. You will receive a message when your job is complete.") or to sending an inquiry message that lets the user choose further program action. The SndUsrMsg command can teach your programs to talk, but the vocabulary associated with this command is specific to these two tasks.

Command SndBrkMsgU gives you a way to shout at users. As with SndUsrMsg, though, you should use SndBrkMsgU primarily as a way to send an urgent informational message to a user.

Now that you know how to train your programs to talk to users, the next challenge is teaching your programs to communicate with each other! You'll be able to master that after we explain how to use the SndPgmMsg (Send Program Message) command, which lets you send messages from program to program with information such as detected program errors and requirements for continued processing.

Chapter 30

Just Between Us Programs

In Chapter 7, we explained that you can use the SndMsg (Send Message), SndBrkMsg (Send Break Message), or SndNetMsg (Send Network Message) command to communicate with someone else on your system. In Chapter 29, we discussed Operational Assistant's QEZSndMg (Send Message) API, along with user-written command SndBrkMsgU (Send Break Message to User), which enhances the API. We showed you how to use command SndUsrMsg (Send User Message) to have a program send a message to a user, and we noted that you can also use SndBrkMsgU in your programs.

But when you want to establish communications between program objects (for this discussion, we use the term "program object" to denote a program or a procedure), none of these commands will do the job. Instead, you need the SndPgmMsg (Send Program Message) and RcvMsg (Receive Message) commands. As an alternative, you can use system APIs to perform these functions, but APIs QMHSndPM (Send Program Message) and QMHRcvPM (Receive Program Message) are typically used by high-level language (HLL) programs. In this chapter, we talk about the SndPgmMsg command. For a discussion of the RcvMsg command, see Chapter 31.

Program messages are normally used for one of two reasons: to send error messages to a calling program or procedure (so it knows when a function has not been successfully completed) or to communicate the status or successful completion of a process to a calling program or procedure. In this chapter, you'll learn how a job stores messages, how to have one program object send a message to another, what types of messages a program object can send, and what actions those messages can require a job to perform. But first, you need to understand the importance of call message queues.

Call Message Queues

All messages on the iSeries must be sent to and received from a message queue. User-to-user and program-to-user messages are exchanged primarily via non-call message queues (i.e., a workstation message queue or a user message queue). OS/400 creates a non-call message queue when a workstation device or a user profile is created. You can also use the CrtMsgQ (Create Message Queue) command to create non-call message queues. For example, you might want to create a message queue for communication between program objects that aren't part of the same job. Or you might want to create a central message queue to handle all print messages. Both users and program objects can send messages to and receive messages from non-call message queues.

Although program objects can use non-call message queues to communicate with other program and procedures, OS/400 provides a more convenient means of communication between program objects in the same job. For each job on the system, OS/400 automatically creates call message queues. These consist of an external message queue (*Ext, through which a program object communicates with the job's user) and a message queue associated with each call stack entry (program or procedure) in that job. (For an introduction to the call stack, see Chapter 21.)

Note

Now is a good time to point out the fact that although we discuss Integrated Language Environment (ILE) concepts here, we limit examples to the Original Program Model (OPM) environment. We do so because our goal is to introduce you to sending program messages rather than to overwhelm you. Because ILE is more comprehensive than OPM, it's also more complex. Once you have a handle on sending program messages in the OPM environment, you can further explore ILE.

Figure 30.1 illustrates a sample call message queue.

FIGURE 30.1
Sample Call Message Queue Structure

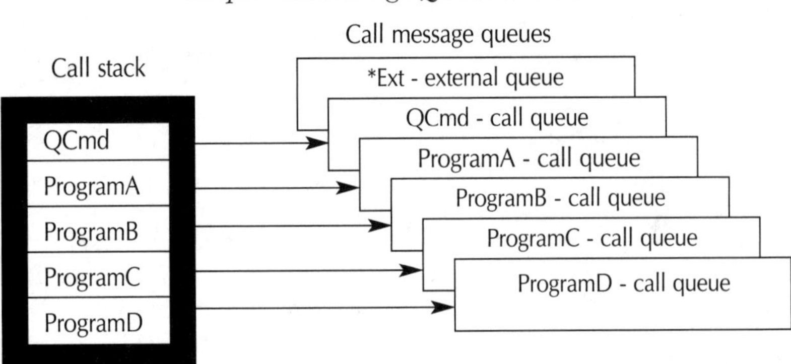

Note: Not actual size. This is a simplified call stack without system programs and ILE procedures.

OS/400 creates an external message queue when a job is initialized and deletes this queue when the job ends. OS/400 also creates a call message queue for each entry in the call stack and deletes it when the entry is removed from the call stack (i.e. when the program or procedure ends). The call message queue becomes the basis for the job log produced when a job is completed. The job log includes all messages from the call message queue, as well as other essential job information. (For more information about job logs, see Chapter 9. In addition, "Understanding Job Logs" on page 487 reviews some key points and provides additional details.)

Understanding Job Logs

During job execution, OS/400 logs informational, completion, diagnostic, and other messages into the job's message queue (the external message queue and the various call message queues associated with the job). When the job is finished, OS/400 creates a spooled file that lists these messages as well as the CL commands executed during the job's execution. This spooled file is commonly known as the job log. Every job, whether interactive or batch, generates a job log that records the job's activities and varies in content (both in the number and type of messages) depending on the job attributes associated with the job.

During a job's execution, you can use the DspJob (Display Job) or DspJobLog (Display Job Log) command to view the job log while the system creates it, accessing, in effect, a window to the job's active message queue.

Enough Is Enough

At times you may want to control the generation of or contents of job logs. For instance, you may not want to generate logs for jobs that are completed normally; conversely, you may want to generate the maximum amount of information in the job log for jobs that are experiencing frequent problems. Or you may want to exclude from the log messages that are only informational in nature.

Job attributes control the creation and contents of the job log. The Log (Message logging) attribute consists of three values: *message level* and *message severity*, both of which control the type and number of messages the system writes to a job log, and *message text level*, which controls the amount of message text written to the job log when the job encounters a message that meets the requirements of the first two values.

The message level value specifies one of the following five logging levels:

Level	***Description***
1	No data is logged.
2	Only messages logged sent to the job's external message queue with a severity greater than or equal to the specified message severity are logged.
3	All level 1 messages are logged, plus the following: • any requests or commands from a CL program that cause the system to issue a message with a severity level that exceeds or equals the severity specified in the Log attribute • all messages associated with a request or command from a CL program that results in a high-level message (i.e., one sent to the receiving program's message queue) with a severity at least equal to the specified severity
4	All messages logged by level 2 are logged, plus the following: • all requests or commands from a CL program • all messages associated with a request or command that results in a high-level message with a severity at least equal to the message severity specified
5	The following information is logged: • all requests or commands logged from a CL program • all messages, including trace messages, with a severity at least equal to the specified severity

continued

(Understanding Job Logs *Continued*)

Every iSeries message has an associated severity (i.e., priority). The message severity determines which messages are logged and which are ignored. Messages with a severity greater than or equal to the severity specified in the Log attribute are logged according to the specified logging level. Messages essential to the system's operation (e.g., inquiry messages that must be answered) have the highest severity, 99. Informational messages (e.g., messages that tell you a function is in progress) have a severity of 00.

A value of *Msg for the message text level portion of the Log attribute specifies that the system should write only first-level message text to the job log. A value of *SecLvl specifies that the system write both the first-level message and the help text (defined as second-level text in the message description) to the job log.

By setting the message text level attribute value to *NoList, you can ensure that the job doesn't generate a job log when it ends normally. Jobs that end abnormally always generate a job log with both first- and second-level message text (as if you specified *SecLvl for the message text level). Eliminating job logs for jobs that are completed normally can greatly reduce the number of spooled and printed logs.

Logging CL Commands

Jobs also include the LogCLPgm attribute, for which a value of *Yes instructs the system to write any loggable CL commands to the job log. (You must also specify Log(*Job) or Log(*Yes) as an attribute of the CL program.) A value of LogCLPgm(*No) specifies that commands in a CL program are not logged to the job log. Using LogCLPgm(*Yes) differs from using the Log attribute, which controls logging only of CL commands that generate a message with a severity at least equal to the severity identified in the Log attribute. LogCLPgm(*Yes) lets you force OS/400 to log all CL commands issued during job execution.

The SndPgmMsg Command

Figure 30.2 shows the parameters associated with the SndPgmMsg command. You can use this command in a CL program to send a program message to a non-call or a call message queue.

For the Msg (Message text) parameter, you can enter an impromptu message (up to 512 characters long), or you can use the MsgID (Message identifier), MsgF (Message file), and MsgDta (Message data field values) parameters to send a predefined message. (To review predefined messages, see Chapter 29.) The system routes messages sent using the SndPgmMsg command based on values you specify in the ToPgmQ (Call stack entry message queue), ToMsgQ (Send to non-program message queue), and ToUsr (To user profile) parameters.

FIGURE 30.2
SndPgmMsg Command Parameters

```
                     Send Program Message (SNDPGMMSG)

 Type choices, press Enter.

 Message text, or . . . . . . . . MSG            ________________________________
 ________________________________________________________________________________
 ________________________________________________________________________________
 ________________________________________________________________________________
 ________________________________________________________________________________
 ________________________________________________________________________________
 ________________________________________________________________________________
__...
 Message identifier . . . . . . . MSGID          _______
 Message file . . . . . . . . . . MSGF           __________
   Library  . . . . . . . . . . .                  *LIBL_____
 Message data field values  . . . MSGDTA         *NONE___________________________
 ________________________________________________________________________________
 ________________________________________________________________________________
 ________________________________________________________________________________
 ________________________________________________________________________________
 ________________________________________________________________________________
 ________________________________________________________________________________
__...
 Call stack entry message queue:  TOPGMQ
   Relationship . . . . . . . . .                *PRV_
   Call stack entry identifier:
   Call stack entry . . . . . . .                *_______________________________
 ________________________________________________________________________________
 ________________________________________________________________________________
 ___________________________________________________________________
   Module . . . . . . . . . . . .                *NONE_____
   Bound program  . . . . . . . .                *NONE_____
 Send to non-pgm message queue  . TOMSGQ         *TOPGMQ___
   Library  . . . . . . . . . . .                  __________
                        + for more values        __________
                                                   __________
 To user profile  . . . . . . . . TOUSR          __________
 Message type . . . . . . . . . . MSGTYPE        *INFO__
 Message queue to get reply . . . RPYMSGQ        *PGMQ_____
   Library  . . . . . . . . . . .                  __________
 CL var for KEYVAR        (4) . . KEYVAR         __________

                          Additional Parameters

 Coded character set ID . . . . . CCSID          *JOB_______
```

The ToPgmQ parameter is unique to the SndPgmMsg command and identifies the call message queue to which the message will be sent. The message queue can be the external message queue (*Ext) or a message queue associated with a call stack entry. Parameter ToPgmQ consists of two elements, Relationship and Call stack entry identifier, that are used in determining the message queue to which the message will be sent.

ToPgmQ's first element specifies the relationship between the target program object and the sending program object. For this element, you can specify the following values:

- *Ext — The message is to go to the job's external message queue.
- *Prv — The message is to go to the message queue of the call stack entry immediately preceding the one identified by ToPgmQ's second element. If this preceding message queue is for an ILE program entry procedure (PEP), the message is sent to the message queue that precedes the PEP message queue in the call stack.
- *Same — The message is to be sent to the message queue of the call stack entry identified by ToPgmQ's second element.

ToPgmQ's second element has three elements: Call stack entry, Module, and Bound program. These items determine the exact call message queue to receive the message. The Call stack entry item identifies the program or procedure name used to identify the call message queue. Special value * (asterisk) indicates that the call stack entry is the program or procedure issuing the SndPgmMsg command. In ILE, it's possible to have duplicate procedure names in the call stack; hence, procedure name alone may not be sufficient to identify the correct procedure. In such a case, you can use the Module and Bound program items to further identify, or qualify, the exact procedure. The Module item identifies the module into which the procedure was compiled, and the Bound program item identifies the program into which the procedure was bound.

With SndPgmMsg's ToMsgQ parameter, you can send a message to non-program message queues, or you can use special value *ToPgmQ (the default) to instruct the system to refer to the ToPgmQ parameter to determine the message destination.

Let's look at the job message queues shown in Figure 30.1. Assuming that ProgramD is the active program, let's suppose ProgramD executes the following SndPgmMsg command:

```
SndPgmMsg Msg('Test message')  +
          ToMsgQ(*SysOpr)      +
          MsgType(*Info)
```

ProgramD sends the message "Test message" to the system operator's message queue (QSys/QSysOpr) because the value *SysOpr is specified for the ToMsgQ parameter.

In the following SndPgmMsg command

```
SndPgmMsg Msg('Test message') +
          ToPgmQ(*Same *)     +
          ToMsgQ(*ToPgmQ)     +
          MsgType(*Info)
```

the parameter ToMsgQ(*ToPgmQ) tells OS/400 to use the ToPgmQ parameter to determine the message destination. Because ToPgmQ specifies *Same for the relationship and * for the call-stack-entry identifier, the system sends the message "Test message" to call message queue ProgramD.

Now, consider the command

```
SndPgmMsg Msg('Test message') +
          ToPgmQ(*Prv *)      +
          MsgType(*Info)
```

In this case, the message is sent to call message queue ProgramC because ProgramC is ProgramD's calling program (*Prv). (Notice that this time we chose not to specify the ToMsgQ parameter but let it default to *ToPgmQ.)

The SndPgmMsg command's ToUsr parameter instructs the system to send the message to the message queue specified in the named user profile. You can also select from special values that instruct the system to send the message to the system operator (*SysOpr), to the user profile requesting that the message be sent (*Requester), or to the user message queue of all users with a currently running interactive job (*AllAct).

Message Types

The next parameter on the SndPgmMsg command is MsgType (Message type). You may recall that with the SndMsg and SndUsrMsg commands you can send two types of messages: informational (*Info) and inquiry (*Inq). SndPgmMsg supports both of these message types as well as six additional ones. Figure 30.3 lists the message types and describes the limitations (message content and destination) and normal uses of each. Each message type has a distinct purpose and communicates specific kinds of information.

FIGURE 30.3
Message Types

Message type	*Use of Msg or MsgID*	*Message queues*	*Typical use*
*Info	Both	All	To send a message containing descriptive information about a process
*Inq	Both	Non-call, external	To prompt a user for a reply needed to complete a process
*Comp	MsgID	All	To inform the calling program or the user that requested work has been successfully completed
*Diag	MsgID	All	To describe errors detected during program execution
*Rqs	Msg	All	To send a command string (i.e., a request) to a request message processing program
*Escape	MsgID	All[1] except external	To state specifically an error condition that caused the sending program to fail
*Status	MsgID	Call and external	To describe the current status of a process
*Notify	MsgID	All	To describe a condition that exists in the sending program that requires correction or a reply

[1] Escape messages are typically sent to call-stack-entry message queues to terminate program objects. If you send an escape message to a non–call-stack-entry message queue, no processes are terminated.

You can send an *informational message* (*Info) to any message queue. Because *inquiry messages* (*Inq) expect a reply, you can send an inquiry message only to a non–call-stack-entry message queue (i.e., a user or workstation message queue) or to the current job's external message queue.

A *completion message* (*Comp) is usually sent to inform the calling program object that the requested work is complete. It can be sent to any message queue or to the job's external message queue.

Diagnostic messages (*Diag) can be sent to any message queue but typically are sent to call-stack-entry message queues or to the external message queue to describe errors detected during program execution. Typically, escape messages follow diagnostic messages, telling the calling program object that diagnostic messages are present and that the requested function has failed.

You can send a *request message* (*Rqs) to any message queue as a command request. You must use an impromptu message on the Msg parameter to send the request.

An *escape message* (*Escape) specifically identifies the error that caused the sending program to fail. Although you can send an escape message to message queues other than call-stack-entry message queues, there is no need to do so and the system behaves differently. An escape message's function is to terminate one or more processes immediately. For this to happen, the message must be sent to a call-stack-entry message queue. If the message is sent to some other type of message queue, no processes are terminated. An escape message terminates the program objects that are below the receiving program object in the call stack. Control returns to the program object receiving the message, where the exception can be handled. If the exception is not handled, the receiving program object fails. MsgType(*Escape) cannot be specified if the Msg parameter is specified — in other words, all escape messages must be predefined and you cannot send an escape message to the external message queue.

Status messages (*Status) describe the status of the work that the sending program object performs. When a program sends a status message to an interactive job's external message queue, the message is displayed on the workstation screen, processing continues, and the sending program object does not require a response. When a status message is sent to a call-stack-entry message queue, the message functions as a warning message. If the program object receiving the message monitors for this message (for instance, using the MonMsg, or Monitor Message, command in CL programs), the message functions as an escape message. If the program receiving the status message does not monitor for that message, the system immediately returns control to the sending program object.

OS/400 uses *notify messages* (*Notify) to describe a condition in the sending program object that requires a correction or a reply. If the notify message is sent to an interactive job's external message queue, the message acts like an inquiry message and waits for a reply, which the sending program object can then receive. When a notify message is sent to a call-stack-entry message queue, the message functions as a warning.

If the program object receiving the notify message monitors for it, control is returned to the receiving program object after any necessary call stack entries are removed. If the receiving program object doesn't monitor for the message, or if the message is sent to a batch job's external message queue, the default reply for that message is sent and control returns to the sending program object. You can either define the default reply in the message description or specify it on the system reply list.

The Receiving End

The next parameter on the SndPgmMsg command is RpyMsgQ (Message queue to get reply), which lets you specify the message queue to which the system sends a reply for an inquiry or status message. The only valid values are *PgmQ, which specifies that the reply is to go to the message queue associated with the call stack entry of the program or procedure issuing the SndPgmMsg command, or a qualified non-call message queue name.

You can receive or remove a specific message by using a key value to identify that message. The KeyVar (CL variable for KEYVAR) parameter specifies the CL return variable to contain the message key value of the message sent by the SndPgmMsg command. To understand how key variables work, examine the following CL statement:

```
SndPgmMsg Msg('Test message') +
          ToPgmQ(*Prv *)      +
          MsgType(*Info)      +
          KeyVar(&MsgKey)
```

The SndPgmMsg command places the message on the message queue associated with the previous call stack entry, and OS/400 assigns to that message a unique message identifier that is returned in the &MsgKey variable. In the following example

```
RmvMsg PgmQ(*Prv *)    +
       MsgKey(&MsgKey) +
       Clear(*ByKey)
```

the RmvMsg (Remove Message) command uses the &MsgKey value to remove the correct message from the message queue. In CL, the return variable must be defined as Type(*Char) with Len(4).

Program Message Uses

Now that you're acquainted with SndPgmMsg parameters, let's look at a few examples that demonstrate how to use this command. The following command sends a sample diagnostic message:

```
SndPgmMsg MsgID(CPF9898)                 +
          MsgF(QSys/QCPFMsg)             +
          MsgDta('Output queue' *BCat +
                 &OutQLib       *TCat +
                 '/'            *Cat  +
                 &OutQ          *BCat +
                 'not found')         +
          ToPgmQ(*Prv *)              +
          MsgType(*Diag)
```

In this example, we've concatenated constants ('Output queue', '/', and 'not found') and two variables (&OutQLib and &OutQ) to construct the diagnostic message "Output queue *YourLib/YourOutQ* not found." The current program sends this message to the calling program, which upon receiving control again can receive the message from the message queue associated with its call stack entry.

As we mentioned in the discussion of the MsgType parameter, you must supply a valid message ID for the MsgID keyword when you send certain message types. (To review which types require a message ID, see Figure 30.3.) Because this means you can't simply use the Msg parameter to construct text for these message types, OS/400 provides two special message IDs, CPF9897 and CPF9898, to handle this particular requirement. The message text for these messages is almost identical. The message text for CPF9897 — &1 — means that substitution variable &1 will supply the message text, which you can construct using the MsgDta parameter. Message CPF9898 functions exactly the same way, except that its message text adds a period at the end!

Notice in the preceding example that we constructed the message text in the MsgDta parameter. When the program sends the message, the MsgDta text becomes the message through substitution into the &1 data variable. (For a more complete explanation of substitution variables, see Chapter 29.)

The next example constructs an escape message that might follow such a diagnostic message:

```
SndPgmMsg MsgID(CPF9898)                         +
          MsgF(QSys/QCPFMsg)                     +
          MsgDta('Operations ended in error.' *BCat +
                 'See previously listed messages')  +
          ToPgmQ(*Prv *)                         +
          MsgType(*Escape)
```

OS/400 uses an escape message to terminate program objects when it encounters an error. When a program sends an escape message, control returns to the program object to which the message is sent after programs below the receiving program object in the call stack are ended and removed from the call stack.

In the following example, the current program sends a completion message to the calling program to confirm the successful completion of a task.

```
SndPgmMsg MsgID(CPF9898)                            +
          MsgF(QSys/QCPFMsg)                        +
          MsgDta('Copy of spooled files is complete') +
          ToPgmQ(*Prv *)                            +
          MsgType(*Comp)
```

The following sample status message goes to the job's external message queue and tells the job's external user what progress the job is making.

```
SndPgmMsg MSGID(CPF9898)                            +
          MsgF(QSys/QCPFMsg)                        +
          MsgDta('Copy of spooled files in progress') +
          ToPgmQ(*Ext)                              +
          MsgType(*Status)
```

When you send a status message to an interactive job's external message queue, OS/400 displays the message on the screen until another program message replaces it or until the message line on the display is cleared.

Although you may now be ready to send messages to another program, you have only half the picture. In Chapter 31, you'll learn how programs receive and manipulate messages, and we'll give you some sample code that contains helpful messaging techniques.

Chapter 31

Hello, Any Messages?

On the iSeries, sending and receiving program messages functions much like voice mail. Within a job, each program object, as well as each job, has its own "mailbox." One program or procedure within the job can leave a message for another program or procedure or for the job. Each program object or job can "listen" to messages in its mailbox, and programs or procedures can remove old messages from their mailboxes.

In Chapter 30, we explained how program objects can send messages to message queues associated with call stack entries and to a job's external message queue. In this chapter, we discuss the "listening" side of the equation: the RcvMsg (Receive Message) and MonMsg (Monitor Message) commands.

As was the case with the previous chapter, the information in this chapter is intended as an introduction only. We therefore touch on the Integrated Language Environment (ILE) but focus on CL programs in the Original Program Model (OPM) environment.

Receiving the Right Message

You can use the RcvMsg command in a CL program to receive a message from a message queue and copy the message contents and attributes into CL variables. Why would you want to do this? You may want to look for a particular message in a message queue to trigger an event on your system. Or you may want to look for messages that normally would require an operator reply and instead have your program supply the reply. Or you may want to log specific messages received at a message queue. Whatever the reason, the place to begin is the RcvMsg command.

Figure 31.1 shows the RcvMsg command parameters. The first seven parameters — PgmQ (Call stack entry message queue), MsgQ (Message queue), MsgType (Message type), MsgKey (Message key), Wait (Wait time), Rmv (Remove message), and CCSID (Coded character set ID) — determine which message your program will receive, the message queue from which the message will be received, and how your program processes the message.

Figure 31.2 (page 499) illustrates a call message queue made up of a job's external message queue and five call message queues. For our purposes, each message queue contains one message.

FIGURE 31.1
RcvMsg Command Parameters

```
                        Receive Message (RCVMSG)

 Type choices, press Enter.

 Call stack entry message queue:  PGMQ
   Relationship . . . . . . . . .                *SAME
   Call stack entry identifier:
   Call stack entry . . . . . . .                *____________________________
_______________________________________________________________________________
_______________________________________________________________________________
_________________________________________________________________
   Module . . . . . . . . . . . .                *NONE_____
   Bound program  . . . . . . . .                *NONE_____
 Message queue  . . . . . . . . . MSGQ           __________
   Library  . . . . . . . . . . .                  *LIBL_____
 Message type . . . . . . . . . . MSGTYPE        *ANY__
 Message key  . . . . . . . . . . MSGKEY         *NONE
 Wait time  . . . . . . . . . . . WAIT           0_________
 Remove message . . . . . . . . . RMV            *YES_____
 Coded character set ID . . . . . CCSID          *JOB_______
 CL var for KEYVAR          (4) . . KEYVAR       ___________
 CL var for 1st level text  . . . MSG            ___________
 CL var for MSGLEN        (5 0) . . MSGLEN       ___________
 CL var for 2nd level text  . . . SECLVL         ___________
 CL var for SECLVLLEN     (5 0) . . SECLVLLEN    ___________
 CL var for msg data  . . . . . . MSGDTA         ___________
 CL var for MSGDTALEN     (5 0) . . MSGDTALEN    ___________
 CL var for MSGID           (7) . . MSGID        ___________
 CL var for SEV           (2 0) . . SEV          ___________
 CL var for SENDER         (80) . . SENDER       ___________
 Sender format  . . . . . . . . . SENDERFMT      *SHORT
 CL var for RTNTYPE         (2) . . RTNTYPE      ___________
 CL var for ALROPT          (9) . . ALROPT       ___________
 CL var for MSGF           (10) . . MSGF         ___________
 CL var for MSGFLIB        (10) . . MSGFLIB      ___________
 CL var for SNDMSGFLIB     (10) . . SNDMSGFLIB   ___________
 CL var for text CCSID    (5 0) . . TXTCCSID     ___________
 CL var for data CCSID    (5 0) . . DTACCSID     ___________
```

Let's suppose that ProgramD is the active program and that it issues the following command:

```
RcvMsg
```

Because no specific parameter values are provided, OS/400 would use the following default values for the command's first seven parameters:

```
RcvMsg PgmQ(*Same (* *None *None)) +
       MsgQ(*PgmQ)                 +
       MsgType(*Any)               +
       MsgKey(*None)               +
       Wait(0)                     +
       Rmv(*Yes)                   +
       CCSID(*Job)
```

FIGURE 31.2
Sample Call Message Queues with Messages

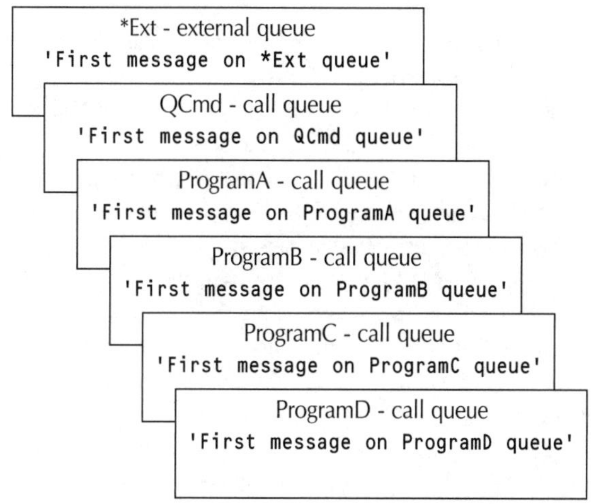

Note: Not actual size. This is a simplified call stack without system programs and ILE procedures.

The PgmQ and MsgQ parameters function the same way as the SndPgmMsg (Send Program Message) command's ToPgmQ (Call stack entry message queue) and ToMsgQ (Send to non-program message queue) parameters, respectively (see Chapter 30 for details). In the example above, because the PgmQ value is

```
(*Same (* *None *None))
```

ProgramD would receive a message from its own (i.e., the ProgramD) call queue. According to Figure 31.2, there is only one message to receive: "First message on ProgramD queue."

In the example, the value MsgType(*Any), combined with the value MsgKey(*None), instructs the program to receive the first message of any message type found on the queue, regardless of the key value. (For more information about the MsgType and MsgKey parameters, see "RcvMsg and the MsgType and MsgKey Parameters," page 500.)

The value Wait(0) tells the program to wait zero (0) seconds for a message to arrive on the message queue. You can use parameter Wait to specify a length of time in seconds that RcvMsg will wait for the arrival of a message, or you can specify *Max, which instructs the program to wait indefinitely to receive a message. If RcvMsg finds a message immediately, or finds one before the number of seconds specified in the Wait value elapse, RcvMsg receives the message. If RcvMsg finds no message on the queue during the Wait period, it returns blanks or zeroed values for any return variables.

RcvMsg and the MsgType and MsgKey Parameters

The RcvMsg (Receive Message) command can use its MsgType (Message type) and MsgKey (Message key) parameters to determine which message or type of message the command will receive. Here are some guidelines for using these parameters:

- If RcvMsg specifies only the MsgType parameter (using the default value of *None for the MsgKey parameter) and one of the message types specified for MsgType is *Comp, *Diag, *Info, *Inq, *Rpy, *Copy, or *Rqs, RcvMsg will receive a new message of that specific type in first-in, first-out (FIFO) order. However, if RcvMsg uses the MsgType value *Excp, the command will receive messages in last-in, first-out (LIFO) order.
- If RcvMsg specifies only the MsgKey parameter (using the default value of *Any for the MsgType parameter) and a message exists on the message queue with that message reference key, RcvMsg receives that message. If both an original inquiry message and a reply exist with that reference key (both messages will have the same message reference key), the program will receive the reply message. If the reply is not yet available in the message queue, RcvMsg will receive no message. Note: If your program tries to receive a message by key and the message can't be found on the message queue, an escape message is sent to your program.
- If RcvMsg specifies neither the MsgType nor the MsgKey parameter, the default MsgType(*Any) is used and the first new message in the queue is received.
- If RcvMsg specifies MsgType(*Copy) and MsgKey(&MsgKey), RcvMsg will receive the sender's copy of an inquiry message, if available.
- If RcvMsg specifies both the MsgType and MsgKey parameters and a message of that type exists, RcvMsg receives that message. When the reference key is correct and the message type is not, OS/400 sends an error message to the program that executed RcvMsg.
- If RcvMsg specifies MsgType(*Next), the MsgKey parameter must have a valid reference key value. RcvMsg then receives the next message following the message with that reference key.
- If RcvMsg specifies MsgKey(*Top) along with MsgType(*Next), RcvMsg receives the first message on the message queue.

The Rmv parameter value of *Yes tells the program to delete the message from the queue after processing the command. You can use Rmv(*No) to instruct OS/400 to leave the message on the queue after RcvMsg receives the message; OS/400 then marks the message as an "old" message on the queue. A program can receive an old message again only by using the specific message key value to receive the message or by using the value *First, *Last, *Next, or *Prv for the MsgType parameter. You can also specify special value *KeepExcp for the Rmv parameter to instruct the system to leave any unhandled exception message on the queue as a new message. If you specify *KeepExcp and the message is not an exception message or is an exception message that has been handled already, the system leaves the message in the message queue as an old message.

Receiving the Right Values

The remaining RcvMsg parameters listed in Figure 31.1 provide CL return variables to hold copies of the actual message data or message attributes. You typically use the RcvMsg command to retrieve the actual message text or attributes in order to evaluate the message and then take appropriate actions. For example, the command

```
RcvMsg MsgQ(MyMsgQ)        +
       MsgType(*Comp)      +
       Rmv(*No)            +
       Msg(&Msg)           +
       MsgDta(&MsgDta)     +
       MsgID(&MsgID)       +
       Sender(&Sender)
```

retrieves the actual message text, the message data, the message identifier, and the message sender data into return variables &Msg, &MsgDta, &MsgID, and &Sender, respectively. After a program executes a RcvMsg command, it can use these return variables. For example, the program may be looking for a particular message identifier. In the example, the current program might be looking for a particular completion message on a non-program message queue (MyMsgQ) to determine whether a job has been completed before starting another job.

Retrieving Message Sender Data

Notice the Sender parameter used in the example above. When you create a return variable for the Sender parameter, the variable should be at least 80 characters long when the SenderFmt (Sender format) parameter value is *Short (or a minimum of 720 characters if the format is *Long). When you use SenderFmt(*Short) — the default and most often used format — the following information is returned:

Positions 1–26 identify the sending job:
1–10 — job name
11–20 — user name
21–26 — job number

Positions 27–42 identify the sending program:
27–38 — program name
39–42 — statement number

Positions 43–55 provide the date and timestamp of the message:
43–49 — date (*cyymmdd*)
50–55 — time (*hhmmss*)

Positions 56–69 identify the receiving program (when the message is sent to a program message queue):
56–65 — program name
66–69 — statement number

Positions 70–80 are reserved for future use.

The Sender return variable can be helpful when processing messages. For example, during the execution of certain programs, it's helpful to know the name of the calling program without having to pass this information as a parameter or code the name of the program into the current program. You can use the technique shown in Figure 31.3 to retrieve that information.

FIGURE 31.3

Using RcvMsg to Retrieve the Previous Program's Name

```
/*  ================================================================  */
/*  =  Variable declarations                                       =  */
/*  ================================================================  */

    Dcl         &MsgKey      *Char       (    4     )
    Dcl         &Sender      *Char       (   80     )
    Dcl         &PrvPgm      *Char       (   10     )

/*  ================================================================  */
/*  =  Retrieve previous program's name                            =  */
/*  ================================================================  */

    SndPgmMsg   Msg( 'Any message will do' )                             +
                ToPgmQ( *Prv * )                                         +
                KeyVar( &MsgKey )

    RcvMsg      PgmQ( *Prv ( * ) )                                       +
                MsgKey( &MsgKey )                                        +
                Rmv( *Yes )                                              +
                Sender( &Sender )

    ChgVar      &PrvPgm      ( %Sst( &Sender 56 10 ) )
```

The current program sends a message to the calling program and then immediately uses the RcvMsg command to receive from the *Prv message queue the message just sent. Positions 56–65 of the &Sender return value contain the name of the program that received the original message; thus, you have the name of the calling program.

Retrieving the Message Return Type

Another RcvMsg command parameter you might find useful is RtnType (Return message type). When you use RcvMsg to receive messages with MsgType(*Any), your program can use a return variable to capture and interrogate the message type value. For instance, in the command

```
RcvMsg PgmQ(*Same (* *None *None)) +
       MsgType(*Any)               +
       Msg(&Msg)                   +
       RtnType(&RtnType)
```

the variable &RtnType returns a code that provides the type of the message that RcvMsg is receiving.

The possible codes returned are

Code	*Message type*
01	Completion
02	Diagnostic
04	Information
05	Inquiry
06	Copy
08	Request
10	Request with prompting
14	Notify (exception already handled)
15	Escape (exception already handled)
16	Notify (exception not already handled)
17	Escape (exception not already handled)
21	Reply (not checked for validity)
22	Reply (already checked for validity)
23	Reply (message default used)
24	Reply (system default used)
25	Reply (from system reply list)

As you can see, IBM didn't choose to return the "word" values (e.g., *DIAG, *ESCAPE, *NOTIFY) that are used with the MsgType parameter on the SndPgmMsg command but instead chose to use codes. When you write a CL program that must test the &RtnType return variable, you might want to avoid writing code that looks like this:

```
If (&RtnType *Eq 'Ø2')      +
  Do
  .
  .
  .
  EndDo
Else If (&RtnType *Eq '15') +
  Do
  .
  .
  .
  EndDo
```

Instead, you'll find your CL program easier to read and maintain if you use a standard list of variables, such as those defined by the CL code shown in Figure 31.4.

FIGURE 31.4

Declare Statements for Return Types

```
/*  ============================================================  */
/*  =  Variable declarations                                   =  */
/*  ============================================================  */

  Dcl        &RtnType     *Char     (    2    )
  Dcl        &Comp        *Char     (    2    )   ( 'Ø1' )
  Dcl        &Diag        *Char     (    2    )   ( 'Ø2' )
  Dcl        &Info        *Char     (    2    )   ( 'Ø4' )
  Dcl        &Inquiry     *Char     (    2    )   ( 'Ø5' )
  Dcl        &Copy        *Char     (    2    )   ( 'Ø6' )
  Dcl        &Request     *Char     (    2    )   ( 'Ø8' )
  Dcl        &RequestPmt  *Char     (    2    )   ( '1Ø' )
  Dcl        &NotifyHd    *Char     (    2    )   ( '14' )
  Dcl        &EscapeHd    *Char     (    2    )   ( '15' )
  Dcl        &NotifyNtHd  *Char     (    2    )   ( '16' )
  Dcl        &EscapeNtHd  *Char     (    2    )   ( '17' )
  Dcl        &ReplyNtChk  *Char     (    2    )   ( '21' )
  Dcl        &ReplyChk    *Char     (    2    )   ( '22' )
  Dcl        &ReplyMDft   *Char     (    2    )   ( '23' )
  Dcl        &ReplySDft   *Char     (    2    )   ( '24' )
  Dcl        &ReplyRpyL   *Char     (    2    )   ( '25' )
```

With this approach, you can change the code above to appear as

```
If (&RtnType *Eq &Diag)            +
  Do
  .
  .
  .
  EndDo
Else If (&RtnType *Eq &EscapeNtHd) +
  Do
  .
  .
  .
  EndDo
```

Monitoring for a Message

The MonMsg command is available only in CL programs. It provides a technique for trapping error and exception conditions by monitoring for escape, notify, and status messages. MonMsg also provides a way to direct the execution of a program based on the particular error conditions detected. Figure 31.5 shows the MonMsg command parameters.

You can use the MsgID (Message identifier) parameter to name from one to 50 specific or generic message identifiers for which the command will monitor. A specific message identifier is a message ID that represents only one message, such as CPF9802, which is the message ID for the message "Not authorized to object &2 in &3." A generic message identifier is a message ID that represents a group of messages, such as CPF9800,

FIGURE 31.5
MonMsg Command Parameters

```
                        Monitor Message (MONMSG)

 Type choices, press Enter.

 Message identifier . . . . . . . MSGID          _______
                       + for more values         _______
 Comparison data  . . . . . . . . CMPDTA         *NONE____________________

 Command to execute . . . . . . . EXEC           _________________________
_____________________________________________________________________________
_____________________________________________________________________________
___________________________________________________________________
```

which includes all messages in the CPF9801 through CPF9899 range. Thus, the command

```
MonMsg (CPF9802) Exec(GoTo Error)
```

monitors for the specific message CPF9802, whereas the command

```
MonMsg (CPF9800) Exec(GoTo Error)
```

monitors for all escape, notify, and status messages in the CPF9801 through CPF9899 range.

The second parameter on the MonMsg command is the CmpDta (Comparison data) parameter. You can use this parameter to specify comparison data that will be used to check against the message data of the message trapped by the MonMsg command. If the message data matches the comparison data (actually, only the first 28 positions are compared), the MonMsg command is successful and the action specified by the Exec (Command to execute) parameter is taken. For example, the command

```
MonMsg (CPF9802) CmpDta('MAINMENU') Exec(Do)
```

monitors for message identifier CPF9802 but executes the command found in the Exec parameter only if the CmpDta value 'MAINMENU' matches the first eight positions of the actual message data of the trapped CPF9802 message.

The Exec parameter lets you specify a CL command that is processed when MonMsg traps a valid message. If no Exec value is found, the program simply continues with the next statement found after the MonMsg command.

Command-Level Message Monitoring

You can use the MonMsg command to monitor for messages that might occur during the execution of a single command. This form of MonMsg use is called a command-level message monitor. You place the command immediately after the CL command that might generate the message. It might appear as

```
ChkObj &ObjLib/&Obj &ObjType
MonMsg (CPF9801) Exec(GoTo NotFound)
MonMsg (CPF9802) Exec(GoTo NotAuth)
```

The MonMsg commands here monitor only for messages that might occur during the execution of the ChkObj (Check Object) command. You should use this implementation to anticipate error conditions in your programs. When a command-level MonMsg traps a message, you can then take the appropriate action in the program to continue or end processing. For example, to monitor for the "CPF2105 File not found" message, you might code the following:

```
DltF   QTemp/WorkF
MonMsg (CPF2105)
```

In this example, if error CPF2105 is found, the program simply continues processing as if no error occurred. That may be appropriate for some programs.

Now, examine the following code:

```
ChkObj QTemp/Work *File
MonMsg (CPF9801) Exec(Do)
  CrtPF  File(QTemp/Work) RcdLen(80)
  EndDo
ClrPFM QTemp/Work
```

This code uses the MonMsg command to determine whether a particular file exists. If the file does not exist, the program uses the CrtPF (Create Physical File) command to create the file. The program then uses the ClrPFM (Clear Physical File Member) command to clear the existing file (if the program just created the new file, the member will already be empty).

Global Message Monitoring

In addition to using a command-level message monitor to plan for errors from specific commands, you can use another form of MonMsg to catch other errors that might occur. This form of MonMsg use is called a program-level, or global, message monitor. You must position a global message monitor immediately after the last Dcl (Declare) statement and before any executable CL commands. Figure 31.6 illustrates the placement of a global message monitor.

FIGURE 31.6
Global Message Monitor

```
Pgm

/*  ==============================================================  */
/*  =  Variable declarations                                     =  */
/*  ==============================================================  */

  Dcl         &Obj         *Char      (   10    )
  Dcl         &ObjLib      *Char      (   10    )
  Dcl         &ObjType     *Char      (    8    )

/*  ==============================================================  */
/*  =  Global error monitor                                      =  */
/*  ==============================================================  */

  MonMsg      ( CPF0000 MCH0000 ) Exec(                                +
    GoTo        Error                )
  .
  .
  .
```

There are two schools of thought concerning which message IDs a global message monitor should monitor for. One method monitors for CPF0000 and MCH0000 (and potentially other generic message IDs), while the other monitors for CPF9999. We'll describe the major differences, and you can decide which method suits you best.

When a global MonMsg command monitors for CPF0000 and MCH0000, it receives control when your program receives any CPF*xxxx* or MCH*xxxx* exception message that isn't trapped by a specific MonMsg following the command that caused the exception. The result is that the last exception message in the message queue is the message related to the error. Your program can then easily receive this message and present it in whatever manner you prefer (e.g., resend it up the call stack, display it in a message subfile). With this method, if messages with other prefixes are of concern, you need to add a generic message to the list of global messages to be monitored.

If you instead implement your global message monitor so that it monitors for CPF9999, the monitor gains control when the program receives a CPF9999 escape message. Any unhandled exceptions generate a CPF9999 message, so your program will still trap all exceptions, but it will do so later in the game. Proponents of this method cite two potential advantages: You need only list the CPF9999 message on the global MonMsg command, and the CPF9999 message data contains the number of the statement where the error occurred. The disadvantage of this method is that the CPF9999 message becomes the most recent exception message in the message queue. You must therefore add logic to try to mine the actual message from all the messages in the message queue — and there may be many! Even though the original error message still exists in the message queue, it's sometimes very difficult to determine what the actual error is by retrieving and examining the messages. Therefore, presentation isn't as easy as when you monitor for CPF0000 and MCH0000.

We prefer to monitor for CPF0000 and MCH0000, and that is the method used in the examples presented here. Whichever method you choose, use it consistently.

Message Processing in Action

Figure 31.7 shows a sample program that demonstrates message processing.

FIGURE 31.7

Examples of Message Processing

```
/*  ================================================================  */
/*  =  Sample message processing                                   =  */
/*  ================================================================= */

  Pgm

/*  ================================================================  */
/*  = Variable declarations                                        =  */
/*  ================================================================  */

  Dcl         &MsgID       *Char      (    7    )
  Dcl         &MsgDta      *Char      (  256    )
  Dcl         &MsgF        *Char      (   10    )
  Dcl         &MsgFLib     *Char      (   10    )
  Dcl         &Error       *Lgl

/*  ================================================================  */
/*  = Global error monitor                                         =  */
/*  ================================================================  */

  MonMsg      ( CPF0000 MCH0000 ) Exec(                               +
    Goto        Error                  )

/*  ================================================================  */
/*  = Try to delete a nonexistent file and trap errors             =  */
/*  ================================================================  */

  DltF        QTemp/DummyF1
  MonMsg      ( CPF2105 )

/*  ================================================================  */
/*  = Try to delete a nonexistent file and do not trap errors      =  */
/*  ================================================================  */

  DltF        QTemp/DummyF2

/*  ================================================================  */
/*  = Send completion message                                      =  */
/*  ================================================================  */

  SndPgmMsg   MsgID( CPF9897 )                                        +
              MsgF( QSys/QCPFMsg )                                    +
              MsgDta( 'Example completed normally.' )                 +
              ToPgmQ( *Prv ( * ) )                                    +
              MsgType( *Comp )
```

continued

FIGURE 31.7 CONTINUED

```
/*  ================================================================  */
/*  = Exit program                                                 =  */
/*  ================================================================  */

  Return

/*  ================================================================  */
/*  = Error handler                                                =  */
/*  ================================================================  */

Error:

  If         ( &Error )                                                +
    Do
      SndPgmMsg  MsgID( CPF9897 )                                      +
                 MsgF( QSYS/QCPFMSG )                                  +
                 MsgDta( 'Unexpected error occurred. See job log.' )   +
                 MsgType( *Escape )
      MonMsg     ( CPF0000 MCH0000 )
      Return
    EndDo

  ChgVar     &Error      ( '1' )

  RcvMsg     MsgType( *Excp )                                          +
             MsgDta( &MsgDta )                                         +
             MsgID( &MsgID )                                           +
             MsgF( &MsgF )                                             +
             MsgFLib( &MsgFLib )

  MonMsg     ( CPF0000 MCH0000 )

  SndPgmMsg  MsgID( &MsgID)                                            +
             MsgF( &MsgFLib/&MsgF )                                    +
             MsgDta( &MsgDta )                                         +
             MsgType( *Escape )

  MonMsg     ( CPF0000 MCH0000 )

/*  ================================================================  */
/*  = End of program                                               =  */
/*  ================================================================  */

  EndPgm
```

The program begins by declaring variables used with error handling. Next, you see a global error monitor that monitors for any CPF*xxxx* and MCH*xxxx* exceptions. If such an exception occurs, control is passed to the error handler at label Error. The program then attempts to delete a nonexistent file, DummyF1 in library QTemp. Because this command is followed by a MonMsg command that traps the error, the program continues. Next, the program tries to delete yet another nonexistent file, DummyF2 in library QTemp. Because this DltF command is not followed by a specific MonMsg command, the global monitor gains control and in turn passes control to the error handler at label Error. Notice that following the attempt to delete file DummyF2 is a SndPgmMsg command to send a completion message indicating successful completion. The program does not execute this command because the global error handler gains control before the program ever reaches this point.

The global error handler appears at label Error. It first checks to see whether the error handler has already been entered (i.e., whether logical variable &Error is true). This happens only if some unexpected error occurs in the global error handler itself. If &Error is true, the program sends an escape message indicating that an unexpected error occurred. For precaution's sake, the program also includes a MonMsg command and a Return command in case the SndPgmMsg command fails.

The remainder of the global error handler is the portion that executes under normal error-handling circumstances (i.e., when &Error is false). This section first sets logical variable &Error to true ('1') to indicate that the error-handling section has been entered. Next, the program receives the most recent exception message using the RcvMsg command and resends the message up the call stack as an escape message using the SndPgmMsg command.

What Else Can You Do with Messages?

Now that you understand the mechanics, you may want to know what else you can do with messages. Here are three possible solutions using messages:

- Create a message break-handling program for your message queue. (For more information, see Chapter 8.)
- Create a request message processor (a command processor like QCmd). (For more information, see *OS/400 CL Programming*, SC41-5721.)
- Use the SndPgmMsg and RcvMsg commands to send and receive data strings between programs. For instance, you might send a string of order data to a message queue where the order print program uses RcvMsg to receive and print the order data. This approach avoids the need to submit a job or call a program. The order print program simply waits for messages to arrive on the queue. The process functions similarly to data queue processing but is simpler because you can display message information (you can't display a data queue without writing a special program to perform that task).

These are only a few examples of how you might use messages to perform tasks on the system. With the mechanics under your belt, it's time for you to explore how you can use messages to enhance your own applications.

Chapter 32

OS/400 Commands

OS/400 commands — friend or foe? That's the big question for anyone new to the iSeries. It's certainly understandable to look at the IBM-supplied system commands and wonder just how many there are, why so many are needed, and how you're ever going to remember them all!

The good news is that you don't need to remember all these commands. You do need a modicum of familiarity with them, though. In this introduction to OS/400 commands, we give you a few helpful tips and suggestions for using and customizing system commands.

Commands: The Heart of the System

The command is at the heart of the iSeries operating system. Whether you're working with an output queue, creating an object, displaying messages, or creating a subsystem, you are using an OS/400 command. When you select an option from an OS/400 menu or from a list panel display, you're usually executing a command. Let us give you a couple of examples.

Figure 32.1 shows the iSeries USER (User Tasks) menu. Next to each menu option, we've listed the command that the system executes when you select that option. You can simply key in the named command to achieve the same results as the menu option.

Figure 32.2 shows the familiar Work with Output Queue display. After the screen format, we've listed the available options and the command that the system executes for each one. For instance, if you enter **6** (Release) next to a spooled file entry on the list, the system releases that spooled file. If you're familiar with the system commands, you can enter **RlsSplF** on a command line (to execute the Release Spooled File command), request prompting for the command, and fill in the appropriate parameters to accomplish the same thing. Obviously, typing in the RlsSplF command is much more time-consuming than entering a 6 in the appropriate blank. However, this example isn't typical of all OS/400 commands. In many cases, keying in the command is quicker and easier than using the menus. To know which technique to use, it's helpful to have a firm grasp of how commands are organized and how they can be used and to know which commands are important to remember.

FIGURE 32.1
User Tasks Menu and System Commands Panel

```
USER                                  User Tasks
                                                          System:   AS400
Select one of the following:

     1. Display or change your job                  (WrkJob)
     2. Display messages                            (DspMsg)
     3. Send a message                              (SndMsg)
     4. Submit a job                                (SbmJob)
     5. Work with your spooled output files         (WrkSplF)
     6. Work with your batch jobs                   (WrkSbmJob)
     7. Display or change your library list         (EdtLibL)
     8. Change your password                        (ChgPwd)
     9. Change your user profile                    (ChgUsrPrf)

    60. More user task options

    90. Sign off

Selection or command
===> ____________________________________________________________

F3=Exit   F4=Prompt   F9=Retrieve   F12=Cancel   F13=Information Assistant
F16=AS/400 Main menu
(C) COPYRIGHT IBM CORP. 1980, 1999.
```

FIGURE 32.2
Work with Output Queue Panel

```
                        Work with Output Queue

Queue:   PRT01          Library:   QUSRSYS        Status:   RLS

Type options, press Enter.
  1=Send   2=Change   3=Hold   4=Delete   5=Display   6=Release   7=Messages
  8=Attributes        9=Work with printing status

Opt  File        User       User Data   Sts   Pages   Copies  Form Type   Pty
 _   QSYSPRT     QSYSOPR    PRT01       WTR       3        1  *STD          5
 _   PRINTKEY    QSYSOPR    PRT01       RDY       1        1  *STD          5
 _   QQRYPRT     GGUTHRIE   PRT01       HLD      23        2  *STD          5
 _   QPDSPLIB    QSECOFR    PRT01       HLD      70        1  *STD          5
 _   ARLIST      KNIELSEN   PRT01       SAV      31        3  *STD          5



                                                                       Bottom
Parameters for options 1, 2, 3 or command
===> ____________________________________________________________
F3=Exit   F11=View 2   F12=Cancel   F20=Writers   F22=Printers
F24=More keys
```

continued

FIGURE 32.2 *CONTINUED*

Command invoked for each Work with Output Queue option

Option	*OS/400 command*	*Command function description*
1=Send	SndNetSplF	Send Network Spooled File
2=Change	ChgSplF	Change Spooled File Attributes
3=Hold	HldSplF	Hold Spooled File
4=Delete	DltSplF	Delete Spooled File
5=Display	DspSplF	Display Spooled File
6=Release	RlsSplF	Release Spooled File
8=Attributes	WrkSplFA	Work with Spooled File Attributes
9=Work with printing status	WrkPrtSts	Work with Printing Status

Before we continue with this chapter, let us say something about how system commands are organized and named. OS/400 commands consist basically of a verb and a noun — for example, the CrtOutQ command is made up of the verb "Create" and the noun "Output Queue." More than two-thirds of the existing commands are constructed using just 10 verbs: Add, Chg, Cpy, Crt, Dlt, Dsp, End, Rmv, Str, and Wrk. This is good news if you're worried about remembering commands. We recommend you first familiarize yourself with the various objects that can exist on the system. Once you understand most of those objects, you can quickly figure out what verbs can operate on each object type. For example, you can't delete a job, but you can end one.

For help identifying and using OS/400 commands, try using one or more of the following resources:

- On any command line, press F4 (Prompt). OS/400 will present you with a menu of the major command groups. You can choose menu options to find and select the command you need.
- On any command line, type **Go Cmd*xxx***, filling in the *xxx* with either a verb or an object — for example, **Go CmdPTF** for PTF-related commands or **Go CmdWrk** for "work with" commands. OS/400 will present you with a list of those commands.
- Type a generic name directly on the command line (e.g., Wrk*, Str*, CrtDev*) and press Enter. OS/400 will present you with a list of commands that start with the same letters you specified before the asterisk.
- Type a command on the command line, and press F1 (Help). OS/400 offers online help for all system commands.

Note

You can also execute the SltCmd (Select Command) command to find commands using a generic name (e.g., Str*, Wrk*). We don't recommend using this command, though; it's too easy to accidentally type D instead of S as the first character in the command — that's right, DltCmd Wrk*! Oops!!

Tips for Entering Commands

Put a little time and effort into learning a few phrases in this new language, and you'll be comfortably productive with day-to-day tasks on the iSeries. Once you've acquainted yourself with some of the most frequently used commands, it's often easier to key them in on the system command line than it is to go through the menus. Follow these tips for entering commands to help ensure correct syntax and get up to speed:

- Be sure to enter values for required parameters.
- When entering parameter values positionally (i.e., without keywords), key them in the same order as they appear in the CL documentation's command syntax diagram. If you exceed the number of allowed parameters, the system issues an error message. The syntax diagram uses a P in a box to designate the number of allowed positional parameters. If this symbol doesn't appear in the syntax diagram, you can code all parameters positionally.
- Specify values for positional parameters unless you want to use the default values.

Keeping these guidelines in mind, let's practice a few commands. First, consider the DspObjD (Display Object Description) command. Type **DspObjD** and press F4 to prompt the command. In the resulting screen (Figure 32.3), the line next to "Object" will be in bold, indicating that parameter Object is a required parameter.

FIGURE 32.3
DspObjD Command Panel

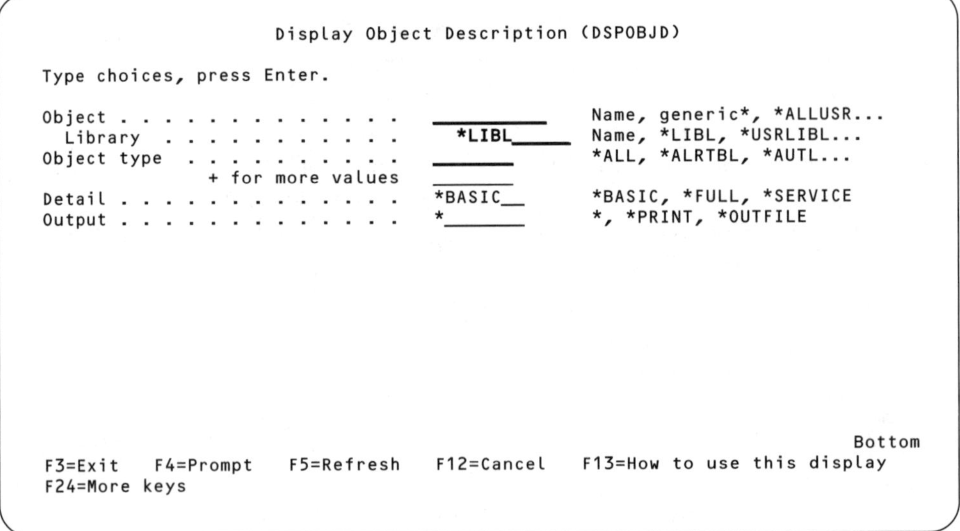

```
                    Display Object Description (DSPOBJD)

Type choices, press Enter.

Object . . . . . . . . . . . . . .   __________    Name, generic*, *ALLUSR...
  Library  . . . . . . . . . . . .     *LIBL_____  Name, *LIBL, *USRLIBL...
Object type  . . . . . . . . . . .   _______       *ALL, *ALRTBL, *AUTL...
               + for more values     _______
Detail . . . . . . . . . . . . . .   *BASIC__      *BASIC, *FULL, *SERVICE
Output . . . . . . . . . . . . . .   *_______      *, *PRINT, *OUTFILE

                                                                     Bottom
F3=Exit   F4=Prompt   F5=Refresh   F12=Cancel   F13=How to use this display
F24=More keys
```

Now press F11, and you'll see the screen shown in Figure 32.4.

FIGURE 32.4
DspObjD Command Panel with Keywords

```
                     Display Object Description (DSPOBJD)

Type choices, press Enter.

Object . . . . . . . . . . . . . OBJ          __________
  Library  . . . . . . . . . . .                *LIBL______
Object type  . . . . . . . . . . OBJTYPE      _______
                       + for more values      _______
Detail . . . . . . . . . . . . . DETAIL       *BASIC__
Output . . . . . . . . . . . . . OUTPUT       *_______









                                                                    Bottom
F3=Exit   F4=Prompt   F5=Refresh   F12=Cancel   F13=How to use this display
F24=More keys
```

Notice that the keywords now appear beside each field (e.g., OBJ for object name, OBJTYPE for object type). The Obj keyword requires a qualified value, which means you must supply the name of the library in which the object is found. The default value *LibL displayed on the screen indicates that if you don't enter a specific library name, the system will search for the object in the job's library list.

You'll also see that the entry fields for keywords DETAIL and OUTPUT do not appear in bold; this means they are optional parameters. The default value for Detail is *Basic, indicating that basic object information should be displayed. The default value for Output is * (asterisk), which instructs the system to display the results of the command on the screen.

Now, key in the values QGPL and QSys for the object name and library name, respectively, and enter the value *Lib for the ObjType parameter. Press Enter, and the screen will display the object description for library QGPL, which exists in library QSys.

Next, using only the command line, type in the same command as either

```
DspObjD QSys/QGPL *Lib
```

or

```
DspObjD QGPL *Lib
```

Either command meets the syntax requirements. Keywords aren't needed because all the parameters used are positional and the order of the values is correct. Suppose you type

```
DspObjD QGPL *Lib *Full
```

Will this work? Sure. In this example, you've entered, in the correct order, values for the two required parameters and a value (*Full) for the optional, positional parameter (Detail).

What if you want to direct the output to the printer and you type

```
DspObjD QGPL *Lib *Full *Print
```

Will this work? No! You have to use the keyword (Output) in addition to the value (*Print), because Output is beyond the positional coding limit.

Let's say you skip *Full and just enter

```
DspObjD QGPL *Lib Output(*Print)
```

Because you haven't specified a value for the positional parameter Detail, you'll get the description specified by the default value (*Basic).

Most of the time, you'll probably prompt commands, but learning how to enter a few frequently used commands with minimal keystrokes can save you time. For example, which would be faster: to prompt the WrkOutQ (Work with Output Queue) command just to enter the output queue name or to enter

```
WrkOutQ OutQName
```

Should you prompt the WrkJobQ (Work with Job Queue) command just to enter the job queue name, or should you simply enter

```
WrkJobQ JobQName
```

In both cases, you'll save yourself a step (or more) by simply entering the entire command.

Customizing Commands

Taking our discussion one step further, let's explore how you might create friendlier versions of certain useful system commands. Why would you want to? Well, some (translation: "many") IBM-supplied commands are long, requiring multiple keystrokes. You might want to shorten the commands you use most often. For example, you could shorten the command WrkSbmJob (Work with Submitted Jobs) to WSJ or Jobs. The command WrkOutQ could become WO, and the command DspMsg (Display Messages) could become Msg. How can you accomplish this without renaming the actual IBM commands or having to create your own command to execute the real system command? Easy! Just use the CrtDupObj (Create Duplicate Object) command.

Before trying this command, first create a library to hold all your new customized versions of IBM-supplied commands.

Caution

Don't place the new command in library QSys or any other system-supplied library. New releases of OS/400 replace these libraries, and your modified command will be lost when that happens. Give your new library a name that describes the library's purpose (e.g., AltSys), and include (before QSys) the new library in the system portion of the library list of those users who will use your modified commands.

When the destination library is ready, use the CrtDupObj command to copy the commands you want to customize into the new library. CrtDupObj lets you duplicate individual objects, or you can duplicate objects generically (i.e., using an initial character string common to a group of objects followed by an asterisk), all objects in a particular library, or multiple object types.

To rename the WrkOutQ command, you could enter

```
CrtDupObj WrkOutQ QSys *Cmd AltSys WO
```

In this example, WrkOutQ, QSys, and *Cmd are values for required parameters that specify the object, the originating library, and the object type, respectively. If you prompt for the parameters, enter

```
CrtDupObj Obj(WrkOutQ)   +
          FromLib(QSys) +
          ObjType(*Cmd) +
          ToLib(AltSys) +
          NewObj(WO)
```

Either of these commands places the new command (WO) into library AltSys.

When you duplicate an object, all the object's attributes are duplicated. This means that the command processing program for WO is the same as for WrkOutQ, so the new command functions just the same as the IBM-supplied command.

Changing Default Values

The final touch for tailoring commands is to modify certain parameter default values when you know you'll normally use different standard values for those parameters. You may want to change default values for the Crt*Xxx* (Create) commands especially. For example, for every physical file created, you may want to specify the Size (Member size) parameter as (1000 1000 999). Or you may want the WaitRcd (Maximum record wait time) parameter to contain the value 30 rather than the IBM-supplied default value of 60. You can change these defaults using one of two methods.

The first method requires that everyone who uses a command remember to specify the desired values instead of the defaults for certain parameters. Although you can place such requirements in a data processing handbook or a standards guide, this method relies on your staff to either remember the substitute values or look up the values each time they need to key them in.

The other method for changing the default values of IBM-supplied commands is to use the ChgCmdDft (Change Command Default) command. ChgCmdDft simply changes the default values that will be used when the command is processed. For instance, to make the changes mentioned above for the CrtPF (Create Physical File) command, you'd type

```
ChgCmdDft Cmd(CrtPF)                                 +
          NewDft('Size(1000 1000 999) WaitRcd(30)')
```

You could also use ChgCmdDft to enhance the WO command we created earlier. Suppose you usually use the WO command to work with your own output queue. Why not change the default value of *All for the OutQ parameter to be the name of your own output queue? Then, rather than having to type

```
WO YourOutQ
```

you could simply type WO (of course, this personalized command should exist only in your library list). If you want to work with another output queue, you can still type in the queue name to override the default value. See? Commands can be fun!

To change system command parameter defaults using the ChgCmdDft command, you should duplicate the command into a different library. Then change the command defaults and, if you have retained the CL command names rather than renaming the commands, list the library before QSys on the system library list.

Tip

When you use the ChgCmdDft or CrtDupObj command to customize CL commands, you should create a CL source program that performs those changes. Then whenever a new release of OS/400 is installed, you should run the CL program, thus duplicating or modifying the new version of the system commands. The system commands on the new release might have new parameters, different command processing programs, or new default values.

Using ChgCmdDft is an effective way to control standards. However, you should be cautious when using this command because it affects all uses of the changed command. (For example, a vendor-supplied software package might be affected by a change you make.) You might want to use a good documentation package to find all uses of specific commands and evaluate the risk of changing certain default values.

You can change your user profile attribute UsrOpt (User options) to include the value *CLKwd if you want the CL keywords to be displayed automatically when you prompt commands (rather than having to press F11 to see them). To change this attribute, someone with the proper authority should enter the ChgUsrPrf (Change User Profile) command as follows:

```
ChgUsrPrf UserProfile UsrOpt(*CLKwd)
```

Some users, notably some programmers, find this option useful.

The iSeries provides a function-rich command structure that lets you maneuver through the operations of your system. We don't happen to believe that everyone should be able to enter every command without prompting or using any keywords. But we're convinced that having a good working knowledge of the available OS/400 commands will not only help you save time but also make you more productive on the system.

Chapter 33

It's Gotta Be TCP/IP, If You Wanna Talk with Me

It's virtually impossible to have a computer today without the need to use Transmission Control Protocol/Internet Protocol (TCP/IP). It seems that no matter where you turn, TCP/IP is being used for something. TCP/IP arose out of the need for dissimilar systems to share information and resources across a network. You need only think of the Internet for a good example.

TCP and IP, separate protocols, are only two in a set of several protocols that provide the support for sharing information and resources across your local area network (LAN) or even around the world on the Internet. However, because TCP and IP are the foundation protocols of the set, the industry simply refers to the entire set as TCP/IP.

OS/400 contains basic communications support for TCP/IP on the iSeries, and many iSeries installations are putting TCP/IP to use. In fact, we can't recall the last time we saw an iSeries or AS/400 installation that wasn't using TCP/IP. One reason for this is the fact that, in most cases, installations are using Client Access Express for display sessions, and Client Access Express works only with TCP/IP connectivity. TCP/IP does a lot more, though, and with licensed program 5769-TC1, it provides support for several applications and functions.

For instance, TCP/IP includes applications such as

- Telnet (TELetypewriter NETwork) — lets users on one system sign on to another system
- FTP (File Transfer Protocol) — sends files from one system to another
- SMTP (Simple Mail Transfer Protocol) — exchanges e-mail between systems
- POP server (Post Office Protocol) — the iSeries implementation of POP3 that lets iSeries systems act as POP servers for clients that support the POP mail interface
- REXEC server (Remote EXECution) — lets clients submit system commands to remote servers
- LPR/LPD (Line Printer Requester/Line Printer Daemon) — sends printer files to and receives printer files from remote systems
- SNMP (Simple Network Management Protocol) — supports the industry-standard management protocol that originated for TCP/IP networks
- HTTP server (HyperText Transfer Protocol) — serves multimedia objects such as Hypertext Markup Language (HTML) documents to Web browsers
- SSL (Secure Sockets Layer) — provides secure public encryption for HTML, Telnet, and FTP

In addition to these applications, TCP/IP supports functions such as

- BOOTP server (BOOTstrap Protocol) — lets workstations without media request IPL code from a server
- RouteD server (Route Daemon) — supports Routing Information Protocol (RIP), the most commonly used routing protocol
- SLIP (Serial Line Internet Protocol) — provides dial-up TCP/IP support
- PPP (Point-to-Point Protocol) — provides dial-up TCP/IP support
- TFTP server (Trivial File Transfer Protocol) — permits unauthenticated basic file transfer using a simple protocol

Although this isn't a complete list of TCP/IP applications and functions, it should make clear the fact that TCP/IP has considerable substance.

To administer TCP/IP on your system, you need a basic understanding of a few TCP/IP concepts. In this chapter, we introduce you to those concepts and discuss a commonly used iSeries TCP/IP configuration: TCP/IP over Ethernet.

Networks and Internetworks

An important aspect of TCP/IP is that in addition to supporting networks, TCP/IP supports *internetworks*. An internetwork is actually a collection of multiple individual networks that, to the attached computers, appears to be a single large network. The Internet, composed of thousands of networks, is the quintessential example of an internetwork.

Even though the networks that make up an internetwork can be of differing physical types (e.g., Ethernet, Token-Ring), through the magic of TCP/IP, interaction between the systems on the internetwork is possible. Before we discuss how internetworks send information from one attached system to another, we want to briefly touch on the way in which information gets from one attached system to another on a network.

Figure 33.1A shows an Ethernet network that we refer to as network A.

FIGURE 33.1A
Ethernet Network A

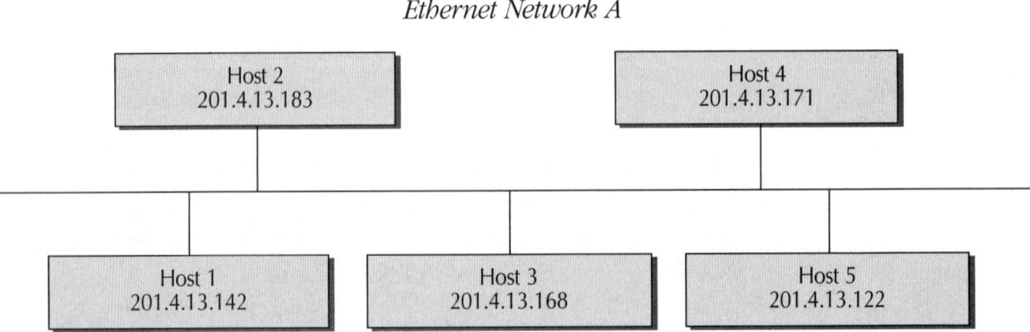

This network has five attached computers (hosts), each with an IP address unique to the network. The uniqueness of the IP address makes it possible to route information to a particular host on the network. For example, host 2 could send information to host 4 by directing the information to IP address 201.4.13.171. We discuss IP addressing in more detail later; for now, simply note that an IP address consists of four bytes most often represented in *dotted-decimal notation*, as the examples show. Dotted-decimal notation represents each byte as a decimal number in the range 0–255, separated by periods.

Figure 33.1B represents yet another network, network B.

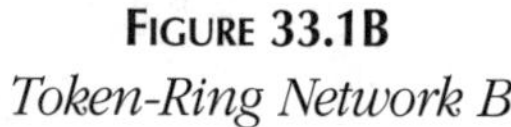
FIGURE 33.1B
Token-Ring Network B

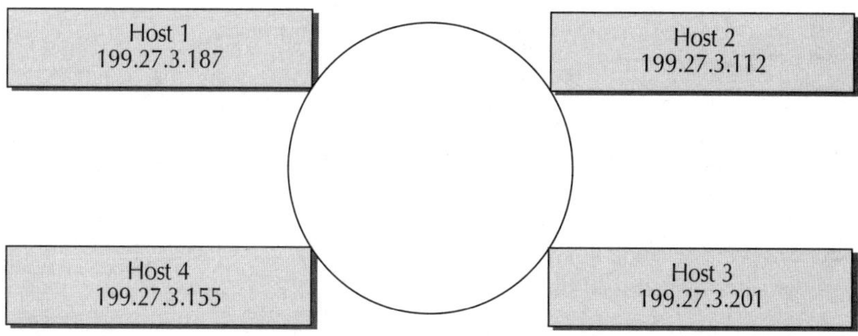

Notice that this network is a Token-Ring network with four attached hosts. Again, each attached host has an IP address that uniquely identifies the host to the network. Just as any host on network A can send information to any other host on network A, so can any host on network B send information to any other of network B's hosts.

An internetwork might connect LANs within a building or campus, or it might be a wide area network (WAN) connecting far-flung LANs. Each network connects to the internetwork via a special device called a *gateway* or *router*. The terms are used interchangeably, but usually a gateway is a computer running special software, called *routing software*, while a router is a dedicated hardware device devoted to providing an interface with the internetwork.

With an internetwork, any host can send information to any other host, regardless of the network containing the host. All one machine has to know is that a destination IP address isn't local — it then sends the traffic for that IP address to the gateway or router, which figures out how to get the traffic to the final destination. This process is called *routing*.

Figure 33.2 represents an internetwork connecting the local area networks network A and network B. Notice that network A and network B each have their own IP router devices. When hosts on network A want to exchange data, they do so directly across the network A LAN. But when a host on network A wants to talk to one on network B, the network A host sends its traffic to the router. For example, host 2 on network A could send information to host 3 on network B (199.27.3.201) by directing the information to the

FIGURE 33.2
Internetwork

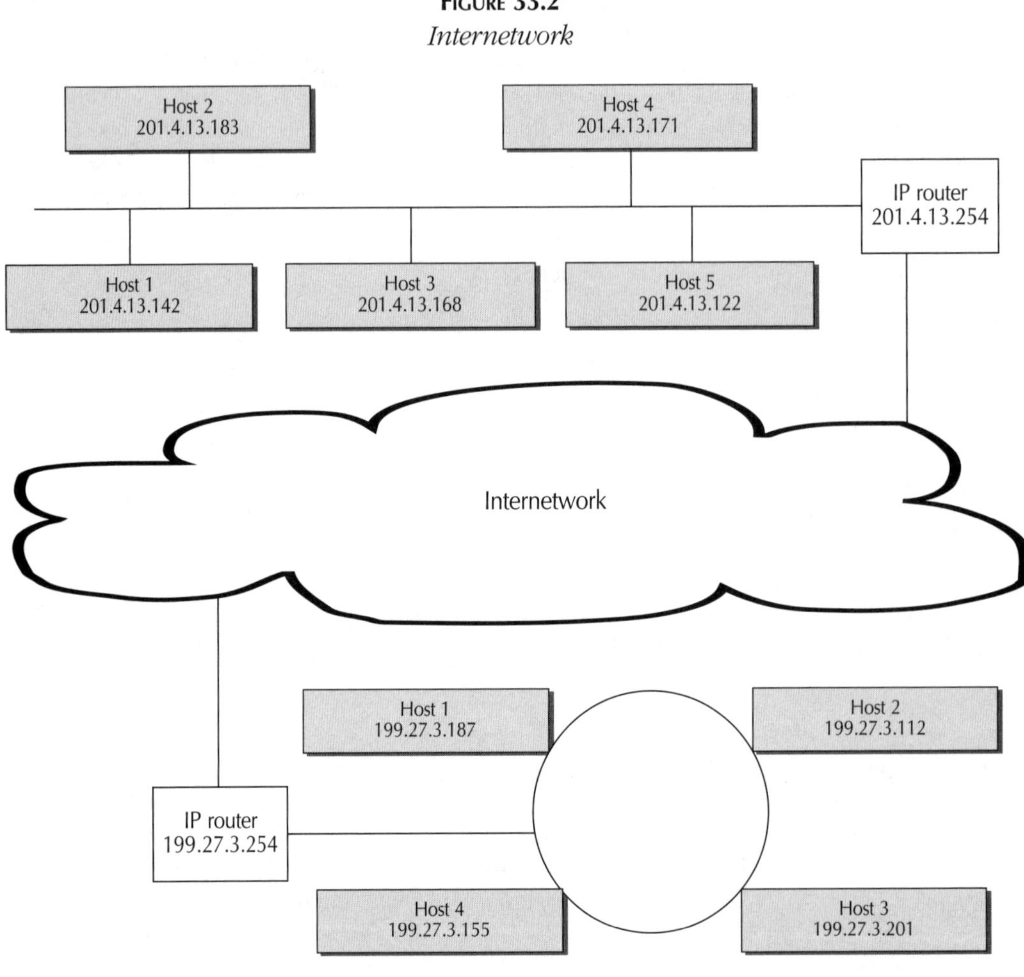

router on network A at IP address 201.4.13.254. This router then sends the information to the network B IP router at address 199.27.3.254, which in turn forwards the information to destination IP address 199.27.3.201, host 3 on network B. The response from host 3 on network B follows the reverse path. How does host 2 know that host 3 is on a distant network? The answer is the IP address, as you'll see shortly.

TCP/IP traffic from one host to another can travel through numerous routers before reaching its final destination. So how does TCP/IP know when the information has reached the destination? TCP/IP sends information in *packets*, and these packets contain not only data but also the destination IP address. As a system receives packets, it compares its own IP address (the system could actually have multiple IP addresses) to the destination IP address in the packet. When these addresses match, the packet has reached its destination and the system doesn't forward it to any other systems.

That's the simple version, anyhow. Considering that the Internet has millions of attached hosts, what do you think would happen if when one host sent information to another, all of the Internet's hosts had to determine whether the information was for them? The answer is nothing! The internetwork would exhaust its resources trying to determine destinations. You might think, then, that it obviously doesn't work like this. Essentially, it *does* work this way, but not without optimization.

That optimization is the routing process, which keeps track of the best path to any destination from any other given destination. The wonderful thing about TCP/IP routing is that if a path to a destination becomes unavailable (perhaps someone inadvertently cuts a fiber optic cable), TCP/IP routing will find an alternative path and immediately switch to it without interrupting user sessions. This self-healing aspect of TCP/IP is what makes the Internet practical. In reality, the Internet is never running completely — there are always some routers in the Internet broken at any given time. However, TCP/IP routes around this damage so that most users never see the problem. The only time TCP/IP routing fails is when no alternative path to a given destination exists. For example, if your company has a single link to the Internet and that link goes down, nobody on the Internet can reach you until that link is repaired.

You've seen that each host on an internetwork has a unique address. What we've not yet told you is that each network also has a unique address. This network address makes it possible for the internetwork to determine a more direct route to a system when sending information to it. This reduces the number of routing decisions the internetwork must make, improving internetwork performance.

You also know how to specify a host's unique IP address, but you may be wondering how you specify the network address. As it turns out, the network address is part of the IP address you specify for your host. That is, an IP address contains both the network address (or *network ID*) *and* the host address (or *host ID*), with the network address preceding the host address. An IP address can therefore be represented with these two portions as

[Network ID][Host ID]

As a quick illustration, consider three hosts, with IP addresses 192.168.0.1, 192.168.0.5, and 192.168.120.1. If the network part of the address is the first three bytes, the first two hosts are on the same network — the 192.168.0.0 network. The third host is on a completely different network — the 192.168.120.0 network. In a minute, you'll see how to tell the network part of the address from the host part. In the meantime, keep this important rule in mind: *For a host in one network to talk to a host in another network, the networks must be connected through a router.* This key concept will save you many headaches when you work on your own network designs. With that in mind, it's time to turn our attention to IP addressing to get a closer look at how things work.

IP Addressing

If you want to understand TCP/IP, one of the first things you must understand is a few IP addressing concepts. You need to know more than the fact that IP addresses normally appear in dotted form and that IP addresses contain both a network ID and a host ID.

TCP/IP is for use by small networks with only a few hosts as well as by very large networks that have tens of thousands of hosts. In addition, internetworks such as the Internet use TCP/IP. When you consider the variable sizes and complexities of these arrangements, you may begin to wonder just how TCP/IP divides the IP address into the network ID and host ID portions. With all these different types of networks, it's not possible to divide an IP address into its network ID and host ID portions with a single fixed method. Instead, two methods have evolved, called *classful* and *classless* IP addressing. The first method, classful addressing, is older and falling into disuse, primarily because it allocates IP addresses inefficiently and the rapid growth of the Internet is quickly depleting the available addresses. The classless method of IP addressing is what is primarily used today, but to understand classless addressing, you first need to appreciate classful addressing. The good news is that classless addressing is much simpler than classful addressing!

Classful IP Addressing

In classful addressing, TCP/IP defines five classes of networks. Primarily, the size characteristics of a network determine its class, as Figure 33.3 shows.

FIGURE 33.3
Network Classes

Network class	*Beginning value*	*Network ID (N) and host ID (h)*	*Maximum networks*	*Maximum hosts*
A	1–127[1]	NNN.hhh.hhh.hhh	127	16,777,214
B	128–191	NNN.NNN.hhh.hhh	16,383	65,534
C	192–223	NNN.NNN.NNN.hhh	2,097,151	254
D	224–239			Multicast
E	240–255[2]			Reserved

[1]Value 127 is reserved for loopback addresses used in testing TCP/IP.
[2]With the exception of broadcast address 255.255.255.255, this range is not supported by the iSeries.

The first three classes in the figure (A, B, and C) are the most commonly used classes and are the subject of this discussion. You can see that IP addresses that begin with a value between 1 and 127 belong to class A, between 128 and 191 to class B, and so on. The last two columns in the figure show the maximum number of networks and the maximum number of hosts that each class can have. With a maximum of more 16 million hosts, class A networks were intended for the largest of organizations.

The third column in the figure shows how TCP/IP divides the IP address into its respective network ID and host ID. Notice that the scheme differs for each of the classes A, B, and C. With class A networks, the first byte of the IP address defines the network

ID, and the last three bytes define the host ID. With class B networks, the first two bytes define the network ID, and the last two bytes define the host ID. Class C networks follow this pattern, with the first three bytes defining the network ID and the last byte defining the host ID.

If you're wondering how this scheme works, it may help you to think of the IP address in terms of binary, as TCP/IP does. Let's begin by looking at how TCP/IP determines the maximum number of hosts for a class C network. The third column in Figure 33.3 shows that TCP/IP specifies the host ID in the last byte of the IP address for a class C network. In binary format, the minimum possible value appears as

```
 Bits: 0123 4567
Value: 0000 0000
```

for a decimal value of 0. The maximum possible decimal value of 255 appears in binary format as

```
 Bits: 0123 4567
Value: 1111 1111
```

Between decimal values 0 and 255, there are 256 distinct values or possible combinations of bits. It may therefore seem that there is a maximum of 256 hosts allowed for a class C network. Figure 33.3, however, lists the maximum as 254 hosts. TCP/IP doesn't allow the host ID portion of an IP address to be all binary 0s or all binary 1s. Therefore, decimal value 0 (binary value 0000 0000) and decimal value 255 (binary value 1111 1111) can't be used. Removing these two values from the list of possible values yields a maximum of 254 hosts for a class C network.

To calculate the maximum number of hosts for a network class, you can use the formula

$$2^n - 2$$

where n is the number of *bits* allocated for the host ID. The formula adjusts for the two disallowed host ID values (all binary 0s and all binary 1s). With class B networks, 16 bits are allocated to the host ID, so there is a maximum of $2^{16} - 2$, or 65,534, class B hosts. Likewise, the maximum number of class A hosts is $2^{24} - 2$, or 16,777,214.

The simplest mathematical formula for calculating the maximum number of networks for a network class is

$$128^n - 1$$

where n is the number of *bytes* allocated for the network ID. You must reduce the number by 1 to adjust for a value of decimal 0 (all binary 0s). Therefore, class A networks have a maximum number of 127 ($128^1 - 1$), class B networks have a maximum of 16,383 ($128^2 - 1$), and class C networks have a maximum of 2,097,151 ($128^3 - 1$) networks.

Earlier, we said that network addresses (network IDs) reduce the number of routing decisions an internetwork must make by providing more direct routes to systems. We also mentioned that IP routers join networks together. Remember, the Internet is simply many networks connected by IP routers to form what appears to be a single, very large network. Because an association exists between an IP router and a network ID, a large internetwork such as the Internet is able to move information from system to system in an efficient way.

Classless Addressing and Subnetworks

Now that you have a handle on classful IP addressing and how it relates to network IDs and host IDs, it's time to muddy the waters again. Don't worry — everything clears up by the end!

A problem arose with the classful addressing scheme in that the three different network sizes it supports don't fit all organizations, or even most organizations, very well. A Class B network, for example, allows 65,534 hosts. How many companies do you know that have this many hosts on their network? Yet the next smaller size, the Class C network of 254 hosts, may well be too small for many organizations. Worse, the standard of many companies today, concerned about security, is to use only *private* IP addresses internally — these addresses aren't visible to the outside world at all. These organizations usually need only a handful of IP addresses — one for each public server or firewall. The servers and firewalls take care of translating IP addresses for the private IP users on the company's internal LAN. For these reasons, TCP/IP supports the splitting of networks into subnetworks, or *subnets*. This technique is called classless IP addressing because it circumvents the limitations of network classes. Let's look at a few reasons for creating subnets, along with the details about how to do so.

Consider class A and class B networks for a moment. Both of these classes have a large number of available host IDs — nearly 17 million in the case of class A networks! Chances are excellent that an organization won't have 17 million hosts on a single network. Subnetting, using classless IP addressing, provides a way to avoid wasting these IP addresses by letting you change the way your system determines the network portion and host portion of your IP addresses. In other words, you can divide the host ID, reassigning some of the host space to network space. Reassigning host space to network space is referred to as creating a subnet, or *subnetting*.

Recall that earlier we represented the fact that an IP address is made up of the network ID followed by the host ID as

[Network ID][Host ID]

With subnetting, the representation would be

[Network ID][Subnet ID][Host ID]

Consider a class B network with a network ID of 153.47 as a candidate for subnetting. Remember, a class B network has 16 bits allocated for the network ID and 16 bits allocated for the host ID as

16 bits	*16 bits*
Network ID	Host ID

In classless addressing, a Class B network is renamed — it's called a /16 network, because the network part of the address is 16 bits. We can reallocate some of the host ID space to the subnet. To make the example simple, we'll reallocate a full byte (eight bits) of host space to the subnet. We now have 24 bits total allocated to the network portion of the IP address and eight bits allocated to the host portion as

16 bits	*8 bits*	*8 bits*
Network ID	Subnet ID	Host ID
Subnetwork		Host ID

In classless notation, this is a /24 network. Because only eight bits are allocated for the host ID, each subnet can now have only 254 hosts. However, there can now be 254 subnets of the original /16 network. (Keep in mind that each of these networks requires a router to communicate with the other networks!)

You're probably now wondering how you go about reassigning host space to network space. It's done using a *subnet mask.* A subnet mask is simply a string of binary 1s and binary 0s (32 bits' worth) that map out the network space and the host space. A value of 1 indicates the bit is allocated to network space, and a value of 0 represents host space. Figure 33.4 shows the classes of networks with their associated subnet masks.

FIGURE 33.4

Network Classes and Associated Subnet Masks

Network class	*Beginning value*	*Network ID (N) and host ID (h)*	*Subnet mask*
A	1–127[1]	NNN.hhh.hhh.hhh	255.0.0.0
B	128–191	NNN.NNN.hhh.hhh	255.255.0.0
C	192–223	NNN.NNN.NNN.hhh	255.255.255.0

[1] Value 127 is reserved for loopback addresses used in testing TCP/IP.

The values in this table are fairly straightforward because we're dealing with whole bytes. Decimal value 255 is equivalent to eight bits of binary 1, and decimal value 0 is equivalent to eight bits of binary 0. Therefore, when decimal value 255 is the subnet mask, all bits are 1 and the entire byte to which the mask is applied is network space. Likewise, when decimal value 0 is the subnet mask, all bits are 0 and the entire byte to which the mask is applied is host space.

Perhaps we can make this a little clearer by showing you the following subnet mask information with each of the four bytes clearly delineated:

```
Decimal:      255        255        255          0
 Binary: 11111111   11111111   11111111   00000000
```

It should be clearer now that a subnet mask of 255.255.255.0 indicates that the first three bytes of the IP address are network space and the last byte is host space. Note that, at a minimum, a subnet mask *must* mask off the network ID portion of the IP address. In other words, a class A network must specify a value of 255 for the first byte of the subnet mask, a class B network must specify a value of 255 for both the first and second bytes of the subnet mask, and a class C network must specify a value of 255 for the first three bytes of the subnet mask.

The subnet mask notation is still the most common way of indicating subnets, but it's rapidly being replaced by the classless notation, which is both more compact and easier to understand. For example, you could specify a complete IP address for a host as

153.47.1.4 with a subnet mask of 255.255.255.0

Or you could specify it more concisely, and more clearly, using classless notation:

153.47.1.4/24

The formal term for classless notation is *Classless Internet Domain Routing*, or *CIDR*. If someone asks you for the CIDR address of your host, you know that they want it in classless notation.

Let's look at examples of applying a subnet mask and deciphering the result. For the first example, let's use our class B network with an IP address of 153.47.21.209 and apply the associated subnet mask from Figure 33.4 (255.255.0.0). To apply a subnet mask, you perform a logical AND with the IP address (a logical AND states that if both bits are 1, the result is 1; otherwise, the result is 0).

```
Subnet mask: 11111111  11111111  00000000  00000000
 IP address: 10011001  00101111  00010101  11010001
     Subnet: 10011001  00101111  00000000  00000000
```

In this case, the subnet ID is 153.47 (drop trailing 0 values). Notice that this is the same value as the network ID, so there is no subnet. You extract the host ID from the original IP address beginning at the bit beyond the point where the subnet ID ends and ending with the last bit (bit 32). In this case, that is bits 17–32, or bytes 3 and 4. The host ID is therefore 21.209, the same as in the original IP address. We could have stopped extracting information once we determined there was no subnet because without a subnet, the network ID and host ID can be easily extracted from the IP address based on the class of network.

For our second example, let's allocate the first byte of the host ID portion of the IP address (the third byte in the IP address) to a subnet. Remember that to allocate a whole byte to a subnet, we simply set the subnet mask for that byte to value 255. Let's use our new subnet mask of 255.255.255.0 and see what the logical AND yields for a subnet.

```
Subnet mask: 11111111  11111111  11111111  00000000
 IP address: 10011001  00101111  00010101  11010001
     Subnet: 10011001  00101111  00010101  00000000
```

In this example, the subnet ID is 153.47.21, and the value 209 remains for the host ID. Again, this example is fairly straightforward because we're dealing with whole bytes and subnet mask values of 255 and 0.

Let's look now at an example that allocates bits to a subnet on a boundary other than a whole-byte boundary. In this example, let's allocate the first byte plus the first two bits of the host ID to a subnet.

```
Subnet mask: 11111111 11111111 11111111 11000000
 IP address: 10011001 00101111 00010101 11010001
     Subnet: 10011001 00101111 00010101 11000000
```

Here, the subnet mask is 255.255.255.192. The resulting subnet ID is 153.47.21.192 (notice that the value of the fourth byte of the subnet is the same as the value of the fourth byte of the subnet mask). The host ID in this example is contained in bits 27–32 because bits 25 and 26 were allocated to the subnet. Extracting bits 27–32 of the original IP address yields a value of 17 for the host ID. This shows that a class B network with a network ID of 153.47 and a subnet mask of 255.255.255.192 will resolve to subnet 153.47.21.192 host ID 17 when presented with 153.47.21.209 for an IP address.

Now that we've taken you through all these calculations, you may notice when you examine the IP address and the subnet mask that 209 minus 192 is 17. We didn't want to deprive you of any fun! Actually, we wanted you to have an understanding of how things are really working. Figure 33.5 will help you translate bit configurations to the decimal values used in subnet masks.

FIGURE 33.5

Commonly Used Values in Subnet Masks

Binary	*Decimal*
00000000	0
10000000	128
11000000	192
11100000	224
11110000	240
11111000	248
11111100	252
11111110	254
11111111	255

Peaceful Coexistence

For any network, when you assign IP addresses, you must remain aware of a few things. First, you must heed matters of correctness, such as maintaining address uniqueness as well as assigning addresses that are appropriate for the network to which your system is connected. You must also remain cognizant of any special circumstances or restrictions that might apply. For example, all networks use IP addresses beginning with 127 for loopback purposes. You should therefore refrain from assigning these addresses to hosts within your network.

With a private network — one within your enterprise — you have control over the IP addresses you assign. Other than the concerns we just mentioned, you're virtually restriction-free. Public networks, such as the Internet, require that a central authority assign any addresses that are to be detectable by the network in order to maintain uniqueness. How long do you think it would take for a duplicate address issue to arise if everyone on the Internet assigned their own addresses?

When you architect a network, you need to carefully consider not only your current needs but also what the future may hold for your network. If today's private network is tomorrow exposed to a public network, there will be problems unless you've designed your private network in a way that avoids conflict with the public network.

To help prevent problems and to promote peaceful coexistence, The Internet Assigned Numbers Authority (IANA) has designated blocks of IP addresses for use in private networks. These blocks are

10.0.0.0 to 10.255.255.255
172.15.0.0 to 172.31.255.255
192.168.0.0 to 192.168.255.255

IANA guarantees that IP addresses from these blocks are not valid host addresses for use on the Internet. We strongly suggest that for your private networks, you use IP addresses from these blocks of numbers. Doing so will prevent any problems if, in the future, these networks are exposed to the Internet. Of these blocks, the IP addresses beginning with 10 and those beginning with 192.168 are the most commonly used for private networks.

A Simple iSeries Configuration

Many users create a TCP/IP network solely to use with Client Access in accessing the iSeries from their PCs. This private network is most often an Ethernet network and makes for a good sample configuration, introducing you to the mechanics of TCP/IP configuration on an iSeries.

You should start by gathering a couple of pieces of information you'll use in configuring TCP/IP. First, determine the system name. You can find the current system name using command DspNetA (Display Network Attributes).

Next, you need to determine whether a line description exists that is associated with your communications adapter (your Ethernet card). To do so, from the command line, enter command **Go Hardware** and press Enter to display the HARDWARE (Hardware Resources) menu. From menu HARDWARE, select option 1 to work with communication resources. On the resulting Work with Communication Resources panel, locate the appropriate Ethernet adapter, and note the resource name. To determine whether a line exists for the adapter, use option 5 to work with configuration descriptions. The resulting Work with Configuration Descriptions panel displays the line information. If a line description exists, note its name; otherwise, create a line description using the following instructions:

> On the Work with Configuration Descriptions panel, type 1 in the Opt field and press Enter. The CrtLinEth (Create Line Description (Ethernet)) command prompt will be displayed. Specify a line description name. You can choose any name you like. We prefer to give the line description the same name as the resource; this makes it easy to correlate a line description with its associated resource. In addition to the line description name, you must specify the previously determined resource name.
>
> You can accept most of the default parameter values, but we suggest you page down to the AutoCrtCtl (Autocreate controller) parameter and change its value from *No to *Yes. This lets the system handle some of the additional configuration tasks. You can also enter descriptive text for the Text (Text 'description') parameter. Once you've entered all the information, press Enter to create the line description. After confirming that the system successfully created the line description, you have completed the preparatory steps.

Menus TCPADM (TCP/IP Administration, shown in Figure 33.6) and CFGTCP (Configure TCP/IP, shown in Figure 33.7) contain administration and configuration options. You'll be using options from these menus to configure your network. (For an introduction to the options these menus provide, see "TCP/IP Administration and Configuration Options," page 536.)

FIGURE 33.6

TCP/IP Administration Menu

```
TCPADM                         TCP/IP Administration
                                                              System:   AS400
Select one of the following:

     1. Configure TCP/IP
     2. Configure TCP/IP applications
     3. Start TCP/IP
     4. End TCP/IP
     5. Start TCP/IP servers
     6. End TCP/IP servers
     7. Work with TCP/IP network status
     8. Verify TCP/IP connection
     9. Start TCP/IP FTP session
    10. Start TCP/IP TELNET session
    11. Send TCP/IP spooled file

    20. Work with TCP/IP jobs in QSYSWRK subsystem


Selection or command
===> ________________________________________________________________________

F3=Exit   F4=Prompt   F9=Retrieve   F12=Cancel
```

FIGURE 33.7
Configure TCP/IP Menu

```
CFGTCP                          Configure TCP/IP
                                                              System:    AS400
Select one of the following:

     1. Work with TCP/IP interfaces
     2. Work with TCP/IP routes
     3. Change TCP/IP attributes
     4. Work with TCP/IP port restrictions
     5. Work with TCP/IP remote system information

    10. Work with TCP/IP host table entries
    11. Merge TCP/IP host table
    12. Change TCP/IP domain information

    20. Configure TCP/IP applications
    21. Configure related tables
    22. Configure point-to-point TCP/IP

Selection or command
===> ____________________________________________________________________________

F3=Exit   F4=Prompt   F9=Retrieve   F12=Cancel
```

With the simple network you're configuring, you have only two tasks to complete to begin communicating with TCP/IP. You must define the iSeries to the network by specifying its IP address, and you must specify your domain information.

For our sample network, we'll use a class A IP address from the block of reserved private addresses beginning with 10. We'll also create a subnet, in light of the fact that a class A address has space for a few million more addresses than we really need! This will also give us flexibility for future networking needs within the organization. In the example, we'll allocate a full byte for the subnet ID portion of our IP address. We'll therefore select an IP address of 10.1.0.1 for the iSeries, with a value of 255.255.0.0 for the subnet mask.

You specify the system's IP address by defining a TCP/IP interface. We'll use option 1 from menu CFGTCP, Work with TCP/IP interfaces, to perform this task. Figure 33.8 shows the Work with TCP/IP Interfaces panel you'll see when you select option 1 from menu CFGTCP.

If TCP/IP has never been configured on your system, you'll probably see that a single interface with an IP address of 127.0.0.1 already exists. This is a special address for loopback functions used in testing TCP/IP. Using option 1 (Add) from the Work with TCP/IP Interfaces panel, we'll add our network's interface information. This option prompts the AddTCPIfc (Add TCP/IP Interface) command as shown in Figure 33.9.

FIGURE 33.8
Work with TCP/IP Interfaces Panel

```
                    Work with TCP/IP Interfaces
                                                     System:   AS400
Type options, press Enter.
  1=Add   2=Change   4=Remove   5=Display   9=Start   10=End

     Internet          Subnet              Line        Line
Opt  Address           Mask                Description Type
___  ______________
___  127.0.0.1         255.0.0.0           *LOOPBACK   *NONE















                                                          Bottom
F3=Exit      F5=Refresh   F6=Print list   F11=Display interface status
F12=Cancel   F17=Top      F18=Bottom
```

FIGURE 33.9
AddTCPIfc (Add TCP/IP Interface) Command Prompt

```
                  Add TCP/IP Interface (ADDTCPIFC)

Type choices, press Enter.

Internet address . . . . . . . . > ' '______________
Line description . . . . . . . .   __________    Name, *LOOPBACK...
Subnet mask  . . . . . . . . . .   _________________
Associated local interface . . .   *NONE
Type of service  . . . . . . . .   *NORMAL       *MINDELAY, *MAXTHRPUT...
Maximum transmission unit  . . .   *LIND         576-16388, *LIND
Autostart  . . . . . . . . . . .   *YES          *YES, *NO
PVC logical channel identifier                   001-FFF
               + for more values
X.25 idle circuit timeout  . . .   60            1-600
X.25 maximum virtual circuits  .   64            0-64
X.25 DDN interface . . . . . . .   *NO           *YES, *NO
TRLAN bit sequencing . . . . . .   *MSB          *MSB, *LSB




                                                          Bottom
F3=Exit   F4=Prompt   F5=Refresh   F12=Cancel   F13=How to use this display
F24=More keys
```

You need specify only the first three values with following information:

Internet address: `10.1.0.1`
Line description: *`YourLineDescriptionName`*
Subnet mask: `255.255.0.0`

where *YourLineDescriptionName* is the line description you identified earlier. You can accept the default values for all other parameters. After you've supplied the necessary values, simply press Enter, and you've assigned the TCP/IP address for your system.

Last, we'll define the network's *domain* information. The domain name has two parts: the local domain name and the local host name. The qualified domain name (often referred to as the *host name*) by which your system is known to the network is the combination of these two parts. You can use any names you like for these values, but we suggest a standard: For local host name, we suggest you use the system name you retrieved earlier during the preparatory phase. For local domain name, use a value that is descriptive of your organization. A local domain name consists of labels separated by periods, such as iseries.ibm.com where iseries defines a domain within another domain named ibm. The .com portion simply follows Internet conventions to signify that the organization is a commercial enterprise.

Once you decide which local domain name you'd like to use, you can use option 12, Change TCP/IP domain information, from menu CFGTCP to enter your domain information. Figure 33.10 shows the Change TCP/IP Domain panel, where you can enter your chosen domain information.

FIGURE 33.10
ChgTCPDmn (Change TCP/IP Domain) Command

```
                    Change TCP/IP Domain (CHGTCPDMN)

Type choices, press Enter.

Host name . . . . . . . . . .   'AS400'_______________________________
_______________________________
Domain name . . . . . . . . .   'QUINTESSENCE.COM'____________________
______________________________________________________________________
______________________________________________________________________
_______________________________________________
Host name search priority . . .   *REMOTE       *REMOTE, *LOCAL, *SAME
Domain name server:
  Internet address . . . . . . .   *NONE__________
                                   _______________
                                   _______________

                                                                Bottom
F3=Exit   F4=Prompt   F5=Refresh   F10=Additional parameters   F12=Cancel
F13=How to use this display        F24=More keys
```

Starting TCP/IP

Your iSeries now has a TCP/IP configuration capable of communicating with other hosts on the network. Before it can do so, however, you must start TCP/IP processing. You can start TCP/IP using option 3 from menu TCPADM. This option starts TCP/IP processing as well as TCP/IP interfaces and server jobs that are configured to start automatically. After starting TCP/IP and waiting for a brief time, you can check the TCP/IP jobs in subsystem QSysWrk using option 20, Work with TCP/IP jobs in QSYSWRK subsystem, from menu TCPADM. Job QTCPIP should be in the list of active jobs, as well as TCP/IP server jobs for applications such as FTP, SMTP, and Telnet (potentially).

Tip

You can end TCP/IP processing explicitly using the EndTCP (End TCP/IP) command, implicitly by ending subsystem QSysWrk, or implicitly with a system IPL. To once again use TCP/IP, you must start TCP/IP processing again. We suggest you add command StrTCP (Start TCP/IP) to your system start-up program so TCP/IP processing starts each time you IPL the system.

Once job QTCPIP is started, you can verify that TCP/IP is functioning properly. Menu TCPADM's option 8, Verify TCP/IP connection, issues a ping to test connections. You can test TCP/IP connections at various levels as follows:

- To test connections without sending anything out of the Ethernet adapter, specify Loopback for the RmtSys (Remote system) parameter on the VfyTCPCnn (Verify TCP/IP Connection) command, as shown in Figure 33.11.
- To verify that the line description and TCP/IP interface are functioning correctly, specify your system's IP address (10.1.0.1) for the RmtSys parameter.
- To test connection to the network, specify the IP address of another host in the network (if one currently exists) for the RmtSys parameter.

Examine the resulting messages to determine whether your connections are functioning properly. If everything is fine, your system is ready to run TCP/IP applications.

FIGURE 33.11
VfyTCPCnn (Verify TCP/IP Connection) Command

```
                    Verify TCP/IP Connection (VFYTCPCNN)

 Type choices, press Enter.

 Remote system . . . . . . . . .   LOOPBACK______________________________________
________________________________________________________________________________
________________________________________________________________________________
__________________________________________









                                                                         Bottom
 F3=Exit   F4=Prompt   F5=Refresh   F10=Additional parameters   F12=Cancel
 F13=How to use this display        F24=More keys
```

TCP/IP Administration and Configuration Options

You should familiarize yourself with the TCP/IP administration and configuration options available on menus TCPADM (TCP/IP Administration) and CFGTCP (Configure TCP/IP). Here is a brief introduction to the functions these options provide.

Menu TCPADM — TCP/IP Administration

1. **Configure TCP/IP**
   This option displays menu CFGTCP.
2. **Configure TCP/IP applications**
   This option displays options for configuring TCP/IP applications.
3. **Start TCP/IP**
   This option issues the StrTCP (Start TCP/IP) command, which initializes and activates TCP/IP processing, starts the TCP/IP interfaces, and starts the TCP/IP server jobs.
4. **End TCP/IP**
   This option issues the EndTCP (End TCP/IP) command, which ends all TCP/IP processing.
5. **Start TCP/IP servers**
   This option issues the StrTCPSvr (Start TCP/IP Server) command, which starts the TCP/IP application servers.
6. **End TCP/IP servers**
   This option issues the EndTCPSvr (End TCP/IP Server) command, which ends the TCP/IP application servers.
7. **Work with TCP/IP network status**
   This option issues the WrkTCPSts (Work with TCP/IP Network Status) command, which lets you view and manage the status of your TCP/IP interfaces, routes, and connections. WrkTCPSts is the OS/400 version of the TCP/IP NetStat (Network Status) command (OS/400 also has a NetStat command).

continued

8. **Verify TCP/IP connection**
   This option issues the VfyTCPCnn (Verify TCP/IP Connection) command, which tests the TCP/IP connection between your system and a remote system. VfyTCPCnn is the OS/400 version of the TCP/IP Ping command (OS/400 also has a Ping command).
9. **Start TCP/IP FTP session**
   This option issues the StrTCPFTP (Start TCP/IP FTP) command, which transfers a file. StrTCPFTP is the OS/400 version of the TCP/IP FTP command (OS/400 also has a FTP command).
10. **Start TCP/IP TELNET session**
   This option issues the StrTCPTelN (Start TCP/IP Telnet) command, which starts a client session with a remote system, letting you sign on to the remote system. StrTCPTelN is the OS/400 version of the TCP/IP Telnet command (OS/400 also has a Telnet command).
11. **Send TCP/IP spooled file**
   This option issues the SndTCPSplF (Send TCP/IP Spooled File) command, which sends a spooled file to a remote system. SndTCPSplF is the OS/400 version of the TCP/IP LPR (Line Printer Requester) command (OS/400 also has an LPR command).
20. **Work with TCP/IP jobs in QSYSWRK subsystem**
   This option lets you work with the active TCP/IP jobs in subsystem QSysWrk (using the WrkActJob, or Work with Active Jobs, command).

Menu CFGTCP — Configure TCP/IP

1. **Work with TCP/IP interfaces**
   This option lets you add, display, change, print, or delete TCP/IP interface information. You can also start or end an interface.
2. **Work with TCP/IP routes**
   This option lets you add, display, change, print, or delete TCP/IP route information.
3. **Change TCP/IP attributes**
   This option issues the ChgTCPA (Change TCP/IP Attributes) command, which lets you change attributes that relate to TCP/IP.
4. **Work with TCP/IP port restrictions**
   This option lets you add, display, print, or delete TCP/IP port restrictions.
5. **Work with TCP/IP remote system information**
   This option lets you add, print, or delete X.25 data network addresses.
10. **Work with TCP/IP host table entries**
   This option lets you add display, change, print, rename, or delete host table entries.
11. **Merge TCP/IP host table**
   This option issues the MrgTCPHT (Merge TCP/IP Host Table) command, which lets you merge or replace a local host table.
12. **Change TCP/IP domain information**
   This option lets you add or change TCP/IP domain information.
20. **Configure TCP/IP applications**
   This option lets you configure TCP/IP applications.
21. **Configure related tables**
   This option lets you configure tables related to TCP/IP.
22. **Configure point-to-point TCP/IP**
   This option lets you define, display, or change your TCP/IP point-to-point (SLIP) configuration.

Identifying Other Hosts in Your Network

To communicate with other hosts in your network, you need to identify them. So far, we've seen that you identify hosts by their unique IP address. Although you can use IP addresses for identification, doing so is unwieldy at best. It's simply not practical to try to remember the IP address for all your hosts, not to mention the fact that identification by IP address is certain to introduce errors.

To alleviate these problems, you can give your hosts names you can use in identifying them. There's no doubt that names are easier to remember. With a *host table*, you can associate a host name with a host address. When you then communicate with a host by name, the system retrieves that host's corresponding IP address from the host table.

You can store a host table on your iSeries system (a local host table), or you can store it on a remote name server in your network. In fact, you can have multiple remote name servers in your network. Although you can use both a local host table and remote name servers concurrently, you typically use one method or the other. Each method has its advantages and disadvantages, which we'll point out.

You usually use a local host table when your network is small with relatively few hosts. A local host table's advantage is that because it's local, it is always available and can be searched quickly. The local host table approach suffers the disadvantage that each host in your network must maintain its own host table. With every change to a host table, the change must be replicated on all your hosts.

A remote name server, more often referred to as a *domain name server (DNS)*, maintains host table information for the entire TCP/IP domain. This method has the obvious, and significant, advantage of eliminating the need to maintain a host table on each host in your network. Its disadvantage is that it requires more in-depth experience to administer than local host tables. Your network must also have a system that can act as a domain name server, and it's possible that at times outages will render this system inaccessible. Larger networks invariably use this approach to maintaining host table information.

Because our sample configuration is for a small network without a domain name server, we show you how to build a local host table. The iSeries lets you associate up to four host names with an IP address. This association is referred to as a *host table entry*. You can add a host table entry to the local host table using CFGTCP option 10, Work with TCP/IP host table entries. Figure 33.12 shows the Work with TCP/IP Host Table Entries panel. This panel's option 1 (Add) prompts the AddTCPHTE (Add TCP/IP Host Table Entry) command. Figure 33.13 shows the AddTCPHTE command with host table entry information entered.

FIGURE 33.12
Work with TCP/IP Host Table Entries Panel

```
                    Work with TCP/IP Host Table Entries
                                                      System:   AS4ØØ
Type options, press Enter.
  1=Add   2=Change   4=Remove   5=Display   7=Rename

     Internet          Host
Opt  Address           Name
_    _______________
_    127.Ø.Ø.1         LOOPBACK
                        LOCALHOST

                                                                 Bottom
F3=Exit   F5=Refresh   F6=Print list   F12=Cancel   F17=Position to
```

FIGURE 33.13
AddTCPHTE (Add TCP/IP Host Table Entry) Command

```
                    Add TCP/IP Host Table Entry (ADDTCPHTE)

 Type choices, press Enter.

 Internet address . . . . . . . . > '1Ø.1.Ø.2'_______
 Host names:                        _
   Name . . . . . . . . . . . . . > PCØØ2________________________________
________________________________________________________________________
________________________________________________________________________
__________________________________________________
                + for more values _
 Text 'description' . . . . . . .  'PCØØ2   Room 147, Slot 9'__________
___________________________________

                                                                  Bottom
 F3=Exit   F4=Prompt   F5=Refresh   F12=Cancel   F13=How to use this display
 F24=More keys
```

Notice that we've entered the host name as PC002. This name is known as a *short name* because it doesn't specify domain information. A common practice is to specify both a short name and a long name (which includes domain information). You can do this by keying the plus sign (+) for more values and entering a value such as

```
PC002.Quintessence.com
```

for the long name. Remember, you can enter up to four host names for a single IP address.

The Real World

In a full-fledged TCP/IP environment, there are many considerations above and beyond those we've discussed in this chapter. From issues such as address manipulation with network address translation (NAT) to security, the list of topics is significant.

We hope we've given you a foundation upon which you can build your TCP/IP knowledge. You can find IBM documentation for TCP/IP with the iSeries in *TCP/IP Fastpath Setup* (SC41-5430) and *TCP/IP Configuration and Reference* (SC41-5420).

Chapter 34

Operations Navigator

Full of functions of interest to iSeries administrators, operators, and users, Operations Navigator (commonly referred to as OpsNav) is increasingly becoming an integral part of system interaction. If you've not yet looked at OpsNav, now is a good time to see how its many features simplify the administration of one or more iSeries systems in a network. The Explorer-like appearance of this Windows-based graphical user interface (GUI) minimizes the need to learn the OS/400 command interface.

OpsNav is an optionally installable component of Client Access with a user interface that will be familiar to those who use any of the Windows operating systems. For instance, you'll find such customary features as help windows, drag-and-drop functions, pull-down menus, fly-over help, and configuration wizards. Many find this graphical interface more productive than the system's traditional command-line interface.

In this chapter, we highlight some of the major functions supported by OpsNav. We also introduce you to a few navigational techniques you'll use in moving around within OpsNav.

OpsNav Components

In addition to base support that provides its basic functions (such as the user interface), OpsNav consists of several optionally installable components. These components include

- Basic Operations
- Job Management
- Configuration and Service
- Network
- Security
- Users and Groups
- Database
- File Systems
- Multimedia
- Backup
- Application Development
- Management Central
- Application Administration

Figure 34.1 shows the main OpsNav window with two systems, named As400 and Thumper.

FIGURE 34.1
Main Operations Navigator Window

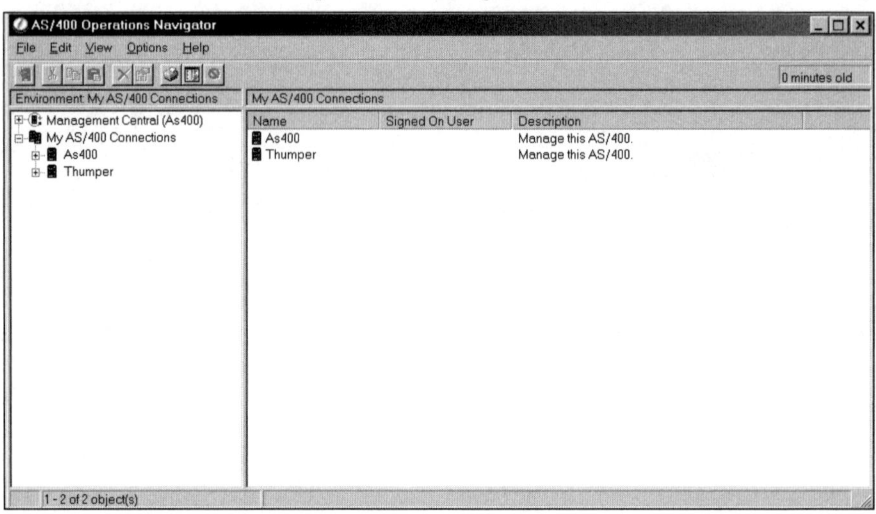

To see the OpsNav components available for a system, you simply expand the system's information by clicking the plus sign (+ symbol) beside the system in the left-hand pane of this window. Figure 34.2 shows the components for system As400.

FIGURE 34.2
Operations Navigator Components

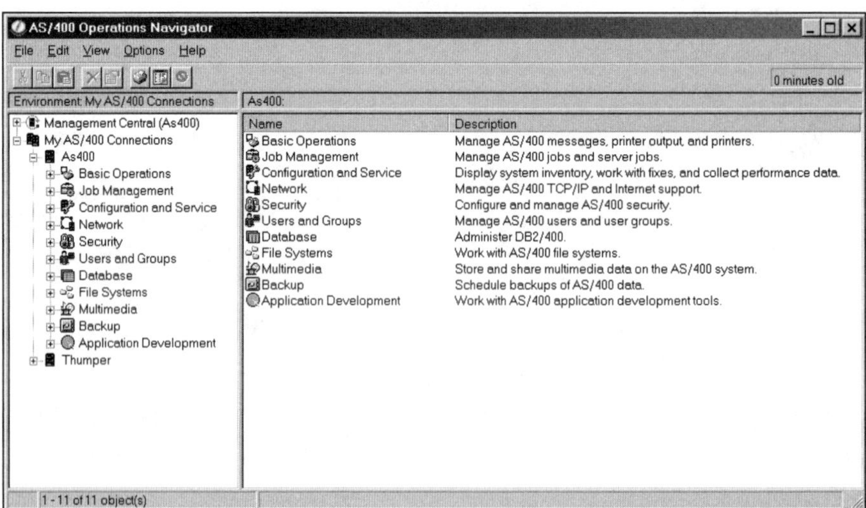

You may notice that the Management Central component appears before the list of systems. That's because Management Central applies to *all* systems in your network. You may also notice that the Application Administration component doesn't appear at all. Application Administration is a property of a system and therefore is accessible by right-clicking the system and selecting Application Administration from the pop-up menu.

To effectively use OpsNav, you need to know the functions it provides as well as a few navigational techniques you use to access information. To give you a jump start with navigational techniques, we provide several examples for, and discuss in greater detail, the first component, Basic Operations. Then we briefly introduce you to the other OpsNav components.

Basic Operations

OpsNav's Basic Operations component contains functions for working with perhaps the most common of day-to-day operations. Expanding the view for Basic Operations (Figure 34.3) reveals that this component includes functions for working with Messages, Printer Output (spooled files), and Printers.

FIGURE 34.3
Basic Operations

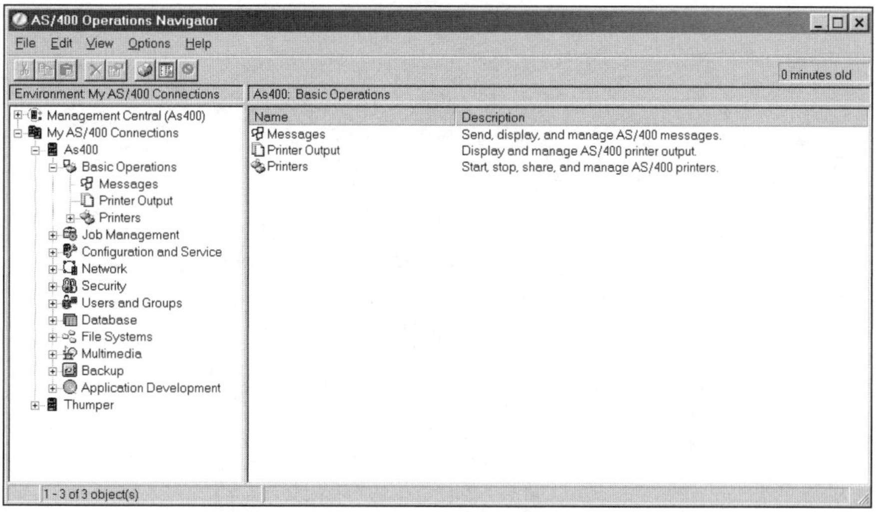

You select Messages to perform message management functions, such as displaying messages, sending messages, and replying to messages. Figure 34.4 shows the window that results when you select Messages. In this example, the message queue contains a single, yet important, message. The security officer wants to know where to have lunch!

You can view the message details by double-clicking the From user entry to the left of the message or by right-clicking the entry and selecting Details from the resulting context-sensitive pop-up menu. Figure 34.5 shows the window that displays message details.

FIGURE 34.4
Messages

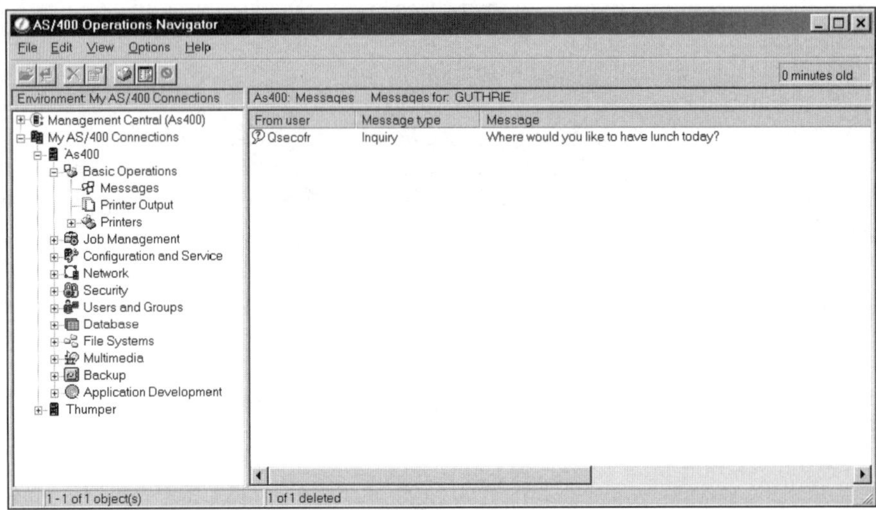

FIGURE 34.5
Message Details

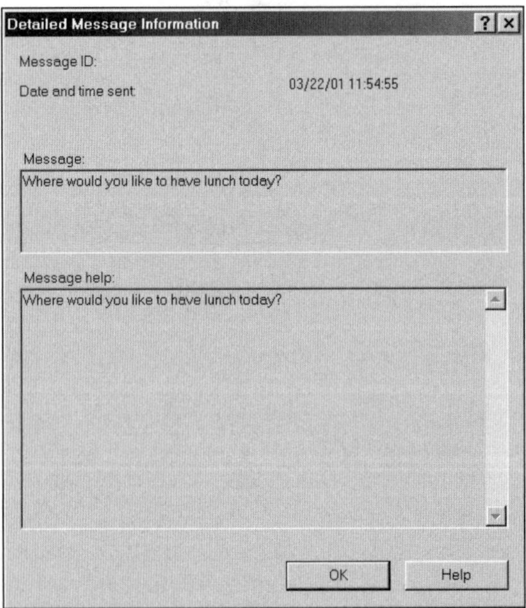

In this example, the section for Message help simply shows the message text because this message is an ad hoc message and, hence, has no associated second-level text. When the message is a predefined message from a message file, the Message help section displays the message's second-level text.

Look again at Figure 34.4 and notice that the Message type associated with the message from the security officer is Inquiry. To reply to this message, you right-click the From user entry and select Reply from the pop-up menu. Figure 34.6 shows the window from which you reply to an inquiry message.

FIGURE 34.6

Reply to a Message

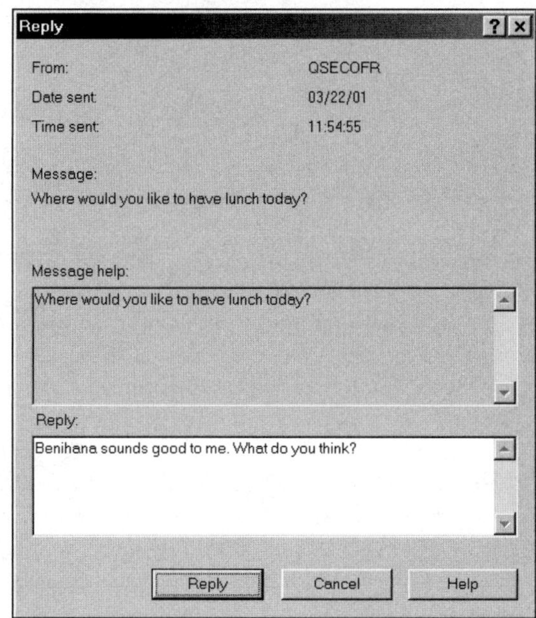

After you type the reply, a simple click of the Reply button sends it.

By now, you should be noticing that right-clicking an entity is important to understanding how to perform various tasks related to that entity. This point is true throughout OpsNav.

You can set the frequency with which the system refreshes the OpsNav Messages window. If you forget to do this, you may wonder where your messages are! To set the frequency, you right-click Messages in the left-hand pane and select Properties from the pop-up menu. Figure 34.7 shows the resulting Properties window, where you can enter the automatic refresh properties you want to use.

FIGURE 34.7
Setting Refresh Frequency for Messages

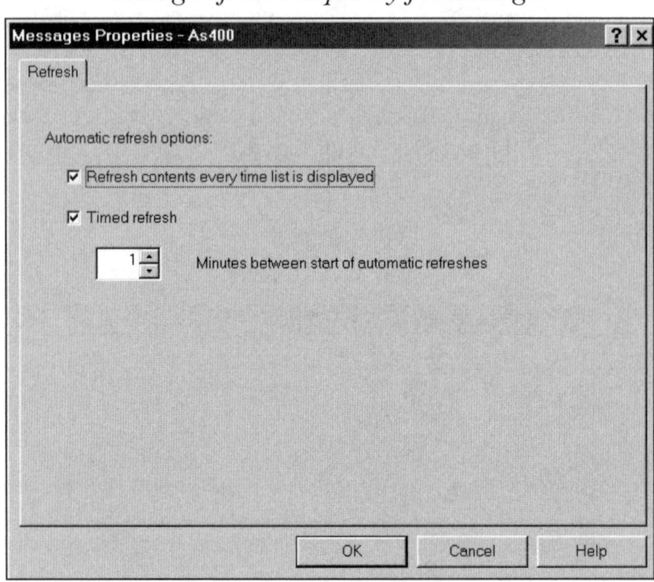

The Printer Output entry in Basic Operations is another important day-to-day task that OpsNav addresses. This option lets you work with spooled files. Figure 34.8 shows the window you see when you select Printer Output. You can see that the user has two spooled files.

As with messages, you can obtain further information by right-clicking a spooled file entry and selecting Properties from the pop-up menu. Figure 34.9 shows the resulting window. From here, you can click the various tabs to obtain additional attribute information.

You can display a spooled file by double-clicking its entry or by right-clicking its entry and selecting Open from the pop-up menu. Figure 34.10 shows the job log that is in the current user's list of spooled files. You can use drag-and-drop to copy or move a spooled file from one printer to another. The target printer can even be on a different system! You can also use drag-and-drop to copy a spooled file to the PC desktop or a Windows folder. This action creates an ASCII text file, ignoring any graphics that the spooled file may contain.

The last of the Basic Operations options, Printers, lets you work with your printers. Figure 34.11 shows the window you see when you select Printers. With this option, you can perform a variety of printer management functions. For instance, you can display a list of spooled files for a printer by selecting that printer from the list of printers in Printers. Figure 34.12 shows the result.

FIGURE 34.8
Printer Output

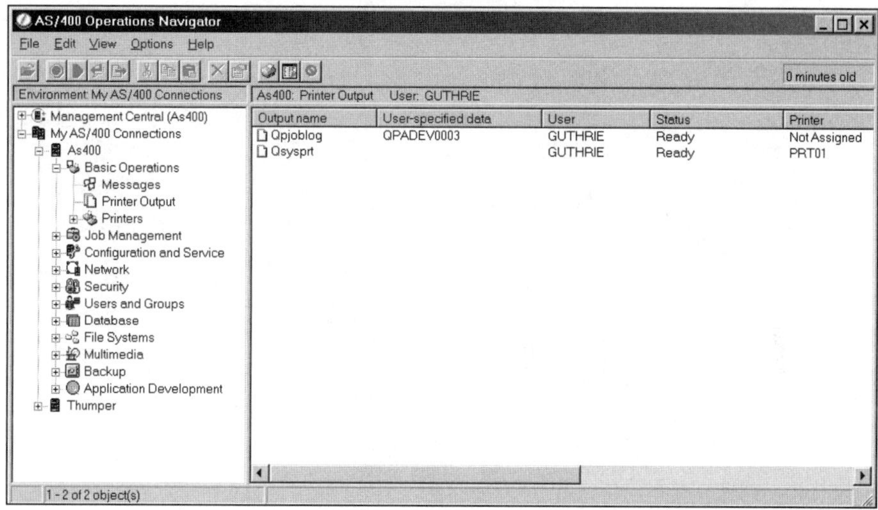

FIGURE 34.9
Spooled File Properties

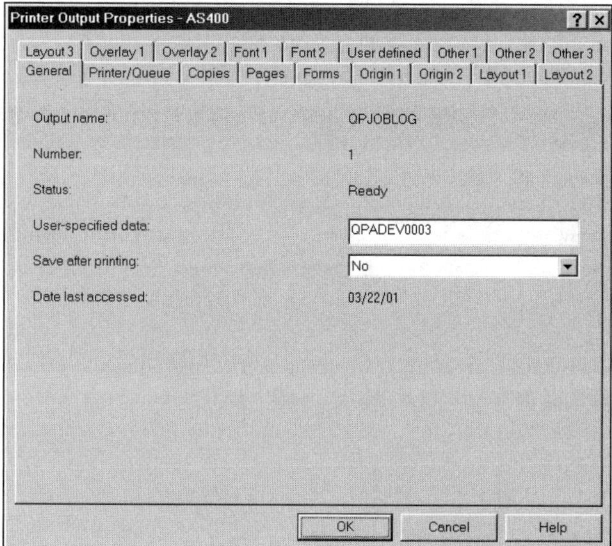

FIGURE 34.10
Displaying a Spooled File

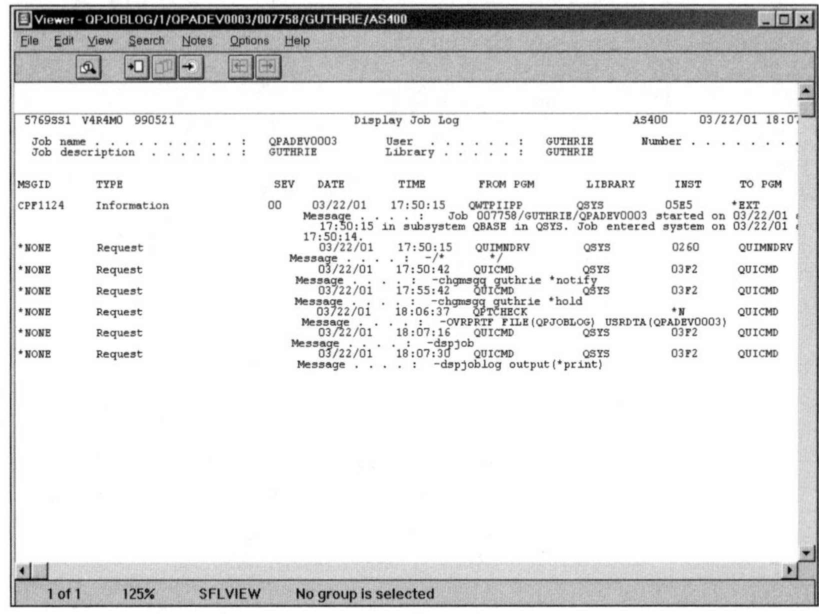

FIGURE 34.11
Printers

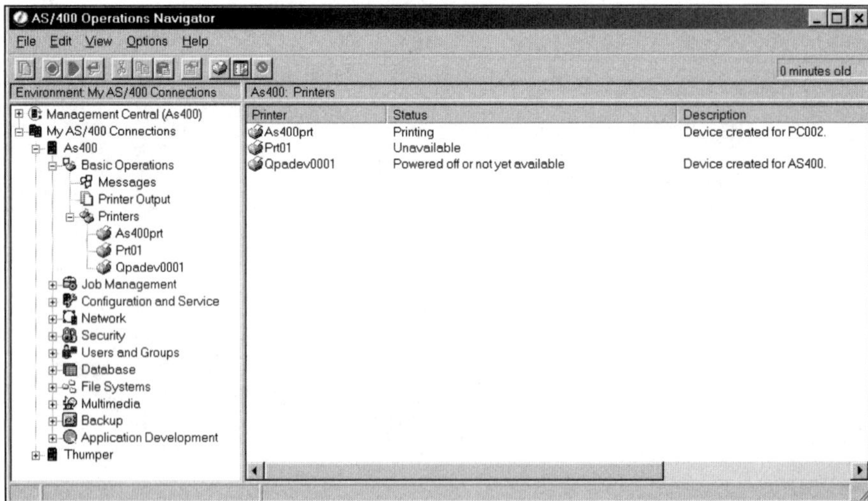

FIGURE 34.12
Displaying the List of Spooled Files for a Printer

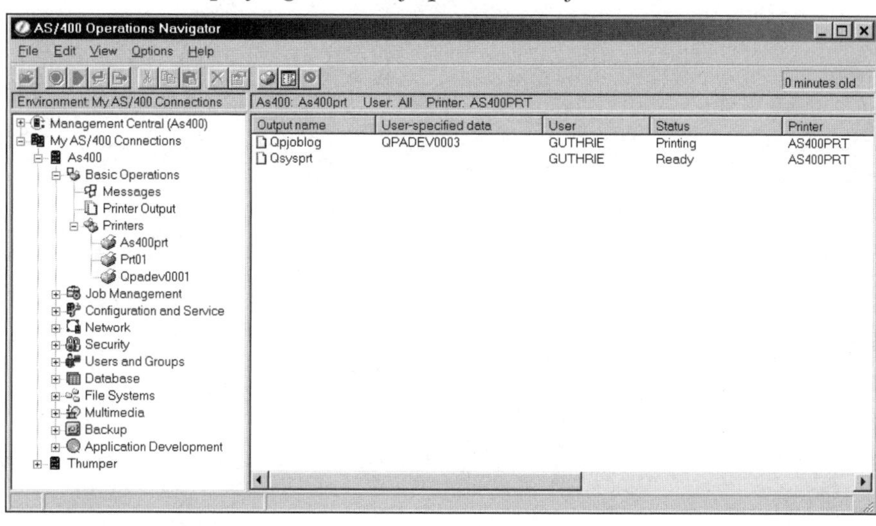

Other functions include those to start and stop printers, hold and release printers, vary off and on printers, and reply to printer messages. Practice your navigational techniques and determine what mouse action gives you access to these functions.

Job Management

With OpsNav's Job Management component, you can work with Jobs and Server Jobs for a selected system. Server jobs are those jobs performing work for a particular OS/400 server. Some of the supported functions include those to display jobs, hold jobs, and delete jobs.

You can tailor the look of the job information displayed using the Options pull-down menu. For example, you can select Sort to sort the list of jobs by one or more columns, select Columns to specify the columns you want to display and the order in which you want to arrange them, and select Include to specify which information you want to include.

Configuration and Service

The Configuration and Service component of OpsNav lets you work with Hardware Inventory, Software Inventory, Fixes Inventory (PTFs), and Collection Services (performance data from multiple systems). For instance, you can view a list of hardware resources and their operational status with the Hardware Inventory entry. One handy feature of Hardware Inventory is the ability to manage disk units and auxiliary storage pools, as you can with System Service Tools (using command StrSST, or Start System Service Tools).

With the Software Inventory entry, you can view a list of the software resources on your system, along with the version and release level of each resource and the installed options.

The Fixes Inventory entry gives you a way to display and manage PTFs on your system. This option provides some very handy features. For instance, you can run wizards to compare and update fixes on a group of systems against those on a model system, send fixes to and install them on other systems, permanently install fixes, temporarily install fixes, and remove fixes. Also among the features presented by Fixes Inventory is one for cleaning up the save files and cover letters associated with fixes.

The Collection Services entry lets you work with performance data. You can collect performance data for multiple systems, view the data, and view the status on one or more systems or groups of systems.

Network

The Network component contains many functions that let you work with network-related issues. OpsNav categorizes these functions into various entries in Network.

With the IP Security entry, you can work with items such as IP filtering and network address translation (NAT). IP Security also lets you set up Virtual Private Networking (VPN).

The Point-to-Point entry provides a way for you to work with connection profiles. This ability includes Point-to-Point Protocol (PPP) and Serial Line Internet Protocol (SLIP). Using the Modem entry in Point-to-Point, you can also work with modems and their properties. With Point-to-Point's Connection Profiles entry, you can perform such tasks as work with the Point-to-Point attributes for TCP/IP.

The Protocols entry contains basic TCP/IP functions as well as TCP/IP connection wizards. You can access the wizards by right-clicking TCP/IP in the right pane and then clicking New Interfaces. The Protocols entry provides functions such as setting TCP/IP properties, running TCP/IP utilities, starting and stopping TCP/IP, verifying TCP/IP connections, and working with and monitoring TCP/IP interfaces.

With the Servers entry, you can work with servers on your system, including TCP/IP and Client Access servers. You can perform such functions as configuring servers, starting and stopping servers, and checking server status.

The IBM Network Stations entry lets you work with IBM Network Stations and IBM Network Station users. With this option, you can perform setup and management functions.

The Internet entry provides a list of Internet functions you can access from within OpsNav. In addition to launching Internet applications, you can access the home page for Internet-related functions installed on your system. The Firewall home page lets you set up and monitor an Internet firewall. With the IBM HTTP Server home page, you can configure the HTTP server and Secure Sockets Layer (SSL) support. The IBM Payment Server home page lets you configure and manage the payment server. The Digital Certificate Manager home page lets you manage the certificates used by your secure applications and users. Using the Net.Commerce home page, you can configure the Net.Commerce server.

Security

You use OpsNav's Security component to secure your system. This entry contains functions for using the Security Wizard, managing security and auditing settings, working with security and auditing policies, and working with authorization lists.

The Security Wizard makes it easy to secure your system. To access the Security Wizard, right-click Security and select Configure. Simply follow the instructions to configure your system security.

The Authorization Lists entry in Security lets you work with authorization lists. You can perform such tasks as creating and changing authorization lists, adding users and groups to authorization lists, and displaying the objects secured by authorization lists.

With the Security Policies entry in Security, you can set audit policies as well as security policies. Policies are overriding values used as defaults in processing.

Users and Groups

The Users and Groups component contains functions that let you manage users and groups. You can filter the list of users using the entries in Users and Groups. You can select All Users, Groups, or Users Not in a Group.

Using Users and Groups, you can create, change, and delete users; add users to groups; copy users to other systems; and create and change groups. You can use drag-and-drop to perform tasks such as adding users to groups, moving users to different groups, removing users from groups, and adding users to another system.

Database

The Database component gives you an extensive array of functions you can use to manage DB2 database objects such as journals, tables, and views. The Database entry also contains functions for working with services such as Open Database Connectivity (ODBC), running Structured Query Language (SQL) statements, and monitoring SQL performance. This entry also supports drag-and-drop.

Among the many functions provided by the Database component are the ability to create libraries, journals, tables, views, aliases, functions, procedures, and types; to display libraries; to display, edit, and reorganize tables; and to delete database objects. You'll find these functions in the Libraries entry in Database.

With the ODBC Data Sources entry, you can manage ODBC data sources. You can create data sources, change data sources, and delete data sources.

The SQL Performance Monitors entry gives you a way to track resources used by SQL statements. You can use the resource usage information to determine whether your SQL statements are performing as they should or need fine-tuning. This entry includes functions to create SQL monitors, delete SQL monitors, end SQL monitors, pause SQL monitors, and analyze the results of SQL monitors.

File Systems

The File Systems component functions let you administer integrated file system (IFS) objects as well as file shares. Selecting the File Systems entry displays a list of file systems to which you are authorized.

The Integrated File Systems entry in File Systems provides functions to accomplish tasks such as browsing file systems, setting permissions to objects, and creating and managing file shares. You can drag and drop files within a system or between systems and the PC desktop.

The File Shares entry in File Systems lets you work with NetServer file shares. You can configure NetServer by right-clicking File Shares and selecting Open NetServer from the pop-up menu. In addition to opening and exploring file systems, you can map network drives to your file shares.

Multimedia

The Multimedia component of OpsNav lets you use the Ultimedia System Facilities (USF) application to store and share multimedia objects (e.g., video, audio, and graphic objects) on the iSeries. Using the Ultimedia System Facilities entry in Multimedia, you can perform such functions as creating, copying, and deleting multimedia objects.

Backup

With the Backup component, you can schedule and administer backup services. This entry provides access to backup options that correspond to those on the OS/400 Backup menu.

The Policies entry in Backup includes functions for setting general backup options and for working with daily, weekly, and monthly backups. You can define what, when, and where the system backs up data. In addition to defining daily, weekly, and monthly backups, you can view them.

Application Development

The Application Development component contains functions for working with application development tools. The Interprocess Communication entry in Application Development lets you view the types of Interprocess Communication (IPC) objects on your system. These IPC objects include such items as Kernel Message Queues, Shared Memory, and Semaphore sets.

The IPC properties help you identify and locate a selected IPC object. To view these properties, click Kernel Message Queues, click Shared Memory, or expand Semaphores. These entries all appear in Interprocess Communication.

Management Central

The Management Central component of OpsNav is a collection of system management functions that let you more easily manage multiple systems. Because Management Central entails a considerable number of features, we provide only a glimpse of this component here. (For tips on obtaining more detailed information about Management Central, see More About OpsNav," page 554.)

To use Management Central, you define a managing, or central, system whose function it is to store Management Central data. This system connects to the PC and communicates with the endpoint systems. Endpoint systems are the other systems in your network that you choose to manage through the central system using Management Central. You can define a system that serves as a repository for information (e.g., fixes, files, folders) that you want to send to other systems. You can also define groups of systems with which Management Central can work.

Management Central works in conjunction with other OpsNav components. It lets you perform tasks such as working with hardware, software, and fixes inventories; working with fixes (PTF) management; working with collection services (performance data); working with packages (collections of files and objects) that you can send to other systems; scheduling tasks; working with command definitions (used in running commands on multiple systems); and working with performance monitors.

You can even access Management Central information remotely using a Web browser, a Personal Digital Assistant (PDA) with a wireless modem, or an Internet telephone. For instance, you could remotely check systems availability or check active monitors.

Application Administration

The Application Administration component lets you control the availability of OpsNav functions to users. You can also use this component to control the availability of functions in other applications if those applications have defined functions that Application Administration can manage.

We've already mentioned that Application Administration is a property of a system and therefore is accessible by right-clicking the system and selecting Application Administration from the pop-up menu. You can also access Application Administration through Management Central by right-clicking Management Central and selecting Application Administration from the pop-up menu. You then select the function with which you want to work.

Plug-in Support

You can enhance OpsNav by adding plug-ins — your own custom tools or applications — to the OpsNav hierarchy. Programs written in C++, Java, or Visual Basic can take advantage of the application programming interfaces (APIs) that IBM provides for use with plug-ins. For instance, Lotus Domino provides a plug-in for managing Domino servers. When installed, this plug-in appears in the Network component as an entry in the Servers entry.

Once you develop a plug-in, you can take advantage of support provided by Client Access Selective Setup to distribute the plug-in to users. Whether distributing to users within your own organization or to customers, distribution and installation of your plug-in is simple.

If you're interested in trying your hand at writing OpsNav plug-ins, see "More About OpsNav" for further reading options.

More Than Just a Pretty Face

You can see that OpsNav does indeed provide support for many OS/400 operational procedures and in many cases greatly simplifies the tasks at hand. As you explore OpsNav more closely, you'll soon realize that we've touched only the tip of the iceberg. There really is something in OpsNav for all classes of users!

IBM recommends you use OpsNav and is committed to continued support. With each new release of the operating system, it's probably safe to expect significant OpsNav enhancements. So, does OpsNav equate to the beginning of a GUI for the iSeries? Let's hope so!

More About OpsNav

One option you might find useful when working with Operations Navigator (OpsNav) is its own Welcome window (Figure 34.A). This is the OpsNav portal to help! The Welcome window is displayed each time you start OpsNav unless you've indicated that the window is not to be displayed at start-up time. You can also access the Welcome window by selecting Help Topics from the Help pull-down menu on the OpsNav toolbar.

FIGURE 34.A
Operations Navigator Online Help

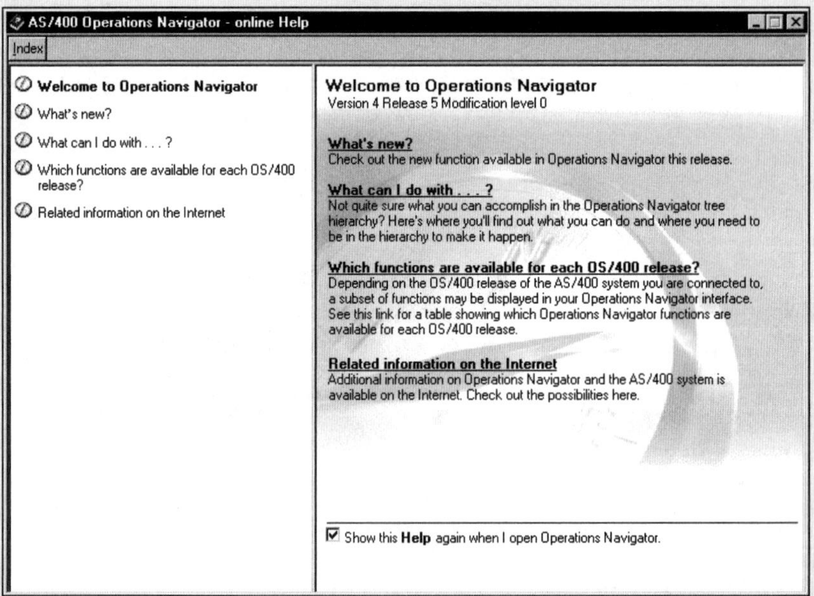

continued

OpsNav: Further Reading

You can find additional OpsNav information on the Internet. Following are some of the locations you may want to visit.

Caution

IBM is notorious for changing documentation locations. We hope the URLs listed here still work as advertised when you try them. If they don't, call IBM, not us!

iSeries Information Center

http://www.iseries.ibm.com/infocenter

IBM's iSeries Information Center is available on CD-ROM and on the Internet. You can access the Information Center from the OpsNav Help pull-down menu found on the OpsNav toolbar, as well as through hyperlinks found within Client Access and OpsNav help topics. You identify the location (CD-ROM or Internet) that you want to use when accessing the Information Center using the OpsNav Help pull-down menu. Click the link for Information Center, and then select Location; you can opt to use the Internet, or you can specify the path for accessing information from the CD-ROM (or disk if you copied the CD-ROM to disk).

Online Library

http://publib.boulder.ibm.com/pubs/html/as400/online/homeeng1.htm (for English)

http://publib.boulder.ibm.com/pubs/html/as400/onlinelib.htm (to select a language of your choice)

You can search IBM's online library for publications containing OpsNav information. For instance, one good source of information is the Redbook *Managing AS/400 V4R4 with Operations Navigator* (SG24-5646). Even though this book is geared to V4R4, it's still a good source of general OpsNav information. Note that the URLs given above for the Online Library aren't prefixed with "www". You can also access the Online Library using links found at the Information Center.

Technical Studio

http://www.as400.ibm.com/tstudio

You can search IBM's Technical Studio for OpsNav information. You can also access Technical Studio using links found at the Information Center.

Operations Navigator home page

http://www.as400.ibm.com/oper_nav

For the latest Operations Navigator information, visit this page.

continued

(More About OpsNav *Continued*)

Management Central home page

http://www.as400.ibm.com/sftsol/mgmtcentral.htm

For the latest Management Central information, visit this page.

Plug-Ins: Further Reading

You can find additional information for creating OpsNav plug-ins on the Internet. Here are some of the locations you may want to visit.

Third-Party Plug-in Support page

http://www.as400.ibm.com/oper_nav/pluginpage.htm

This page is a good source of information useful for working with plug-ins.

"Operations Navigator Plug-in Support"

http://www.as400.ibm.com/tstudio/opsnav/plugin/pludex.htm

This Tech Studio document provides information to help you create your own OpsNav plug-ins.

Further Reading

IBM Manuals

In the list below, documents followed by "InfoCenter" rather than an IBM document number can be viewed online at IBM's iSeries Information Center, *http://publib.boulder.ibm.com/pubs/html/as400/infocenter.htm.* The references with document numbers are available online at IBM's Online Library site, *http://publib.boulder.ibm.com/pubs/html/as400/online/homeeng1.htm* (for English) or *http://publib.boulder.ibm.com/pubs/html/as400/onlinelib.htm* (to select a language of your choice). Most cited references are for V4R5; however, a few are located in the V4R4 section of the Online Library. If you have trouble locating a reference using the document number given here, check the AS400 Network's Index400 facility (*http://www.as400network.com/index400*), which provides a directory of IBM documentation organized by topics, with links to the latest location of the documentation on the Web.

Backup, Recovery and Media Services (SC41-5345)

Basic System Operation, Administration, and Problem Handling (SC41-5206)

DB2 UDB for AS/400 Database Programming (InfoCenter)

DDS Reference (InfoCenter)

File Management (InfoCenter)

OS/400 Backup and Recovery (SC41-5304)

OS/400 CL Programming (SC41-5721)

OS/400 CL Reference – Part 2 (SC41-5724)

OS/400 CL Reference – Part 4 (SC41-5726)

OS/400 Communications Configuration (SC41-5401)

OS/400 Security – Reference (SC41-5302)

OS/400 Work Management (SC41-5306)

OS/400 Work Management APIs (SC41-5878)

Security – Enabling for C2 (SC41-5303)

Software Installation (SC41-5120)

System API Reference (SC41-5801)

TCP/IP Configuration and Reference (SC41-5420)

TCP/IP Fastpath Setup (SC41-5430)

Tips and Tools for Securing Your AS/400 (SC41-5300)

IBM Redbooks

IBM's Redbooks are available online at *http://www.redbooks.ibm.com.*

AS/400 Internet Security: Protecting Your AS/400 from HARM on the Internet (SG24-4929)

An Implementation Guide for AS/400 Security and Auditing: Including C2, Cryptography, Communications, and PC Connectivity (GG24-4200)

Managing AS/400 V4R4 with Operations Navigator (SG24-5646)

IBM Web Sites

Backup, Recovery and Media Services (BRMS)
http://www.as400.ibm.com/service/brms.htm

Client Access
http://www.as400.ibm.com/clientaccess

Global Services (AS/400 Alert)
http://www.ibm.com/services

iSeries and AS/400 Information Center
http://publib.boulder.ibm.com/pubs/html/as400/infocenter.htm

iSeries and AS/400 Technical Support
http://www.as400service.ibm.com

Management Central
http://www.as400.ibm.com/sftsol/mgmtcentral.htm

Online Library
http://publib.boulder.ibm.com/pubs/html/as400/online/homeeng1.htm (for English)
http://publib.boulder.ibm.com/pubs/html/as400/onlinelib.htm (to select a language of your choice)

Operations Navigator
http://www.as400.ibm.com/oper_nav

"Operations Navigator Plug-in Support"
http://www.as400.ibm.com/tstudio/opsnav/plugin/pludex.htm

Security Advisor
http://www.as400.ibm.com/tstudio/secure1/index_av.htm

Technical Studio
http://www.as400.ibm.com/tstudio

Third-Party Operations Navigator Plug-in Support
http://www.as400.ibm.com/oper_nav/pluginpage.htm

Articles

For a searchable archive of articles providing more detail on the topics covered in this book, see the *NEWS/400* article database at *http://www.as400network.com* (in the Tech Resources section).

Books

Conte, Paul. *Database Design and Programming for DB2/400.* 29th Street Press, 1996.

Cravitz, Mike. *ILE by Example.* NEWS/400 Books, 2000.

Dawson, Mike, and Mike Manto. *OPNQRYF by Example.* NEWS/400 Books, 1999.

Fottral, Jerry. *Mastering the AS/400,* 3rd ed. 29th Street Press, 2000.

Meyers, Bryan, and Dan Riehl. *Control Language Programming for the AS/400,* 2nd ed. 29th Street Press, 1997.

Nelson, Lynn. *Creating CL Commands by Example.* NEWS/400 Books, 1999.

Rothenbuehler, Heidi, and Patrice Gapen. *Introduction to AS/400 System Operations,* 2nd ed. 29th Street Press, 2000.

Ryan, Michael. *TCP/IP and the AS/400.* NEWS/400 Books, 1999.

Woodbury, Carol, and Wayne Madden. *Implementing AS/400 Security,* 4th ed. NEWS/400 Books, 2000.

Index

A

B

C

D

I

J

P

Q

S

W

X

New Books in the 29th Street Press® and NEWS/400 Books™ Library

CREATING CL COMMANDS BY EXAMPLE

By Lynn Nelson

Learn from an expert how to create CL commands that have the same functionality and power as the IBM commands you use every day. You'll see how to create commands with all the function found in IBM's commands, including parameter editing, function keys, F4 prompt for values, expanding lists of values, and conditional prompting. Whether you're in operations or programming, *Creating CL Commands by Example* can help you tap the tremendous power and flexibility of CL commands to automate tasks and enhance applications. 134 pages.

DOMINO R5 AND THE AS/400

By Justine Middleton, Wilfried Blankertz, Rosana Choruzy, Linda Defreyne, Dwight Egerton, Joanne Mindzora, Stephen Ryan, Juan van der Breggen, Felix Zalcmann, and Michelle Zolkos

Domino R5 and the AS/400 provides comprehensive installation and setup instructions for those installing Domino R5 "from scratch," upgrading from a previous version, or migrating from a platform other than the AS/400. In addition, you get detailed explanations of SMTP in Domino for AS/400, dial-up connectivity, directory synchronization, Advanced Services for Domino for AS/400, and Domino administration strategies, including backup strategies. 512 pages.

E-BUSINESS

Thriving in the Electronic Marketplace

By Nahid Jilovec

E-Business: Thriving in the Electronic Marketplace identifies key issues organizations face when they implement e-business projects and answers fundamental questions about entering and navigating the changing world of e-business. A concise guide to moving your business into the exciting world of collaborative e-business, the book introduces the four e-business models that drive today's economy and gives a clear summary of e-business technologies. It focuses on practical business-to-business applications. 172 pages.

ILE BY EXAMPLE

A Hands-on Guide to the AS/400's Integrated Language Environment

By Mike Cravitz

Learn the fundamentals of the AS/400's Integrated Language Environment (ILE) by following working examples that illustrate the ins and outs of this powerful programming model. Major topics include ILE program structure, bind by copy, ILE RPG subprocedures, service programs, activation groups, ILE condition handling and cancel handling, and more. A CD contains all sample programs discussed in the book, as well as a sample ILE condition handler to address record locks and ILE RPG software to synchronize system clocks using the Internet SNTP protocol. 165 pages.

IMPLEMENTING AS/400 SECURITY, FOURTH EDITION

By Carol Woodbury and Wayne Madden

For years, AS/400 professionals have depended on earlier editions of *Implementing AS/400 Security* to learn and implement essential AS/400 security concepts. This latest edition not only brings together in one place the fundamental AS/400 security tools and experience-based recommendations you need but also includes specifics on the security enhancements available in OS/400 V4R5. In addition, you'll find expanded coverage of network, communications, and Internet security — including thwarting hacker activities — as well as updated chapters covering security system values, user profiles, object authorization, database security, output-queue and spooled-file security, auditing, contingency planning, and more. 454 pages.

INTRODUCTION TO AS/400 SYSTEM OPERATIONS, SECOND EDITION

By Heidi Rothenbuehler and Patrice Gapen

Here's the second edition of the textbook that covers what you need to know to become a successful AS/400 system operator or administrator. *Introduction to AS/400 System Operations, Second Edition* teaches you the basics of system operations so that you can manage printed reports, perform regularly scheduled procedures, and resolve end-user problems. New material covers the Integrated File System (IFS), AS/400 InfoSeeker, Operations Navigator, and much more. 182 pages.

MASTERING THE AS/400, THIRD EDITION

A Practical, Hands-On Guide

By Jerry Fottral

The latest edition of this best-selling introduction to AS/400 concepts and facilities takes a utilitarian approach that stresses student participation. The book emphasizes mastery of system/user interface, member-object-library relationship, use of CL commands, basic database concepts, and program development utilities. The text prepares students to move directly into programming languages, database management, and system operations courses. Each lesson includes a lab that focuses on the essential topics presented in the lesson. 553 pages.

PROGRAMMING IN RPG IV, SECOND EDITION

By Bryan Meyers and Judy Yaeger

This textbook provides a strong foundation in the essentials of business programming, featuring the newest version of the RPG language: RPG IV. Focusing on real-world problems and down-to-earth solutions using the latest techniques and features of RPG, this book provides everything you need to know to write a well-designed RPG IV program. The second edition includes new chapters on defining data with D-specs and modular programming concepts, as well as an RPG IV summary appendix and an RPG IV style guide. An instructor's kit is available. 408 pages.

RPG IV JUMP START, THIRD EDITION

By Bryan Meyers

RPG IV Jump Start presents RPG IV from the perspective of a programmer who already knows RPG III, pointing out the differences between the two languages and demonstrating how to take advantage of the new syntax and function. This third edition is fully updated for V4R4 and includes information about the latest H-spec keywords, built-in functions, opcodes, and data types. Also included are expanded coverage of RPG's pointer support, new chapters on RPG programming style, and what's in store for the future of RPG. 234 pages.

SQL/400 DEVELOPER'S GUIDE

By Paul Conte and Mike Cravitz

SQL/400 Developer's Guide provides start-to-finish coverage of SQL/400, IBM's strategic language for the AS/400's integrated database. This textbook covers database and SQL fundamentals, SQL/400 Data Definition Language (DDL) and Data Manipulation Language (DML), and database modeling and design. Throughout the book, coding suggestions reinforce the topics covered and provide practical advice on how to produce robust, well-functioning code. Hands-on exercises reinforce comprehension of the concepts covered. 508 pages.

Also Published by 29th Street Press® and NEWS/400 Books™

THE AS/400 EXPERT: READY-TO-RUN RPG/400 TECHNIQUES

By Julian Monypenny and Roger Pence

Ready-to-Run RPG/400 Techniques provides a variety of RPG templates, subroutines, and copy modules, sprinkled with fundamental advice, to help you write robust and effective RPG/400 programs. Highlights include string-handling routines, numeric editing routines, date routines, error-handling modules, and tips for using OS/400 APIs with RPG/400. The tested and ready-to-run code building blocks — provided on an accompanying CD — easily snap into existing RPG code and integrate well with new RPG/400 projects. 203 pages.

THE A TO Z OF EDI AND ITS ROLE IN E-COMMERCE, SECOND EDITION

By Nahid Jilovec

E-commerce expert Nahid Jilovec gives you the practical details of EDI implementation. Not only does this book show you how to cost justify EDI, but it also gives you job descriptions for EDI team members, detailed criteria and forms for evaluating EDI vendors, considerations for trading-partner agreements, an EDI glossary, and lists of EDI organizations and publications. The second edition includes new information about EDI and the Internet, system security, and auditing. 221 pages.

CONTROL LANGUAGE PROGRAMMING FOR THE AS/400, SECOND EDITION

By Bryan Meyers and Dan Riehl

This CL programming textbook offers students comprehensive knowledge of the skills they will need in today's MIS environment. Chapters progress methodically from CL basics to more complex processes and concepts, guiding students toward a professional grasp of CL programming techniques and style. In this second edition, the authors have updated the text to include discussion of the Integrated Language Environment (ILE) and the fundamental changes ILE introduces to the AS/400's execution model. 522 pages.

DATABASE DESIGN AND PROGRAMMING FOR DB2/400

By Paul Conte

This textbook is the most complete guide to DB2/400 design and programming available anywhere. The author shows you everything you need to know about physical and logical file DDS, SQL/400, and RPG IV and COBOL/400 database programming. Clear explanations illustrated by a wealth of examples demonstrate efficient database programming and error handling with both DDS and SQL/400. 610 pages.

DATA WAREHOUSING AND THE AS/400

By Scott Steinacher

In this book, Scott Steinacher takes an in-depth look at data warehousing components, concepts, and terminology. After laying this foundation, Scott presents a compelling case for implementing a data warehouse on the AS/400. Included on an accompanying CD are demos of AS/400 data warehousing software from several independent software vendors. 342 pages.

DDS KEYWORD REFERENCE

By James Coolbaugh

Reach for the *DDS Keyword Reference* when you need quick, at-your-fingertips information about DDS keywords for physical files, logical files, display files, printer files, and ICF files. In this no-nonsense volume, author Jim Coolbaugh gives you all the keywords you'll need, listed alphabetically in five sections. He explains each keyword, providing syntax rules and examples for coding the keyword. *DDS Keyword Reference* is a friendly and manageable alternative to IBM's bulky DDS reference manual. 212 pages.

DDS PROGRAMMING FOR DISPLAY AND PRINTER FILES, SECOND EDITION

By James Coolbaugh

DDS Programming for Display and Printer Files, Second Edition helps you master DDS and — as a result — improve the quality of your display presentations and your printed jobs. Updated through OS/400 V4R3, the second edition offers a thorough, straightforward explanation of how to use DDS to program display files and printer files. It includes extensive DDS programming examples for CL and RPG that you can put to use immediately because a companion CD includes all the DDS, RPG, and CL source code presented in the book. 429 pages.

DEVELOPING YOUR AS/400 INTERNET STRATEGY

By Alan Arnold

This book addresses the issues unique to deploying your AS/400 on the Internet. It includes procedures for configuring AS/400 TCP/IP and information about which client and server technologies the AS/400 supports natively. This enterprise-class tutorial evaluates the AS/400 as an Internet server and teaches you how to design, program, and manage your Web home page. 248 pages.

DOMINO AND THE AS/400

Installation and Configuration

By Wilfried Blankertz, Rosana Choruzy, Joanne Mindzora, and Michelle Zolkos

Domino and the AS/400: Installation and Configuration gives you everything you need to implement Lotus Domino 4.6 on the AS/400, guiding you step by step through installation, configuration, customization, and administration. Here you get an introduction to Domino for AS/400 and full instructions for developing a backup and recovery plan for saving and restoring Domino data on the AS/400. 311 pages.

ESSENTIALS OF SUBFILE PROGRAMMING

and Advanced Topics in RPG/400

By Phil Levinson

Essentials of Subfile Programming and Advanced Topics in RPG/400 teaches you to design and program subfiles, offering step-by-step instructions and real-world programming exercises that build from chapter to chapter. You learn to design and create subfile records; load, clear, and display subfiles; and create pop-up windows. In addition, the advanced topics help you mine the rich store of data in the file-information and program-status data structures, handle errors, improve data integrity, and manage program-to-program communications. An instructor's manual is available. 260 pages.

ESSENTIALS OF SUBFILE PROGRAMMING

and Advanced Topics in RPG IV

By Phil Levinson

This textbook provides a solid background in AS/400 subfile programming in the newest version of the RPG language: RPG IV. Subfiles are the AS/400 tool that lets you display lists of data on the screen for user interaction. You learn to design and program subfiles via step-by-step instructions and real-world programming exercises that build from chapter to chapter. A section on the Integrated Language Environment (ILE), introduced concurrently with RPG IV, presents tools and techniques that support effective modular programming. An instructor's kit is available. 293 pages.

ILE: A FIRST LOOK

By George Farr and Shailan Topiwala

This book begins by showing the differences between ILE and its predecessors and then goes on to explain the essentials of an ILE program — using concepts such as modules, binding, service programs, and binding directories. You'll discover how ILE program activation works and how ILE works with its predecessor environments. The book covers the APIs and debugging facilities and explains the benefits of ILE's exception-handling model. You also get answers to the most commonly asked questions about ILE. 183 pages.

IMPLEMENTING WINDOWS NT ON THE AS/400

Installing, Configuring, and Troubleshooting

By Nick Harris, Phil Ainsworth, Steve Fullerton, and Antoine Sammut

Implementing Windows NT on the AS/400: Installing, Configuring, and Troubleshooting provides everything you need to know about using NT on your AS/400, including how to install NT Server 4.0 on the Integrated Netfinity Server, synchronize user profiles and passwords between the AS/400 and NT, administer NT disk storage and service packs from the AS/400, back up NT data from the AS/400, manage NT servers on remote AS/400s, and run Windows-based personal productivity applications on the AS/400. 393 pages.

INSIDE THE AS/400, SECOND EDITION

Featuring the AS/400e series

By Frank G. Soltis

Learn from the architect of the AS/400 about the new generation of AS/400e systems and servers and about the system features and capabilities introduced in Version 4 of OS/400. Dr. Frank Soltis demystifies the system, shedding light on how it came to be, how it can do the things it does, and what its future may hold. 402 pages.

JAVA AND THE AS/400

Practical Examples Using VisualAge for Java

By Daniel Darnell

This detailed guide takes you through everything you need to know about the AS/400's implementation of Java, including the QShell Interpreter and the Integrated File System (IFS), and development products such as VisualAge for Java (VAJ) and the AS/400 Toolbox for Java. The author provides several small application examples that demonstrate the advantages of Java programming for the AS/400. The companion CD contains all the sample code presented in the book and full-version copies of VAJ Professional Edition and the AS/400 Toolbox for Java. 300 pages.

JIM SLOAN'S CL TIPS & TECHNIQUES

By Jim Sloan

Written for those who understand CL, this book draws from Jim Sloan's knowledge and experience as a developer for the System/38 and the AS/400 and his creation of QUSRTOOL's TAA tools, to give you tips that can help you write better CL programs and become more productive. The book includes more than 200 field-tested techniques, plus exercises to help you understand and apply many of the techniques presented. 564 pages.

MASTERING AS/400 PERFORMANCE

By Alan Arnold, Charly Jones, Jim Stewart, and Rick Turner

If you want more from your AS/400 — faster interactive response time, more batch jobs completed on time, and maximum use of your expensive resources — this book is for you. In *Mastering AS/400 Performance*, the experts tell you how to measure, evaluate, and tune your AS/400's performance. From their experience in the field, the authors give you techniques for improving performance beyond simply buying additional hardware. 259 pages.

OPNQRYF BY EXAMPLE

By Mike Dawson and Mike Manto

The OPNQRYF (Open Query File) command is the single most dynamic and versatile command on the AS/400. Drawing from real-life, real-job experiences, the authors explain the basics and the intricacies of OPNQRYF with lots of examples to make you productive quickly. An appendix provides the UPDQRYF (Update Query File) command — a powerful addition to AS/400 and System/38 file update capabilities. CD included. 216 pages.

PROGRAMMING IN RPG/400, SECOND EDITION

By Judy Yaeger

The second edition of this textbook refines and extends the comprehensive instructional material contained in the original textbook and features a new section that introduces externally described printer files, a new chapter that highlights the fundamentals of RPG IV, and a new appendix that correlates the key concepts from each chapter with their RPG IV counterparts. The book includes everything you need to learn how to write a well-designed RPG program, from the most basic to the more complex. An instructor's kit is available. 481 pages.

PROGRAMMING SUBFILES IN COBOL/400

By Jerry Goldson

Learn how to program subfiles in COBOL/400 in a matter of hours! This powerful and flexible programming technique no longer needs to elude you. You can begin programming with subfiles the same day you get the book. You don't have to wade through page after page, chapter after chapter of rules and parameters and keywords. Instead, you get solid, helpful information and working examples that you can apply to your application programs right away. 204 pages.

RPG IV BY EXAMPLE

By George Farr and Shailan Topiwala

RPG IV by Example addresses the needs and concerns of RPG programmers at any level of experience. The focus is on RPG IV in a practical context that lets AS/400 professionals quickly grasp what's new without dwelling on the old. Beginning with an overview of RPG IV specifications, the authors prepare the way for examining all the features of the new version of the language. The chapters that follow explore RPG IV further with practical, easy-to-use applications. 488 pages.

RPG ERROR HANDLING TECHNIQUE

Bulletproofing Your Applications

By Russell Popeil

RPG Error Handling Technique teaches you the skills you need to use the powerful tools provided by OS/400 and RPG to handle almost any error from within your programs. The book explains the INFSR, INFDS, PSSR, and SDS in programming terms, with examples that show you how all these tools work together and which tools are most appropriate for which kind of error or exception situation. It continues by presenting a robust suite of error/exception-handling techniques within RPG programs. Each technique is explained in an application setting, using both RPG III and RPG IV code. Diskette included. 163 pages.

SQL/400 BY EXAMPLE

By James Coolbaugh

Designed to help you make the most of SQL/400, *SQL/400 by Example* includes everything from SQL syntax and rules to the specifics of embedding SQL within an RPG program. For novice SQL users, this book features plenty of introductory-level text and examples, including all the features and terminology of SQL/400. For experienced AS/400 programmers, *SQL/400 by Example* offers a number of specific examples that will help you increase your understanding of SQL concepts and improve your programming skills. 204 pages.

SUBFILE TECHNIQUE FOR RPG/400 PROGRAMMERS

By Jonathan Yergin, CDP, and Wayne Madden

Here's the code you need for a complete library of shell subfile programs: RPG/400 code, DDS, CL, and sample data files. There's even an example for programming windows plus some "whiz bang" techniques that can add punch to your applications. The book explains the code in simple, straightforward style and tells you when each technique should be used for best results. 3.5-inch PC diskette included. 326 pages.

TCP/IP AND THE AS/400

By Michael Ryan

Transmission Control Protocol/Internet Protocol (TCP/IP) is fast becoming a major protocol in the AS/400 world because of TCP/IP's ubiquity and predominance in the networked world, as well as its being the protocol for the Internet, intranets, and extranets. *TCP/IP and the AS/400* provides background for AS/400 professionals to understand the capabilities of TCP/IP, its strengths and weaknesses, and how to configure and administer the TCP/IP protocol stack on the AS/400. It shows TCP/IP gurus on other types of systems how to configure and manage the AS/400 TCP/IP capabilities. 362 pages.

USING QUERY/400

By Patrice Gapen and Catherine Stoughton

This textbook, designed for any AS/400 user from student to professional with or without prior programming knowledge, presents Query as an easy and fast tool for creating reports and files from AS/400 databases. Topics are ordered from simple to complex and emphasize hands-on AS/400 use; they include defining database files to Query, selecting and sequencing fields, generating new numeric and character fields, sorting within Query, joining database files, defining custom headings, creating new database files, and more. An instructor's kit is available. 92 pages.

VISUALAGE FOR RPG BY EXAMPLE

By Bryan Meyers and Jef Sutherland

VisualAge for RPG (VARPG) is a rich, full-featured development environment that provides all the tools necessary to build Windows applications for the AS/400. *VisualAge for RPG by Example* brings the RPG language to the GUI world and lets you use your existing knowledge to develop Windows applications. Using a tutorial approach, *VisualAge for RPG by Example* lets you learn as you go and create simple yet functional programs from start to finish. The accompanying CD offers a scaled-down version of VARPG and complete source code for the sample project. 236 pages.

Talk to Us!

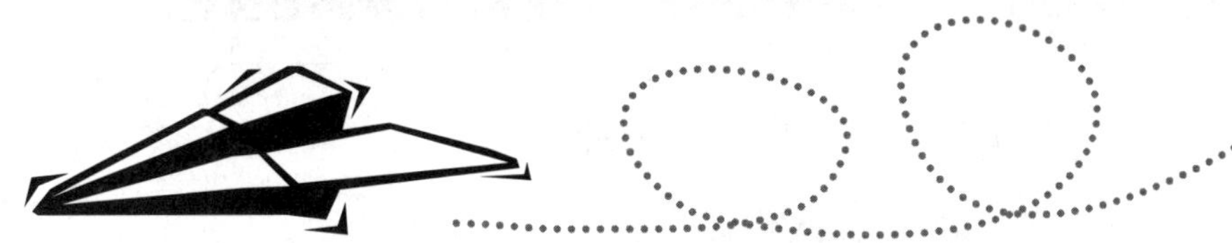

Complete this form to join our network of computer professionals

e'll gladly send you a ***free*** copy of

- ❑ *NEWS/400*
- ❑ *Selling eServer Solutions*
- ❑ *Business Finance*
- ❑ *Windows 2000 Magazine*
- ❑ *SQL Server Magazine*
- ❑ *Group Computing Magazine*

Providing help — not hype.

29th Street PRESS®

Publisher of practical, hands-on technical books for AS/400 computer professionals.

Name ______________________________

Title ____________________ Phone ____________

Company ______________________________

Address ______________________________

City/State/Zip ______________________________

E-mail ______________________________

Where did you purchase this book?

❑ Trade show ❑ Computer store ❑ Internet ❑ Card deck

❑ Bookstore ❑ Magazine ❑ Direct mail catalog or brochure

What new applications do you expect to use during the next year?

____

____

How many times this month will you visit one of our Web sites (29th Street Press®, AS400 Network, *Selling eServer Solutions*, *Business Finance*, *Windows 2000 Magazine*, *SQL Server Magazine*, or *Group Computing Magazine*)? ____________

Please share your reaction to *Starter Kit for the IBM iSeries and AS/400*. ____________

____

____

____

____

❑ YES! You have my permission to quote my comments in your publications (initials) ________

[BX001X1A]

Copy this page and mail to

29th Street Press • 221 East 29th Street • Loveland, CO 80538

OR **Fax to (970) 667-4007**

OR **Visit our Web site at www.as400networkstore.com**

WE'RE VERY RESOURCE-FULL!

Join the AS400 Network — your complete AS/400 resource!

The AS400 Network
AS400 iSeries NETWORK

NewswatchHeadlines

- Cybercrime Laws All Over the Map
- Microsoft Jumps the Java Ship, While IBM Stays the Course
- IBM WebSphere Help Program Tries for Good 1st Impression
- Tune In This Week
- Shield Delivers iSeries System Management Utility Suite
- More news and the weekly tech tip inside!

Read-Up, Ask Questions, Download System Management Products - and More!
(2/1/01)
We've launched our new System Management Microsite. It's packed with system management-specific articles, and we'll be adding more in the days ahead. Plus, you can download

Your Professional Membership Includes:

- ✓ ***NEWS/400***, the #1 AS/400 magazine worldwide, 14 times per year
- ✓ **Tech Resources:** Web-exclusive articles, downloadable code and tutorials, and the *NEWS/400* archive
- ✓ **Member Communities:** AS/400-specific forums
- ✓ **Solution Center:** AS/400 vendors, buyers guides, product reviews, and screen tours
- ✓ **IBM Connection:** Find what you need at ibm.com
- ✓ **News & Analysis:** AS/400 news updated daily
- ✓ **Jobs400:** To hire or be hired
- ✓ **Worldwide Events:** AS/400 events searchable by subject or location
- ✓ **NEWSWire/400:** E-mail newsletters on AS/400 products, news, tips, and techniques
- ✓ **Discounts on *NEWS/400* products:**
  - 25% off book purchases of $99 or less
  - 30% off book purchases of $100 or more

ASSOCIATE MEMBERSHIP
Includes e-mail newsletters & access to much more!

Click on www.as400network.com and find out what the buzz is all about!

❒ **Yes,** sign me up for the AS400 Network as a Professional Member for US$149/year in the U.S. and Canada. Elsewhere US$199/year. Additional Professional Memberships US$39/year in the U.S. and Canada. Elsewhere US$89/year.

COPY THIS PAGE AND MAIL TO:

NEWS/400
221 E. 29th St.
Loveland, CO 80538

or fax to
970/663-4007

or subscribe on the Web at
www.as400network.com

Name

Title

Company

Address

City/State/Zip

Phone Fax

E-mail [BX001X1A]

NEWS/400